The Individual in the International Legal System

Kate Parlett's study of the individual in the international legal system examines the way in which individuals have come to have a certain status in international law, from the first treaties conferring rights and capacities on individuals through to the present day. The analysis cuts across fields including human rights law, international investment law, international claims processes, humanitarian law and international criminal law in order to draw conclusions about structural change in the international legal system. By engaging with much new literature on non-state actors in international law, the author seeks to dispel myths about state-centrism and the direction in which the international legal system continues to evolve.

KATE PARLETT is an Associate in the public international law and arbitration groups of the Paris office of Freshfields Bruckhaus Deringer LLP. She was previously a research fellow of the Lauterpacht Centre for International Law at the University of Cambridge.

CAMBRIDGE STUDIES IN INTERNATIONAL AND COMPARATIVE LAW

Established in 1946, this series produces high quality scholarship in the fields of public and private international law and comparative law. Although these are distinct legal sub-disciplines, developments since 1946 confirm their interrelation.

Comparative law is increasingly used as a tool in the making of law at national, regional and international levels. Private international law is now often affected by international conventions, and the issues faced by classical conflicts rules are frequently dealt with by substantive harmonisation of law under international auspices. Mixed international arbitrations, especially those involving state economic activity, raise mixed questions of public and private international law, while in many fields (such as the protection of human rights and democratic standards, investment guarantees and international criminal law) international and national systems interact. National constitutional arrangements relating to 'foreign affairs', and to the implementation of international norms, are a focus of attention.

The Board welcomes works of a theoretical or interdisciplinary character, and those focusing on the new approaches to international or comparative law or conflicts of law. Studies of particular institutions or problems are equally welcome, as are translations of the best work published in other languages.

A list of books in the series can be found at the end of this volume.

The Individual in the International Legal System

Kate Parlett's study of the individual in the international legal system examines the way in which individuals have come to have a certain status in international law, from the first treaties conferring rights and capacities on individuals through to the present day. The analysis cuts across fields including human rights law, international investment law, international claims processes, humanitarian law and international criminal law in order to draw conclusions about structural change in the international legal system. By engaging with much new literature on non-state actors in international law, the author seeks to dispel myths about state-centrism and the direction in which the international legal system continues to evolve.

KATE PARLETT is an Associate in the public international law and arbitration groups of the Paris office of Freshfields Bruckhaus Deringer LLP. She was previously a research fellow of the Lauterpacht Centre for International Law at the University of Cambridge.

CAMBRIDGE STUDIES IN INTERNATIONAL AND COMPARATIVE LAW

Established in 1946, this series produces high quality scholarship in the fields of public and private international law and comparative law. Although these are distinct legal sub-disciplines, developments since 1946 confirm their interrelation.

Comparative law is increasingly used as a tool in the making of law at national, regional and international levels. Private international law is now often affected by international conventions, and the issues faced by classical conflicts rules are frequently dealt with by substantive harmonisation of law under international auspices. Mixed international arbitrations, especially those involving state economic activity, raise mixed questions of public and private international law, while in many fields (such as the protection of human rights and democratic standards, investment guarantees and international criminal law) international and national systems interact. National constitutional arrangements relating to 'foreign affairs', and to the implementation of international norms, are a focus of attention.

The Board welcomes works of a theoretical or interdisciplinary character, and those focusing on the new approaches to international or comparative law or conflicts of law. Studies of particular institutions or problems are equally welcome, as are translations of the best work published in other languages.

A list of books in the series can be found at the end of this volume.

The Individual in the International Legal System: Continuity and Change in International Law

Kate Parlett

CAMBRIDGE
UNIVERSITY PRESS

CAMBRIDGE UNIVERSITY PRESS
Cambridge, New York, Melbourne, Madrid, Cape Town,
Singapore, São Paulo, Delhi, Mexico City

Cambridge University Press
The Edinburgh Building, Cambridge CB2 8RU, UK

Published in the United States of America by Cambridge University Press, New York

www.cambridge.org
Information on this title: www.cambridge.org/9780521196666

First published 2011
Reprinted 2012

A catalogue record for this publication is available from the British Library

Library of Congress Cataloguing in Publication Data
Parlett, Kate.
The individual in the international legal system : continuity and change in
international law / Kate Parlett.
p. cm. – (Cambridge studies in international and comparative law ; 75)
ISBN 978-0-521-19666-6 (hardback)
1. Persons (International law) I. Title.
KZ3920.P37 2011
346.01′2–dc22

2010036888

ISBN 978-0-521-19666-6 Hardback

For Ruth Parlett

For Ruth Parlett

Contents

Foreword *page* xiii
Acknowledgements xv
Select list of abbreviations xviii
Table of cases xx
Table of treaties xxxiii

Part I: The Framework 1

1. Structures of the international legal system 3
   1.1 Introduction 3
   1.2 Methodology: a rules-based approach 7
   1.3 The engagement of individuals in the international legal system: structural issues 10
      (a) Prelude: differing legal structures in the early period 10
      (b) The long nineteenth century 13
      (c) The inter-war period 16
      (d) The post-1945 international legal system 26
   1.4 International legal personality as the measure of engagement in the international legal system 29
      (a) Development of the doctrine of subjects: the *Reparations* Opinion 30
      (b) *Sui generis* subjects of international law 32
      (c) The individual as a 'subject' of international law 36
   1.5 Challenges to the centrality of states in the international legal system: alternative approaches 38
      (a) Positivism in its classical and modern forms 40
      (b) Process approaches 42
      (c) 'Cosmopolitanism' 43

Part II: The Individual in International Law 45

2. The individual and international claims 47
 2.1 Introduction 47
 2.2 Doctrine and practice pre-1914 48
  (a) Vattel's articulation 49
  (b) The practice 50
   (i) Arbitration of specifically defined diplomatic protection claims 52
   (ii) Claims tribunals and commissions 54
    (A) Control of the claim 55
    (B) Payment of awards 57
    (C) Binding effect of the decision on an inter-state basis 58
    (D) Standing before the International Prize Court and the Central American Court of Justice 60
  (c) Conclusions 62
 2.3 Doctrine and practice in the inter-war period 65
  (a) The development of doctrine 65
  (b) The practice of international claims tribunals 71
   (i) Mixed arbitral tribunals after the First World War 72
    (A) The mixed arbitral tribunals under the Peace Treaties 72
    (B) The US Mixed Claims Commissions 73
    (C) The Upper Silesian Mixed Commission and Arbitral Tribunal 74
   (ii) Mexican Claims Commissions 1923–1932 77
  (c) Conclusions 83
 2.4 Diplomatic protection and individual claims after 1945 85
  (a) The development of doctrine 85
   (i) Diplomatic protection 85
   (ii) Individual rights 94
  (b) International claims tribunals and commissions 97
   (i) Post-Second World War commissions and tribunals 97
   (ii) The Iran–US Claims Tribunal 98
   (iii) The UN Compensation Commission 101
  (c) Investment treaty arbitration 103
  (d) Conclusions 119

2.5 Conclusions: the position of the individual relative to international claims 120
Appendix I Arbitration of diplomatic protection claims 1794–1914 124
Appendix II International claims tribunals and commissions 1794–1914 134
Appendix III International claims tribunals and commissions 1919–1939 162

3. The individual in international humanitarian law 176
3.1 Introduction 176
3.2 The individual in international armed conflict 177
(a) Regulation of international war pre-1914 177
(b) Developments in the inter-war period 180
(c) The individual in international armed conflict after 1945 181
(i) The 1949 Geneva Conventions 182
(ii) Additional Protocol I of 1977 189
(iii) Customary international humanitarian law 191
(iv) International human rights law applicable in international armed conflict 193
3.3 The individual in internal armed conflict 196
(a) Regulation of civil war pre-1914 198
(b) The inter-war period 206
(c) The individual in internal armed conflict after 1945 208
(i) Common Article 3 of the Geneva Conventions 208
(ii) Additional Protocol II 213
(iii) Customary international humanitarian law 219
(iv) International human rights law applicable in non-international armed conflict 222
3.4 Conclusions: the position of the individual in international humanitarian law 224

4. The individual in international criminal law 229
4.1 Introduction 229
4.2 Individual responsibility before 1919 230
4.3 The inter-war period: the Kaiser and the Leipzig trials 234
4.4 Individual responsibility after 1945 241
(a) Post-Second World War prosecutions 241
(i) The Nuremberg Tribunal 241
(ii) The Tokyo Tribunal 249

(iii) Control Council Law No. 10 trials and military commissions in the Pacific 251
(b) The 'Nuremberg Principles' 253
(c) Development of substantive international criminal law in the United Nations 258
(d) International criminal tribunals and courts 260
(i) Ad hoc international tribunals 261
(ii) The International Criminal Court 267
(iii) International crimes before 'hybrid' and domestic courts 271
4.5 Conclusions: the position of the individual in international criminal law 274

5. The individual in international human rights law 278
5.1 Introduction 278
5.2 Antecedents: the case of slavery 279
5.3 Protection of individuals during the inter-war period 282
(a) Minorities 282
(b) Inhabitants of mandated territories 287
(c) Refugees 291
(d) The International Labour Organisation 294
(e) Conclusions 295
5.4 International protection of human rights after 1945 296
(a) Human rights rhetoric during the Second World War 296
(b) Preparation for an international bill of rights 299
(c) The United Nations Charter: a promise postponed 301
(d) The Universal Declaration of Human Rights 306
(e) From moral imperative to legal articulation: state obligations, individual rights and international enforcement in the European system 307
(f) Human rights and state obligations in the UN system 312
(i) Subject-specific conventions 313
(ii) The International Covenants 315
(iii) Declarations of specific rights 320
(iv) Special procedures before the Human Rights Commission (now the Human Rights Council) 321
(g) Customary international human rights law: from soft to hard law? 322
(h) *Jus cogens* human rights norms 326

(i) The evolution of enforcement mechanisms: the regional systems
(j) Conclusions 327
5.5 Conclusions: the position of the individual in international human rights law 337

Part III: Reassessing the Framework 341

6. Reflections on the structures of the international legal system 343
6.1 Introduction 343
6.2 Historical development of the position of the individual in the international legal system 343
(a) The nineteenth century international legal system 343
(b) The inter-war period 346
(c) The post-1945 international legal system 349
6.3 International legal personality as the measure of engagement: the case of the individual 353
(a) 'Subjects' versus 'objects' 353
(b) Locating individuals: rights, obligations and capacities 358
(c) Moving from the actor to the action? The notion of international law relationships 363
6.4 Reflections on structural transition in the international legal system: the case of the individual 365
(a) Relative openness and flexibility of the system 365
(b) Forces for structural change: solutions above theories 367
(c) States in the international legal system 369

Bibliography 373
Index 394

Foreword

The reach of the international legal system beyond traditional inter-state relations has been the subject of much writing in recent times. Work lamenting the inability of the international legal system to address the challenges of non-state actors obscures, in large part, the reality that the system has come a long way in a short time. Sir Hersch Lauterpacht, one of the first and most fervent advocates for recognition of individuals as subjects of international law,[1] wrote in 1947 that '[a]s a rule, the subjects of the rights and duties arising from the Law of Nations are States solely and exclusively'.[2] Only a few years later, the International Court of Justice recognised that the United Nations was an international legal person;[3] within a decade one could hardly doubt that the individual had a certain standing in international law, albeit in a specialised way. The international legal system, although principally controlled by states, now encompasses a broad range of actors, including with increasing regularity, individuals.

Kate Parlett's study examines afresh one of the classical topics of public international law: the position of the individual in the international legal system. This is – remarkably – the first general work on the individual's standing in international law since the 1960s, and the first study which addresses the topic in a systematic and comprehensive way, explaining how the individual engages and is engaged by international law across a number of fields, covering those areas of international law which are the most significant for individuals.

[1] See, e.g., H. Lauterpacht, *An International Bill of the Rights of Man* (New York, Columbia University Press, 1945).

[2] H. Lauterpacht (ed.), *International Law: A Treatise, by L. Oppenheim* (6th edn, London, Longmans, 1947), 19 (§13).

[3] *Reparations for Injuries Suffered in the Services of the United Nations, ICJ Reports 1949*, p. 174.

The book quite properly takes a historical approach to the subject. Indeed it is hard to imagine not doing so, given the rather fortuitous and episodic character of the various developments. A highlight in that regard is Dr Parlett's account of the PCIJ's famous dictum in *Danzig Railway Officials* – a dictum which not only challenged the received wisdom in general, but specifically appeared to contradict the strongly dualist views of President Anzilotti. Willy-nilly, the system changed from one seen as limited to inter-state relations in the nineteenth century through to the present day where things are much more variegated, not to say confused (confused in that states retain many of their monopolies despite the variegation).

Dr Parlett illustrates the changing scene by focusing on four areas of international law which have the clearest potential to engage individuals, whether as beneficiaries or rights-holders. These are:

- *international claims*, covering diplomatic protection and claims brought directly to an international forum by individuals;
- *international humanitarian law*, covering both international and internal armed conflict;
- *international criminal law*, focusing on the responsibility of individuals directly under international law; and
- *international human rights law*, covering both doctrine and practice and international claims in human rights courts and supervisory bodies.

The book thus reflects on issues relating to structural change and development in the international legal system, building on historical research to dispel certain generally accepted myths. It is a valuable addition to the literature on the doctrine of subjects in international law. In particular it suggests that analysing the relation of particular entities to the international legal system requires a more nuanced and sophisticated approach than the binary – and hoary – categories of 'subjects' and 'objects' permit.

James Crawford
Lauterpacht Centre for International Law
University of Cambridge
12 February 2011

Acknowledgements

This book began with a quizzical inquiry, after the English High Court had held that a bilateral investment treaty which had not been incorporated into English law could nevertheless form the basis of a domestic law claim. This decision stood in contrast to the treatment of human rights treaties: a solid line of authority held that prior to the incorporation of the European Convention on Human Rights by the Human Rights Act 1998, that Convention created no justiciable rights for individuals. This differential treatment may have been explicable on technical bases under domestic law, but it indicated an inherent and more general uncertainty about the relationship of individuals to international law. In an effort to bring clarity to this question, this book explores how the international legal system has changed from the exclusive inter-state Vattelian construct to a system in which individuals have a certain status, and aims to identify more clearly what that status is.

This book is based on my doctoral thesis completed at the University of Cambridge, under the supervision of Professor James Crawford SC. The experience of a doctoral thesis is an inherently solitary one, but the difficulty of embarking on such a project was considerably eased by the supportive and vibrant research community in international law in Cambridge, fostered by the Lauterpacht Centre. It is a testament to Sir Elihu Lauterpacht and a fitting tribute to him and his father, the late Sir Hersch Lauterpacht, that the Centre provides such a welcoming environment for Cambridge students and visitors, and that it fosters academic community in international law. I am grateful to the fellows of the Centre for allowing me to participate in and contribute to the life of the Centre over my five years of residence in Cambridge. My research benefitted from discussions with many of its resident and visiting members and my well-being benefitted from the many friendships formed over morning coffee and cake: in particular I am grateful to Joanna Gomula, Thomas Grant, Penelope Nevill, Roger O'Keefe and Guglielmo Verdirame. I also thank the community of doctoral students in the Faculty of Law; my own research benefitted from their diverse and informed perspectives.

It is to my supervisor, James Crawford, that I am most indebted. He patiently encouraged the project from its inception to its conclusion; he permitted me to indulge my interest in history and discovery and has guided that interest into a coherent work; and he provided comments and guidance in an extraordinarily timely fashion. He combined interest with a scepticism which challenged me to paradigmatically adjust my uncertain optimism for the (possible) futures of the international legal system – at least a little! The book is much better for his input, and I hope it goes some way to meet his expectation.

A number of friends from Cambridge and elsewhere provided comments and advice for which I am grateful: Anita Coles, Anthony Cullen, Kate Gibson, Tom Grant, Megan Hirst, Sarah Joseph, Daniel Joyce, Jonathan Ketcheson, Marcelo Kohen, Conor McCarthy, Sarah Nouwen, Melissa Perry, Anthea Roberts, Sandy Sivakumaran and Kylie Weston-Scheuber. Arnoldo Brenes, Siobhan McKeering, Federica Paddeu and Natalie Vasey kindly assisted with translations. Jonathan Ketcheson also provided technical and helpful assistance with the production of the Appendices to Chapter 2. At Jesus College, Andrew Johnston and Zachary Douglas both provided guidance and welcome advice. Anthony and Nicky Cassimatis, Megan Hirst, Conor McCarthy, Stacy Burgess, Lee Schab and Justice Margaret White provided support and encouragement for the completion of the thesis as well as the book, and I am indebted to them. I am also grateful to Caroline Gill and Charlie Detmold, who warmly welcomed me to Paris as this book was nearing completion and encouraged me to the finish.

My research in Cambridge was supported by the Cambridge Commonwealth Trust, the Gates Trust, Jesus College, the Yorke Fund and the Robbie Jennings Fund. Part of the research was conducted from the University of Melbourne Law School, in the (antipodean) summers of 2008 and 2010, kindly hosted by Associate Professor Andrew Mitchell and Dr Margaret Young. Sharon Burchell, Lucy Kirwan, Verity Quinn and Penny Gleeson provided hospitality in Melbourne and assistance across the miles. My colleagues at the Lauterpacht Centre, in the Costa Rican Foreign Ministry and at Freshfields in Paris were accommodating and encouraging.

My thesis examiners, Professor Christine Gray and Professor Robert McCorquodale, challenged me to make this a better work and I am grateful to them for their very useful feedback. I am also grateful to the anonymous reviewers of my book proposal for their insightful comments. I am indebted to both Finola O'Sullivan and Nienke van Schaverbeke of Cambridge University Press, for supporting the publication of this book and for their efficiency. Richard Woodham, Elizabeth Davison and Rosina Di Marzo were helpful and accommodating through the production process and I am grateful to them.

I am blessed with a wonderful and supportive family, led by my father Peter Parlett, who together with my late mother, Ruth, instilled in me the value of education and that of hard work. Both values have been indispensable to the completion of this book. Natalie, Peter, Holly, Russell, James, Julie, Neil, Marnie and Tamara all provided invaluable support and expressed welcome interest.

I dedicate any good parts in this work to the memory of my mother, Ruth Parlett, who was interested in life, in learning and above all in people.

Kate Parlett
Paris 1 May 2010

Select list of abbreviations

ACHPR	African [Banjul] Charter on Human and Peoples' Rights
ACHR	American Convention on Human Rights
Additional Protocol I	Protocol I Additional to the 1949 Geneva Conventions and Relating to the Protection of Victims of International Armed Conflicts
Additional Protocol II	Protocol II Additional to the 1949 Geneva Conventions and Relating to the Protection of Victims of Non-International Armed Conflicts
BIT	bilateral investment treaty
CAT	Convention Against Torture and Other Cruel, Inhuman or Degrading Treatment or Punishment
CEDAW	Convention on the Elimination of All Forms of Discrimination Against Women
CERD	International Convention on the Elimination of all Forms of Racial Discrimination
CROC	Convention on the Rights of the Child
CTS	Consolidated Treaty Series
ECHR	European Convention for the Protection of Human Rights and Fundamental Freedoms
ECOSOC	United Nations Economic and Social Council
ECT	Energy Charter Treaty
ECtHR	European Court of Human Rights
GA	UN General Assembly
Geneva Convention I	Geneva Convention I for the Amelioration of the Condition of the Wounded and Sick in Armed Forces in the Field

Geneva Convention II	Geneva Convention II for the Amelioration of the Condition of Wounded, Sick and Shipwrecked Members of Armed Forces at Sea
Geneva Convention III	Geneva Convention III Relative to the Treatment of Prisoners of War
Geneva Convention IV	Geneva Convention IV Relative to the Protection of Civilian Persons in Time of War
ICC	International Criminal Court
ICCPR	International Covenant on Civil and Political Rights
ICESCR	International Covenant on Economic, Social and Cultural Rights
ICJ	International Court of Justice
ICRC	International Commission for the Red Cross
ICSID	International Centre for the Settlement of Investment Disputes
ICTR	International Criminal Tribunal for Rwanda
ICTY	International Criminal Tribunal for the former Yugoslavia
ILC	International Law Commission
LNTS	League of Nations Treaty Series
NGO	non-governmental organisation
PCA	Permanent Court of Arbitration
PCIJ	Permanent Court of International Justice
SC	UN Security Council
UDHR	Universal Declaration of Human Rights
UNRIAA	United Nations Reports of International Arbitral Awards
UNTS	United Nations Treaty Series
UNWCC	United Nations War Crimes Commission

Table of cases

Abbasi and another v. *Secretary of State for Foreign and Commonwealth Affairs* [2003] UKHRR 76 *page* 89
Access to German Minority Schools in Upper Silesia, PCIJ Rep. ser. A/B no. 40 (1931) 285
Acquisition of Polish Nationality, Advisory Opinion, PCIJ Rep. ser. B no. 7 (1923) 285
Administrative Decision No. II, German-US Mixed Claims Commission, 1 November 1923, VII UNRIAA 23 74
Administrative Decision No. V, German-US Mixed Claims Commission, 31 October 1924, VII UNRIAA 119 68, 74
Administrator of Germany Property v. *Knoop* [1932] 1 Ch. 439 72
Ahmadou Sadio Diallo (Republic of Guinea v. *Democratic Republic of the Congo)*, Preliminary Objections, ICJ, 24 May 2007 85–6, 93, 106
Akdivar v. *Turkey*, Just Satisfaction, Grand Chamber, 1 April 1998, ECtHR, 23 EHRR 365 332
Albert and LeCompte v. *Belgium*, Judgment, 10 February 1983, ECHR ser. A no. 58 330
Aloeboetoe et al. v. *Suriname, Reparations and Costs*, 10 September 1993, Inter-Am. Ct HR ser. C no. 15 104
American Manufacturing and Trading, Inc. v. *Republic of Zaire*, Award, 21 February 1997, 5 ICSID Rep. 11 59
Antoine Fabiani, French-Venezuelan Commission of 1902, 31 July 1905, X UNRIAA 83 70, 266
Appeal from a Judgment of the Hungaro-Czechoslovak Mixed Arbitral Tribunal (Peter Pázmány University v. *State of Czechoslovakia)*, PCIJ ser. A/B no. 61 (1933) 66

Archer Daniels Midland Company and Tate & Lyle Ingredients Americas, Inc. v. *United Mexican States*, ICSID Case no. ARB (AF)/04/01, Award, 21 November 2007 4, 114, 116–18

Armed Activities on the Territory of the Congo (Democratic Republic of the Congo v. *Uganda)* [2005] ICJ Rep. 116 194

Arrest Warrant of 11 April 2000 (Democratic Republic of Congo v. *Belgium)*, Preliminary Objections and Merits, Judgment [2002] ICJ Rep. 3 85, 325

Asian Agricultural Products Ltd v. *Republic of Sri Lanka*, Award, 27 June 1990, 4 ICSID Rep. 254 104

Association of Italian Knights of the Order of Malta v. *Piccoli*, Italian Court of Cassation, 6 June 1974, 65 ILR 308 33–4

Attorney General (Israel) v. *Adolf Eichmann*, Israeli Supreme Court sitting as a Court of Criminal Appeal (1962) 36 ILR 5 272

Avena and Other Mexican Nationals (Mexico v. *United States)* [2004] ICJ Rep. 12 85, 95–6, 112

Baboeram et al v. *Suriname*, Human Rights Committee, Communication no. 154/83, 10 April 1984 222

Bámaca-Velásquez v. *Guatemala*, Merits, 25 November 2000, Inter-Am. Ct HR ser. C no. 70 222

Banković and others v. *Belgium and others*, Admissibility, Application no. 52207/99, ECtHR, 19 December 2001 194

Barberà, Messengué and Jabardo v. *Spain*, Judgment, 6 December 1988, ECHR ser. A. no. 146 93, 311

Barcelona Traction, Light and Power Co. Ltd (Belgium v. *Spain)* [1970] ICJ Rep. 4 85, 88, 91, 323, 326

B. E. Chattin (United States) v. *United Mexican States*, US-Mexican General Claims Commission, 23 July 1928, IV UNRIAA 284 79

Beaumartin v. *France*, Application no. 15287/89, ECtHR, 25 November 1994, [1994] ECHR 40 89

Bodenkreditbank in Basel and the Swiss Confederation v. *Gebrüder Roher GMBH and the German Federal Republic*, Mixed Commission for the Agreement on German External Debts, 7 November 1956, 25 ILR 326 98

Bouzari v. *Islamic Republic of Iran*, Court of Appeal of Ontario, 30 June 2004, 128 ILR 586 326

Broniowski v Poland, Application no. 31443/96, ECtHR, Judgment, 22 June 2004 333

Campbell v. *MGN* [2003] 1 WLR 740 337
Cape Law Society v. *Van Aardt* (1926) South African Law Reports CPD 312; (1925–6) 3 ILR 43 291
Captain W. H. Gleadell (Great Britain) v. *United Mexican States*, British-Mexican Claims Commission, reported in G. H. Hackworth, *Digest of International Law* (Washington, US Government Printing Office, 1943), vol. 5, p. 805 69
Československá Obchodni Banka AS v. *Slovak Republic*, Decision on Objections to Jurisdiction, 24 May 1999, 14 ICSID Rev. 251 113
Civilian War Claimants' Association v. *The King* [1932] AC 14 72
CMS Gas Transmission Company v. *Republic of Argentina*, ICSID Case no. ARB/01/8, Decision on Annulment, 25 September 2007 110
Coard and others v. *United States*, Inter-American Commission on Human Rights, 29 September 1999, 123 ILR 156 194
Community of Heirs of the Late Fritz Cahn v. *Federal Republic of Germany and Pensionsverein*, Mixed Commission for the Agreement on German External Debts, 12 November 1964, 35 ILR 253 98
Compañía Aguas del Acquija SA and Vivendi Universal v. *Argentine Republic*, Decision on Annulment, 3 July 2002, 6 ICSID Rep. 340 111
Competence of the ILO to Regulate Agricultural Production, PCIJ Rep. ser. B no. 3 (1922) 31
Competence of the ILO to Regulate Conditions of Labour in Agriculture, PCIJ Rep. ser. B no. 2 (1922) 31
Corn Products International, Inc. v. *United Mexican States*, ICSID Case no. ARB(AF)/04/01, Decision on Responsibility, 15 January 2008 4, 114, 116–18
Costello-Roberts v. *United Kingdom*, ECtHR, 1993, ser. A no. 247-C 337
Cyprus v. *Turkey*, Application no. 25781/94, ECtHR, 10 May 2001 194
Dallal v. *Bank Mellat*, HC, 26 July 1985, QB Division, 75 ILR 151 101, 103
Dames and Moore v. *Regan*, 2 July 1981, US Supreme Court, 72 ILR 271 100
Décision et demande en vue d'obtenir l'identification, la localisation, le gel et la saisie des biens et avoirs adressées à la république Portguaise (in prosecution of Jean-Pierra Bemba Gombo), ICC-01/05-01/08, International Criminal Court, 27 May 2008 271

Decision No. 1, Criteria for Expedited Processing of Urgent Claims: For Individuals under Categories A, B and C, UN Compensation Commission, 1991, UN Doc. S/AC.26/1991/1(1991) 102
Decision No. 18 on Distribution of Payments and Transparency, UN Compensation Commission, 1994, UN Doc. S/AC.26/Dec18 (1994) 102
Decision on State Succession to the Obligations of the Former Yugoslavia under the International Covenant on Civil and Political Rights, Human Rights Committee, 19 October 1992, (1992) 15 EHRR 234 223
Delgado Paéz v. *Colombia*, Human Rights Committee, Communication no. 195/1985, 12 July 1990 337
Denise Matthews v. *United Kingdom*, Application no. 24833/94, ECtHR, 18 February 1999 337
Dickson Car Wheel Company (USA) v. *United Mexican States*, US-Mexican General Claims Commission, July 1931, IV UNRIAA 669 81
Doninelli v. *Ebeling*, Mixed Commission for the Agreement on German External Debts, 28 October 1965, 35 ILR 261 98
Douglas v. *Hello!; Venables* v. *News Group* [2002] 2 WLR 992 337
Douglas G. Collie MacNeill (Great Britain) v. *United Mexican States*, British-Mexican Claims Commission, 22 July 1931, V UNRIAA 135 80
EG v. *Poland*, Application no. 50425/99, ECtHR, 23 September 2008 333
Egduardo Trucco, Decision No. 1 (unpublished), Italian-Mexican Claims Commission, cited in A. H. Feller, *The Mexican Claims Commissions 1923–1934: A Study in the Law and Procedure of International Tribunals* (New York, Macmillan Company, 1935), p. 96 69
El Oro Mining and Railway Company (Great Britain) v. *United Mexican States*, British-Mexican Claims Commission, 18 June 1931, V UNRIAA 191 81
Elettronica Sicula SPA (ELSI) (United States v. *Italy)* [1980] ICJ Rep. 15 85, 92
Employment of Women during the Night, PCIJ Rep. ser. A/B no. 50 (1932) 31
Eritrea's Claims 2, 4, 6, 7, 8 and 22, Central Front, Eritrean-Ethiopian Claims Commission, The Hague, Partial Award, 28 April 2004, available at www.pca-cpa.org 192

Eritrea's Claims 15, 16, 23 and 27–32, Civilians Claims, Eritrean-Ethiopian Claims Commission, The Hague, Partial Award, 17 December 2004, available at www.pca-cpa.org 192
Eritrea's Claim 17, Prisoners of War, Eritrean-Ethiopian Claims Commission, The Hague, Partial Award, 1 July 2003, available at www.pca-cpa.org 192
Esphahanian v. *Bank Tejarat*, Case no. 157, Award no. 31-157-2 (1983-I) 2 Iran-US CT Rep. 157 99
Ethiopia's Claim 2, Central Front, Eritrean-Ethiopian Claims Commission, The Hague, Partial Award, 28 April 2004, available at www.pca-cpa.org 192
Ethiopia's Claim 4, Prisoners of War, Eritrean-Ethiopian Claims Commission, The Hague, Partial Award, 1 July 2003, available at www.pca-cpa.org 192
Ethiopia's Claim 5, Civilians Claims, Eritrean-Ethiopian Claims Commission, The Hague, Partial Award, 17 December 2004, available at www.pca-cpa.org 192
Eureko v. *Poland*, Partial Award, 19 August 2005, 12 ICSID Rep. 335 111
European Commission on the Danube, Advisory Opinion, PCIJ Rep. ser. B no. 14 (1927) 31
Exchange of Greek and Turkish Populations, Advisory Opinion, PCIJ Rep. ser. B no. 10 (1925) 22, 285
Factory at Chorzów (Claim for Indemnity), Merits, PCIJ ser. A no. 17 (1928) 70, 105, 271
Fifield v. *The Insurance Co. of the State of Pennsylvania*, 47 PA 166 (1864) 201
Fisheries Jurisdiction (Spain v. *Canada)* [1998] ICJ Rep. 432 85
Free Zones of Upper Savoy and the District of Gex, PCIJ Rep. ser. A/B no. 46 (1932) 96 25
Frelinghuysen v. *Key*, 110 US 63 (1884) 58
F. W. Flack, on behalf of the Estate of the Late D. L. Flack (Great Britain) v. *United Mexican States*, British-Mexican Claims Commission, Decision no. 10, 6 December 1929, V UNRIAA 61 69–70
German Settlers in Poland, Advisory Opinion, PCJ Rep. ser. B no. 6 (1923) 285
H v. *Belgium*, ECtHR, Judgment, 30 November 1987, ECHR ser. A no. 127-B 93, 311

Håkansson and Sturesson v. *Sweden*, ECtHR, Judgment, 21 February 1990, ECHR ser. A. no. 171-A 93, 311
Herrera Rubio v. *Colombia*, Human Rights Committee, Communication no. 161/83, Views of 2 November 1987 222
Ilaşcu and others v. *Moldova*, Application no. 48787/99, ECtHR, 8 July 2004 222
Interhandel (Switzerland v. *United States)*, Preliminary Objections [1959] ICJ Rep. 6 85, 92
International Fisheries Company (United States) v. *United Mexican States*, US-Mexican General Claims Commission, July 1931, IV UNRIAA 691 80
International Status of South-West Africa, Advisory Opinion [1950] ICJ Rep. 128 289
Interoceanic Railway of Mexico (Acapulco to Veracruz) (Ltd), Mexican Eastern Railway Company (Ltd) and Mexican Southern Railway (Ltd) (Great Britain) v. *United Mexican States*, British-Mexican Claims Commission, 18 June 1931, V UNRIAA 178 80
Interpretation of Article 3, Paragraph 2, of the Treaty of Lausanne, PCIJ Rep. ser. B no. 12 (1925) 291
Interpretation of Peace Treaties with Bulgaria, Hungary and Romania, Advisory Opinion [1950] ICJ Rep. 71 305
Interpretation of the Greco-Turkish Agreement of December 1st, 1926, PCIJ Rep. ser. B no. 16 (1928) 285
Interpretation of the Statute of the Memel Territory, PCIJ Rep. ser. A/B no. 49 (1932) 294 24
Islamic Republic of Iran v. *United States*, Case nos. A/15 (IV) and A/24, Award No. 590-A15(IV)/A24-FT, (1998) 34 Iran-US CT Rep. 105 98, 99
Islamic Republic of Iran v. *United States*, Case no. A/18 (1984-I) 5 Iran-US CT Rep. 251 99
Islamic Republic of Iran v. *United States*, Case no. A/21 (1987-I) 14 Iran-US CT Rep. 324 99
ISSA and others v. *Turkey*, Application no. 31821/96, ECtHR, 16 November 2004 222
Ituango Massacres v. *Colombia*, Preliminary Objections, Merits, Reparations and Costs, 1 July 2006, Inter-Am. Ct HR ser. C no. 148 222
Jerusalem, Jaffa District Governor v. *Suleiman Murra* (1926) ER Appeal Cases 321 291

Juridical Condition and Rights of the Undocumented Migrants, OC-18/03, Inter-American Court of Human Rights, Advisory Opinion, 17 September 2003 326
Jurisdiction of the Courts of Danzig (Pecuniary Claims of Danzig Railway Officials who have Passed into the Polish Service, Against the Polish Railways Administration), PCIJ Rep. ser. B no. 15 (1928) 17, 19–26, 28–9, 71, 96, 218, 266, 347, 359–60
Khatsiyeva and others v. *Russia*, Application no. 5108/02, ECtHR, 17 January 2008 222
LaGrand (Germany v. *United States)* [2001] ICJ Rep. 466 85, 94–5, 349, 360
Lanco International Inc. v. *Argentina*, Preliminary Decision on Jurisdiction, 8 December 1998, 5 ICSID Rep. 11 104
Las Palmeras v. *Colombia*, Preliminary Objections, 4 February 2000, Inter-Am. Ct HR ser. C no. 67 222
Lederer v. *German Government*, Anglo-German Mixed Arbitral Tribunal, *Recueil des Décisions des Tribunaux Arbitraux Mixtes* (Paris, 1924) 762 73
Legal Consequences for States of the Continued Presence of South Africa in Namibia, Advisory Opinion [1971] ICJ Rep. 6 304
Legal Consequences of the Construction of a Wall in the Occupied Palestinian Territory, Advisory Opinion [2004] ICJ Rep. 36 193, 195, 318
Legal Status and Human Rights of the Child, Inter-American Court of Human Rights, Advisory Opinion OC-17/02, 28 August 2002, (2004) 11 IHRR 510 359
LG&E Energy Corp., LG&E Capital Corp. and LG&E International Inc. v. *Argentina*, ICSID Case no. ARB/02/1, Decision on Liability, 3 October 2006 110, 112
LG&E Energy Corp., LG&E Capital Corp. and LG&E International Inc. v. *Argentine Republic*, ICSID Case no. ARB/02/1, Award, 3 October 2006 116
Lonrho Exports Ltd v. *Export Credits Guarantee Department* [1996] 4 All ER 673 72
Lord Corporation (a claim of less than US $250,000 presented by the United States, Claimant v. *Iran Helicopter Support and Renewal Co., Respondent*, Award no. 346-10973-2 (1988-I) 18 Iran-US CT Rep. 377 99
Lundevall v. *Sweden*, ECtHR, Judgment, 12 November 2002 (unreported) 93, 312

Maffezini (Emilio Agustín) v. *Kingdom of Spain*, Decision on Objections to Jurisdiction, 25 January 2000, 5 ICSID Rep. 396 113

Mamatkulov and Askarvo v. *Turkey*, Application nos. 46827/99 and 46951/99, ECtHR Grand Chamber, 4 February 2005 334

Mapiripán Massacre v. *Colombia*, Merits, Reparations and Costs, 15 September 2005, Inter-Am. Ct HR ser. C no. 134 222, 330

Maria Guadalupe A. Vve. Markassuza, Sentence No. 38 (unpublished), French-Mexican Claims Commission, cited in A. H. Feller, *The Mexican Claims Commissions 1923–1934: A Study in the Law and Procedure of International Tribunals* (New York, Macmillan Company, 1935), p. 97 69

Mavrommatis Palestine Concessions, Judgment no. 2, PCIJ ser. A no. 2 (1924) 65–6, 70, 291

McGonnell v. *United Kingdom*, ECtHR, Judgment, 8 February 2000, ECHR Rep. 2000-II 93, 311

Melczer Mining Company (USA) v. *United Mexican States*, US-Mexican General Claims Commission, 30 April 1929, IV UNRIAA 481 82

Mexican Union Railway (Ltd) (Great Britain) v. *United Mexican States*, British-Mexican Claims Commission, Decision no. 21, February 1930, V UNRIAA 115 82

Mexico City Bombardment Claims (Great Britain) v. *United Mexican States*, British-Mexican Claims Commission, Decision no. 12, 15 February 1930, V UNRIAA 76 81

Ministry of Finance v. *Association of Italian Knights of the Order of Malta*, Italian Court of Cassation, 3 May 1978, 65 ILR 320 34

Minnie Stevens Eschauzier (Great Britain) v. *United Mexican States*, British-Mexican Claims Commission, Decision no. 64, 24 June 1931, V UNRIAA 207 69

Minority Schools in Albania, PCIJ Rep. ser. A/B no. 64 (1935) 285

Mondev International Ltd v. *United States*, Award, 11 October 2002, 6 ICSID Rep. 192 105

Nanni v. *Pace and the Sovereign Order of Malta*, Italian Court of Cassation, 13 March 1935, 8 ILR 2 33

Nationality Decrees Issued in Tunis and Morocco, Advisory Opinion PCIJ Rep. ser. B no. 4 (1923) 309

North American Dredging Company of Texas (United States) v. *United Mexican States*, US-Mexican General Claims Commission, 31 March 1926, IV UNRIAA 26 80

Oberschlick v. *Austria*, ECtHR, Judgment, 23 May 1991, ECHR ser. A no. 204 93, 311
Oil Platforms (Iran v. *United States)* [2003] ICJ Rep. 161 85
Pailot v. *France*, ECtHR, 22 April 1998, ECHR Rep. 1998-II 311
Panevezys-Saldutikis Railway (Estonia v. *Lativa)*, PCIJ ser. A/B no. 76 (1939) 66–8, 91
Payment of Various Serbian Loans Issued in France/Payment in Gold of Brazilian Federal Loans Issued in France, PCIJ ser. A nos. 20/21 (1929) 66–7
Personal Work of Employers, PCIJ Rep. ser. B no. 13 (1926) 31
Pfeifer and Plankl v. *Austria*, ECtHR, Judgment, 25 February 1992, ECHR ser. A no. 227 312
Piccoli v. *Association of the Italian Knights of the Order of Malta*, Court of Appeal, Rome, 23 January 1978, 77 ILR 613 34
Piracy Jure Gentium, In re [1934] AC 586 232
Private Armed Brig of War General Armstrong, Report of the US Court of Claims, 1 February 1858, S. Mis. Doc. 142, 35 Cong. 1 sess. 106–16 53–4
Prize Cases (1862) 2 Black 635, 17 L 459 200
Prosecutor v. *Blagojoe Simic, Milan Simic, Miroslav Tadic, Stevan Todorovic, Simo Zaric*, Case no. IT-95-P, ICTY Trial Chamber, Decision on the Prosecution Motion under Rule 73 for a Ruling concerning the Testimony of a Witness, 27 July 1999 34, 36
Prosecutor v. *Delalić, Mucić, Delić and Landžo* (*Celebici* case), Case no. IT-96-21-A, Appeals Chamber, 20 February 2001 221, 251
Prosecutor v. *Delalić, Mucić, Delić and Landžo*, Case no. IT-96-21-T, Judgment, 16 November 1998 209, 326
Prosecutor v. *Furundžija*, Case no. IT-95-21-T, Judgment, 10 December 1998, (1999) 38 ILM 317 209, 326
Prosecutor v. *Kanyabashi*, Case no. ICTR-96-15-T, Decision on the Defence Motion on Jurisdiction, 18 June 1997 265–6
Prosecutor v. *Kunarac, Kovać and Vuković*, Case no. IT-96-23-T, Judgment, 22 February 2001 326
Prosecutor v. *Moinina Fofana*, Case no. SCSL-2004-14-AR72(E), Appeals Chamber, Decision on Preliminary Motion on Lack of Jurisdiction Ratione Materiae: Nature of the Armed Conflict, 25 May 2004 273
Prosecutor v. *Rutaganda*, Case no. ICTR-96-3, Judgment, 6 December 1999, (2000) 39 ILM 557 209

Prosecutor v. *Tadić*, Case no. IT-94-1-AR72, Appeal on Jurisdiction, 2 October 1995, (1996) 35 ILM 32 189, 209, 220–1, 261, 264–5, 270
Prosecutor v. *Tadić*, Case no. IT-94-1-AR72, Trial Chamber, Decision on Defence Motion on Jurisdiction (Rule 73), 10 August 1995 264
Quirin, Ex Parte, 317 US 1 (1942) 242
Reparations for Injuries Suffered in the Services of the United Nations [1949] ICJ Rep. 174 30–2, 354, 356–7
Republic of Ecuador v. *Occidental Exploration and Production Company*, High Court Queen's Bench Division [2005] EWHC 774 (Comm) 107
Republic of Ecuador v. *Occidental Exploration and Production Company*, Court of Appeal (Civil Division) [2006] 1 QB 432 107–8, 111
Rex v. *Christian* (1924) South African Law Reports 101 291
Salas v. *United States*, Inter-American Commission on Human Rights, 14 October 1993, 123 ILR 117 194
Salman v. *Turkey*, Merits, ECtHR Grand Chamber, 27 June 2000, 34 EHRR 17 332
Saluka Investments BV v. *Czech Republic*, Decision on Jurisdiction over the Czech Republic's Counterclaim, 7 May 2004, 1 ICSID Rep. 543 104
Sanjuan Arevalo v. *Colombia*, Human Rights Committee, Communication no. 181/84, 3 November 1989 222
Santullo v. *Uruguay*, Human Rights Committee, Communication no. 9/1977, 20 February 1977 337
Schöps v. *Germany*, ECtHR, Judgment, 13 February 2001, ECHR Rep. 2001-I 312
Sejdovic v. *Italy*, Application no. 56581/00, ECtHR, 10 November 2004 333
Serrano-Cruz Sisters v. *El Salvador*, Preliminary Objections, 23 November 2004, Inter-Am. Ct HR ser. C no. 118 222
SGS Société Générale de Surveillance SA v. *Islamic Republic of Pakistan*, Decision on Objections to Jurisdiction, 6 August 2003, 8 ICSID Rep. 383 112
SGS Société Générale de Surveillance SA v. *Republic of the Philippines*, Decision on Objections to Jurisdiction, 29 January 2004, 8 ICSID Rep. 515 112–13

Siderman de Blake v. *Republic of Argentina*, US Court of Appeals (Ninth Circuit), 22 May 1992, 103 ILR 472 326
Siemens AG v. *Argentine Republic*, Decision on Jurisdiction, 3 August 2004, 12 ICSID Rep. 174 113
Sigwald Charles v. *Germany*, French-German Mixed Arbitral Tribunal, 27 August 1926, 4 ILR 337 73
Smith v. *Brown* (1705) 91 ER 566 281
Somerset v. *Stewart* (1772) 98 ER 499 281
Sosa v. *Alvarez-Machain*, 124 S. Ct 2739 (2004) 325
Sovereign Order of Malta v. *Brunelli, Tacali and others*, Italian Court of Cassation, 17 December 1931, 6 ILR 46 34
Sovereign Order of Malta v. *Société Anonyme Commerciale*, Tribunal of Rome, 3 November 1954, 22 ILR 1 34
SS Lotus, PCIJ Rep. ser. A no. 10 (1927) 41
Steiner and Gross v. *Polish State*, Upper Silesian Arbitral Tribunal, 30 March 1928, 4 ILR 291 76, 232
Suresh v. *Canada*, Supreme Court of Canada, 11 January 2002, 124 ILR 344 326
Tangiora v. *Wellington District Legal Services Committee*, Privy Council (1999) 124 ILR 570 371
The Ambrose Light, 25 Fed. Rep. 44 203
The Anzures Land Company (Ltd) (Great Britain) v. *United Mexican States*, British-Mexican Claims Commission, Decision no. 62, 24 June 1931, V UNRIAA 207 81
The Hiawatha, 12 Fed. Cas. 95 (DC SD NY, 1861) 201
The Loewen Group Inc. and Raymond L. Loewen v. *United States*, Award, 26 June 2003, 7 ICSID Rep. 421 107
The Right to Information on Consular Assistance in the Framework of the Guarantees of the Due Process of Law, Advisory Opinion OC-16/99, Inter American Court of Human Rights, 1 October 1999 94
The Three Friends, 166 US 1 (1897) 203
Thornington v. *Smith*, 75 US (8 Wall) 1 (1868) 201
Tokios Tokelès v. *Ukraine*, Decision on Jurisdiction, 29 April 2004, 20 ICSID Rep. 205 113
United Kingdom in re Hong Kong and Shanghai Banking Corporation v. *Japan*, Anglo-Japanese Property Commission, 21 November 1960, 29 ILR 383 98
United Kingdom in re International Electrolytic Plant Company Ltd v. *Japan*, Anglo-Japanese Property Commission, 30 November 1960, 29 ILR 308 98

United Kingdom in re Struthers and others v. *Japan*, Anglo-Japanese Property Commission, 30 November 1960, 29 ILR 389 98
United States v. *Altstoetter* (1951) III Trials of War Criminals Before the Nuernberg Military Tribunals under Control Council Law No. 10 968 252
United States v. *Freidrich Flick* (1950) VI Trials of War Criminals Before the Nuernberg Military Tribunals under Control Council Law No. 10 1187 252
United States v. *La Abra Silver Mining Co.*, 29 US Court of Claims 432 (1899) 58
United States v. *Otto Ohendorf* (1950) VI Trials of War Criminals Before the Nuernberg Military Tribunals under Control Council Law No. 10 411 252
United States v. *Wilhelm von Leeb* (1950) XI Trials of War Criminals Before the Nuernberg Military Tribunals under Control Council Law No. 10 462 252
United States ex rel Boynton v. *Blaine*, 139 US 306 (1891) 58
United States, on behalf of US nationals and Islamic Republic of Iran, Award on Agreed Terms no. 483, Claims of less than US$250,000/86/B38/B76/B77-FT, 22 June 1990 (1990-II) 25 Iran-US CT Rep. 327 99
United States Diplomatic and Consular Staff in Tehran (United States v. *Iran)*, Merits [1980] ICJ Rep. 3 85, 304, 323
Velásquez Rodríguez v. *Honduras*, Inter-American Court of Human Rights, 29 July 1988, ser. C no. 4, (1988) 9 HRLJ 212 337
Velásquez Rodríguez (Interpretation of Compensatory Damages), Judgment, 17 August 1990, Inter-Am. Ct HR ser. C no. 9 (1990) 330
Vienna Convention on Consular Relations (Paraguay v. *United States)* [1998] ICJ Rep. 248 85
Victims of the Tugboat '13 de Marzo' v. *Cuba*, Case no. 11.436, Inter-American Commission of Human Rights, 16 October 1996, Report no. 47/96, Inter-Am.CHR,OEA/Ser.L/V/II.95 Doc. 7 rev. (1997) 326
Waite and Kennedy v. *Germany*, Application no 26083/94, ECtHR, Judgment, 18 February 1999 337
Wellington District Legal Services Committee v. *Tangiora*, New Zealand Supreme Court (1997) 115 ILR 655 371
William A. Parker (USA) v. *United Mexican States*, US-Mexican General Claims Commission, 31 March 1926, IV UNRIAA 35 81

William E. Bowerman and Messrs Burberry's (Ltd) (Great Britain) v. *United Mexican States*, British-Mexican Claims Commission, Decision no. 18, 15 February 1930, V UNRIAA 104 81
Witkowska-Tobola v. *Poland*, Application no. 11208/02, ECtHR, 4 December 2007 333
Wolkenberg and others v. *Poland*, Application no. 50003/99, ECtHR, 4 December 2007 333
Yamashita, In re, 66 Sup. Ct 340 (1946) 242
Zoppot Street Crossing, Danzig High Court, 16 January 1934, 7 ILR 269 22

Table of treaties

First Treaty of Partition between France, Great Britain and the Netherlands, signed at Loo/The Hague, 24 September/11 October 1698, 22 CTS 197 *page* 12

Second Treaty of Partition between France, Great Britain and the Netherlands, signed at London/The Hague, 13/25 March 1700, 22 CTS 471 12

US–Great Britain, 19 November 1794, Moore (1898), vol. I, p. 271 50–1, 55, 57, 134

Spain–US, 27 October 1795, Malloy (1910), vol. I, p. 1013, Moore (1898), vol. II, p. 991 51, 55, 57, 134

US–France, 30 April 1803, Moore (1898), vol. V, p. 4434 135

US–Great Britain, 30 June/12 July 1822, Moore (1898), vol. I, p. 363 55, 124

Mexico–US, 11 April 1839, Malloy (1910), vol. I, p. 1101; Feller (1935), p. 3; Moore (1898), vol. II, p. 1229 135

Great Britain–France, 14 November 1842, Moore (1898), vol. V, p. 4936 52, 124

France–Spain, 15 February 1851, 105 CTS 153, de Clerq (1864), vol. VI, p. 81 52, 125

US–Portugal, 28 February 1851, Moore (1898), vol. II, p. 1092 52, 53, 125

US–Great Britain, 8 February 1853, Moore (1898), vol. I, p. 391 50, 56–7, 59, 137

Great Britain–Portugal, [date of treaty unknown, award given in 1856], Moore (1898), vol. V, 4979 52, 126

US–New Granada, 10 September 1857, Moore (1898), vol. II, p. 1361 56–7, 138

Brazil–Great Britain, 2 June 1858, 119 CTS 91, XLVIII BFSP 18 56, 59, 138
US–Chile, 10 November 1858, Moore (1898), vol. II, p. 1460 126
US–Paraguay, 4 February 1859, Moore (1898), vol. II, p. 1485 52, 53, 126
US–Costa Rica, 2 July 1860, Moore (1898), vol. II, p. 1551 56, 139
Great Britain–Portugal, [date of treaty unknown, award given in 1861], Moore (1898), vol. V, p. 4984 126
Ecuador–US, 25 November 1862, Moore (1898), vol. II, p. 1569 140
US–Peru, 23 December 1862, Moore (1898), vol. II. p. 1610 52, 126
US–Peru, 12 January 1863, Moore (1898), vol. II, p. 1613 56, 140
Great Britain–US, 1 July 1863, Moore (1898), vol. I, p. 237 52, 53, 127
Great Britain–Peru, [date of treaty unknown, award given in 1864], Moore (1898), vol. V, 4967 52, 127
US–Colombia, 10 February 1864, Moore (1898), vol. II, p. 1361 56, 141
France–Mexico, 10 April 1864, 54 BFSP 926; Feller (1935), p. 9 141
Geneva Convention for the Amelioration of the Wounded, 22 August 1864 (entry into force 22 June 1865), 129 CTS 361 179, 231
US–Venezuela, 25 April 1866, Malloy (1910), vol. II, p. 1856; Moore (1898), vol. II, p. 1659 56–7, 59, 141
Great Britain–Mexico, 26 June 1866, Feller (1935), pp. 9–11; Moore (1898), vol. V, p. 4948 56, 59, 141
Great Britain–Spain, 4 March 1868 (1867–8) LVIII BFSP 2; Moore (1898), vol. V, p. 5018 52, 53, 126
US–Salvador, 4 May 1868, Moore (1898), vol. II, p. 1857 127
Mexico–US, 4 July 1868, Malloy (1910), vol. I, p. 1128; Moore (1898), vol. II, p. 1659 56, 59, 143
Great Britain–Venezuela, 21 September 1868, Moore (1898), vol. V, p. 5017 144
Peru–US, 4 December 1868, Moore (1898), vol. II, p. 1639 144
Declaration Renouncing the Use, in Time of War, of Explosive Projectiles under 400 Grammes Weight, 11 December 1868 (entry into force 11 December 1868), IXIV UKPP (1869) 659 178
US–Brazil, 14 March 1870, Moore (1898), vol. II, p. 1733 52, 126
Spain–US, 16 June 1870, Moore (1898), vol. II, p. 1007 52, 53, 128
Spain–US, 12 February 1871, Moore (1898), vol. II, p. 1019; Malloy (1910), vol. I, p. 1661; (1871–2) 147 CTS 1 55, 57, 59, 145
Great Britain–US, 8 May 1871, Moore (1898), vol. I, pp. 495 and 683; de la Pradelle (1955), vol. III, p. 41 56–7, 59, 146

Brazil–Paraguay, 9 January 1872, 144 CTS 149 147
Great Britain–Colombia, 14 December 1872, Moore (1898), vol. II, p. 2050 52, 128
Japan–Peru, June 1873, Moore (1898), vol. II, p. 5034 52, 129
Great Britain–France, 23 July 1873, Moore (1898), vol. V, p. 4938; LXIII BFSP 207–13 52, 53, 129
US–Colombia, 17 August 1874, Moore (1898), vol. II, p. 1421 52, 53, 129
France–US, 15 January 1880, Moore (1898), vol. II, p. 1133 56–7, 147
Netherlands–Dominican Republic, 26 March 1881, Moore (1898), vol. V, p. 5036 52, 129
Haiti–US, 1883, Moore (1898), vol. II, p. 1860 52, 129
Great Britain–Chile, 4 January 1883, Moore (1898), vol. V, p. 4928 147
Chile–France, 1883/1884, Moore (1898), vol. V, p. 4929 148
Chile–Italy, 1883/1884, Moore (1898), vol. V, p. 4929 148
US–China, 1884, Moore (1898), vol. II, p. 1858 52, 130
Haiti–US, 24 May 1884, Moore (1898), vol. II, p. 1749 130
Belgium–Chile, 30 August 1884, 164 CTS 283; LXXV BFSP 495 148
Spain–US, 1885, Moore (1898), vol. II, p. 1811 130
US–Venezuela, 5 December 1885, Malloy (1910), p. 1858; Moore (1898), vol. II, p. 1665 56–7, 148
Guatemala–Mexico, 26 January 1888, 170 CTS 467 56, 59, 149
US–Haiti, 24 May 1888, Moore (1898), vol. II, p. 1811 52, 131
US–Denmark, 6 December 1888, Moore (1898), vol. II, p. 1185 52, 131
Great Britain–Haiti, 1890, Moore (1898), vol. V, p. 4947 150
Italy–Persia, 5 June 1890, Moore (1898), vol. V, p. 5018 52, 131
US–Great Britain–Portugal, 13 June 1891, Moore (1898), vol. II, p. 1865 52–3, 131
Italy–Portugal, 1 September 1891, Moore (1898), vol. V, p. 5021 131
US–Venezuela, 1 January 1892, Moore (1898), vol. II, p. 1693 52–3, 56, 131
Chile–US, 7 August 1892, Moore (1898), vol. II, p. 1469 56–7, 150
US–Ecuador, 28 February 1893, Moore (1898), vol. II, p. 1587 52, 132
Chile–Great Britain, 26 September 1893, Moore (1898), vol. V, p. 4930 151
Great Britain–Netherlands, 16 May 1895, Moore (1898), vol. V, p. 4948 52–3, 132
Chile–Sweden/Norway, 6 July 1895, Moore (1989), vol. V, p. 4935 151

US–Great Britain, 8 February 1896, Moore (1898), vol. I, p. 960 56, 151
Brazil–Italy, 12 February 1896, Moore (1898), vol. V, p. 5018 152
US–Siam, 1896–7, Moore (1898), vol. II, p. 1863 52, 132
US–Siam, 1896–7, Moore (1898), vol. II, p. 1899 52, 133
Hague Declaration II Concerning Asphyxiating Gases, 29 July 1899 (entry into force 4 September 1900), 187 CTS 435 178
Hague Declaration III Concerning Expanding Bullets, 29 July 1899 (entry into force 4 September 1900), 187 CTS 459 178
Convention Extending the 1864 Geneva Convention of 1864 to Maritime War, 29 July 1899, 187 CTS 443 179
France–Venezuela, 19 February 1902, X UNRIAA 11 152
US–Mexico, 22 May 1902, Wilson (1915), p. 1 132
Great Britain–Russia, 1 June 1902, IX UNRIAA 51 52, 133
Germany–Venezuela, 13 February 1903, IX UNRIAA 359 56–7, 154
Italy–Venezuela, 13 February 1903, X UNRIAA 479 56, 154
Mexico–Venezuela, 13 February 1903, X UNRIAA 695 56, 59, 150
US–Venezuela, 13 February 1903, 1010 BFSP 646, IX UNRIAA 115 56, 59, 155
Venezuela–Great Britain, 13 February 1903, IX UNRIAA 351 56–7, 153
France–Venezuela, 27 February 1903, X UNRIAA 3 56, 59, 176
Netherlands–Venezuela, 28 February 1903, X UNRIAA 709 56–7, 59, 157
Belgium–Venezuela, 7 March 1903, IX UNRIAA 321 56, 59, 157
Sweden/Norway–Venezuela, 10 March 1903, X UNRIAA 763 56, 59, 157
Spain–Venezuela, 2 April 1903, X UNRIAA 737 56, 59, 158
Brazil–Bolivia, 17 November 1903, 194 CTS 249 159
Brazil–Peru, 12 July 1904, 196 CTS 106 57, 59, 159
Convention for the Amelioration of Wounded and Sick in Armies, 9 July 1906 (entry into force 9 August 1907), 202 CTS 144 179, 231
Hague Convention IV Respecting the Laws and Customs of War on Land, 18 October 1907 (entry into force 26 January 1910), 205 CTS 277 178–9
Annex to the Hague Convention IV, Regulations Respecting the Laws and Customs of War on Land, 18 October 1907, 205 CTS 277 178
Hague Convention XII Relative to the Creation of an International Prize Court, The Hague, 18 October 1907 (not yet in force), reproduced in (1908) 2 *AJIL* 174 60, 160

El Salvador–Nicaragua–Costa Rica–Honduras–Guatemala, 20 December 1907, (1908) 2 *AJIL* 231 61, 160, 344
London Naval Conference, 26 February 1909 (not yet in force), reproduced in (1909) 3 *AJIL Supplement* 179 61
Additional Protocol to the Convention Relative to the Establishment of an International Court of Prize, signed at The Hague, 19 September 1910 (not yet in force), reproduced in (1911) 5 *AJIL Supplement* 95 60
Treaty of Peace between the United States, the British Empire, France, Italy and Japan, and Poland, 28 June 1919 (entry into force 10 January 1920), 225 CTS 412 75, 283–4
Covenant of the League of Nations, 28 June 1919 (entry into force 10 January 1920), 108 LNTS 188 282, 287, 289
Treaty of Versailles, 28 June 1919, UKTS 4 (Cmd 153) 19, 72–3, 162, 236, 238, 240–1, 283, 294, 349
Treaty of St Germain-en-Laye, 10 September 1919, UKTS 11 (Cmd 400) 72–3, 163, 283
Treaty of Neuilly, 27 November 1919, UKTS 5 (Cmd 522) 72–3, 163, 283
Treaty of Trianon, 4 June 1920, UKTS 10 (Cmd 896) 72–3, 163, 283
US–Peru, 21 May 1921, I UNRIAA 347 71
US–Norway, 30 June 1921, I UNRIAA 309 71, 164
Great Britain–Costa Rica, 12 January 1922, I UNRIAA 371 71
Treaty Relating to the Use of Submarines and Noxious Gases in Warfare, Washington, DC, 6 February 1922 (not yet in force), 25 LNTS 202 181
Germany–Poland, Geneva Convention Concerning Upper Silesia, 15 May 1922, 9 LNTS 466 75–6, 164
Arrangement with regard to the Issue of Certificates of Identity to Russian Refugees, 5 July 1922, 355 LNTS 238 292
Germany–US, 10 August 1922, 48 LNTS 69 74, 165
Treaty of Lausanne, 24 July 1923, UKTS 16 (Cmd 1929) 72–3, 167, 238
US–Mexico, General Claims Convention, 8 September 1923, Feller (1935), Appendix 77–83, 167–8
US–Mexico, Special Claims Convention, 10 September 1923, Feller (1935), Appendix 77–83, 169
Canada–US, 23 January 1924, III UNRIAA 1610 71, 169
France–Mexico, 24 September 1924, Feller (1935), Appendix 70, 77–83, 170

US–Austria–Hungary, 26 November 1924, 48 LNTS 69 74, 171
Germany–Mexico, 16 March 1925, Feller (1935), Appendix 77, 171
Geneva Protocol for the Prohibition of the Use in War of Asphyxiating, Poisonous or Other Gases, and of Bacteriological Methods of Warfare, 17 June 1925 (entry into force 8 February 1928), 126 BFSP (1927) 324 181
Spain–Mexico, 25 November 1925, Feller (1935), Appendix 77–83, 172
Panama–US, 28 July 1926, 138 LNTS 119 71–2, 172
Slavery Convention, 25 September 1926 (entry into force 9 March 1927), 60 LNTS 253 281, 344
Great Britain–Mexico, 19 November 1926, Feller (1935), Appendix 70, 77–83, 173
Italy–Mexico, 13 January 1927, Feller (1935), Appendix 77–83, 173
Belgium–Mexico, 14 May 1927, Feller (1935), Appendix 77–83, 173
Great Britain–Ethiopia, 13 September 1927, II UNRIAA 823 71
Arrangement Concerning the Extension to Other Categories of Refugee of Certain Measures Taken in Favour of Russian and Armenian Refugees, 30 June 1928, 2006 LNTS 65 292
Arrangement Relating to the Legal Status of Russian and Armenian Refugees, 30 June 1928, 89 LNTS 53 292
Geneva Convention for the Amelioration of the Condition of the Wounded and Sick in Armies in the Field, 27 July 1929 (entry into force 19 June 1931), 118 LNTS 303 180
Geneva Convention on Prisoners of War, 27 July 1929 (entry into force 19 June 1931), 118 LNTS 343 35, 180, 184
US–Guatemala, 2 November 1929, II UNRIAA 1081 71
France–Great Britain, 4 March 1930, II UNRIAA 1114; (1932) 26 *AJIL* 804 71
Convention no. 29 Concerning Forced Labour, 28 June 1930 (entry into force 1 May 1932), available at www.unhchr.ch/html/menu3/b/31.htm 294
Great Britain–Portugal, 1 August 1930, II UNRIAA 1146, 7 ILR 261 71
Sweden–US, 17 December 1930, II UNRIAA 1241 71
US–Egypt, 20 January 1931, II UNRIAA 1163 71
Finland–Great Britain, 30 September 1932, III UNRIAA 1480 71
Great Britain–Panama, 15 October 1932, III UNRIAA 1440 71
Convention Relating to the International Status of Refugees, 28 October 1933 (entry into force 13 June 1935), 159 LNTS 3663 293

Provisional Arrangement Concerning the Status of Refugees Coming from Germany, 4 July 1936, 3952 LNTS 77 293
Convention Concerning the Status of Refugees Coming from Germany, 10 February 1938, 4461 LNTS 61 293
Mexico–US, 11 April 1939, Malloy (1910), vol. I, p. 1103; Moore (1898), vol. II, p. 1229 55
Additional Protocol Concerning the Status of Refugees Coming from Germany, 14 September 1939, 4634 LNTS 142 293
London Agreement for the Prosecution and Punishment of the Major War Criminals of the European Axis Powers and Charter of the International Military Tribunal, 8 August 1945 (entry into force 8 August 1945) 8 UNTS 279 244–5, 247
Special Proclamation, Establishment of an International Military Tribunal for the Far East, 19 January 1946, IAS no. 1589, 3 249–50
Italy–United Nations (US, UK, the Netherlands, France), 10 February 1947, 49 UNTS 126, XIV UNRIAA 1 97
Convention on the Prevention and Punishment of the Crime of Genocide, 1 January 1948 (entry into force 12 January 1951), 78 UNTS 277 258–9, 313
Universal Declaration of Human Rights, 10 December 1948, UN GA Res. 217A(III) 282, 306–7, 336
Convention Against Torture and Other Cruel, Inhuman or Degrading Treatment or Punishment, 10 December 1948 (entry into force 26 June 1987), 1465 UNTS 85 258
Geneva Convention I for the Amelioration of the Condition of the Wounded and Sick in Armed Forces in the Field, 12 August 1949 (entry into force 21 October 1950), 75 UNTS 31 35, 182–4, 188, 191, 350
Geneva Convention II for the Amelioration of the Condition of Wounded, Sick and Shipwrecked Members of Armed Forces at Sea, 12 August 1949 (entry into force 21 October 1950), 75 UNTS 85 35, 182–4, 188, 191, 350
Geneva Convention III Relative to the Treatment of Prisoners of War, 12 August 1949 (entry into force 21 October 1950), 75 UNTS 135 35, 183–4, 188, 191, 350
Geneva Convention IV Relative to the Protection of Civilian Persons in Time of War, 12 August 1949 (entry into force 21 October 1950), 75 UNTS 287 35, 182–4, 188, 191, 350

European Convention for the Protection of Human Rights and Fundamental Freedoms, 4 November 1950 (entry into force 3 September 1953), 87 UNTS 103 282, 309–10
Japan–Allied Powers, Treaty of Peace, 8 September 1951, 136 UNTS 46 97
Japan–Allied Powers, Agreement for Settlement of Disputes, 12 June 1952, 138 UNTS 183, XIV UNRIAA 447 97
Allied Powers–Germany, 27 February 1953, 333 UNTS 2–263 98
Supplementary Convention on the Abolition of Slavery, the Slave Trade, and Institutions and Practices Similar to Slavery, 7 September 1956 (entry into force 30 April 1957), 266 UNTS 3 281
Austria–Germany, 15 June 1957, reproduced in Oellers-Frahm (1984), p. 784 98
Convention no. 105 Concerning the Abolition of Forced Labour, 25 June 1957 (entry into force 17 January 1959), available at www.unhchr.ch/html/menu3/b/32.htm 294
Convention on the Settlement of Investment Disputes between States and Nationals of Other States, 18 March 1965 (entry into force 14 October 1966), 575 UNTS 159 103–4
International Convention on the Elimination of All Forms of Racial Discrimination, 21 December 1965 (entry into force 4 January 1969), 660 UNTS 195 313–14, 315
International Covenant on Civil and Political Rights, 16 December 1966 (entry into force 23 March 1976), 999 UNTS 171 316
International Covenant on Economic, Social and Cultural Rights, 19 December 1966 (entry into force 3 January 1976), 993 UNTS 3 317–18
Vienna Convention on the Law of Treaties, 22 May 1969 (entered into force 27 January 1980) 1155 UNTS 331 25
American Convention on Human Rights, 22 November 1969 (entry into force 18 July 1978), 1144 UNTS 123 328–9, 330, 336
International Convention on the Suppression and Punishment of the Crime of Apartheid, 30 November 1973 (entry into force 18 July 1976), 1015 UNTS 243 315
Protocol I Additional to the Geneva Conventions of 12 August 1949 and Relating to the Protection of Victims of International Armed Conflicts, 8 June 1977 (entry into force 7 December 1978), 1125 UNTS 3 189–91, 213, 217, 270

Protocol II Additional to the Geneva Conventions of 12 August 1949 and Relating to the Protection of Victims of Non-International Armed Conflicts, 8 June 1977 (entry into force 7 December 1978), 1125 UNTS 606 191, 213, 350
Convention on the Elimination of All Forms of Discrimination Against Women, 18 December 1979 (entry into force 3 September 1981), 1249 UNTS 13 314
Convention on Prohibitions or Restriction on the Use of Certain Conventional Weapons which May be Deemed to be Excessively Injurious or to Have Indiscriminate Effects, 10 October 1980 (entry into force 2 December 1983), 1342 UNTS 137 182
African (Banjul) Charter on Human and Peoples' Rights, 27 June 1981 (entry into force 21 October 1986), 21 ILM 58 328, 330, 336
Declaration of the Government of the Democratic and Popular Republic of Algeria Concerning the Settlement of Claims by the Government of the United States of America and the Government of the Islamic Republic of Iran, 19 January 1981, (1981) 20 ILM 230 99–100
ASEAN Agreement for the Promotion and Protection of Investments, 15 December 1987, reproduced in 27 ILM 612 108
Convention on the Rights of the Child, 20 November 1989 (entry into force 2 September 1990), 1577 UNTS 3 314
Second Optional Protocol to the International Covenant on Civil and Political Rights, Aiming at the Abolition of the Death Penalty, 15 December 1989 (entry into force 11 July 1991), 29 ILM 1464 316
International Convention on the Protection of the Rights of All Migrant Workers and Members of Their Families, 18 December 1990 (entry into force 1 July 2003), 2220 UNTS 93 315
North American Free Trade Agreement, 17 December 1992 (entry into force 1 January 1994), (1993) 32 ILM 612 106, 109
Protocol no. 11 to the Convention for the Protection of Human Rights and Fundamental Freedoms, Restructuring the Control Machinery Established Thereby, 11 May 1994 (entry into force 1 November 1998, ETS no. 5 332
Arab Charter on Human Rights, adopted by the Council of the League of Arab States by Resolution 5437, 15 September 1994 (not yet in force), reproduced in (1997) 18 *HRLJ* 151 328

Energy Charter Treaty, 17 December 1994 (entry into force 16 April 1998), 2080 UNTS 100 106
Protocol to the African Charter on Human and Peoples' Rights on the Establishment of an African Court on Human and Peoples' Rights, 9 June 1998 (entry into force 25 January 2004), OAU Doc. OAU/LEG/EXP/AFCHPR/PROT(III) 331
Rome Statute of the International Criminal Court, 17 July 1998 (entry into force 1 July 2002), 2187 UNTS 3 222, 268–71
Optional Protocol to the Convention on the Elimination of Discrimination Against Women, 10 December 1999 (entry into force 22 December 2000), GA/Res/54/4 315
Agreement between the Government of the Federal Democratic Republic of Ethiopia and the Government of the State of Eritrea, Algiers, Algeria, 12 December 2000, available at www.pca-cpa.org/upload/files/Algiers%20Agreement.pdf 192
Protocol no. 14 to the Convention for the Protection of Human Rights and Fundamental Freedoms, Amending the Control System of the Convention, 13 May 2004 (not yet in force), ETS no. 194 333–4
International Convention on the Protection and Promotion of the Rights and Dignity of Persons with Disabilities, 13 December 2006 (not yet in force), 46 ILM 443 315
Optional Protocol to the International Convention on the Protection and Promotion of the Rights and Dignity of Persons with Disabilities, 13 December 2006 (not yet in force), 46 ILM 443 315
Optional Protocol to the International Covenant on Economic, Social and Cultural Rights, 10 December 2008 (not yet in force), GA/Res/63/117 319–20

PART I

The Framework

1 Structures of the international legal system

1.1 Introduction

At least by the nineteenth century, international law was generally conceived as a body of rules and forms of conduct applicable to states in their relations with each other.[1] During the twentieth century, a more multifaceted and cosmopolitan view of legal relations in international law emerged. It is widely thought that individuals now have a certain status in international law as the beneficiaries of rights and the bearers of obligations, although they are not subjects of international law of the same kind or to the same extent as states. There has thus been a significant shift in attitudes towards the individual and individual rights over the period since Vattel.[2] But while in some fields of international law it is uncontroversial to treat individuals as holding rights (for example, in international human rights law) and bearing obligations (in international criminal law), in other fields there is uncertainty about the status of the individual. Moreover, although it is now accepted that individuals are 'subjects' in some sense, there is little consensus about what that means for the extent to which individuals *engage* in the international legal system and are engaged by it.

In the relatively open and flexible international system of the twenty-first century, the formal status of entities may seem to have little significance. Whether an individual is a direct right-bearer or an indirect beneficiary of an inter-state obligation may seem to be a distinction

[1] See H. Grotius, *The Rights of War and Peace* (1625, R. Tuck (ed.), Indianapolis, Liberty Fund, 2005), bk I, ch. I, XIV (p. 162).

[2] E. de Vattel, *The Law of Nations or, Principles of the Law of Nature Applied to the Conduct and Affairs of Nations and Sovereigns* (1758, B. Kapossy and R. Whatmore (eds.), Indianapolis, Liberty Fund, 2008), Introduction, para. 3 (p. 67).

without a difference for the operation of the primary rules of international law: either way, the individual benefits from some substantive right, held either directly or through its state of nationality. But when it comes to the operation of secondary rules, the distinction assumes practical significance. If a bilateral investment treaty (BIT) is terminated while an individual investor has a pending claim for breach of a standard of treatment required by the BIT, the question whether the individual investor holds direct substantive rights of protection under the BIT may well be relevant in determining whether the termination of the BIT entails termination of the claim. Again in the context of investment protection, if a state claims a right to non-forcible countermeasures concerning its obligations to accord certain treatment to investments under a treaty, the position of the individual investor will be relevant to the question whether a defence of countermeasures against another state precludes wrongfulness of the breach of treaty.[3] These issues are not limited to investment protection regimes; they may arise in any circumstance in which individuals have capacity to bring international claims.

Moreover, an inquiry into the position of the individual in the international legal system can provide insight into structural change in the international legal system. Accounts of the development of the international legal order commonly present international law as historically confined to the activities of sovereign states, but as tending, more or less inevitably, towards a more inclusive system which takes account of a multiplicity of actors, including individuals.[4] By undertaking a thorough examination of the way in which the international legal system developed to take account of individuals and individuals' interests, this book examines the extent to which this common account is reflected in the historical record. As will be explained, this book adopts a 'rules-based' approach to the engagement of individuals in the international system; focussing on the question of the law as it is rather than normative arguments as to what the law should be.

For the purpose of this book, individuals are defined as natural human persons. The discussion and analysis are focussed on

[3] For an example, see *Corn Products International, Inc.* v. *United Mexican States*, (ICSID Case no. ARB(AF)/04/01), Decision on Responsibility, 15 January 2008; *Archer Daniels Midland Company and Tate & Lyle Ingredients Americas, Inc.* v. *United Mexican States* (ICSID Case no. ARB (AF)/04/05), Award, 21 November 2007; see discussion in 2.4(c) below.

[4] See e.g., C. Grossman and D. D. Bradlow, 'Are We Being Propelled Towards a People-Centred Transnational Legal Order?' (1993–4) 9 *Am. U J Int'l L and Pol'y* 1; C. Ochoa, 'The Individual and Customary International Law Formation' (2007) 48 *Virginia JIL* 119.

individuals, rather than groups, corporations, intergovernmental organisations or non-governmental organisations. The tendency to class together all non-state entities as 'non-state actors' has been severely criticised in the literature, and rightly so.[5] To divide the world into opposed categories of states and 'non-states' is an oversimplification and risks overlooking significant differences between the rules applicable to specific categories of non-state actors. Even if it were possible to generalise aspects of the analysis to a broader range of non-state entities, it is beyond the scope of this book to examine the position of other non-state entities. While some of the material covered in Part II of the book may be applicable to certain other entities, and it may draw upon treatment of other entities for purposes of drawing analogies or examining general aspects of procedure,[6] the analysis is focussed on the question of the position of human persons in the international legal system.

The book is structured in three parts. Part I examines the framework of the international legal system. This Chapter 1 makes a general overview of the framework over three specified periods: these are, roughly speaking, the period beginning in the nineteenth century and ending in 1914; the inter-war period; and the period from 1945 to the present. In each of these periods, the orthodox account of the position of the individual in the international legal system is summarised. Chapter 1 then examines the concept of international legal personality, as the principal traditional measure of engagement of entities in the international legal system. Chapter 1 concludes with an examination of the challenges to state-centrism in international law presented by some of the relevant alternative theoretical approaches. As explained in the section on methodology below, this book takes an approach consistent with a 'rules-based' approach to international law and does not necessarily take a position on one or other theoretical approaches to international law. But to the extent that particular theoretical approaches

[5] See e.g., P. Alston, 'The "Not-a-Cat" Syndrome: Can the International Human Rights Regime Accommodate Non-State Actors?' in P. Alston (ed.), *Non-State Actors and Human Rights* (Oxford, Oxford University Press, 2005), pp. 3–36.

[6] For example, international investment treaties may confer a right to arbitrate on an 'investor' which is either a natural or legal entity. Moreover, some of the practice examined relates to tribunals and commissions with jurisdiction *ratione personae* which includes both natural and legal persons. Where decisions relating to claims brought by legal persons are referred to in this context, these are cited for generalised points reliant to procedure which are also revealing with respect to the treatment of natural persons.

claim that structural change in the international legal system is motivated by or results in an increased role for individuals, it is possible that the material under examination in this book could be informed by and directly address such claims. To this end the final section of this chapter sets out some critiques of state-centrism which will be examined in Part III of the book, in light of the material examined in Part II.

Having set out the structural elements in Chapter 1, Part II (Chapters 2–5) surveys developments relating to individuals in four areas of international law, roughly organised to correspond to the three historical periods surveyed in Chapter 1. In each of the areas, the intention is to explore (a) whether and to what extent the developments in doctrine and practice correspond to the orthodox accounts of the framework of the international legal system outlined in Part I; and (b) whether and to what extent the current framework reflects existing doctrine and practice. Chapter 2 covers international claims: it examines the development of diplomatic protection claims in doctrine and practice, and the practice of 'mixed' or 'international' claims, defined as claims brought by individuals against a state. Chapter 3 examines international humanitarian law. It is divided to reflect the two strands of humanitarian law: international and internal armed conflict. Chapter 4 explores international criminal law, focussing on the criminal responsibility of individuals directly under international law. Chapter 5 deals with international human rights law, considering both doctrine and practice, including capacity to bring individual claims.

These four areas have been selected because they are the areas of international law which have the clearest potential to engage individuals, whether as beneficiaries or as right-holders. Other areas of international law could have been chosen – refugee law, environmental law and aspects of international institutional law. These have been excluded for practical reasons, but also because they do not contain new or different structural elements which are not already covered by the areas under examination. For example, refugee law is largely defined by the 1951 Refugees Convention, which confers rights on categories of individuals using the same structural devices as those used to confer rights on minorities in the League period or by human rights treaties in the UN period, both canvassed in Chapter 5. Other inter-state obligations which might have the effect of benefiting or punishing individuals operate through the same techniques as the rules applicable in international armed conflict which are designed to protect individuals from the effects of warfare, through limitations on either methods or means of warfare. Since the excluded areas do not evidence any different treatment of individuals in the international legal system, the areas examined in Part II may be taken as representative.

In Part III of the book, the material examined in Part II is used to reassess the framework of the international legal system. In Chapter 6, the analysis in each of these four areas is drawn together to reach conclusions about the individual in the international legal system as a whole. Chapter 6 also critiques the use of the doctrine of international legal personality and suggests that analysing the relations of particular entities to the international legal system requires a more nuanced approach than the binary categories of 'subjects' and 'objects' permit. It reflects on ideas of flexibility and openness in the international legal system, and seeks to dispel certain myths about the structural development of the international legal system. Chapter 6 also examines challenges to state-centrism in the international legal system and reflects on the extent to which the case of the individual supports claims that the international legal system is turning away from a state-centric model towards a more cosmopolitan ideal.

1.2 Methodology: a rules-based approach

The approach to the international legal system articulated in this chapter, and which forms the basis of the examination of law and practice in Part II of the book, is consistent with a 'rules-based' approach to international law and possibly also with positivism as a legal theory (depending on the definition one adopts of positivism). Something should be said about each of these.

Traditionally positivism has been associated with an emphasis on state will: in the absence of central authority, law can only be based on the consent of states.[7] As a legal theory positivism emphasises the distinction between the law in force, according to the recognised, consent-based sources of law, from non-legal factors including morality and 'natural law'.[8]

7 For example, see G. Jellinek, *Die Rechtliche Natur der Staatenvertrage* (Vienna, Alfred Hölder, 1880), pp. 2, 42–9, 56–8; S. R. Ratner and A.-M. Slaughter, 'Appraising the Methods of International Law: A Prospectus for Readers' (1999) 93 *AJIL* 291, 293.

8 B. Simma and A. L. Paulus, 'The Responsibility of Individuals for Human Rights Abuses in Internal Conflicts: A Positivist View' (1999) 93 *AJIL* 302, 304; C. Tomuschat, 'International Law: Ensuring the Survival of Mankind on the Eve of a New Century' (1999) 281 *RdC* 9, 26–7.

A 'rules-based' approach finds resonance in positivism because it is focussed on discerning the existence of legal rules on the basis of the sources of international law. In this sense, a rules-based approach also distinguishes between the law as it is (*lege lata*) and normative arguments as to what the law should be (*lege ferenda*).[9] However, a rules-based approach does not necessarily indicate that law emanates exclusively from state consent. It may take account of a broader range of law-makers but it still emphasises the idea of law as a system of rules.[10]

This book is concerned with the development of law and practice *de lege lata* and with explaining that development; in doing so it takes a rules-based approach. The starting point for determining those sources is Article 38(1) of the Statute of the International Court of Justice, but there may be other sources of international law which are recognised as binding by the international community. In this way a rules-based approach is not necessarily wedded to state consent as the only basis for generating rules of international law. Neither does it exclude the possibility that individuals and other non-state entities may have a role or participate in the international legal system, provided that role or participation is supported by rules generated according to the recognised sources of law. Since the aim of the book is to explain the development of law (in the sense of the generally accepted rules), it is justifiable to take a rules-based approach while remaining open to the possibility that there may be rules which emanate from sources other than the traditional source of state-based consent.

As such, it is not necessary to take a position on theoretical approaches to international law, including positivism. Other theoretical approaches can generally be characterised as more focussed on normative arguments than with the existing state of the law.[11] Some (e.g., the New Haven School) emphasise process rather than content; some (e.g., feminist theories) are concerned to critique 'the law as it is' from the perspective of groups or persons disempowered by it; others (including critical legal studies) take a more or less rule-sceptical approach.

[9] Simma and Paulus, 'The Responsibility of Individuals', 304; P. Weil, 'Towards a Relative Normativity in International Law' (1983) 77 *AJIL* 415, 416–17.

[10] For a discussion of the rules-based approach, see M. Koskenniemi, 'International Legal Theory and Doctrine' in R. Wolfrum (ed.), *The Max Planck Encyclopedia of Public International Law* (Oxford, Oxford University Press, 2008, online edition, www.mpepil.com), para. 29.

[11] Koskenniemi, 'International Legal Theory and Doctrine', para. 21.

To the extent that these alternative theoretical approaches make arguments *de lege ferenda*, in support of their normative claims, they are of little assistance in achieving the objective of this book, which is to examine the development of law and practice in concrete terms. However, these theoretical approaches might assist in two ways. First, they may suggest an adjustment of the traditional view of the sources of international law or the accepted categories of participants or subjects in the international legal system (see 1.5 below). For example, the claim of the process approach that a multiplicity of actors other than states influence the development of the law, may lead to an adjustment of the recognised sources of international law. In this respect, the examination of law and practice in Part II will be undertaken with a view open to the claims presented by proponents of these different theoretical approaches, bearing in mind the focus here is on *de lege lata*. Secondly, and more generally, they may challenge the traditional state-centric view of the international legal system reflected in orthodox doctrine, which is discussed further in section 5 of this chapter.

It is beyond the scope of this book to examine more generally the normative claims of alternative theoretical approaches to the law as it should be. This is in part for practical reasons: an examination of normative claims would require examination of political and sociological factors which are difficult to assess in the absence of a more generalised study. But since the primary goal of the book is to shed light on the position of the individual in the international legal system *in its own terms*, and on the basis of that examination to discuss structural change in the international legal system, the claims of the differing theoretical approaches are of limited relevance. A focus on the development of the rules according to generally recognised sources of international law (which falls within a general understanding of the rules-based approach) can shed light on the question identified for study, without preferring one or other theoretical approach. It is enough to posit that international law exists as a more or less determinate system, that its processes are, in some meaningful way, rule-based, and that changes in rules and processes can be identified with sufficient certainty. No doubt each of these positions would require to be established at a more basic level, but the assumptions identified here seem reasonable and workable. The enterprise of international law may be flawed, even radically flawed, but that it is an enterprise in its own terms does not seem open to doubt.

1.3 The engagement of individuals in the international legal system: structural issues

This section sketches the structural aspects of the international legal system which will be the focus of further reflection in Part II. The emphasis is on the way in which the international legal system takes account of individuals, rather than substantive rights and duties of individuals, or any specific procedural capacities. The dominant doctrine in each of the relevant periods is examined, together with relevant developments in practice and doctrine which later came to be conceived as effecting structural change in the international legal system.

(a) Prelude: differing legal structures in the early period

It was with the work of Emer de Vattel in the mid-eighteenth century that 'the law of nations' came to be seen as a law between states. Before Vattel, writers on the law of nations had a broader conception of the *jus gentium*. Hugo Grotius (1583–1645) in *De jure belli ac pacis libri tres* referred to the 'law of nations' or *jus gentium*; he did not envisage a law exclusively concerned with relations between states, but rather a law between the rulers of nations – those exercising public power – and between groups of citizens or private individuals not in a domestic relation to each other.[12] Grotius did not see the state as a separate juridical entity, but as a 'body of free Persons, associated together'[13] under the personal leadership of the ruler.[14] Grotius' law of nations was not an inter-state law, but an inter-individual law, applicable on a

[12] P. Haggenmacher, *Grotius et la doctrine de le guerre juste* (Paris, Presses Universitaires de France, 1983), pp. 541–3; E. Jouannet, *Emer de Vattel et l'émergence doctrinale du droit international classique* (Paris, Pedone, 1998), pp. 263, 361; J. Crawford, *International Law as an Open System* (London, Cameron May, 2002), p. 19. Hugo Grotius is often said to be the founder of modern international law: see L. Oppenheim, *International Law: A Treatise* (London, Longmans, Green & Co, 1905), p. 77; H. Lauterpacht (ed.), *International Law: A Treatise, by L. Oppenheim* (8th edn, London, Longmans, 1955), p. 91; H. Lauterpacht, 'The Grotian Tradition in International Law' (1946) 23 *BYIL* 1, 51. But more recently this has been subject to criticism and dismissed as an exaggeration: see R. Jennings and A. Watts, *Oppenheim's International Law* (9th edn, London, Longmans, 1992), p. 4; H. Waldock (ed.), *J L Brierly, The Law of Nations: An Introduction to the International Law of Peace* (6th edn, Oxford, Clarendon Press, 1963), p. 28; Crawford, *International Law as an Open System*, p. 19; D. Kennedy, 'Primitive Legal Scholarship' (1986) *Harvard International Law Journal* 1, 77.

[13] Grotius, *The Rights of War and Peace*, bk I, ch. I, XIV (p. 162).

[14] Haggenmacher, *Grotius et la doctrine de le guerre juste*, pp. 541–3; Jouannet, *Emer de Vattel*, pp. 261–4.

universal basis.[15] In this respect his work followed a leading tradition of medieval scholastic thought. Medieval natural law was seen to be all-embracing; it regulated the natural and social life of all, applying between rulers as well as between private individuals.[16] Similarly, Vitoria's idea of an international society was based on the concept of a universal community which encompassed all mankind, an organised community of peoples which were themselves constituted politically as states.[17] Suárez conceived of a rational basis of the law of nations as the moral and political unity of the human race.[18] The sources of this law of nations were believed to be natural law principles, which were merely supplemented by tacit or express agreements between sovereign princes, which bound them in a personal capacity.[19] The law of nations as conceived by these early writers was all-embracing in character.[20]

In his widely circulated treatise *Le droit des gens, ou principes de la loi naturelle appliqués à conduite aux affaires des nations et des souverains* of 1758, Vattel defined the law of nations as 'the science which teaches the rights subsisting between nations or states, and the obligations correspondent to those rights'.[21] His separation of the law of nature, which was applicable to individuals, from the law of nations, which was applicable to states, resulted in a conception of the law of nations as inter-state law, rather than as a law for individuals or for a society of humankind.[22] Vattel regarded the state as a separate person with its own will,

15 M. Koskenniemi, *From Apology to Utopia* (Cambridge, Cambridge University Press, 2005), p. 98.

16 S. C. Neff, 'A Short History of International Law' in M. Evans (ed.), *International Law* (2nd edn, Oxford, Oxford University Press, 2006), pp. 29, 32.

17 W. G. Grewe, *The Epochs of International Law* (M. Byers (trans.), Berlin, Walter de Gruyter, 2000), pp. 145–6.

18 F. Suárez, *On Laws and God the Lawgiver* (1612, G. L. Williams (trans.), Oxford, Clarendon Press, 1944), bk II, ch. 19.9 (pp. 348–9).

19 F. de Vitoria, *Political Writings* (A. Pagden and L. Jeremy (eds.), Cambridge, Cambridge University Press, 1991), Relectio De Indis Question 3 Article 1, para. 4 (pp. 280–1), Relectio De Potestate Civili Question 3 Article 1 paras. 15–17 (pp. 32–6); Grotius, *The Rights of War and Peace*, bk I, ch. I, XIV (p. 162). See also R. Lesaffer, 'The Grotian Tradition Revisited: Change and Continuity in the History of International Law' (2002) 73 *BYIL* 103, 123–4.

20 Kennedy, 'Primitive Legal Scholarship', 16–17, 42–5, 62–5 and 81–3; see also Koskenniemi, *From Apology to Utopia*, pp. 98–9; A. Nussbaum, *A Concise History of the Law of Nations* (New York, Macmillan, 1964), pp. 86–7 and 108–9.

21 Vattel, *The Law of Nations*, Introduction, para. 3 (p. 67).

22 See generally, P. Remec, *The Position of the Individual in International Law according to Grotius and Vattel* (The Hague, Martinus Nijhoff, 1960), p. 199.

distinguishable from the will of its members as individuals:[23] 'The law of nations is the law of sovereigns: free and independent states are moral persons, whose rights and obligations we are to establish in this treatise.'[24]

Vattel's work can be related to a wider intellectual development from the mid-seventeenth century which elaborated contractual theories of the state as an entity separated in varying degrees from both the personal ruler and citizens. Thomas Hobbes introduced the concept of an 'artificial personality', although closely attached to the person of the ruler.[25] Samuel Pufendorf saw the state as having a personality distinct from both its citizens and its ruler, though he considered that the organs ruling the state were the sovereign.[26] In Christian Wolff's writings, the artificial person of the state acquired sovereignty, which could be passed to the person ruling the state.[27] But in Vattel's view the state was a separate and distinct entity and it was the only sovereign.[28]

Positive international law, according to Vattel, was created by the separate personality of the state, rather than by princes or personal rulers. Consistent with an emerging practice whereby treaties referred to states as parties, it was the separate and distinct entity of the state which entered into international agreements.[29] Vattel distinguished three forms of positive law of nations: conventional law, resulting from the express will of states; customary law resulting from their

[23] Vattel, *The Law of Nations*, Préliminaires, para. 2 (p. 1). See Jouannet, *Emer de Vattel*, p. 319, and S. Beaulac, *The Power of Language in the Making of International Law: The Word 'Sovereignty' in Bodin and Vattel and the Myth of Westphalia* (Leiden, Martinus Nijhoff, 2004), pp. 138, 143–9; Remec, *The Position of the Individual*, pp. 160–2.

[24] Vattel, *The Law of Nations*, ch. I, para.12, (p. 85).

[25] T. Hobbes, *Leviathan* (R. Tuck (ed.), Cambridge, Cambridge University Press, 1996), Pt II, ch. XVII (pp. 120–1); see also D. Boucher and P. Kelly, 'The Social Contract and its Critics: An Overview' in D. Boucher and P. Kelly (eds.), *The Social Contract from Hobbes to Rawls* (London, Routledge, 1994), pp. 1, 15.

[26] S. Pufendorf, *De Jure Naturae et Gentium Libra Octo* (J. B. Scott (ed.), C. H. and W. A. Oldfather (trans.), Oxford, Clarendon Press, 1934), bk VII, ch. VI, paras. 7–8 (p. 1063); see also Jouannet, *Emer de Vattel*, pp. 295–9.

[27] C. Wolff, *Jus Gentum Methodo Scientifica Pertractatum* (J. B. Scott (ed.), J. H. Drake (trans.), Oxford, Clarendon Press, 1934), vol. II, ch. 4, para. 368 (p. 181); see also Jouannet, *Emer de Vattel*, p. 316.

[28] Vattel, *The Law of Nations*, Préliminaires, para. 2 (p. 1).

[29] *Ibid*. Preliminaries, para. 24 (p. 77); Lesaffer, 'The Grotian Tradition Revisited', 130–1. See e.g., First Treaty of Partition between France, Great Britain and the Netherlands, signed at Loo/The Hague, 24 September/11 October 1698, 22 CTS 197; Second Treaty of Partition between France, Great Britain and the Netherlands, signed at London/The Hague, 13/25 March 1700, 22 CTS 471.

tacit or implicit consent; and voluntary law, the law which was presumed to reflect the will of the states in order to preserve basic principles of the international community. Alongside these forms of positive law, Vattel regarded fundamental principles of natural law applied to states as part of the law of nations, called the 'necessary' law of nations.[30] State-made law, the positive law of nations, could not contradict this necessary law of nations.[31] Thus, states could create law, but they were constrained by natural law principles.

In Vattel's doctrine, the scope of application of the law of nations narrowed to sovereign states as separate entities from their personal rulers, their citizens and private individuals. The law of nations, insofar as it was created by agreement, was the product of the will of the states, not of the individuals comprising the state.

(b) The long nineteenth century

The Vattelian premise that the law of nations applied between states as separate legal persons came to occupy a dominant position in doctrine from the late eighteenth until the mid-nineteenth century.[32] This coincided with and was related to the dominance of the positivist school, with its central belief in law as a human institution, an emanation of the will. Vattel's emphasis on the creation of law by states was a clear antecedent of positivism, but nineteenth century positivism saw the voluntary law as the only source of law. The insistence on states as the fundamental unit of law also led to abandonment of the natural law, replaced by an instrumentalist view of the law as servant of the will of states. In the major treatises of the time, this was evidenced by an emphasis on state practice rather than on statements of general principle, still less natural-law doctrine.[33] Some writers attempted to reconcile positivism and naturalism: for example, Lorimer accepted that the law of nations comprised treaty and custom, but argued that the overall purpose of the law of nations was securing and furthering liberty, a purpose derived from the law of nature.[34] But the most influential writers, such as Westlake and Hall, were emphatically positivist. The influence of the positivist school

[30] Vattel, *The Law of Nations*, Preliminaries, para. 7 (p. 70) and paras. 27–8 (pp. 78–9).

[31] *Ibid.* Preliminaries para. 7 (p. 70) and paras. 27–8 (pp. 78–9); see also Jouannet, *Emer de Vattel*, p. 93.

[32] See e.g., Nussbaum, *A Concise History of the Law of Nations*, p. ix.

[33] See e.g., R. Phillimore, *Commentaries upon International Law* (3rd edn, London, Butterworths, 1879), vol. I, pp. 14–29.

[34] J. Lorimer, *The Institutes of the Law of Nations* (Edinburgh, Blackwood, 1883), p. 23.

was such that in 1908, Lassa Oppenheim wrote that 'we are no longer justified in teaching a law of nature and a "natural" law of nations'.[35]

It is useful to attempt to analyse the position of the individual in the international legal system according to international legal doctrine in the late nineteenth century. By the end of the nineteenth century there was general agreement on the scope and subjects of international law, which implied interrelated doctrines of legal personality and designated the individual as an object of international law. Oppenheim's *International Law* provides the clearest and the most influential expression in English of these doctrines.[36]

The relevant points are as follows.

(1) International law was the law between civilised nations.[37] The rules of international law were based on the common consent of those states who were members of the society of nations.[38]

(2) Subjects of rights and duties under international law were states 'solely and exclusively'.[39] International law was a law 'for the international conduct of States, and not of their citizens'.[40] Individuals and groups were not subjects of international law and had no rights as such under international law.[41]

(3) While international law regulated relations between member states of the society of nations, municipal law regulated relations between individuals and relations between individuals and states.[42]

(4) Any rights and duties which might have appeared to have been granted to individual human beings by international law were not international law rights and duties, but rather were rights and duties derived from municipal law. In this context, Oppenheim referred to rights granted to monarchs, other heads of state, diplomatic envoys and citizens on foreign territory, and suggested that international law

[35] L. Oppenheim, 'The Science of International Law: Its Task and Method' (1908) 2 *AJIL* 313, 328.

[36] This approach has been used in the leading treatise on statehood: J. Crawford, *The Creation of States in International Law* (2nd edn, Oxford, Oxford University Press, 2006), pp. 14–16. Similar principles can be derived from other texts: for example, H. Wheaton, *Elements of International Law 1866 Edition* (R. H. Dana (ed.), Oxford, Clarendon Press, 1936); W. E. Hall, *A Treatise on International Law* (3rd edn, Oxford, Clarendon Press, 1890).

[37] Oppenheim, *International Law: A Treatise*, 1, para.1. See also Hall, *A Treatise on International Law*, 1.

[38] Oppenheim, *International Law: A Treatise*, pp. 16–17, para.12; see also Crawford, *The Creation of States*, p. 14.

[39] Oppenheim, *International Law: A Treatise*, pp. 18–19, para.13.

[40] *Ibid.*

[41] See also Crawford, *The Creation of States*, p. 15.

[42] Oppenheim, *International Law: A Treatise*, p. 26, para. 20.

imposed a direct obligation on states to confer these rights on individuals by their domestic law.

If we look more closely into these rights, it becomes quite obvious that they are not given to the favoured individuals by the law of nations directly. For how could international law, which is a law between states, give rights to individuals concerning their relations to a state?[43]

Instead, Oppenheim argued, the law of nations imposed a duty on states to grant certain rights to individuals; states granting these rights did so by their municipal law, and 'these rights are, therefore, not international rights, but rights derived from Municipal laws'.[44] These rights did not exist unless states create them by their own municipal law. In this context, treaties which spoke of rights which individuals should have derived from the treaties themselves were dismissed as 'nothing more than an inaccuracy of language'.[45] The treaties only imposed a duty upon contracting states to create these rights for individuals in their domestic law.

(5) Since individuals were not subjects of international law, they could only be objects of international law.[46] Individuals were objects of international law in the same way as a state's territory was, since international law recognised the personal supremacy of every state over its subjects at home and abroad.[47]

(6) Because individuals were not subjects but objects of international law, the only link between individuals and international law was through nationality.[48] The function of nationality could most clearly be seen in respect of the right of protection over nationals abroad which every state held and could assert against other states.[49] Individuals who did not possess any nationality had no international protection.[50] The assertion that all individuals, including stateless persons, enjoyed some fundamental rights under international law was not accepted.[51]

[43] *Ibid*. p. 342, para. 289; see also pp. 18–19, para.13.

[44] *Ibid*. p. 342, para. 289; see also pp. 18–19, para.13.

[45] *Ibid*. p. 343, para. 289.

[46] See generally, G. Manner, 'The Object Theory of the Individual in International Law' (1952) 46 *AJIL* 428, 428–9.

[47] Oppenheim, *International Law: A Treatise*, p. 344, para. 290.

[48] *Ibid*. pp. 344–7, paras. 291–2.

[49] *Ibid*. p. 349, para. 294.

[50] *Ibid*. pp. 344–7, paras. 291–2. Oppenheim referred to two exceptional cases in which individuals might come under the international protection of a state without really being its subjects: first, where a state undertakes by international agreement to exercise diplomatic protection of another state's citizens abroad, for example, where a small state has no diplomatic envoy in a foreign country; and secondly, where a state promises diplomatic protection of 'natives' in the service of its embassy or consulate: *ibid*. pp. 350–1, para. 295.

[51] *Ibid*. p. 346, para. 292.

Further, the determination of nationality was a matter for municipal law, not for international law.[52]

(7) Every state held a right of protection over its citizens abroad corresponding to the duty of every state to treat foreigners with a certain consideration.[53] This right of protection could be exercised by the state of nationality when one of its subjects suffered injury abroad. The state of nationality could insist by diplomatic channels on the wrongdoers being punished; it could take reprisals in order to make the foreign state comply with its demands; and it could even go further and intervene by force when necessary.[54]

The nineteenth century framework of the international legal system reflected Vattel's state-centrism: international law was the law regulating the relations between sovereign states, who were the exclusive subjects of international law. The relations of individuals were governed by municipal law; if international law dictated standards or rules as to their treatment at all, it only imposed an obligation on states to create rights for individuals through their domestic law. The spheres of application of international law and domestic law were thus sharply defined; international law could regulate matters which concerned individuals only indirectly, since that regulation would necessarily be implemented through domestic law.

(c) *The inter-war period*

In the inter-war period, international legal doctrine as reflected in the texts was in principle unchanged. One issue which surfaced but was never definitively settled[55] was the status of the League of Nations. McNair's fourth edition of *Oppenheim* stated that the League of Nations, which had 'distinctive international rights and duties', was a *sui generis* international person; the only international person apart from sovereign states.[56] But the same treatise reiterated the nineteenth century view that individuals could not be subjects of international law, nor

[52] *Ibid.* p. 348, para. 293; see also pp. 352–7, paras. 297–302.

[53] *Ibid.* pp. 374–7, paras. 319–22. [54] *Ibid.* p. 375, para. 319.

[55] J. F. Williams, *Some Aspects of the Covenant of the League of Nations* (London, Oxford University Press, 1934), p. 43; A. Zimmern, *The League of Nations and the Rule of Law 1918–1935* (London, Macmillan and Co., 1936), pp. 277–85; J. L. Brierly, 'The Covenant and the Charter' (1946) 23 *BYIL* 83, 85.

[56] A. McNair, *Oppenheim's International Law* (4th edn, London, Longmans, 1928), vol. I, pp. 133–4. This view was consistent with that of Oppenheim writing before the Covenant had come into force: see L. Oppenheim, 'Le Caractère essentiel de la Société des Nations' (1919) *RGIDP* 234; for a different view see P. E. Corbett, 'What is the League of Nations?' (1924) 5 *BYIL* 119.

could they acquire rights and duties under international law: the latter was 'untenable as a general proposition . . . for international rights and duties can only exist between States, or between the League of Nations and States'.[57] During the inter-war period the idea that the League could be an international legal person does not appear to have been applied more broadly to other entities: for example, when the Bank for International Settlements was created in 1930, it was doubted that a bank could be created at the international level; instead it was constituted as a Swiss entity, with treaty guarantees that Switzerland would not exercise control which amounted to interference with the Bank's activities.[58] But at least the discussion suggested that nothing in the character of the international legal system prevented the creation of international legal persons which were not states.

Also during the inter-war period, the opinion of the Permanent Court of International Justice (PCIJ) in *Jurisdiction of the Court of Danzig*[59] dealt with the question whether individuals could be granted rights by treaty. The Court held:

> It may be readily admitted that, according to a well established principle of international law, the [treaty], being an international agreement, cannot, as such, create direct rights and obligations for private individuals. But it cannot be disputed that the very object of an international agreement, according to the intention of the contracting Parties, may be the adoption by the Parties of some definite rules creating individual rights and obligations and enforceable by the national courts.[60]

This Opinion of the PCIJ warrants detailed examination for two reasons. First, it was the first authoritative statement that individuals can bear direct rights under treaties, and it is now commonly cited to that effect.[61] But also, the question whether the PCIJ's Opinion held that

57 McNair, *Oppenheim's International Law*, vol. I, p. 520.

58 H. Coing, 'Bank for International Settlements' in R. Bernhardt (ed.), *Encyclopedia of Public International Law* (Amsterdam, Elsevier Science Publishers, 1992), vol. I, p. 342. In 1987, the Bank for International Settlements was reconstituted as an international legal person.

59 *Jurisdiction of the Courts of Danzig (Pecuniary Claims of Danzig Railway Officials who have passed into the Polish Service, Against the Polish Railways Administration)*, PCIJ Rep. ser. B no. 15 (1928) 3.

60 *Ibid.* 17–18.

61 For examples, see R. McCorquodale, 'The Individual and the International Legal System' in M. Evans (ed.), *International Law* (2nd edn, Oxford, Oxford University Press, 2006), pp. 307, 312; C. M. Vázquez, 'Treaty Based Rights and Remedies of Individuals' (1992) 92 *Colum. L Rev* 1083, 1087; P. K. Menon, 'The International Personality of Individuals in International Law: A Broadening of the Traditional Doctrine' (1992) *Journal of Transnational Law and Policy* 151, 163–4; H. Lauterpacht, 'The Subjects of the Law of Nations, Part I' (1947) 63 *LQR* 460, 456; H. Lauterpacht, 'The Subjects of the Law of

individuals could bear rights under treaties without a need for those rights to be incorporated into municipal law was very much disputed at the time of the Opinion, a dispute which has never clearly been resolved. Hersch Lauterpacht argued that it was 'difficult to exaggerate the bearing' of the PCIJ's Opinion on the principle that states only and exclusively are subjects of the law of nations.[62] He described the Opinion as an 'affirmation by the [PCIJ] of the right of individuals to acquire rights directly under treaties' and said 'it laid down, in effect, that no considerations of theory can prevent the individual from becoming the subject of international rights if States so wish'.[63] On the other hand, the then-President of the PCIJ, Dionisio Anzilotti, took a narrow view of the scope of the Opinion, stating extra-judicially that:

> The opinion of the PCIJ does not say that a treaty, as such, can create rights and obligations for individuals, without the need for the rules and those things associated with the rules to be incorporated into internal law; it says only that the intention of the contracting parties can be that of adopting definite rules creating rights and obligations for individuals and capable of being applied by national tribunals.
>
> If, in this particular case, the Court did not consider it necessary to examine whether the rules outlined in the agreement had effectively been adopted, it is because the Court considered that the party which was obliged to adopt the said rules was not able, in any case, to take advantage of the fact that it had not executed its obligation, in order to avoid the duties imposed on it by the agreement as regards the other party.[64]

Beckett took the point even further, stating that the PCIJ held that the effect of the treaty was 'that one of the states should take the necessary steps to create certain rights and obligations for individuals' in municipal law, that Poland was bound to take such steps to create the rights under municipal law, and the Court had held that 'in the circumstances it was not open to Poland to rely on her own failure to fulfil her

Nations, Part II' (1948) 64 *LQR* 97, 97–9. See also *Republic of Ecuador* v. *Occidental Exploration and Production Company* [2006] 1 QB 432 (CA (Civ.)).

62 H. Lauterpacht, *The Development of International Law by the Permanent Court of International Justice* (London, Longmans, 1934), pp. 50–2.

63 Lauterpacht, 'The Subjects of the Law of Nations, Part II', 98.

64 D. Anzilotti, *Cours de droit International* (Paris, Librairie de Recueil Sirey, 1929), pp. 407–8 and 133–4 (author's own translation). For discussion of Anzilotti's dualist approach to international law, see G. Gaja, 'Positivism and Dualism in Dionisio Anzilotti' (1992) 3 *EJIL* 123; and generally J. M. Ruda, 'The Opinions of Judge Dionisio Anzilotti at the Permanent Court of International Justice' (1992) 3 *EJIL* 100, 102; A. P. Sereni, *The Italian Conception of International Law* (New York, Columbia University Press, 1943), esp. pp. 213–44.

obligation to do so as an argument in her favour in the case'.[65] He concluded:

One of the time-honoured theoretical questions as to which publicists have indulged in controversy is the question whether individuals are subjects or only objects of international law. A sturdy minority of writers has stoutly maintained that individuals directly acquired rights under international law, and has quoted in support of its views the redress of their grievances by diplomatic action and international tribunals. The Permanent Court have most clearly expressed their view in the contrary sense.[66]

The relevant treaty before the PCIJ was a 1921 Agreement between the governments of Poland and the Free City of Danzig dealing with the treatment of railway officials.[67] This treaty, which provided for the administration of part of the railway system in Danzig by Poland, was one of a number of arrangements set in motion by the Treaty of Versailles relating to the newly independent Polish state and the internationalised territory in Danzig.[68] The 1921 Agreement provided that personnel who were transferred into the Polish service would retain their acquired rights to, *inter alia*, claims and candidatures for posts, and all arrangements in force for the promotion of their welfare. The provisions of the 1921 Agreement were not incorporated into Polish law nor into the law of the Free City.[69]

Subsequently, railway officials who had been transferred into the Polish service brought pecuniary claims in the courts of the Free City against the Polish Railways Administration (PRA), basing them in part on the 1921 Agreement. Poland disputed the jurisdiction of the Danzig courts and that claims could be brought by individuals based on the 1921 Agreement. The dispute between Poland and Danzig was referred to the High Commissioner for the Free City[70] who held: first, that Danzig railway officials were entitled to bring actions against the Polish authority in the Danzig courts; but second, that claims for

65 W. E. Beckett, 'Decisions of the Permanent Court of International Justice on Points of Law and Procedure of General Application' (1930) 11 *BYIL* 1, 4.

66 *Ibid.* See also M. O. Hudson, *The Permanent Court of International Justice: A Treatise* (New York, Macmillan, 1934), pp. 530–1.

67 Final Agreement reproduced in *Jurisdiction of the Courts of Danzig (Actions by Certain Railway Officials Against the Polish Administration)*, PCIJ Rep. ser. C no. 14-I (1928) 152–7.

68 Treaty of Versailles, 28 June 1919, UKTS 4 (Cmd 153), Arts. 100, 102 and 103.

69 See K. Parlett, 'The PCIJ's Opinion in *Jurisdiction of the Courts of Danzig*: Individual Rights under Treaties' (2008) 10 *JHIL* 119, 128.

70 In accordance with Treaty of Versailles, Art. 103, 28 June 1919, UKTS 4 (Cmd 153).

payment could not be based on the 1921 Agreement, because it was 'an international treaty concluded between . . . two States, an international act which establishes reciprocal legal relations between governments' and as such, it did not 'confer direct rights on individuals'.[71] The Free City appealed the High Commissioner's decision to the Council of the League, who sought an advisory opinion from the PCIJ as to whether the decision on the second point – that pecuniary claims could not be brought by individuals based on the 1921 Agreement – was legally well-founded.[72]

The PCIJ first considered whether Danzig had complied with international law in allowing claims based on the 1921 Agreement to be brought before its courts. Poland argued that the Agreement created rights and obligations between the contracting parties only; that it could not, failing incorporation into Polish national legislation or the provision of a direct right of claim against the state in an international court, create direct rights for individuals; and that if Poland had not fulfilled its obligations under the Agreement it would only be liable to Danzig, not directly to individuals.[73] Danzig argued that the contracting parties had clearly intended to establish direct and personal rights for individuals and the Polish authority, and the fact that they were found in an international agreement was irrelevant as their character ought to be determined by their content and not by the form in which they were drawn up.[74] On the key question whether the international agreement formed part of the contract of service of the Danzig officials, the PCIJ considered 'the intention of the contracting Parties' to be paramount. Thus, the Court recognised an exception to the general principle that an

[71] *Jurisdiction of Danzig Courts in Actions Brought by Railway Officials Against the Railway Administration*, Decision of the High Commissioner, 8 April 1927, English translation reproduced in *Jurisdiction of the Courts of Danzig (Pecuniary Claims of Danzig Railway Officials who have passed into the Polish Service, Against the Polish Railways Administration)*, PCIJ Rep. ser. B no. 15 (1928), Annex I, 28, 29.

[72] *Ibid.* 5.

[73] *Jurisdiction of the Courts of Danzig (Actions by Certain Railway Officials Against the Polish Administration)*, Reply of the Polish Government to the Appeal by the Senate of the Free City of Danzig, PCIJ Rep. ser. C no. 14-I (1928) 137. In its submissions, Poland suggested that a claim based on the 1921 Agreement would require legislation in both Poland and the Free City, in order to give the courts 'jurisdiction'.

[74] *Jurisdiction of the Courts of Danzig (Actions by Certain Railway Officials Against the Polish Administration)*, Appeal by the Government of the Free City of Danzig, PCIJ Rep. ser. C no. 14-I (1928) 115. See also *Jurisdiction of the Courts of Danzig (Pecuniary Claims of Danzig Railway Officials who have Passed into the Polish Service, Against the Polish Railways Administration)*, PCIJ Rep. ser. B no. 15 (1928) 3, 17.

international agreement cannot 'create direct rights and obligations' for individuals, where the 'object' of an international agreement was 'the adoption ... of some definite rules creating individual rights and obligations and enforceable by the national courts'. The Court's formulation of 'adoption of definite rules creating individual rights' was a different formulation from the 'creation of direct rights' for individuals. But the adoption of these 'definite rules' must be taken to have occurred at the international level, since the 1921 Agreement had not been incorporated into domestic law. In the absence of incorporation of the treaty into domestic law, the treaty was still taken to have created rights for individuals.

In the second part of its Opinion, the PCIJ then considered whether Poland was obliged to recognise and enforce decisions of the Danzig courts based on the 1921 Agreement.[75] The Court framed this as a discussion about applicable law: the extent of Poland's obligation to recognise the jurisdiction of the Danzig courts depended upon the substantive law which could lawfully be applied, a question of the character and extent of the jurisdiction of the Danzig courts in relation to the PRA. Since the PRA was subject to the civil and criminal courts of Danzig, the Court considered that if the Danzig courts were acting within their jurisdiction by applying the 1921 Agreement, and in so doing was not acting contrary to any rule of international law binding upon Danzig, Poland was bound to recognise and enforce those judgments.[76]

The PCIJ first held that the Danzig courts were acting within their jurisdiction in applying the 1921 Agreement. It noted that if Poland had contended that the Danzig courts could not apply the 1921 Agreement because its provisions 'were not duly inserted in the Polish national law', the Court would have to observe that Poland could not avail itself of this objection, which would amount to relying on the non-fulfilment of its own obligation imposed by an international agreement.[77] This was

[75] *Jurisdiction of the Courts of Danzig (Pecuniary Claims of Danzig Railway Officials who have Passed into the Polish Service, Against the Polish Railways Administration)*, PCIJ Rep. ser. B no. 15 (1928) 3, 5.

[76] *Ibid.* 25.

[77] *Ibid.* 26–7. Danzig had raised this issue in its observations, submitting that Poland had 'made itself guilty of an omission, and to plead this omission in dealing with cases brought by officials would, according to generally recognized legal principles, be fraudulent and therefore inadmissible': *Jurisdiction of the Courts of Danzig (Actions by Certain Railway Officials Against the Polish Administration)*, Observations of the Danzig Senate Regarding the Polish Reply, PCIJ Rep. ser. C no. 14-I (1928) 144–5. The PCIJ had

the only mention of the principle that a state cannot rely on non-fulfilment of an obligation to raise an objection to its liability, and it arose in the context of the Court's consideration of whether Poland was bound to accept the jurisdiction of the Danzig courts and to enforce its judgments. It was separate from the Court's findings on the question whether the 1921 Agreement conferred direct rights on individuals. The Court held that Poland could not argue that it was not obliged to accept the jurisdiction of the Danzig courts and enforce its judgments because the 1921 Agreement was not part of its domestic law.

Accordingly, the PCIJ concluded that the High Commissioner's decision, insofar as it did not comply with the requests of Danzig, was not legally well-founded.[78] Subsequently, the courts of Danzig continued to hear claims based on the 1921 Agreement, relying on the PCIJ's Opinion.[79] For example, in the *Zoppot Street Crossing* case, the High Court of Danzig held that international agreements made supplementary to the 1921 Agreement conferred direct rights on third persons. (In that case, the plaintiff sought to obtain performance of a contract concluded with the Prussian railway administration; the supplementary agreements provided for the PRA to be joined as a party in pending actions by or against the former administration of the railways; hence the High Court held that the private persons who had pending claims against the Prussian railway administration had a claim enforceable against the PRA.) The High Court there emphasised that the question whether the international agreements had been incorporated into Danzig municipal law was irrelevant, since international legal obligations were created by the treaty and those obligations vested in third persons as against Poland.

An examination of the PCIJ's Opinion in its historical context leads to two conclusions. First, as a matter of practical effect the PCIJ found that

previously stated that it was self-evident that a state which had assumed valid international obligations was bound to make modifications in its legislation as necessary to ensure the fulfilment of its international obligations: *Exchange of Greek and Turkish Populations*, Advisory Opinion, PCIJ Rep. ser. B no. 10 (1925) 6.

78 *Jurisdiction of the Courts of Danzig (Pecuniary Claims of Danzig Railway Officials who have Passed into the Polish Service, Against the Polish Railways Administration)*, PCIJ Rep. ser. B no. 15 (1928) 3, 27. Both Poland and the Free City had agreed to accept the PCIJ's Opinion in advance and on 6 March 1928, the two governments signed an agreement to the effect that the Council of the League should be asked not to place the question on its agenda because the parties had agreed to accept the Opinion. On 9 March 1928, the Council took formal note of the Opinion and of the parties' agreement: (1928) *League of Nations Official Journal* (April) 433.

79 For example, *Zoppot Street Crossing*, Danzig High Court, 16 January 1934, 7 ILR 269.

individuals held substantive rights which originated in the treaty. Second, in the circumstances the treaty had not been incorporated into domestic law, and consequently the rights must have been created by an international agreement – and hence by international law, rather than domestic law. Thus, the PCIJ held that an international treaty can confer rights on individuals directly. Yet this conclusion seems to contradict the Court's express statement that an international treaty 'cannot, as such, create direct rights and obligations for private individuals'.[80]

The first part of the Opinion, which establishes that Danzig courts have jurisdiction in pecuniary claims based on the terms of the treaty, seems to indicate that a treaty may confer rights on an individual but do so indirectly: the state parties may adopt 'definite rules creating individual rights and obligations'. The interpretation advocated by Anzilotti and Beckett was that the adoption of those rules could only occur through domestic law. As such, the individual obtains rights under domestic law and the dualist approach is maintained: states have rights and obligations under international law; individuals have rights and obligations under domestic law. The difficulty with this interpretation is that the PCIJ held that the individual rights existed despite the fact that the relevant rules had not been adopted in either the domestic law of Poland or the Free City. A categorical distinction between two legal orders – the international and the domestic – thus becomes more difficult to maintain.

Anzilotti and Beckett sought to overcome this difficulty by reference to the argument that Poland could not base its objection to the exercise of jurisdiction by the Danzig courts on its failure to fulfil its obligation to incorporate the relevant rights into domestic law. The attractive symmetry of this approach at first glance is lessened when the PCIJ's statements are considered in their context. The Court referred to the principle that a state could not rely on non-fulfilment of an obligation to raise an objection to its liability in the context of considering whether Poland was bound to accept the jurisdiction of the Danzig courts and enforce its judgments, having already held that the Danzig courts had substantive jurisdiction in the relevant claims. Essentially, in the first part of its Opinion (jurisdiction) the Court was considering whether

80 *Jurisdiction of the Courts of Danzig (Pecuniary Claims of Danzig Railway Officials who have Passed into the Polish Service, Against the Polish Railways Administration)*, PCIJ Rep. ser. B no. 15 (1928) 3, 17–18.

Danzig was in breach of international law by permitting claims to be brought in its courts by individuals based on the treaty; and in the second part (applicable law), it was considering whether Poland was obliged under international law to recognise and enforce the judgments based on that jurisdiction. Poland's objection to liability based on its failure to fulfil its obligations under the treaty to incorporate its provisions in domestic law arose in the second part because it dealt with Poland's obligations, whereas the first part dealt with Danzig's rights and obligations. The approach of Anzilotti and Beckett makes the PCIJ's conclusions in the first part (jurisdiction) subject to its conclusions in the second part (applicable law). But the Court had already concluded that the treaty constituted part of the contract of service and that judgments based on the agreement should be recognised and executed by the PRA, and although it noted that its conclusions in the second part confirmed its conclusions in the first part, it is clear that the Court's conclusions in the first part were not dependent on its findings in the second part. A careful reading of the Opinion supports the opposite view: that the PCIJ's conclusion that the legal effect of the 1921 Agreement is such that individuals derived rights stands independently from its consideration of the applicable law.

This conclusion is affirmed by a second consideration. The interpretation offered by Anzilotti and Beckett implies a kind of wilful blindness on the part of the PCIJ: that the Court ignored the fact that the treaty had not been incorporated into domestic law and still concluded that individuals derived rights under domestic law. The reasoning implicit in this approach must be as follows:

(a) rights for individuals which originate in a treaty can only exist if they are incorporated into domestic law;
(b) Poland was obliged to incorporate those rights into domestic law;
(c) Poland could not argue that the rights did not exist in domestic law because of its failure to comply with its obligation to incorporate them into domestic law; and
(d) the Court must therefore ignore that the rights were not incorporated into domestic law; rather it should apply the international law priority rule against Poland.

A careful reading of the Opinion does not support such an interpretation.[81]

[81] Some support for this conclusion can be taken from the PCIJ's later decision in *Interpretation of the Statute of the Memel Territory*, PCIJ Rep. ser. A/B no. 49 (1932) 294, 336.

Having discarded the approach which assumes incorporation into domestic law, it remains to consider what meaning the PCIJ's Opinion bears in its context. The practical effect of the Court's conclusion is that individuals held substantive rights which originated in the treaty. Since these rights were not incorporated into domestic law, it also follows that they were created by an international treaty, on the plane of international law.

Why, then, might the PCIJ have been at such pains to say that a treaty 'cannot, as such, create direct rights' for individuals, but rather that the object of a treaty 'may be the adoption by the [state] Parties of some definite rules creating individual rights'?[82] If the PCIJ had not expressly stated that a treaty cannot create direct rights for individuals, it would have been evident that that was exactly what the Court had intended. Effectively the Court advocated an intermediate step, thus preserving its view that in cases of doubt, treaties do not create rights for third parties.[83] In order to do so, states must clearly *intend* to adopt rules conferring rights on individuals via treaty. But it is clear from the Opinion that the 'adoption' of rules conferring rights on individuals can occur at the international level and the individual rights are created by treaty, that is, by international law, rather than by municipal law.[84] The emphasis on clear intention of states parties to a treaty reinforced the position of states in the international legal system, as any rights for individuals were premised on clear state consent, and states thus retained their monopoly on access to the international system and their status as gatekeepers of international rights and duties.

In circumstances where there was an obligation to incorporate a treaty into municipal legislation, but a failure to do so, the PCIJ did not imply that there had been incorporation of the treaty into domestic law.

82 *Jurisdiction of the Courts of Danzig (Pecuniary Claims of Danzig Railway Officials who have Passed into the Polish Service, Against the Polish Railways Administration)*, PCIJ Rep. ser. B no. 15 (1928) 3, 17–18.

83 This is consistent with the position under the Vienna Convention on the Law of Treaties in respect of rights created for third parties under treaties: see Vienna Convention on the Law of Treaties, Art. 36(1), 23 May 1969 (entered into force 27 January 1980), 155 UNTS 331; *Free Zones of Upper Savoy and the District of Gex*, Judgment, PCIJ Rep. ser. A/B no. 46 (1932) 96, 147–8. See discussion in A. Aust, *Modern Treaty Law and Practice* (Cambridge, Cambridge University Press, 2000), p. 208; P. Reuter, *Introduction to the Law of Treaties* (London, Pinter, 1989), p. 79.

84 Lauterpacht suggested that the ambiguity was deliberate, stating that the PCIJ's 'departure from the established view was effected with such ingenious restraint that some have been led to believe that the decision of the Court amounts to a solemn affirmation of the established doctrine': see Lauterpacht, *The Development of International Law*, p. 52.

Like the question of the personality of the League of Nations, the question of the effect of the PCIJ's Opinion vis-à-vis individual rights was not definitively resolved in the inter-war period and certainly it was not reflected in a shift in traditional doctrine providing for a different position for individuals: for example, there was no mention of the *Danzig* Opinion in Arnold McNair's 1930 edition of *Oppenheim*, although later PCIJ decisions were referenced,[85] and it was maintained that it was impossible for individuals to bear rights and duties under international law.[86] The Opinion did not have an immediate transformative effect on the position of the individual in the international legal system; there was not even general agreement that it provided for individual rights directly under international law in a way which was inconsistent with the generally-accepted framework of the international legal system. Nevertheless, it later came to be cited in support of both of those claims.

International legal doctrine during the inter-war period suggested that the framework of the international legal system remained essentially unchanged: in particular, subjects of international law were states exclusively; and individuals, as objects of international law, did not obtain rights and duties directly from international law. But during the inter-war period some developments laid the ground for future amendment of both of these aspects of the framework: recognition that there could be subjects of international law apart from states; and recognition that individuals could be granted rights directly under international treaties.[87] At the time, these developments were not acknowledged as having any transformative effect.

(d) The post-1945 international legal system

The framework of the international legal system in the post-1945 period reflects the core of the state-centrism that had long characterised the international legal system, but in several respects there have been significant changes to the traditional framework. It is useful to refer

[85] See e.g., the reference to the April 1928 Judgment of *German Minority Schools in Polish Upper Silesia*: McNair, *Oppenheim's International Law*, vol. I, p. 584, para. 340d.

[86] McNair repeats the statement found in the first edition, that the assertion that individuals can 'acquire rights and duties from International Law, is untenable as a general proposition': see McNair, *Oppenheim's International Law*, vol. I, p. 520, para. 289.

[87] As will be discussed in Part II, a number of practical developments also introduced or predicated elements of structural change in the inter-war period: these include the mandates system (see 5.3(b) below); the system for protection of minorities (see 5.3(a) below); and the International Labor Organisation (see 5.3(d) below).

to *Oppenheim*, this time in the ninth edition, published in 1992.[88] *Oppenheim* has been selected not only because of useful symmetry with its first edition, but because it remains one of the most influential texts. A similar exercise could be undertaken with other leading texts, including Brownlie,[89] Shaw[90] or Evans.[91]

The relevant points are as follows.

(1) International law primarily consists of the rules binding on states in their relations with each other.[92] These rules are based on the common express or tacit consent of states.[93]

(2) States are the principal subjects of international law and international law does not normally impose duties or confer rights directly upon individuals.[94] Although individuals can enjoy certain rights and duties in conformity with, or according to international law, in most cases it is the state to which those individuals belong in which the relevant right is vested, and by international law it is that state which has the right to require that other states grant rights to those individuals while they are in their territories.[95] Those individuals do not thereby become subjects of international law.

(3) States are primarily but not exclusively the subjects of international law. To the extent that other entities 'directly possess' rights, powers and duties in international law they may be regarded as subjects of international law and as possessing international personality. The question whether a particular entity is a subject of international law and what rights, powers and duties they possess is a matter for inquiry in each case.[96]

(4) States can and occasionally do confer upon individuals 'international rights *stricto sensu*, i.e. rights which they acquire without the

88 Jennings and Watts, *Oppenheim's International Law*.

89 I. Brownlie, *Principles of Public International Law* (7th edn, Oxford, Oxford University Press, 2008).

90 M. Shaw, *International Law* (6th edn, Cambridge, Cambridge University Press, 2008).

91 M. Evans (ed.), *International Law* (2nd edn, Oxford, Oxford University Press, 2006).

92 Jennings and Watts, *Oppenheim's International Law*, p. 4, para. 1; p. 16, para. 6.

93 *Ibid.* p. 14, para. 5. See also Shaw, *International Law*, pp. 2, 5–6, 45, 130; Brownlie, *Principles of Public International Law*, p. 289; C. Warbrick, 'States and Recognition in International Law' in M. Evans (ed.), *International Law* (2nd edn, Oxford, Oxford University Press, 2006), pp. 217, 217–18; McCorquodale, 'The Individual and the International Legal System', 308.

94 Jennings and Watts, *Oppenheim's International Law*, p. 16, para. 5; p. 846, para. 374.

95 *Ibid.* pp. 846–7, para. 374. See also Shaw, *International Law*, pp. 1, 197; Brownlie, *Principles of Public International Law*, pp. 58–9; McCorquodale, 'The Individual and the International Legal System', 308–9.

96 Jennings and Watts, *Oppenheim's International Law*, p. 16, para. 7. See also Shaw, *International Law*, pp. 196–7, 260–4; Brownlie, *Principles of Public International Law*, p. 65; McCorquodale, 'The Individual and the International Legal System', 308–9, 312–15.

intervention of municipal legislation and which they can enforce in their own name before international tribunals' (citing the PCIJ's Opinion in *Jurisdiction of the Courts of Danzig*).[97] Thus, in certain spheres, individuals can enter into direct legal relationships on an international plane with states and, as such, have rights and duties flowing directly from international law, and these rights and duties may exist and be enforceable without having been previously incorporated in municipal law.[98] To the extent that states treat individuals as directly endowed with international rights and duties, individuals are subjects of international law.[99] '[T]here is an increasing disposition to treat individuals, within a limited sphere, as subjects of international law.'[100]

(5) To the extent that individuals are subject to international duties, they may commit international wrongs. The Nuremberg Tribunal held its provisions relating to individual responsibility to be declaratory of a principle of international law. Since 1946 there has been an increasing trend towards the expansion of individual criminal responsibility directly under international law.[101]

(6) To the extent that individuals are not subjects of international law, nationality is the link between individuals and international law. It is through nationality that individuals 'can normally enjoy benefits from international law'.[102] If individuals who possess nationality are wronged abroad, as a rule, it is the state of nationality which has an exclusive right to ask for redress; 'individuals themselves have no such [international] right'.[103] Individuals who do not possess any nationality enjoy only limited protection. Apart from obligations expressly laid down by treaty and obligations to respect human rights and fundamental freedoms, as far as international law is concerned there is 'no restriction upon a state maltreating ... stateless individuals'.[104] In principle, subject to any particular applicable international obligation, 'it is

97 Jennings and Watts, *Oppenheim's International Law*, p. 847, s.375; p. 17, para. 7.

98 *Ibid.* p. 17, para. 7.

99 *Ibid.* p. 16, para. 7.

100 *Ibid.* pp. 847–9, para. 375, esp. p. 849, para. 375. See also Shaw, *International Law*, p. 259; McCorquodale, 'The Individual and the International Legal System', pp. 312–15.

101 Jennings and Watts, *Oppenheim's International Law*, pp. 506–8, para. 148. See also Shaw, *International Law*, pp. 259, 357, 400–1; Brownlie, *Principles of Public International Law*, pp. 35, 587–8; McCorquodale, 'The Individual and the International Legal System', 314–15.

102 Jennings and Watts, *Oppenheim's International Law*, p. 847, para. 376; see also pp. 857–9, para. 379.

103 *Ibid.* p. 849, para. 376.

104 *Ibid.* p. 849, para. 376, see also pp. 886–7, para. 397.

not for international law but for the internal law of each state to determine who is, and who is not, to be considered its national'.[105]

(7) Every state has a right to protect its nationals abroad, which provides a means to enforce the obligations of other states to treat aliens on their territory in accordance with certain legal rules and principles. International law imposes no duty upon a state to protect its nationals abroad; this is a matter within the discretion of every state, and no national has an international law right to demand protection from his state of nationality, although such a right may exist under municipal law.[106]

When compared to the propositions set out in respect of the nineteenth century framework, it can be seen that the post-1945 framework differs in two significant respects. First, states may confer rights and duties upon individuals, and the capacity to enforce those rights and duties, without the interposition of municipal law. This is traced to the Opinion of the PCIJ in *Danzig*. Second, it is accepted that there may be a broader range of subjects in the international legal system: entities other than states may be subjects of international law. This specific development is addressed in some detail in the following section on the development of doctrine relating to international legal personality.

1.4 International legal personality as the measure of engagement in the international legal system

Since at least the end of the nineteenth century the device used to explain the relationship of entities to the international legal system has been the doctrine of the subjects of international law, which divides entities into either 'subjects' or 'objects'. The distinction, or lack thereof, between the terms 'subjects' and 'international legal personality' has led to much confusion in the literature. In early treatises, it appears that the term 'subjects' was used to denote full members of the international community, on whom rights were conferred and obligations imposed; whereas 'international persons' encompassed a broader

105 *Ibid.* p. 852, para. 378. See also Shaw, *International Law*, pp. 258, 808–9; Brownlie, *Principles of Public International Law*, pp. 402–3; McCorquodale, 'The Individual and the International Legal System', 316.

106 Jennings and Watts, *Oppenheim's International Law*, p. 934, para. 410; see also pp. 910–11, para. 405; pp. 511–15, para.150. See also Shaw, *International Law*, pp. 809–11; Brownlie, *Principles of Public International Law*, p. 478; P. Okowa, 'Issues of Admissibility and the Law of International Responsibility' in M. Evans (ed.), *International Law* (2nd edn, Oxford, Oxford University Press, 2006), pp. 479, 483–4.

category of entities who were treated as subjects in some more limited sense.[107] The concepts were, however, conflated by the International Court of Justice (ICJ) in its 1949 Advisory Opinion in the *Reparations* case. The ICJ there held that the UN was an 'international person', meaning that 'it is a subject of international law'.[108] It is now generally common to use the terms interchangeably, although some writers continue to perpetuate the distinction.[109]

(a) Development of the doctrine of subjects: the Reparations *Opinion*

In the nineteenth century international legal system, it was said that subjects of international law were states 'solely and exclusively'.[110] In the inter-war period the possibility of the League of Nations being a subject of international law since it had 'distinctive international rights and duties' was raised but not resolved.[111] In the post-1945 international legal system it has been accepted that to the extent that entities other than states 'directly possess' rights, powers and duties in international law they may be regarded as subjects of international law.[112] This proposition is traced to the 1949 Advisory Opinion of the ICJ in the *Reparations* case, an Opinion which also brought some clarity to the question of the characteristics or definition of 'subjects' of international law.[113] As such it is worth examination in some detail.

[107] 'Full Sovereign States are perfect, not-full Sovereign States are imperfect International Persons, for not-full Sovereign States are for some parts only subjects of International Law': Oppenheim, *International Law: A Treatise*, p. 99.

[108] *Reparations for Injuries Suffered in the Services of the United Nations* [1949] ICJ Rep. 174, 179.

[109] The Restatement (Third) suggests that 'persons under international law' are those that 'have legal status, personality, rights, and duties under international law and whose acts and relationships are the principal concerns of international law', whereas the term 'subjects' connotes entities that 'have only rights and obligations': *Restatement of the Law: Third, Foreign Relations Law of the United States* (The American Law Institute, 1987), I, p. 70. Jan Klabbers suggests there is a more fundamental distinction: 'To be a subject of international law is to be given an academic label: a subject of international law is the legitimate subject of international legal research and reflection . . . [While] personality is, in principle at any rate, a status conferred by the legal system.' J. Klabbers, *An Introduction to International Institutional Law* (Cambridge, Cambridge University Press, 2002), p. 43. See generally, H. Mosler, 'Subjects of International Law' (1984) IV *MPIL* 710, 711; J. Klabbers, 'The Concept of Legal Personality' (2005) *Ius Gentium* 35.

[110] Oppenheim, *International Law: A Treatise*, pp. 18–19, para.13.

[111] McNair, *Oppenheim's International Law*, vol. I, pp. 133–4.

[112] Jennings and Watts, *Oppenheim's International Law*, p. 16, para. 7.

[113] *Reparations for Injuries Suffered in the Services of the United Nations* [1949] ICJ Rep. 174. The question of international personality for international organisations was not directly addressed by the PCIJ, although in its Advisory Opinion in *European Commission on the*

The relevant question put to the ICJ was whether the UN had 'the capacity to bring an international claim' against a state in circumstances involving the responsibility of that state,[114] which the Court interpreted as asking whether the UN had international legal personality. Since this question was not settled explicitly in the UN Charter, the Court considered what characteristics states had intended to give to the UN through its Charter. The ICJ introduced a variegated approach to the subject categorisation, stating:

> The subjects of law in any legal system are not necessarily identical in their nature or in the extent of their rights, and their nature depends upon the needs of the community. Throughout its history, the development of international law has been influenced by the requirements of international law, and the progressive increase in the collective activities of States has already given rise to instances of action upon the international plane by certain entities which are not States. This development culminated in the establishment in June 1945 of an international organization whose purposes and principles are specified in the Charter of the United Nations. But to achieve these ends the attribution of international personality is indispensable.[115]

After examining factors surrounding the establishment of the UN, provisions of its Charter which set out its functions and subsequent practice of the international community, in particular of concluding conventions to which the UN is a party, the ICJ unhesitatingly held that the UN was an international legal person with capacity to bring an international claim:

Danube, the Court compared the commission to a state and regarded it as being able to perform functions with international consequences: see *European Commission on the Danube*, Advisory Opinion, PCIJ Rep. ser. B no. 14 (1927) 64. In the several cases in which the PCIJ dealt with disputes about the powers of the International Labor Organization (ILO), the issue of personality was not directly raised but it repeatedly held that the ILO was able to exercise certain powers under its constitution, which suggests that the ILO was acting as a separate legal person rather than through its constituent members: *Employment of Women During the Night*, PCIJ Rep. ser. A/B no. 50 (1932); *Competence of the ILO to Regulate Conditions of Labour in Agriculture*, PCIJ Rep. ser. B no. 2 (1922); *Competence of the ILO to Regulate Agricultural Production*, PCIJ Rep. ser. B no. 3 (1922); *Personal Work of Employers*, PCIJ Rep. ser. B no. 13 (1926). See generally, F. Seyersted, 'International Personality of Intergovernmental Organizations: Do their Capacities Really Depend upon their Constitutions?' (1964) 4 *Ind. JIL* 1; P. H. F. Bekker, *The Legal Position of Intergovernmental Organizations: A Functional Necessity Analysis of their Legal Status and Immunities* (Dordrecht, Martinus Nijhoff, 1994).

114 *Reparations for Injuries Suffered in the Services of the United Nations*, Advisory Opinion [1949] ICJ Rep. 175.

115 *Ibid.* 178.

the Organization was intended to exercise and enjoy, and is in fact exercising and enjoying functions and rights which can only be explained on the basis of the possession of a large measure of international personality and the capacity to operate upon an international plane ... Accordingly, the Court has come to the conclusion that the Organization is an international person.[116]

The ICJ emphasised that this did not mean that its legal personality and rights and duties were equivalent to those of a state, but it meant that the UN was 'a subject of international law and capable of possessing international rights and duties, and [it had] capacity to maintain its rights by bringing international claims'.[117] Furthermore, the Court held that the UN could bring a claim against a state which was not a UN member, since the UN had 'objective international legal personality'.[118]

Four general points about international legal personality may be taken from the *Reparations* Opinion. First, while states possess the full range of rights and duties under international law, with attendant capacity, other subjects of international law may have different rights, duties and capacities. Second, being a subject of international law entails the possession of international rights and duties, and the capacity to bring international claims. Third, capacities of an entity may be inferred from functional necessity and practice and need not be expressly or directly conferred by a constituent instrument. Finally, 'the vast majority' of states may create an entity with objective international personality, which therefore can bring international claims against any state.

(b) Sui generis *subjects of international law*

Characterising international organisations as subjects of international law marked a clear departure from nineteenth century doctrine, but even then the international legal order was conceived as being within the exclusive *control* of states, because international organisations are created by states. Similar control can be seen in the case of entities which are *sui generis* subjects of international law by virtue of their recognition by states. Two of these, the Holy See[119] and the Order of St

116 *Ibid.* 179.

117 *Ibid.* 179. This was affirmed in the work of the International Law Commission: see (1985) II *Yearbook of the International Law Commission* Pt 1, p. 107.

118 *Reparations for Injuries Suffered in the Services of the United Nations*, Advisory Opinion, [1949] ICJ Rep. 175, 185. For criticism, see G. Schwarzenberger, *International Law* (3rd edn, London, Stevens, 1957), vol. I, pp. 128–9, 469–71, 523 and 596; cf. Jennings and Watts, *Oppenheim's International Law*, p. 18, para. 7; p. 1203, para. 583; p. 1263, para. 627.

119 The Holy See is the central authority and administrative organ of the Catholic Church.

John of Malta,[120] had historical claims to territory, and might be explained as near-states, at least in their origins.

Before 1870, the international capacity of the Holy See was associated with the government of the Papal states, but even after the annexation of the Papal states, states continued to accredit envoys to receive Legates from the Holy See and the Pope continued to make concordats with foreign states.[121] Since 1929, the State of the City of the Vatican City and the Holy See achieved general recognition as two distinct legal persons, in practice and in the literature,[122] and although the exact relationship between the two entities is unclear,[123] it is generally accepted that after 1929 the Holy See retained a measure of international personality separate from its personality attendant to its position as the independent government of the Vatican City.

The Order of St John of Malta, an organisation formed around 1100 and dedicated to the provision of medical and religious care, was sovereign over the islands of Rhodes (1310–1528) and Malta (1520–1798): the latter was ceded to Napoleon by treaty[124] and subsequently ceded by France to Great Britain by the Treaty of Peace of 1814.[125] In 1879, the Order established headquarters in Rome.[126] The Order exchanges envoys with or is otherwise recognised by more than eighty states;[127]

120 The Sovereign Military Order of St John of Jerusalem, of Rhodes and of Malta is an ancient organisation dedicated to the provision of medical and religious care.

121 R. A. Graham, *The Rise of the Double Diplomatic Corps in Rome: A Study in International Practice* (The Hague, Martinus Nijhoff, 1952); G. Arangio-Ruiz, 'On the Nature of the International Personality of the Holy See' (1996) 29 *Revue Belge de Droit International* 354, 360–1.

122 Crawford, *The Creation of States*, pp. 226–7; both entities are parties to a number of multilateral treaties. See also generally, J. Duursma, *Fragmentation and the International Relations of Microstates* (Cambridge, Cambridge University Press, 1996), pp. 386–7.

123 See e.g., Duursma, *Fragmentation and the International Relations of Microstates*, pp. 386–7; Crawford, *The Creation of States*, pp. 230–1.

124 53 CTS 375.

125 56 CTS 289. Britain treated Malta as a possession, in violation of the Treaty of Amiens of 1802, by which Britain undertook to restore Malta to the Order on the same conditions as existed prior to 1798 (56 CTS 389); the Order was unable to obtain a reversal of this state of affairs at the Congress of Vienna: C. D'Oliver Farran, 'The Sovereign Order of Malta in International Law' (1954) 3 *ICLQ* 211, 221.

126 D'Oliver Farran, 'The Sovereign Order of Malta in International Law', 221.

127 Crawford, *The Creation of States*, p. 231; D'Oliver Farran, 'The Sovereign Order of Malta in International Law', 222–7; H. J. A. Sire, *The Knights of Malta* (New Haven, Conn., Yale University Press, 1994), pp. 271, 285. The Order had been recognised by the Italian courts as a subject of international law as early as 1935: see *Nanni* v. *Pace and the Sovereign Order of Malta* (1935–7) ILR 2 (Italian Court of Cassation, 13 March 1935); *Association of Italian Knights of the Order of Malta* v. *Piccoli* (1984) 65 ILR 308 (Italian Court of

those states which recognise it also accord it immunity for acts *jure imperii*;[128] in Italy it is exempt from taxation on the basis that it is a subject of international law[129] and judgments of its courts are treated like those of a foreign state.[130] In 1994, the Order was granted observer status at the UN General Assembly.[131] Its Charter asserts that it is 'a subject of international law and exercises sovereign functions',[132] but in practice its functions are limited and specific.

By contrast, a third *sui generis* subject of international law, the International Committee for the Red Cross (ICRC), has no historical or current connection to territory, nor any aspirations to statehood. Rather, it came to be recognised as having a measure of international personality in view of its special status under international humanitarian law.[133] The ICRC was formed in 1862 by Henry Dunant as a humanitarian initiative. It was established as a Swiss association and has legal personality under Swiss law.[134] Its work has been recognised in all the major international conventions regulating armed conflict

Cassation, 6 June 1974). See generally, A. C. Breycha-Vauthier, 'The Order of St John in International Law: A Forerunner of the Red Cross' (1954) 48 *AJIL* 554.

128 *Sovereign Order of Malta* v. *Brunelli, Tacali and others* (1931) 6 ILR 46 (Court of Cassation); *Sovereign Order of Malta* v. *Soc An Commerciale* (1954) 22 ILR 1.

129 *Ministry of Finance* v. *Association of Italian Knights of the Order of Malta* (1978) 65 ILR 320, 323 (Court of Cassation).

130 *Piccoli* v. *Association of the Italian Knights of the Order of Malta* (1978) 77 ILR 613, 615 (CA, Rome).

131 Observer Status for the Sovereign Military Order of Malta in the General Assembly, GA/Res/48/265, 24 August 1994, esp. Preamble, para. 2. The documentation on the granting of observer status indicated that sixty-four member states of the UN had recognised the Order's 'full sovereignty as an equal member of the international community' and noted that the Order is represented by accredited delegations to numerous international agencies, including the UN Offices at Geneva and Vienna, the Commission of the European Union and the Council of Europe: Request for the Inclusion of an Additional Item in the Agenda of the Forty-Eighth Session, GA/46/957 (29 June 1994), and GA/46/957/Add.1 (22 July 1994), Annex, paras. 1, 8.

132 Constitutional Charter and Code 1961, revised 28–30 April 1997: N. Cox, 'The Acquisition of Sovereignty by Quasi-States: The Case of the Order of Malta' (2002) 6 *Mountbatten J of Legal Studies* 26, 40–1.

133 See generally, C. Dominicé, 'La personalité juridique internationale du CICR' in C. Swinarski (ed.), *Studies and Essays on International Humanitarian Law and Red Cross Principles in Honour of Jean Pictet* (The Hague, Martinus Nijhoff, 1984), pp. 663, 663–73. See also Reuter, *Introduction to the Law of Treaties*, pp. 783–91; G. Rona, 'The ICRC Privilege Not to Testify: Confidentiality in Action' (2002) 845 IRRC 207; *Prosecutor* v. *Blagojoe Simic, Milan Simic, Miroslav Tadic, Stevan Todorovic, Simo Zaric*, Case no. IT-95-P, ICTY Trial Chamber, Decision on the Prosecution Motion under Rule 73 for a Ruling concerning the Testimony of a Witness, 27 July 1999.

134 Y. Sandoz, *The International Committee of the Red Cross as Guardian of International Humanitarian Law* (Geneva, ICRC, 1998), p. 4.

since the 1929 Geneva Convention on Prisoners of War, which gave it a power of initiative in relation to a central agency for information regarding prisoners of war and recognised its 'humanitarian work'.[135] Its public functions were developed in Protocol I of 1977.[136] The Statute of the ICRC, which has been adopted by the states parties to the 1949 Geneva Conventions,[137] designates it as an 'independent humanitarian organisation having a status of its own'. Further, the ICRC has concluded headquarters agreements with seventy-four states to facilitate the independence of the ICRC and its delegates, which are plainly treaties under international law.[138] Some of these agreements expressly or implicitly refer to the international personality of the ICRC.[139] The vast majority of them grant the ICRC immunity, inviolability of premises and exemption from taxes.

135 Geneva Convention on Prisoners of War, 27 July 1929 (entry into force 19 June 1931), 118 LNTS 343, Arts. 79 and 88. These provisions were substantially reinforced in the 1949 Geneva Conventions. Article 129 of the Third Geneva Convention gives ICRC delegates 'the same prerogatives' as those of the Protecting Power to visit places of detention and interview detainees: Geneva Convention III Relative to the Treatment of Prisoners of War, 12 August 1949 (entry into force 21 October 1950), 75 UNTS 13; see also Geneva Convention IV Relative to the Protection of Civilian Persons in Time of War, Art. 143, 12 August 1949 (entry into force 21 October 1950), 75 UNTS 287. Article 88 of the 1929 Geneva Convention is also repeated in common Art. 9/9/9/10 of the 1949 Geneva Conventions, as well as in Geneva Convention III, Art. 123 and Geneva Convention IV, Art. 140. Common Art. 3 specifically designates the ICRC as an 'impartial humanitarian body' which may offer its services to the parties to a conflict. Geneva Convention III, Art. 125 provides that the 'special position' of the ICRC 'shall be recognized and respected at all times'; see also Geneva Convention IV, Art. 142.

136 Article 5 develops the potential role of the ICRC as a substitute Protecting Power, and reflects the key characteristic of the ICRC: impartiality. Further, Art. 81(1) provides that parties to the conflict 'shall grant to the [ICRC] all facilities within their power so as to enable it to carry out the humanitarian functions' assigned to it by the Geneva Conventions and the Protocol.

137 Sandoz, *The International Committee of the Red Cross*, p. 4.

138 ICRC Annual Report 2003, p. 21, available at www.icrc.org/Web/Eng/siteeng0.nsf/htmlall/section_annual_report_2003www.icrc.org/Web/Eng/siteeng0.nsf/htmlall/section_annual_report_2003; Dominicé, 'La personalité juridique internationale du CICR', 668–9; Reuter, *Introduction to the Law of Treaties*, p. 789.

139 For example, Art. 1 of the Agreement with Switzerland states: 'The Federal Council recognizes the international legal personality and the legal capacity in Switzerland of the International Committee of the Red Cross.' Agreement between the International Committee of the Red Cross and the Swiss Federal Council to Determine the Legal Status of the Committee in Switzerland (1993) 293 IRRC 152. Under the terms of the Agreement, the ICRC is granted inviolability of premises and archives and immunity from legal process and execution and from taxation: Arts. 1, 3, 4 and 5. Other agreements recognise the ICRC's status in a functional way without express reference to its international legal personality.

That the ICRC has a measure of international personality is also affirmed by the fact that it has been recognised as having a specific right to non-disclosure in the context of international criminal law. In 1999, the Trial Chamber of the International Criminal Tribunal for the former Yugoslavia (ICTY) held that the ICRC had a right to non-disclosure in judicial proceedings because it was necessary for the effective discharge of the ICRC's mandate under the Geneva Conventions, and the parties to the Geneva Conventions and Protocols had assumed a conventional obligation corresponding to the ICRC's right to non-disclosure. The Tribunal held further that the ICRC had a correlative right under customary international law.[140] This has been codified in the International Criminal Court (ICC) Rules of Procedure and Evidence, which provide that ICRC information is privileged and is therefore not subject to disclosure unless the ICRC waives its privilege or the information is included in public statements and documents.[141] Further, the ICRC has observer status in the General Assembly, in consideration of 'the special role carried on accordingly by the [ICRC] in international humanitarian relations'.[142]

The existence of *sui generis* subjects of international law which are not states and are not composed of nor created by states signifies a certain openness of the international legal system but it also affirms state authority over the entry of new international legal persons. The creation of *sui generis* subjects of international law is linked to recognition by states, which retain a monopoly on control of access to the international legal system, as gatekeepers of that system.

(c) The individual as a 'subject' of international law

The traditional doctrine which asserted that states were the exclusive subjects of international law also asserted that individuals were 'objects' of international law:

[140] *Prosecutor* v. *Blagojoe Simic, Milan Simic, Miroslav Tadic, Stevan Todorovic, Simo Zaric*, Case no. IT-95-P, ICTY Trial Chamber, Decision on the Prosecution Motion under Rule 73 for a Ruling concerning the Testimony of a Witness, 27 July 1999, paras. 73–4.

[141] International Criminal Court, Rules of Procedure and Evidence, adopted by the Assembly of State Parties, 3–10 September 2002, ICC_ASP/1/3, rule 73(4).

[142] Observer Status for the International Committee of the Red Cross, GA/Res/45/6, 16 October 1990. In 1994, the International Federation of the Red Cross and Red Crescent Societies was also given observer status: Observer Status for the International Federation of the Red Cross, GA/Res/49/2, 19 October 1994. See Statement of Ambassador J. Moore, Alternate Representative of the United States, UNGA 45, 31st Mtg, 16 October 1990.

> The designating of States as 'subjects' within the international legal system in turn led to an embracing . . . of the position that under a legal system there exist only 'objects' and 'subjects'. . . [T]o the positivist there is no permissive rule of international law that allows individuals to be bearers of rights and duties. They must, therefore, be *objects*: that is to say, they are like 'boundaries' or 'rivers' or 'territory' or any of the other chapter headings found in the traditional textbooks.[143]

The 'object theory' of the individual in international law was premised above all on the assertion that individuals have no rights or duties under international law, and are therefore unable to invoke this law for their protection or to violate its rules.[144] It is clearly open to challenge on the basis that individuals may, in current doctrine and practice, bear rights, obligations and capacities under international law.

The broadening of the doctrine of subjects has made it possible for individuals to become subjects of international law. Whether this has in fact occurred will depend on their functions and capacities in the international legal system. It requires an inquiry into those functions and capacities, which necessarily begins with the question whether individuals have rights, obligations and capacities under international law.

The broadening of the doctrine of subjects has also opened the way for critiques of that doctrine. The variegated approach to subjects of international law has the consequence that there are qualitatively different subjects: those which have the full range of rights, obligations and capacities; and those which have one or more right, obligation or capacity. There are significant qualitative differences between the wide range of entities which are now apt to be described as subjects: from states at one end of the spectrum, to entities such as non-governmental organisations with standing before a single intergovernmental organisation at the other. Perhaps it would be difficult to find any entity which has no claim to be a subject of international law in at least one area of international law.[145] Yet, in orthodox doctrine there are no criteria for locating subjects according to the measure of their rights,

143 R. Higgins, *Problems and Process: International Law and How We Use It* (Oxford, Oxford University Press, 1994), p. 49.

144 Manner, 'The Object Theory', 428–9.

145 Although there is literature which contests the ability of corporations to have international legal personality, even corporations may have international rights: in the context of foreign investment, bilateral investment treaties (BITs) may permit companies to bring claims: see 2.4(c) above.

obligations and capacities. Thus, the variegated approach to the doctrine of subjects has exposed a fundamental deficiency of the doctrine: that the identifier 'subject' has no objective and meaningful content, since it denotes no particular capacities: hence it fails to provide any revealing description of the relationship of the entity to the international legal system. Critics of the concept of international legal personality have proposed various alternatives, drawing upon concepts such as participation,[146] capacities,[147] functions[148] and 'international legal relationships'[149] to provide a new measure for the engagement of entities in the international legal system. These critiques will be examined in more detail in Part III, drawing upon Part II, which examines the extent to which individuals are engaged in the international legal system.

1.5 Challenges to the centrality of states in the international legal system: alternative approaches

Much of the literature which examines the engagement of non-state actors in the international legal system denounces principles which might be characterised as the cornerstones of the international legal system, at least as it is recounted in orthodox doctrine. Commonly the 'state' and 'state sovereignty' are characterised as the 'archaic nemes[e]s'[150] to progression in international legal scholarship. It is claimed that although the international legal system of the past was overly concerned with states, or was excessively 'state-centric',[151] the international legal system of the future must be one more concerned with a multiplicity of actors and interests, driven by factors including increased privatisation of public functions, the movement of power

[146] Higgins, *Problems and Process*, p. 49; McCorquodale, 'The Individual and the International Legal System', 311; R. McCorquodale, 'An Inclusive International Legal System' (2004) 17 *LJIL* 477, 481.

[147] D. P. O'Connell, *International Law* (2nd edn, London, Stevens and Sons, 1970), vol. I, p. 83.

[148] C. Schreuer, 'The Waning of the Sovereign State: Towards a New Paradigm for International Law' (1994) 4 *EJIL* 447, 453.

[149] C. Walter, 'Subjects of International Law' in R. Wolfrum (ed.), *The Max Planck Encyclopedia of Public International Law* (Oxford, Oxford University Press, 2008, online edition, www.mpepil.com).

[150] See discussion in D. Kennedy, 'A New World Order: Yesterday, Today, and Tomorrow' (1994) 4 *Transnat'l Law and Contemporary Problems* 329, 363.

[151] For a general discussion of the pejorative use of the term 'state-centrism', see S. Marks, 'State-Centrism, International Law, and the Anxieties of Influence' (2006) 19 *LJIL* 339.

away from the entity of the sovereign state and towards private entities, and globalisation, with its de-emphasising of state boundaries.

These general views, which use 'state-centrism' in a pejorative way, are more specifically manifested in claims about the position of individuals in the international legal system. It is commonly claimed that, historically, international law, being exclusively concerned with the rules applicable in inter-state relations, rarely engaged with individuals, but that, over time, the international legal system has moved away from a state-centred approach to engage with a wider range of actors, including individuals. While at first glance this account rings true, the assumptions underlying it are open to question. In particular, the extent to which there has been, in practice, a move away from state-centrism in international law or a move towards individualism is open to question. Rather, there may be other possible explanations. One view might be that far from moving away from state-centrism and towards individualism, the creation of law and processes which provide very limited protection for individuals – and which are created exclusively by states – could be seen as directed to preserving the centrality of states in the international legal order, to the greatest extent possible, taking account of political realities. The question can be asked in this way: is the account commonly given of a natural and almost inevitable turn away from an overly state-centric international legal system towards a less state-centric system consistent with the historical record, at least so far as individuals are concerned? These are some of the questions which will be addressed in Part III, taking account of the material covered in Part II. To facilitate discussion of these issues, this section briefly and broadly surveys critiques of state-centrism in international law.

Critiques of state-centrism in international law are most often linked to critiques based on particular theoretical approaches which are opposed to positivism. As already explained, it is not strictly necessary to take a position on theoretical approaches to international law for the purposes of determining the existence of legal rules on the basis of the generally accepted sources of international law. However, alternative theoretical approaches are, broadly speaking, of interest to the question of what the case of the individual reveals about the extent to which the international legal system has been transformed from a state-centric system to a more multifaceted or cosmopolitan system.

In this part, discussion of the challenges to state-centrism is organised in categories corresponding to the theoretical approaches which address, in some meaningful way, the question of actors in the international legal system. These have been identified as positivism, in both its classical and 'modern' forms; process approaches; and what might be loosely termed 'cosmopolitanism'. Like the critiques of international legal personality, these critiques of state-centrism will be discussed and evaluated in Part III, drawing upon the material examined in Part II.

It should be noted at the outset that the intention is not to produce a catalogue of theoretical approaches in international law, but rather to focus on those approaches which clearly manifest a view on state-centrism in international law, and seek to construct an approach which engages in some meaningful way with individuals. Any omissions can be explained on this basis. For example, international relations theory seeks to make normative recommendations based on perceived political realities, explaining how interests, power and governance structures of states and other actors, information, ideas and understandings on which they operate, and the institutions within which they interact shape the law.[152] It does not assert that non-state actors have a particular status under the present international legal system.[153] Similarly, critical approaches (which can be used to describe critical legal studies as well as more specialised critiques, including feminist and so-called 'post-colonial' approaches) embark on a rather different enterprise, a by-product of which may be a normative argument against the centrality of states, but not asserting a particular status for other non-state actors.

(a) *Positivism in its classical and modern forms*

There is no settled or accepted definition of 'positivism' as a method or theory of international law but there are two characteristics which are broadly accepted to constitute a classical or traditional positivist approach. The first is that positivism associates law with an emanation of state will, which is also referred to as 'voluntarism'.[154] That is, international law consists of rules created by the consent of states. This finds expression in the famous *Lotus* judgment of the PCIJ:

> International law governs relations between independent States. The rules of law binding upon States therefore emanate from their own free will as

[152] K. W. Abbott, 'International Relations Theory, International Law, and the Regime Governing Atrocities in Internal Conflicts' (1999) 93 *AJIL* 361, 362.

[153] See e.g., P. J. Spiro, 'Globalization, International Law, and the Academy' (2000) 32 *New York University Journal of International Law and Politics* 852.

[154] Simma and Paulus, 'The Responsibility of Individuals', 303–4.

expressed in conventions or by usages generally accepted as expressing principles of law and established in order to regulate the relations between these co-existing independent communities or with a view to the achievement of common aims. Restrictions upon the independence of States cannot therefore be presumed.[155]

As described in one critique, '[f]or positivists, international law is no more or less than the rules to which states have agreed through treaties, custom, and perhaps other forms of consent'.[156]

The second basic characteristic of classical positivism is that it is focussed on describing the law as it is, distinguished from moral or ethical arguments.[157] It is concerned with a system of rules rather than non-legal factors. This implies that these rules are derived from one of the traditional sources of international law; in this way the second basic characteristic of positivism is related to the first, although a preoccupation with describing the law as it is may exist independently of a narrow conception of the sources of international law.

Classical positivism can be accurately described as 'state-centric' because of its close association between the rules of international law and consent of states. However, more modern forms of positivism have disassociated the second basic characteristic of classical positivism from the first, resulting in an approach where the primary concern is still deriving a rule, but where that rule may be derived from sources of law which are not necessarily strictly wedded to the consent of states. Modern positivism would take account, for example, of generally accepted sources of international law which might develop in the absence of a close connection to state consent. Simma and Paulus give as an example a widening view of evidence of 'state practice', which would incorporate not only interactions between states, but also domestic legislation, judicial decisions, diplomatic despatches, internal government memoranda and ministerial statements.[158] Another example is the practice of international organisations, which might directly contribute to the development of a rule of customary international law. So in this way modern positivism is less open to being described as 'state-centric', while still being

155 *S. S. Lotus (France* v. *Turkey)*, PCIJ Rep. ser. A no. 10 (1927) 18.

156 Ratner and Slaughter, 'Appraising the Methods of International Law', 293.

157 *Ibid.* 293; Simma and Paulus, 'The Responsibility of Individuals', 304; see also generally, Tomuschat, 'International Law', 25–9.

158 Simma and Paulus, 'The Responsibility of Individuals', 306–7.

concerned to examine generally accepted sources of law. The extent to which those sources of law are, in doctrine and practice, connected with state consent is, at least theoretically, incidental to the inquiry.

(b) Process approaches

The process approach incorporates those who see law mainly as a constant process of decisions rather than a system of rules. It can be divided into two broad categories: the policy-oriented approach and the international legal process approach. Both strands of the process approach seek to take account of the participation of a wider range of actors apart from states, as decision-makers exerting influence on the development of law.

The policy-oriented approach sees law as 'the process through which members of a community seek to clarify and secure their common interest'[159] and as made by 'authorised decision-makers' which may be any person who is expected to make such decisions 'in accordance with criteria expected by community members, in established structures of authority, with sufficient bases in effective power to secure consequential control and by authorized procedures'.[160] These potential participants in decision-making may include:

> Besides the traditional nation-state, whether independent or associated with another actor, the world social and decision processes include intergovernmental organizations, non-self governing territories, autonomous regions, and indigenous and other peoples, as well as private entities such as multinational corporations, media, nongovernmental organizations, private armies, gangs and individuals. An actor with actual or potential influence is a candidate for participation in the decision process.[161]

While the policy-oriented approach is clearly less state-centric than classical positivism, its leading proponents acknowledge that these 'authorized decision-makers are dominated by state actors',[162] and

[159] S. Wiessner and A. R. Willard, 'Policy-Oriented Jurisprudence and Human Rights Abuses in Internal Conflict: Toward a World Public Order of Human Dignity' (1999) 93 *AJIL* 316, 319. See also H. D. Lasswell and M. S. McDougal, *Jurisprudence for a Free Society: Studies in Law, Science and Policy* (Dordrecht, Nijhoff, 1992); M. W. Reisman, *Jurisprudence: Understanding and Shaping Law* (New Haven, New Haven Press, 1987).

[160] Wiessner and Willard, 'Policy-Oriented Jurisprudence and Human Rights Abuses in Internal Conflict', 319.

[161] *Ibid.* 323. [162] Higgins, *Problems and Process*, p. 39.

that the most important decision-makers are state officials. But they argue that this category is not necessarily closed to non-state actors, which would include individuals.[163]

The international legal process approach (at least in its 'new' incarnation)[164] emphasises understanding how international law works by how it is used by makers of foreign policy, and advocates certain normative values by which international institutions ought to have authority to make decisions in support of those values.[165] International legal process more clearly focusses on normative arguments[166] than the process-oriented approach, while drawing from the latter in respect of its basic method. Its preoccupation is with foreign policy-makers rather than states as such. Formally, it might be described as less state-centric than classical positivism but the extent to which the relevant actors (foreign policy-makers) are in practice disassociated from the state as such is open to question.

(c) 'Cosmopolitanism'

The concept of 'cosmopolitanism' is less well-known as a category of a theoretical approach to international law than as a political philosophy. It is used here to designate legal approaches which can be seen to derive from or incorporate elements of cosmopolitanism as it is known in political philosophy.[167] The basic premise of cosmopolitanism can be seen in this extract of Kant's essay on perpetual peace:

> The peoples of the earth have entered in varying degrees into a universal community, and it has developed to the point where a violation of the rights in *one* part of the world is felt *everywhere*. The idea of a cosmopolitan right is therefore not fantastic and overstrained; it is a necessary complement to the unwritten code of political and international right, transforming it into a universal right of humanity. Only under this condition can we flatter ourselves that we are continually advancing toward a perpetual peace.[168]

[163] Wiessner and Willard, 'Policy-Oriented Jurisprudence and Human Rights Abuses in Internal Conflict', 323.

[164] M. E. O'Connell, 'New International Legal Process' (1999) 93 *AJIL* 334, 339.

[165] *Ibid.* 388; H. Koh, 'Transnational Legal Process' (1996) 75 *Nebraska Law Review* 181, 188.

[166] O'Connell, 'New International Legal Process', 345.

[167] Cosmopolitanism has been associated with the Stoics and a number of liberal philosophers including Kant, Locke and Rawls.

[168] I. Kant, *Political Writings* (H. Reiss (ed.), H. B. Nisbet (trans.), 2nd edn, Cambridge, Cambridge University Press, 1991), pp. 107–8.

Cosmopolitanism has been associated with ideas about globalisation, global citizenship, internationalism and individualism.[169] As a political philosophy, cosmopolitanism de-emphasises traditional organising units for society such as tribes, ethnic, cultural or religious communities and nations or states and focusses instead on individuals as the basic unit, organised only by reference to a global, all-encompassing order. In literal terms it might be manifest in a world government with global citizenship.[170]

Ideas associated with cosmopolitanism as a political philosophy have been incorporated into approaches to international law which de-emphasise states and focus on a global order which refers directly to individuals. Argument about the role of transnational networks or global civil society might incorporate some aspects of cosmopolitanism. Some parallels can be drawn between these kind of approaches and the process approach.[171] Usually cosmopolitan international law approaches focus on normative arguments rather than the law *de lege lata*.[172] The focus here is on existing law and practice, and to that extent normative claims do not hold much interest. However, where cosmopolitan approaches suggest that rights, obligations and capacities (and even law-making capacities) have devolved to individuals in a manner which has transformed the international legal order in a particular way, these claims are of interest in the present context; the extent to which such claims are reflected in existing law and practice will be assessed in Part III of this book.

169 See e.g., N. Feldman, 'Cosmopolitan Law?' (2006) 116 *Yale Law Journal* 101, 102–3; J. Goldsmith, 'Liberal Democracy and Cosmopolitan Duty' (2002–3) 55 *Stanford Law Review* 1667, 1670; and T. Pogge, 'Cosmopolitanism and Sovereignty' (1992) 103 *Ethics* 48, 48–9.

170 See discussion in Feldman, 'Cosmopolitan Law?', 102–3.

171 Wiessner and Willard, 'Policy-Oriented Jurisprudence and Human Rights Abuses in Internal Conflict'.

172 See e.g., C. Ochoa, 'Towards a Cosmopolitan Vision for International Law: Identifying and Defining CIL Post *Sosa v Alvarez-Machain*' (2005–6) 74 *University of Cincinnati Law Review* 105; Ochoa, 'The Individual and Customary International Law Formation'.

PART II

The Individual in International Law

2 The individual and international claims

2.1 Introduction

The doctrine of diplomatic protection has been accepted since the nineteenth century. It provides that an injury to an individual by a foreign state is actionable by that individual's state of nationality. Diplomatic protection, often referred to as a 'fiction', transposes wrongs against individuals into wrongs against their state of nationality. But there is also a body of practice in which individuals have been permitted access to international forums to bring a direct claim against a state, without the interposition of their state of nationality. This practice is often referred to as 'mixed claims'.

Both diplomatic protection and mixed claims practice relate to the protection of individuals, but the two practices engage individuals in the international legal system in fundamentally different ways. This chapter surveys the development of the doctrine and practice of both types of claims over the same three historical periods set out in Part I. In each of these periods, the means and extent to which individuals have been engaged in the international legal system is investigated and assessed against the orthodox accounts of the international legal system examined in Part I. In accordance with the approach taken throughout the book, this chapter is focussed on doctrine, practice and procedure in relation to natural persons, i.e. individuals. Nevertheless, there is occasional reference to claims brought by other entities, including companies. Where these claims are referred to, they are discussed for the purpose of elucidation of the practice and procedure of particular claims processes which are equally applicable to natural persons: for example, where in a claim brought by a company a tribunal explains that the claim is a diplomatic protection claim in which the substantive rights at issue are states' rights, the same analysis is taken to have applied to claims brought by individuals, unless there are specific reasons for drawing a distinction between claims by natural or legal persons. As explained in Chapter 1, the examination of the position of entities other than natural persons is beyond the scope of this book, although some of the analysis might be equally applicable to such other persons.

This chapter is concerned with all international claims practice and is not limited to the law and practice relating to treatment of aliens. Before there was a developed conception of the international minimum standard of treatment of aliens there was practice which addressed claims which did not necessarily fall within the substantive content of the international minimum standard. And although the content of customary international obligations in respect of the minimum standard of treatment of aliens is now highly developed, treaties which provide for international claims do not necessarily incorporate this standard. Taking account of a broader range of practice permits a broader and more representative analysis of the position of the individual in international claims.[1]

2.2 Doctrine and practice pre-1914

The protection of aliens through a process of what came to be known as diplomatic protection began in the late eighteenth century. There was an earlier practice of issuing letters of reprisal (or letters of marque) to private individuals who had suffered damage at the hands of a foreign state or its nationals.[2] The ancient practice of reprisals had a purely private character: letters of reprisal authorised an individual who had suffered a wrong at the hands of another private party to recover property to repair the injury. Later reprisals were limited to cases of

[1] For example, it might exclude prize claims (which were referred to the Jay Treaty commissions in 1794) and contract claims (such as those dealt with by the Venezuelan Claims Commissions). See Appendix II below for further information about these processes.

[2] A. A. Cançado Trindade, 'Origin and Historical Development of the Rule of Exhaustion of Local Remedies in International Law' (1976-I) XII) *Revue Belge de droit International* 499; Y. de la Brière, 'Évolution de la Doctrine et de la Pratique en Matière de Représailles' (1928-II) *RdC* 237, 253–8; H. W. Spiegel, 'Origin and Development of Denial of Justice' (1938) *AJIL* 64; G. Clark, 'The English Practice with regard to Reprisals by Private Persons' (1933) *AJIL* 694; A. McNair, *International Law Opinions: Selected and Annotated* (Cambridge, Cambridge University Press, 1956), vol. II, pp. 297–304.

denial of justice: where there was a failure on the part of the sovereign or state to render justice to an alien against injury which was inflicted either by a private party or that sovereign. Although eventually abandoned, the practice of reprisals resembled diplomatic protection in that it entailed the proposition that a dispute between an alien and a host state (or its national) was also, in some measure, a dispute between the host state and state of nationality. Thus it was an antecedent of diplomatic protection.

(a) Vattel's articulation

The basic premise of diplomatic protection is traced to Vattel, who wrote:

> Whoever uses a citizen ill, indirectly offends the state, which is bound to protect this citizen; and the sovereign of the latter should avenge his wrongs, punish the aggressor, and, if possible, oblige him to make full reparation; since otherwise the citizen would not obtain the great end of the civil association, which is safety.[3]

Vattel thus expressed diplomatic protection as an obligation of the sending state to protect its citizens when they are injured abroad: 'Whoever uses a citizen ill, indirectly offends the State, which is bound to protect this citizen'.[4] Vattel began with the proposition that a grant of entrance to territory by a sovereign implies a condition that aliens will be subject to the local laws: consistent with the general proposition that individuals were governed by municipal rather than international law. In that context he referred to disputes between foreigners, or between foreigners and citizens, as being within the remit of the local courts, and required that the foreigner first have recourse to all peaceful means of obtaining reparation for the injury.[5] This was a corollary of a nation's territorial jurisdiction, which was to be respected by other states, and foreign states could only interfere in limited circumstances: where there was a denial of justice; the decision was clearly and palpably unjust; the proper procedure had not been observed; or

[3] E. de Vattel, *The Law of Nations or, Principles of the Law of Nature Applied to the Conduct and Affairs of Nations and Sovereigns* (1758, B. Kapossy and R. Whatmore (eds.), Indianapolis, Liberty Fund, 2008), bk II, ch. VI, para. 71 (p. 298).

[4] *Ibid.* para. 71 (p. 298). Vattel's formulation joined the view that it was the duty of the sending state to protect its citizens injured abroad to the view that the sending state was thereby vindicating its own rights.

[5] *Ibid.* para. 84 (p. 304); see also para. 338 (p. 458).

foreigners had been discriminated against.[6] Consistent with Vattel's conception of the law of nations as the law of sovereigns, he referred in this context to 'the rights and obligations of sovereigns' in respect of the protection of citizens, implying that the relevant rights were state rights, not individual rights.[7]

Vattel's proposition that an injury to an individual is an injury to his state of nationality became basic to the practice of diplomatic protection. It has been suggested that Vattel's thesis derived either from feudal law under which the lord's protection was given in return for allegiance of his subjects, or as an extension of 'social contract' theories, popular at the time to legitimise the state, which linked social peace with recognition of sovereign authority;[8] it might also have been inspired by the earlier practice of letters of reprisal. The fiction of diplomatic protection as suggested by Vattel was concerned with the treatment of individuals but referred only to inter-state rights and inter-state relations; the interests of individuals could only be protected through an inter-state process.

(b) The practice

The first recorded treaty referring an inter-state dispute to arbitration, the 1794 Jay Treaty between the US and Great Britain, established two arbitration commissions to settle the claims of British subjects for confiscated pre-war debts and claims of US nationals relating to seizures of US vessels by British cruisers and the capture of British vessels by French ships armed in US ports.[9] The Treaty did not specify whether and to what extent these claims related to any internationally wrongful act: no mention was made of any standard of treatment of aliens or obligation under the law of nations. Nor was there any suggestion that British and US nationals had international law rights.[10] The Treaty provided

[6] *Ibid.* para. 84 (p. 304). [7] *Ibid.* para. 71 (p. 298).

[8] See International Law Commission, *Preliminary Report on Diplomatic Protection*, A/CN.4/484 (Mohamed Bennouna, Special Rapporteur, 4 February 1998), p. 3, para. 7.

[9] US–Great Britain, 19 November 1794, J. B. Moore, *History and Digest of the International Arbitrations to which the United States has been a Party* (Washington, DC, Government Printing Office, 1898), vol. I, p. 271 *et seq.* In his Preliminary Report, Bennouna suggests that the first international claims commission was the commission established by the US–Great Britain Treaty of 8 February 1853 (Moore, *International Arbitrations*, vol. I, p. 391) but this is clearly incorrect: *Preliminary Report on Diplomatic Protection*, A/CN.4/484 (Mohamed Bennouna, Special Rapporteur, 4 February 1998), p. 12, para. 41.

[10] US–Great Britain, 19 November 1794, Moore, *International Arbitrations*, vol. I, p. 271, Arts. 6 and 7. The commission examining the claims of British subjects was to apply 'justice and equity' in determining the claims; whereas the commission examining the claims of US nationals was to apply 'the law of nations, justice and equity'.

that compensation was not to be awarded where there had been a failure to pursue local remedies.[11] Claims were presented by states at their discretion and individual claimants had no standing.[12] Although the Treaty expressly provided that the two governments would pay any awards directly to the claimants,[13] the British claims were subsequently settled by lump sum paid to the British government,[14] suggesting that the claims were conceived as inter-state claims.

The following year, a commission was established by Spain and the US, which provided that all losses of US citizens consequent upon their vessels and cargoes having been taken by subjects of Spain during the war between Spain and France would be referred to a commission composed of three members. Like the claims under the Jay Treaty for seizure and capture of vessels, the applicable law was designated as 'justice, equity and the law of nations',[15] but there was no mention of individual rights or specification of an internationally wrongful act. Awards were payable directly to the claimants or their representatives. The commission operated for two years from 1797 and issued forty awards amounting to some US$325,000.[16]

Throughout the nineteenth century diplomatic protection claims were asserted frequently, and two mechanisms for their resolution developed: first, specifically defined claims were submitted to arbitration, usually by a sole arbitrator; and second, classes of claims were referred to commissions or tribunals usually consisting of three members, one appointed by each government and the third by agreement or by nomination of an independent sovereign. These two kinds of dispute settlement mechanism are discussed in the remainder of this Part, with particular emphasis on whether and to what extent these mechanisms

[11] *Ibid.* Art. 6. In 1793, the US Secretary of State wrote to the British Minister that 'a foreigner, before he applies for extraordinary interposition, should use his best endeavours to obtain the justice he claims from the ordinary tribunals of the country': J. B. Moore, *A Digest of International Law* (Washington, DC, Government Printing Office, 1906), p. 259.

[12] US–Great Britain, 19 November 1794, Moore, *International Arbitrations*, vol. I, p. 271, Arts. 6 and 7.

[13] *Ibid.*

[14] Moore, *International Arbitrations*, vol. I, p. 298. It is not known whether this lump sum was paid on to the individual claimants.

[15] Spanish-US commission, 27 October 1795; W. M. Malloy, *Treaties, Conventions, International Acts, Protocols and Agreements between the United States of America and Other Powers 1776–1909* (Washington, DC, Government Printing Office, 1910), vol. I, p. 1013; Moore, *International Arbitrations*, vol. II, p. 991, Art. XXI.

[16] *Ibid.*

took account of individual claimants and how the relationship of individuals to the claim and to the respondent state was conceptualised.

(i) Arbitration of specifically defined diplomatic protection claims

Specifically defined claims which were submitted to arbitration involved a variety of subject matter. A list of reported arbitrations in the nineteenth and early twentieth centuries is included in Appendix I below.[17] Claims relating to treatment of nationals which were referred to arbitration included disputes over naval captures;[18] claims relating to treatment of vessels,[19] including fishing disputes;[20] claims relating to the imposition of excessive customs duties;[21] claims concerning the treatment of nationals (for example, regarding arrest or imprisonment);[22] claims relating to the expropriation of property;[23] and claims relating to breach of contract by a state.[24] The treaties referring these claims to arbitration did not specifically identify the internationally wrongful act as a violation of a state right or an individual right.

[17] Where the practice and procedure of tribunals and commissions in respect of claims brought by claimants other than natural persons (i.e. by legal persons) is set out in Appendix I below, these decisions are considered to the extent that they provide insight into the procedure and practice which is also applicable to claims by natural persons.

[18] France–Spain, 15 February 1851, 105 CTS 153, A. de Clerq (ed.), *Recueil des Traités de la France* (Paris, Arynot, 1864), vol. VI, p. 81; see also US–Peru, 23 December 1862, Moore, *International Arbitrations*, vol. II, p. 1610; US–Brazil, 14 March 1870, *ibid.* vol. II, p. 1733; Spain–US, 16 June 1870, *ibid.* vol. II, p. 1007; Japan–Peru, June 1873, *ibid.* vol. II, p. 5034; US–Colombia, 17 August 1874, *ibid.* vol. II, p. 1421; Netherlands–Dominican Republic, 26 March 1881, *ibid.* vol. V, p. 5036; Haiti–US, 24 May 1884, *ibid.* vol. II, p. 1749 (the claim of Antonio Pelletier); US–Denmark, 6 December 1888, *ibid.* vol. II, p. 1185; Venezuela–US, 1 January 1892, *ibid.* vol. II, p. 1693.

[19] Great Britain–France, 14 November 1842, *ibid.* vol. V, p. 4936; Great Britain–Portugal, 14 November 1842, *ibid.* vol. V, p. 4979 (Award); Great Britain–Spain, 4 March 1868, *ibid.* vol. V, p. 5018; US–Brazil, 14 March 1870, *ibid.* vol. II, p. 1007; US–Denmark, 6 December 1888, *ibid.* vol. II, p. 1185; US–Portugal, 28 February 1851, *ibid.* vol. II, p. 1092.

[20] US–China, 1884; Moore, *International Arbitrations*, vol. II, p. 1858.

[21] Great Britain–France, 23 July 1873, *ibid.* vol. V, p. 4938, LXIII BFSP 207–13; Italy–Persia, 5 June 1890, Moore, *International Arbitrations*, vol. V, p. 5018.

[22] Great Britain–Peru, 1864, Moore, *International Arbitrations*, vol. V, p. 4967; Spain–US, 16 June 1870, *ibid.* vol. II, p. 1007; Great Britain–Colombia, 14 December 1872, *ibid.* vol. II, p. 2050; US–Haiti, 24 May 1888, *ibid.* vol. II, p. 1811; US–Ecuador, 28 February 1893, *ibid.* vol. II, p. 1587; Great Britain–Netherlands, 16 May 1895, *ibid.* vol. V, p. 4948; US–Siam, 1896, *ibid.* vol. II, p. 1863; Great Britain–Portugal, 14 November 1842, *ibid.* vol. V, p. 4979.

[23] Great Britain–Russia, 1 June 1902, IX UNRIAA 51.

[24] US–Paraguay, 4 February 1859, Moore, *International Arbitrations*, vol. II, p. 1485; Great Britain–US, 1 July 1863, *ibid.* vol. I, p. 237; Haiti–US, *ibid.* vol. II, p. 1749; US–Great Britain–Portugal, 13 June 1891, *ibid.* vol. II, p. 1865; US–Siam, 1896, *ibid.* vol. II, p. 1899.

The procedures used in these arbitrations, such as they may be discerned from archive material and documentation, suggest that the claims were conceptualised as inter-state claims, rather than as individual claims. In this respect, it is relevant that the claims were submitted and presented by the two governments and any award issued was payable to the government.[25] A right of the individual national to appear or be represented was exceptional,[26] as was payment of the award directly to the claimant, rather than to the state of nationality.[27] Generally it appears that the state of nationality did not consult the individual claimants about the agreement to arbitrate.[28] In an arbitration between the US and Portugal, the claimants and owners of the vessel protested after their claim was dismissed, arguing that the US government had no authority to submit their claim to arbitration without their consent. The US Court of Claims dismissed their protest, holding that the submission of the claim was a matter falling entirely within the discretion of the US government and that the claimants had no right to be consulted.[29] The court noted:

as soon as our government was induced by the claimants to interfere, the controversy became an affair of state, to be treated as between the two

25 In one case the award stipulated that the claimant state would deliver the proceeds of the award to the individual claimant: US–Great Britain–Portugal, 13 June 1891, *ibid.* vol. II, p. 1865.

26 For example, in US–Paraguay, 4 February 1859, *ibid.* vol. II, p. 1485, counsel for the Paraguay Navigation Company (a US company) was permitted to appear before the commissioners; in Great Britain–US, 1 July 1863, *ibid.* vol. I, p. 237, counsel for the claimants appeared before the commission (as did counsel for the US) and filed their own memorials; it appears that the claimants counsel were permitted to appear before the arbitrator in Great Britain–France, 23 July 1873, *ibid.* vol. V, p. 4938, LXIII BFSP 207, since there was an order refusing their costs; in Venezuela–US, 1 January 1892, Moore, *International Arbitrations*, vol. II, pp. 1693, 1711, 1722, the US agent presented special counsel for the claimants to the commission and they made final arguments on behalf of the US government; and in Great Britain–Spain, 4 March 1868, *ibid.* vol. V, p. 5018 the claimants appear to have been represented before the commission and were entitled to submit evidence to the commission.

27 Great Britain–Netherlands, 16 May 1895, Moore, *International Arbitrations*, vol. V, p. 4948; Great Britain–Spain, 4 March 1868, (1867–8) LVIII BFSP 2 (Art. IV).

28 There were two exceptions: one where the owner of a seized steamer suggested that the dispute be submitted to arbitration (Spain–US, 16 June 1870, Moore, *International Arbitrations*, vol. II, pp. 1007, 1013) and one where the state of nationality consulted the claimants before accepting the respondent state's proposal to arbitrate (US–Colombia, 17 August 1874, *ibid.* vol. II, pp. 1421, 1425).

29 US–Portugal, 28 February 1851, *ibid.* vol. II, pp. 1092, 1098 *et seq.* esp. p. 1106; *Private Armed Brig of War General Armstrong*, Report of the US Court of Claims, 1 February 1858, S. Mis. Doc. 142, 35 Cong. 1 sess. 106–16.

governments as other differences between nations are treated; that is to say, by negotiation, arbitration, and such other modes as are recognized by the law of nations.[30]

Thus, the arbitral practice for specific diplomatic protection claims in the nineteenth and early twentieth centuries reflected the Vattelian approach: the claim was treated as an inter-state claim and the international dispute mechanism did not allow for direct participation of the injured individual, the state having control of the claim. Procedures which took account of individuals by permitting them to be represented or to directly receive the proceeds of award were exceptional and limited; they did not displace the conception of claims as inter-state claims, espoused by the state of nationality. Moreover, the claims were treated as deriving from inter-state rights in relation to treatment of that state's nationals. There was no suggestion that individuals derived rights from international law.

(ii) Claims tribunals and commissions

International claims tribunals operating in this period had varying degrees of success and had differing approaches to the involvement of individual claimants. However, three aspects of the practice and procedure weigh in favour of characterising the bulk of claims as inter-state claims rather than as direct claims by an individual against a state. These three aspects will be addressed in turn: first, the control of the claim; second, the payment of awards; and finally, the binding effect of the decisions on the states parties to the convention. In addition to these measures of procedure, it is notable that none of the claims conventions referred to individual rights; rather, the rights at stake were treated as inter-state rights and obligations. Procedurally, two exceptional tribunals provided for direct claims by individuals: the International Prize Court proposed under the Hague Convention of 1907 and the Central American Court of Justice which operated from 1908 to 1918. A summary of all the international claims tribunals discussed in this part is at Appendix II below.[31]

[30] *Private Armed Brig of War General Armstrong*, *ibid.*, reproduced in Moore, *International Arbitrations*, vol. II, p. 1106.

[31] Where the practice and procedure of tribunals and commissions in respect of claims brought by claimants other than natural persons (i.e. by legal persons) is set out in Appendix I below, these decisions are considered to the extent that they provide insight into the procedure and practice which is also applicable to claims by natural persons.

(A) Control of the claim

In most tribunals and commissions the state of nationality had control over the presentation of a claim and the submission of evidence in support of the claim. Where claimants were entitled to direct representation, it was for limited purposes: individuals could not institute proceedings by filing a claim and did not have general control over the presentation of a case.[32] The question of access of claimants was the subject of controversy in the 1839 commission established to determine the claims of US citizens against Mexico. The commission was empowered to determine its own rules of procedure,[33] although Article IV of the convention establishing the commission provided that all relevant documents in the possession of the US Department of State ought to be delivered to the commissioners, as would any documents and explanation by the Mexican government.[34] At its first session, the American commissioners presented draft rules to permit the claimants and their representatives to communicate directly with and appear before the commission.[35] They argued that in the cases before the commission each claimant was 'the *actor* or plaintiff, the state of Mexico the *reus* or defendant, and the board of commissioners the *judex* or judge' and that it was 'the right of both parties to be heard, each by his agent or counsel (if he shall so choose), in writing or *viva voce*, as he may select'.[36] The Mexican commissioners disagreed, insisting that pursuant to Article IV, the commission could not receive documents from any persons other than the two governments. The dispute was eventually resolved by a compromise under which claimants could present written explanations, documents and petitions only through their government.[37] Thus, the claimants were informed as to how they could present their cases to and communicate with the commission (effectively by submitting documents to the Department of State), but they were denied personal access to the commission and were not permitted to be represented in any oral hearings (in any event, no oral hearings were held;

[32] For example, Arts. 6 and 7, US-Great Britain, 19 November 1794, Moore, *International Arbitrations*, vol. I, pp. 271, 277 and 322; Spain-US Treaty, 27 October 1795, Malloy, *Treaties, Conventions, International Acts*, vol. I, p. 1013; Moore, *International Arbitrations*, vol. II, p. 991; US-Great Britain, 12 July 1822, *ibid.* vol. I, pp. 363, 365.

[33] Mexico-US, 11 April 1939, Malloy, *Treaties, Conventions, International Acts*, vol. I, p. 1103; Moore, *International Arbitrations*, vol. II, p. 1229.

[34] Mexico-US, 11 April 1939, Malloy, *Treaties, Conventions, International Acts*, vol. I, p. 1103.

[35] Draft Rules of Procedure, 31 August 1840, Moore, *International Arbitrations*, vol. II, p. 1224.

[36] *Ibid.* pp. 1227–8 (emphasis in original).

[37] *Ibid.* p. 1229.

the commission disposed of cases on the papers.)[38] Moreover, there was no suggestion that the US representatives could be compelled to pass on any documents received from individual claimants.

Subsequently, commissions commonly made provision to hear one representative on each separate claim, but only received evidence from agents of the relevant states.[39] Some commissions permitted individual claimants to be represented by their own counsel, provided they were introduced by the agent of their government, but required that all evidence be received through the government;[40] or permitted claimants to be represented by counsel but required their claims to be formally presented by the agent of their government.[41] The war claims commission set up by the US and Great Britain after the American Civil War permitted the claimants to file their own memorials, but they do not seem to have been given rights of appearance.[42] The commission established by the US and Costa Rica in 1860 allowed counsel for the claimants to appear;[43] and although there was no express prohibition of counsel for the claimants introducing evidence, there is no record of

[38] See description of disposition of cases in *ibid.* p. 1230.

[39] US–Great Britain, 8 February 1853, *ibid.* vol. I, p. 391; Brazil–Great Britain, 2 June 1858, 119 CTS 91, XLVIII BFSP 18; US–Peru, 12 January 1863, Moore, *International Arbitrations*, vol. II, pp. 1613, 1616; US–Venezuela, 25 April 1866, Malloy, *Treaties, Conventions, International Acts*, vol. II, p. 1856; Moore, *International Arbitrations*, vol. II, p. 1659; Mexico–US, 4 July 1868, Malloy, *Treaties, Conventions, International Acts*, vol. I, p. 1128; Moore, *International Arbitrations*, vol. II, p. 1659; Spain–US, 12 February 1871, Moore, *International Arbitrations*, vol. II, p. 1019; Malloy, *Treaties, Conventions, International Acts*, vol. I, p. 1661, (1871–72) 147 CTS 1; France–US, 15 January 1880, Moore, *International Arbitrations*, vol. II, pp. 1133, 1156–8; US–Venezuela, 5 December 1885, Malloy, *Treaties, Conventions, International Acts*, vol. II, p. 1858; Moore, *International Arbitrations*, vol. II, p. 1665; Guatemala–Mexico, 26 January 1888, 170 CTS 467; Chile–US, 7 August 1892, Moore, *International Arbitrations*, vol. II, p. 1469; US–Great Britain, 8 February 1896, Moore, *International Arbitrations*, vol. I, p. 960; Venezuela–Great Britain, 13 February 1903, IX UNRIAA 351; Germany–Venezuela, 13 February 1903, IX UNRIAA 359; Italy–Venezuela, 13 February 1903, X UNRIAA 479; US–Venezuela, 13 February 1903, 1010 BFSP 646, IX UNRIAA 115; Mexico–Venezuela, 13 February 1903, X UNRIAA 695; France–Venezuela, 27 February 1903, X UNRIAA 3; Netherlands–Venezuela, 28 February 1903, X UNRIAA 709; Belgium–Venezuela, 7 March 1903, IX UNRIAA 321; Sweden/Norway–Venezuela, 10 March 1903, X UNRIAA 763; Spain–Venezuela, 2 April 1903, X UNRIAA 737.

[40] US–Great Britain, 8 February 1853, Moore, *International Arbitrations*, vol. I, pp. 391 404, 406; US–Venezuela, 1 January 1892, *ibid.* vol. II, p. 1693 (the commission was authorised at its discretion to hear counsel other than agents of the governments).

[41] US–New Granada, 10 September 1857, *ibid.* vol. II, pp. 1361, 1381; US–Colombia, 10 February 1864, *ibid.* vol. II, p. 1361.

[42] Great Britain–US, 8 May 1871, *ibid.* vol. I, p. 683.

[43] US–Costa Rica, 2 July 1860, Moore, *International Arbitrations*, vol. II, p. 1551.

any counsel having done so. Some of the Venezuelan claims commissions in the early twentieth century received declarations from claimants or their agents[44] and permitted claimants to be present for the hearing,[45] sometimes subject to express permission from the commission[46] or from government agents.[47]

(B) Payment of awards

The majority of claims conventions provided for payment of the awards to the state of nationality.[48] Several commissions issued claimants with certificates of the awards in order for them to be reimbursed when the total award was paid to the state of nationality, but the conventions did not specify that these certificates conferred a right on individuals to receive corresponding payment.[49] The only two commissions which provided for payment directly to the claimants were those mentioned above: the commissions established by the 1794 Jay Treaty between the US and Great Britain and the 1795 Treaty between Spain and the US.[50]

The suggestion that a claimant state was obliged to pay the proceeds of an award to the relevant individual claimant was rejected by the US Supreme Court on two occasions. Mexico alleged that two awards of the 1868 Mexican-US Claims Commission, *Weil* and *La Abra*, had been obtained fraudulently.[51] At the time the allegation of fraud was raised, the awards had been issued and Mexico had paid part of the award to

[44] Germany–Venezuela, 13 February 1903, IX UNRIAA 359; Italy–Venezuela, 13 February 1903, X UNRIAA 479.

[45] Netherlands–Venezuela, 28 February 1903, X UNRIAA 709.

[46] Venezuela–Great Britain, 13 February 1903, IX UNRIAA 351.

[47] Chile–US, 7 August 1892, Moore, *International Arbitrations*, vol. II, pp. 1469, 1474.

[48] US–Great Britain, 8 February 1853, Moore, *International Arbitrations*, vol. I, pp. 391, 406; Spain–US, 12 February 1871, *ibid.* vol. II, p. 1019, (1871–2) 147 CTS 1; Great Britain–US, 8 May 1871, Moore, *International Arbitrations*, vol. I, p. 683; A. G. de la Pradelle and N. S. Politis, *Recueil des arbitrages internationaux* (Paris, Editions Internationales, 1955), vol. III, p. 41; France–US, 15 January 1880, Moore, *International Arbitrations*, vol. II, p. 1133 (Arts. I–IV); Brazil–Peru, 12 July 1904, 196 CTS 106.

[49] US–New Granada, 10 September 1857, Moore, *International Arbitrations*, vol. II, p. 1361, Art. III; US–Venezuela, 25 April 1866, *ibid.* vol. II, p. 1856; US–Venezuela, 5 December 1885, Malloy, *Treaties, Conventions, International Acts*, vol. II, p. 1858; Moore, *International Arbitrations*, vol. II, p. 1665.

[50] US–Great Britain, 19 November 1794, Moore, *International Arbitrations*, vol. I, 271 *et seq.*, Arts. 6 and 7; Spain–US Treaty, 27 October 1795, reproduced in Malloy, *Treaties, Conventions, International Acts*, vol. I, p. 1013; Moore, *International Arbitrations*, vol. II, p. 991, Art. XXI.

[51] Moore, *International Arbitrations*, vol. II, pp. 1324–58.

the US government under an instalment arrangement. One of the assignees of the *Weil* award sought to compel the Secretary of State to distribute the instalment received by the US government from the Mexican government. Before the US Supreme Court the petition was dismissed. The Court held that the treaty 'represents a compact between the [two] governments' and that citizens of the US having claims against Mexico 'were not parties to this convention'. In circumstances where a US national presented a fraudulent claim, the US was not obliged to deliver the proceeds of an award to that national.[52] Subsequently, a second assignee of part of the *Weil* award made a further application. The Supreme Court again refused to order the Secretary of State to distribute the proceeds. Chief Justice Fuller for the Court stated that the award was not a final and conclusive adjudication between the individual claimant and Mexico, but rather an adjudication between the two states, the US having made the claim its own:

> As between nations, the proprietary right in respect to those things belonging to private individuals or bodies corporate within a nation's territorial limits is absolute, and the rights of Weil cannot be regarded as distinct from those of his government. The government assumed the responsibility of presenting his claim, and made it its own in seeking redress in respect to it.[53]

In December 1892, Congress referred the two cases to the Court of Claims which found that the charges of fraud were well-founded; subsequently the US refunded the instalment payments to the Mexican government.[54]

(C) Binding effect of the decision on an inter-state basis

Finally, several of the claims conventions expressly stated that the high contracting parties (i.e. the states) agreed that decisions of the commission would be a full and final settlement of each claim of a government

[52] *Frelinghuysen* v. *Key*, 110 US 63 (1884), extracted in Moore, *International Arbitrations*, vol. II, pp. 1338–9.

[53] *United States ex rel. Boynton* v. *Blaine*, 139 US 306 (1891), extracted in Moore, *International Arbitrations*, vol. II, pp. 1345–7.

[54] Moore, *International Arbitrations*, vol. II, p. 1347; F. S. Dunn, *The Diplomatic Protection of Americans in Mexico* (New York, Columbia University Press, 1933), p. 98. The decision of the Court of Claims is reported as *United States* v. *La Abra Silver Mining Co.*, 29 Court of Claims 432 (1899).

upon the other within the jurisdiction of the commission.[55] That the clause referred to the claim of each government upon the other indicates that the claims were conceptualised as inter-state claims rather than as individual claims against a state.

The conventions did not expressly stipulate that the decisions were binding with respect to any corresponding private law claim between an individual and the respondent state or its national. However, some decisions indicate that any private claim was expunged through the inter-state process. In the *Antoine Fabiani* case, the French-Venezuelan Commission suggested that any private law claim between an individual and a state did not survive once those claims had been espoused by the individual's state of nationality. The umpire held that when France intervened, Fabiani's claims against Venezuela relating to denial of justice 'were no longer individual and private claims; they became national'. Once those claims had either been addressed through the agreed inter-state process or surrendered by France, 'if Fabiani has a claim it is against his own Government, not against Venezuela'.[56] The umpire did not specify as to the basis of any claim against the French government; it would necessarily be a domestic law claim, not an international claim, a claim of a national against his own state. The implication is that any international claim could only be addressed on an inter-state basis and that once a claim had been taken up by the national state, the claim ceased to be individual and that any private claim became a national (or state-owned) claim.[57] Thus, the decision of the commission had binding effect on any private law dispute between

[55] US–Great Britain, 8 February 1853, Moore, *International Arbitrations*, vol. I, pp. 391, 413; Brazil–Great Britain, 2 June 1858, 119 CTS 91, XLVIII BFSP 18 (Art. V); US–Venezuela, 25 April 1866, Malloy, *Treaties, Conventions, International Acts*, vol. II, 1865, Moore, *International Arbitrations*, vol. II, p. 1659 (Art. V); Mexico–US, 4 July 1868, Malloy, *Treaties, Conventions, International Acts*, vol. I, p. 1128, Moore, *International Arbitrations*, vol. II, p. 1659; Spain–US, 12 February 1871, Malloy, *Treaties, Conventions, International Acts*, vol. I, p. 1661, Moore, *International Arbitrations*, vol. II, p. 1019, (1871–2) 147 CTS 1; Great Britain–US, 8 May 1871, Moore, *International Arbitrations*, vol. I, p. 683; Guatemala–Mexico, 26 January 1888, 170 CTS 467. See also US–Venezuela, 13 February 1903, 1010 BFSP 646, IX UNRIAA 115; Mexico–Venezuela, 13 February 1903, X UNRIAA 695; France–Venezuela, 27 February 1903, X UNRIAA 3; Netherlands–Venezuela, 28 February 1903, X UNRIAA 709; Belgium–Venezuela, 7 March 1903, IX UNRIAA 321; Sweden/Norway–Venezuela, 10 March 1903, X UNRIAA 763; Spain–Venezuela, 2 April 1903, X UNRIAA 737; Brazil–Peru, 12 July 1904, 196 CTS 106.

[56] *Antoine Fabiani* case, French-Venezuelan commission of 1902, 31 July 1905, X UNRIAA 83, 127.

[57] *Ibid.* 127.

the claimant individual and the respondent state; there may have been a residual private law claim between the individual claimant and the national state but it would be a domestic (not international) law claim, and its existence was dependent on the applicable domestic law.

(D) Standing before the International Prize Court and the Central American Court of Justice

Two early twentieth century tribunals gave individuals standing to bring claims before an international forum: the proposed International Prize Court and the Central American Court of Justice. The 1907 Hague Convention for an International Prize Court was never ratified and the Court never came into operation. Had it done so, individual subjects of a contracting power could have appealed judgments of national prize courts, provided that their state of nationality did not veto the claim.[58] There was provision for individuals to participate fully in proceedings,[59] although in light of the provision for the national state to veto any claim (without reasons or limitation) it is questionable whether the Court would have provided an effective independent individual right of claim. Two aspects of the convention became controversial and eventually prevented the creation of the Court. The first was the applicable law: Great Britain sought agreement on rules to determine the law 'where no generally recognised rule exists' in order to withdraw from the Court a right to 'give judgment in accordance with the general principles of justice and equity'.[60] The second was the right of appeal: the US argued that it was unable to ratify a convention which permitted an appeal from a decision of its Supreme Court, as this was incompatible with the US Constitution.[61] The second aspect was resolved by an Additional Protocol of 1910 which allowed states to enter a reservation limiting the competence of the Court to awarding compensation, thus excluding the possibility of annulment of a decision of the relevant domestic court.[62] Subsequently, the US Senate

[58] Hague Convention XII Relative to the Creation of an International Prize Court, Arts. 3–5, The Hague, 18 October 1907 (not yet in force), reproduced in (1908) 2 *AJIL* 174.

[59] *Ibid.* Arts. 28–50.

[60] J. B. Scott, 'The Declaration of London of February 26, 1909' (1914) 8 *AJIL* 274, 285; British parliamentary papers, Miscellaneous, no. 5 (1909), p. xix.

[61] A. P. Higgins, *The Hague Peace Conferences* (Cambridge, Cambridge University Press, 1909), pp. 443–4; J. B. Scott, 'The International Court of Prize' (1911) 5 *AJIL* 302.

[62] Additional Protocol to the Convention Relative to the Establishment of an International Court of Prize, signed at The Hague, 19 September 1910 (not yet in force), reproduced in (1911) 5 *AJIL Supplement* 95; see also G. C. Butte, 'The "Protocole Additionell" to the

consented to ratification of the convention and its Additional Protocol.[63] The first problem was resolved in part by the 1909 Declaration of London, which set out the principles of law to be applied by the Court.[64] However, the Declaration was not ratified by Great Britain;[65] the other signatories to the convention were unwilling to create the Court without the cooperation of Great Britain,[66] and when the First World War broke out in 1914, no action had been taken to establish the Court. The project was not taken up again after the War.

The second tribunal, the Central American Court of Justice, established by El Salvador, Nicaragua, Costa Rica, Honduras and Guatemala in 1907, had jurisdiction over cases of an international character or concerning violations of a treaty, between the contracting states and individuals of another state, provided the claimant individual had exhausted local remedies or showed a denial of justice.[67] The convention enabled individuals to seise the Court with questions of 'violation of treaties or conventions' without requiring that the claimant individual be a victim of a violation of a treaty or that the relevant treaty contain any individual right. Five cases were brought by individuals during the ten years the Court was in operation, but none were successful: four were dismissed for jurisdictional reasons,[68] and the one case which proceeded to the merits was decided in favour of the respondent state.

In the single case brought which proceeded to the merits, Nuñez, a Nicaraguan national who had been expelled from Costa Rica, argued that his expulsion was not justified under either national or international law.[69] Nuñez was a Costa Rican resident who had been granted asylum. Subsequently, he organised a rebellion into Nicaragua, and

International Prize Court Convention' (1912) 6 *AJIL* 799; London Naval Conference, 26 February 1909 (not yet in force), reproduced in (1909) 3 *AJIL Supplement* 179, 184.

63 Scott, 'The Declaration of London', 279.

64 London Naval Conference, 26 February 1909 (not yet in force), reproduced in (1909) 3 *AJIL Supplement* 179.

65 See www.icrc.org/ihl.nsf/INTRO/255?OpenDocument; see generally, C. Martin, 'The Declaration of London: A Matter of Operational Capability' (2008) *Historical Research* 1, 31; Scott, 'The Declaration of London', 275.

66 Scott, 'The Declaration of London', 275.

67 El Salvador–Nicaragua–Costa Rica–Honduras–Guatemala, Art. 2, 20 December 1907, (1908) 2 *AJIL* 231.

68 See M. O. Hudson, *International Tribunals* (Washington, DC, Carnegie, 1944), p. 34. One case asking for declaration of nullity of an election in Costa Rica was dismissed because it was not international in character; another case brought by Díaz (Nicaraguan) against Guatemala for wrongful arrest was dismissed for failure to exhaust local remedies.

69 The Court's decision was not reported and the author has been unable to locate a copy of the original. This analysis is based upon a commentary to the case by the former

when it failed he sought to return to Costa Rica. A Costa Rican decree prohibited the entry of any person involved in revolutionary movements; on the basis that he had previously been resident, Nuñez was permitted to return to the country temporarily but he was later expelled to Panama. Nuñez argued before the Court that his expulsion was not justified on the basis that he was entitled to certain rights under a 1871 Central American Peace Treaty, which imposed an obligation on states parties to confine persons involved in revolutionary movements to their capital cities.[70] The Court held that Costa Rica was entitled to deny asylum and/or expel Nuñez, on the basis that it was in accordance with international and national law. It noted that states had an 'undisputed faculty' to deny asylum to aliens, although this faculty had to be exercised in conformity with international law.[71] The Court did not agree with the claimant that international treaties conferred upon him any right to asylum, rather it interpreted that provision as conferring upon states a right to apply measures to nationals of any Central American state. The Court stated: '[t]hat article [17] did not seek to guarantee the right to asylum of persons, but the high public interest in the maintenance of peace of states [parties] and to prevent revolutions'.[72] The main focus of the Court's decision was whether Nuñez was entitled to national treatment under domestic law: the Court held he was not; moreover, the Court held that the treatment accorded to him was in accordance with the applicable domestic law.[73] Thus, the Court did not refer to individual rights under international law or treaties; rather it focussed on two issues: whether the respondent state had complied with its international law obligations and whether the treatment accorded to the claimant was in accordance with domestic law.

(c) Conclusions

The doctrine of diplomatic protection, first enunciated by Vattel as including the basic fiction of injury to the state and as dictating certain requirements to establish nationality, was entrenched in international practice by the early twentieth century. State practice in seeking redress for injury to individuals operated generally within the confines of the doctrine of diplomatic protection, so that where a claim was determined either by resort to arbitration in a specific instance or by the

Costa Rican Foreign Minister (in Spanish): C. J. Gutiérrez, *La Corte de Justicia CentroAmericana* (Tegucigalpa, Biblioteca del Pensamiento Centroamericano, 1957).

[70] Article 17, reproduced in *ibid.* (unnumbered, above footnote 49).

[71] *Ibid.* (unnumbered, above footnote 49). [72] *Ibid.* [73] *Ibid.*

establishment of an international claims tribunal and its decision, it was conceived of as a claim by one state against another, for the injury suffered by the state in the person of its national. This is particularly clear in the arbitral practice of specific claims in the nineteenth and early twentieth centuries, which without exception conceptualised claims belonging to the state of nationality and which did not permit injured individuals to participate in proceedings.

International claims tribunals operating in the ninteenth and early twentieth centuries took account of individuals in a haphazard manner, a fact which is unsurprising given that the practice was experimental. The weight of practice derived from the procedure of these tribunals supports characterisation of claims as inter-state claims, rather than claims by an individual against a foreign state. The practice suggests that states were bringing claims for the injury which the state itself suffered in the fact of injury to a national, essentially on the basis of diplomatic protection. The vast majority of the claims conventions provided that awards were payable directly to the state of nationality and only the first two tribunals paid awards directly to individual claimants. Individual claimants were unable to compel states to distribute awards made to their state of nationality which corresponded to the injury suffered by individuals. In the majority of tribunals, claims and evidence were presented by the state of nationality, a procedure consistent with conceptualisation of claims as inter-state claims. Some commissions and tribunals permitted individuals to be represented in a limited capacity: either by their designation as a person to be heard on behalf of the government, by permitting claimants to be represented but requiring claims to be formally presented by an agent of the government, or by permitting individuals to file declarations or memorials but not to fully participate in proceedings nor to institute proceedings. Finally, several of the claims conventions expressly stated that the decisions of the commission would be a full and final settlement of all claims of each government on the other, a stipulation consistent with conceptualisation of the claims as inter-state claims brought on the basis of an inter-state dispute.

Although the weight of practice and procedure before international claims tribunals supports characterisation of the claims as diplomatic protection claims, some tribunals engaged individuals in specific ways: for example, by permitting them to be represented in a limited capacity. Thus, even where claims were brought on the basis of diplomatic protection, on occasion individuals were permitted some involvement or given some capacity, presumably in recognition of their interest in the claim. These procedural aspects of the nineteenth century practice suggest that it might be preferable to view international claims procedures as fitting somewhere along a spectrum, from claims prosecuted strictly as diplomatic protection claims, through an exclusive inter-state process, to claims which were prosecuted directly by individuals.

It appears to have been accepted that individuals could possess a private law claim against a foreign state: the commissions determined, for example, claims relating to excessive imposition of customs duties or for contractual debts owed by foreign states to claimant nationals. However, there was no suggestion in this early period that any such claims derived from any international law rights owed directly to individuals. It was not contemplated that individuals could derive direct rights from international law; the practice was consistent with the understanding of the day that international law did not confer rights on individuals, whose rights were exclusively derived from domestic law.

Individuals were given capacity to directly pursue their own claims for breach of international law to an international court in only one instance, before the Central American Court of Justice, which operated for ten years from 1907, but which on the whole dealt unfavourably with individual claimants. Although the jurisdictional provisions of the Central American Court permitted individuals to invoke international treaties, its Statute did not suggest that individuals derived direct rights from any treaty. The proposed International Prize Court, which never came into existence, would also have given individuals capacity to bring direct claims. This kind of direct access for, and control by, individual claimants was exceptional.

International claims practice in the ninteenth and early twentieth centuries was generally consistent with the then-accepted framework of international law. In particular, two points can be highlighted. First, individuals had no general independent capacity to pursue claims against states in an international forum; rather, any capacity to bring any claim was dependent on an agreed regime between the injuring state and the state of nationality. Second, any claims concerning the treatment of individuals were made on the basis of diplomatic protection, effectively as inter-state claims. Individuals were treated as though they had no direct rights, substantive or procedural, in international law. The prevailing approach was that a state invoked its own international rights in respect of treatment of its national. Any capacity of individuals in the international system was exceptional: only the Central American Court of Justice gave individuals exclusive control of claims. Even before that Court, individuals were not treated as having substantive rights under international law: rather, in the only individual application which proceeded to the merits, the Court held that the relevant individual derived no direct rights from international law. Individuals possessed only a procedural right for the assessment of a state's conduct in accordance with its international obligations. The vast majority of claims during the pre-1914 period were prosecuted by states on an inter-state basis.

2.3 Doctrine and practice in the inter-war period

In the inter-war period, the Permanent Court of International Justice (PCIJ) affirmed the doctrine of diplomatic protection and also held that individuals could be granted rights under treaties. These two propositions are reflected in the practice of international claims tribunals in this period, some of which operated on the basis of diplomatic protection and some of which gave individuals direct rights of recourse.

(a) The development of doctrine

The classical formulation of the doctrine of diplomatic protection is to be found in the decision of the PCIJ in 1924 in the *Mavrommatis* case. The Court recognised Greece as a proper claimant against Great Britain in respect of a claim that Mavrommatis, a Greek subject, had been treated by the British authorities in Palestine in a matter incompatible with certain international obligations they were bound to observe. Thus, the dispute fell within the jurisdiction of the PCIJ which, pursuant to Article 34 of the Court's Statute, was limited to disputes between states or members of the League. The Court said:

> It is true that the dispute was at first between a private person and a State – i.e., between M. Mavrommatis and Great Britain. Subsequently the Greek Government took up the case. The dispute then entered upon a new phase; it entered the domain of international law, and became a dispute between two States. Henceforward therefore it is a dispute which may or may not fall under the jurisdiction of the Permanent Court of International Justice.[74]

[74] *Mavrommatis Palestine Concessions*, Judgment no. 2, PCIJ Rep. ser. A no. 2 (1924) 12.

The Court stated further, in point of principle:

It is an elementary principle of international law that a State is entitled to protect its subjects, when injured by acts contrary to international law committed by another State, from which they have been unable to obtain satisfaction through ordinary channels. By taking up the case of one of its subjects and by resorting to diplomatic protection or international judicial proceedings on his behalf, a State is in reality asserting its own rights – its right to ensure, in the person of its subjects, respect for the rules of international law.[75]

The basic requirement of nationality of claims followed from this principle: a state could only protect a person (natural or legal) from breaches of international law if that person was a national of that state at the relevant times. More generally, the *Mavrommatis* formulation was consistent with a conception of international law as exclusively concerned with inter-state rights and obligations; the rights pursued by a state through diplomatic protection were state rights, not individual rights.

The PCIJ elaborated this principle in later cases, in particular, *Serbian Loans* (1929) and the *Panevezys-Saldutikis Railway* case (1939).[76] In *Serbian Loans*,[77] the questions put to the PCIJ by special agreement related to the form of payment of certain loans by the Serb-Croat-Slovene government to French bondholders. The French bondholders had requested the intervention of their government to resolve the dispute as to whether the loans ought to be paid in gold rather than French francs. In considering whether the matter fell within its jurisdiction, the Court examined the question whether the dispute was a dispute between two states, or merely one with the French bondholders. The Court noted that the dispute related to the obligations between the borrowing state and private persons, relations which were 'within the domain of municipal law'.[78] However, a second controversy elevated the claim to the plane of international law: when the holders of the Serbian loans appealed to the French government and it intervened on their behalf,

[75] *Ibid.*

[76] In other decisions the Permanent Court indirectly affirmed the doctrine of diplomatic protection. For example, in 1933 the Court affirmed that the dispute between the two states was distinct from the dispute between an injured individual and the respondent state (*Appeal from a Judgment of the Hungaro-Czechoslovak Mixed Arbitral Tribunal (Peter Pázmány University* v. *State of Czechoslovakia)*, PCIJ Rep. ser. A/B no. 61 (1933) 221).

[77] *Payment of Various Serbian Loans Issued in France/Payment in Gold of Brazilian Federal Loans Issued in France*, PCIJ rep. ser. A nos. 20/21 (1929).

[78] *Ibid.* 18.

the Court considered that a distinct difference of opinion arose between the two states which 'though fundamentally identical with the controversy already existing between the Serb-Croat-Slovene government and its creditors, is distinct therefrom'.[79] Thus, the PCIJ held the claim admissible.[80]

The question of the relevant time for determining the nationality of a claim arose in the *Panevezys–Saldutikis Railway* case.[81] Estonia had brought a claim against Lithuania regarding the latter's refusal to recognise rights claimed by an Estonian company in respect of the Panevezys–Saldutikis Railway, which had been seized.[82] Lithuania raised a preliminary objection on the basis that Estonia had not observed the rule of international law that 'a claim must be a national claim not only at the time of its presentation but also at the time when the injury was suffered'.[83] The PCIJ held that Estonia 'must prove that at the time when the injury occurred which is alleged to involve the international responsibility of Lithuania the company suffering the injury possessed Estonian nationality'.[84] In the view of the Court, this was a corollary of the character of diplomatic protection, by which a state was 'in reality asserting its own right, the right to ensure in the person of its nationals respect for the rules of international law'.[85]

[79] *Ibid.* 18.

[80] *Ibid.* 17–18. Two judges dissented on this point. Judge M. Pessôa stated that the Court had no jurisdiction because there was no distinction between the state–state difference of opinion and the dispute between the Serb-Croat-Slovene government and the French bondholders. Judge M. Novacovitch suggested that the Court had no jurisdiction because it was not a 'public international law controversy'. He stated that although a dispute between states may originate in a controversy between a state and an individual, all disputes previously considered by the Court concerned the application of treaties between states and the protection of the interests of the individuals only came into question as a consequence of the application of a treaty. There was no contention that the Serb-Croat-Slovene government had violated an international treaty or violated a rule of international law, and hence the Court had no jurisdiction.

[81] *Panevezys-Saldutikis Railway (Estonia* v. *Lativa)*, PCIJ Rep. ser. A/B no. 76 (1939).

[82] *Ibid.* Although this claim related to a company rather than a natural person, it is cited here for its treatment of the confines of diplomatic protection, which is equally applicable to claims relating to natural persons.

[83] *Ibid.* 6.

[84] *Ibid.* 16–17. However, in the circumstances the Court held that it could not admit the objection since the grounds on which Lithuania disputed Estonia's right to take up the case could not be separated from those on which Lithuania disputed the company's alleged right to ownership of the railway (17–18). It upheld Lithuania's second objection, that Estonia had failed to exhaust local remedies, and therefore the claim was dismissed at the preliminary objections phase (22).

[85] *Ibid.* 16.

There was no dispute that nationality was possessed at the time of filing of the claim in this case, and the Court appears to have accepted that nationality was also required at the time of presentation of the claim.[86]

The question whether nationality was required at the time of filing of the claim, or at any subsequent time was addressed by several of the post-war arbitral tribunals and commissions operating during the interwar period. Their treatment of the question can be summarised in three positions.

First, some of the commissions required continuity of nationality until the date the treaty came into force. In 1924, the German-US Mixed Claims Commission held, in an often-quoted decision of Umpire Parker, that to fall within the jurisdiction of the commission, the claims must have had American nationality '(1) on the date when the loss, damage, or injury occurred and (2) on [the date] when the Treaty [establishing the commission] became effective'. Further, the commission noted that if nationality was established on both of those dates, then it 'need not concern itself with any subsequent devolution of interest either voluntary or involuntary'.[87] Thus, nationality was required at the time of the injury and the time the obligations of the defendant state became absolute.[88] This did not coincide with the date of presentation of the claim to the commission; rather, it was the date on which Germany 'accorded to the United States ... rights in behalf of American nationals which had no prior existence but which were created by the treaty'[89] – it then assumed contractual obligations to the US to make compensation in respect of claims within the ambit of the treaty.[90]

Second, some of the commissions required continuity of nationality until the date of presentation of the specific claim.[91] This position was

[86] This appears also to have been accepted by Judge van Eysinga in dissent: *ibid.* 34–5.

[87] *Administrative Decision no. V*, German-US Mixed Claims Commission, 31 October 1924, VII UNRIAA 119, 150.

[88] The German agent had argued before the umpire that it was an established rule of international law that no state would assert a claim of a private character against another state unless it possessed the relevant nationality continuously from its origin to the time of its presentation, and even until final adjudication by the relevant tribunal: *ibid.* 140.

[89] *Ibid.* 147–8. [90] *Ibid.* 148–9.

[91] This position was also incorporated in Art. VIII of Project no. 16 on Diplomatic Protection by the American Institute of International Law (reproduced in (1956) II *Yearbook of the International Law Commission* 227); in Art. 15 of the 1929 Harvard Draft Convention on the Responsibility of States for Damage Done in Their Territory to the Person or Property of Foreigners (reproduced in *ibid.* 229). However, in 1932 the Institute of International Law refused to approve a draft put forward by Borchard

adopted by several of the Mexican claims commissions. The Rules of Procedure of those commissions suggested that the date of filing was relevant by specifying that the nationality of the relevant individuals from the time of injury to the date of filing was to be included in the memorial.[92] The British-Mexican Commission expressed the position as follows:

a claim must be founded upon an injury or wrong to a citizen of the claimant Government, and . . . the title to that claim must have remained continuously in the hands of citizens of such Government until the time of its presentation for filing before the Commission.[93]

Thus, a claim for injury suffered by a British national which had been passed by will to a Mexican national before it was filed was rejected;[94] as was a claim in respect of an Italian national who had become a naturalised Mexican between the injury and filing of the claim.[95]

Third, some of the commissions required continuity of nationality until the date of the award.[96] Both the British- and French-Mexican Commissions[97] made decisions requiring continuity of nationality until the date of the award, the British Commission finding that 'it would hardly be just to obligate the respondent Government to pay compensation to a citizen of a country other than that with which it entered into a convention'.[98] These decisions are curious for two reasons: first, in respect of the British Commission, this decision was somewhat of an anomaly since other decisions of the commission required

incorporating this position (see (1932) *Annuaire de l'Institut de Droit International* (Oslo session) 487–8); for commentary see E. M. Borchard, 'The Protection of Citizens Abroad and Change of Original Nationality' (1933–4) 43 *Yale Law Journal* 359.

92 A. H. Feller, *The Mexican Claims Commissions 1923–1934: A Study in the Law and Procedure of International Tribunals* (New York, Macmillan Company, 1935), p. 232.

93 *F. W. Flack, on behalf of the Estate of the Late D. L. Flack (Great Britain)* v. *United Mexican States*, British-Mexican Claims Commission, Decision no. 10, 6 December 1929, V UNRIAA 61, 62.

94 *Captain W. H. Gleadell (Great Britain)* v. *United Mexican States*, British-Mexican Claims Commission, reported in G. H. Hackworth, *Digest of International Law* (Washington, DC, US Government Printing Office, 1943), vol. V, p. 805.

95 *Egduardo Trucco*, Decision no. 1 (unpublished), Italian-Mexican Claims Commission, cited in Feller, *The Mexican Claims Commissions*, p. 96.

96 This was the position taken by the Preparatory Committee of the 1930 Hague Codification Conference in Basis of Discussion no. 28 (reproduced in (1956) II *Yearbook of the International Law Commission* 225).

97 *Maria Guadalupe A. Vve. Markassuza*, Sentence no. 38 (unpublished), French-Mexican Claims Commission, cited in Feller, *The Mexican Claims Commissions*, p. 97.

98 *Minnie Stevens Eschauzier (Great Britain)* v. *United Mexican States*, British-Mexican Claims Commission, Decision no. 64, 24 June 1931, V UNRIAA 207.

nationality only until the date of filing;[99] and second, the relevant conventions provided for payment of an award directly to the state of nationality, not to the claimant individual.[100] Requiring continuous nationality until the date of the award appears inconsistent with the general proposition that once a claim had been taken up by the state of nationality – either through a diplomatic process or through the filing of a claim – that state was 'in reality asserting its own rights'[101] to claim in respect of its own loss. If from the time the state of nationality took up the claim, it was pursuing its own rights and claiming in respect of its own injury, it ought to have been irrelevant whether the individual continued to hold nationality until the date of the award, since the injury would have already been suffered by the state, and the claim would be for the state's own injury.

In *Chorzów Factory* (1928), the PCIJ indirectly affirmed that in a diplomatic protection claim, the rights at issue are states' rights, not individual rights.[102] The Court held that in a dispute between states concerning damage suffered by a national, the applicable rules governing reparation were the rules of international law in force between the two states, not the law governing relations between the state and the injured individual:

> Rights or interests of an individual the violation of which rights causes damage are always in a different plane to rights belonging to a state, which rights may also be infringed by the same act. The damage suffered by the individual is never therefore identical in kind with that which will be suffered by a State; it can only afford a convenient scale for the calculation of the reparation due to the State.[103]

The PCIJ subsequently affirmed that a diplomatic protection claim brought on the basis of injury to a national was a distinct dispute from any dispute between the injured national and the respondent state.[104]

[99] *F. W. Flack, on behalf of the Estate of the Late D. L. Flack (Great Britain)* v. *United Mexican States*, British-Mexican Claims Commission, Decision no. 10, 6 December 1929, V UNRIAA 61, 62.

[100] See France–Mexico, Art. IX, 24 September 1924, Feller, *The Mexican Claims Commissions*, App. and Great Britain–Mexico, 19 November 1926, Art. IX, Feller, *The Mexican Claims Commissions*, App.

[101] *Mavrommatis Palestine Concessions*, Judgment no. 2, PCIJ Rep. ser. A no. 2 (1924) 12.

[102] *Factory at Chorzów (Claim for Indemnity)*, Merits, PCIJ Rep. ser. A no. 17 (1928) 26–8.

[103] *Ibid.* 28.

[104] *Appeal from a Judgment of the Hungaro-Czechoslovak Mixed Arbitral Tribunal (Peter Pázmány University* v. *State of Czechoslovakia)*, PCIJ Rep. ser. A/B no. 61 (1933) 221.

In addition to the development of the doctrine of diplomatic protection during the inter-war period, in 1928 the PCIJ held in *Jurisdiction of the Courts of Danzig* that individuals could be granted rights by international treaty, where the states parties to the treaty clearly intended.[105] It has already been noted that the effect of the PCIJ's Opinion was controversial at the time,[106] although it later came to be cited for the proposition that states may confer international rights upon individuals.

(b) The practice of international claims tribunals

During the inter-war period, in addition to numerous treaties referring particular claims to arbitration,[107] the use of international claims tribunals and commissions reached a peak. There were two significant groups of commissions: the post-war mixed tribunals and commissions; and the claims commissions between several states and Mexico which related in the main to claims arising from the Mexican Revolution between 1910 and 1920. Several other international claims tribunals operated essentially on the basis of diplomatic protection. Before these other tribunals, without exception the relevant state had control of the claims and individual claimants did not have direct access to the tribunal either personally or through their representatives.[108] For example, the 1921 arbitration under the auspices of the Permanent Court of Arbitration (PCA) dealing with the claims of Norwegian subjects against the US was characterised by the tribunal as an inter-state claim: the tribunal noted it was agreed between the parties that the claims were presented by the government of Norway, which 'is the sole claimant before this Tribunal', 'and not the individual claimants'.[109] A further example is the Panama–US Claims Tribunal, where the relevant treaty stipulated that the decisions of the tribunal bound the two states, and

[105] *Jurisdiction of the Courts of Danzig (Pecuniary Claims of Danzig Railway Officials who have Passed into the Polish Service, Against the Polish Railways Administration)*, PCIJ Rep. ser. B no. 15 (1928) 3.

[106] See 1.2(c) above.

[107] For example, US–Peru, 21 May 1921, I UNRIAA 347; Great Britain–Costa Rica, 12 January 1922, I UNRIAA 371; Great Britain–Ethiopia, 13 September 1927, II UNRIAA 823; US–Guatemala, 2 November 1929, II UNRIAA 1081; France–Great Britain, 4 March 1930, II UNRIAA 1114, (1932) 26 *AJIL* 804; Great Britain–Portugal, 1 August 1930, II UNRIAA 1146, 7 ILR 261; Sweden–US, 17 December 1930, II UNRIAA 1241; US–Egypt, 20 January 1931, II UNRIAA 1163; Finland–Great Britain, 30 September 1932, III UNRIAA 1480; and Great Britain–Panama, 15 October 1932, III UNRIAA 1440.

[108] See US–Norway, Art. II, 30 June 1921, I UNRIAA 309; Canada–US, 23 January 1924, III UNRIAA 1610; Panama–US, 28 July 1926, 138 LNTS 119.

[109] US–Norway, 30 June 1921, I UNRIAA 309, 314.

that any awards were payable directly to the state.[110] A list of these tribunals and commissions, together with a description of their basic features, is included in Appendix III below.

(i) Mixed arbitral tribunals after the First World War

There were three sets of post-war tribunals and commissions which dealt with claims for injury to individuals: the mixed arbitral tribunals between the Central and Allied Powers (except the US); the mixed claims commissions between the US and the Central Powers; and the Upper Silesian Mixed Commission and Arbitral Tribunal. Each of these will be addressed in turn, as they each had distinct features and approaches.

(A) The mixed arbitral tribunals under the Peace Treaties

The Peace Treaties between the Allied and Associated Powers and the Central Powers after the First World War made provision for the establishment of mixed arbitral tribunals between each of the Allied and Associated Powers and each of the Central Powers.[111] These mixed arbitral tribunals[112] were in general given jurisdiction over claims relating to contracts;[113] debts;[114] damage to property, rights and interests by

110 Panama–US, 28 July 1926, 138 LNTS 119, Arts. VII and VIII. It was not generally accepted that individual claimants were entitled to the proceeds of diplomatic protection claims made in respect of their injury. In 1932, the House of Lords held that there was no such entitlement under English law. In *Civilian War Claimants' Association* v. *The King* [1932] AC 14, petitioners who had claimed compensation on behalf of civilians who had suffered losses inflicted by German forces during the war sought to compel payment of the reparations settlement reached in Art. 232 of the Treaty of Versailles. They alleged that the Crown had invited them to submit their losses to the Reparations Claims Department, which had taken them into account in the amounts stated in the reparations agreed by Germany. The House of Lords held that the Crown had not constituted itself as agent or trustee of the petitioners in respect of any money received from Germany on account of reparations. This decision was subsequently followed in *Administrator of Germany Property* v. *Knoop* [1932] 1 Ch. 439; see also *Lonrho Exports Ltd* v. *Export Credits Guarantee Department* [1996] 4 All ER 673, 687.

111 The US did not ratify these treaties; it entered into the separate arrangements which are described in the following section.

112 Created by Treaty of Versailles, Art. 304, 28 June 1919, UKTS 4 (Cmd 153); Treaty of St Germain-en-Laye, Art. 256, 10 September 1919, UKTS 11 (Cmd 400); Treaty of Neuilly, Art. 188, 27 November 1919, UKTS 5 (Cmd 522); Treaty of Trianon, Art. 239, 4 June 1920, UKTS 10 (Cmd 896); and Treaty of Lausanne, Art. 92, 24 July 1923, UKTS 16 (Cmd 1929).

113 Treaty of Versailles, Arts. 299–300, 304; Treaty of St Germain-en-Laye, Section V, Art. 256, 10 September 1919; Treaty of Neuilly, Section V, Art. 188; Treaty of Trianon, Section V, Art. 239; Treaty of Lausanne, Art. 92.

114 Treaty of Versailles, Section III, Art. 296; Treaty of St Germain-en-Laye, Section III; Treaty of Neuilly, Section III; Treaty of Trianon, Section III.

the application of certain war measures;[115] compensation;[116] licences for certain property rights;[117] and prejudice suffered in respect of court decisions.[118]

On the whole it appears that individual claimants had control of the claims. Individuals were claimants in proceedings, with state agents present to represent their governments' interests and to supervise the conduct of cases.[119] It appears that the tribunals treated the claims as belonging to the individual claimants rather than to their state of nationality, such that the claims were for direct injury to the individual claimants rather than for any injury suffered by their state of nationality. Awards were paid directly to individual claimants. Although few decisions of the mixed arbitral tribunals referred to the character of the claims, those which did suggested that individuals derived direct rights from the Peace Treaties. Referring to the PCIJ's decision in *Jurisdiction of the Courts of Danzig*, the French-German Mixed Arbitral Tribunal held that the Treaty of Versailles conferred direct international rights on individuals.[120] A specific right to claim compensation was recognised by the Anglo-German Tribunal, which held that '[t]he right to compensation granted by the treaty is granted . . . to the national'.[121] Thus, the mixed arbitral tribunals purported to determine claims of individuals for violation of their own international law rights.

(B) The US Mixed Claims Commissions

The US did not ratify the Peace Treaties but concluded agreements which provided for the establishment of mixed claims commissions to deal with claims of US nationals concerning damage to property, rights

[115] Treaty of Versailles, Arts. 297–8; Treaty of St Germain-en-Laye, Section IV; Treaty of Neuilly, Section IV; Treaty of Trianon, Section IV.

[116] Treaty of Versailles, Art. 305; Treaty of St Germain-en-Laye, Section VII; Treaty of Neuilly, Section VII; Treaty of Trianon, Art. 240.

[117] Treaty of Versailles, Art. 310; Treaty of St Germain-en-Laye, Section VII; Treaty of Neuilly, Section VII; Treaty of Trianon, Section VII; Treaty of Lausanne, Art. 89.

[118] Treaty of Versailles, Art. 305; Treaty of St Germain-en-Laye, Art. 257; Treaty of Neuilly, Art. 189; Treaty of Trianon, Art. 240. In addition to these classes of claims, the treaties of Neuilly and Lausanne made provision for claims relating to prejudice caused in respect of transferred territory: Treaty of Neuilly, Section VIII; Treaty of Trianon, Art. 137.

[119] N. Wühler, 'Mixed Arbitral Tribunals' in R. Bernhardt, *Encyclopedia of Public International Law* (Amsterdam, Elsevier Science, 1997), vol. III, p. 433.

[120] *Sigwald Charles* v. *Germany*, French-German Mixed Arbitral Tribunal, 27 August 1926, 4 ILR 337.

[121] *Lederer* v. *German Government*, Anglo-German Mixed Arbitral Tribunal, (1924) *Recueil des Décisions des Tribunaux Arbitraux Mixtes* 762, 768.

and interests in German territory; loss or damage to persons, property, rights and interests as a consequence of the war; and claims for debts of German nationals or the German government.[122] These mixed claims commissions operated on the basis of diplomatic protection: the claim was brought by the US (as an inter-state claim) for injury suffered by its nationals, to vindicate the state's rights in respect of its nationals. In a preliminary administrative decision the commission held that the proper claimant was the US:

> *The United States is claimant.* Though conducted in behalf of their respective citizens, governments are the real parties to international arbitrations. All claims, therefore, presented to this Commission shall be asserted and controlled by the United States as claimant, either on its own behalf or on behalf of one or more of its nationals. If in the decisions, opinions, and proceedings of the Commission American nationals are referred to as claimants it will be understood that this is for the purpose of convenient designation and that the Government of the United States is the actual claimant.[123]

In a further decision, the commission emphasised that the claim was owned by the US as claimant, the state having 'complete possession and control of the claim', which it prosecuted 'in its own right and not as the agent or trustee of the subordinate claimant' and without accountability to individual claimants for the proceeds of the claim: the state of nationality could return the funds to the nation paying them 'or otherwise dispose of it'. This was justified on the basis that a claim has no 'international status until it is espoused' by a state.[124] The commission also held that continuity of nationality was required until the Treaty entered into force, by which Germany's obligation to the US became absolute, a conclusion which appears consistent with the characterisation of the claim as achieving 'international status' when it was espoused by a state.

(C) The Upper Silesian Mixed Commission and Arbitral Tribunal

The territorial settlement of the area of Upper Silesia was the subject of extended controversy after the First World War. After the territorial

[122] Germany–US, 10 August 1922. Claims of US nationals in respect of Austria and Hungary which came within the terms of the treaties of St Germain-en-Laye and Trianon were also referred to a commissioner by separate agreement: US–Austria–Hungary, 26 November 1924, 48 LNTS 69.

[123] *Administrative Decision no. II*, Germany-US Mixed Claims Commission, 1 November 1923, VII UNRIAA 23, 26.

[124] *Administrative Decision no. V*, Germany-US Mixed Claims Commission, 31 October 1924, VII UNRIAA 119, 126.

division was effected,[125] the Polish portion of Upper Silesia included approximately 300,000 persons of German origin and Poland asserted that German Upper Silesia contained an even greater number of persons of Polish origin.[126] The Conference of Ambassadors decided that the Polish Minorities Treaty[127] was applicable to the Polish portion of Upper Silesia, and to the German portion for at least fifteen years.[128] The Conference provided for the establishment of a mixed commission and an arbitral tribunal to supervise the execution of these measures.[129] On this basis, Germany and Poland signed a convention which provided for special protection of individuals in two ways: first, individuals were given capacity to assert a private dispute against a state (including their own state of nationality) which related to the protection of their rights by treaty before an arbitral tribunal; and second, individuals were given access to a mixed commission in cases where disputes relating to minorities protection had not been satisfactorily resolved.[130]

The Arbitral Tribunal had competence over specified matters, including the payment of indemnities; questions of nationality or right of residence; and interpretation of provisions of the Geneva Conventions.[131] Before the Tribunal, individuals were party to proceedings and were entitled to be represented or to represent themselves. The Rules of Procedure made no distinction between the representatives of governments and private persons, and individuals effectively had full procedural capacity before the Tribunal.[132] In a decision given in 1928,

125 See (1921) *League of Nations Official Journal* (December) 1220–32, esp. 1230–1.

126 J. Stone, *Regional Guarantees of Human Rights: A Study of Minorities Procedure in Upper Silesia* (New York, Macmillan, 1933), p. 3.

127 Treaty of Peace between the US, the British Empire, France, Italy and Japan, and Poland, 28 June 1919 (entry into force 10 January 1920), 225 CTS 412.

128 These provisions were placed under the guarantee of the League in the same manner as those under the Polish Minorities Treaty: see (1921) *League of Nations Official Journal* (December) 1220–32, esp. 1230–1. See discussion in H. Rosting, 'Protection of Minorities by the League of Nations' (1923) 17 *AJIL* 641, 652–3. The minorities system is discussed in 5.2(a) below.

129 (1921) *League of Nations Official Journal* (December) 1231.

130 Germany–Poland, Geneva Convention Concerning Upper Silesia, 15 May 1922, 9 LNTS 466.

131 *Ibid.* Arts. 4–5, 58, 296–8, 313, 368–9 and 588. The latter provision could be invoked by a party to a case before a national court or authority, before the closure of the procedure in the second instance.

132 See generally, G. Kaeckenbeeck, 'The Character and Work of the Arbitral Tribunal of Upper Silesia' (1935) 21 *Transactions of the Grotius Society* 27; G. Kaeckenbeeck, 'Upper Silesia under the League of Nations' (1946) 243 *Annals of the American Academy of Political and Social Science* 129; G. Kaeckenbeeck, *The International Experiment of Upper Silesia:*

the Tribunal held that individuals could bring proceedings before the Tribunal against their own state of nationality, finding that the convention conferred jurisdiction on the Tribunal irrespective of the nationality of the claimants.[133] Thus, individuals were not only permitted to sue a foreign state, but also their own state, in respect of matters falling within the jurisdiction of the Tribunal. The Arbitral Tribunal therefore entertained claims which would not fall within the confines of traditional diplomatic protection claims because they were concerned with a state's treatment of its own nationals. These claims could not have derived from state's rights, since the state of nationality could be the defendant state; rather, the Arbitral Tribunal operated on the basis that the rights it was determining were individual rights under international law.

The Mixed Commission had jurisdiction over disputes relating to minorities protection. Pursuant to the Geneva Conventions, a Minorities Office was set up in both portions of the territory and individuals could, after having filed a complaint with the highest administrative authority, petition the Minorities Office.[134] If the Minorities Office did not succeed in obtaining satisfaction, it transmitted the petition to the President of the Mixed Commission for his opinion, who was to act as an arbitral body.[135] A final appeal was provided for individuals directly to the Council of the League of Nations.[136] The President of the Mixed Commission explained that:

> In this procedure the petitioner is granted the legal status of a litigant party. His adversary is the director of the Minorities Office who represents the authorities. In each case a procedure in writing takes place and, as a rule, hearings. Both parties may present proposals concerning the weighing of evidence and may give all proof which they deem useful. The President may consider the evidence *ex officio*. As a rule, he is not bound by the proposals of the parties.[137]

A Study in the Workings of the Upper Silesian Settlement 1922–1937 (London, Oxford University Press, 1942).

133 *Steiner and Gross* v. *Polish State*, Upper Silesian Arbitral Tribunal, 30 March 1928, 4 ILR 291.

134 Germany–Poland, Geneva Convention Concerning Upper Silesia, Arts. 148, 150, 153–4, 15 May 1922, 9 LNTS 466.

135 *Ibid.* Art. 152; Rules of Procedure of the mixed commission, Arts. 38–48, reproduced in Stone, *Regional Guarantees of Human Rights*, App. II, p. 262.

136 Germany–Poland, Geneva Convention Concerning Upper Silesia, 15 May 1922, 9 LNTS 466, Arts. 149 and 157. For this reason the mixed commission is widely thought to have been the most effective enforcement mechanism for all the minorities treaties: see generally, Stone, *Regional Guarantees of Human Rights*.

137 Cited in Kaeckenbeeck, *The International Experiment of Upper Silesia*, p. x.

Before the Mixed Commission, individuals were parties to disputes with full procedural capacity. The substantive provisions of the minorities treaties, including the provisions applicable to Upper Silesia, were expressed as conferring rights on inhabitants of the relevant territories;[138] thus, it appears that the Mixed Commission was determining individual rights under international law.

(ii) Mexican Claims Commissions 1923–1932

In 1921, after Obregón deposed the Carranza government, the Mexican government contacted the governments of all countries whose nationals might have claims against Mexico (US, Spain, Italy, France, Germany, Norway, Sweden, Denmark, Austria, Great Britain, Cuba, Japan, China and Belgium) to participate in the formation of claims commissions.[139] In 1923, a General Claims Convention and a Special Claims Convention were signed by Mexico and the US. Subsequently, claims conventions were concluded with France, Germany, Great Britain, Italy and Spain.[140] A convention concluded with Belgium provided for the referral of claims to an 'administrative arbitral tribunal' with a simplified procedure, in view of the very small number of Belgian claims.[141]

The Conventions provided for two types of commissions to deal with claims. The US–Mexico General Claims Convention established a commission with jurisdiction over all claims against the US by Mexican citizens, and all claims against Mexico by US citizens, which had arisen since 4 July 1868 (the date of the last claims settlement between the two states). Article I provided that those claims could be for loss or damage to persons or property brought by corporations, companies, associations, partnerships or individuals, and covered claims by US or Mexican nationals who had interests in corporations or companies of a different nationality which had suffered damage. Claims relating to acts incidental to the recent revolution were excluded.[142]

[138] See further discussion in 5.3(a) below.

[139] Reproduced in Feller, *The Mexican Claims Commissions*, p. 19, n. 22. Although some of the decisions discussed in this section derived from claims made by legal persons, these are cited for general points of law and procedure applicable also to claims made by natural persons.

[140] All of these conventions are reproduced in *ibid.* pp. 321–538.

[141] Belgium–Mexico, 14 May 1927, Feller, *The Mexican Claims Commissions*, App., p. 28.

[142] *Ibid.* p. 28.

The US–Mexico Special Claims Convention and the claims conventions with Great Britain, France, Germany, Italy and Spain each established commissions with jurisdiction over claims against Mexico arising from the revolution, and thus were limited *ratione temporis* to claims between 1910 and 1920. The Belgian-Mexican Administrative Arbitral Tribunal was similarly limited to claims relating to the revolution. The conventions covered claims for loss or damage caused by one or any of a number of enumerated 'forces'.[143]

All the commissions were to deal with claims arising out of injuries to individuals: the jurisdictional provisions referred to claims 'against Mexico by citizens' of foreign states for 'losses or damages suffered by persons or by their properties'.[144] The Preamble to the General Claims Convention referred to the desire of the contracting parties 'to settle and adjust amicably *claims by citizens* of each country against the other' and similar statements were made in the Preambles to the other conventions.[145] But the text of the conventions made clear that the state had control over these claims: agents and counsel were to be appointed by governments and there was no provision for individuals to be directly represented.[146] Further, the contracting parties agreed that the decisions of the Commission would be final and binding in full settlement of all claims within their jurisdiction,[147] and payment

[143] In the case of the conventions with European powers, claims for loss or damage caused by civil authorities were covered in certain circumstances.

[144] US–Mexico General Claims Convention, Art. I, 8 September 1923, Feller, *The Mexican Claims Commissions*, App.; similarly in US–Mexico Special Claims Convention, Art. I, 10 September 1923, Feller, *The Mexican Claims Commissions*, App.

[145] US–Mexico General Claims Convention, Preamble, 8 September 1923, Feller, *The Mexican Claims Commissions*, App. (emphasis added). The only exception was the Germany–Mexico convention.

[146] US–Mexico General Claims Convention, Art. III, 8 September 1923, Feller, *The Mexican Claims Commissions*, App.; Germany–Mexico, Art. V, 16 March 1925, Feller, *The Mexican Claims Commissions*, App.; Art. IV of all other conventions, Feller, *The Mexican Claims Commissions*, App.

[147] US–Mexico General Claims Convention, Art. VIII, 8 September 1923, Feller, *The Mexican Claims Commissions*, App.; Germany–Mexico, Art. IX, 16 March 1925, Feller, *The Mexican Claims Commissions*, App.; Art. VIII all other conventions, Feller, *The Mexican Claims Commissions*, App. In the conventions dealing with claims arising out of revolutionary acts (the US Special Claims Commission and all the European Commissions) the parties also agreed that the work of the Commission would be a full, final and perfect settlement of all claims within the jurisdiction of the commission, whether or not all claims had been presented to the commission, provided that the claims which had been presented were examined and decided. No effect was stipulated in respect of any private law claims of individuals.

was to be made directly to the governments and not to individual claimants.[148] The US-Mexican General Claims Commission had jurisdiction to order that property or a right be restored to the claimant in addition to the amount awarded for loss or damage, but was required to specify a value for that property or right and the respondent state could elect to make additional payment of that amount rather than restore the property or right.[149] In this way, there was no recognition of personal or vested individual rights in particular property; rather general principles on inter-state reparation applied. Moreover, there was no suggestion that individuals derived substantive rights from international law directly; rather, the conventions suggested that claims were brought on an inter-state basis to vindicate inter-state rights.

The US-Mexican General Claims Commission held that the right to espouse an international claim was a right held by the state of nationality, in dismissing an argument based on the 'clean hands' principle. In *Chattin*, Mexico argued that because the relevant US national was a 'fugitive from justice', the US government had lost the right to espouse his claim. The Commission held that unlawful conduct of a national did not cause a government to 'los[e] its right to espouse its subject's claim in its discretion'.[150]

The question of the holder of the right to diplomatic protection was also engaged by the issue of validity of 'Calvo clauses' in contracts between aliens and host states. A typical Calvo clause had two parts: it first provided that all disputes concerning the contract would be decided in the courts of the host state; and second, it provided for a complete or partial surrender of rights under international law by the contracting alien and for a waiver of protection by the alien's state of nationality.[151]

148 US-Mexico General Claims Convention, Art. IX, 8 September 1923, Feller, *The Mexican Claims Commissions*, App; Germany-Mexico, Art. X, 16 March 1925, Feller, *The Mexican Claims Commissions*, App.; Art. IX of all other conventions, Feller, *The Mexican Claims Commissions*, App.

149 Apparently the provisions on *restitutio in integrum* were inserted with a view to the settlement of claims relating to Mexican oil and agrarian legislation: Feller, *The Mexican Claims Commissions*, App., p. 36.

150 *B. E. Chattin (United States)* v. *United Mexican States*, US-Mexican General Claims Commission, 23 July 1928, IV UNRIAA 284.

151 See generally, D. R. Shea, *The Calvo Clause: A Problem of International Law and Diplomacy* (Minneapolis, Minn., University of Minnesota Press, 1955), pp. 27–32; A. V. Freeman, 'Recent Aspects of the Calvo Doctrine and the Challenge to International Law' (1946) 40 *AJIL* 121; K. Lipstein, 'The Place of the Calvo Clause in International Law' (1945) 22 *BYIL* 130; A. H. Feller, 'Some Observations on the Calvo Clause' (1933) 27 *AJIL* 461.

In general the Mexican Commissions held that although the first portion of the clause could operate to prevent an alien from presenting his or her claim to the national state for interposition or espousal, the second portion of the Calvo clause, which sought to exclude the protection of the national state, had no effect on the right of the state of nationality to bring a claim.[152] In the *Dredging Co.* case, the US-Mexican General Claims Commission noted that an alien could not 'deprive the Government of his nation of its undoubted right of applying international remedies to violations of international law committed to his damage'.[153] Thus, the international law right of a state to exercise diplomatic protection could not be waived by its national, either expressly by contractual agreement, or implicitly by unlawful conduct.

Consistently with the rules of the 1868 US-Mexican Commission,[154] the Rules of Procedure of the two US Claims Commissions provided that the claims and evidence were to be presented by the governments or their agents[155] and no statements, evidence or documents would be received from individual claimants.[156] These provisions are not found in the Rules of Procedure of other Commissions but it appears that in practice all the Commissions received evidence and documents exclusively through state representatives. The only provision for the role of

[152] *North American Dredging Company of Texas (United States)* v. *United Mexican States*, US-Mexican General Claims Commission, 31 March 1926, IV UNRIAA 26, 29, 34. See also *International Fisheries Company (United States)* v. *United Mexican States*, US-Mexican General Claims Commission, July 1931, IV UNRIAA 691; *Douglas G. Collie MacNeill (Great Britain)* v. *United Mexican States*, British-Mexican Claims Commission, 22 July 1931, V UNRIAA 135; *Interoceanic Railway of Mexico (Acapulco to Veracruz) (Ltd), Mexican Eastern Railway Company (Ltd) and Mexican Southern Railway (Ltd) (Great Britain)* v. *United Mexican States*, British-Mexican Claims Commission, 18 June 1931, V UNRIAA 178. Subsequently, the British-Mexican Claims Commission appeared to limit the circumstances in which the Calvo clause did not apply to a denial of justice: *Mexican Union Railway (Ltd) (Great Britain)* v. *United Mexican States*, British-Mexican Claims Commission, Decision no. 21, February 1930, V UNRIAA 115, paras. 13, 14(d) and (e). Although some of these claims were brought by legal persons rather than natural persons, they are cited for their treatment of diplomatic protection generally, treatment which was equally applicable to claims brought by individuals.

[153] *North American Dredging Company of Texas (United States)* v. *United Mexican States*, US-Mexican General Claims Commission, 31 March 1926, IV UNRIAA 26, 29, 34 (para. 11). On subsequent decisions, see Shea, *The Calvo Clause*, pp. 231–57.

[154] As required by US-Mexican General Claims Commission, Art. III; US-Mexican Special Claims Convention, Art. IV, Feller, *The Mexican Claims Commissions*.

[155] US-Mexican General Rule III, US-Mexican Special Rule III, cited in Feller, *The Mexican Claims Commissions*, App., p. 88.

[156] US-Mexican General Rule VIII; US-Mexican Special Rule VIII, cited in Feller, *The Mexican Claims Commissions*, App., p. 88.

an individual claimant in the rules was a requirement that the memorial be signed by the claimant or his or her attorney.[157] There was no provision in the rules for the participation of individual claimants or their representatives in oral hearings, and permission from the Presiding Commissioner was required for any person other than state agents and representatives to attend a hearing.[158]

The Mexican Claims Commissions dealt with the question of the character of the claims, relative to the position of the individual claimant, in two contexts: first, in describing and explaining how the claims came to be before it; and second, in dealing with the question whether the individual claimant must have consented to the claim as a precondition to the commission's jurisdiction.

In the first of these contexts, the US-Mexico General Claims Commission made comments which, on balance, suggest that the claims before it were brought on the basis of diplomatic protection. In *Dickson Car Wheel Co.*, the Commission held that the claim was an inter-state claim, since in the 'international juridical system' there was no responsibility between a respondent state and an individual 'for the reason that the latter is not subject to international law'.[159] The Commission also applied the continuous nationality rule: in *William A. Parker*, the Commission suggested that the private nature of the claim endured when a claimant state pursued it and therefore the claimant state was required to establish that the individual claimant was its national to bring a claim.[160] The issue in *Parker* was whether the

[157] Feller, *The Mexican Claims Commissions*, App., pp. 233–4. In general this requirement was read broadly and the commissions would admit the memorial whenever it was satisfied that the claimant desired the claim to be submitted (*William E. Bowerman and Messrs Burberry's (Ltd) (Great Britain)* v. *United Mexican States*, British-Mexican Claims Commission, Decision no. 18, 15 February 1930, V UNRIAA 104; *The Anzures Land Company (Ltd) (Great Britain)* v. *United Mexican States*, British-Mexican Claims Commission, Decision no. 62, 24 June 1931, V UNRIAA 207) and only one claim was dismissed for failure to comply with this provision (*Mexico City Bombardment Claims (Great Britain)* v. *United Mexican States*, British-Mexican Claims Commission, Decision no. 12, 15 February 1930, V UNRIAA 76). The British-Mexican Rules permitted the memorial to be signed by the agent alone provided that it contained a statement of claim signed by the claimant. (Again, although some of these claims were initiated by legal rather than natural persons, they are cited to elaborate aspects of procedure which were equally applicable to claims brought by natural persons.)

[158] Feller, *The Mexican Claims Commissions*, p. 248.

[159] *Dickson Car Wheel Company (USA)* v. *United Mexican States*, US-Mexican General Claims Commission, July 1931, IV UNRIAA 669, 678.

[160] *William A. Parker (USA)* v. *United Mexican States*, 31 March 1926, US-Mexican General Claims Commission, IV UNRIAA 35, 36 (emphasis added).

US was required to produce any evidence establishing nationality, it having argued that its espousal of the claim created a presumption of nationality to be rebutted by the respondent state.[161] In contrast to the US-Mexico General Claims Commission, the British-Mexican Commission suggested that the claims before it were of a 'mixed character': they were public claims insofar as they were presented by one state against another; but they were also private claims insofar as they were aimed at granting an award to the benefit of an individual. It was not suggested that the award was paid directly to the individuals, rather it was paid to the state. The Commission stated: '[t]he award is claimed on behalf of' an individual claimant,[162] rather than being claimed by an individual in respect of his or her direct injury. On the whole, the comments of the Commissions as to the character of the claims were supportive of their characterisation as diplomatic protection claims.

The Commissions reached different conclusions on the question whether individual claimants must have consented to the claim as a precondition for the Commission's jurisdiction. The US-Mexican General Claims Commission held that there was no requirement that the claimant state present evidence that the claimant had sought the assistance of his government; all that was required was proof of nationality.[163] But the Italian-Mexican Commission took a different view, holding that it was required that a private claimant initiate the claim under the relevant convention. In circumstances where the claimant refused to sign the memorial and informed the Commission that she did not desire to have the claim presented, the Commission held that it had no jurisdiction.[164] This decision is curious in the absence of an express condition that a private claimant initiate the claim; it may have been more defensible had the Commission disallowed the claim on the basis of a failure to comply with the Rules of Procedure in obtaining the claimant's signature on the memorial, an issue which would go to admissibility rather than jurisdiction.

On balance, the decisions of the Commissions suggest that these claims were brought on the basis of diplomatic protection and as

161 *Ibid.*

162 *Mexican Union Railway (Ltd) (Great Britain)* v. *United Mexican States*, British-Mexican Claims Commission, Decision no. 21, V UNRIAA 115, 120.

163 *Melczer Mining Company (USA)* v. *United Mexican States*, US-Mexican General Claims Commission, 30 April 1929, IV UNRIAA 481.

164 *Emilia Marta Viuda de Giovanni Mantellero*, Decision no. 3, unpublished, extracted in Feller, *The Mexican Claims Commissions*, pp. 90–1.

inter-state claims, the state having control of the claim and individuals taking no part in proceedings apart from a procedural requirement that they indicate consent to the state of nationality espousing the claim.

(c) Conclusions

In this section, two specific developments in doctrine in the inter-war period which relate to individuals and international claims have been identified. First, the doctrine of diplomatic protection was further entrenched by decisions of the PCIJ. Second, the Court recognised that individuals could be recipients of rights under international treaties where the states parties so intended, although commentators were divided as to the effect of the PCIJ's Opinion. The concept of individual rights directly under treaty was invoked in support of the development of a separate line of practice, based on treaty, which endowed individuals with capacity to bring claims against a state in their own right. The structure and practice of international claims tribunals and commissions was about evenly split between those in which individuals directly pursued claims and had control of those claims and those which were brought by states on the basis of diplomatic protection. Where individuals were given capacity to directly participate in claims processes, they were full parties to cases; they were entitled to representation; and the rights they pursued were characterised as their own rights.[165] Where states had control of claims, that control was exclusive and individuals took no part in proceedings, apart from a requirement in some cases to indicate their consent to the claim.[166]

Thus, the practice in this period reflected both aspects of the PCIJ's expositions on diplomatic protection and individual rights under treaties, and developed along parallel lines. Individuals were able to prosecute their own claims before an international tribunal, provided that states had granted individuals specific capacity in an international treaty. In those cases, individuals were given independent capacity to pursue claims against states, but that capacity was preconditioned on the consent of states in a treaty. This practice is consistent with the idea that states may confer upon individuals 'international rights *stricto sensu*, i.e. rights which they acquire without

165 For example, the post-First World War mixed arbitral tribunals with the Allied powers (excluding the US) and the Mixed Commission and Arbitral Tribunal for Upper Silesia.

166 For example, the post-First World War US claims commissions, the Mexican claims commissions, and the tribunals established by Panama and the US, and by Norway and the US.

the intervention of municipal legislation and which they can enforce in their own name before international tribunals',[167] a doctrine which appeared in the orthodox account of the framework of the international legal system in the post-1945 era, traced to the PCIJ's Opinion in *Danzig*.

Thus, the dual doctrines of diplomatic protection and individual rights in the inter-war period were reflected in international claims practice. Diplomatic protection doctrine and practice was consistent with the established understanding of the international legal system at the time: since the nineteenth century it had been accepted that states could bring claims in respect of injury to their nationals, on the basis of inter-state rights. Individual rights doctrine and practice was not, however, reflected in the orthodox account of the international legal system during this period. Although the practice of international claims tribunals which permitted individuals to bring claims in respect of their own rights was supported by the jurisprudence of the PCIJ, at the time this was not generally understood as having a transformative effect on the framework of the international system.

Unlike some of the ninteenth century practice, which was best characterised as diplomatic protection practice but had particular features to take account of an individual's interests, the practice in the inter-war period fits more clearly into the binary categories of diplomatic protection and direct claims. So, for example, where a claim was decided through a process of diplomatic protection, individuals had no rights, limited or otherwise, to representation or to participate in proceedings. The only feature of practice best characterised as diplomatic protection practice which potentially engaged individuals in a limited way was the requirement in the Mexican Claims Commissions that claimants sign the memorial. But even this requirement was not applied strictly; a failure to consent to espousal of the claim was only held to affect the state's ability to bring a claim in one case before the Italian-Mexican Commission. Developments in the inter-war period suggest that it is possible and preferable to categorise claims practice as falling within one of two binary categories of diplomatic protection and direct claims, rather than locating it along a spectrum between the two types of international claims.

[167] R. Jennings and A. Watts, *Oppenheim's International Law* (9th edn, London, Longmans, 1992), p. 847, para. 375; p. 17, para. 7, discussed in 1.2(d) above.

2.4 Diplomatic protection and individual claims after 1945

(a) The development of doctrine

The doctrine of diplomatic protection, which had been affirmed by decisions of the PCIJ in the inter-war period, continued to form the basis of cases and decisions of the Court in the period since 1945. It has also been the focus of work of the International Law Commission (ILC). Relevant aspects of the development of diplomatic protection are outlined in the first section of this Part. In addition, decisions of the International Court of Justice (ICJ) have affirmed that individuals can be granted rights directly under treaty; these are examined in the second section of this Part.

(i) Diplomatic protection

The *Mavrommatis* formulation of diplomatic protection has been affirmed by the ICJ in several cases. In the *Interhandel* case the ICJ stated that in diplomatic protection claims, the applicant state had 'adopted the cause of its national' whose rights had been violated.[168] Cases brought by way of diplomatic protection before the ICJ since *Barcelona Traction* include *Tehran Hostages*;[169] *ELSI*;[170] three matters concerning the application of the Vienna Convention on Consular Relations: *Breard*,[171] *LaGrand*[172] and *Avena*;[173] *Oil Platforms*;[174] *Arrest Warrant*;[175] and *Diallo*.[176]

168 *Interhandel (Switzerland* v. *United States)*, Preliminary Objections [1959] ICJ Rep. 6, 27.

169 *United States Diplomatic and Consular Staff in Tehran (United States* v. *Iran)* [1980] ICJ Rep. 3, 5–6 (para. 8).

170 *Elettronica Sicula Spa (ELSI) (United States* v. *Italy)* [1980] ICJ Rep. 15.

171 *Vienna Convention on Consular Relations (Paraguay* v. *United States)* [1998] ICJ Rep. 248, 250 (para. 5).

172 *LaGrand (Germany* v. *United States)* [2001] ICJ Rep. 466, 472 (para. 10).

173 *Avena and Other Mexican Nationals (Mexico* v. *United States)*, Mexico brought the case by way, *inter alia*, of diplomatic protection, but the Court declined to address the case as such: [2004] ICJ Rep. 12, 36 (para. 40).

174 *Oil Platforms (Iran* v. *United States)*, Separate Opinion of Judge Rigaux, [2003] ICJ Rep. 161, 369–70 (para. 10).

175 Belgium, in *Arrest Warrant of 11 April 2000*, took the position that the case was transformed into one of diplomatic protection after the Foreign Minister of the Democratic Republic of the Congo (DRC) left office. But the DRC had not brought the case by way of diplomatic protection and the Court rejected the Belgian position: [2002] ICJ Rep. 3, 16–17 (paras. 37–40). Cf., implying that the Court (mistakenly) treated Spain's case as one brought by way of diplomatic protection, Dissenting Opinion of Judge Torres Bernárdez, *Fisheries Jurisdiction (Spain* v. *Canada)* [1998] ICJ Rep. 432, 589 (paras. 20–2).

176 *Ahmadou Sadio Diallo (Republic of Guinea* v. *DRC)*, Preliminary Objections, ICJ, 24 May 2007, para. 86.

The suggestion that a state was obliged to exercise its right to diplomatic protection in a particular case was rejected firmly in *Barcelona Traction*: in that case the Court emphasised the discretionary character of the right of diplomatic protection.[177]

In addition to these decisions of the ICJ, the ILC adopted Articles on Diplomatic Protection in 2006.[178] In large measure, the Articles confirmed the traditional parameters of the doctrine. This approach had been encouraged by Special Rapporteur Dugard,[179] who noted:

> diplomatic protection, albeit premised on a fiction, is an accepted institution of customary international law, and one which continues to serve as a valuable instrument for the protection of human rights. It provides a potential remedy for the protection of millions of aliens who have no access to remedies before international bodies and it provides a more effective remedy to those who have access to the often ineffectual remedies contained in international human rights instruments.[180]

Article 1 of the Draft Articles defines diplomatic protection as:

> the invocation by a State, through diplomatic action or other means of peaceful settlement, of the responsibility of another State for an injury caused by an internationally wrongful act of that State to a natural or legal person that is a national of the former State with a view to the implementation of such responsibility.[181]

When the Draft Articles were being formulated by the ILC, developments in respect of individual rights and human rights led some in the

[177] *Barcelona Traction, Light and Power Co. Ltd (Belgium* v. *Spain)* [1970] ICJ Rep. 4, 44 (para. 79).

[178] For Dugard's work on the subject see ILC, *First Report on Diplomatic Protection* (52nd Session, 2000), A/CN.4/506 and Add. 1; ILC, *Second Report on Diplomatic Protection* (53rd Session, 2001), A/CN.4/514; ILC, *Third Report on Diplomatic Protection* (54th Session, 2002), A/CN/523 and Add. 1; ILC, *Fourth Report on Diplomatic Protection* (55th Session, 2003), A/CN.4/530 and Add. 1; ILC, *Fifth Report on Diplomatic Protection* (56th Session, 2004), A/CN.4/538; ILC, *Sixth Report on Diplomatic Protection* (57th Session, 2005), A/CN.4/546; ILC, *Seventh Report on Diplomatic Protection* (58th Session, 2006), A/CN.4/567. See also J. Dugard, 'Diplomatic Protection and Human Rights: The Draft Articles of the International Law Commission' (2005) 24 *Australian YIL* 75. The final Draft Articles on Diplomatic Protection with commentaries are at ILC, *Report of the Fifty-eighth Session* (2006), A/CN.4/L.684. The ILC had taken up the topic of diplomatic protection in 1996: *Official Records of the General Assembly, Fifty-first Session, Supplement No. 1*, A/51/10, para. 249, Annex II, Add. 1; before that it had formed part of the extended study of state responsibility commencing in 1956: *First Report of F.V. García Amador*, A/CN.4/96, reproduced in (1956) II *ILC Yearbook* 173, 192.

[179] ILC, *First Report on Diplomatic Protection* (52nd Session, 2000), A/CN.4/506 and Add. 1, pp. 25–6, paras. 67–73.

[180] *Ibid.* p. 25, para. 64, references omitted.

[181] ILC, *Report of the Fifty-eighth Session* (2006), A/CN.4/L.684, Art. 1.

ILC to argue that diplomatic protection was obsolete.[182] In his First Report, Dugard summarised the argument as follows: the equality of national treatment and international minimum standard of treatment of aliens had been replaced by an international human rights standard for both nationals and aliens, and therefore diplomatic protection claims by a state ought to be limited to cases where there was no method of dispute settlement in place between the alien and the injuring state; in such cases the state would act as agent for the individual and not in its own right. In consequence, 'the right of a state to assert its own right when it acts on behalf of its national is an outdated fiction which should be discarded - except, perhaps, in cases in which the real *national* interest of the State is affected'.[183] The ILC eventually concluded that the current state of international human rights law did not justify discarding diplomatic protection. Dugard noted that, for the vast majority of the world's population, enforcement mechanisms for human rights protection were weak. He concluded that '[a]s long as the State remains the dominant actor in international relations, the espousal of claims by States for the violation of the rights of their nationals remains the most effective remedy for the promotion of human rights'.[184] The extent to which diplomatic protection operates as the more effective alternative to direct claims by individuals can be questioned; nevertheless the ILC's decision that diplomatic protection continues to have a function in the protection of individuals is logical since individuals have no inherent capacity to bring international claims, but only treaty-specific rights in limited circumstances.

The ILC's decision to confine its consideration of the topic to secondary rules, where possible, had the consequence that it did not have to consider whether and to what extent the primary rules of international law confer substantive rights on individuals. The Commentary to the Draft Articles adopted on First Reading states:

Diplomatic protection belongs to the subject of 'Treatment of Aliens'. No attempt is made, however, to deal with the primary rules on this subject - that is, the rules governing the treatment of the person and property of aliens, breach of which gives rise to responsibility to the State of nationality of the

[182] See ILC, *Preliminary Report on Diplomatic Protection*, A/CN.4/484 (Mohamed Bennouna, Special Rapporteur, 4 February 1998) and, for example, statements by Lukashuk and Pellet in A/CN.4/SR.2513, p. 8.

[183] ILC, *First Report on Diplomatic Protection* (52nd Session, 2000), A/CN.4/506 and Add. 1, p. 6, para. 17 (emphasis in original, references omitted).

[184] *Ibid.* p. 10, para. 32.

injured person. Instead the present draft articles are confined to secondary rules only – that is, the rules that relate to the conditions that must be met for the bringing of a claim for diplomatic protection. By and large this means rules governing the admissibility of claims.[185]

It is, of course, understandable that the Commission did not embark on a wholesale examination of the primary rules of international law relating to the treatment of aliens. It is regrettable, however, that the Commission did not consider whether there ought to be a distinction for the purposes of the application of secondary rules between situations where (a) the breached international obligation is an inter-state obligation; and (b) the breached international obligation is an obligation owed directly to an individual. As will be seen, such a distinction might have afforded a more nuanced approach to at least three problematic secondary rules: nationality of claims, exhaustion of local remedies and waiver.

The ILC considered that the right of diplomatic protection belonged to the state, not to the individual. Commentary to Draft Article 2 states:

Article 2 stresses that the right of diplomatic protection belongs to or vests in the State. It gives recognition to the Vattelian notion that an injury to a national is an indirect injury to the State . . .

This view is frequently criticized as a fiction difficult to reconcile with the realities of diplomatic protection, which require continuous nationality for the assertion of a diplomatic claim, the exhaustion of local remedies by the injured national, and the assessment of damages suffered to accord with the loss suffered by the individual. Nevertheless the 'Mavrommatis principle' or the 'Vattelian fiction', as the notion that an injury to a national is an injury to the State has come to be known, remains the cornerstone of diplomatic protection.[186]

Thus, the ILC also confirmed that diplomatic protection was a state right rather than an obligation, consistent with the ICJ's emphasis in *Barcelona Traction* on the discretionary character of diplomatic protection.[187] The Commentary to Draft Article 2 also noted that international law imposed no obligation on a state to exercise its right to diplomatic

[185] ILC, *Report of the Fifty-eighth Session* (2006), A/CN.4/L.684, p. 23, para. 2.
[186] *Ibid.* pp. 27–8, paras. 1–2. Arguably it follows from the recognition of a distinct state right that the equitable principle of 'clean hands' in respect of conduct of the national is inapplicable. The ILC included no provision in relation to that principle in the Draft Articles: see Dugard in ILC, *Sixth Report on Diplomatic Protection* (57th Session, 2005), A/CN.4/546.
[187] *Barcelona Traction, Light and Power Co. Ltd (Belgium v. Spain)* [1970] ICJ Rep. 4, 44 (para. 79).

protection.[188] The implication is that individuals hold no international law right to compel their state of nationality to exercise diplomatic protection.[189] However, in Draft Article 19, entitled 'Recommended practice', the ILC suggested that a state entitled to exercise diplomatic protection should:

(a) give due consideration to the possibility of exercising diplomatic protection, especially where a significant injury has occurred;
(b) take into account, wherever feasible, the views of injured persons with regard to resort to diplomatic protection and the reparation to be sought; and
(c) transfer to the injured person any compensation obtained for the injury from the responsible state subject to any reasonable deductions.

The Commentary to Draft Article 19 noted that these reflected 'practices on the part of States ... which have not yet acquired the status of customary rules', and that they were 'desirable practices ... that add strength to diplomatic protection as a means for the protection of human rights and foreign investment'.[190] In respect of (c), it can be noted that any individual right to compensation in respect of a diplomatic protection claim will ordinarily only arise as a matter of domestic law, but it might also engage international human rights law. In 1994, the European Court of Human Rights held that an international agreement making provision for compensation for claims espoused on the basis of diplomatic protection could give rise to an enforceable right on the part of the injured nationals to compensation. It held that Article 6 of the European Convention on Human Rights (ECHR) was engaged where the French government settled claims of French citizens against the Moroccan government relating to the nationalisation of assets by a lump sum agreement incorporated in a treaty, and subsequently by decree established a national administrative committee to distribute the proceeds of the settlement. The right to compensation was held to be a pecuniary right which was susceptible to determination in accordance with the standards of the ECHR.[191] So at least in circumstances

188 ILC, *Report of the Fifty-eighth Session* (2006), A/CN.4/L.684, pp. 27–8, paras. 1–2.

189 It was held recently in the UK courts that individuals cannot compel their state of nationality to exercise diplomatic protection on their behalf: *Abbasi and another* v. *Secretary of State for Foreign and Commonwealth Affairs* [2003] UKHRR 76.

190 ILC, *Report of the Fifty-eighth Session* (2006), A/CN.4/L.684, Commentary to Art. 19, pp. 94–5.

191 *Beaumartin* v. *France* (Application no. 15287/89), 25 November 1994, [1994] ECHR Rep. 40.

where the ECHR is applicable, individuals may have enforceable rights to the proceeds of a diplomatic protection claim successfully pursued in respect of their injury; whether the incorporation of this recommended practice in the ILC Draft Articles leads to further practice in support of an individual right to the proceeds of such claims (even where the ECHR does not apply) remains to be seen.

In relation to continuity of nationality, the ILC considered that the established rule was that nationality was required at the date of injury and at the date of the official presentation of the claim, noting that this was 'most frequently used in treaties, judicial decisions and doctrine'.[192] The ILC declined to require continuity of nationality to the date of the award, suggesting that it would be 'contrary to the interests of the individual, as many years may pass between the presentation of the claim and its final resolution'.[193] 'In an exercise in progressive development of the law', the ILC drafted the rule to require that the relevant individual be a national continuously between the date of the injury and presentation of the claim, suggesting that it would be incongruous to require nationality to be shown to exist at those two dates, but not continuously.[194] The Draft Articles as adopted create a presumption of continuity if nationality existed at both relevant dates.

The ILC also took the view that there was a need for exceptions to the rule requiring continuity of nationality. The Draft Articles therefore introduced limited exceptions to the requirement that the espousing state be the national state at the time of the injury.[195] These exceptions do not apply in the case of a claim against the state of which the

[192] ILC, *Report of the Fifty-eighth Session* (2006), A/CN.4/L.684, Commentary to Art. 5, p. 37, para. 4. In 1965, the Institute of International Law had adopted a resolution which reaffirmed the traditional rule by requiring nationality at both the date of presentation and of injury, but did not specifically require continuity between those dates: Institute of International Law, 'Resolution on the National Character of an International Claim Presented by a State for Injury Suffered by an Individual, Warsaw Session, 1965', *Resolutions de l'Institut de Droit International, 1957–1991* (1992), pp. 55–6.

[193] ILC, *Report of the Fifty-eighth Session* (2006), A/CN.4/L.684, Commentary to Art. 5, pp. 37–8, para. 5.

[194] *Ibid.* p. 36.

[195] Paragraph 2 of Art. 5 accordingly provides that a state may exercise diplomatic protection in respect of a person who was a national at the date of official presentation of the claim but not at the date of injury provided that three conditions are met: first, the injured person had the nationality of a predecessor state or had lost his or her previous nationality; second, that the injured person acquired the new nationality for a reason unrelated to the bringing of the claim; and third, the new nationality had been acquired in a manner not inconsistent with international law: *ibid.* Art. 5.

individual was a national at the time of the injury.[196] These exceptions, the ILC noted, were intended to introduce an element of flexibility into the continuity rule to avoid unfairness, while retaining safeguards which prevent abuse by individuals and states.[197] The potential for unfairness had been noted by Judge Fitzmaurice in his separate opinion in the *Barcelona Traction* case:

> [T]oo rigid and sweeping an application of the continuity rule can lead to a situation in which important interests go unprotected, claimants unsupported and injuries unredressed, not on account of anything relating to their merits, but because purely technical considerations bring it about that no State is entitled to act. This situation is the less defensible at the present date in that what was always regarded as the other main justification for the continuity rule (and even sometimes thought to be its *fons et origo*), namely the need to prevent the abuses that would result if claims could be assigned for value to nationals of States whose Governments would compel acceptance of them by the defendant State, has largely lost its validity.[198]

The exceptions, which allow a state to espouse a claim in respect of which the relevant individual was its national at the time of official presentation of the claim but not at the time of injury, cannot be said to be codificatory of existing international law. It will be recalled that the PCIJ expressly required nationality to be proved at the time of the injury 'to involve the international responsibility of [the respondent state]'.[199] Introducing exceptions into this rule may well avoid hardship in certain circumstances, but doing so also reveals an underlying confusion about the relation of the injury to the state of nationality. If the Vattelian fiction that an injury to the national is an injury to the state of nationality is accepted at face value, then it logically follows that the injury is suffered by the state immediately at the time of the injury. It should be irrelevant whether nationality is continuously held after that moment. Nevertheless, the ILC decided to retain the continuity rule, albeit in a more flexible form; it remains to be seen whether states accept the ILC's formulation and practice develops in support of a rule in this regard. However, it can be noted that the ILC's treatment of continuity of nationality might have benefited from consideration of the character

196 *Ibid.* Art. 5, para. 3.

197 The Special Rapporteur had suggested that the continuity rule should be abolished altogether: see ILC, First Report on Diplomatic Protection (52nd Session, 2000), A/CN.4/506 and Add. 1, p. 15, para. 24.

198 *Barcelona Traction, Light and Power Co. Ltd (Belgium* v. *Spain)* [1970] ICJ Rep. 4, 23.

199 *Panevezys-Saldutikis Railway (Estonia* v. *Latvia)*, PCIJ Rep. ser. A/B no. 76 (1939) 16–17.

of the underlying right. Where the breached international obligation is owed directly to an individual, nationality at the time of presentation of the claim might assume greater importance, since arguably the claim only becomes an inter-state dispute when it is espoused, or officially presented, on an inter-state basis. Where the breached international obligation is an inter-state obligation, a requirement to retain nationality until the time of presentation of the claim might be of less importance, since when the injury occurs there is a relevant inter-state dispute which might be the subject of an international claim. In this context, examining who holds the right might have allowed the ILC to take a more nuanced approach to the issue at hand, that of continuous nationality.

Nor did the Commission consider who holds the underlying right when it considered the rule on exhaustion of local remedies.[200] Article 14 as adopted requires that local remedies be exhausted in any situation where the claimant state has been injured 'indirectly' through its national.[201] But there must be a distinction between situations where the injury is caused by a violation of domestic law, for which there is a denial of justice; and situations where the injury is caused directly by a violation of international law, whether the obligation is owed to the espousing state or to the injured individual directly.[202] For a claim of denial of justice, where the relevant obligation arises under domestic law, the local remedies requirement would seem to be a valid substantive rule; whereas in respect of a direct violation of international law, international responsibility ought to arise at the time of the injury and any requirement to exhaust local remedies could only be procedural. Consideration of the character of the underlying right (and in particular, identifying the holder of the right) may have contributed to some clarity on the question whether the exhaustion of local remedies was a substantive condition, or a procedural condition going only to the admissibility of a claim.

In the context of the local remedies rule, the Commentary notes that the Draft Articles 'd[o] not take cognizance of the "Calvo Clause"', but

[200] In 1959, in the *Interhandel* case, the ICJ held that the rule that local remedies must be exhausted before international proceedings could be instituted was 'a well-established rule of international law' which had been generally observed where a state had brought a diplomatic protection claim in respect of its national: *Interhandel (Switzerland* v. *United States)*, Preliminary Objections, [1959] ICJ Rep. 6, 27. The ICJ affirmed its status as a principle of customary law in *Elettronica Sicula Spa (ELSI) (United States* v. *Italy)* [1980] ICJ Rep. 15, 42, para. 50.

[201] ILC, *Report of the Fifty-eighth Session* (2006), A/CN.4/L.684, Commentary to Art. 14, p. 74, para. 9.

[202] ILC, *Second Report on Diplomatic Protection* (53rd Session, 2001), A/CN.4/514, p. 15, para. 32.

suggests that the Calvo clause is difficult to reconcile with international law if it constitutes a complete waiver of recourse to international protection where the relevant conduct is an internationally wrongful act or where the injury directly concerns the claimant state. It notes that the objection may be less convincing where the rights are those of the individual and not the claimant state.[203] Apart from this mention of the Calvo clause, the Draft Articles do not address more generally the question of waiver of international rights, either by states or by individuals. In some contexts, where international rights vest in individuals, their ability to waive those rights has been recognised,[204] although there is no consensus on the extent to which a diplomatic protection claim may be encumbered by waiver by individuals. It is regrettable that the Commission did not address more generally the question of waiver, as it is a question to which the Draft Articles could have brought some clarity; again it would seem that consideration of who holds the underlying right is relevant to the question of the validity of any waiver.

Draft Article 16 contains an exclusion clause: the Draft Articles were expressly stated not to apply to any actions or procedures other than diplomatic protection.[205] This was confirmed in the ICJ's decision in preliminary objections in *Diallo*, where the Court rejected an argument that investment tribunal practice had modified the traditional doctrine of diplomatic protection: it held that the practice in the foreign investment context allowing claims by 'substitution' did not reveal 'an exception in customary international law allowing for protection by substitution' in respect of diplomatic protection.[206]

[203] ILC, *Report of the Fifty-eighth Session* (2006), A/CN.4/L.684, Commentary to Art. 14, pp. 73–4, para. 8. See Shea, *The Calvo Clause*, pp. 223–36.

[204] The European Court of Human Rights has held that individuals may validly waive their entitlement to certain of the rights specified in the Convention (such as the right to a public hearing under Art. 6(1)): *Albert and LeCompte* v. *Belgium*, Judgment, 10 February 1983, ECHR ser. A no. 58, para. 35; *H* v. *Belgium*, Judgment, 30 November 1987, ECHR ser. A no. 127-B, para. 54. Any waiver must be 'established in an unequivocal manner' (*Barberà, Messengué and Jabardo* v. *Spain*, Judgment, 6 December 1988, ECHR ser. A no. 146, para. 82; *Oberschlick* v. *Austria*, Judgment, 23 May 1991, ECHR ser. A no. 204, para. 51) and 'not run counter to any important public interest' (*Håkansson and Sturesson* v. *Sweden*, Judgment, 21 February 1990, ECHR ser. A no. 171-A, para. 67; *McGonnell* v. *United Kingdom*, Judgment, 8 February 2000, ECHR Rep. 2000-II, para. 44; *Lundevall* v. *Sweden*, Application no. 38629/97, ECtHR, Judgment, 12 November 2002, para. 34). There are particular considerations in respect of *jus cogens* and non-derogable rights.

[205] See Dugard in ILC, *Fourth Report on Diplomatic Protection*, Add., A/CN.4/530/Add.1, pp. 3–4, paras. 109, 112.

[206] *Ahmadou Sadio Diallo (Republic of Guinea* v. *Democratic Republic of the Congo)*, Preliminary Objections, ICJ, 24 May 2007, paras. 88–9.

(ii) Individual rights

The ICJ has also affirmed that individuals may acquire rights directly under international treaties, particularly in its treatment of the two death penalty cases it has dealt with on the merits. In *LaGrand*, Germany alleged that by breaching its obligation to inform the relevant German nationals of their rights under the Vienna Convention on Consular Relations, the US had violated the individual rights of those nationals.[207] Article 36(1) of the Vienna Convention relevantly provides:

With a view to facilitating the exercise of consular functions relating to nationals of the sending State:

a. . . . ;
b. if he so requests, the competent authorities of the receiving State shall, without delay, inform the consular post of the sending State if, within its consular district, a national of that State is arrested or committed to prison or to custody pending trial or is detained in any other manner. Any communication addressed to the consular post by the person arrested, in prison, custody or detention shall also be forwarded by the said authorities without delay. The said authorities shall inform the person concerned without delay of his rights under this sub-paragraph.

The ICJ concluded that Article 36(1) of the Vienna Convention created individual rights which could be invoked by Germany. It stated:

Article 36, paragraph 1(b), spells out the obligations the receiving State has towards the detained person and the sending State . . . Significantly, [Article 36, paragraph 1(b)] ends with the following language: 'The said authorities shall inform the person concerned without delay of *his rights* under this subparagraph' . . . The clarity of these provisions, viewed in their context, admits of no doubt. It follows . . . that the Court must apply these as they stand. Based on the text of these provisions, the Court concludes that Article 36, paragraph 1, creates individual rights, which . . . may be invoked in this Court by the national State of the detained person. These rights were violated in the present case. (emphasis added)[208]

[207] *LaGrand (Germany* v. *United States)* [2001] ICJ Rep. 466, 481 (para. 38); Memorial of the Government of the Federal Republic of Germany, para. 4.93 (available at www.icj-cij.org/docket/files/104/8552.pdf).

[208] *LaGrand (Germany* v. *United States)* [2001] ICJ Rep. 466, 492–4 (para. 77) (references omitted). The same conclusion concerning the Vienna Convention had been reached by the Inter-American Court of Human Rights in 1999: see *The Right to Information on Consular Assistance in the Framework of the Guarantees of the Due Process of Law*, Advisory Opinion OC-16/99, Inter American Court of Human Rights, 1 October 1999, 48–50 (paras. 80–4).

At the hearings, Germany raised a further argument that the right of the individual to be informed without delay under Article 36(1) was in the character of a human right, which rendered the effectiveness of the provision 'even more imperative'. The ICJ held that, having found that the US had violated the rights accorded by Article 36(1) to the LaGrand brothers, it was not necessary to consider this argument.[209]

Two of the judges entered reservations to the ICJ's conclusion. In his separate opinion, Vice President Shi questioned the Court's conclusion that Article 36(1) created individual rights. He considered the better interpretation to be that the rights of nationals of the sending state to consular notification are derived from the rights of the state party to protect and assist its nationals under the Vienna Convention.[210] In his dissenting opinion, Judge Oda stated that the Vienna Convention did not grant foreign individuals any rights beyond those which could necessarily be implied by the obligations imposed on states under the convention. Judge Oda appears not to have disagreed with the principle that the Vienna Convention granted direct rights to individuals, but thought them to be strictly limited to rights corresponding to the correlative obligations borne by states under the convention.[211]

In *Avena*, the same provision of the Vienna Convention was in dispute, this time between Mexico and the US. Mexico alleged that the US had breached the Vienna Convention in respect of fifty-two of its nationals.[212] The question of the character of the rights under Article 36(1) arose because the US objected to the admissibility of Mexico's application on the ground of a failure to exhaust local remedies.[213] The ICJ agreed with the US that if local remedies remained, Mexico could not espouse the claims of its nationals through diplomatic protection, but noted that Mexico had also asserted its own claims, based on its own direct injury.[214] The Court recalled the finding in the *LaGrand* case that Article 36(1) creates individual rights which may be invoked in the Court by the national state of the detained person, as a violation of the national state's rights. It also noted that the violations of the rights of the individual under Article 36 could entail a violation of the rights of the sending state. The ICJ held that the rights of the state and individual

[209] *LaGrand (Germany* v. *United States)* [2001] ICJ Rep. 466, 492–4 (para. 78).

[210] *Ibid.* Separate Opinion of Vice President Shi, 520–1 (paras. 4–15).

[211] *Ibid.* Dissenting Opinion of Judge Oda, 537 (para. 27).

[212] *Avena and Other Mexican Nationals (Mexico* v. *United States)* [2004] ICJ Rep. 12. The names of the fifty-two Mexican nationals are set out in para. 16.

[213] *Ibid.* 35 (para. 40). [214] *Ibid.* 35 (para. 40).

rights under Article 36(1) of the Vienna Convention were 'interdependent', in circumstances where:

> violations of the right of the individual under Article 36 may entail a violation of the rights of the sending State, and that violations of the rights of the latter may entail a violation of the rights of the former.
>
> In these special circumstances of interdependence of the rights of the State and of individual rights, Mexico may, in submitting a claim in its own name, request the Court to rule on the violation of rights which it claims to have suffered both directly and through the violation of individual rights conferred on Mexican nationals under Article 36, paragraph 1(b). The duty to exhaust local remedies does not apply to such a request.[215]

The approach of the ICJ in both *LaGrand* and *Avena* to the existence of individual rights under treaties can be contrasted with that of its predecessor in *Jurisdiction of the Courts of Danzig*. In *Danzig*, it can be recalled that the PCIJ required that in order to create individual rights, states parties to a treaty must clearly *intend* to adopt rules conferring rights on individuals.[216] In contrast, the ICJ made no inquiry into the intention of the contracting parties to the Vienna Convention, but based its conclusion – that individuals were granted rights by the convention – on a bare reading of its provisions.[217]

The ILC Articles on State Responsibility and the Draft Articles on Responsibility adopted on first reading both contemplate the possibility of enforceable individual rights. Article 33(2) of the Articles on State Responsibility, in the form of a saving clause, envisages that some 'person or entity other than a State' may invoke the international responsibility of a state, and that secondary obligations arising from a breach may be owed directly to the primary right-bearer.[218] This leaves open the possibility that an individual may be entitled to claim reparation in respect of an internationally wrongful act of a state.

[215] *Ibid.* 35 (para. 40). In a separate opinion, President Shi maintained his objection to individual rights under Art. 36(1): see *ibid.* Separate Opinion of President Shi, 74.

[216] *Jurisdiction of the Courts of Danzig (Pecuniary Claims of Danzig Railway Officials who have Passed into the Polish Service, Against the Polish Railways Administration)*, PCIJ Rep. ser. B no. 15 (1928) 17–18. See discussion in 1.2(c) above.

[217] *LaGrand (Germany* v. *United States)* [2001] ICJ Rep. 466, 492–4 (para. 77).

[218] Article 33, reproduced in J. Crawford, *International Law as an Open System* (London, Cameron May, 2002); see also J. Crawford, 'The ILC's Articles on Responsibility of States for Internationally Wrongful Acts: A Retrospect' (2002) 96 *AJIL* 874, 887–8; E.B. Weiss, 'Invoking State Responsibility in the Twenty-First Century' (2002) 96 *AJIL* 798.

(b) International claims tribunals and commissions

In this section the most significant international claims tribunals and commissions operating after 1945 are reviewed: the post-Second World War commissions and tribunals; the Iran–US Claims Tribunal; and the UN Compensation Commission. The work of other administrative bodies and claims processes will not be addressed in any detail.[219] Instead, this section will give a broad overview of three significant international claims processes which have operated since 1945.[220]

(i) Post-Second World War commissions and tribunals

The post-Second World War tribunals and commissions were not uniform in their approach to claims. The Italian and Japanese commissions operated on the basis of diplomatic protection, with states having control of the claim. Proceedings before the Conciliation Commissions established between Italy and the US, the UK, the Netherlands and France were instituted by state agents, who were represented before the Commissions,[221] and the Rules of Procedure of some of the Commissions limited the role of individual claimants to participation as witnesses.[222] Similarly, states were parties in proceedings before the Property Commissions established between Japan and the US, the UK and the Netherlands,[223] and the Rules of Procedure prohibited individual claimants from acting as agent for the claimant state.[224] Proceedings before the Japanese Property Commissions were initiated by state

[219] See e.g., P. Sands, Y. Shany and R. Mackenzie (eds.), *The Manual on International Courts and Tribunals* (London, Butterworths, 1999), which forms part of the Project on International Courts and Tribunals. For a synoptic chart of their work, see www.pict-pcti.org/publications/synoptic_chart/synop_c4.pdf.

[220] Where claims brought by legal rather than natural persons are cited, these elaborate points of procedure and practice which are also applicable to claims brought by natural persons.

[221] Italy–UN (US, UK, the Netherlands, France), 10 February 1947, 49 UNTS 126, XIV UNRIAA 1; see e.g., Rules of Procedure of Anglo-Italian conciliation commission, XIV UNRIAA 6 (Arts. 6–7); Rules of Procedure of Italian-US conciliation commission, XIV UNRIAA 79 (Arts. 4, 7 and 11).

[222] See e.g., Rules of Procedure of Anglo-Italian conciliation commission, XIV UNRIAA 6 (Art. 14).

[223] Japan–Allied Powers, Treaty of Peace, 8 September 1951, 136 UNTS 46; Japan–Allied Powers, Agreement for settlement of disputes, 12 June 1952, 138 UNTS 183, XIV UNRIAA 447. The property commissions were established to determine applications to Japan for the return of any tangible or intangible property, rights or interests of any kind in Japan of each Allied Power and its nationals.

[224] See e.g., Rules of Procedure of US-Japanese property commission, XIV UNRIAA 465 (Art. 6); Rules of Procedure of Netherlands-Japanese property commission, XIV UNRIAA 501

agents[225] and the decisions were reported as inter-state claims between the state of nationality and Japan.[226]

In contrast, the German commissions followed a direct model. Individual claimants could initiate proceedings and participate as parties before the Arbitral Commission on Property Rights and Interests in Germany.[227] Individuals could refer disputes to the Mixed Commission on German external debts[228] provided that their government stated that the question was 'of general importance' for interpretation of the relevant agreement;[229] the relevant individual was then treated as a party to the case.[230] Individuals also could refer disputes to the Austro-German Arbitral Tribunal.[231]

(ii) The Iran–US Claims Tribunal

The Iran–US Claims Tribunal was established by the Claims Settlement Declaration in the Algiers Accords, to settle disputes arising out of the

(Art. 5). In the case of the UK-Japanese property commission, see *United Kingdom in re Struthers and others* v. *Japan*, 29 ILR 389.

225 See e.g., Rules of Procedure of US-Japanese property commission, XIV UNRIAA 465 (Art. 10, see also Art. 16 which provided that all relevant documents were to be signed by the agent of the state); Rules of Procedure of Netherlands-Japanese property commission, XIV UNRIAA 501 (Art. 10).

226 See e.g., *United Kingdom in re International Electrolytic Plant Company Ltd* v. *Japan*, 29 ILR 308; *United Kingdom in re Hong Kong and Shanghai Banking Corp.* v. *Japan*, 29 ILR 383, 385: 'The British Government in supporting this claim . . .'.

227 Germany-Allied Powers (US, UK, Ireland, France, Greece, Belgium, the Netherlands), Convention on settlement of matters arising out of the war and the occupation, 26 May 1952 (entered into force 5 May 1955), 332 UNTS 219; see Rules of Procedure reproduced in *Decisions of the Arbitral Commission on Property, Rights and Interests in Germany* (Koblenz, Directions Press, 1958), vol. I, p. 192 (Arts. 25, 26 and 28). A state was also entitled to be represented in proceedings where its national or resident was a party: see Rules of Procedure, 192 (Art. 51).

228 Allied Powers–Germany, 27 February 1953, 333 UNTS 2.

229 *Ibid.* Art. 31(2)(a).

230 See *Bodenkreditbank in Basel and the Swiss Confederation* v. *Gebrüder Roher GMBH and the German Federal Republic*, Mixed Commission for the Agreement on German External Debts, 7 November 1956, 25 ILR 326: bank treated as applicant. See also *Community of Heirs of the Late Fritz Cahn* v. *Federal Republic of Germany and Pensionsverein*, Mixed Commission for the Agreement on German External Debts, 12 November 1964, 35 ILR 253; *Doninelli v Ebeling*, Mixed Commission for the Agreement on German External Debts, 28 October 1965, 35 ILR 261.

231 Austria–Germany, 15 June 1957, reproduced in K. Oellers-Frahm and N. Wülher, *Dispute Settlement in Public International Law: Text and Materials* (Berlin, Springer-Verlag, 1984), p. 784. This tribunal was established to deal with the settlement of legal property rights of private persons. The right to refer disputes was subject to a preliminary procedure before a conciliation commission and then the domestic court. See generally, I. Seidl-Hohenveldern, *The Austrian-German Arbitral Tribunal* (New York, Syracuse University Press, 1972).

detention of fifty-two US nationals at the US Embassy in Tehran, and the subsequent freeze of Iranian assets by the US. The Tribunal has jurisdiction to decide, *inter alia*, claims of US nationals against Iran and of Iranian nationals against the US, arising out of debts, contracts, expropriations or other measures affecting property rights.

The Claims Settlement Declaration set up a hybrid approach to individual claims. Article III(3) provided:

> Claims of nationals of the United States and Iran that are within the scope of this Agreement shall be presented to the Tribunal either by the claimants themselves or, in the case of claims of less than $250,000, by the government of such national.[232]

It therefore appeared from the Declaration that claims of less than US$250,000 ('small claims') were to be presented by the state of nationality, on a basis which resembled diplomatic protection, while 'large claims', those greater than US$250,000, were to be presented by individuals who presumably would participate as parties to the proceedings; on that basis the procedure for 'large claims' resembled that of a direct claims tribunal. However, the Tribunal held consistently that neither the small or large claims before it were diplomatic protection claims, stating that the Tribunal was a new forum in substitution of diplomatic protection, before which individual claimants vindicated their own rights.[233] The Tribunal rejected the suggestion that it was determining diplomatic protection claims or inter-state disputes, stating that it was determining 'the rights of the claimant, not of his nation'.[234] Thus, in respect of all claims, the Tribunal purported to provide individuals with access to an international forum to vindicate

232 Declaration of the Government of the Democratic and Popular Republic of Algeria Concerning the Settlement of Claims by the Government of the United States and the Government of the Islamic Republic of Iran, 19 January 1981, Art. III(3), (1981) 20 ILM 230.

233 *Esphahanian* v. *Bank Tejarat*, Case no. 157, Award no. 31–157–2 (1983-I) 2 Iran-US CT Rep. 157, 165; Case no. A/18 (1984-I) 5 Iran-US CT Rep. 251, 261–2. See also Case no. A/18 (1984-I) 5 Iran-US CT Rep. 251, Concurring Opinion of Willem Riphagen, 273. This was later affirmed by the Tribunal in Case no. A/21: see *Islamic Republic of Iran* v. *United States*, Case no. A/21 (1987-I) 14 Iran-US CT Rep. 324, 330; see also *Islamic Republic of Iran* v. *United States*, Cases nos. A/15 (IV) and A/24, Award no. 590-A15(IV)/A24-FT (1998) 34 Iran-US CT Rep. 105, 148; cf. dissent of Khalilian in *Lord Corporation (a claim of less than US $250,000 presented by the United States), Claimant* v. *Iran Helicopter Support and Renewal Co., Respondent*, Award no. 346–10973–2 (1988-I) 18 Iran-US CT Rep. 377, Separate Opinion of Khalilian, 385.

234 Case no. A/18 (1984-I) 5 Iran-US CT Rep. 251, 261–2.

their own rights, free from the constraints of the doctrine of diplomatic protection. In fact, most of the small claims were settled by an inter-state lump sum agreement which did not expressly require that the states parties pass on the awards to individual claimants; nor did the Tribunal's notation of the agreement indicate whether the individual claimants had consented to the settlement of the claims.[235] One would expect that where a tribunal was determining claims which belonged to individuals, settlement of those claims by an inter-state agreement would make express provision for payment of the agreed settlement to individual claimants and be conditioned upon their consent to settlement of their claims. The Tribunal's endorsement of the inter-state lump sum settlement was consistent with the terms of the Claims Settlement Declaration, but not with the Tribunal's own statements concerning the character of the claims.

The Claims Settlement Declaration did not confer exclusive jurisdiction on the Tribunal, but once a claim was referred to the Tribunal, Article VII provided that that claim should 'be considered excluded from the jurisdiction of the courts of Iran, or of the United States, or of any other court'.[236] It also provided in general terms that '[a]ll decisions and awards of the Tribunal shall be final and binding'.[237] That exclusion from jurisdiction was effected in the US by Presidential Executive Order providing that claims presented to the Tribunal 'shall have no legal effect in any action now pending in any court of the United States'.[238] Subsequently, the US Supreme Court dismissed a challenge to the constitutionality of that Order.[239]

The extent to which an individual was prevented from pursuing claims which had been dismissed by the Tribunal through domestic courts was also considered by an English court in *Dallal* v. *Bank Mellat*. A US national who had referred his claim to the Tribunal, where it was dismissed, subsequently brought the same claim in the English courts

[235] *United States, on behalf of US nationals and Islamic Republic of Iran*, Award on Agreed Terms no. 483, Claims of less than US$250,000/86/B38/B76/B77-FT, 22 June 1990, (1990-II) 25 Iran-US CT Rep. 327. See also 'Contemporary Practice of the United States' (1990) 84 *AJIL* 890.

[236] Declaration of the Government of the Democratic and Popular Republic of Algeria Concerning the Settlement of Claims by the Government of the United States and the Government of the Islamic Republic of Iran, Art. VII (2), 19 January 1981, (1981) 20 ILM 230.

[237] *Ibid.* Art. IV(1).

[238] Exec. Order no. 1229, 46 Fed. Reg. 14111, cited in *Dames and Moore* v. *Regan*, US Supreme Court, 2 July 1981, 72 ILR 271.

[239] *Ibid.*

against the defendant, who had a place of business and assets in England.[240] The High Court struck out the action as an abuse of process, holding that it would be 'contrary to justice and comity . . . to decline to recognise the decision of the tribunal between the present parties'.[241] In the view of the court, the competence of the Tribunal was derived not only from the inter-state agreement, but from the individual's voluntary submission of his claim to the Tribunal's jurisdiction:

> where two sovereign states have chosen to set up a tribunal to determine disputes between the nationals of their respective states in respect of choses in action for which the situs lies within the jurisdiction of those two states, there can be no warrant for the courts of this country to fail to recognise and treat as fully competent the decisions of that tribunal. It is an *a fortiori* case where the party who is seeking to go behind the decision of such a tribunal is the party who has himself invoked the jurisdiction of that tribunal. I hold that the tribunal was a competent tribunal in respect of the present parties and the present matters.[242]

The implication to be drawn from the High Court's decision is that an individual who voluntarily submits to the jurisdiction of the Tribunal is estopped from subsequently pursuing an alternative claim through domestic courts; the decision of the international tribunal constitutes *res judicata*.[243] The court did not refer specifically to Article VII of the Declaration, but it did refer to the individual's voluntary submission of his claim to the Tribunal, from which the Tribunal derived competence to exclusively determine the claim. Although the decision of the court was based on domestic law, it was consistent with the proposition that Article VII of the Declaration had the effect of making the Tribunal's decision final and binding vis-à-vis the individual claimant.

(iii) The UN Compensation Commission

The UN Compensation Commission was established in 1991 by Security Council Resolution, to process claims and allocate compensation for losses resulting from Iraq's invasion and occupation of Kuwait.[244] It is

240 *Dallal* v. *Bank Mellat*, HC, QB Division, 26 July 1985, 75 ILR 151. 241 *Ibid.* 173.

242 *Ibid.* 173.

243 See J. Crawford, 'Decisions of British Courts during 1985–6' (1986) *BYIL* 410, 411.

244 The UNCC and UN Compensation Fund were established by SC/Res/692 (1991). Compensation is payable from a special fund that receives a percentage of the proceeds from sales of Iraqi oil. This was originally set up by SC/Res/706 (1991) (on the same day as SC/Res/692) but Iraq did not take up the proposed scheme and another scheme only began operating in December 1996. Special lodging procedures were established in respect of stateless persons.

not a court or arbitral tribunal before which parties appear, but 'performs an essentially fact-finding function' in examining claims and determining compensation.[245]

Overall, the characteristics of the procedures before the Compensation Commission indicate that the claims are made on the basis of diplomatic protection. Individual claimants do not have direct access to the Commission: it only receives claims submitted by governments on behalf of victims[246] and all contact with those victims is conducted through the relevant states.[247] But the claims must include a statement of consent from the individual claimant,[248] who may opt to pursue his or her claim in domestic courts rather than before the Commission.[249] Further, the Compensation Commission has held that states must distribute the proceeds of claims in accordance with guidelines issued by the Security Council, which limit the amount governments may deduct from the payments in offset of their costs and which impose reporting requirements on the distribution of awards to individual claimants. Payments not distributed within twelve months must be returned to the Commission.[250] In all material aspects, the Commission appears to operate on the basis of diplomatic protection but with some procedures which ensure that the claims are for the benefit of individual claimants. An individual who did not consent to his or her claim being presented to the Compensation Commission could attempt to pursue it through a domestic court; if a claim presented to the Commission was unsuccessful and the individual claimant

245 SC/Res/687 (1991); *Report of Secretary-General* (3 April 1991), S/22559.

246 Provisional Rules of Procedure, section II, art. 5(1)(a), reproduced in R. B. Lillich (ed.), *The United Nations Compensation Commission: Thirteenth Sokol Colloquium* (New York, Transnational, 1995), pp. 427–43. There is a particular exception in the case of corporations and private legal entities: their claims may be submitted by the government of the state having jurisdiction over the entity at the time of the loss, but where the state fails to submit such a claim, the corporation or entity may itself make a claim to the commission, provided it includes an explanation as to why its claim it not being submitted by a government: Provisional Rules of Procedure, art. 5(3). This exception does not apply to individuals.

247 Provisional Rules of Procedure, Section II, art. 9, Lillich, *The United Nations Compensation Commission*, pp. 427–43.

248 This is clearly stated to be the case for claims under categories A, B and C: see *Criteria for Expedited Processing of Urgent Claims: for Individuals under Categories A, B and C*, Decision No. 1, para. 20, reproduced in Lillich, *The United Nations Compensation Commission*, 399–402.

249 *Report of Secretary-General*, S/22559 (3 April 1991), para. 22.

250 See Decision no. 18 on distribution of payments and transparency, reproduced in Lillich, *The United Nations Compensation Commission*, pp. 452–4. Payments not distributed within twelve months must be returned to the commission.

subsequently commenced proceedings in a domestic court, it is arguable that the decisions of the Commission would constitute *res judicata*, its competence deriving from the Security Council and the claimant's voluntary submission to jurisdiction. In this context some analogy may be drawn with the Iran–US Claims Tribunal,[251] but a point of distinction lies in the fact that the Compensation Commission is not a court or judicial body. The extent to which a claimant's submission to jurisdiction of the Commission would preclude its pursuit of a claim through domestic law would depend on the relevant domestic law.

(c) *Investment treaty arbitration*

A self-contained process of dispute resolution for foreign investment disputes was established in 1965 with the Convention on the Settlement of Investment Disputes between States and Nationals of other States (the 'ICSID Convention').[252] The ICSID Convention does not contain any substantive obligations with respect to foreign investment, but it provides a procedure for the resolution of 'any legal dispute arising directly out of an investment' between a contracting state and a national of another contracting state, which the parties consent to submit to the International Centre for the Settlement of Investment Disputes (ICSID).[253] With the widespread inclusion of substantive investment protection provisions within investment treaties, together with procedural provisions for the submission of investment disputes to arbitration, this form of dispute resolution has grown rapidly. Since 1959 over 2,500 bilateral investment treaties (BITs) have entered into force, as well as several significant multilateral investment treaties.[254] These investment treaties generally impose obligations on a host state to encourage investments; to accord fair and equitable treatment to investments; to accord national or most-favoured-nation treatment to investors and investments; to guarantee unrestricted transfer of investment and returns; not to expropriate investment except for a public interest and

[251] See discussion of *Dallal* v. *Bank Mellat*, HC, QB Division, 26 July 1985, 75 ILR 151, above.

[252] Convention on the Settlement of Investment Disputes between States and Nationals of other States, 18 March 1965 (entry into force 14 October 1966), 575 UNTS 159. The convention set up the International Centre for Settlement of Investment Disputes (ICSID), under the auspices of the World Bank: see http://icsid.worldbank.org/ICSID/Index.jsp.

[253] *Ibid*. Art. 25(1).

[254] See UNCTAD, 'The Entry into Force of Bilateral Investment Treaties (BITs)' (2006) *IIA Monitor* no. 3 , UNCTAD/WEB/ITE/IIA/2006/9 (available at www.unctad.org/en/docs/webiteiia20069_fn.pdf).

on payment of prompt, adequate and effective compensation; and to compensate losses caused by certain circumstances in the host state. A number of BITs also include an 'umbrella clause' by which the host state guarantees its performance of other obligations or commitments.[255]

Most BITs make provision for international arbitration for breaches of its substantive provisions. Commonly, a BIT provides that disputes may be referred to ICSID or to some other institution, or to ad hoc arbitration. In the case of ICSID, the dispute settlement clause in the BIT constitutes an offer to arbitrate, which is perfected when it is accepted by the investor as contemplated in Article 25(1) of the ICSID Convention.[256] The investor-state dispute resolution clause only operates in favour of the investor; it cannot be invoked by a state to bring a claim against an investor,[257] although in the context of a claim brought by an investor it may be possible for the respondent state to make a counterclaim.[258] Since 1987[259] there have been over 200 registered cases before ICSID and perhaps as many investment treaty claims outside it.

In addition to the investor-state dispute resolution mechanism, most BITs contain an arbitration mechanism for inter-state disputes. So far this mechanism has not been invoked to bring a claim on behalf of an investor, but depending on the language of the inter-state dispute resolution clause, it may be applied to this purpose, and this might be particularly useful where there is no investor-state dispute resolution clause.[260] In such circumstances the claim itself would be best

[255] See A. C. Sinclair, 'The Origins of the Umbrella Clause in the International Law of Investment Arbitration' (2004) 20 *Arbitration International* 411. No umbrella clause appears in the US Model BIT: reproduced at www.ustr.gov/assets/Trade_Sectors/Investment/Model_BIT/asset_upload_file847_6897.pdf.

[256] *Lanco International Inc.* v. *Argentina*, Preliminary Decision on Jurisdiction, 8 December 1998, 5 ICSID Rep. 11, paras. 43–4; *American Manufacturing and Trading, Inc.* v. *Republic of Zaire*, Award, 21 February 1997, 5 ICSID Rep. 11, paras. 5.18–5.23.

[257] In a recent award, an ICSID tribunal declined jurisdiction in a claim brought by the government of the Indonesian province of East Kalimantan against foreign investors: *Government of the Province of East Kalimantan* v. *PT Kaltim Prima Coal and others* (ICSID Case no. ARB/07/3), Award, 28 December 2009 (not yet public).

[258] Convention on the Settlement of Investment Disputes between States and Nationals of other States, Art. 46, 18 March 1865, 575 UNTS 159; *Saluka Investments BV* v. *Czech Republic*, Decision on Jurisdiction over the Czech Republic's Counterclaim, 7 May 2004, 1 ICSID Rep. 543, para. 79.

[259] *Asian Agricultural Products Ltd* v. *Republic of Sri Lanka*, Award, 27 June 1990, 4 ICSID Rep. 254.

[260] For example, the Australia–US Free Trade Agreement does not contain an investor-state dispute resolution clause: see Australia–US Free Trade Agreement, 18 May

characterised as a diplomatic protection claim, but the same question arises as to the character of the underlying rights as for investor-state arbitration.

The question of the character of investment treaty arbitration is one which has occupied both scholars and arbitral tribunals. At least three considerations are relevant: first, whether investment arbitration is conducted as a form of direct claim or as a form of diplomatic protection; second, whether investment treaties confer procedural rights on individual investors to bring disputes to arbitration; and third, whether investment treaties confer substantive rights on individual investors corresponding to the host state's obligations of treatment.

As to the character of the arbitration, it is relevant that the investor has exclusive control of the claim which may be presented without the consent of its state of nationality[261] and that damages awards are paid directly to the individual claimant. Further, damages are calculated solely on the basis of the harm caused to the interests of the investor and do not take into account other considerations which may be taken into account in the calculation of damages in a diplomatic protection claim brought on an inter-state basis.[262] These characteristics indicate that the claims are brought as direct claims between the individual and the host state, rather than as diplomatic protection claims on an inter-state basis, at least insofar as the procedure applied to the claim is concerned. The ICJ implied that investment treaty claims were not diplomatic protection claims when it concluded that the practice of the former could not contribute to the creation

2004 (entered into force 1 January 2005) [2005] ATS 1, available at www.ustr.gov/sites/default/files/uploads/agreements/fta/australia/asset_upload_file148_5168.pdf.

261 In some cases the state of nationality has intervened in proceedings to oppose the investor's claim: in *GAMI Inc.* v. *United States of Mexico*, the US intervened pursuant to Art. 1128 of the North American Free Trade Agreement (NAFTA) to argue that the tribunal had no jurisdiction to hear the claims of its national (*GAMI Inc.* v. *United States of Mexico*, see submission of the United States, 30 June 2003, available at www.state.gov/documents/organization/22212.pdf); and in *Mondev International Ltd* v. *United States*, Canada made submissions to the tribunal which supported the conclusion that its national investor's claims ought to be dismissed on the merits (*Mondev International Ltd* v. *United States*, Award, 11 October 2002, 6 ICSID Rep. 192).

262 This can be contrasted with awards in diplomatic protection claims: while the loss to the national most commonly forms the basis for an assessment of damages, other considerations may be taken into account, including the character of the breached international obligation: *Factory at Chorzów (Claim for Indemnity)*, Merits, PCIJ Rep. ser. A no. 17 (1928) 28.

of a rule of customary international law applicable to diplomatic protection claims.[263]

As to the procedural right to commence arbitration, typically the dispute resolution clause in a BIT will constitute an offer to arbitrate, which can be taken up at the election of the investor. It is suggested that the procedural right is a direct individual right for two reasons. First, the language of the dispute resolution clause usually indicates that the individual investor has a procedural right to commence arbitration under the treaty itself. This is most clear where the BIT provides that the investor 'has the right' to submit a dispute to arbitration, but other formulations commonly used suggest that the individual has a right or entitlement to submit a dispute to arbitration: some provide that the dispute shall be submitted 'at the request' of the investor;[264] while others state that either party to a dispute 'may'[265] or 'may choose to' submit the dispute to arbitration.[266] Whether a particular BIT confers a right on an individual investor will depend on its terms, but these representative examples of the language of dispute resolution clauses indicate that the treaty confers a right to submit a dispute to arbitration on the investor directly. Second, that the individual investor has a direct treaty right is consistent with the practical effect of the dispute resolution clause: the individual investor can submit a dispute to arbitration merely by accepting the host state's offer, without requiring the consent of its state of nationality; indeed, its state of nationality cannot prevent the investor's acceptance of the offer to arbitrate, short of terminating the BIT. In the circumstances that an individual investor can independently invoke the dispute resolution clause, it cannot be sustained that the procedural right (under the investor-state dispute resolution clause) is a state right. It is a right independently held by

263 *Ahmadou Sadio Diallo (Republic of Guinea v. Democratic Republic of the Congo)*, Preliminary Objections, ICJ, 24 May 2007, para. 86.

264 For example, Art. 8 of the Sri Lanka Model BIT states that a dispute 'may be submitted upon request of the investor': Sri Lanka Model BIT, reproduced in C. McLachlan, L. Shore and M. Weiniger, *International Investment Arbitration: Substantive Principles* (Oxford, Oxford University Press, 2007), App. 9, p. 427.

265 For example, Art. 1120 of NAFTA provides that 'a disputing investor may submit the claim to arbitration': North American Free Trade Agreement, 17 December 1992 (entry into force 1 January 1994), (1993) 32 ILM 612.

266 See e.g., Energy Charter Treaty (ECT), Art. 26, 17 December 1994 (entry into force 16 April 1998), 2080 UNTS 100.

any individual who qualifies under the BIT.[267] Where there is a state-state dispute resolution clause in the BIT, the national state may have a separate procedural right to submit a dispute to arbitration, which exists and operates independently of the investor-state dispute resolution clause.

That the procedural right to commence arbitration is a right conferred by the BITs on individual investors was the conclusion reached by the English Court of Appeal in *Occidental* v. *Ecuador*.[268] The reasoning of the High Court, affirmed in the Court of Appeal, also supported this interpretation; the High Court made the following observations about the right to arbitrate in the BIT:

> First, ... the State Parties to the BIT intended to give investors the right to pursue, in their name and for themselves, claims against the other State party. Secondly, ... those rights are granted under public international law and must be determined on principles of public international law, as they were by the Tribunal in this case.[269]

It is also consistent with the decision of the NAFTA tribunal in *Loewen* when it affirmed that an individual investor could bring a NAFTA claim on its own behalf. Although the *Loewen* tribunal characterised NAFTA arbitration as a form of delegated diplomatic protection, it acknowledged that an individual claimant had a right to submit the claim to arbitration:

> NAFTA is a treaty intending to promote trade and investment between Canada, Mexico and the United States. Since most international investment occurs in the private sector, investment treaties frequently seek to provide some kind of protection for persons engaging in such investment. ...
>
> Chapter Eleven of NAFTA represents a progressive development in international law whereby the individual investor may make a claim on its own behalf and submit the claim to international arbitration as [the Loewen Group] has done in the instant case.[270]

[267] This question is also discussed in Ole Spiermann, 'Individual Rights, State Interests and the Power to Waive ICSID Jurisdiction under Bilateral Investment Treaties' (2004) 20 *Arbitration International* 179, esp. 183–6.

[268] *Republic of Ecuador* v. *Occidental Exploration and Production Company* [2006] 1 QB 432 (CA (Civ.)).

[269] *Republic of Ecuador* v. *Occidental Exploration and Production Company* [2005] EWHC 774 (Comm) (HC QBD), para. 61.

[270] *The Loewen Group Inc. and Raymond L. Loewen* v. *United States*, Award, 26 June 2003, 7 ICSID Rep. 421, paras. 222–3.

Once the investor invokes its treaty right to take up the host state's offer to arbitrate, a perfected agreement to arbitrate is created in the form of a contract. The agreement to arbitrate is not a treaty;[271] individuals do not acquire treaty-making capacity merely by accepting a treaty offer to arbitrate.[272] But according to *Occidental*, the applicable law of that contract is public international law.

As to the substantive obligations in the BIT to accord the investment certain standards of treatment, the question whether these correspond to individual rights has been more controversial.[273] Again, the inquiry should begin with the text of the BIT. Like the dispute resolution clauses, the language of the substantive treatment provisions varies between BITs. Some clauses provide that the state 'shall accord' to investors or to investments certain treatment;[274] others state that investments 'shall not be' subjected to certain treatment;[275] while others state that 'the investor shall have the right' to certain treatment.[276] It is clear from all of these formulations that the investor has an entitlement to treatment in accordance with the provisions of the BIT. Where the language is that of direct rights (such as the investor

271 Although the proper law of the agreement to arbitrate may be public international law: *Republic of Ecuador* v. *Occidental Exploration and Production Company* [2006] 1 QB 432 (CA (Civ.)), paras. 32–3.

272 See generally, J. Crawford, 'Treaty and Contract in Investment Arbitration' (2008) 24 *Arbitration International* 351, 360–1.

273 For a discussion of the positions, see Z. Douglas, *The International Law of Investment Claims* (Cambridge, Cambridge University Press, 2009), pp. 1–38; Z. Douglas, 'The Hybrid Foundations of Investment Treaty Arbitration' (2003) 74 *BYIL* 151, esp. 162–4.

274 See e.g., US 2004 Model BIT, Art. 3, available at www.ustr.gov/assets/Trade_Sectors/Investment/Model_BIT/asset_upload_file847_6897.pdf; see also US 2004 Model BIT, Art. 4; ECT, Art. 10 ('Each Contracting Party shall endeavour to accord to Investors ... the Treatment'); ECT, Art. 12 ('an Investor ... shall be accorded ... treatment'); NAFTA, Art. 1102 ('Each Party shall accord to investors of another Party treatment'); see also NAFTA, Arts. 1103, 1104 and 1105; ASEAN Agreement for the Promotion and Protection of Investments ('ASEAN Agreement'), Art. III, 15 December 1987, (1998) 27 ILM 612 ('Investments ... shall at all times be accorded ... treatment'); UK Model BIT, Art. 2(2), reproduced in McLachlan, Shore and Weiniger, *International Investment Arbitration*, App. 4, p. 379; and Netherlands Model BIT, Art. 3(2), reproduced in McLachlan, Shore and Weiniger, *International Investment Arbitration*, App. 8, p. 423.

275 See e.g., ECT, Art. 13(1); ASEAN Agreement, Art. VI; UK Model BIT, Art. 5, reproduced in McLachlan, Shore and Weiniger, *International Investment Arbitration*, App. 4, p. 379; Germany Model BIT, Art. 4(2), reproduced in McLachlan, Shore and Weiniger, *International Investment Arbitration*, App. 7, p. 417; Sri Lanka Model BIT, Art. 3(2), reproduced in McLachlan, Shore and Weiniger, *International Investment Arbitration*, App. 9, p. 427.

276 For example, ECT, Art. 13(2).

'shall have the right'), that entitlement to treatment apparently involves an individual right arising directly from the terms of the BIT. Where the language is equivocal (for example, that the host state 'shall accord' treatment to investments), whether the treaty confers a direct and substantive individual right to a qualifying investor is less clear. In some circumstances, determining whether the treaty gives investors direct substantive rights will not be necessary; if the investor is entitled to a certain standard of treatment and the host state has submitted to arbitration for its conduct to be adjudged against that standard, whether the standard of treatment amounts to an individual right will be immaterial for the assessment of violations and damages. Where the question assumes importance is in the application of secondary rules of responsibility, including claims of waiver and circumstances precluding wrongfulness.

It seems clear that there are two constructions which might apply to the entitlement of the investor to treaty-standard treatment. The first construction is that the substantive obligations in the BIT are owed on an inter-state basis; the second is that the substantive obligations in the BIT are owed directly to qualifying investors, as individual rights.

If the substantive obligations in the BIT are owed on an inter-state basis, then the investor's procedural right to arbitrate entitles it to enforce rights which are in origin the rights of its state of nationality. Two possible models which would take account of the inter-state character of the substantive obligations have been discussed by Douglas: what he calls the 'derivative rights theory'; and what might be termed the 'procedural-direct theory'.[277] The derivative rights theory suggests that investment treaty claims are properly characterised as diplomatic protection claims, pursued by individual investors but vindicating the rights of states; under this theory, all obligations in the BIT are owed on an inter-state basis, including the obligation to submit to arbitration on the filing of a request in accordance with the terms of the BIT. This view is most commonly attributed to the *Loewen* tribunal, which stated that NAFTA arbitration permitted individuals 'for convenience to enforce what in origin are the rights of Party states'.[278] It presupposes that (a) investment treaty claims are diplomatic protection claims which are controlled by investors; and (b) that no rights are conferred on

[277] Douglas, *The International Law of Investment Claims*, pp. 11–16.

[278] *The Loewen Group Inc. and Raymond L. Loewen* v. *United States*, Award, 26 June 2003, 7 ICSID Rep. 421, para. 233.

individuals by the BIT; rather, these are exclusively inter-state rights and obligations, including any procedural right to arbitrate. It will be clear from the preceding discussion that neither the language of BITs (which indicate that the right to invoke arbitration is conferred directly on qualifying investors) nor the practice of investment treaty tribunals support this model.

In contrast, the procedural-direct theory suggests that although the substantive treatment obligations in the BIT are owed on an inter-state basis, on the filing of a notice of arbitration (in the exercise of an individual's direct procedural right to invoke a claim before an international tribunal), the claimant investor enters into a legal relationship with the host state in the form of an arbitration agreement, and the claimant 'becomes a counterparty' to the host state's obligation to submit to international arbitration for an assessment of its conduct on the basis of the norms of investment protection set out in the treaty.[279] The obligation to submit to arbitration encompasses a duty to pay compensation where the conduct of the host state is judged to be in violation of the substantive norms; thus, the treaty standards of treatment can be construed as 'the applicable adjudicative standards for the claimant's cause of action rather than binding obligations owed directly to the investor'.[280] The procedural-direct theory allows for the possibility of direct claims, the relevant treaty standards forming part of the legal relationship between the investor and host state which crystallises upon invocation of the dispute resolution clause in the BIT. Prior to that crystallisation of the investor-host state relationship, the substantive obligations in the BIT are owed only on an inter-state basis. The procedural-direct model therefore leaves open the possibility that a state could claim a circumstance precluding wrongfulness (such as countermeasures)[281] which applies to the inter-state relationship in respect of conduct not in conformity with the treaty standard prior to the filing of the notice of arbitration. The procedural-direct model rules

[279] Douglas, *The International Law of Investment Claims*, p. 35; see also Douglas, 'The Hybrid Foundations of Investment Treaty Arbitration',162–4.

[280] Douglas, *The International Law of Investment Claims*, p. 35.

[281] Not all circumstances precluding wrongfulness will raise this issue. For example, the defence of necessity does not require that the wrongful act be necessarily directed at another state: see generally, *LG&E Energy Corp., LG&E Capital Corp. and LG&E International Inc.* v. *Argentine Republic* (ICSID Case no. ARB/02/1), Award, 3 October 2006; *LG&E Energy Corp., LG&E Capital Corp. and LG&E International Inc.* v. *Argentina*, ICSID Case no. ARB/02/1, Decision on Liability, 3 October 2006; *CMS Gas Transmission Co.* v. *Republic of Argentina*, ICSID Case no. ARB/01/8, Decision on Annulment, 25 September 2007.

out the possibility of waiver prior to the crystallisation of the claim by notice of arbitration: only when the investor's procedural right is perfected by the filing of a claim is the investor free to waive its procedural right; prior to that time the substantive treatment cannot be waived by the investor because it does not correspond to a directly vested right. To hold otherwise would be to permit an individual to encumber the state's treaty rights.[282]

If the substantive obligations in the BIT are owed directly to investors (the 'substantive-direct' theory), then the direct legal relationship between an individual and a host state crystallises at the time when the individual qualifies under the BIT as an investor. At that time, the host state owes international treaty obligations directly to an individual investor, who may invoke those obligations before an international tribunal.[283] Because the treaty rights are directly vested in the investor from the moment a qualifying investment exists, it is open to the investor to waive or encumber its rights through an exclusive jurisdiction clause; furthermore, because the investor has direct rights, any circumstance precluding wrongfulness which applies as between the contracting states to the treaty will not apply in the determination of an investor's treaty claim.

The situation assumes a further layer of complexity where contractual claims are involved: that is, a contract between the host state (or para-statal entity) and the claimant investor. Where the BIT provides a basis for invoking an international tribunal's jurisdiction for straightforward contractual claims, independently of any umbrella clause, the rights the tribunal is determining must belong in their origin to the investor, but these are of course contractual not treaty rights.[284] The only relevant treaty right is the investor's right to invoke the jurisdiction of an international tribunal, which is in effect determining a contractual claim in a treaty forum. Where the BIT contains an umbrella clause, the contractual obligations of the host state have the potential to acquire the character of inter-state obligations by virtue of the host state's guarantee of its observance of those

[282] *Eureko* v. *Poland*, Partial Award, 19 August 2005, 12 ICSID Rep. 335, 372.

[283] This was the interpretation favoured by the Court of Appeal in *Republic of Ecuador* v. *Occidental Exploration and Production Company* [2006] 1 QB 432 (CA Civ.), para. 20, citing Douglas, 'The Hybrid Foundations of Investment Treaty Arbitration', 182.

[284] See e.g., Art. 8 of the relevant BIT discussed in the *Vivendi* annulment decision: *Compañía Aguas del Acquija SA and Vivendi Universal* v. *Argentine Republic*, Decision on Annulment, 3 July 2002, 6 ICSID Rep. 340, 356, para. 55.

contractual obligations.[285] In those circumstances, the contractual obligations have the potential to become treaty obligations.[286] Whether the treaty obligation to observe the commitments of the contract is owed directly to the investor or to the state of nationality will depend on the terms of the relevant umbrella clause in the BIT.

The substantive-direct and procedural-direct models represent rather polarised conceptual frameworks for the characterisation of investment treaty rights. It is, of course, possible that some of the substantive rights under a BIT could be characterised as direct rights and others as state rights. A further possibility is that the rights under a BIT could be characterised as *Avena*-style 'interdependent' rights.[287] However, this characterisation seems less likely than one or other of state or individual rights. In *Avena*, the relevant treaty provision, Article 36 of the Vienna Convention, incorporated rights of sending states (for example, to have access to their nationals) and rights of nationals (for example, to have access to the consular post of their sending state) which bear a direct relationship each to the other. In contrast, the substantive treatment provisions of a BIT do not refer to separate rights for states and their nationals, distinct or interdependent, and it is difficult to envisage circumstances where violation of rights of states under a BIT could necessarily entail a violation of the rights of individuals, or vice versa.

Since BITs are not carbon-copied, but differ in their language and context, the question whether investors acquire direct substantive rights from a particular BIT can only be determined on a case-by-case (or BIT-by-BIT) basis. Since the BIT is a treaty, it ought to be interpreted in accordance with treaty interpretation principles: the inquiry should begin with the ordinary meaning of the terms in their context and in

[285] See generally, Crawford, 'Treaty and Contract in Investment Arbitration', 367–9; *LG&E Energy Corp., LG&E Capital Corp. and LG&E International Inc.* v. *Argentina*, ICSID Case no. ARB/02/1, Decision on Liability, 3 October 2006, para. 175; *CMS Gas Transmission Company* v. *Republic of Argentina*, ICSID Case no. ARB/01/8, Decision on Annulment, 25 September 2007, para. 95.

[286] The effect of an umbrella clause was examined by two awards dealing with similar facts. In *SGS Société Générale de Surveillance SA* v. *Islamic Republic of Pakistan*, Decision on Objections to Jurisdiction, 6 August 2003, 8 ICSID Rep. 383, the tribunal took a limited view of the umbrella clause and held that it did not have the effect of elevating contract claims to treaty claims. In *SGS Société Générale de Surveillance SA* v. *Republic of the Philippines*, Decision on Objections to Jurisdiction, 29 January 2004, 8 ICSID Rep. 515, the tribunal held that the umbrella clause conferred jurisdiction on it to adjudicate the contract claims.

[287] *Avena and Other Mexican Nationals (Mexico* v. *United States)* [2004] ICJ Rep. 12, 36 (para. 40).

light of its object and purpose.[288] Some tribunals have suggested in this (and other) contexts that ambiguities in a BIT ought to be resolved in favour of investor protection. In *SGS* v. *Philippines*, the tribunal explained the interpretive presumption as follows:

> The object and purpose of the BIT supports an effective interpretation of Article X(2). The BIT is a treaty for the promotion and reciprocal protection of investments. According to the preamble it is intended 'to create and maintain favourable conditions for investments by investors of one Contracting Party in the territory of the other'. It is legitimate to resolve uncertainties in its interpretation so as to favour the protection of covered investments.[289]

A number of similar statements have been made in the context of determining jurisdiction and in determining violations under substantive provisions of BITs.[290] But, of course, like any treaty, BITs represent a package deal and it is necessary to bear in mind that the broad protection of investors and investments will not always (or perhaps ever) be the sole objective of the compact represented by the treaty. Although the promotion of foreign investment will usually be an objective of the BIT; it is rather more likely that the BIT's objects and purposes involve a number of considerations which include broader public interest objectives.[291] Moreover, in the context of the direct rights inquiry, interpreting BITs in favour of investor's direct rights might increase investment protection in some circumstances (by excluding some circumstances precluding wrongfulness, such as countermeasures defences) but encumber that protection in other circumstances (by permitting individuals to waive BIT protection, even without necessarily being aware of their entitlement to it). Thus, for at least two reasons, an interpretive presumption in favour of direct rights is an oversimplification: because it may fail to take account of the objects and purposes of the BIT as a whole, and because it may not favour investor protection in every

288 Vienna Convention on the Law of Treaties, 22 May 1969 (entry into force 27 January 1980), 1155 UNTS 331, Art. 31.

289 *SGS Société Générale de Surveillance SA* v. *Republic of the Philippines*, Decision on Objections to Jurisdiction, 29 January 2004, 8 ICSID Rep. 515, para. 116.

290 See e.g., *Maffezini (Emilio Agustín)* v. *Kingdom of Spain*, Decision on Objections to Jurisdiction, 25 January 2000, 5 ICSID Rep. 396, paras. 54–6, 64; *Československá Obchodni Banka AS* v. *Slovak Republic*, Decision on Objections to Jurisdiction, 24 May 1999, 14 ICSID Rep. 251, paras. 57 and 64; *Siemens AG* v. *Argentine Republic*, Decision on Jurisdiction, 3 August 2004, 12 ICSID Rep. 174, paras. 85 and 120; *Tokios Tokelės* v. *Ukraine*, Decision on Jurisdiction, 29 April 2004, 20 ICSID Rep. 205, paras. 31–2, 52.

291 See discussion in G. van Harten, *Investment Treaty Arbitration and Public Law* (Oxford, Oxford University Press, 2007), pp. 139–40.

instance. In most BITs the protection of investments will form part of the object and purpose, but that goal does not automatically lead one to conclude that the BIT confers direct substantive rights on investors.

The question of the holder of substantive rights under a BIT has confronted three NAFTA tribunals required to determine a countermeasures defence raised by Mexico. Three separate claims were filed against Mexico by US agricultural companies, relating to the imposition of a 20 per cent tax by Mexico on soft drink bottlers using the sweetener High Fructose Corn Syrup (HFCS). Mexico claimed countermeasures in defence to its alleged violation of the national treatment standard in Article 1102 of NAFTA, claiming that it had imposed the tax as a countermeasure against two violations of NAFTA by the US, relating generally to access of Mexico's surplus sugar produce to the US market. All three NAFTA tribunals have issued redacted awards,[292] but one of the awards, *Cargill* v. *United Mexican States*, is not yet public.

Countermeasures are dealt with in the ILC's Articles on State Responsibility[293] as a circumstance precluding wrongfulness. It was also confirmed by the ICJ in the *Gabčíkovo-Nagymaros Project* case[294] and by the arbitral tribunal in the *United States–France Air Services* case.[295] Article 22 of the ILC Articles provides:

> The wrongfulness of an act of a State not in conformity with an international obligation towards another State is precluded if and to the extent that the act constitutes a countermeasure taken against the latter State in accordance with Chapter II of Part Three.

The objects and limits of countermeasures are elaborated in Article 49, which provides:

> 1. An injured State may only take countermeasures against a State which is responsible for an internationally wrongful act in order to induce that State to comply with its obligations under Part Two.
>
> 2. Countermeasures are limited to the non-performance for the time being of international obligations of the State taking the measures towards the responsible State.

[292] *Corn Products International, Inc.* v. *United Mexican States*, ICSID Case no. ARB(AF)/04/01, Decision on Responsibility, 15 January 2008; *Archer Daniels Midland Co. and Tate & Lyle Ingredients Americas, Inc.* v. *United Mexican States*, ICSID Case no. ARB(AF)/04/05, Award, 21 November 2007.

[293] Articles on the Responsibility of States for Internationally Wrongful Acts, ILC, *Report of the ILC, 53rd Session*, reproduced in (2001) II(2) *ILC Yearbook* 26.

[294] *Gabčíkovo-Nagymaros Project (Hungary/Slovakia)* [1997] ICJ Rep. 7.

[295] (1978) 54 ILR 103, para. 81.

3. Countermeasures shall, as far as possible, be taken in such a way as to permit the resumption of performance of the obligations in question.

Article 49 makes clear that countermeasures must be directed against the state which committed the prior wrongful act. It will not preclude the wrongfulness of a measure taken as against a third party. The ILC Commentary to Article 49 notes:

A second essential element of countermeasures is that they 'must be directed against' a State which has committed an internationally wrongful act and which has not complied with its obligations of cessation and reparation under Part Two of the present articles. The word 'only' in paragraph 1 applies equally to the target of the countermeasures as to their purpose and is intended to convey that countermeasures may only be adopted against a State which is the author of the internationally wrongful act. Countermeasures may not be directed against States other than the responsible State. In a situation where a third State is owed an international obligation by the State taking countermeasures and that obligation is breached by the countermeasure, the wrongfulness of the measure is not precluded as against the third State. In that sense the effect of the countermeasures in precluding wrongfulness is relative. It concerns the legal relations between the injured State and the responsible State.[296]

While this paragraph of the Commentary refers only to the rights of third states, the following paragraph elaborates with respect to the effects of countermeasures as against third states and refers in that context to other parties, contemplating that countermeasures may not preclude the wrongfulness of acts taken in violation of rights of third parties other than states:

This does not mean that countermeasures may not incidentally affect the position of third States or indeed other third parties. For example, if the injured State suspends transit rights with the responsible State in accordance with this Chapter, other parties, including third States, may be affected thereby. If they have no individual rights in the matter they cannot complain. Similarly if, as a consequence of the suspension of a trade agreement, trade with the responsible State is affected and one or more companies lose business or even go bankrupt. Such indirect or collateral effects cannot be entirely avoided.[297]

[296] See Commentary to Art. 49, para. 4, reproduced in J. Crawford, *The International Law Commission's Articles on State Responsibility: Introduction, Text and Commentaries* (Cambridge, Cambridge University Press, 2002), p. 285.

[297] Commentary to Art. 49, para. 5, reproduced in Crawford, *The International Law Commission's Articles on State Responsibility*.

From this Commentary it is clear how a defence based on countermeasures could raise the question whether individual investors derive substantive rights from investment treaties: if they do derive substantive rights, a countermeasures defence cannot preclude the wrongfulness of measures taken as a countermeasure even as against their state of nationality.

Both NAFTA tribunals which have issued public awards rejected the countermeasures defence, but on different grounds. The tribunal in *Archer Daniels Midland Co. and Tate & Lyle Ingredients Americas, Inc.* v. *United Mexican States*[298] ('*ADM*') held that the conditions for the taking of countermeasures were not made out by Mexico; the tribunal in *Corn Products International, Inc.* v. *United Mexican States*[299] ('*CPI*') held that a countermeasures defence was not applicable to claims under Chapter XI of NAFTA.

The central difference between the two tribunals' decisions related to the character of the rights under NAFTA. The tribunal in *ADM* considered that the correct construction of the rights under NAFTA was the procedural-direct model: that individuals derived only a procedural right to arbitrate from the Treaty, and that the remaining rights (including substantive rights of protection) were inter-state rights against which a valid countermeasure could be taken.[300] The *ADM* tribunal effectively adopted the procedural-direct theory, stating that:

> In the Tribunal's view, the obligations under Section A remain inter-state, providing the standards by which the conduct of the NAFTA Party towards the investor will be assessed in the arbitration. All investors have under Section B is a procedural right to trigger arbitration against the host State. What Section B does is to set up the investor's exceptional right of action through arbitration that would not otherwise exist under international law, when another NAFTA Party has breached the obligations of Section A.[301]

In a concurring opinion, Arthur W. Rovine disagreed with the tribunal's conclusion that the substantive obligations of protection owed by the host state corresponded only to substantive rights of protection for

298 *Archer Daniels Midland Co. and Tate & Lyle Ingredients Americas, Inc.* v. *United Mexican States* (ICSID Case no. ARB(AF)/04/05), Award, 21 November 2007.

299 *Corn Products International, Inc.* v. *United Mexican States*, ICSID Case no. ARB(AF)/04/01, Decision on Responsibility, 15 January 2008.

300 *Archer Daniels Midland Co. and Tate & Lyle Ingredients Americas, Inc.* v. *United Mexican States* (ICSID Case no. ARB(AF)/04/05), Award, 21 November 2007, para. 161 *et seq.*

301 *Ibid.* para. 173.

the national state; rather, he considered individual investors derived a substantive legal right to redress from Chapter XI of NAFTA. He stated:

> It is clear that Chapter Eleven, as stated by Brower and Steven, 'creates substantive investment protections that are enforceable in arbitration by the individuals directly impacted by any breach of such protections'. In my view, the substantive investment protections conferred by treaty upon NAFTA investors include the substantive right of legal redress for breaches of Section A of Chapter Eleven.
>
> Why is the right to legal redress a substantive rather than a procedural right? In my view, the logic of the law, both internal and international, necessarily entails that a claimant with a right to file a claim and be awarded damages for breach of an obligation by defendant, should claimant prevail, has an individual right, owed to him directly, and underlying the right to file and collect damages, not to have that obligation breached by defendant . . .
>
> . . . To have the right to bring the claim, in addition to having the possibility or reality of satisfying that claim, demonstrates an enforceable right and remedy. Again, legal redress for the wrong committed is a substantive right.[302]

In contrast to the majority in *ADM*, the tribunal in *CPI* considered that the correct construction of rights under NAFTA was a substantive-direct model, that 'NAFTA confers upon investors substantive rights separate and distinct from those of the State of which they are nationals'.[303] The tribunal considered that a central purpose of Chapter XI was to 'remove [investor] claims from the inter-State plane and to ensure that investors could assert rights directly against a host State'.[304] Noting that individuals and corporations may possess rights under international law, the tribunal stated:

> In the case of rights said to be derived from a treaty, the question will be whether the text of the treaty reveals an intention to confer rights not only upon the Parties thereto but also upon individuals and/or corporations.
>
> In the case of Chapter XI of NAFTA, the Tribunal considers that the intention of the Parties was to confer substantive rights directly upon investors. That follows from the language used and is confirmed by the fact that Chapter XI confers procedural rights upon them. The notion that Chapter XI conferred upon investors a right, in their own name and for their own benefit, to institute

302 *Ibid.* Concurring Opinion of Arthur W. Rovine, Issues of Independent Investor Rights, Diplomatic Protection and Countermeasures, para. 67.

303 *Corn Products International, Inc.* v. *United Mexican States*, ICSID Case no. ARB(AF)/04/01, Decision on Responsibility, 15 January 2008, para. 168.

304 *Ibid.* para. 161.

proceedings to enforce rights which were not theirs but were solely the property of the State of their nationality is counterintuitive.[305]

The *CPI* tribunal therefore rejected Mexico's countermeasures defence as inapplicable to claims made by investors under Chapter XI of NAFTA.[306] Its determination of direct substantive rights was not premised on an interpretive presumption in favour of individual rights but rather on the text of the provisions of the BIT taken in their context (although in the determination of countermeasures such a presumption would have indicated the same conclusion as that reached by the tribunal). The *CPI* tribunal's reasoning can be distinguished from that of Rovine in *ADM*: the latter referred to the right of redress (i.e. enforcement) as a substantive right which would have the effect of precluding a countermeasures defence, whereas the decision of the *CPI* tribunal suggested that the substantive rights of protection (for example, the right of national treatment) accrued directly to individual investors.

Two uncontroversial points can be made about investment treaty arbitration. First, investment treaty arbitration is conducted on the basis of direct claims (that is, pursued directly by an individual against a state), like some of the earlier practice which permitted individuals to pursue claims against a foreign state in an international forum. Second, it is clear that where a BIT contains an investor-state dispute resolution clause in the usual terms, individuals who qualify as investors have a procedural treaty right to refer a dispute to arbitration. Whether the right to refer a dispute to arbitration infers a substantive right of redress held by the investor, or whether the underlying substantive rights of protection are held directly by the investor, are more controversial. Each provision of a BIT will need to be examined in accordance with the ordinary principles of treaty interpretation in order to determine whether it confers direct rights on individuals: the inquiry should begin with the ordinary meaning of the terms in their context and in light of their object and purpose. While there is an emerging tendency to favour protection of investment by applying an interpretive presumption on the basis that investment protection is the object or purpose of a BIT, a general health warning is warranted against the generalised application of interpretive presumptions in the determination of the character of

305 *Ibid.* paras. 168–9. In his separate opinion, Andreas Lowenfeld agreed with the tribunal's conclusion on this point but argued that aspects of its discussion 'blur[red] the message' about the essence of investor-state arbitration (para. 5).

306 *Ibid.* paras. 191–2.

investment treaty rights. Such interpretive presumptions may oversimplify the objects and purposes of the BIT as a whole; moreover, interpreting BITs as conferring direct rights may increase investor protection in one context, but limit it more severely in other contexts. In most BITs the protection of investments will form part of the object and purpose of the BIT, but that goal should not automatically lead one to conclude that the BIT confers direct substantive rights on investors.

(d) Conclusions

The structure and practice of international claims tribunals and investment treaty arbitration after 1945 have in general continued along the same lines as practice in the inter-war period, reflecting diplomatic protection, on the one hand, and providing individuals with direct rights of access, on the other hand. Individuals are thus permitted to prosecute their own claims before international tribunals, and in their own right, provided that states consent to this procedure. Individual capacity to act depends on the relevant instruments. This is seen clearly in the practice of the major international claims tribunals and commissions operating in this period. A number of tribunals have operated on the basis of diplomatic protection, while others have provided for direct claims by individuals. Investment arbitration, which has been used with increasing frequency in recent years, operates as a form of direct claims process, with individuals pursuing claims independently, without the consent or assistance of their state of nationality. The question of the underlying substantive rights in investment arbitration has given rise to conflicting decisions. In this context, the implications of the position of the individual for the application of the secondary rules of responsibility have been borne out in a number of issues, including circumstances precluding wrongfulness and waiver. It is suggested that the question can only be resolved by an examination of each treaty (and each relevant provision within that treaty). An interpretive presumption in favour of investor protection may in some circumstances suggest direct substantive rights, but in other circumstances direct substantive rights may not favour investor protection. Moreover, such interpretive presumptions have the potential to oversimplify the purposes of BITs, which may incorporate a broader range of public interest objectives than simply encouraging and protecting foreign investment.

Some of the claims processes used in this period are reminiscent of the nineteenth century practice, in that they fall within the category of diplomatic protection, but employ procedures which take account of the interest of individuals. One example is the requirement that awards be distributed to claimants by states under the UN Compensation Commission procedures. These kind of features suggest that international claims practice might be viewed as falling in one of either binary category of diplomatic protection and direct claims, or it might fall somewhere in between, taking account of individuals and engaging them without detracting from the primarily inter-state character of the claim.

In the post-1945 period, the traditional confines of the doctrine of diplomatic protection have been affirmed, particularly by decisions of the ICJ and the work of the ILC in its Draft Articles. Although the ILC accepted that the 'fiction' of diplomatic protection had continued to have relevance in this period, its treatment of several issues revealed an underlying confusion about the relation of the injury to the state of nationality. It was perpetuated by the failure of the Draft Articles to examine the character of the relevant primary rules, which might have afforded a more nuanced approach to the application of the secondary rules. In particular, whether the underlying right is an individual right or a state right should inform the application of rules relating to continuity of nationality, waiver and exhaustion of local remedies.

It has been the established understanding in the post-1945 period that individuals can bear direct rights under international law. The ICJ has shown less reluctance to recognise that individuals may be the recipient of rights under international treaties than the PCIJ, holding that treaties may confer direct rights on individuals in circumstances where the language of the treaty is clear, without inquiring into the intention of the states parties. A number of tribunals have reached the same conclusion in respect of treaty rights, while others have referred to the intention of states parties to support their conclusion that a treaty confers direct rights on individuals.

2.5 Conclusions: the position of the individual relative to international claims

Since at least the inter-war period, the dual doctrines of diplomatic protection and individual rights under treaties have been reflected in two strands of international practice: diplomatic protection claims for injuries to nationals, which remain within the control and discretion of the state of nationality; and direct claims by individuals before international tribunals in circumstances where states have created capacity for individuals to so act by treaty.

From the nineteenth century until the mid-twentieth century, the vast majority of international claims practice operated on the basis of diplomatic protection, so that where a claim was determined either by resort to arbitration in a specific case or by the establishment and operation of an international claims tribunal, it was conceived of as a claim by one state against another for injury suffered by the state in the person of its national. Moreover, tribunals were determining states rights, rather than individual international law rights. Various characteristics of the international claims tribunals weigh in favour of this characterisation of the claims, including that awards were paid directly to the state of nationality rather than the injured individuals; that the state had exclusive control of the claim including its presentation and argument; and that the decisions were designated as final and binding in respect of the dispute between states. In addition, where the character of the claims was examined by the relevant tribunal, the control of the state was emphasised and it was stated that the true claimant before the tribunal was the state on behalf of its national. Two exceptional cases in the early twentieth century have been identified: first, the proposed International Prize Court would have permitted direct access for individuals but required the state of nationality in effect to consent to the claim; and second, the Central American Court of Justice permitted cases to be brought by individuals against a state alleging violation of treaty, but there were few cases and none were decided in favour of the individuals. Thus, in the early period individuals were only protected through the exclusive conception of diplomatic protection; individuals held no independent substantive or procedural rights in the international legal system which would enable them to seek recourse against violations of international law or secure their own protection.

In the inter-war period, the doctrine of diplomatic protection was further entrenched by decisions of the PCIJ affirming its existence and parameters. In the same period, the Court held that individuals may be the recipient of rights under international treaties where the states parties so intended, in a statement which was controversial at the time. These two doctrines were manifested in dual strands of practice in international claims tribunals. In diplomatic protection practice, states were claimants before international claims tribunals; in other cases, individuals were given capacity to directly assert claims in their own right against states. These direct claims were often pursued to assert what were characterised as the individual's own international law rights. Thus, in the inter-war period individuals could be protected both by their state of nationality, through diplomatic protection, and by independent capacity to assert claims to vindicate treaty-granted individual rights. This practice is consistent with the idea that states may confer upon individuals 'international rights *stricto sensu*, i.e. rights which they acquire without the intervention of municipal legislation and which they can enforce in their own name before international tribunals',[307] which only appeared in the orthodox account of the international legal system after 1945. The acquisition and enforcement of rights remained within the monopoly of states, as capacity to bear and enforce rights was dependent on a specific grant in a treaty.

After 1945 these dual strands have continued in both doctrine and practice, reflecting diplomatic protection, on the one hand, and providing individuals with direct rights of access, on the other hand. Individuals are thus permitted to prosecute their own claims before international tribunals, and in their own right, provided that states consent, but that capacity remains dependent on the relevant constituent instrument. In the field of foreign investment protection, individuals have procedural capacity to enforce what may be best characterised as their own substantive rights against states. Nevertheless, this is considered to be *lex specialis* and has not impacted upon the traditional doctrine of diplomatic protection. The two strands of practice reflect parallel doctrines, and although there may be a majority of practice in which individuals have distinct capacities, it is not to the extent that it has overtaken the practice of diplomatic protection: the ILC's Draft Articles and the ICJ decision in *Diallo* affirm its continued relevance. The practice of international claims after 1945 is consistent with the established understanding of the international legal framework in this period. Individuals may be granted rights enforceable before international courts by states: but capacity to present international claims and to possess international rights is dependent on a specific grant of capacity by states. Individuals have some independence in that they may choose to utilise an international process for pursuit of their rights or not; but it is a handicapped independence since individuals cannot create their own capacity to pursue a claim.

[307] Jennings and Watts, *Oppenheim's International Law*, p. 847, para. 375; p. 17, para. 7, discussed in 1.2(d) above.

In general, international claims practice has been considered as falling within one or other of the binary categories of direct claims or diplomatic protection claims. There may be room for viewing this practice as fitting somewhere between these two polarised categories: some of the nineteenth century practice and some of the post-1945 practice might fall somewhere in between diplomatic protection and direct claims, taking account of the interest of individuals in claims without detracting from the primarily inter-state character of the claims. There is a tendency to view this practice as diplomatic protection practice and fail to take account of the fact that it does engage individuals in various ways. The ICJ's approach in *Avena* suggests that there is room for some middle-ground views, and although the interdependent rights analysis might not be apt to describe modern international claims practice, a more nuanced approach to the categorisation of international claims practice might suggest that individuals have been engaged in international claims since the nineteenth century, even though that engagement might not have amounted to meaningful participation until some of the processes put in place after the First World War.

Appendix I
Arbitration of diplomatic protection claims 1794–1914

	Parties	Date of Instrument	Reference	Description	Outcomes	Relevant characteristics
1	US–Great Britain	30 June 1822	Moore (1898), vol. I, p. 363	Referral to a board of enumerated list of individual claims relating to slaves and other private property for which US citizens claimed indemnity relating to war of 1812.	Appears that the board issued no decisions. On 13 November 1826 new convention provided for lump sum settlement of all claims, annulling 1822 Convention. US created national claims commission to distribute sum.	Board authorised to receive evidence and argument from individual claimants. Claims settled by lump sum agreement in inter-state convention with no obligation to pay the proceeds to individual claimants; however, it appears that the proceeds were distributed through a national commission.
2	Great Britain–France	14 November 1842	Moore (1898), vol. V, p. 4936	Claims of British subjects arising from measures adopted by France in 1834–5 on coast of Portendic submitted to arbitrator to determine question of indemnity. Claims to be submitted to mixed commission for liquidation.	Award reproduced in Moore (1898), vol. V, pp. 4937–8.	Appears to have operated on the basis of diplomatic protection.

3	France–Spain	15 February 1851	105 CTS 153; de Clerq (1864), vol. VI, p. 81	King of Netherlands as sole arbitrator given limited competence over disputed naval captures.	Award appears to have been given on 13 April 1852 but cannot be located.	Appears to have operated on the basis of diplomatic protection.
4	US–Portugal	28 February 1851	Moore (1898), vol. II, p. 1092	Public law questions relating to the destruction in Portugal by British vessels of the US vessel *General Armstrong* submitted to arbitration. All other claims settled by lump sum.	Claim dismissed by arbitrator. In 1878, the claim was revived and subsequently paid. As to lump sum settlement, under domestic arrangements the Secretary of State was required to examine the claims and to settle them in accordance with principles of justice and equity.	Arbitration appears to have operated on the basis of diplomatic protection. The claimants protested to Congress that they had no knowledge of, and had not consented to, the submission of their claims to arbitration. The protest was referred to the court of claims, which rejected the submission that the US government had no authority to submit the case to arbitration: 'as soon as our government was induced by the claimants to interfere, the controversy became an affair of state, to be treated of between the two governments as other differences between nations are treated; that is to say, by negotiation, arbitration, and such other modes as are recognized by

	Parties	Date of Instrument	Reference	Description	Outcomes	Relevant characteristics
						the law of nations': Blackford J (in majority with Scarburgh J, Gilchrist CJ dissenting).
5	Great Britain–Portugal	Unknown; award given in 1856	Moore (1898), vol. V, p. 4979	Claim concerning refusal of patent registration by Peru submitted to arbitration.	Claim dismissed.	Appears to have operated on the basis of diplomatic protection.
6	US–Chile	10 November 1858	Moore (1898), vol. II, p. 1460	Claim against Chile concerning US vessel *Macedonian* submitted to arbitration.	Award of US$42,400 plus interest.	Appears to have operated on the basis of diplomatic protection. Arguments were presented by the governments.
7	US–Paraguay	4 February 1859	Moore (1898), vol. II, p. 1485	Claim of Paraguay Navigation Company (US) against Paraguay referred to 2 commissioners.	Claim dismissed.	Permitted counsel for the company to appear before commission.
8	Great Britain–Portugal	Unknown; award given in 1861	Moore (1898), vol. V, p. 4984	Claim against Portugal by Great Britain in respect of its subjects.	Unknown as award was not published.	Appears to have operated on the basis of diplomatic protection.
9	US–Peru	20 December 1862	Moore (1898), vol. II, p. 1610	Claims of *Georgiana* and *Lizzie Thompson* (US) with respect to seizure/confiscation by Peru referred to arbitrator.	The King of Belgium declined to arbitrate and US abandoned claims.	Appears to have contemplated arbitration on the basis of diplomatic protection. States were to have control of the claims.

10	Great Britain–US	1 July 1863	Moore (1898), vol. I, p. 237	Claims of Hudson's Bay and Puget's Sound Companies submitted to commission for arbitration. Treaty of 1 July 1846 provided substantive protection.	Award of US $450,000 to Hudson's Bay Company and US $200,000 to Puget's Sound.	Counsel for claimants appeared before the commission, as did counsel for the US government; claimants filed own memorials.
11	US–Salvador	4 May 1864	Moore (1898), vol. II, p. 1857	Claim of Henry Savage (US) against Salvador submitted to referees for arbitration.	Awarded US $4,497.50 with interest.	Unknown.
12	Great Britain–Peru	Unknown; award given in 1864	Moore (1898), vol. V, p. 4967	Claim against Peru relating to the arrest of Captain T. Melville White, a British subject, referred to arbitration.	Claim dismissed.	Unknown.
13	Great Britain–Spain	4 March 1868	Moore (1898), vol. V, p. 5016; (1867–8) LVIII BFSP 2	Compensation claims relating to Spanish authorities firing at British schooner *Mermaid* referred to mixed commission.	Unknown.	Commission was to receive and consider evidence submitted by owners of schooner and the government of Spain (Art. III). The claimants appear to have been represented before the commission for the oral hearing. Award to be paid directly to claimants (Art. IV).
14	US–Brazil	14 March 1870	Moore (1898), vol. II, p. 1733	Case of US vessel *Canada* referred to arbitration to	Award held Brazil liable to US as compensation for	Appears to have operated on the basis of diplomatic protection; in particular

Parties	Date of Instrument	Reference	Description	Outcomes	Relevant characteristics
			determine whether US claim time-barred; whether vessel was lost and voyage determined by illegal interference of Brazilian officials; and any amount of damage.	owners of *Canada* for US $100,740.04.	the two governments had control of the claims.
15 Spain–US	16 June 1870	Moore (1898), vol. II, p. 1007	Claim of US for damage to owners of steamer *Lloyd Aspinal* on account of seizure by Spanish man-of-war and detention at Havana referred to arbitration.	Award of 18 November 1870 was in amount of US$19,702.50 in gold.	Appears to have operated on the basis of diplomatic protection. The owners of the steamer had suggested that the claim be submitted to arbitration.
16 Great Britain–Colombia	14 December 1872	Moore (1898), vol. II, p. 2050	Claim of British nationals referred to arbitration to determine whether Colombia was bound to grant indemnity and, if so, the amount.	Award of US$50,000 for actual loss of the claimants.	Appears to have operated on the basis of diplomatic protection.

17	Japan–Peru	June 1873	Moore (1898), vol. V, p. 5034	Claims relating to Peruvian vessel *Maria Luz* against Japan referred to arbitration.	Held that Japan not responsible.	Appears to have operated on the basis of diplomatic protection.
18	Great Britain–France	23 July 1873	Moore (1898), vol. V, p. 4938; LXIII BFSP 207–13	Claims for alleged excessive duties charge in France on British mineral oils referred to 2 commissioners.	Award in favour of Great Britain for 314,393.33 francs.	Appears to have operated on the basis of diplomatic protection. No allowance given for claimants' counsel fees or costs of submitting their claims to the commission.
19	US–Colombia	17 August 1874	Moore (1898), vol. II, p. 1421	Claims of US citizens against Colombia relating to steamer *Montijo* submitted to arbitration.	Umpire rendered award in favour of US claimants for US$33,401. Award paid in full.	Appears to have operated on the basis of diplomatic protection but US consulted claimants before accepting proposal to arbitrate. The claimants were paid the amount of the award less expenses.
20	Netherlands–Dominican Republic	26 March 1881	Moore (1898), vol. V, p. 5036	Difference relating to confiscation of Dutch vessel *Havana Packet* referred to arbitration.	Award in favour of Netherlands for 140,000 francs.	Appears to have operated on the basis of diplomatic protection.
21	Haiti–US	1883	Moore (1898), vol. II, p. 1860	Claims against Haiti for injury to US citizens relating to riots referred to mixed commission.	Award US$5,700 for 4 claims. Final 2 claims settled by the parties for US $9,000.	Appears to have operated on the basis of diplomatic protection.

	Parties	Date of Instrument	Reference	Description	Outcomes	Relevant characteristics
22	Haiti–US	24 July 1884 Extended by supplementary Protocol.	Moore (1898), vol. II, p. 1749	Claims of US citizens, Antonio Pelletier (contractual claim) and A. H. Lazare (arrest of vessel), against Haiti referred to arbitration.	Award in Lazare claim of US $117,500 plus interest. Award in Pelletier claim of US$57,250.	Appears to have operated on the basis of diplomatic protection. The papers and evidence were presented by the two governments. After Haiti protested against awards on the basis of new evidence, the US declined to enforce the award.
23	US–China	1884	Moore (1898), vol. II, p. 1858	Claim of Ashmore (US) against China relating to a fishery.	Award of US$4,600.	Appears to have operated on the basis of diplomatic protection.
24	Spain–US	1885	Moore (1898), vol. II, p. 1060	Sum of indemnification payable by Spanish treasury to US owners of *Masonic* submitted to arbitration.	Award of US $51,674.07 inclusive of interest.	Appears to have operated on the basis of diplomatic protection; evidence was presented by two governments.
25	US–Haiti	24 May 1888	Moore (1898), vol. II, p. 1811	Claim against Haiti for imprisonment of US citizen, Van Bokkelen, referred to arbitration.	Award of US$60,000 against Haiti on basis that imprisonment violated a treaty. Paid in full by 1895.	Appears to have operated on the basis of diplomatic protection; counsel appear to have acted on behalf of the governments.

26	US–Denmark	6 December 1888	Moore (1898), vol. II, p. 1185	Claim for seizure and detention of vessels and related claims referred to arbitration.	Claim dismissed.	Appears to have operated on the basis of diplomatic protection.
27	Italy–Persia	5 June 1890	Moore (1898), vol. V, p. 5019	Difference between Persian customs and Italian subject, Joseph Consonno, on account of importation of merchandise submitted to arbitration.	Award of 78,000 francs and interest to M. Consonno.	Award was in favour of the individual claimant; in other respects the arbitration appears to have operated on the basis of diplomatic protection.
28	US–Great Britain–Portugal	13 June 1891	Moore (1898), vol. II, p. 1865	Claim for seizure by Portugal of Delagoa Bay Railway referred to arbitration.	Award provided for Portugal to pay to US and Great Britain 15,314,00 francs in addition to £28,000 paid on account in 1890.	Appears to have operated on the basis of diplomatic protection. The Award required Portugal to pay directly to the two governments who received the Award 'on behalf of' the relevant individuals.
29	Italy–Portgual	1 September 1891	Moore (1898), vol. V, p. 5021	Claim against Portugal of Italian subject, Lavarello, submitted to arbitration.	Award of 12,347.68 lires plus interest to Lavarello.	Award was in favour of the individual claimant; in other respects the arbitration appears to have operated on the basis of diplomatic protection.
30	US–Venezuela	1 January 1892	Moore (1898), vol. II, p. 1693	Question whether indemnity should be paid by Venezuela for treatment of	Award of US $141,500 to US (p. 1724).	Appears to have operated on the basis of diplomatic protection. The commission heard one

Parties	Date of Instrument	Reference	Description	Outcomes	Relevant characteristics
			vessels referred to arbitration.		representative of either government and was authorised to hear other counsel. The US agent presented counsel for claimants, who made the closing argument for the US.
31 US–Ecuador	28 February 1893	Moore (1898), vol. II, p. 1587	Claim on behalf of Julio Santos, US citizen, for injuries to person and property related to arrest and imprisonment by Ecuador submitted to arbitration.	Award in favour of claimant of US $40,000, payable to US government.	Appears to have operated on the basis of diplomatic protection. Award paid directly to state.
32 Great Britain–the Netherlands	16 May 1895	Moore (1898), vol. V, p. 4948	Claims relating to arrest and detention in the Netherlands Indies of Carpenter (Master of *Costa Rica Packet*) referred to arbitration.	Award required indemnity to be paid to Carpenter, to the officers and crew and to the owners of the vessel.	Appears to have operated on the basis of diplomatic protection, although indemnity was paid directly to the relevant individuals.
33 US–Siam	1896/7	Moore (1898), vol. II, p. 1863	Claim against Siam concerning personal injury and arrest of	Award provided for expression of official regret and	Appears to have operated on the basis of diplomatic protection.

				US citizen, Kellett, referred to arbitration.	reprimand of those involved.	
34	US–Siam	1896–7	Moore (1898), vol. II, p. 1899	Claim of US citizen, Cheek, regarding contractual dispute against Siam submitted to arbitration.	Unknown as award was not published.	Unknown.
35	US–Mexico	22 May 1902	Wilson (1915), p. 1; I RIAA 1	Claim of 'Pious Funds of the Californias' for annuities payable by Mexico.	Held that claim of the US was *res judicata* by virtue of the earlier arbitral award. Mexico was required to pay unpaid annuities.	Appears to have operated on the basis of diplomatic protection.
36	Great Britain–Russia	1 June 1902	IX UNRIAA 51	Claims relating to expropriated British property at British concession at Tientsin referred to commission.	Unknown	Appears to have operated on the basis of diplomatic protection.

Appendix II International claims tribunals and commissions 1794–1914

	Parties	Date of Instrument	Reference	Description	Outcomes	Relevant characteristics
1	US–Great Britain	19 November 1794 (Jay Treaty)	Moore (1898), vol. I, p. 271	Two commissions were established: a commission of 5 to ascertain losses and damages for non-payment of pre-war debts owed to British nationals (Art. 6); a commission of 5 to assess loss and damage suffered by US nationals relating to capture of British vessels by French ships in US ports (Art. 7).	Art. 6 commission operated from 1796 to 1799, when proceedings were suspended. British claims settled by lump sum agreement in 1802 Convention. Art. 7 Commission operated from 1796 to 1799 and 1802 to 1804, dealing with all claims referred to it.	Individuals were not claimants before the commissions. Agents of the state had the function of representing government interests and the claims of its citizens, though individuals could be compelled to give testimony. Awards were final and binding between the two states. The claimant state was obliged to make payment directly to claimant individuals. Pursuant to a treaty between the US and Great Britain, British claims were settled by lump sum agreement with no obligation to pay the proceeds to individual claimants.
2	Spain–US	27 October 1795	Moore (1898), vol. II, p. 991.	Differences on account of losses of US citizens resulting	Operated from 1797 to 1799, issuing 40 awards. Total	Commissioners authorised to receive all complaints and applications within 18

			Treaty reproduced in Malloy (1910), vol. I, p. 1013.	from seizure of vessels and cargoes by Spanish subjects referred to commission to decide 'according to the merits of the several cases, and to justice, equity, and the laws of nations' (Art. XXI).	amount awarded US$325,440.07 ½. The records of the commission have not been located.	months. Power to examine persons before them and to receive in evidence all testimony they think proper to require or admit. Awards payable directly to the claimant and delivered to the claimant or his representative.
3	US–France	30 April 1803	Moore (1898), vol. V, p. 4434	Commission of three to determine debts due by France to US citizens. The US provided an indemnity limited to 20,000,000 francs.	Final disposition of claims was controversial.	Appears that states presented arguments but there were measures for individuals to notify claims. Rules required that no determination would be finally made without giving reasonable notice to claimant and his attorney, if known to be in Paris (Art. 4). Rules provided that copy of award to be given to claimant (Art. 5).
4	Mexico–US	11 April 1839	Malloy (1910), vol. I, p. 1101; Feller (1935), p. 3; Moore (1898),	Mixed commission with jurisdiction over claims by US citizens against Mexico, which had been presented to State Department or	Commission made 11 awards and rejected 4 claims. The umpire made 53 awards and rejected four claims.	The convention was not clear as to the involvement of individual claimants in proceedings. Art. IV provided that documents in the possession of states ought to be delivered to the

Parties	Date of Instrument	Reference	Description	Outcomes	Relevant characteristics
		vol. II, p. 1229	the US diplomatic agent in Mexico prior to the signature of the convention (Art. I). Matters would be referred to umpire if the commission was unable to reach a decision.	1843 Convention postponed payment of awards; subsequently a 1848 peace treaty provided that the US would pay all liquidated claims under the 1839 Convention and discharge Mexico from all claims It required the US to create a board of commissioners, to which individuals presented claims. The board awarded more than US $3,208,000 in 198 claims.	commissioners. When the commission came to formulate rules of procedure there was a dispute as to whether individuals could provide documents and evidence directly. The Mexican commissioners argued that claimants could not; the US commissioners argued that each claimant was 'the *actor* or plaintiff' and that individuals had a right to be heard. It was eventually agreed that all documents would be presented through the state agents. That the US subsequently assumed liability for the claims and agreed to establish a domestic claims process suggests that the claims were direct claims by individuals against Mexico. If these were inter-state claims, the US could simply have waived them.

5	US–Great Britain	8 February 1853 Extended by convention 17 July 1854	Moore (1898), vol. I, p. 391	Mixed commission for all outstanding claims between the two countries, which had been presented since the 1814 Treaty of Ghent and remained unsettled, or any other such claims as may be presented within time limit (Art. I). Claims arising out of transactions prior to 24 December 1814 were inadmissible. In the event of disagreement in the commission, claims were to be referred to an umpire.	Commission settled 115 claims. Of 75 British claims 19 allowed (9 awards by commission and 10 by umpire), 52 dismissed and 4 withdrawn. Awards included the *McLeod* case, and others involved issues of domicile/ nationality. Of 40 US claims 12 allowed (2 awards by commission and 10 by umpire), 27 dismissed and 1 withdrawn, relating to customs duties; seizure of vessels in connection with slave trade and fisheries; capture of US vessel by British warship.	The convention provided that the commission could hear one person on behalf of each government on each separate claim. In various cases the commissioners heard private counsel of the claimants, introduced by the agents. The commission could only receive evidence from the two states. Awards were paid to the states. Decisions of the commission were stated to be a full, final and perfect settlement of every claim upon either government.

	Parties	Date of Instrument	Reference	Description	Outcomes	Relevant characteristics
6	US–New Granada	10 September 1857	Moore (1898), vol. II, p. 1361	Claims of US citizens presented prior to 1 September 1859, especially for damage caused by a riot in Panama, for which New Granada admitted liability, referred to board of 2 commissioners and, in case of disagreement, to an umpire. Claims to be decided according to justice and equity.	Commission operated 1861–2 and of the 218 claims presented, 109 cases settled by awards, 2 by partial award and 2 in overlapping cases. 107 were not settled. In total US $496,235.47 awarded. Unsettled claims referred to the 1864 Colombian-US Commission (see below).	Claims were presented by US government (Art. II). Claimants were often represented by their own attorneys before the commission. Full amount was to be paid to the US government, but claimants were given certificate of awards (Art. III).
7	Brazil–Great Britain	2 June 1858	119 CTS 91; XLVIII BFSP 18	Claims of corporations, companies and private individuals presented to either government since Declaration of Independence of Brazil, which	9 of 157 claims submitted to the commission were determined. Great Britain objected to the competence of the commission,	Evidence was presented by states. Awards were payable to states (Art. IV). Decisions of the commission were a full and final settlement of all claims between the states (Art. V).

				remained unsettled referred to a commission of 2 and to an umpire in case of disagreement.	which was terminated after diplomatic relations between the two states interrupted.	
8	US–Costa Rica	2 July 1860	Moore (1898), vol. II, p. 1551	Claims of US citizens against Costa Rica arising from injury to persons or property, presented to US prior to date of signature of convention, referred to a board of 2 commissioners (in case of disagreement, to be referred to umpire). No claims by US citizen proved to have been a belligerent during occupation of Nicaragua by Costa Rican troops were to be considered. Applicable law was principles of justice and equity and stipulations of treaty.	The commission operated in 1862; of the 35 claims, 13 were rejected by the commissioners, 22 were referred to the umpire who made 13 awards and rejected 9 claims. The total amount awarded was US$24,704.14.	The Secretary of the Commission was authorised to allow claimants and counsel to examine the papers and opinions of commissioners in their respective cases. It appears that counsel for claimants appeared before commission.

	Parties	Date of Instrument	Reference	Description	Outcomes	Relevant characteristics
9	Ecuador–US	25 November 1862	Moore (1898), vol. II, p. 1569	Claims of corporations, companies or citizens of one state against the other referred to board of 2 commissioners and to an umpire in case of disagreement. Claims to be decided according to justice in compliance with convention.	Commission operated 1864–5. Of the 14 claims presented against Ecuador, 5 were dismissed, 9 awards were issued (8 by umpire and 1 by commission) and US$94,799.56 was paid by Ecuador. No claims against US.	Appears that the states had control of the claims and that the awards were paid directly to the state.
10	US–Peru	12 January 1863	Moore (1898), vol. II, pp. 1613–15	Claims of citizens of one state against other state submitted for interposition prior to signature of convention submitted to mixed commission of 4 (in case of disagreement,	The commission operated in 1863. Of the 4 claims against the US, 2 were dismissed and 2 resulted in awards. Of the 19 claims against Peru, 11 were dismissed and 8 resulted in	It appears that the states had control of the claims: the commission heard one person on behalf of each government on each separate claim.

				referred to umpire). Commission to decide according to principles of justice, equity, international law and treaty stipulations.	awards. Work continued by 1868 Commission (see below).	
11	US–Colombia	10 February 1864	Moore (1898), vol. II, p. 1361	Convention provided for adjustment of undecided claims under 1857 New Granada Convention.	5 of the awards contested by Colombia were reconsidered by 1864 Commission.	Appears to have used the same procedure as 1857 Commission. Claims presented by US government. Claimants were often represented by their own attorneys before the commission. Awards paid to US government, but claimants were given certificates of awards.
12	France–Mexico	10 April 1864; 27 September 1865 provided for payment	54 BFSP 926; Feller (1935), p. 9	Claims of French nationals against Mexico for injuries referred to commission of 3 nationals of either state and then to another commission for liquidation.	First instalment of fixed sum was paid to French government. The convention was repudiated by Juárez government in 1867.	Awards paid directly to French government.
13	US–Venezuela	25 April 1866	Malloy (1910), vol. II, p. 1856;	Claims of US citizens against Venezuela, which had been	Commission dealt with 49 claims in 24 awards; 245	The convention provided that commission could hear one person for each

	Parties	Date of Instrument	Reference	Description	Outcomes	Relevant characteristics
			Moore (1898), vol. II, p. 1659	presented to US or its legation, submitted to commission of 2 and, in the event of disagreement, to an umpire.	claims rejected. In 1869 Venezuela protested on the basis of an irregularity in umpire's appointment and fraud in the proceedings. The US accepted that these protests were not without foundation and sought to conclude new claims convention (see 1885 US-Venezuelan Commission below).	government on each claim and governments could provide documents and evidence. The convention provided commission could issue certificates of awards to claimants; full amount to be paid directly to the US government.
14	Great Britain–Mexico	26 June 1866	Feller (1935), pp. 9–11. Moore (1898),	Commission of 5 to determine British claims for which Mexico responsible	Sat from August 1866 to March 1867. Issued no awards, Juárez	Unknown.

			vol. V, p. 4948	in accordance with international law.	government repudiated convention in 1867.	
15	Mexico–US	4 July 1868 Extended by supplementary Protocol.	Malloy (1910), vol. I, p. 1128; Moore (1898), vol. II, p. 1659	Claims by companies, corporations or private individuals of one state against the government of the other arising from injury to person or property which had been presented to either government since the 1848 treaty and remain unsettled, as well as other claims presented in specified time, were referred to commission.	Commission operated from 1871 to 1876 and dealt with over 2,000 claims. Claims against Mexico: 186 awards; 831 rejected. Claims against US: 167 awards; 831 rejected. Mexico made payments but later alleged fraud in two large cases and the funds transferred in part-payment of those awards were eventually refunded to Mexico.	The convention provided that claims and evidence were to be presented by government. The commission could hear a person for each government on each claim. The convention provided that the decisions of the commission were a final settlement of every claim upon either government, and for lump sum payment to government after offset. 2 awards for which there was alleged fraud (*Weil* (1889) and *La Abra* (1899)) were the subject of two US Supreme Court cases. The claimants sought to compel the US to distribute proceeds. In *Frelinghuysen* v. *Key*, 110 U.S. 63 (1884), the Court stated that the inter-state treaty was an agreement between the

	Parties	Date of Instrument	Reference	Description	Outcomes	Relevant characteristics
						two states and it did not give rise to any obligation to collect for claimaints. In *United States ex rel Boynton* v. *Blaine*, 139 U.S. 306 (1891), the Court noted that the award was an adjudication between the two states rather than an adjudication between the individual claimant and Mexico.
16	Great Britain–Venezuela	21 September 1868	Moore (1898), vol. V, p. 5017	Tribunal with umpire to sit as mixed commission to fix amount of British claims pending against Venezuela.	The tribunal sat in 1869 and decided 79 claims.	Unknown
17	Peru–US	4 December 1868	Moore (1898), vol. II, p. 1639	Claims of citizens of one state against the other state arising out of any transaction prior to 30 November 1863	Commission operated 1869 to 1870 and gave 23 awards. In the one claim against the US umpire issued award of US	Appears that the states had control of the claims; the commission notified claimants of its meetings.

				were referred to commission.	$57,040. Of the 22 claims against Peru 15 awards made totalling US $194,417.62 and 7 dismissed.	
18	Spain–US	12 February 1871. Extended by Protocol. Wound up by agreement of 2 June 1883.	Moore (1898), vol. II, p. 1019; Malloy (1910), p. 1661; (1871–2) 147 CTS 1	Claims of US citizens or their heirs against Spain for wrongs and injuries to person or property in Cuba (or within maritime jurisdiction) since specified date submitted to 2 arbitrators and, in case of disagreement, claims referred to umpire.	Tribunal operated 1871 to 1883. Of 140 claims, 105 were dismissed and 35 awards given, total amount awarded was US $1,293,450.55. Spain paid awards from 1877. Initially 5% was reserved by State Department until the commission made ruling regarding arbitration expenses. This was invested and eventually paid to claimants without interest.	Appears that the state had control of the claims: each government named an advocate to appear before arbitrators or umpire to represent the interests of the parties (Art. 3); all claims and testimony in favour of them was presented only through the US government (Art. 4). The awards were final and conclusive as between the two states (Art. 7). As to 5% of awards withheld, claimant sought mandamus to compel Secretary of State to pay the interest: *United States ex rel Angarica* v. *Bayard, Secretary of State*, 127 U.S. 251 (1888) (esp. 259). The US Supreme Court held that in the absence of

	Parties	Date of Instrument	Reference	Description	Outcomes	Relevant characteristics
						express statutory provision, the US government was not liable to pay interest on claims.
19	Great Britain–US	8 May 1871	Moore (1898), vol. I, pp. 495 and 683 *et seq.*; de la Pradelle (1955), vol. III, p. 41	*Alabama claims*: tribunal of 5 to determine claims relating to acts of vessels. *Civil war claims*: mixed commission to determine claims of US citizens and British subjects arising out of civil war; North Atlantic fisheries; navigation of certain rivers, canals and Lake Michigan; system of bonded transit; certain features of the coasting trade; exemption from duty of lumber cut on American territorial	*Alabama claims*: tribunal awarded US$15,500,000 compensation for all Alabama claims. *Civil war claims*: mixed commission sat 1871–3. Of the 478 claims filed by the British: 29 dismissed; 260 disallowed on merits; 8 withdrawn; 181 awards were given, amounting to US$1,929,819. Of the 19 claims filed by the US, all	*Alabama claims*: appears that states had control of the claims: each state named one person as agent (Art. II); written case of each party was delivered to arbitrators (Art. III). Award in gross sum to be paid by British government to US (Art. VII). Decisions of the tribunal were full, perfect, final settlement of all claims between the two states (Art. XI). *Civil war claims*: appears that the states had control of the claims: each state named one person to present claims and to respond to claims. It appears that claimants

				waters by St John and floated down that river to the US; and the San Juan boundary.	were dismissed. Full amount of award duly paid to British government: 1874 FRUS 570–2.	presented memorials. Decisions of the commissioners were absolutely final and conclusive upon each claim as between the two states. Award provided for payment of full amount by US to British government.
20	Brazil–Paraguay	9 January 1872	144 CTS 149	Mixed commission of 2 to examine and liquidate indemnities given by Paraguay for expenses of war and damage to Brazilian citizens (referred to umpire in case of disagreement).	The commission apparently operated 1872–81. Results are unknown.	Unknown.
21	France–US	15 January 1880 Extended by supplementary Protocol.	Moore (1898), vol. II, p. 1133	Claims of corporations, companies or citizens of one state against the other state referred to 3 commissioners.	The commission operated 1880–4 and decided 745 claims. It made awards in favour of nationals of both parties.	It appears that the state had control of the claims: the two governments were represented before the commission and the claimants were not otherwise represented. Awards were paid directly to the governments.
22	Great Britain–Chile	4 January 1883	Moore (1898), vol. V, p. 4928	Claims of British subjects arising from acts of Chilean land	Commission dealt with 118 claims: 97 were disposed	Appears that states had control of the claims. Some

	Parties	Date of Instrument	Reference	Description	Outcomes	Relevant characteristics
				and maritime forces in Peru and Bolivia from 14 February 1879 to Treaty of Peace referred to mixed commission of 3.	of and 21 withdrawn or settled by two governments. Total amount awarded appears to have been about US $275,000.	of the claims were settled by bilateral agreement.
23	Chile–France	1883/1884	Moore (1898), vol. V, p. 4929	Similar to commission established by 1883 Great Britain–Chile Treaty.	Unknown.	Appears to have had the same procedure as the British-Chile Commission.
24	Chile–Italy	1883/1884	Moore (1898), vol. V, p. 4929	Similar to commission established by 1883 Great Britain–Chile Treaty.	Unknown.	Appears to have had the same procedure as the British-Chile Commission.
25	Belgium–Chile	30 August 1884	164 CTS 283; LXXV BFSP 495	Similar to commission established by 1883 Britain–Chile Treaty.	Unknown.	Appears to have had the same procedure as the British-Chile Commission.
26	US–Venezuela	5 December 1885 Additional convention to clarify in 1888.	Malloy (1910), vol. II, pp. 1858, 1865; Moore	Claims presented to or within jurisdiction of 1866 Commission were resubmitted to	Commission operated 1889–90 and dealt with 63 claims. The	Convention provided commission could receive evidence from two governments and, if

			(1898), vol. II, p. 1665	a new commission of 3 members for reconsideration.	commission awarded US $980,572.60 in substitution of US $1,253,310.30 awarded by 1866 Commission.	required, hear one person from each government on each claim. The convention stipulated that claimants could offer evidence through their government. The convention provided for a certificate of amount to be issued to individual claimants and total amount paid directly to the US. The commission held that the failure of claimant or representative to appear did not prevent it from exercising jurisdiction since parties to claim were the two governments. When a claim was pressed by a state it ceased to be an individual and became a national claim: see *Opinion of Commission on general questions*.
27	Guatemala–Mexico	26 January 1888	170 CTS 467	Claims of corporations, companies or citizens of one state against the other submitted to	The commission rendered awards in favour of nationals of both parties.	The states had control over the claims. The claims and evidence in support were presented by the governments. The

	Parties	Date of Instrument	Reference	Description	Outcomes	Relevant characteristics
				commission of 2 and, in case of disagreement, referred to umpire. For claims relating to real property, rights to be proved in accordance with law of country where property held.		convention provided that the results were a definite arrangement with respect to all claims within jurisdiction of the commission.
28	Great Britain–Haiti	1890	Moore (1898), vol. V, p. 4947	Claims of British subjects against Haiti within specified period referred to mixed commission of 3.	The commission sat in 1892. Results are unknown.	Unknown.
29	Chile–US	7 August 1892	Moore (1898), vol. II, p. 1469	Claims of corporations, companies or citizens of US against Chile arising out of acts committed against persons or property not in aid of enemies of Chile and all claims of Chilean	Commission rendered awards in favour of nationals of both parties. 40 claims were presented by US and 3 by Chile. 6 awards were made against	The state had control of the claims. Each government had agent for prosecution of claims. In first claim against Chile, agent of Chile consented to brief being filed by private counsel for claimants, but later moved that it be

				citizens against US referred to 3 commissioners.	Chile totalling US $240,564.35. 1 claim against US dismissed and 2 were undetermined.	struck as containing offensive language. The commission ordered it be withdrawn and that the briefs of private counsel be considered only when presented with approval and upon responsibility of government agents.
30	Chile–Great Britain	26 September 1893	Moore (1898), vol. V, p. 4930	Claims of British subjects arising out of operations by Chilean land and sea forces during civil war, and for subsequent events for which Chilean government might be held responsible referred to mixed commission of 3.	The commission operated 1894–6 and considered 101 claims. Outcomes unknown.	Unknown.
31	Chile–Sweden/ Norway	6 July 1895	Moore (1898), vol. V, p. 4935	Claims of subjects of Sweden and Norway against Chile referred to Anglo-Chilean tribunal of 1893.	2 claims were submitted. Amount of 251,179 pesos 95 centavos plus interest awarded.	Unknown.
32	US–Great Britain	8 February 1896	Moore (1898), vol. I, p. 960	British claim relating to Bering Fur Seal	Results unknown.	States had control of the claims: counsel before

	Parties	Date of Instrument	Reference	Description	Outcomes	Relevant characteristics
				Arbitration referred to commission of 2.		commission were agents of the two governments.
33	Brazil–Italy	12 February 1896	Moore (1898), vol. V, p. 5018	Claims of Italian subjects against Brazil to be arbitrated by US President and claims of Italian subjects against Brazil for requisition of animals, merchandise and valuables to be dealt with by a mixed commission.	Arbitral tribunal and mixed commission considered 439 claims in total.	Unknown.
34	France–Venezuela	19 February 1902	X UNRIAA 11	Claims of French nationals against Venezuela arising from 1892 insurrection and all events prior to 23 May 1899, when insurrection led by Castro began,	Some decisions are reported in X UNRIAA. The overall results of the commission are unknown.	Claims treated as diplomatic protection claims. In *Antonie Fabiani*, the commission held that when France intervened, the claim became a national claim. In *French Company of Venezuelan Railroads*, the commission held only claims central to

				referred to mixed commission.		a contract were subject to an exclusive jurisdiction clause in the contract. A claim for rescission of contract was subject to the clause; whereas an international tribunal could determine a claim for damages ulterior to contract.
35	Venezuela–Great Britain	13 February 1903 Additional Protocol of 7 May 1903.	IX UNRIAA 351	Convention provided for all claims of British citizens against Venezuela, including those of railway companies, unless otherwise satisfied, referred to a mixed commission of 2 (in case of disagreement to be decided by the umpire). In respect of claims to injury to or wrongful seizure of property, Venezuela admitted liability in principle. Commission to	Commission sat 1903–4. Some of the results are reported in IX UNRIAA.	It appears that the states had control of claims. The convention provided that the commissioner was bound to receive evidence from the governments and to hear oral or written arguments of their agents. The Rules of Procedure provided that claimants or their representatives required authorisation to attend any hearing. Decisions of the commission were final and conclusive as regards the dispute between the two states. Great Britain sought to bring a claim (*Stevenson*)

	Parties	Date of Instrument	Reference	Description	Outcomes	Relevant characteristics
				decide the claims on the basis of equity.		concerning a deceased British subject whose successors were not British. The umpire held that he had no jurisdiction, since it was not a claim of a British subject.
36	Germany–Venezuela	13 February 1903 Additional Protocol of 7 May 1903.	X UNRIAA 359	Convention provided for all claims of German subjects referred to mixed commission of 2 (in case of disagreement, referred to umpire). Venezuela admitted liability for property claims. Commission to decide claims on the basis of equity.	Some of the results are reported in X UNRIAA.	Appears that states had control of the claims. The Additional Protocol provided that claims, evidence and documents were to be presented by claimant government, but provided that the commission was authorised to receive declarations of claimants or their agents.
37	Italy–Venezuela	13 February 1903 Additional Protocol of 7 May 1903.	X UNRIAA 479	The convention provided for all claims of Italian subjects referred to mixed commission	Some of the results are reported in X UNRIAA.	Appears states had control of the claims. Additional Protocol provided that claims, evidence and documents were to be

				of 2 (in case of disagreement, referred to umpire). Venezuela admitted liability for property claims. Commission to decide claims on the basis of equity.		presented by claimant government, but commission was authorised to receive declarations of claimants or their agents. In *Miliani*, the umpire rejected a claim in respect of Italian-Venezuelan dual national. In *Martini*, the commission held that the convention superseded existing contractual arrangements, including exclusive jurisdiction clauses.
38	US–Venezuela	13 February 1903	101 BFSP 646; IX UNRIAA 115	Claims by US citizens against Venezuela not settled by diplomatic agreement or arbitration referred to mixed commission of 2 (in case of disagreement, referred to umpire). The applicable law was justice and provisions of the convention.	Some of the results are reported in IX UNRIAA.	It appears that the states had control of the claims. Under the convention, the commission was bound to receive evidence from the governments, to hear oral or written arguments of agents of government and to decide claims solely on evidence provided by the governments. The Rules provided that claims/briefs were to be filed by claimant government. Decisions of the commission were final and conclusive.

	Parties	Date of Instrument	Reference	Description	Outcomes	Relevant characteristics
39	Mexico–Venezuela	13 February 1903	X UNRIAA 695	Claims by Mexican citizens against Venezuela to be decided by a mixed commission of 2. Applicable law was justice and the convention. Jurisdiction of commission extended to claims against Mexico by Venezuelan nationals.	Some of the results are reported in X UNRIAA.	It appears that the states had control of the claims. Under the convention the commission was bound to receive evidence from governments and to hear oral or written arguments of agents of government and the commission was to decide claims solely on evidence provided by the governments. The Rules provided that claims/briefs were to be filed by claimant government. Decisions of the commission were final and conclusive.
40	France–Venezuela	27 February 1903	X UNRIAA 3	Claims by French citizens against Venezuela not settled by arbitration or diplomatic agreement (and not within terms of 1902 Protocol) to be	Some of the results are reported in X UNRIAA.	It appears that the states had control of the claims. Under the convention the commission was bound to receive evidence from governments and to hear oral or written arguments of agents of government

				decided by mixed commission of 2 (in case of disagreement, referred to umpire). Applicable law was justice and provisions of the convention.		and the commission was to decide claims solely on evidence provided by the governments. The Rules provided that claims/briefs were to be filed by claimant government. Decisions of the commission were final and conclusive.
41	Netherlands–Venezuela	28 February 1903	X UNRIAA 709	Claims by citizens of the Netherlands against Venezuela referred to mixed commission. Applicable law was justice and the convention.	Some of the results are reported in X UNRIAA.	It appears that the states had control of the claims. Rules provided that claims/briefs were to be filed by claimant government but that claimants or their representatives could attend hearings. Decisions of the commission were final and conclusive.
42	Belgium–Venezuela	7 March 1903	IX UNRIAA 321	Claims by Belgian citizens referred to mixed commission. Applicable law was justice and convention.	Some of the results are reported in IX UNRIAA.	It appears that the states had control of the claims. Under the convention the commission was bound to receive evidence from governments, to hear oral or written arguments of agents of government and to decide claims solely on evidence provided by governments. Rules

	Parties	Date of Instrument	Reference	Description	Outcomes	Relevant characteristics
						provided that claims/briefs to be filed by claimant government. Decisions of commission final and conclusive.
43	Sweden/Norway–Venezuela	10 March 1903	X UNRIAA 763	Claims by citizens of Sweden and Norway against Venezuela referred to mixed commission. Applicable law was justice and convention.	Some of the results are reported in X UNRIAA.	Appears that the states had control of the claims. Under the convention the commission was bound to receive evidence from governments, to hear oral or written arguments of agents of government and to decide claims solely on evidence provided by the governments. Rules provided that claims/briefs were to be filed by claimant government. Decisions of commission were final and conclusive.
44	Spain–Venezuela	2 April 1903	X UNRIAA 737	Claims by Spanish citizens against Venezuela referred to mixed	Some of the results are reported in X UNRIAA.	Appears that the states had control of the claims. Under the convention the commission was bound to

				commission. Applicable law was justice and convention.		receive evidence from governments, to hear oral or written arguments of agents of government and to decide claims solely on evidence provided by the governments. Rules provided that claims/briefs were to be filed by claimant government. Decisions of commission were final and conclusive.
45	Brazil–Bolivia	17 November 1903	194 CTS 249	Claims arising from administrative acts and events in exchanged territories submitted to arbitral tribunal of 3, which appeared to have jurisdiction for claims against either state.	Unknown.	Unknown.
46	Brazil–Peru	12 July 1904	196 CTS 106	Complaints by citizens of either state for damage or violence in Alto Juruá and Alto Purús since 1902 submitted to tribunal of 2 members (referred to umpire	Tribunal operated from 1907–10 and issued 91 awards.	Convention provided that the states agreed that the awards were perfect, final and binding, the claimants being bound beforehand to accept them as definite. It is not clear whether the 'claimants' here referred to

	Parties	Date of Instrument	Reference	Description	Outcomes	Relevant characteristics
				in case of disagreement).		were individuals or the state (see Art. IV). Awards were paid direct to governments.
47	Hague Convention XII of 1907	Adopted 18 October 1907; never came into force	(1908) 2 AJIL 174	Individual subjects of contracting states given right to appeal from judgments of national courts to International Prize Court. Appeals could be brought if a judgment injuriously affected a claimant's property. State of nationality could forbid claimant bringing case (Arts. 3–5).	The proposed International Prize Court never came into existence because the requisite number of ratifications were not obtained.	There was provision for individual claimants to fully participate in proceedings. They had control of the claim (see Arts. 28–50).
48	El Salvador–Nicaragua–Costa Rica–Honduras–Guatemala	20 December 1907	(1908) 2 AJIL 231	Central American Court of Justice established with jurisdiction over cases between contracting parties	Court operated for 10 years. 5 cases were brought by individuals, but none were successful. 4 were	Case brought by Díaz (Nicaraguan) against Guatemala for wrongful arrest dismissed for failure to exhaust local remedies. Case brought asking for

and individual of another state if case was of international character, or if it concerned violations of a treaty or convention, provided that local remedies had been exhausted or a denial of justice was shown: see Art. 2.	dismissed for lack of jurisdiction and in the fifth case, the Court decided against individual.	declaration of nullity of election in Costa Rica dismissed because it was not international in character. The Court heard case brought by Nuñez asking whether Costa Rica could expel Nicaraguan citizen for reason of his having formed part of armed expedition against Nicaragua. The Court held that the expulsion was lawful.

Appendix III
International claims tribunals and commissions 1919–1939

	Parties	Date of Instrument	Reference	Description	Outcomes	Relevant characteristics
1	Germany–Portugal–Romania–France–Greece–Italy–Great Britain–Japan–Czechoslovakia–Yugoslavia–Siam–Poland–Belgium	28 June 1919 (Treaty of Versailles)	UKTS 4 (Cmd. 153)	Established mixed arbitral tribunals between each of the Allied and Associates Powers and Germany, with jurisdiction to decide disputes relating to: debts to or from German nationals; compensation for damage to property, rights or interests by application of war measures; contracts, prescriptions and judgments; and licence of industrial, literary or artistic property.	First decision issued by French-German tribunal on 21 July 1920. Settled by Hague Convention of 20 January 1903, 104 LNTS 243.	Individual claimants had control of the claims. See Art. 304 Annex pt (3); Wühler (1997), p. 433. French-German Mixed Arbitral Tribunal held that Treaty of Versailles conferred rights on individuals: *Sigwald, Charles* v. *Germany*, 27 August 1926, 3 ILR 337. Anglo-German tribunal held that an individual's right to claim compensation was independent from the discretion of their state of nationality, granted directly to a national: *Lederer* v. *German Government*, (1924) Recueil des Décisions des Tribunaux Arbitraux Mixtes 762, 768.

						It was also held that a Calvo clause in a contract did not defeat the tribunal's jurisdiction, as was clearly intended in the Peace Treaties: *Wauquier et Compagnie* v. *(1) Governor-General of the Vilayet and the Municipality of Sivas (2) Turkey* (1930) 5 ILR 434.
2	Austria–France–Greece–Yugoslavia–Belgium–Romania–Great Britain–Italy	10 September 1919 (Treaty of St Germain-en-Laye)	UKTS 11 (Cmd. 153)	Established mixed arbitral tribunal with same jurisdiction as the tribunal established under the Treaty of Versailles (see above).		Appears to have operated on the same basis as the mixed arbitral tribunals established by the Treaty of Versailles.
3	Bulgaria–Great Britain–Greece–Yugoslavia–Belgium–Romania–Italy	27 November 1919 (Treaty of Neuilly)	UKTS 5 (Cmd. 522)	Established mixed arbitral tribunal with same jurisdiction as the tribunal established under the Treaty of Versailles (see above).		Appears to have operated on the same basis as the mixed arbitral tribunals established by the Treaty of Versailles.
4	Hungary–Romania–Great Britain–Belgium–	4 June 1920 (Treaty of Trianon)	113 BFSP 486; UKTS 10 (Cmd. 896)	Established mixed arbitral tribunal with same jurisdiction as the tribunal		Appears to have operated on the same basis as the mixed arbitral tribunals

	Parties	Date of Instrument	Reference	Description	Outcomes	Relevant characteristics
	Czechoslovakia–Yugoslavia–Italy			established under the Treaty of Versailles (see above).		established by the Treaty of Versailles.
5	US–Norway	30 June 1921	I UNRIAA 309	Claims of Norwegian subjects against US concerning requisitions by US Shipping Board Emergency Fleet Corp. referred to PCA arbitration. Claims determined in accordance with principles of law and equity. Arbitrators also had jurisdiction over claims by Page Brothers (US).	Awards were made in each of the 15 claims against US. US claimed US $22,800 in respect of Page Brothers; disallowed as against Norway but amount retained as against 1 of the claims.	States had control of the claims (Art. II). Tribunal held that it was the governments 'not the individual claimants' who were the claimants before the tribunal. In the case of the Page Brothers (US), the claim was essentially between two subjects (Art. I). Tribunal conditioned the award in *Page Brothers* on the assumption that the amount retained by US for Page Brothers would be passed on to the Page Brothers as claimant.
6	Germany–Poland	15 May 1922 (Geneva Convention)	9 LNTS 466; ILR 3, 4, 6, 7, 8	Decision of Conference of Ambassadors established two bodies: Upper	Mixed Commission dealt with 2,283 cases. It was widely thought to	Before the Mixed Commission, individuals had control of their claims. The Commission's

				Silesian Mixed Commission with jurisdiction over disputes relating to minorities protection; and Arbitral Tribunal with competence over specified matters including payment of indemnities, questions of nationality or right of residence, and any dispute relating to the interpretation of the Geneva Convention.	have been the most effective mechanism for enforcement of minorities protection. Arbitral Tribunal sat from 1922–37.	President explained that the 'petitioner is granted the legal status of a litigant party': Official Collection of Opinions of the President of the Upper Silesian Mixed Commission. Before the mixed arbitral tribunal, individuals controlled their claims. They were entitled to be represented on the same footing as governments. Parties could be represented by barristers or professors of law, or represent themselves. Individuals were also permitted to bring an action against their state of nationality: *Steiner and Gross* v. *Poland*, Upper Silesian Arbitral Tribunal, 30 March 1929, 4 ILR 291.
7	Germany–US	10 August 1922 Extended by supplementary Protocol.	8 ILR 8, 480, 482, 483 See also 48 LNTS 69	Established mixed claims commissions to determine amounts due by Germany in relation	Operated 1923–33; considered about 20,000 claims, issued about 7,000 awards in the	Operated on the basis of diplomatic protection. Claims were brought by the US, which had control over claims. Rules appear

Parties	Date of Instrument	Reference	Description	Outcomes	Relevant characteristics
			to claims of US citizens for damage to or seizure of property, rights or interests; and debts owing to US citizens by German government or by German nationals. These commissions were established separately because the US did not ratify the Treaty of Versailles.	amount of approximately US $181,000,000.	to refer to claims being presented by agents of the states. The commission held that the US was the proper claimant: Administrative Decision No. II, VII UNRIAA 23, 26. In a further decision, the commission emphasised that the US had 'complete possession and control of the claim', which it prosecuted 'in its own right and not as the agent or trustee of the subordinate claimant' and without accountability to individual claimants for the proceeds of the claim, on the basis that a claim has no 'international status unless it is espoused' by a state: see Administrative Decision No. V, VII UNRIAA 19, 126.

8	Turkey–Great Britain–France–Italy–Japan–Greece–Romania–Serb–Croat–Slovene State	24 July 1923 (Treaty of Lausanne)	UKTS 16 (Cmd. 1929)	Established mixed arbitral tribunals between Turkey and each Allied Power with competence relating to restitution of property in Turkey belonging to Allied nationals; certain contractual disputes; mortgages and debts; licences for industrial property, reproduction of literary or artistic works; orders and decisions of occupying power at Constantinople; and damages resulting from civil decisions.	Unknown.	Appears that individuals before the mixed arbitral tribunals had control of their claim, like the other Allied mixed arbitral tribunals established under the Peace Treaties.
9	Mexico–US (general claims)	8 November 1923 Extended by supplementary Protocol. Further two Protocols expedited claims.	Feller (1935), Appendix	Claims by nationals of a state party against other state for loss or damage to persons or property of companies, corporations, associations,	General claims commission operated 1926–31; over 3,000 claims were submitted but the commission only dealt with a small	States controlled claims. The convention provided for appointment of agents and counsel by governments who were to present evidence and arguments orally or in writing. Rules provided that all claims,

Parties	Date of Instrument	Reference	Description	Outcomes	Relevant characteristics
			partnerships or individuals (including interests in companies or corporations of different nationality) between 4 July 1868 and 3 years after commission's first meeting referred to general claims commission. Acts relating to recent revolution excluded. Applicable law was principles of international law, justice and equity.	percentage of these. 2,781 claims were filed by US: 89 awards; 50 rejected. 836 claims were filed by Mexico: 5 awards; 4 rejected. Protocols of 1932 and 1934 simplified procedures and changed organisation of commission. Final results unknown.	documents and evidence were to be filed by governments and agents. However, memorial was to be signed by individual claimant or their attorney. Commission held that a state could press claim on mere proof of nationality and the individual need not have sought aid of government: *Melczer Mining Company*. Awards were to be paid in lump sum to government after offset. Decisions of commission on character of claims suggested that these were diplomatic protection claims. In *Dickson Car Wheel Co.*, the commission held that the injury is wrongful act against state of nationality. In *William A. Parker*, the commission held that the private claim

						was not property of nation but it was controlled by state when espoused.
10	Mexico–US (special claims)	10 September 1923 Supplementary Protocol extending was not ratified; 1934 convention provided for lump sum settlement.	Feller (1935), Appendix	Claims against Mexico by US nationals arising from 1910–20 revolution, caused by any of enumerated 'forces' referred to a special claims commission. Applicable law stated as principles of international law, justice and equity.	Commission operated 1926–34, receiving 3,176 claims (2 were rejected). There were problems between the commissioners. 1934 convention provided for lump sum payment calculated by reference to awards of other commissions, then referred to domestic claims commission.	States had control of the claims. The convention provided for appointment of agents and counsel by governments who were to present evidence and arguments orally or in writing. Rules provided that all claims, documents and evidence were to be filed by governments and agents. The memorial was to be signed by individual claimant or attorney. Awards payable directly (in lump sum) to US government. Outstanding claims were settled by lump sum payable direct to the US government. Decisions were specified to be final and conclusive in respect of the dispute between states.
11	Canada–US	23 January 1924	III UNRIAA 1610	Claims by British vessels for compensation on	In case of the SS *I'm Alone* commissioners	Operated on the basis of diplomatic protection: state had control of claims.

	Parties	Date of Instrument	Reference	Description	Outcomes	Relevant characteristics
				grounds of improper exercise of treaty rights referred to 2 persons and, if disagreement, to claims commission under 1910 convention.	held no compensation payable for loss of ship or cargo; but specified compensation payable to benefit of captain and crew.	
12	France–Mexico	24 September 1924 Extended by supplementary Protocol and exchange of notes; 1930 convention provided for expedition of proceedings.	Feller (1935), Appendix	Claims against Mexico by French nationals arising from 1910–20 revolution, caused by any of enumerated 'forces', referred to claims commission. Also covered claims for loss or damage for acts caused by civil authorities relating to revolution by enumerated forces. Applicable law was principles of justice and equity.	Operated 1928–29, issuing 3 awards. Mexican Commissioner then withdrew and 23 awards issued in his absence. 1930 convention created new commission, which dealt with those 23 awards and all claims listed in Appendix. It dealt	State had control of claims. Convention provided for appointment of agents and counsel by governments who were to present evidence and arguments orally or in writing. Memorial was to be signed by individual claimant or attorney. Decisions were final and conclusive in respect of the dispute between states. Awards were to be paid in lump sum directly to US government.

					with 251 claims: 108 withdrawn; 50 rejected; and 93 resulted in awards.	
13	US–Austria–Hungary	26 November 1924	48 LNTS 69; 4 ILR 262, 543	Commissioner to decide claims for loss, damage or injury suffered by US or its nationals falling within terms of US–Austria Treaty of 24 August 1921, the Treaty of 29 August 1921 between Hungary and the US and/or Treaties of St Germain-en-Laye and Trianon.	Operated 1927–29.	States had control of the claims: the governments could designate counsel and agents to appear before commissioner (see Art. IV).
14	Germany–Mexico	16 March 1925 Extended by three supplementary Protocols.	Feller (1935), Appendix	Claims against Mexico by German nationals arising from 1910–20 revolution and caused by enumerated ‘forces’ or acts of civil authorities related to revolution referred to claims commission.	Commission operated 1926–30, dealing with 140 claims: 68 withdrawn, 38 rejected; 34 awards.	States had control of claims. The convention provided for the appointment of agents and counsel by governments who were to present evidence and arguments orally or in writing. Memorial was to be signed by individual claimant or attorney. The decisions were final

	Parties	Date of Instrument	Reference	Description	Outcomes	Relevant characteristics
				Applicable law was principles of justice and equity.		and conclusive in respect of the dispute between states.
15	Spain–Mexico	25 November 1925 Extended by supplementary Protocol.	Feller (1935), Appendix	Claims of Spanish nationals against Mexico arising from 1910–20 revolution, caused by enumerated 'forces' or acts by civil authorities related to revolution referred to claims commission. Applicable law was principles of justice and equity.	Commission received 1,268 claims. No awards were issued during first term of 3.5 years. Awards were eventually issued but never published.	States had control of claims. The convention provided for the appointment of agents and counsel by governments who were to present evidence and arguments orally or in writing. Memorial was to be signed by individual claimant or attorney. Decisions were final and conclusive in respect of the dispute between states.
16	Panama–US	28 July 1926 Extended by supplementary Protocol.	138 LNTS 119; 7 ILR 253, 254, 259, 439, 479, 482, 478, 480, 254, 256, 257	Claims arising since 3 November 1903 of citizens of one state against other for loss or damage suffered by person or property (excluding fire claims by US	Commission operated in 1933.	Appears that states had control of claims. Decisions were to be final and conclusive in respect of each and every claim within the commission's jurisdiction. Awards paid

				citizens) referred to commission of 3 for decision on basis of principles of international law, justice and equity.		directly to governments, after offset.
17	Great Britain–Mexico	19 November 1926 Extended by supplementary Protocol and exchange of notes.	Feller (1935), Appendix	Claims by British nationals against Mexico arising from 1910–20 revolution, caused by enumerated 'forces' referred to claims commission. Also covered loss or damage for acts caused by civil authorities related to revolution. Applicable law was stated as principles of justice and equity.	Commission operated 1929–32, receiving 110 claims: 18 were withdrawn; 60 were rejected; and 50 awards were issued. Under Supplementary Convention of 1930 claims relating to acts of Huerta forces were excluded from jurisdiction.	States had control of the claims. The convention provided for the appointment of agents and counsel by governments who were to present evidence and arguments orally or in writing. Memorial was to be signed by claimant or attorney; or by agent of government if memorial contained statement of claim signed by claimant. Decisions were final and conclusive as between the two states. Commission considered the claims to be of 'mixed character': 'they were public claims insofar as they were presented by one state against another; but they were also private claims insofar as they were

	Parties	Date of Instrument	Reference	Description	Outcomes	Relevant characteristics
						aimed at granting an award to an individual': *Case of Mexican Union Railway*.
18	Italy–Mexico	13 January 1927 Extended by agreement as to interpretation.	Feller (1935), Appendix	Claims by Italian nationals against Mexico arising from 1910–20 revolution, caused by enumerated 'forces' or acts of civil authorities related to revolution referred to claims commission. Also covered loss or damage. Applicable law was stated as principles of justice and equity.	Operated until 1932. Commission received 157 claims: 51 withdrawn; 63 rejected; 43 awards.	States had control of the claims. Convention provided for the appointment of agents and counsel by governments who were to present evidence and arguments orally or in writing. Memorial was to be signed by claimant or attorney; or by agent of government if memorial contained statement of claim signed by claimant. Decisions were final and conclusive as between the two states. Commission held that it was a condition that private claimant initiate claim under convention and the government could only prosecute claim as

						representative of convention party. A claim was disallowed where the claimant refused to sign memorial and informed commission she did not want claim to be examined: *Emilia Marta Viuda de Giovanni Mantellero* (unpublished, extracted in Feller (1935), pp. 90–1).
19	Belgium–Mexico	14 May 1927	Feller (1935), Appendix	Claims of Belgium nationals against Mexico relating to revolution referred to administrative arbitral tribunal with simplified procedure.	Very few Belgian claims. Outcomes unknown.	Unknown.

3 The individual in international humanitarian law

3.1 Introduction

International humanitarian law, a relatively modern term, is now used to refer to the principal body of law which governs the conduct of armed conflict: the former phrase, the 'laws of war', implied a much more inter-state focus. International regulation of the conduct of inter-state war dates to the mid-nineteenth century. Similarly, international regulation of civil strife began with practice in the mid-nineteenth century.

In international armed conflict, rules which limit the conduct of armed forces have the potential to engage individuals in the international legal system. In internal armed conflict, the extension of belligerent rights and obligations to armed opposition groups effectively engages individuals. This chapter surveys the development of international humanitarian law with respect to individuals in both spheres. The extent to which individuals have been engaged in the international legal system will be assessed against the orthodox accounts of the international legal system examined in Part I. In recent scholarship it has been suggested that there is convergence in humanitarian law applicable in international and non-international armed conflicts;[1] but in this chapter they are addressed separately for several reasons, including the diversity in the historical development of the applicable rules in each type of conflict.

In the post-1945 period, there has been significant development of individual responsibility for international crimes, including war

[1] See e.g., E. Crawford, 'Unequal Before the Law: The Case for the Elimination of the Distinction between International and Non-International Armed Conflicts' (2007) 20 *LJIL* 441.

crimes. Individuals have been held responsible under international law for acts which amount to violations of international humanitarian law. In this chapter, the provisions which implicate individual responsibility for violations of the laws and customs of war are noted in both international and internal armed conflict, but they are explored in more detail in Chapter 4, which examines individual criminal responsibility under international law.

3.2 The individual in international armed conflict

(a) *Regulation of international war pre-1914*

The regulation of international armed conflict has roots in practices emerging in the late Middle Ages; in particular codes of conduct for participants in armed conflict.[2] The idea of generalised rules regulating the means and methods of warfare gained traction with the development of the voluntary law through the work of Wolff and Vattel in the late eighteenth century,[3] coinciding with the professionalisation of war around the same period. Vattel urged that the 'regular armies' ought to refrain from acts of hostility against 'the people, the peasantry, the towns-folk'.[4] By the nineteenth century there were moves towards the

[2] As to developments in the Middle Ages, see M. H. Keen, *The Laws of War in the Late Middle Ages* (London, Keegan Paul, 1965), pp. 156–85; M. H. Keen, *Chivalry* (New Haven, Conn., Yale University Press, 1984), p. 221. An early example was produced by Florence in 1369. King Charles V of France promulgated a code in 1371 and King Richard II of England issued ordinances on war in 1385, which were replaced by Henry V in 1419 with a set of 'Statutes and Ordinances to be Kept in Time of War'. In 1432, Holy Roman Emperor Sigismund issued a code of conduct for the imminent campaign against the Hussite forces in Bohemia. A set of rules on war was promulgated by Charles the Bold of Burgundy in 1473.

[3] Vattel's voluntary law was that positive law which was presumed to reflect the will of states in order to preserve the basic principles of the international community: E. de Vattel, *The Law of Nations or, Principles of the Law of Nature Applied to the Conduct and Affairs of Nations and Sovereigns* (1758, B. Kapossy and R. Whatmore (eds.), Indianapolis, Liberty Fund, 2008), Preliminaries para. 7 (p. 70) and paras. 27–8 (pp. 78–9); see 1.2(a) above. Grotius illustrated the difference between the natural law and the voluntary law in reference to the capture of enemy property. According to the voluntary law, soldiers on both sides obtained 'external' legal title to captured property; but the soldiers on the unjust side were under a natural law moral duty to restore the property to the original owner: H. Grotius, *The Rights of War and Peace* (1625, R. Tuck (ed.), Indianapolis, Liberty Fund, 2005), bk II, ch. XIII, I–II (pp. 1475–6).

[4] de Vattel, *The Law of Nations*, bk III, ch. VIII, para. 147 (p. 550).

imposition of specific rules regulating the means and methods of warfare by international treaty.[5]

The first treaties governing the conduct of warfare were framed as prohibitions imposed upon states parties to a conflict which operated to benefit individuals, rather than as obligations imposed or rights conferred on individuals. The 1868 St Petersburg Declaration, which banned the use of certain projectiles, provided that the 'Contracting Parties engage mutually to renounce, in case of war among themselves', the employment of the specified weapons.[6] The Hague Declaration of 1899 concerning asphyxiating gases expressed its prohibition as the agreement of the 'Contracting Powers ... to abstain from the use' of such gases;[7] the Hague Declaration concerning expanding bullets[8] used similar language. The Hague Regulations were also expressed in language suggestive of obligations on the belligerents: for example, Article 22 affirmed that the 'right of belligerents to adopt means of injuring the enemy is not unlimited'.[9] Hague Convention IV imposed an obligation on contracting powers to issue instructions to their armed land forces in conformity with the annexed Hague Regulations,[10] and provided that in case of violation of the provisions of the Regulations, the contracting belligerent party would be responsible for acts committed by persons forming part of its armed forces, and would be liable to pay compensation.[11] The specification of state responsibility was consistent with a conception of these rules comprising inter-state obligations rather than rights conferred or obligations imposed on individuals. They involved obligations of mutual inter-state restraint in inter-state armed conflict.

Similarly, initiatives directed towards relieving the suffering of victims of war were characterised as protective obligations on parties to the conflict, rather than rights conferred on individuals. The first Geneva

[5] C. von Clausewitz, *On War* (J. J. Graham (trans.), London, Kegan Paul, 1908), pp. 69, 87, 149 and 605.

[6] Declaration Renouncing the Use, in Time of War, of Explosive Projectiles under 400 Grammes Weight, 11 December 1868 (entry into force 11 December 1868), (1869) LXIV UKPP 659.

[7] Hague Declaration II Concerning Asphyxiating Gases, 29 July 1899 (entry into force 4 September 1900), 187 CTS 435.

[8] Hague Declaration III Concerning Expanding Bullets, 29 July 1899 (entry into force 4 September 1900), 187 CTS 459.

[9] Annex to Hague Convention IV, Regulations respecting the Laws and Customs of War on Land, 18 October 1907, 205 CTS 277.

[10] Hague Convention IV Respecting the Laws and Customs of War on Land, Art. I, 18 October 1907 (entry into force 26 January 1910), 205 CTS 277.

[11] *Ibid.* Art. 3.

Convention concluded under the auspices of the International Committee of the Red Cross (ICRC) in 1864 provided that ambulances and military hospitals should be 'protected and respected by the belligerents' and that wounded and sick combatants 'shall be collected and cared for'.[12] The 1907 Hague Regulations provided for certain standards of treatment for prisoners of war, also expressed as obligations incumbent upon the contracting states, who would be responsible for acts of its armed forces in violation of those obligations.[13]

Hague Convention II of 1899 and Hague Convention IV of 1907 both included the so-called 'Martens' clause, which stated that:

> Until a more complete code of the laws of war has been issued, the High Contracting parties deem it expedient to declare that, in cases not included in the Regulations adopted by them, the inhabitants and the belligerents remain under the protection and the rule of the principles of the law of nations, as they result from the usages established among civilized peoples, from the laws of humanity, and the dictates of the public conscience.[14]

The Martens clause acknowledged that other principles of international law might apply to protect individuals and to limit permissible conduct of belligerents in conflict. It was originally intended to provide for the application of residual rules for the protection of the population in occupied territories.[15] But it did not suggest a different normative framework for the application of those principles than that already applicable under treaty rules: that is, the Martens clause did not suggest that any international rights were conferred on individuals, in contradistinction to obligations of inter-state restraint.

In this early period, rules relating to both methods and means of warfare and humanitarian relief were conceived as imposing obligations upon states parties to the conflict, to the benefit of individuals.

12 Geneva Convention for the Amelioration of the Wounded, 22 August 1864 (entry into force 22 June 1865), 129 CTS 361, Arts. 1 and 6. This convention was extended to cover maritime warfare by the Hague Peace Conference in 1899 and supplemented by further arrangements in 1906: Convention Extending the 1864 Geneva Convention of 1864 to Maritime War, 29 July 1899, 187 CTS 443; Convention for the Amelioration of Wounded and Sick in Armies, 9 July 1906, 202 CTS 144.

13 Hague Convention IV Respecting the Laws and Customs of War on Land, 18 October 1907 (entry into force 26 January 1910), 205 CTS 277.

14 Reproduced and translated in J. B. Scott (ed.), *The Hague Convention and Declarations of 1899 and 1907* (New York, Oxford University Press, 1915), pp. 101–2.

15 A. Cassese, 'The Martens Clause: Half a Loaf or Simply Pie in the Sky?' (2000) 11 *EJIL* 187; T. Meron, 'The Martens Clause, Principles of Humanity, and Dictates of Public Conscience' (2000) 94 *AJIL* 78.

They were consistent with the orthodox account of the framework of the international legal system as a system of rules between states and a system which did not confer rights or impose duties on individuals.

(b) Developments in the inter-war period

After the First World War, it was generally acknowledged that the existing Geneva law was inadequate in its protection of civilians and persons *hors de combat*. In 1929, the Geneva Conventions were redrafted, resulting in two conventions: the Convention Relative to the Treatment of Prisoners of War[16] and the Convention for the Amelioration of the Condition of the Wounded and Sick in Armies in the Field.[17] A majority of the provisions of the 1929 Prisoners of War Convention expressed inter-state obligations to accord certain treatment to qualifying persons. For example, Article 7 provided that prisoners of war 'shall be evacuated'; Article 9 provided that they 'may be interned'; Article 12 required that certain items 'shall be supplied to prisoners of war' and Article 16 required that prisoners of war 'shall be permitted' freedom of religion. However, some of the provisions used language suggestive of individual rights: prisoners of war 'shall have the right' in certain circumstances. For example, Article 42 stated that '[p]risoners of war shall have the right' to bring petitions relating to their conditions of captivity and Articles 62 and 64 referred to 'rights' to procedural protections in judicial proceedings.[18] The 1929 Wounded and Sick Convention used language indicative of inter-state obligations to accord certain standards of treatment;[19] the exception was Article 23, which provided that medical units belonging to neutral countries 'shall ... have the right' to fly their national flag. The two 1929 Geneva Conventions were the first humanitarian law treaties to refer to rights for individuals. But it was not clear that these were international law rights: the language 'shall have the right' was broad enough to

[16] Geneva Convention on Prisoners of War, 27 July 1929 (entry into force 19 June 1931), 118 LNTS 343. See generally, Gustav Rasmussen, *Code des Prisonniers de Guerre: Commentarie de la Convention du 27 Juillet 1929 Relative au Traitement des Prisonniers de Guerre* (Copenhagen, Leven and Munksgaard, 1931).

[17] Geneva Convention for the Amelioration of the Condition of the Wounded and Sick in Armies in the Field, 27 July 1929 (entry into force 19 June 1931), 118 LNTS 303.

[18] Geneva Convention on Prisoners of War, Arts. 62 and 64, 27 July 1929 (entry into force 19 June 1931), 118 LNTS 343.

[19] Geneva Convention for the Amelioration of the Condition of the Wounded and Sick in Armies in the Field, Arts. 1, 5, 9 and 12, 27 July 1929 (entry into force 19 June 1931), 118 LNTS 30.

encompass either the direct creation of individual rights by treaty or a requirement that individual rights be created under domestic law. It will be recalled that the PCIJ affirmed that treaties could create direct rights for individuals in 1928, but when the Geneva Conventions were concluded in 1929 it had not been generally accepted that this was the effect of the Court's Opinion: international legal doctrine still maintained that individuals could not bear rights and obligations under international law.[20] Reading the oblique references to 'rights' in the 1929 Geneva Conventions in the context of their other provisions, the vast majority of which referred to treatment rather than rights, suggests that these provisions were not conceived, at least at the time, as creating international law rights for individuals. Thus, what is indicated is a normative framework of inter-state rights and obligations, consistent with the established understanding of the international legal system during this period.

In addition to the 1929 Geneva Conventions, treaties governing the conduct of warfare used language suggestive of injunctions for states parties rather than obligations or rights for individuals. The 1925 Geneva Protocol stated that 'the High Contracting Parties ... accept th[e] prohibition' relating to the use of certain gases and bacteriological warfare,[21] and similar language was used in other Hague treaties concluded in the inter-war period.[22] These treaties were consistent with the established understanding of international law during this period, as exclusively concerned with rights and obligations of states.

(c) The individual in international armed conflict after 1945

Since 1945, Geneva law has been developed in two waves: the first immediately after the Second World War, resulting in the four Geneva Conventions of 1949; the second in the 1970s, producing the two Additional Protocols of 1977. The treatment of individuals in international armed conflict is supplemented by customary international humanitarian law and applicable international human rights law. In addition to Geneva law, in the period since 1945 there have been several treaties progressing Hague law; like the early Hague treaties, these

[20] See 1.2(c) above.

[21] Geneva Protocol for the Prohibition of the Use in War of Asphyxiating, Poisonous or Other Gases, and of Bacteriological Methods of Warfare, 17 June 1925 (entry into force 8 February 1828), (1927)126 BFSP 324.

[22] See e.g., Treaty Relating to the Use of Submarines and Noxious Gases in Warfare, Washington, DC, 6 February 1922 (not yet in force), 25 LNTS 202.

conventions indicate obligations imposed on states rather than individual rights.[23]

(i) The 1949 Geneva Conventions

The substantive provisions of the four Geneva Conventions generally express the protection of individuals as protective obligations on state parties to a conflict, rather than as specific rights conferred directly on individuals. Common Article 1 of each of the Geneva Conventions states that the high contracting parties 'undertake to respect and to ensure respect for the present Convention in all circumstances'. Additionally, the first and second Geneva Conventions provide that '[e]ach Party to the conflict . . . shall ensure the detailed execution' of the provisions of those conventions.[24] The provisions relating to execution in all four conventions refer exclusively to obligations incumbent upon states.[25]

The vast majority of the provisions of the conventions which provide for the protection of various categories of individuals are expressed in terms which indicate that obligations are imposed on states parties to a conflict, rather than rights directly conferred on the relevant individuals. The provisions of the first and second Geneva Conventions, which apply to the wounded and sick in armed forces in the field and the wounded, sick and shipwrecked members of armed forces at sea respectively, express the relevant obligations as obligations imposed on states parties, either as injunctions directed to the parties to a conflict,[26] or

[23] For example, the Convention on Prohibitions or Restriction on the Use of Certain Conventional Weapons which May be Deemed to be Excessively Injurious or to Have Indiscriminate Effects, 10 October 1980 (entry into force 2 December 1983), 1342 UNTS 137 prohibits the use of any weapons 'the primary effect of which is to injure by fragments which in the human body escape detection by X-rays'.

[24] Geneva Convention I for the Amelioration of the Condition of the Wounded and Sick in Armed Forces in the Field, Art. 46, 12 August 1949 (entry into force 21 October 1950), 75 UNTS 31; Geneva Convention II for the Amelioration of the Condition of Wounded, Sick and Shipwrecked Members of Armed Forces at Sea, Art. 46, 12 August 1949 (entry into force 21 October 1950), 75 UNTS 85.

[25] Geneva Convention I, Arts. 45–53; Geneva Convention II, Arts. 46–53; Geneva Convention III Relative to the Treatment of Prisoners of War, Arts. 126–32, 12 August 1949 (entry into force 21 October 1950), 75 UNTS 135; Geneva Convention IV Relative to the Protection of Civilian Persons in Time of War, Arts 142–9, 12 August 1949 (entry into force 21 October 1950), 75 UNTS 28. The possibility that common Article 3 imposes obligations on individuals in internal armed conflict is discussed in section 2 of this chapter.

[26] For example, Art. 15 of Geneva Convention I states that 'Parties to a conflict shall, without delay, take all possible measures to search for and collect the wounded and sick'. Similar expression is found in Art. 18 of Geneva Convention II.

protective obligations which express a benefit to certain of the wounded and sick without reference to their 'rights'.[27] Geneva Convention III relating to prisoners of war uses similar language: for example, it provides that '[p]risoners of war must at all times be humanely treated' and 'must at all times be protected';[28] in other provisions the relevant detaining power 'shall be bound' to comply with certain standards.[29] Finally, many of the provisions of Geneva Convention IV Relative to the Protection of Civilian Persons also impose obligations on parties to the conflict.[30] Some of the provisions require parties to the conflict to grant rights to specified categories of persons: for example, Article 38 provides that parties to the conflict shall grant various rights to aliens in the territory of a party to the conflict.[31]

Some of the provisions of the third and fourth Geneva Conventions use language suggestive of individual rights, although it is not clear that these are international law rights, as opposed to rights which states are required to create by their domestic law. In the third Geneva Convention, the language of rights is used in two contexts. First, Article 78 provides that prisoners of war shall have a right of complaint in relation to conditions of captivity, expressed as 'the unrestricted right to apply to the representatives of the Protecting Power either through their prisoners' representatives or, if they consider it necessary, direct'.[32] Second, the provisions relating to judicial proceedings refer to a 'right of appeal or petition from any sentence'[33] and require that prisoners be advised of their 'rights' in relation to the procedure of any trial.[34] The fourth Geneva Convention relevantly provides that internees 'shall have the right' to petition authorities in respect of the conditions of their internment;[35] that in case of trial the relevant persons 'shall not be deprived of the rights of fair and regular trial prescribed by the present Convention';[36] that accused persons 'shall have the right' to present evidence;[37] and that convicted persons 'shall have the right of appeal'.[38]

27 For example, Art. 12 of Geneva Convention I states that 'Members of the armed forces and other persons mentioned in the following Article, who are wounded or sick, shall be respected and protected in all circumstances'. Similarly, Art. 12 of Geneva Convention II provides that the relevant persons 'shall be treated humanely and cared for by the Parties to the conflict in whose power they may be, without any adverse discrimination'.

28 Geneva Convention III, Art. 13. 29 For example, *ibid.* Art. 29.

30 For example, Geneva Convention IV, Arts. 13, 14 and 18. 31 *Ibid.* Art. 38.

32 Geneva Convention III, Art. 78. 33 *Ibid.* Art. 106. 34 *Ibid.* Art. 105.

35 Geneva Convention IV, Art. 101. 36 *Ibid.* Art. 5. 37 *Ibid.* Art. 72. 38 *Ibid.* Art. 73.

Each of the four conventions contains a saving clause and a non-renunciation clause which refer to rights under the convention. The savings provisions state that no special agreement concluded between the high contracting parties shall adversely affect the situations of protected persons 'as defined by the present Convention, nor restrict the rights which it confers upon them'.[39] Although it is not entirely clear, the 'it' in the latter part of the provision appears to refer to the convention itself (rather than the special agreement); the savings clauses therefore appear to refer to rights conferred upon relevant persons by the conventions. In contrast, the non-renunciation clauses prohibit renunciation of 'the rights secured to' the relevant individuals by the conventions;[40] their language is more equivocal as rights could be 'secured' either directly through the conventions or indirectly through domestic law. On the basis of the language of the savings provisions it might be argued that the conventions confer direct rights on individuals. Although the non-renunciation provisions also refer to 'rights', like other provisions of the third and fourth Geneva Conventions which use the language of rights, the non-renunciation provisions leave open the possibility that these rights would be secured through domestic law, rather than international law.

The savings clauses can be contrasted with Article 83 of the 1929 Prisoners of War Convention,[41] which contemplated special agreements between states to vary the terms of the convention and derogate from its provisions. During the Second World War, this type of provision was open to manipulation by strong states, leaving prisoners of war in a vulnerable position. An example is the agreement by which Vichy France agreed to some prisoners of war held by Germany being treated as civilian workers not entitled to the protection of the 1929 Geneva Convention.[42] Bearing in mind that the purpose of the savings clauses was to prevent this kind of derogation, these provisions could be

[39] Geneva Convention I, Art. 6; Geneva Convention II, Art. 6; Geneva Convention III, Art. 6; Geneva Convention IV, Art. 7.

[40] Geneva Convention I, Art. 7; Geneva Convention II, Art. 7; Geneva Convention III, Art. 7; Geneva Convention IV, Art. 8. The ICRC Commentaries to the Geneva Conventions suggest that these prohibitions were directed against the possibility of coercive renunciation of rights: J. Pictet (ed.), *Commentary of the Geneva Conventions of 12 August 1949*, vol. III, *Geneva Convention III Relative to the Treatment of Prisoners of War* (Geneva, ICRC, 1960) (hereinafter *ICRC Commentary to Geneva Convention III*), pp. 87–92.

[41] Geneva Convention on Prisoners of War, 27 July 1929, 118 LNTS 343.

[42] See the Scapini–Hitler Agreement of 16 November 1940 and the Laval–Sauckel Agreement of April 1943, cited in R. J. Wilhelm, 'La Caractère droits accordés à l'individu dans les Conventions de Genève' (1950) *Revue International de la Croix-Rouge* 561, 588.

interpreted as either a prohibition on the waiver of the rights of protected persons by states or a statement that the Geneva Conventions establish a minimum standard of treatment from which no derogation is permitted.

The non-renunciation provision, which had no antecedent in the 1929 Geneva Conventions, differs from the initial Red Cross draft which provided for the possibility of a waiver by protected persons in the absence of undue pressure or coercion. A direct power of waiver vested in individuals would be suggestive of direct rights. At the Geneva Conference, a prohibition of renunciation was preferred because the validity of a waiver would have been difficult to assess.[43] The ICRC Commentary justifies the prohibition of waiver on the ground that protected persons are not in a position to freely assess whether a waiver is in their best interests.[44]

The records of the Diplomatic Conference, which may assist in interpretation of the provisions of the Geneva Conventions as they constitute the *travaux préparatoires*, do not indicate that the difference of language between the savings and non-renunciation clauses was intended to be material, and more generally the records do not assist in interpreting the character of the rights and obligations provided for in the conventions. In respect of the savings clauses, a proposal to replace the phrase 'the rights which it confers upon them' in the savings clause with 'the rights which it stipulates on their behalf' was defeated,[45] but without discussion as to the character of the rights. A further proposal to limit the savings clauses to the restriction of 'fundamental rights' was also rejected, on the basis that it would be difficult to distinguish between rights which were fundamental and those which were not.[46]

The ICRC Commentaries to the Geneva Conventions might also assist in interpretation of the conventions: while they do not constitute a binding interpretation of the conventions, their provisions or their objects, the close involvement of the ICRC in the negotiation and conclusion of the Geneva Conventions (and in recording the Diplomatic

43 *Final Record of the Diplomatic Conference of Geneva of 1949* (New York, William S. Hein & Co. Inc., 2004), vol. II, sec. B, pp. 17–18.

44 J. Pictet (ed.), *Commentary of the Geneva Conventions of 12 August 1949*, vol. IV, *Geneva Convention IV Relative to the Protection of Civilian Persons in Time of War* (Geneva, ICRC, 1958) (hereinafter *ICRC Commentary to Geneva Convention IV*), p. 75.

45 *Final Record of the Diplomatic Conference of Geneva of 1949* (New York, William S. Hein & Co. Inc., 2004), vol. II, sec. B, p. 76.

46 *Ibid.* pp. 3–74; see also *ICRC Commentary to Geneva Convention III*, p. 85.

Conference) place it in a unique position to provide comment on the specific provisions. Based on the savings and non-renunciation clauses, the ICRC Commentaries suggest that the Geneva Conventions 'affirmed' the existence of rights for protected persons[47] and that the reference to 'rights' referred to 'the whole body of safeguards which the Convention affords to protected persons'.[48] The Commentary states:

> The initiators of the Geneva Conventions wished to safeguard the dignity of the human person, in the profound conviction that imprescriptible and inviolable rights are attached to it [*sic*] even when hostilities are at their height.
>
> At the outset, however, the treatment which belligerents were required to accord to persons referred to in the Convention was not presented, nor indeed clearly conceived, as constituting a body of 'rights' to which they were automatically entitled ... It was not ... until the Conventions of 1949 (in particular [the non-renunciation and savings clauses]) that the existence of 'rights' conferred on [protected persons] was affirmed.[49]

In explaining the 'nature of the rights conferred upon protected persons', the Commentaries suggest that the language of the savings provision which was contained in the draft prepared by the ICRC was influenced by the 'theoretical trends which also resulted in the Universal Declaration of Human Rights'.[50] The ICRC Commentaries also suggest that the Geneva Conventions provided mechanisms for individuals to enforce their rights. In this respect, the Commentaries referred to the obligations incumbent on all states parties to punish breaches of the conventions, to the role of the Protecting Power, and to the possibility of protected persons appealing to the Protecting Power or to the ICRC under Geneva Convention III.[51] The Commentaries conclude:

[47] J. Pictet (ed.), *Commentary of the Geneva Conventions of 12 August 1949*, vol. I, *Geneva Convention I for the Amelioration of the Condition of the Wounded and Sick in Armed Forces in the Field* (Geneva, ICRC, 1952) (hereinafter *ICRC Commentary to Geneva Convention I*), p. 82; J. Pictet (ed.), *Commentary of the Geneva Conventions of 12 August 1949*, vol. II, *Geneva Convention II for the Amelioration of the Condition of Wounded, Sick and Shipwrecked Armed Forces at Sea* (Geneva, ICRC, 1960) (hereinafter *ICRC Commentary to Geneva Convention II*), p. 59; *ICRC Commentary to Geneva Convention III*, p. 91; *ICRC Commentary to Geneva Convention IV*, p. 77.

[48] *ICRC Commentary to Geneva Convention I*, p. 74; *ICRC Commentary to Geneva Convention II*, p. 52; *ICRC Commentary to Geneva Convention III*, p. 85; *ICRC Commentary to Geneva Convention IV*, p. 70.

[49] *ICRC Commentary to Geneva Convention III*, pp. 90–1.

[50] *ICRC Commentary to Geneva Convention I*, pp. 77–8.

[51] *ICRC Commentary to Geneva Convention IV*, pp. 78–9; *ICRC Commentary to Geneva Convention III*, pp. 91–2; *ICRC Commentary to Geneva Convention II*, pp. 58–9; *ICRC Commentary to Geneva Convention I*, pp. 83–4.

Undoubtedly, owing to the still undeveloped character of international law, the safeguards protecting the rights conferred on persons to whom the Convention relates are by no means as complete, effective or automatic as those of national legislation. Nevertheless, [the non-renunciation provision] is of the greatest assistance to all protected persons. It allows them to claim the protection of the Convention, not as a favour, but as a right, and in case of violation, it enables them to employ any procedure available, however rudimentary, to demand respect for the Convention's terms.[52]

While the ICRC's Commentaries are not apt to be dismissed lightly, the claim that the Geneva Conventions 'affirmed' the existence of individual rights in respect of all of the safeguards afforded to protected persons finds little support in the text of the Conventions themselves. It has already been noted that apart from the common savings and non-renunciation clauses, only the third and fourth Geneva Conventions use the language of 'rights' and that even these references to rights are not definitively international law rights, rather than rights which are to be created and conferred by domestic law. It is equally arguable that the conventions prescribe standards of treatment rather than individual rights.[53] Moreover, an interpretation of the conventions as establishing standards of treatment and protective obligations for states is easier to reconcile with the content of the non-renunciation and savings clauses, which by their terms prohibit both states and individuals from waiving the standards prescribed by the conventions; moreover, it is consistent with a normative (not to say factual) framework in which individuals have no meaningful capacity to exercise their 'rights'.

The only Geneva Convention which refers to obligations for individuals is Geneva Convention III Relative to Prisoners of War. Article 17 provides that when questioned on the subject, a prisoner of war 'is bound to give only' certain information, and that wilful infringement of this rule may render the prisoner 'liable to the restriction of the privileges accorded to his rank and status'. Similar language is used in Article 21, which expresses that prisoners of war who are paroled 'are bound on their personal honour' to fulfil the engagements of their paroles or promises. Article 39 provides that 'Prisoners of war, with the exception of officers, must salute and show ... the external marks of respect' to the camp

[52] *ICRC Commentary to Geneva Convention IV*, p. 79; very similar wording is found in *ICRC Commentary to Geneva Convention III*, p. 92; *ICRC Commentary to Geneva Convention II*, p. 59; and *ICRC Commentary to Geneva Convention I*, p. 84.

[53] See generally, F. Hampson, 'Human Rights Law and Humanitarian Law: Two Coins or Two Sides of the Same Coin?' (1991) 1 *Bull. Hum. Rts* 46, 49.

commander and officers of a higher rank of the detaining power. These are the only provisions of the Geneva Conventions which use language indicative of obligations of individuals; like the oblique references to 'rights' they do not conclusively indicate that these obligations are imposed directly under international law; they may equally be interpreted as establishing standards of treatment of individuals by states.

More generally, the third Geneva Convention states that prisoners of war 'shall be subject to' the laws in force in the armed forces of the detaining power[54] and refers to punishments which may be imposed under penal or disciplinary proceedings.[55] In this way, the convention provides for the application of domestic laws to individuals, since individuals may be subject to and punished for violations of the law of the detaining power. Therefore, this provision does not have the effect of conferring substantive obligations on individuals directly under international law. Similar language is used in the provisions dealing with the application of laws to protected persons in occupied territory[56] and internees[57] in the fourth Geneva Convention.

In principle, the question of individual criminal responsibility is addressed in Chapter 4. However, some comments relating to the grave breaches regime established by the Geneva Conventions are necessary here. The grave breaches provisions do not expressly refer to individual obligations. Each of the conventions imposes two specific obligations on states with respect to grave breaches: 'to enact any legislation necessary to provide effective penal sanctions for persons committing, or ordering to be committed' grave breaches; and to search for such persons and to bring them before its own courts or to extradite such persons.[58] There is no express statement in the conventions which imposes a direct obligation on individuals not to commit grave breaches. In these circumstances, it seems clear that the conventions themselves do not impose direct obligations on individuals not to commit grave breaches. The only positive obligations referred to in these provisions establishing the grave breaches regime are obligations on states. Rather than a system of individual obligations, the grave breaches regime is better characterised as a regime of mandatory

[54] Geneva Convention III, Art. 82. [55] Geneva Convention III, Arts. 82–108.
[56] Geneva Convention IV, Arts. 64–78. [57] *Ibid.* Arts. 117–26.
[58] Geneva Convention I, Art. 49; Geneva Convention II, Art. 50; Geneva Convention III, Art. 129; Geneva Convention IV, Art. 147. Each of the Geneva Conventions defined grave breaches separately: see Geneva Convention I, Art. 50; Geneva Convention II, Art. 51; Geneva Convention III, Art. 130; and Geneva Convention IV, Art. 147.

universal jurisdiction in international armed conflict for which individual obligations would be imposed through domestic processes and law, including military law. This is confirmed by the statement of the Appeals Chamber of the International Criminal Tribunal for the former Yugoslavia (ICTY) in *Tadić*, as follows:

> The grave breaches of the Geneva Conventions established a twofold system: there is on the one hand an enumeration of offences that are regarded [as] so serious as to constitute 'grave breaches'; closely bound up with this enumeration a mandatory enforcement mechanism is set up, based on the concept of a duty and a right of all Contracting States to search for and try or extradite persons allegedly responsible for 'grave breaches'. The international armed conflict element generally attributed to the grave breaches provisions of the Geneva Conventions is merely a function of the system of universal mandatory jurisdiction that those provisions create. The international armed conflict requirement was a necessary limitation on the grave breaches system in light of the intrusion on State sovereignty that such mandatory universal jurisdiction represents. State parties to the 1949 Geneva Conventions did not want to give other States jurisdiction over serious violations of international humanitarian law committed in their internal armed conflicts - at least not the mandatory universal jurisdiction involved in the grave breaches system.[59]

(ii) Additional Protocol I of 1977

The first Additional Protocol of 1977 supplemented the obligations of states parties relating to the protection of victims of international armed conflict. Like the majority of the provisions of the Geneva Conventions, the provisions of Protocol I are expressed in terms which suggest the imposition of obligations upon states rather than the grant of direct rights to individuals. Article 1 includes an undertaking by states parties 'to respect and to ensure respect' for the Protocol. Additionally, in the execution provisions the Protocol requires that states parties 'take all necessary measures for the execution of their obligations under the Conventions and this Protocol'.[60] The provisions which relate to protection of individuals are either expressed as obligations on states parties[61] or as benefits to the relevant persons without

59 *Prosecutor* v. *Tadić*, Case no. IT-94-1-AR72, Appeal on Jurisdiction, Judgment, 2 October 1995, (1996) 35 ILM 32, para. 80.

60 Protocol I Additional to the Geneva Conventions of 12 August 1949 and Relating to the Protection of Victims of International Armed Conflicts, 8 June 1977 (entry into force 7 December 1978), 1125 UNTS 3 (hereinafter 'Additional Protocol I'), Art. 80(1).

61 For example, *ibid.* Art. 74: 'The High Contracting Parties and the Parties to the conflict shall facilitate . . .'.

express reference to the conferral of direct rights.[62] The only specific reference to a 'right' for individuals is found in Article 43, which specifies that members of the armed forces of a party to the conflict 'have the right to participate directly in hostilities'.[63] Thus, the only 'right' expressly provided for in the Protocol relates not to the protection of victims of war, but rather to the right of armed forces to participate in armed conflict! In contrast to the Geneva Conventions, Protocol I does not include a savings or non-renunciation clause. The absence of these provisions explains why the ICRC Commentary to Protocol I is silent as to whether individuals are the subjects of direct rights.[64]

In terms of individual responsibility, Additional Protocol I added various violations to the grave breaches regime established by the Geneva Convention and specified that these grave breaches were to be regarded as war crimes.[65] Like the conventions, the Protocol does not contain a provision expressly imposing obligations not to commit grave breaches. However, the Protocol includes a provision entitled 'Duty of commanders' which provides that high contracting parties 'shall require military commanders' to suppress and report breaches of the conventions and this Protocol and that the parties 'shall require that ... commanders ensure that members of the armed forces under their command are aware of their obligations under the Conventions and this Protocol'; and 'shall require any commander ... to initiate such steps as are necessary to prevent such violations'.[66] The language used in respect of commanders indicates that the obligation is on the (state) party to require its commanders to do certain acts, but this provision does refer to 'their obligations under the Conventions and this Protocol' in respect of members of the armed forces. It implies that members of the armed forces bear obligations under the conventions and the Protocol. But like the conventions, the Protocol fails to refer expressly to the imposition of any obligations on individuals.

[62] For example, *ibid.* Art. 75(1) provides that the relevant persons 'shall be treated humanely in all circumstances and shall enjoy, as a minimum, the protection provided by this Article without any adverse discrimination'; Art. 15(1) provides that 'Civilian medical personnel shall be respected and protected'.

[63] *Ibid.* Art. 43(2). See also Art. 46 which provides that persons engaged in espionage 'shall not have the right of the status of prisoner of war'.

[64] There is no discussion of the point in the Commentary: see Y. Sandoz, C. Swinarski and B. Zimmermann (eds.), *Commentary on the Protocol Additional to the Geneva Conventions of 12 August 1949, and Relating to the Protection of Victims of International Armed Conflicts* (Geneva, ICRC/Martinus Nijhoff, 1987).

[65] Additional Protocol I, Art. 85.

[66] *Ibid.* Art. 87.

(iii) Customary international humanitarian law

In addition to treaty law applicable in international armed conflict, some rules have acquired the status of customary international law.[67] The ICRC Customary Law Study asserts the customary status of certain general principles relating to the treatment of individuals, drawing upon the provisions of the Geneva Conventions and Protocol I, and on an extensive study of state practice.[68] These principles are expressed in language which refers to obligations for 'parties to the conflict'[69] or which refers to a standard of treatment applicable to individuals without direct reference to the conferral of rights.[70] The Customary Law Study does not express a position on the question whether customary international humanitarian law confers direct rights on individuals, but the way in which rules are expressed is consistent with the majority of the provisions of the Geneva Conventions and the Additional Protocol, which refer to obligations for states.

The Customary Law Study did not include any analysis of the Martens clause[71] nor did it pay attention to the possibility that the Martens clause suggests a less formalistic approach to the assessment of custom, at least in respect of 'principles of humanity and dictates of public conscience'.[72] In substance, the Martens clause (which was restated in the 1949 Geneva Conventions and the 1977 Additional Protocols in a modified form)[73] does not suggest a separate or different normative framework but it does confirm that the protection of individuals is at least one goal of humanitarian law. The ICJ has affirmed that the Martens clause itself reflects a rule of customary law.[74]

[67] The ICJ noted that all states were bound by the rules of Additional Protocol I which were the expression of customary international law: *Nuclear Weapons*, Advisory Opinion [1996] ICJ Rep. 226, 260 (para. 87).

[68] J. M. Henckaerts and L. Doswald-Beck, *International Committee of the Red Cross: Customary International Humanitarian Law*, vol. I, *Rules* (Cambridge, Cambridge University Press, 2005) (hereinafter *ICRC Customary Law Study*), see e.g., Rules 89–105, 109–11.

[69] For example, *ibid.* Rules 109–11.

[70] For example, *ibid.* Rule 87 states: 'Civilians and persons *hors de combat* must be treated humanely'; Rule 90 states: 'Torture, cruel or inhumane treatment . . . are prohibited.'

[71] *Ibid.* Introduction, p. xxx.

[72] E. Wilmshurst, 'Conclusions' in E. Wilmshurst and S. Breau (eds.), *Perspectives on the ICRC Study on Customary International Humanitarian Law* (Cambridge, Cambridge University Press, 2007), pp. 401, 402.

[73] Geneva Convention I, Art. 63; Geneva Convention II, Art. 62; Geneva Convention III, Art. 142; Geneva Convention IV, Art. 158; Additional Protocol I, Art. 1(2); Additional Protocol II, Preamble, para. 4.

[74] *Nuclear Weapons*, Advisory Opinion [1996] ICJ Rep. 226, 249 (para. 84).

The expression of customary international humanitarian law as inter-state obligations and standards of treatment for individuals rather than individual rights is consistent with the decisions of the Eritrea-Ethiopia Claims Commission. The Claims Commission was established by treaty, with jurisdiction to determine claims for loss, damage or injury related to the conflict and resulting 'from violations of international humanitarian law ... or other violations of international law'.[75] The claims were brought on an inter-state basis for losses to each state as well as to their nationals. Eritrea acceded to the Geneva Conventions from 14 August 2000; hence the conventions were not applicable from the outbreak of the conflict in May 1998 to 14 August 2000. In the circumstances, the Commission held that the applicable law for events prior to 14 August 2000 was customary international law.[76] The Commission issued awards in relation to the treatment of prisoners of war, the treatment of civilians and the conduct of the conflict and held repeatedly that provisions of the Geneva Conventions and Additional Protocol I had acquired the status of customary international law obligations.[77] The Commission treated these obligations as state obligations to accord certain standards of treatment, rather than individual rights.[78]

[75] Agreement between the Government of the Federal Democratic Republic of Ethiopia and the Government of the State of Eritrea, Art. 5, Algiers, Algeria, 12 December 2000, available at www.pca-cpa.org/upload/files/Algiers%20Agreement.pdf.

[76] *Prisoners of War, Ethiopia's Claim 4*, The Hague, Partial Award, 1 July 2003, paras. 24–9; *Prisoners of War, Eritrea's Claim 17*, The Hague, Partial Award, 1 July 2003, paras. 33–41; *Civilians Claims, Eritrea's Claims 15, 16, 23 and 27–32*, The Hague, Partial Award, 17 December 2004, paras. 28–31; *Civilians Claims, Ethiopia's Claim 5*, The Hague, Partial Award, 17 December 2004, para. 23; *Central Front, Ethiopia's Claim 2*, The Hague, Partial Award, 28 April 2004, para. 15; *Central Front, Eritrea's Claims 2, 4, 6, 7, 8 and 22*, The Hague, Partial Award, 28 April 2004, para. 21 (all available at www.pca-cpa.org/showpage.asp?pag_id=1151).

[77] *Prisoners of War, Ethiopia's Claim 4*, The Hague, Partial Award, 1 July 2003, paras. 32, 53–4, 61; *Prisoners of War, Eritrea's Claim 17*, The Hague, Partial Award, 1 July 2003, paras. 33–41; *Civilians Claims, Eritrea's Claims 15, 16, 23 and 27–32*, The Hague, Partial Award, 17 December 2004, paras. 28–31; *Civilians Claims, Ethiopia's Claim 5*, The Hague, Partial Award, 17 December 2004, paras. 23–25; *Central Front, Ethiopia's Claim 2*, The Hague, Partial Award, 28 April 2004, paras. 17–18; *Central Front, Eritrea's Claims 2, 4, 6, 7, 8 and 22*, The Hague, Partial Award, 28 April 2004, paras. 21–3 (all available at www.pca-cpa.org/showpage.asp?pag_id=1151).

[78] See e.g., *Prisoners of War, Ethiopia's Claim 4*, The Hague, Partial Award, 1 July 2003, paras. 68, 70, 74; *Prisoners of War, Eritrea's Claim 17*, The Hague, Partial Award, 1 July 2003, paras. 64–5, 73, 87–8; *Civilians Claims, Ethiopia's Claim 5*, The Hague, Partial Award, 17 December 2004, para. 52; *Central Front, Ethiopia's Claim 2*, The Hague, Partial Award, 28 April 2004, para. 35; *Central Front, Eritrea's Claims 2, 4, 6, 7, 8 and 22*, The Hague, Partial Award, 28 April 2004, para. 37 (all available at www.pca-cpa.org/showpage.asp?pag_id=1151).

In respect of individual responsibility, the ICRC Study suggests that '[i]ndividuals are criminally responsible for war crimes they commit'[79] and asserts that the principle of command responsibility is also customary law.[80] It defines war crimes as '[s]erious violations of international humanitarian law'.[81] As mentioned above, the development of individual criminal responsibility is dealt with in Chapter 4.

(iv) International human rights law applicable in international armed conflict

International human rights law may also be applicable in armed conflict. The question of the applicability of international human rights law in international armed conflict was raised by the 1968 International Conference on Human Rights in Tehran. The first resolution of the Conference called on Israel to apply the Universal Declaration and the Geneva Conventions in the occupied territories.[82] A further resolution entitled 'Respect for human rights in armed conflict' referred to 'humanitarian principles' in armed conflicts.[83] Subsequently, the General Assembly affirmed that '[f]undamental human rights, as accepted in international law and laid down in international instruments, continue to apply fully in situations of armed conflict'.[84] In 1996, the ICJ stated in its *Nuclear Weapons* Advisory Opinion that human rights obligations '[do] not cease in times of war' except where there is a valid derogation in times of national emergency.[85] In the *Wall* Opinion in 2004, the Court reiterated the principle expressed in *Nuclear Weapons*, concluding that Israel's human rights obligations applied in the occupied territories.[86] In *DRC* v. *Uganda* in 2005, the ICJ held that the conduct of Ugandan forces during its occupation of Congolese territory

79 *ICRC Customary Law Study*, Rule 151. 80 *Ibid.* Rule 152.

81 *Ibid.* Rule 156. It has been suggested that the term 'serious violations' would include but not be limited to grave breaches of the Geneva Conventions and Additional Protocol I: see e.g., Charles Garraway, 'War Crimes' in E. Wilmshurst and S. Breau (eds.), *Perspectives on the ICRC Study on Customary International Humanitarian Law* (Cambridge, Cambridge University Press, 2007), p. 385.

82 *Final Act of the International Conference on Human Rights, 22 April–13 May 1968*, UN Doc. A/Conf.32/41 (12 May 1968).

83 *Ibid.*

84 UN GAOR, 29th Sess., Supp. No. 31. See also GA/Res/2444 (1968), 19 December 1968, at pp. 50–1; and the Secretary-General's two reports entitled *Respect for Human Rights in Armed Conflict*, UN Doc. A/7720 (1969); UN Doc. A/8052 (1970).

85 *Nuclear Weapons*, Advisory Opinion [1996] ICJ Rep. 226, 240 (para. 25).

86 *Legal Consequences of the Construction of a Wall in the Occupied Palestinian Territory*, Advisory Opinion [2004] ICJ Rep. 36, paras. 134, 137.

constituted violations of Uganda's human rights and humanitarian law obligations.[87] That human rights obligations continue to apply in armed conflict has been affirmed by the Human Rights Committee,[88] the European Court of Human Rights[89] and the Inter-American Commission of Human Rights.[90]

The relationship between international humanitarian law and international human rights law has generally been considered through the interpretative maxim of *lex specialis derogate legi generali*[91] – that international humanitarian law constitutes a regime more tailored to a particular context, and therefore it takes precedence over generally applicable law, in the form of international human rights law.[92] In its *Nuclear Weapons* Advisory Opinion, the ICJ noted that, except to the extent permitted by lawful derogation, international human rights standard remained applicable in armed conflict, but that 'the test of what is an arbitrary deprivation of life ... falls to be determined by the applicable *lex specialis*'.[93] In the *Wall* Opinion, the ICJ affirmed that humanitarian law constituted *lex specialis*:

> As regards the relationship between international humanitarian law and human rights law, there are thus three possible situations: some rights may be exclusively matters of international humanitarian law; others may be exclusively matters of human rights law; yet others may be matters of both those branches of international law. In order to answer the question put to it, the Court will have to take into consideration both these branches of international

[87] *Armed Activities on the Territory of the Congo (Democratic Republic of the Congo* v. *Uganda)* [2005] ICJ Rep. 2005 116, paras. 219, 345.

[88] Human Rights Committee, General Comment No. 31, *The Nature of the General Legal Obligation Imposed on State Parties to the Covenant*, CCPR/C/74/CRP.4/Rev.6 (29 March 2004); see also Human Rights Committee, *Concluding Observations, Norway*, CCPR/C/NOR/CO/5 (26 April 2006).

[89] *Banković and others* v. *Belgium and others*, Admissibility, Application no. 52207/99, ECtHR, 19 December 2001; *Cyprus* v. *Turkey*, Application no. 25781/94, ECtHR, 10 May 2001.

[90] *Salas* v. *United States*, Inter-American Commission on Human Rights, 14 October 1993, 123 ILR 117; *Coard and others* v. *United States*, Inter-American Commission on Human Rights, 29 September 1999, 123 ILR 156.

[91] See generally, ILC, *Fragmentation of International Law: Difficulties Arising from the Diversification and Expansion of International Law*, Report of the Study Group of the International Law Commission, A/CN.4/L.682 (13 April 2006), pp. 34–65 (hereinafter *ILC Report on Fragmentation*).

[92] A. Aust, *Modern Treaty Law and Practice* (Cambridge, Cambridge University Press, 2000), pp. 200–1.

[93] *Nuclear Weapons*, Advisory Opinion [1996] ICJ Rep. 226, 240 (para. 25).

law, namely human rights law and, as *lex specialis*, international humanitarian law.[94]

The ICJ's approach does not suggest that humanitarian law obligations will necessarily take precedence over human rights obligations, and neither should they. The relationship between the two bodies of law requires a rather more nuanced approach and depends upon the particular context. While during an active armed conflict humanitarian law is likely to constitute the *lex specialis*, in other situations in which the rules of humanitarian law apply, it is possible that human rights standards will be better tailored to the specific context. Human rights law might therefore constitute the more specialised regime in a particular context. The most obvious example is that of military occupation, where issues of maintaining security, public order and law enforcement will be better addressed by human rights law than by humanitarian law.[95]

An aspect of the relationship between humanitarian law and human rights law which has received less attention is the question of conflict between two distinct normative or conceptual frameworks.[96] The normative framework of international humanitarian law applicable in armed conflict presents as one which imposes obligations on states to accord standards of treatment to individuals, but does not confer direct corresponding rights on individuals. In contrast, the normative framework of international human rights law imposes obligations on states and correlative rights on individuals, those rights being direct international law rights.[97] So there is a conceptual problematic where a human rights court, for example, uses international humanitarian law to interpret human rights law where it amounts to that court converting the benefit individuals might derive from a state's humanitarian law obligations into individual rights.[98] There is also a difficulty where an individual human right, such as the right to life, is curtailed in

[94] *Legal Consequences of the Construction of a Wall in the Occupied Palestinian Territory*, Advisory Opinion [2004] ICJ Rep. 178, para. 106.

[95] C. McCarthy, 'Legal Reasoning and the Applicability of International Human Rights Standards during Military Occupation' in N. Quenivet and R. Arnold (eds.), *International Humanitarian Law and Human Rights Law: Towards a New Merger in International Law* (Leiden, Martinus Nijhoff, 2008), p. 121.

[96] This question was flagged in the *ILC Report on Fragmentation* but did not receive attention outside of the treatment of self-contained regimes: see *ibid.* p. 31 (para. 48).

[97] See discussion in Chapter 5 (particularly 5.4(f) below).

[98] C. McCarthy, 'Human Rights and the Laws of War under the American Convention on Human Rights' (2008) *EHRLR* 762, 779.

humanitarian law by a state's right to kill in circumstances of necessity.[99] It is not a question of normative conflict between two individual rights: the human right to life and a humanitarian law right not to be killed in certain circumstances; rather, it is a conflict between an individual right and a state liberty or right to kill in certain circumstances (or an individual entitlement to treatment), the latter operating to limit the former. Where there is only a curtailment of a human right, it is possible to conceptualise the humanitarian law rights of states as having a limiting effect on an individual right, but in circumstances where an individual human right is replaced wholesale by a state obligation of treatment, there is a more obvious conflict between normative frameworks and the position of the individual as right-bearer might be relegated to an entitlement to treatment. This question has received little attention, probably because there are few aspects of humanitarian law which are directly justiciable by individuals, but the increasing willingness of human rights courts to determine the content of individual human rights by reference to state's obligations in humanitarian law risks supplanting the normative framework of humanitarian law as one of entitlement to treatment and replacing it with an individual rights framework, or at least misinterpreting the normative framework applicable to benefits derived from humanitarian law.

It has been suggested that human rights has influenced the development of humanitarian law: for example, Article 75 of Additional Protocol I resembles Article 14 of the ICCPR; and undoubtedly there has been some cross-pollination. But even where the influence of human rights on the substantive humanitarian law standards is discernible, international humanitarian law continues to use the language of treatment, not rights. The application of human rights law to situations of armed conflict has not had a transformative effect on the way in which humanitarian law structurally engages with individuals.

3.3 The individual in internal armed conflict

As mentioned above, it is desirable to consider international law in international armed conflict and internal armed conflict separately

[99] The ICRC has recently argued that a permissible attack against a person not entitled to protection 'must not exceed what is actually necessary to accomplish a legitimate military purpose in the prevailing circumstances': see ICRC, *Interpretive Guidance on the Notion of Direct Participation in Hostilities under International Humanitarian Law* (Geneva, ICRC, 2009), p. 77 (Rule IX).

because of their separate and distinct historical origins. It is also useful to consider the position of the individual in internal armed conflict separately because an interesting juridical question arises in this context which does not appear in a conflict between states. Since one or more parties to internal conflict will be a non-state actor, international law applicable in internal conflict must engage with non-state actors (either as individuals or in some group formation) to regulate the conduct of both parties to the conflict.

Whether the law applicable in internal armed conflict interacts directly with individuals who form part of insurgent or armed groups, or whether it engages with a separate legal and juridical entity constituted by the group as such is an open question. There are at least four possible constructions of the extension of the rules of humanitarian law to rebels, insurgents or armed opposition groups. First, the group may have separate and distinct legal personality as an artifice (in the same way that a state is conceived as having legal personality distinct from its nationals) and the group itself may acquire rights and obligations separately from its members. On this construction the development of the law would hold little interest for the question of the position of the individual, since it would only indirectly engage with individuals (in the same way that the laws governing the conduct of international armed conflict might engage with members of a state's armed forces). This first construction, which presupposes that there is a category of international legal persons constituted by armed opposition groups which meet certain threshold requirements, is supported by recent literature which argues in favour of recognising a separate and distinct entity constituted by the group.[100] A second possible construction is that the group itself may have no separate and distinct legal personality; rather, rights and obligations would be directly acquired by the individuals who constitute the group. If this were the position, the development of the law would be of central interest to the position of the individual, as the law would directly engage with individuals. A third possibility is that there is no clear conceptual division between an insurgent or rebel group and its members; in that case, the development of the law is of interest to the position of the individual since members of a group will in practice be treated as though they are engaged directly. Fourth,

[100] For example, L. Zegfeld, *Accountability of Armed Opposition Groups in International Law* (Cambridge, Cambridge University Press, 2002); L. Moir, *The Law of Internal Armed Conflict* (Cambridge, Cambridge University Press, 2002); S. Sivakumaran, 'Binding Armed Opposition Groups' (2006) 55 *ICLQ* 369.

even if armed opposition groups have now acquired separate legal status, this may not have always been the case; instead, some of the early developments might have imposed obligations and conferred rights on the constituent individual members of a group or as a collective of individuals without ascribing the group as such separate legal personality. Bearing in mind these possible constructions of the structural engagement of the law applicable in internal armed conflict with non-state groups and individuals, the remainder of this part examines the development of that law from the nineteenth century through to the present day.

(a) Regulation of civil war pre-1914

Towards the end of the eighteenth century Vattel urged that the laws of war be observed in 'civil wars'. Wolff distinguished a rebellion from civil war properly speaking on the basis that the latter was a justified struggle against an oppressive sovereign. Elaborating on Wolff's work, Vattel developed the category of 'true civil war', where rebellious subjects reject the right of the ruler to govern them and their goal is to supplant the sovereign or to secede. He described this as a 'public war between two different Nations'.[101] Vattel argued that in the case of true civil war, the laws of war ought to apply, on the basis that it 'breaks the bonds of society and government . . .; it gives rise, within the Nation, to two independent parties'. It was therefore necessary to regard the two parties as forming at least two distinct nations 'which enter into a dispute and, being unable to agree, have recourse to arms'. In such circumstances, the established laws of war should be observed by both sides in a civil war, for the same reason they ought to apply in a conflict between two nations.[102] Vattel's approach was not to accord rights and duties to individuals within a state, but rather to treat an internal conflict as an inter-state conflict.

In practice, civil conflict caused problems for naval states when either or both of the lawful government and the insurgents claimed belligerent rights at sea; of the most powerful naval states, the practice of the United States and Britain had the greatest impact on the development of doctrine. In response to the practical difficulties raised by the assertion of belligerent rights, naval states began to recognise belligerent rights in civil conflict. From the late eighteenth century to the early nineteenth century, recognition of belligerent rights was linked to recognition of independence. This was most commonly implied from the invocation of the law of

[101] de Vattel, *The Law of Nations*, bk III, ch. XVIII, paras. 292, 295 (pp. 644–5, 647–8).
[102] *Ibid.* bk III, ch. XVIII, paras. 293–4 (pp. 645–6).

neutrality (under which a third state was obliged not to interfere in a conflict between states) but there are also examples of express recognition of particular belligerent rights. During the American independence conflict (1775–83), Britain invoked its law of neutrality in cautioning third states against providing aid to the insurgents;[103] this invocation of the law of neutrality had the effect of designating the enemy as a separate state.[104] Britain expressly recognised the right of the parties in the Spanish American independence conflict (1814–25) 'to exercise the ordinary privileges of War in maritime capture':[105] in 1823, Foreign Secretary Canning justified Britain's recognition of belligerent rights on the basis that it was necessary 'to treat the colonies as actually independent of Spain' since the law of nations 'was entirely silent' as to the course to be taken in such circumstances.[106] In both of these cases, the insurgent rebels were assimilated to states in order to justify the conferral of belligerent rights.

Subsequently, recognition of belligerency was detached from recognition of independence or statehood. In its treatment of the Greek rebellion against Turkey (1821–25), the British government claimed that the law of nations required it to recognise the free exercise of belligerent rights to Greek subjects of Turkey, separately from any obligation to recognise Greece as an independent state.[107] Britain took

[103] 17 Geo. 3 c. 9.

[104] The fact that recognition of statehood was considered to be the basis of the acquisition of rights of belligerents in this early practice is also seen from an arbitration between the US and Chile concerning the application of neutrality: see *The Macedonian* report in J. B. Moore, *History and Digest of the International Arbitrations to which the United States has been a Party* (Washington, DC, Government Printing Office, 1898), vol. II, p. 1449 *et seq.* See discussion in A. McNair, 'The Law Relating to the Civil War in Spain' (1937) 53 *LQR* 471, 479. The recognition of belligerent rights and obligations was affirmed by a further statute in 1777, which set out a British policy to detain US privateers captured on the high seas 'in safe custody': J. B. Moore, *A Digest of International Law* (Washington, DC, Government Printing Office, 1906), vol. II, p. 1076, citing 31 Pickering's Statutes 312.

[105] Robinson, Opinion of 14 September 1822, reproduced in H. A. Smith (ed.), *Great Britain and the Law of Nations*, vol. I, *States* (London, P. S. King & Son Ltd, 1932), p. 279.

[106] George Canning, *The Speeches of the Right Honourable George Canning with a Memoir of his Life* (2nd edn, R. Therry (ed.), London, J. Ridgway, 1830), vol. V, p. 40; see also p. 43. See also generally, R. Oglesby, *Internal War and the Search for Normative Order* (The Hague, Martinus Nijhoff, 1971), pp. 72–83.

[107] Dispatch from Canning to Wellesley at Vienna, 31 December 1824, reproduced in Smith, *Great Britain and the Law of Nations*, vol. I, *States*, pp. 294–7, esp. 295. See discussion in H. Lauterpacht, *Recognition in International Law* (Cambridge, Cambridge University Press, 1947), pp. 178–9, also p. 188. See also Opinion of Stephen Lushington, Doctors' Commons, 29 May 1823, reproduced in Smith, *Great Britain and the Law of Nations*, vol. I, *States*, pp. 291–3; Opinion of Stephen Lushington, Doctors' Commons, 26 June 1823, reproduced in *ibid.* pp. 293–4.

the same position in relation to the Portuguese rebellion (1820–34): the King's Advocate advised that although Britain 'may not be at present prepared to admit the right of [Don Miguel] to the title of king', it could not 'refuse to acknowledge the validity of a Blockade, declared by him ... without departing from that system of neutrality to which it has expressed its determination strictly to adhere, between the contending Parties in Portugal'.[108] In accordance with this opinion, the British government recognised that Don Miguel was entitled to belligerent rights.[109] Thus, the practice suggested that entities not assimilated to states could be the subject of belligerent rights.

Britain took the same approach to the American Civil War (1861–5). When news of Lincoln's blockade of insurgent ports reached Britain, naval commanders were immediately instructed that 'a state of actual War' existed and that both parties were entitled to exercise belligerent rights within the limits of international law.[110] Initially, the US objected to Britain's recognition of belligerent rights for Confederate states on the basis that 'a concession of belligerent rights' by Great Britain to the Confederate states would 'be liable to be construed' as recognition of their independence.[111] Although the US Congress recognised the conflict as a 'civil war', it refused to admit the full attribute of belligerent rights for the Confederates:[112] it treated captured insurgents in land

108 Opinion of Herbert Jenner, 13 August 1828, reproduced in Smith, *Great Britain and the Law of Nations*, vol. I, *States*, p. 299; see also A. McNair, *International Law Opinions: Selected and Annotated* (Cambridge, Cambridge University Press, 1956), vol. II, pp. 376–7.

109 Notification of the British government, Foreign Office, 13 August 1828, Notifications respecting the Blockade of Funchal, in Madeira, by a Portuguese Naval Force, July to September 1828, (1827–8) XV BFSP 1093.

110 FO 97/47 and 83/221, cited in Smith, *Great Britain and the Law of Nations*, vol. I, *States*, p. 302. See also Proclamation of Neutrality in Contest between United States and Confederate States, 13 May 1861, (1860–1) 51 BFSP 165. Lauterpacht suggests that in declaring its neutrality the British government may have considered the proclamation by the lawful government of a blockade *jure gentium* as a recognition by that government of a state of belligerency: see Lauterpacht, *Recognition in International Law*, p. 178. The instructions to naval commanders were in accordance with Foreign Office advice: Letter from Lord John Russell to Lord Lyons, Foreign Office, 6 May 1861, reproduced in McNair, *International Law Opinions*, vol. I, p. 138.

111 Seward's instructions to Adams, 21 May 1861, (1861) FRUS 87–90, reproduced in Moore, *A Digest of International Law*, vol. I, p. 184. This was also emphasised in instructions to the Minister of France of 30 May 1861: *ibid.* p. 185. Correspondence is published in 51 BFSP 173; 55 BFSP 723; 57 BFSP 1119; and 59 BFSP 21. The US position is elaborated in correspondence reproduced in (1861) FRUS 71–181.

112 The US Supreme Court held in 1862 that the proclamation of a blockade was sufficient to declare the existence of a war, without express recognition: see *Prize Cases* (1862) 2 Black 635, 17 L. 459, 477. That the US was under no legal obligation to apply the rules

warfare as prisoners of war, stating that this was done on the basis of humanitarian policy rather than legal obligation,[113] but did not extend that same treatment to forces captured at sea, who were prosecuted for piracy.[114] Britain's consistent position was that the US itself could not claim the rights of a belligerent (which it did on its first declaration of a blockade in April 1861) without at the same time conceding to all other states the rights of neutrals, and to its enemy the rights of belligerents.[115] The US argued that the mere assertion of belligerent rights did not necessitate recognition of belligerent rights for the insurgents; rather a broader range of matters ought to be considered: the extent of the territory, population and resources of the rebellion; the existence of its completely organised state and general governments; its unequivocal determination to treat any acts of authority by the lawful government as war; a long antecedent history and preparations for the rebellion; that there was little prospect of termination of the struggle; and the certainty of the magnitude and extent of the war.[116] After the war, the US sought to include claims relating to the 'premature recognition of the Confederate States as a belligerent Power' in the *Alabama Claims* arbitration.[117] Britain refused to included the question of recognition in the matters to be arbitrated, but in the course of argument the US referred to the British position as evidence of hostility;[118] the British case made a full statement of the facts which compelled it to recognise the Confederacy and cited historical precedents to justify its position.[119] The award of the tribunal made no reference to the dispute over

of war to rebels was reflected in Art. 152 of the Lieber Code: reproduced in D. Schindler and J. Toman (eds.), *The Laws of Armed Conflicts: A Collection of Conventions, Resolutions and Other Documents* (3rd edn, Dordrecht, Nijhoff, 1988), p. 3.

113 See *Fifield* v. *The Insurance Co. of the State of Pennsylvania*, 47 PA 166 (1864) and *Thornington* v. *Smith*, 75 US (8 Wall) 1 (1868). This was consistent with the Lieber Code, Arts. 152 and 153. See generally, Q. Wright, 'The American Civil War, 1861–1865' in R. A. Falk (ed.), *The International Law of Civil War* (Baltimore, Md, Johns Hopkins Press, 1971), p. 30.

114 See C. B. Swisher, *The Taney Period* (New York, Macmillan, 1974), pp. 866–76. There was judicial authority to the effect that the US government had a free choice whether to pursue force as a matter of sovereign right or of belligerent right: see *The Hiawatha*, 12 Fed. Cas. 95 (DC SD NY, 1861).

115 See Opinion of Atherton, Palmer and Phillimore, 16 September 1863, reproduced in McNair, *International Law Opinions*, vol. I, pp. 139–40, esp. 140.

116 Correspondence between Adams and Russell, cited in H. Wheaton, *Elements of International Law, 1866 Edition* (R. H. Dana (ed.), Oxford, Clarendon Press, 1936), para. 23, note 32.

117 A general account of the history of the Geneva arbitration is found in Moore, *International Arbitrations*, vol. I, pp. 496–682.

118 See *United States, Recognition of Belligerency*, *ibid.* pp. 562–3.

119 See *Britain, Proclamation of Neutrality*, *ibid.* p. 595.

recognition but it assumed that the *Alabama* and other vessels were duly commissioned ships of war, which could only be the case if the Confederate states possessed belligerent rights.[120]

After the American Civil War, the British practice was generally consistent: where the lawful government asserted belligerent rights, that assertion compelled recognition of belligerent rights for the insurgents without further inquiry;[121] in circumstances where the lawful government had not asserted belligerent rights, whether a state of war existed justifying recognition of belligerent rights was a matter to be determined by the foreign state in its discretion. In the latter cases, factors to be considered included whether the conflict was protracted; the number, order and discipline of the rebel forces; their subordination to a *de facto* government capable of maintaining relations with foreign states; and the actions taken by the lawful government.[122] In contrast, the US denied that the mere assertion of belligerent rights by the lawful government compelled recognition; rather, in each and every situation a state had discretion to recognise belligerent rights. Relevant factors in the exercise of that discretion included the extent of the conflict; the existence of a *de facto* insurgent government; the territory, population and resources of the rebellion; and whether there was any immediate prospect of termination of the struggle.[123] The US also encompassed a separate category of recognition of insurgency, which granted parties partial rights of belligerency in circumstances where some but not all of the criteria for recognition of belligerency were met. This was applied in respect of the insurrection in Cuba, on the basis that the insurrection

[120] Decision and Award is reproduced in *ibid.* p. 653.

[121] For example, response to Spanish proclamation of blockade of Dominican coast in 1864 ((1863–4) 54 BFSP 845; Report of 22 August 1864 by Palmer, Collier and Phillimore, reproduced in Smith, *Great Britain and the Law of Nations*, vol. I, *States*, pp. 313–19, esp. 314); the blockade announced by the Venezuelan Government in 1871 (Opinion of Travers Twiss, 28 June 1871, reproduced in Lauterpacht, *Recognition in International Law*, pp. 202–3, esp. 203); a proposed blockade of the ports of Northern Spain in 1874 (Telegram from Lord Granville to Mr Layard at Madrid, 13 February 1874, reproduced in Smith, *Great Britain and the Law of Nations*, vol. I, *States*, p. 321); and a blockade by the Haitian Government in 1876 (Opinion of John Holder, Hardinge S. Giffard, J. Parker Deane, 6 May 1876, reproduced in Lauterpacht, *Recognition in International Law*, pp. 210–11).

[122] Opinion of Karslake, Selwyn and Phillimore, 14 August 1867, reproduced in McNair, *International Law Opinions*, vol. I, pp. 143–5, esp. p. 144. A consistent approach is evidenced in the British treatment of the rebellious Kerais against Japan in 1868: see Lauterpacht, *Recognition in International Law*, p. 189.

[123] Correspondence between Adams and Russell, cited in Wheaton, *Elements of International Law*, para. 23, note 32.

did not possess the character and resources to constitute it as a state,[124] and in respect of the insurrection in Colombia in 1885.[125]

In the late nineteenth century, however, the British and US practice began to converge. This was evident in the treatment of the Brazilian rebellion of 1893, in which both the US and British governments refused to recognise belligerent rights for the rebels on the basis that they had not *de facto* established a government.[126] By 1900, the prevailing view in the literature was that if objective criteria for recognition of belligerency were met, then foreign states were permitted to recognise belligerency, but not compelled to do so; mere assertion of belligerent rights by either the lawful government or the insurgents did not compel recognition, nor was it sufficient to justify recognition.[127] This approach was approved in the civil war resolution adopted by the Institute of International Law in 1900.[128] The conditions by which

[124] President Grant, Special Message, 13 June 1870, reproduced in Moore, *A Digest of International Law*, vol. I, pp. 194–6, esp. pp. 194–5. He restated this position in President Grant, Seventh Annual Message, 7 December 1875, reproduced in *ibid.* pp. 196–8. In 1869, the President recognised a condition of insurrection; on that basis the US Supreme Court held the neutrality laws applicable: *The Three Friends* 166 US 1, 63 (1897).

[125] Letter of T. F. Bayard, Secretary of State to Garland, Attorney-General, 1 July 1885, reproduced in Moore, *A Digest of International Law*, vol. I, p. 200; F. Wharton, 'Insurgents as Belligerents' (1886) 33 *Albany Law Journal* 125, 126; *The Ambrose Light*, 25 Fed. Rep. 44.

[126] Moore, *A Digest of International Law*, vol. I, p. 202; Instructions to Mr Thompson, US Minister at Rio de Janeiro, 25 October 1893, (1893) FRUS 63, reproduced in Moore, *A Digest of International Law*, vol. I, p. 202; Letter from Mr Gresham, Secretary of State, to Messrs. Lanham and Kemp, 2 November 1893, reproduced in *ibid.* p. 203; Opinion of Russell and Rigby, 13 October 1893, reproduced in McNair, *International Law Opinions*, vol. II, p. 393. Agreeing in respect of blockades, see Gresham, Secretary of State, to Mr Thompson, Minister to Brazil, 11 January 1893, (1893) FRUS 99, reproduced in Moore, *A Digest of International Law*, vol. I, p. 204. The commanders of the German, British, French, Portuguese, American and Italian naval forces made a joint communication to the insurgent forces rejecting any asserted rights of belligerency: (1893) FRUS 95, reproduced in Moore, *A Digest of International Law*, vol. I, p. 203. In February 1894, the insurgents again requested recognition of their belligerency which was denied by the US on the grounds that they had no 'absolute control' of any state and 'their provisional government was not intact and was not improving either in its organization or effectiveness': see Cable from Mr Thompson to Mr Gresham, 5 February 1894, reproduced in Moore, *A Digest of International Law*, vol. I, p. 205.

[127] See W. E. Hall, *A Treatise on International Law* (3rd edn, Oxford, Clarendon Press, 1890), pp. 33–5; K. Bluntschli, *Le Droit International codifié* (M. C. Lardy (trans.), Paris, Guillaumin, 1870), pp. 272–2; L. Oppenheim, *International Law: A Treatise* (1st edn, London, Longmans, Green & Co., 1905), pp. 65–6, 86.

[128] Rights and Duties of Foreign States in Case of an Insurrection, Institute of International Law, Neuchâtel, 8 September 1900, original in (1900) XVIII *Annuaire de l'Institut de droit international* 227; English translation in Institute of International Law, *Resolutions of the Institute of International Law Dealing with the Law of Nations: With an*

recognition of belligerency could be granted by third states were set out in Article VIII as follows:

Third Powers cannot recognize the character of belligerent in a revolutionary party:

(1) If it has not acquired a distinct territorial existence through the possession of a definite portion of the national territory;
(2) If it has not the elements of a regular government exercising in fact the manifest rights of sovereignty over this portion of the territory;
(3) If the fight is not carried on in its name by organized troops, subject to military discipline and conforming to the laws and customs of war.[129]

In addition to convergence around a doctrine of recognition of belligerency, a doctrine of recognition of insurgency developed, stemming from the US practice. In these cases, full belligerent rights were not recognised, but certain more limited rights were acknowledged. The reasons for recognising insurgency rather than belligerency were that the conditions for full rights of belligerency were not fulfilled, or that recognition of belligerent status was undesirable for some other reason.[130] Recognition of insurgency was not the subject of specified conditions and did not have generally applicable consequences.[131] Legal rights and duties existed as between insurgents and foreign states only insofar as they were expressly conceded and agreed upon as matters of convenience, humanity or economic interest. The consequences ranged from a mere decision not to treat the insurgents as law-breakers to regular relations with insurgents as a *de facto* government within a portion of territory. It was possible that the concessions to the insurgents would be so comprehensive as to amount to *de facto* recognition of full belligerent rights, although if accompanied by an express refusal to

Historical Introduction and Explanatory Notes (J. B. Scott (ed.), New York, Oxford University Press, 1916).

[129] Institute of International Law, *Resolutions of the Institute of International Law*. The Resolution did not include a requirement that the recognising state's interests be affected to the extent to which a definition of its relationship to the insurgents is required, which would correlate to Dana's reference to the 'relations of the foreign state'. In practice this requirement was not emphasised, although Lauterpacht concedes that it is an additional condition for recognition of belligerency: See Lauterpacht, *Recognition in International Law*, p. 176. This is difficult to reconcile with a duty of recognition and the position that belligerency is a condition which arises from certain facts.

[130] See generally, E. Castrén, 'Recognition of Insurgency' (1965) *Indian Journal of International Law* 443; E. H. Riedel, 'Recognition of Insurgency' in R. Bernhardt, *Encyclopedia of Public International Law* (Amsterdam, Elsevier, 2000), p. 54.

[131] See discussion in Lauterpacht, *Recognition in International Law*, pp. 270–1.

recognise their belligerency, the relationship would be characterised as one of insurgency rather than belligerency.[132]

The practice of recognition of belligerency and insurgency bears out a marked uncertainty on the part of states as to what was actually occurring. Reflecting that uncertainty, there was a lack of consensus in the literature as to the implications in terms of international legal personality for rebel insurgents. In 1890, Hall suggested that the discretionary character of recognition of belligerency was a consequence of the absence of legal personality on the part of the insurgents:

> As a belligerent community is not itself a legal person, a society claiming only to be belligerent, and not to have permanently established its independence, it can have no rights under that law. It cannot, therefore, demand to be recognized upon legal grounds, and recognition, when it takes place, either on the part of the foreign government, or of that against which the revolt is directed, is from the legal point of view a concession of pure grace.[133]

The question whether there was a duty of recognition or whether recognition of belligerency was entirely within state discretion was never entirely resolved. However, once belligerent rights had been recognised, the belligerent community must have acquired a measure of international legal personality in consequence of bearing rights and obligations under international law.[134] It is not clear whether this was achieved through the conferral of rights and obligations on the belligerents as a group or collective, or whether it involved the recognition of individual rights and obligations. Either construction was possible and in practice it appears that members of the group were treated as having international law rights. The early practice referred to the bearing of international legal personality as a consequence of recognition of belligerency: it overcame the conceptual hurdle by assimilating the non-state

132 Lauterpacht states that 'international law knows of no "recognition of insurgency" as an act conferring upon insurgents international rights flowing from a well-defined status. That insurgency has been recognized in a given case means that specific rights have been conceded or particular municipal enactments brought into being. It does not create a status from which further and more general rights can be deduced.' See *ibid.* pp. 270–1; affirmed in T.-C. Chen, *The International Law of Recognition* (London, Stevens & Sons Ltd, 1951), pp. 398–407; see also Castrén, 'Recognition of Insurgency', 445–9; P. K. Menon, *The Law of Recognition in International Law: Basic Principles* (New York, Edwin Mellen Press, 1994). As to the consequences of recognition of insurgency, see H. Silvanie, 'Responsibility of States for Acts of Insurgent Governments' (1939) 33 *AJIL* 78.

133 Hall, *A Treatise on International Law*, p. 35.

134 Chen, *The International Law of Recognition*, p. 306; E. Castrén, *Civil War* (Helsinki, Soumalainen Tiedeakatemia, 1966), pp. 136–67.

belligerents to states. The later practice recognised belligerent capacity as a separate category without much engagement with the consequences of that separate category, and in particular how it could be reconciled with the orthodox understanding of the international legal system as exclusively concerned with the rights and duties of states.

The practice of recognition of belligerency and insurgency during this early period reflect the orthodox account of the post-1945 international legal system. The recognition (or conferral) of belligerent rights and obligations depended on a positive intentional act of recognition on the part of a state, either the lawful government in whose territory the conflict occurred or a foreign state. This is consistent with the post-1945 understanding of the Opinion of the Permanent Court in *Jurisdiction of the Court of Danzig*: that states may create international rights for individuals under treaty where they clearly intend to do so. It is also consistent with the framework of the post-1945 international legal system in that recognition of belligerency conferred direct obligations on non-state actors. Neither of these possibilities reflected the established understanding of the international legal system pre-1945. It can also be noted that belligerent rights and obligations were conferred without requiring an express acceptance of those rights and obligations by the insurgent rebels. Generally, it was considered that the acquisition of belligerent rights was desirable and none of the conditions included reference to the intention or desires of the parties themselves, or required their agreement to be bound. This is also consistent with the post-1945 international legal system which recognises that states may confer rights and obligations on individuals without conditioning that conferral on an individual's consent or acceptance.

(b) The inter-war period

After the First World War, the practice of recognition of belligerency and insurgency declined to the point of virtual obsolescence. In part this must have been caused by deficiencies in the discretionary approach to recognition.[135] The approach to the Spanish Civil War (1936–9) was strongly criticised as an example of the doctrines being used for political purposes rather than in accordance with legal processes.[136] Initially, European states had signed a non-intervention agreement in respect of the revolt

[135] See generally, Oglesby, *Internal War*, pp. 100–14. Oglesby suggests that belligerent recognition passed into desuetude after 1945: at pp. 112–13.

[136] See H. A. Smith, 'Some Problems of the Spanish Civil War' (1937) 18 *BYIL* 17; V. A. O'Rourke, 'Recognition of Belligerency and the Spanish War' (1937) 31 *AJIL* 398; A. Van Wynen Thomas and A. J. Thomas Jr, 'International Legal Aspects of the Civil War in

(which was consistent with an invocation of the law of neutrality), but when it became clear that a number of states had breached the agreement and had intervened in the conflict, Britain offered to recognise the belligerency of both parties upon condition of the withdrawal of foreign forces, which was refused.[137] The rebels insisted on recognition of belligerency without conditions, based on (a) their control over a majority of the national Spanish territory; (b) the existence of a government exercising rights inherent in sovereignty over that territory; and (c) their possession of a regular land and air army, organised and subject to military discipline.[138] Despite their insistence, states refused to recognise the belligerency of the rebels, but a number of states recognised a state of insurgency: no attempt was made to interfere with naval or aerial operations on the high seas or in territorial waters and official intercourse was maintained for certain purposes.[139] The controversial treatment of the Spanish Civil War provided impetus for the development of more objective criteria for the application of the laws of war in civil conflict which occurred after the Second World War.

During the inter-war period, the ICRC also pressed for the application of humanitarian relief in civil conflict. The ICRC and National Red Cross societies had been attempting, on an ad hoc basis, to render humanitarian assistance in civil insurrections.[140] However, the ICRC considered that legal regulation was desirable in order to limit states' discretion, and to make states more receptive to the provision of humanitarian assistance in civil conflict.[141] In 1921, the ICRC adopted a modest resolution drawing the attention of 'all peoples, all governments and all political parties of national or other character, to the fact that the state of civil war cannot justify violation of international law'.[142] In 1928, the Statutes of the ICRC asserted for it a role in civil

Spain, 1936–1939' in R. A. Falk (ed.), *The International Law of Civil War* (Baltimore, Johns Hopkins Press, 1971), p. 111.

137 See Lauterpacht, *Recognition in International Law*, pp. 251–2.

138 This Note of 2 August 1938 is printed in *The Times*, 22 August 1938, and extracted in Lauterpacht, *Recognition in International Law*, p. 251.

139 See discussion in Lauterpacht, *Recognition in International Law*, pp. 2–273.

140 For an account of these activities, see J. Moreillon, *Le CICR et la protection des détenus politiques* (Geneva, Henry Dunant Institute, 1973).

141 See R. Abi-Saab, 'Humanitarian Law and Internal Conflicts: The Evolution of Legal Concern' in A. J. M. Delissen and G. J. Tanya (eds.), *Humanitarian Law of Armed Conflict: Challenges Ahead, Essays in Honour of Frits Kalshoven* (Dordrecht, Martinus Nijhoff, 1991), pp. 211–12.

142 Resolution 4 of the 10th International Red Cross Conference, Geneva, 1921, reproduced in A. Schlögel, 'La guerre civile' (1970) 617 *Revue International de la Croix-Rouge* 137, 139–40. Author's own translation from the original French.

conflict.[143] On the basis of these provisions, the Red Cross induced both sides in the conflict in Spain and Upper Silesia to give undertakings to respect the Geneva Conventions. A more substantial resolution was passed in 1938 which 'urged . . . the application of all essential humanitarian principles' of the 1929 Geneva Conventions to internal conflicts including 'humane treatment' and 'respect for the life and liberty of non-combatants'.[144] The ICRC had planned a conference to address civil conflicts when the Second World War broke out, and the question came to be addressed when that Conference was eventually convened after the war.

(c) The individual in internal armed conflict after 1945

(i) Common Article 3 of the Geneva Conventions

The fundamental review of the Geneva Conventions after the Second World War gave the ICRC an opportunity to press for the international regulation of civil conflict on more objective and concrete factual criteria than the process of recognition of belligerency and insurgency had allowed. Initially, the ICRC sought to apply the entirety of the Conventions to internal conflicts on the basis of reciprocity between the parties.[145] However, from the beginning of the Diplomatic Conference there was a marked reluctance by governments to take such an approach. One of the issues raised was the basis upon which rights and obligations could be imposed on a non-assenting entity, i.e. the rebel insurgents, but there was no serious discussion of the question.[146] The outcome of the Conference, common Article 3, was accepted by the ICRC as a compromise solution which would ensure 'in the case of civil war, at least the application of the humanitarian rules which are recognized by all civilized peoples'.[147]

143 Article 4 of the ICRC Statute of 1928 provides: 'The special role of the ICRC shall be . . . (d) to take action in its capacity as a neutral institution, especially in case of war, civil war or internal strife.'

144 Resolution XIV of the 16th International Red Cross Conference, London, 1938, reproduced in Schlögel, 'La guerre civile', 141. Author's own translation from the original French.

145 Schlögel, 'La guerre civile', 142–3.

146 See summary in D. A. Elder, 'The Historical Background of Common Article 3 of the Geneva Conventions of 1949' (1979) 11 *Case Western Reserve Journal of International Law* 37, 43–4; *ICRC Commentary to Geneva Convention II*, pp. 120–1; *ICRC Commentary to Geneva Convention III*, pp. 32–3.

147 *Final Record of the Diplomatic Conference of Geneva of 1949* (New York, William S. Hein & Co. Inc., 2004), vol. II, sec. B, p. 335.

Common Article 3 applies '[i]n the case of armed conflict not of an international character occurring in the territory of one of the High Contracting Parties'. Parties to the conflict 'should further endeavour to bring into force, by means of special agreements, all or part of the other provisions' of the Geneva Conventions. Common Article 3 expressly provides that: 'The application of the preceding provisions shall not affect the legal status of the Parties to the conflict.'

The circumstances required to trigger the application of common Article 3 are not set out in that provision; rather, it refers only to armed conflict 'not of an international character' in the territory of a state party to the conventions. Because the ICRC was in favour of applying common Article 3 'as widely as possible' to all civil conflicts,[148] the ICRC Commentaries do not clearly set out what is required; rather, they outline 'non-obligatory' criteria which reflect what was required for recognition of belligerency. Their list of non-obligatory criteria include: that the insurgents possess an organised military force and an authority responsible for its acts; that they act within a determinate territory and have the means of respecting and ensuring respect for the Convention; that the insurgents have an organisation purporting to have the characteristics of a state; that the insurgent civil authority exercises *de facto* authority over persons within a determinate territory; that the armed forces act under direction of the organised civil authority and are prepared to observe the ordinary laws of war; and that the insurgent civil authority agrees to be bound by the provisions of the Convention.[149] These criteria suggest that what is relevant is the status and capacities of the insurgent group as such, rather than the individuals within that group.

When the Appeals Chamber of the ICTY addressed the question of the threshold of applicability for common Article 3 in *Tadić*, the threshold of application required was merely a state of 'protracted armed violence between governmental authorities and organized armed groups or between such groups within a State'.[150] The tribunal made no reference to requirements that insurgents exercise territorial control or that they conduct their operations in accordance with the laws and customs of war. Thus, in comparison with the traditional criteria for recognition of

148 *ICRC Commentary to Geneva Convention I*, p. 50; there is a similar statement in the *ICRC Commentary to Geneva Convention IV*, p. 36.

149 *ICRC Commentary to Geneva Convention I*, pp. 49–50.

150 *Prosecutor* v. *Tadić*, Case no. IT-94-1-AR72, Appeal on Jurisdiction, Judgment, 2 October 1995, (1996) 35 ILM 32, para. 70.

belligerency and the non-obligatory criteria identified by the ICRC, the threshold of application for common Article 3 is much less stringent. The Appeals Chamber's definition in *Tadić* has been applied in subsequent ICTY[151] and International Criminal Tribunal for Rwanda (ICTR)[152] decisions.

Common Article 3 requires that 'each Party to the conflict shall be bound to apply, as a minimum' certain specified provisions. As an injunction addressed to the parties to the conflict, its terms suggest that the entity bound is the 'party' to the conflict – a term which might be interpreted as either the insurgent group or its constituent members. The terms of common Article 3 did not address the question raised at the Conference of the jurisprudential basis for the imposition of duties and assumption of rights by a non-state entity, and discussions of the issue in the ICRC Commentaries and in the literature refer to either the group itself or the individual members as being directly bound. The ICRC Commentary notes that this question was important:

> [U]ntil recently it would have been considered impossible in law for an international Convention to bind a non-signatory Party – a Party, moreover, which was not yet in existence and which was not even required to represent a legal entity capable of undertaking international obligations.[153]

The position taken in the ICRC Commentary to the first Geneva Convention is that rebels are bound because they are a 'responsible authority' in fact exercising effective sovereignty:

> [I]f the responsible authority at [the insurgents'] head exercises effective sovereignty, it is bound by the very fact that it claims to represent the country, or part of the country. The 'authority' in question can only free itself from its obligations under the Convention by following the procedure for denunciation laid down in Article 63.[154]

The Commentary dealt only superficially with this issue, suggesting that since the application of common Article 3 is desirable, the issue has no practical significance:

151 *Prosecutor* v. *Delalić, Mucić, Delić and Landžo*, Case no. IT-96-21-T, Judgment, 16 November 1998, para. 183; *Prosecutor* v. *Furundžija*, Case no. IT-95-21-T, Judgment, 10 December 1998, (1999) 38 ILM 317, para. 59.

152 *Prosecutor* v. *Rutaganda*, Case no. ICTR-96-3, Judgment, 6 December 1999, (2000) 39 ILM 557, para. 91.

153 *ICRC Commentary to Geneva Convention I*, p. 51.

154 *Ibid.* This was repeated in the *ICRC Commentary to Geneva Convention III*, p. 37.

> If an insurgent party applies Article 3, so much the better for the victims of the conflict. No one will complain. If it does not apply it, it will prove that those who regard its actions as mere acts of anarchy or brigandage are right.[155]

The ICRC Commentary to the second Geneva Convention repeated the idea of effective sovereignty, but also contained a further possible justification: incorporation of common Article 3 into domestic law:

> Some doubt has been expressed as to whether insurgents can be legally bound by a Convention which they have not themselves signed. The answer is provided in most national legislations; by the fact of ratification, an international convention becomes part of law and is therefore binding upon all the individuals of that country. But this system is not universal. However that may be and without embarking on a discussion of international law which cannot be settled in the same way everywhere, one may state this: if the responsible authority at the head of the insurgents exercises effective sovereignty, it is bound by the very fact that it claims to represent the country, or part of the country.[156]

During the Conference,[157] the Greek delegate had offered the same justification of automatic incorporation into domestic law but also referred to the binding force of the conventions for nationals of signatory states as an additional basis, an explanation which seems to assume that individuals are bound directly by the provisions:[158]

> [The Greek delegate] was of the view that from the legal standpoint, [insurgents] should be considered bound by the Convention; failure by the insurgents to accede to the Conventions was not an insurmountable obstacle; he based his arguments on two reasons:
>
> (a) The Conventions which were being drafted could and should be considered as law making conventions, i.e., as rules which should be applicable not only on behalf of or against the contracting Parties, but also in circumstances which were analogous to those governed by the said Conventions;
>
> (b) Insurgents and even bandits were obviously nationals of some State, and were thereby bound by the obligations undertaken by the latter,

155 *ICRC Commentary to Geneva Convention I*, p. 52. See generally, Castrén, *Civil War*, pp. 84–7.

156 *ICRC Commentary to Geneva Convention II*, p. 34.

157 The record of the Conference may assist in interpretation as *travaux préparatoires*.

158 In the literature the Greek delegate is commonly credited with referring to the American law principle of 'legislative jurisdiction' but reference to the statement of the delegate reveals no reference to this principle and there is no mention of the legislative competence of states to bind their nationals. The argument which is made is the simpler one, that of the binding nature of treaties for nationals of a state. However, no authority is given in support of this argument, as will be discussed below.

> since practically all civilized States would sign the Conventions which were being drawn up, it therefore follows that, subject to exceptions, any insurgent or bandit would be a national of a Signatory State, and would *ipso facto* be bound by the Convention. This legal interpretation enabled insurgents to be considered as automatically bound by the Convention - the aim of the rules which were being drawn up - since the *de jure* governments would apply the humanitarian principles even without being bound by the Conventions to do so; it was mainly insurgents which should be required to observe a humane attitude.[159]

This second basis was seized upon as avoiding complex questions, as noted by Draper. In consequence, common Article 3 could be interpreted as directly binding individual members and the problem of construing the group as the legal person obliged under the provision could then be avoided:

> Who are the 'Parties to the conflict' and to whom do they owe the obligations imposed in Article 3? It would seem that these obligations are international and not municipal. Does the article have the effect of attributing a functional 'semi-personality' upon an association of individuals operating as Governmental and rebel groups? The entity is not a Party to the Conventions, nor does it exist until there is a conflict. A possible solution avoiding that complexity and artificiality is to consider that the obligations imposed by the article devolve upon the whole of the population of the State concerned, at any time, so that any person taking part in an internal conflict on either side is exposed to the risk of being in breach of an international obligation if he acts in violation of Article 3. This would, if correct, be an instance of obligations, international in nature, inhering directly in individuals.[160]

The question of the jurisprudential basis of the imposition of duties upon insurgents under common Article 3 was not resolved and it resurfaced during negotiation of the Additional Protocols. The practical application of common Article 3 was widely considered to be disappointing, and during discussions at the Diplomatic Conference of 1974–7 several delegates pointed out the failure to apply the Article despite the occurrence of numerous civil wars which passed the minimum threshold.[161]

[159] *Final Record of the Diplomatic Conference of Geneva of 1949* (New York, William S. Hein & Co. Inc., 2004), vol. II, sec. B, p. 94; G. I. A. D. Draper, 'The Geneva Conventions of 1949' (1965) 114-I *RdC* 60, 96; cited in *ICRC Commentary to Geneva Convention II*, p. 34 (this was the final commentary to be published).

[160] Draper, 'The Geneva Conventions of 1949', 96.

[161] See e.g., *Official Records of the Diplomatic Conference on the Reaffirmation and Development of International Humanitarian Law Applicable in Armed Conflicts, Geneva, (1974–1977)* (Bern, Federal Political Department, 1978), vol. XIV, p. 313 (Mr Reed).

(ii) Additional Protocol II

In terms of the law applicable to civil conflicts, the Additional Protocols developed the existing law in two significant aspects. First, certain wars of national liberation were classified as international armed conflicts under Additional Protocol I,[162] and the rules which governed international armed conflict in Protocol I therefore applied to those conflicts. Second, Additional Protocol II[163] supplemented the applicable law in civil conflicts and defined its own threshold for application independently of common Article 3.

In respect of national liberation movements, the ICRC had been arguing, since at least 1969,[164] that 'freedom fighters' ought at least be entitled to treatment as prisoners of war.[165] Moreover, developments within the UN relating to the right to self-determination, in particular recognition of self-determination as a legal right in the 1970 Friendly Relations Declaration,[166] had the consequence of conferring an international character on armed conflicts arising from a struggle to achieve a right of self-determination or conflicts resulting from its forcible denial.[167] At the Diplomatic Conference for the 1977 Protocols, a number of states proposed amendments to Article 1 of Protocol I which would apply the whole of the Geneva Conventions and Protocol I to wars of national liberation.[168] This proposal was eventually adopted with eighty-seven votes in favour, one against and eleven abstentions,[169] reflected in Article 1(4) as follows:

162 Additional Protocol I, Art. 1(4).

163 Protocol II Additional to the Geneva Conventions of 12 August 1949 and Relating to the Protection of Victims of Non-International Armed Conflicts, 8 June 1977 (entry into force 7 December 1978), 1125 UNTS 606 (hereinafter 'Additional Protocol II').

164 Sandoz, Swinarski and Zimmermann, *Commentary on the Protocol Additional to the Geneva Conventions*, p. 48 (para. 91).

165 See e.g., ICRC, *Protection of Victims of Non-International Conflicts*, Report submitted at the XXIst International Conference of the Red Cross, Istanbul, 1969 (ICRC, Geneva, 1969), pp. 7–8. See discussion in H. A. Wilson, *International Law and the Use of Force by National Liberation Movements* (Oxford, Clarendon Press, 1988), pp. 163–4.

166 Declaration on Principles of International Law concerning Friendly Relations and Co-operation among States in Accordance with the Charter of the United Nations, GA/Res./2625 (XXV), 24 October 1970, Annex.

167 See discussion in full in G. Abi-Saab, 'Wars of National Liberation' (1979-IV) 165 *RdC* 353, 369–72; cf Wilson, *International Law and the Use of Force by National Liberation Movements*, pp. 98–9.

168 Abi-Saab, 'Wars of National Liberation', 372–92.

169 Vote against: Israel; abstentions: Monaco, UK, Ireland, Federal Republic of Germany, Canada, Spain, US, France, Italy, Japan and Guatemala: *ibid.* 392.

4. The situations [to which this Protocol, which supplements the Geneva Conventions of 1949, shall apply] include armed conflicts in which people are fighting against colonial domination and alien occupation and against racist regimes in the exercise of their right of self-determination, as enshrined in the Charter of the United Nations and the Declaration on Principles of International Law Concerning Friendly Relations and Cooperation among States in accordance with the Charter of the United Nations.

While paragraph 4 refers to 'people', it is unclear whether the rights and obligations which accrue to parties to the conflict are attributed to the national liberation movement as such or directly on its members. However, Article 1(4) is supplemented by Article 96, entitled 'treaty relations upon entry into force of this Protocol'. Paragraph 3 of Article 96 refers to acceptance of the rights and obligations by an 'authority' representing a people, in the following terms:

The authority representing a people engaged against a High Contracting Party in an armed conflict of the type referred to in Article 1, paragraph 4, may undertake to apply the Conventions and this Protocol in relation to that conflict by means of a unilateral declaration addressed to the depositary. Such declaration shall, upon its receipt by the depositary, have in relation to that conflict the following effects:

(a) the Conventions and this Protocol are brought into force for the said authority as a Party to the conflict with immediate effect;
(b) the said authority assumes the same rights and obligations as those which have been assumed by a High Contracting Party to the Conventions and this Protocol; and
(c) the Conventions and this Protocol are equally binding upon all Parties to the conflict.

While the phrase 'authority representing a people' is not determinative of the question whether the relevant rights and obligations are conferred on the movement as such (as a group) or upon its constituent members, it is clear that some kind of group formation is essential to qualification of a conflict as a national liberation conflict, and hence to the application of the Geneva Conventions and Protocol I to the parties to that conflict. But crucially, the relevant authority must make an express declaration undertaking to apply the Geneva Conventions and Protocol I; in contrast to applicable provisions in respect of any other civil conflict (including common Article 3 and Protocol II), where there is no requirement of acceptance of any rights and obligations by the relevant non-state party or parties.

In respect of all other civil conflicts, in its draft Article 1 of Protocol II submitted to the Diplomatic Conference, the ICRC proposed that the

Protocol apply broadly, to situations where there are hostilities between armed forces or other organised armed groups under responsible command.[170] During the Conference it was suggested that the threshold of application be raised either by a requirement that the government of the territorial state recognise the applicability of the Protocol,[171] or by requiring a high intensity conflict with territorial control.[172] The latter was preferred and Article 1 as adopted provides that Protocol II applies to all armed conflicts not covered by Protocol I which:

> take place in the territory of a High Contracting Party between its armed forces and dissident armed forces or other organized armed groups which, under responsible command, exercise such control over a part of its territory as to enable them to carry out sustained and concerted military operations and to implement this Protocol.

Paragraph 2 of Article 1 expressly excludes 'situations of internal disturbances and tensions, such as riots, isolated and sporadic acts of violence and other acts of a similar nature'.

The phrase 'parties to the conflict', as used in common Article 3, was deliberately omitted from Protocol II as a result of the concern of delegates not to confer a legal status on insurgents. Consequently, Article 1 read as obligations addressed exclusively to governments.[173] Several delegations argued that the Protocol only imposed obligations on contracting states parties. The Italian delegation stated during the Diplomatic Conference:

> In ratifying this instrument, the High Contracting Parties will assume obligations, not toward rebel forces (which are neither subjects of international law nor Parties to Protocol II), but towards the other Contracting Parties, the international community and world opinion. Clearly, therefore, each Contracting Party's obligation to respect Protocol II cannot be conditioned or modified by the conduct of rebel forces.[174]

170 *Official Records of the Diplomatic Conference on the Reaffirmation and Development of International Humanitarian Law Applicable in Armed Conflicts, Geneva, (1974–1977)* (Bern, Federal Political Department, 1978), vol. III, p. 204.

171 *Official Records of the Diplomatic Conference on the Reaffirmation and Development of International Humanitarian Law Applicable in Armed Conflicts, Geneva, (1974–1977)* (Bern, Federal Political Department, 1978), vol. IV, p. 7 (Romania).

172 *Ibid.* p. 6 (Pakistan).

173 G. Abi-Saab, 'Non International Armed Conflicts' in UNESCO, *International Dimensions of Humanitarian Law* (Geneva, Henry Dunant Institute, 1988), pp. 217, 231.

174 *Official Records of the Diplomatic Conference on the Reaffirmation and Development of International Humanitarian Law Applicable in Armed Conflicts, Geneva, (1974–1977)* (Bern, Federal Political Department, 1978), vol. VII, pp. 107, 122.

The Zairean delegation agreed:

Only a sovereign State can claim to have international legal personality and, as such, it enjoys all the prerogatives of sovereignty, including that of entering into international agreements and conventions, that is to say, of becoming a party to them. Accordingly, dissident armed forces are ... rebels with no international legal personality. Their only legal status is that granted them under the domestic laws of their national State. To claim otherwise is to place a sovereign State on the same footing as a rebel movement, and that would imply *de facto* recognition of the movement.[175]

Other delegations argued in support of a broader approach to the obligations under the Protocol but, within the traditional framework of international law, saw the obligations for insurgents deriving from national law. Belgium and the Soviet Union stated:

Once adopted, the text would become a national law imposing an obligation on all persons within the territory of the State in question. Any international instrument signed by a Government was binding on all those within its territory ... Some delegations had thought that the text in question would impose an obligation on Governments only. That would be a serious mistake. The obligation was in fact valid for all citizens.[176]

The deletion of the phrase 'parties to the conflict' from the text of Protocol II[177] and protests from states against the acquisition of rights and imposition of obligations on insurgents did not change the legal structure of the Protocol as applying equally to states and insurgents in armed conflicts meeting its conditions for application. But the failure to address the injunctions clearly to a specified party did not assist in clarifying whether the rights and obligations were held by the insurgent group as such, or its composite individuals. Like the debate over the jurisprudential basis for the imposition of duties and assumption of rights by insurgents in respect of common Article 3, the basis of the binding character of Protocol II for insurgents was not resolved and no common view is evident in the views of delegations to the Diplomatic Conference. The ICRC Commentary to the Protocol suggested that

[175] *Ibid.* pp. 85, 104.

[176] *Official Records of the Diplomatic Conference on the Reaffirmation and Development of International Humanitarian Law Applicable in Armed Conflicts, Geneva, (1974–1977)* (Bern, Federal Political Department, 1978), vol. XVI, pp. 309, 314.

[177] The ICRC Commentary to Additional Protocol II notes that this deletion 'does not change [the instrument's] structure from a legal point of view': Sandoz, Swinarski and Zimmermann, *Commentary on the Protocol Additional to the Geneva Conventions*, p. 1345, para. 4442.

insurgents were bound as nationals of a contracting state (suggesting that the relevant bound entities are the individual members of the group rather than the group as such) and that the fact of application was not challenged by states:

> The question is often raised how the insurgent party can be bound by a treaty to which it is not a High Contracting Party. It may therefore be appropriate to recall here the explanation given in 1949: the commitment made by a State not only applies to the government but also to any established authorities and private individuals within the national territory of that State and certain obligations are therefore imposed upon them. The extent of the rights and duties of private individuals is therefore the same as that of the rights and duties of the State. Although this argument has occasionally been questioned in legal literature, the validity of the obligation imposed upon insurgents has never been contested.[178]

The leading article on the question of the application of the provisions of the Protocol to non-state entities by Cassese concluded that the Protocol applied to insurgents on the basis of the effects of treaties for third parties, in accordance with the rules in the Vienna Convention on the Law of Treaties, which applied, on his argument, to any international subject taking the position of a third party vis-à-vis a treaty.[179] On that basis, the relevant armed opposition group would have to consent to be bound by the Additional Protocol, which consent must be ascertained in each individual conflict. This argument is entirely consistent with the provisions applicable to national liberation movements, which as noted require an express declaration from the authority representing the non-state party to the conflict undertaking to apply the Conventions and Protocol I to bring the Conventions and the Protocol into force for all parties to the conflict.[180]

Alternative bases have also been discussed in the literature.[181] First, justifications have been put forward on the basis of the type of rule, either as principles of customary international law or as general principles of law. This justification, however, fails to put forward a positive basis for the assertion that either customary principles or general principles automatically and directly bind individuals, in the absence of

178 *Ibid.* p. 1345, para. 4444 (references omitted).

179 A. Cassese, 'The Status of Rebels under the 1977 Geneva Protocol on Non-International Armed Conflicts' (1981) 30 *ICLQ* 416, 423.

180 Additional Protocol I, Art. 96(3).

181 The main discussions occur in Cassese, 'The Status of Rebels'; Zegfeld, *Accountability of Armed Opposition Groups*, pp. 15–18; Moir, *The Law of Internal Armed Conflict*, pp. 96–9; Sivakumaran, 'Binding Armed Opposition Groups'.

incorporation or reception into domestic law. It also encounters the difficulty of establishing that all the relevant provisions of Additional Protocol II form part of customary international law or reflect general principles of international law.

Second, it has been suggested that the provisions of Additional Protocol II bind armed opposition groups through the principle of succession: treaties bind the state and not only the signatory government, and therefore armed opposition groups are bound either if they become the *de facto* and *de jure* government or have some aspiration of so doing. This extension of the principle of succession to international obligations is also problematic: apart from assuming that all armed opposition groups aspire to become or in fact become the lawful government, it does not explain how an aspiration to become a state binds individuals to treaty obligations. If an armed opposition group does become the successor government, they will be so bound by the state's international obligations, but during the conflict there will not have been any succession. It is in fact a significant and unreasoned extension of the principle of succession.

Third, it is argued that the principle of 'legislative jurisdiction' provides a basis for the application of Additional Protocol II to insurgent groups. It appears that this term has been used to cover three distinct doctrines. First, it refers to a US domestic principle which noted the competence of a federal state to legislate for all its nationals.[182] Second, it refers to the idea that all insurgents would be bound as nationals of some signatory state.[183] Third, it is used to refer to an extension of the principle stated by the PCIJ in *Jurisdiction of the Courts of Danzig*,[184] arguing that the contracting states parties to Protocol II intended to create direct obligations for individuals and that occurs without any need for incorporation of the Protocol in domestic law.[185]

The first two doctrines, which have been cast together as 'legislative jurisdiction', confront difficulties. First, the domestic principle of

182 *Final Record of the Diplomatic Conference of Geneva of 1949* (New York, William S. Hein & Co. Inc., 2004), vol. II, sec. B, p. 94.

183 This was suggested by the Greek delegate at the Diplomatic Conference for the Geneva Conventions in respect of common Article 3 and is reflected in the ICRC Commentary to Protocol II: *Final Record of the Diplomatic Conference of Geneva of 1949* (New York, William S. Hein & Co. Inc., 2004), vol. II, sec. B, p. 94.

184 *Jurisdiction of the Courts of Danzig (Pecuniary Claims of Danzig Railway Officials who have Passed into the Polish Service, Against the Polish Railways Administration)*, PCIJ Rep. ser. B no. 15 (1928) 3.

185 Sivakumaran, 'Binding Armed Opposition Groups', 381 et seq.

legislative jurisdiction does not explain how the provisions of a treaty come to have a direct effect on individuals in the absence of incorporation of that treaty into domestic law. Second, the argument put forward by the Greek delegate, that all insurgents would be bound as nationals of some signatory state, assumes without explanation or justification that the Protocol directly binds the nationals of signatory states. The third doctrine is more promising. In the *Danzig* Opinion, the PCIJ acknowledged that treaties could confer rights on individuals; as discussed in Chapter 1, the ICJ has more recently affirmed that treaties may do so by their plain language.[186] In principle it appears that this doctrine might also be extended to the imposition of obligations on individuals, where it is clear from a plain reading that this is the effect of the relevant treaty. It seems arguable on this basis that common Article 3 and the provisions of Additional Protocol I impose obligations on parties to the conflict. It also seems arguable that the *Danzig* principle is apt to be applied to the conferral of rights and obligations on other entities; treaties could confer rights and obligations on armed opposition groups as such, rather than conferring them directly on the composite members of the relevant groups. The terms of Additional Protocol I are not expressed as injunctions specifically to the parties to the conflict, and thus are not of assistance in determining whether they are addressed to the relevant group as such or to its individual members directly.

(iii) Customary international humanitarian law

During drafting of Additional Protocol II there was a marked reluctance on the part of states to accept that customary rules governing internal armed conflict existed: consequently the Martens clause in Protocol II makes no reference to 'the principles of international law derived from established custom'.[187] However, the ICJ confirmed the existence of customary principles when it held in 1986 that common Article 3 reflected elementary considerations of humanity applicable to all armed conflicts.[188] The ICRC's Customary Law Study did not deal with the question of the definition of a non-international armed conflict or

[186] See 1.2(d) above.
[187] T. Meron, *Human Rights and Humanitarian Norms at Customary Law* (Oxford, Clarendon Press, 1989), p. 73; Sandoz, Swinarski and Zimmermann, *Commentary on the Protocol Additional to the Geneva Conventions of 12 August 1949*, p. 1340.
[188] *Military and Paramilitary Activities in and Against Nicaragua (Nicaragua* v. *United States)*, Merits, [1986] ICJ Rep. 14, 114 (para. 218).

the threshold for application of the relevant customary rules. It identified 147 rules applicable in all situations of armed conflict, covering both international and non-international conflicts. The assertion that these rules for non-international armed conflict have acquired customary status has been subject to criticism by both states[189] and writers,[190] although it is generally acknowledged that there is some developing convergence in the applicable rules.

The ICTY has also concluded that principles of customary international law applicable in internal armed conflict exist independently of common Article 3 and Additional Protocol II.[191] When the ICTY Statute was drafted, the UN Secretary-General had explained that Article 3 of the Tribunal's Statute was based on Hague Convention IV of 1907 and its annexed Regulations, and the Nuremberg Tribunal's interpretation of those provisions.[192] At the time of adoption of the Statute, the US representative suggested that the phrase 'laws and customs of war' in Article 3 included 'all obligations under humanitarian law agreements in force in the territory of the former Yugoslavia at the time the acts were committed'.[193] Similar statements were made by France and the UK.[194] In light of these remarks, the ICTY Appeals Chamber held that Article 3 of its Statute encompassed all violations of humanitarian law not covered by other provisions of the Statute, including violations of Hague law on internal armed conflicts, violations of provisions of the Geneva Conventions other than grave breaches, violations of common Article 3 and other customary rules governing internal armed conflict, and violations of agreements binding on parties to the conflict under treaty.[195] It held that the principal rules of customary international law governing internal armed conflict were:

[189] Letter from John Bellinger III, Legal Adviser, US Department of State, and William J. Haynes, General Counsel, US Department of Defense, to Dr Jakob Kellenberger, President, International Committee of the Red Cross, regarding Customary International Law Study, 3 November 2006, (2007) 46 ILM 514, at pp. 4, 6, 11.

[190] See e.g., Wilmshurst, 'Conclusions', 406–7.

[191] *Prosecutor* v. *Tadić*, Case no. IT-94-1-AR72, Appeals Chamber, Judgment on Jurisdiction, 2 October 1995.

[192] *Secretary-General's Report on Aspects of Establishing an International Tribunal for the Prosecution of Persons Responsible for Serious Violations of International Humanitarian Law Committed in the Territory of the Former Yugoslavia*, UN Doc. S/25704 (3 May 1993), (1993) 32 ILM 1159.

[193] Security Council, Provisional Verbatim Record of the 3217th Meeting, UN Doc. S/PV.3217 (25 May 1993), p. 15.

[194] *Ibid.* pp. 11, 19.

[195] *Prosecutor* v. *Tadić*, Case no. IT-94-1-AR72, Appeal Chamber, Judgment on Jurisdiction, 2 October 1995, (1996) 35 ILM 32, para. 89.

[t]he protection of civilians from hostilities, in particular from indiscriminate attacks, the protection of civilian objects, in particular cultural property, protection of all those who do not (or no longer) take active part in hostilities, as well as prohibition of the means of warfare proscribed in international armed conflicts and ban of certain methods of conducting hostilities.[196]

The Appeals Chamber denied that it was applying the laws governing international armed conflict to internal conflict on a wholesale basis, but argued that 'the general essence of those rights' had become applicable to internal conflict.[197] The decision was criticised on the basis that it was over-inclusive in its assessment of customary law applicable to non-international armed conflicts.[198] However, the point of principle that internal armed conflict was governed by customary international law met little criticism.

In terms of individual criminal responsibility, the grave breaches regime established by the Geneva Conventions applies only in international armed conflict. The terms of common Article 3 of the Geneva Conventions, cast as obligations on contracting states parties, do not indicate that individual obligations, criminal or otherwise, attach to breaches of its terms and common Article 3 was not included in the grave breaches regime. No grave breaches provisions were included in Additional Protocol II and it was widely accepted until around 1990 that the law of war crimes did not apply in internal armed conflict.[199] However, through the jurisprudence of the ICTY[200] and the statutes of the ICTR[201]

196 *Ibid.* para. 127. 197 *Ibid.* para. 126.

198 T. Meron, 'The Continuing Role of Custom in the Formation of International Humanitarian Law' (1996) 90 *AJIL* 238, 243.

199 See ICRC DDM/JUR442b (25 March 1993), para. 4; cited in *Prosecutor* v. *Tadić*, Case no. IT-94-1-AR72, Appeal on Jurisdiction, Judgment, 2 October 1995, (1996) 35 ILM 32, Separate Opinion of Judge Li, para. 7; D. Plattner, 'The Penal Repression of Violations of International Humanitarian Law' (1990) 30 *IRRC* 409.

200 *Prosecutor* v. *Tadić*, Case no. IT-94-1-AR72, Appeal on Jurisdiction, Judgment, 2 October 1995, (1996) 35 ILM 32, paras. 89, 130–2, 134. See also *Prosecutor* v. *Delalić, Mucić, Delić and Landžo* (*Celebici* case), Case no. IT-96-21-A, Appeals Chamber, 20 February 2001, paras. 163–4, 171.

201 ICTR Statute, Art. 4, available at www.un.org/ictr/statute.html. In his first Report on implementation of Security Council Resolution 955 establishing the Rwandan Tribunal, the UN Secretary-General stated that Art. 4 of the ICTR Statute 'for the first time criminalizes common article 3 of the four Geneva Conventions': UN Doc. S/1995/134 (13 February 1995), para. 12. A footnote in the Report added: 'Although the question of whether common article 3 entails the individual criminal responsibility of the perpetrator of the crime is still debatable, some of the crimes included therein, when committed against the civilian population, also constitute crimes against humanity and as such are customarily recognized as entailing the criminal responsibility of the individual.'

and the ICC,[202] the idea of individual criminal responsibility for violations of humanitarian law in internal armed conflict has developed. For reasons already explained, the development of individual criminal responsibility is addressed in Chapter 4.

(iv) International human rights law applicable in non-international armed conflict

International human rights law remains applicable in non-international armed conflict: it is uncontroversial that it continues to bind states and may thereby confer direct rights on individuals.[203] The Human Rights Committee, the European Court of Human Rights, and the Inter-American Court of Human Rights have affirmed that human rights law is applicable in non-international armed conflict.[204] Whether armed opposition groups are bound by international human rights law is more controversial.

There is some practice which suggests that armed opposition groups are bound by human rights law. This has emerged from four categories of sources. First, the UN Security Council and the General Assembly have occasionally called upon parties to civil conflict, including opposition groups, to observe human rights obligations.[205] Second, the

[202] Rome Statute of the International Criminal Court, Art. 8(1), (2), 17 July 1998 (entry into force 1 July 2002), 2187 UNTS 3. Article 8(2)(d) expressly states that these apply to 'armed conflicts not of an international character' thus excluding 'situations of internal disturbances and tensions, such as riots, isolated and sporadic acts of violence or other acts of a similar nature'.

[203] See e.g., Moir, *The Law of Internal Armed Conflict*, p. 194.

[204] For the Human Rights Committee: *Herrera Rubio* v. *Colombia*, HRC, Communication no. 161/83, Views of 2 November 1987, para. 10.2; also *Baboeram and others* v. *Suriname*, HRC, Communication no. 154/83, 10 April 1984,; *Sanjuan Arevalo* v. *Colombia*, HRC, Communication no. 181/84, 3 November 1989; for the ECtHR: *ISSA and others* v. *Turkey*, Application no. 31821/96, 16 November 2004; *Ilaşcu and others* v. *Moldova*, Application no. 48787/99, 8 July 2004; *Khatsiyeva and others* v. *Russia*, Application no. 5108/02, 17 January 2008; for the Inter-American Court of Human Rights: see *Las Palmeras* v. *Colombia*, Preliminary Objections, 4 February 2000, Inter-Am. Ct HR ser. C no. 67; *Serrano-Cruz Sisters* v. *El Salvador*, Preliminary Objections, 23 November 2004, Inter-Am. Ct HR ser. C no. 118; *Bámaca-Velásquez* v. *Guatemala*, Merits, 25 November 2000, Inter-Am. Ct HR ser. C no. 70; *Mapiripán Massacre* v. *Colombia*, Merits, 15 September 2005, Inter-Am. Ct HR ser. C no. 134; *Ituango Massacres* v. *Colombia*, Preliminary Objections, Merits, Reparations and Costs, 1 July 2006, Inter-Am. Ct HR ser. C no. 148. On the Inter-American Court, see McCarthy, 'Human Rights and the Laws of War'.

[205] SC/Res/1214 (1998), 8 December 1998, para. 12 (Afghanistan); SC/Res/1216 (1998), para. 5 (Guinea-Bissau); SC/Res/1270 (1999), 22 October 1999 (Sierra Leone); SC/Res/1509 (2003), para. 10 (Liberia); SC/Res/1479 (2003), para. 8 (Côte d'Ivoire); GA/Res/54/182, 17 December 1999 (Sudan); GA/Res/54/185, 17 December 1999 (Afghanistan).

Human Rights Committee has suggested that where an armed opposition group is in control of a territory, it might be asked to explain how it has complied with human rights obligations.[206] Third, truth and reconciliation commissions in Guatemala[207] and Sierra Leone[208] determined that insurgent rebels owed human rights obligations. Finally, UN Special Rapporteurs have suggested that armed opposition groups have human rights obligations on the basis that 'insofar as [armed groups] aspire to represent a people before the world, the international community will evaluate their conduct according to the Universal Declaration's "common standard of achievement".'[209] In some cases, effective control over territory has been emphasised, leading some scholars to suggest that rebel movements may be bound by human rights obligations where they act as *de facto* governments.[210] In other cases, human rights standards have been invoked against groups with limited or no control over territory.[211] Broadly, there is some practice

[206] *Decision on State Succession to the Obligations of the Former Yugoslavia under the International Covenant on Civil and Political Rights*, Human Rights Committee, 19 October 1992, reproduced in (1992) 15 EHRR 234.

[207] Guatemalan Historical Clarification Commission, Guatemala Memory of Silence, Executive Summary Conclusions and Recommendations, UN Doc. A/53/928 (27 April 1999), Annex, paras. 127–8.

[208] See Sierra Leone Truth and Reconciliation Commission, 2004 Report,, vol. 2, ch. 2, paras. 106–7, 115–72, available at http://trcsierraleone.org/drwebsite/publish/v2c2.shtml.

[209] UN Doc. E/CN.4/2006/53/Add.5 (27 March 2005) (references omitted). See also the joint report on Lebanon and Israel: UN Doc. A/HRC/2/7 (2 October 2006), para. 19; UN Commission on Human Rights, E/CN.4/1989/24, para. 68 (Report on the Situation in Afghanistan by the Special Rapporteur, F. Ermacora, 16 February 1989). See also Institute of International Law, 'The Application of International Humanitarian Law and Fundamental Human Rights, in Armed Conflicts in which Non-State Entities are Parties', Berlin Session, 25 August 1999, Art. II.

[210] C. Tomuschat, 'The Applicability of Human Rights Law to Insurgent Movements' in H. Fischer, U. Froissart, U. Heintschel von Heinegg and C. Raap (eds.), *Krisensicherung und Humanitärer Schutz (Crisis Management and Humanitarian Protection): Festschrift für Dieter Fleck* (Berlin, Berliner Wissenschafts-Verlag, 2004), pp. 573, 587–8. See also N. Rodley, 'Can Armed Opposition Groups Violate Human Rights Standards?' in K. H. Mahoney and P. Mahoney (eds.), *Human Rights in the Twenty-First Century* (The Hague, Martinus Nijhoff, 1993), pp. 307, 313. In practice there has been a marked reluctance on the part of the existing government to acknowledge that insurgent forces are operating as *de facto* government: see Zegfeld, *Accountability of Armed Opposition Groups*, p. 152.

[211] See e.g., the Human Rights Commission's resolution regarding Somalia, where many of the relevant groups lacked any control over territory or persons: Human Rights Commission Resolution 1997/47, 11 April 1997, para. 3,; and SC/Res//70 (1998), 21 April 1998, paras. 2 and 4 (Afghanistan), where the Security Council called upon 'Afghan factions' some of which had no control over territory.

which suggests that it can no longer be assumed that armed opposition groups are not bound by human rights obligations.[212] However, the practice in support of obligations for such groups cannot be said to have reached a level of consistency as to support a generally applicable principle of customary international law. A customary rule requiring armed opposition groups to observe at least core human rights obligations may yet emerge, but at present the practice is sporadic rather than consistent, even in respect of conflicts where insurgents exercise elements of governmental authority. It might also be argued that, in any event, common Article 3 and applicable provisions of Protocol I (in particular, Article 4) bind insurgent groups to observe standards which reflect in substance fundamental human rights.[213] Where there is some conceptual similarity between the content of the humanitarian law obligations and states' obligations in human rights law, the latter might be used to clarify or interpret the former.[214] The extent to which international human rights law imposes obligations on individuals more generally is addressed in Chapter 5.

3.4 Conclusions: the position of the individual in international humanitarian law

Many of the rules governing international armed conflict are directed to the protection of individuals: this is true of both Geneva and Hague law. However, the normative framework of international humanitarian law applicable in international armed conflict is one which establishes standards of treatment for individuals rather than creating direct rights for individuals. In this way the vast majority of conventional and customary law applicable in international armed conflict is consistent with

[212] See generally, A. Clapham, 'Human Rights Obligations of Non-state Actors in Conflict Situations' (2006) 88 *IRRC* 491; A. Clapham, *Human Rights Obligations of Non-State Actors* (Oxford, Oxford University Press, 2006), pp. 271–85.

[213] See e.g., H.-P. Gasser, 'International Humanitarian Law' in H. Haug (ed.), *Humanity for All: The International Red Cross and Red Crescent Movement* (Berne, P. Haupt, 1993), pp. 491, 566; Moir, *The Law of Internal Armed Conflict*, pp. 197–231. This does not exclude both human rights and humanitarian law being applicable: either regime may have particular strengths which serve to protect individuals: in favour of human rights law see Clapham, *Human Rights Obligations of Non-State Actors*, p. 285; in favour of humanitarian law see M. Sassoli and A. Bouvier (eds.), *How Does Law Protect in War* (2nd edn, Geneva, ICRC, 2006), pp. 342–53; L. Doswald-Beck and S. Vité, 'International Humanitarian Law and Human Rights Law' (1993) *IRRC* 94.

[214] See e.g., Moir, *The Law of Internal Armed Conflict*, pp. 196–7.

the nineteenth century framework of the international legal system. Humanitarian law applicable in international armed conflict is expressed as inter-state obligations which create a benefit for individuals. Although human rights law might also be applicable in international armed conflict, and thus may create direct rights for individuals, it has not influenced humanitarian law to the extent that humanitarian law also confers direct rights on individuals; that is to say, it has not impacted upon the normative framework of humanitarian law. It does not necessarily follow that humanitarian law provides less effective means for the protection of individuals: rather, in conflict situations, where recourse to judicial supervision is often impracticable or impossible, a framework of normative standards may be more effective than an individual rights framework in ensuring the protection of individuals.[215] Although the Geneva Conventions and Additional Protocol I do not expressly refer to individual obligations, nevertheless individual criminal responsibility for certain acts in violation of humanitarian law is now firmly established. The question of the source of the obligation, if any, which gives rises to individual criminal responsibility for acts in violation of international humanitarian law will be addressed in Chapter 4.

International humanitarian law applicable in international armed conflict remains consistent with the nineteenth century framework of the international legal system, as a system which creates only inter-state rights. However, individual criminal responsibility for violations of international humanitarian law is suggestive of direct obligations imposed on individuals, which is consistent with the post-1945 international legal system. Individual criminal responsibility is explored in Chapter 4. For present purposes it may be suggested that international humanitarian law applicable in international armed conflict creates a hybrid framework: on the one hand, it establishes standards of treatment rather than direct rights; on the other hand, it may impose obligations on individuals.

In internal armed conflict the situation is more complex because of the question of the status of insurgent groups and members of insurgent groups. International regulation of civil conflict has occurred in two distinct phases: first, through the practice of recognition of belligerency and insurgency, which reached a peak in the early twentieth

[215] See generally, discussion in R. Provost, *International Human Rights and Humanitarian Law* (Cambridge, Cambridge University Press, 2002), pp. 54–6.

century; and second, through the application of aspects of international humanitarian law to non-international armed conflict, first by common Article 3 to the Geneva Conventions and then by Additional Protocol II.

Traditionally civil conflict was considered as a matter falling within the domestic reserve of the conflicted state, and beyond the remit of international regulation. However, civil conflict became a problem internationally through the assertion of belligerent rights at sea. The practice of recognising belligerent rights in civil conflict began in the early nineteenth century, led by Britain. Initially the conferral of belligerent rights was based on assimilating the insurgent rebels to a separate state: like Vattel, the approach was not to accord rights and duties to individuals, but rather to treat an internal conflict as if it were for the time being an inter-state conflict. Subsequently recognition of belligerency was detached from recognition of statehood, suggesting that entities not assimilated to states could bear belligerent rights, and consequently held at least a measure of international legal personality. By the end of the nineteenth century a reasonably coherent doctrine had developed along these lines, subject to a deliberate act of recognition by the lawful government or foreign state(s). This doctrine was consistent with the post-1945 account of the framework of the international legal system, since it allowed states to confer direct rights and obligations on individuals by a positive intentional act. But there was no generally accepted basis by which this practice could be reconciled with the prevailing understanding of the international legal system in the nineteenth and early twentieth centuries: it seems to have been accepted as a pragmatic compromise.

After the Second World War, the practice of recognition of belligerency was effectively abandoned in favour of a system which defines when the rules of international humanitarian law become applicable to civil conflict, and what those rules are. This process began with an extension of minimum humanitarian protection in common Article 3 of the Geneva Conventions and was expanded and strengthened by rules in Additional Protocol II of 1977. During the drafting of common Article 3, the question of the basis upon which rights and obligations could be imposed on insurgents was raised but not resolved. The issue resurfaced during the drafting of Protocol II, with several states arguing that the only status which rebel insurgents could claim was under domestic law, and that they became bound by the terms of the Protocol once it was either signed by their national state or incorporated into domestic law. But there was no common view emerging from the debates concerning the basis upon which insurgents became bound by its provisions. In respect of national liberation movements, Protocol I classified armed conflicts involving a national liberation movement as international conflicts to which the Geneva Conventions and Protocol I applied – subject to an express declaration from the non-state party or parties to the conflict undertaking to apply the Geneva Conventions and the Protocol. For national liberation movements at least, the application of the rights and obligations applicable in international armed conflict is predicated on their express consent, but there is no such requirement for the application of relevant rules to other internal conflicts. In the literature, several alternative bases have been put forward to assert the direct application of rights and obligations to insurgents through international law rather than as a matter of domestic law. Some are more consistent with conventional doctrine or supported by precedent and practice than others. But the conclusion that must be drawn is that there was no clear or accepted view about the conceptual basis for the conferral of direct rights and obligations on insurgents in internal armed conflict. Furthermore, there is an absence of debate on this question at the Diplomatic Conferences for the Geneva Conventions and Protocol II. Neither is it clear from the text and the commentaries whether the rights and obligations are conferred on an armed opposition group as such, or directly on individuals constituting its membership. Although common Article 3 was addressed as injunctions to the parties to the conflict, suggesting that the group itself was the relevant obliged entity, discussion of the jurisprudential basis for the conferral of rights and obligations on a non-state entity in the ICRC Commentaries and in the literature elide the question of the relevant bound entity. The provisions of Additional Protocol II are not clear in the entities to which they are addressed, since the phrase 'parties to the conflict' does not appear in the text. Whether the relevantly bound entity is the armed opposition group as such or the individuals constituting the group cannot be determined on the basis of these texts; rather, it seems there is no clear conceptual division between the group and its membership and individual members of the group are in practice treated as though they are directly and personally bound.

Since the end of the nineteenth century, states conferred direct rights and obligations on insurgent groups and individuals through a deliberate act of recognition of belligerency or insurgency. This practice is consistent with the post-1945 framework of the international legal system, although it developed into a consistent practice much earlier.

Although the doctrines of recognition have been replaced with conventional rules in common Article 3 and Additional Protocol II, and also by customary rules, these rules also confer direct rights and obligations on insurgents, engaging individuals in a manner consistent with the post-1945 framework of the international legal system.

In the development of international humanitarian law, the means and extent to which individuals are engaged in international law does not necessarily correspond to the understanding of the framework of the international legal system prevailing at the time. The protection of individuals in international armed conflict is to the present day effected by a framework consistent with nineteenth century international law; while since the nineteenth century civil conflict has been regulated by a framework consistent with the post-1945 international legal system. While these potential conflicts with the established understanding of the engagement of individuals were noted at the time, the inconsistency of the rules with the prevailing framework did not prevent these rules from being effected in practice; in some instances that practice then was cited to overcome or to minimise the significance of the conceptual questions raised by the conflict.

The position of the individual in international humanitarian law depends upon the type of conflict and it is difficult to make generalisations across both types of conflict. In both international and internal armed conflicts, individuals are protected by rules which establish standards for their treatment without conferring direct rights upon them. In internal armed conflicts, individuals who form part of insurgent groups also have direct rights under international humanitarian law. In both types of conflicts, individuals may be subject to direct obligations, a question which is explored in Chapter 4.

4 The individual in international criminal law

4.1 Introduction

It is now widely acknowledged that individual criminal responsibility is imposed on individuals through international criminal law. This is most often traced to the famous statement of the International Military Tribunal at Nuremberg in 1946 that:

> crimes against international law are committed by men, not abstract entities, and only by punishing individuals who commit such crimes can the provisions of international law be enforced . . . individuals have duties which transcend the national obligations of obedience imposed by the individual state.[1]

This chapter explores the development of individual criminal responsibility under international law. The first section of the chapter looks at often-cited 'antecedents' of individual responsibility for international crimes; the second section examines individual criminal responsibility in the inter-war period; and the third section traces the evolution of individual criminal responsibility since 1945.

The term 'international criminal law' is used in a broader sense by some scholars to include international crimes of states; crimes established by treaty regimes which require states to prohibit conduct in their domestic law; aspects of procedural law applicable in international tribunals; and transnational or inter-state cooperation in criminal matters, including through extradition law.[2] Although these types of rules may have relevance for individuals, the primary inquiry of this chapter is

[1] International Military Judgment (Nuremberg), Judgment and Sentences, 1 October 1946, reproduced in (1947) 41 *AJIL* 172, 220–1.

[2] See e.g., R. Cryer, *Prosecuting International Crimes: Selectivity and the International Criminal Law Regime* (Cambridge, Cambridge University Press, 2005), pp. 2–3.

the extent to which international law imposes obligations on individuals which result in individual criminal responsibility. The focus here is on the principle of individual criminal responsibility in international law, rather than on these other aspects of international crimes.

4.2 Individual responsibility before 1919

Before 1919, and arguably before 1945, there was no developed conception of individual criminal responsibility under international law. However, three categories of practice are often cited as antecedents of individual criminal responsibility under international law: first, individual responsibility for war crimes under national law; second, the 'international crime' of piracy; and third, internationalised courts for the prosecution of individuals. Although these practices may have claims as conceptual antecedents of international crimes, treating them as antecedents of individual responsibility under international law is questionable.

The first category of practice covers the prosecution of war crimes or violations of the laws of war in national courts and tribunals. Examples of these prosecutions can be traced to the late Middle Ages:[3] in 1268 in Naples, Conradin von Hohenstafen was tried, convicted and sentenced to death for 'initiating an unjust war';[4] in 1305, the Scot William Wallace was tried and convicted for excesses in war 'sparing neither age nor sex, monk nor nun'.[5] In the fourteenth and fifteenth centuries, the 'law of arms', a generally applicable law of knights, was used by domestic tribunals to prosecute offences committed not only against the power trying the individual knight, but also for offences committed against the enemy.[6] For example in 1346, Walter de Selby, an English

[3] T. Meron, *War Crimes Law Comes of Age: Essays* (Oxford, Clarendon Press, 1998), pp. 1–2.

[4] M. C. Bassiouni, *Crimes Against Humanity in International Law* (Dordrecht, Martinus Nijoff, 1992), p. 154.

[5] G. Schwarzenberger, 'The Judgment of Nuremberg' (1947) 21 *Tulane L Rev.* 329. In 1279, the Statute of Westminster authorised the Crown to 'punish soldiers according to the law and customs of the realm': J. W. Bishop Jr, *Justice Under Fire: A Study of Military Law* (New York, Charterhouse, 1974), p. 4.

[6] In 1367, it was agreed that a dispute between the Black Prince and the Marshal d'Audreham concerning a violation of parole by the Marshal as a prisoner should be dealt with by a panel of twelve knights because it was 'a matter of knights of and of war'. It was alleged that the Marshal, in breaching his personal obligation to refrain from taking up arms, had committed the crime of treason. He was acquitted on a technical point: the Marshal was fighting on the wages of Pedro of Castile who was in battle against Don Pedro, for whom the Prince was fighting as a private person and not as a public person; therefore the Marshal had not armed himself against the Prince: see M. H. Keen, *The Laws of War in the Late Middle Ages* (London, Keegan Paul, 1965), pp. 50–3.

captain, was captured by the Scots and was tried and put to death for treason which had been committed against the English.[7] It appears that the offences under the law of arms also constituted domestic crimes under ordinary criminal law and that this was the basis on which prosecutions were brought and the basis upon which individuals incurred responsibility. In the seventeenth and eighteenth centuries, national codes of conduct in war became increasingly prevalent;[8] these codes often included disciplinary offences prosecutable in national courts and tribunals.[9] Similarly, the 1863 Lieber Code provided that individuals were criminally responsible;[10] individuals were prosecuted in US military tribunals for breaches of its provisions.[11] In 1880, the Institute of International Law affirmed that belligerents had a right to prosecute violations of the laws of war[12] and in 1906, the 1864 Geneva Convention was updated to include an article requiring states parties to ensure their criminal laws covered violations of the Convention.[13] This category of practice has limited precedential value for international criminal law. On the one hand, it demonstrates that conduct in armed conflict could amount to a prosecutable offence, but on the other hand, individual responsibility arose exclusively under national law and was implemented through national processes. It is consistent with the nineteenth century framework of the international legal system,

[7] Keen, *The Laws of War in the Late Middle Ages*, pp. 45–6. Another example is that of Jean d'Angennes, a Frenchman, who was tried under the law of arms by Henry V for surrendering Cherbourg to Humphrey of Gloucester, an act which benefitted the English: *ibid.* pp. 46–7.

[8] T. H. McCormack, 'From Sun Tzu to the Sixth Committee: The Evolution of an International Criminal Law Regime' in T. H. McCormack and G. Simpson (eds.), *The Law of War Crimes: National and International Approaches* (The Hague, Kluwer, 1997), pp. 31, 40.

[9] Cryer, *Prosecuting International Crimes*, pp. 24–5. See also G. Parker, 'Early Modern Europe' in M. Howard, G. J. Andreopoulos and M. Schulman (eds.), *The Laws of War: Constraints on Warfare in the Western World* (New Haven, Conn., Yale University Press, 1994), pp. 40, 52.

[10] *General Order No. 100* (New York, van Nostrand, 1863); G. B. Davis, 'Doctor Francis Lieber's Instructions for the Government of Armies in the Field' (1907) 1 *AJIL* 13.

[11] In 1863, Henry Wirz, commander of the Confederate prisoner of war camp in Andersonville, was tried before a US military tribunal and found guilty of causing the deaths of many Union prisoners through criminal negligence: see R. K. Woetzel, *The Nuremberg Trial in International law* (London, Stevens & Sons Ltd, 1962), pp. 26–7.

[12] Institute of International Law, *Manual of the Law of War on Land* (Oxford, Institute of International Law, 1880).

[13] Convention for the Amelioration of Wounded and Sick in Armies, Art. 28(1), 9 July 1906 (entry into force 9 August 1907), 202 CTS 144; cf. Geneva Convention for the Amelioration of the Wounded, 22 August 1864 (entry into force 22 June 1865), 129 CTS 361.

which suggested that individual obligations could only be derived from municipal law.

The second category of practice often cited as antecedent to international criminal law is the so-called 'international crime' of piracy (piracy *jure gentium*).[14] This is based on a misconception of piracy, which was 'not a legal crime or offence under the law of nations' but rather a 'special ground of state jurisdiction'.[15] The pirate was designated as *hostis humani generis*, enemy of all mankind,[16] and could be taken to have 'disclaimed all state allegiance'.[17] Furthermore, piracy was committed on the high seas, outside the jurisdiction of any one state.[18] On that basis, the pirate was subject to the jurisdiction of any state, which could prosecute the offence under its municipal law.[19] But pirates were tried by national courts and punished under national law, not international law: international law simply endorsed piracy as a special source of national jurisdiction.

The third category of practice is the use of internationalised processes for the treatment of individuals. The most commonly-cited example of an international trial is that of Peter von Hagenbach in 1474.[20] Von Hagenbach, a knight, was appointed by Charles the Bold as governor of the Burgundian city of Breisach. He instituted a regime of terror in the city in order to annex it for Charles. After a coalition was formed by Austria, France and the towns and knights of the Upper Rhine to overthrow the regime, von Hagenbach was captured.[21] Upon order of the Archduke of Austria, von Hagenbach was tried in the marketplace of Breisach before a bench comprised of judges from Austria and the Allied cities, and sixteen knights representing the order of knighthood.[22] The

14 See e.g., G. Komarow, 'Individual Responsibility under International Law: The Nuremberg Principles in Domestic Legal Systems' (1980) 29 *ICLQ* 21, 22.

15 'Harvard Research Draft on Piracy' (1932) 26 *AJIL Supplement* 739, 759.

16 See e.g., Opinion of Judge Moore in *SS Lotus* (1927) PCIJ ser. A no. 10 (1927). See generally, A. P. Rubin, *The Law of Piracy* (2nd edn, Newport, Naval War College Press, 1998), p. 17 n. 61.

17 'Harvard Research Draft on Piracy' (1932) 26 *AJIL Supplement* 739, 823.

18 See *In re Piracy Jure Gentium* [1934] AC 586, Viscount Sankey LC.

19 'Harvard Research Draft on Piracy' (1932) 26 *AJIL Supplement* 739, 754, 757.

20 G. Schwarzenberger, *International Law as Applied by International Courts and Tribunals*, vol. II, *The Law of Armed Conflict* (London, Stevens, 1968), pp. 462–6.

21 For a general history of von Hagenbach, see H. Brauer-Gramm, *Der Landrogt Peter von Hagenbach: Die burgundische Herrschaft am Oberrhein 1469–1474* (Göttingen, Musterschmidt-Verlag, 1957). For the citation of this as a precedent, see Woetzel, *The Nuremberg Trial in International Law*, pp. 19–20.

22 See A. G. de Barante, *Histoire des Ducs de Bourgogne de la Maison de Valois, 1364–1477* (Brussels, JP Meline, 1839), vol. IX, pp. 289, 405; G. Claerr-Stamm, *Pierre de Hagenbach: Le destin tragique d'un chevalier sundgauvien au service de Charles le Téméraire* (Altkirch, Société

trial was held in public and had a vast number of spectators.[23] Von Hagenbach was charged with both direct crimes and crimes committed by persons under his command, including murder, rape and perjury. His defence was based primarily on superior orders, his representative arguing that '[h]e had no right to question the orders which he was charged to carry out, and it was his duty to obey'.[24] Von Hagenbach addressed the tribunal himself on this point, requesting an adjournment to obtain the necessary confirmation from his master.[25] The tribunal refused to grant an adjournment and rejected the defence of superior orders, stating that to accept his defence would be contrary to the law of God.[26] It found von Hagenbach guilty and sentenced him to death. Before he was executed, he was deprived of his knighthood.[27]

In order to assess the precedential value of the von Hagenbach trial, it is necessary to consider the law under which his individual responsibility arose. However, the applicable law of the trial is not clear. That the defendant was deprived of his knighthood suggests that it was brought under the law of arms, but the leading authority on the laws of war in the late Middle Ages, Maurice Keen, does not refer to the trial.[28] Von Hagenbach was also convicted of ordinary crimes (rape, murder, etc.) as perpetrator and commander. Like other trials in which violations of the law of arms were prosecuted, all of the offences may have been prosecuted as ordinary criminal offences under domestic law. Nor is it clear how the international panel was constituted: whether it was an international court in the modern sense,[29] or whether it was a domestic court which happened to be constituted by members of different nationalities. In another trial, that of Barbasan before Henry V for the murder of

d'Histoire du Sundgau, 2005), p. 175; R. Vaughan, *Charles the Bold: The Last Valois Duke of Burgundy* (London, Longman, 1973), pp. 268–86.

[23] Claerr-Stamm, *Pierre de Hagenbach*, p. 175. Von Hagenbach was subjected to severe torture in the proceedings leading to his formal accusation, producing confessions later withdrawn in the oral proceedings.

[24] de Barante, *Histoire des Ducs de Bourgogne de la Maison de Valois, 1364–1477*, vol. IX, p. 16.

[25] Claerr-Stamm, *Pierre de Hagenbach*, pp. 177–80.

[26] de Barante, *Histoire des Ducs de Bourgogne de la Maison de Valois, 1364–1477*, vol. IX, p. 17.

[27] *Ibid.* p. 19.

[28] No reference to the von Hagenbach trial can be found in either of Keen's works on the subject: Keen, *The Laws of War in the Late Middle Ages* and M. H. Keen, *Nobles, Knights and Men-At-Arms in the Middle Ages* (London, Hambledon Press, 1996).

[29] Schwarzenberger argued that the tribunal was a real international court on the basis that the Holy Roman Empire had degenerated to the point that relations among its different entities had an international character: Schwarzenberger, *International Law as Applied by International Courts and Tribunals*, vol. II, p. 15.

John the Fearless, apparently Barbasan successfully appealed his sentence to an international panel of heralds.[30] Other cases in which reference to the law of arms was made involved only a domestic tribunal or court.[31] In some ways, the von Hagenbach trial bears some resemblance to modern international criminal law, in its use of an internationalised process for prosecutions with (possibly) the applicable law being a form of international rules, albeit rules which applied to a certain class of persons (knights). But it seems to have been regarded as the end of an old era, not the beginning of a new.

A lack of clear information about these processes makes it difficult to assess whether they can be regarded as individual prosecutions before international courts and thus as antecedents to modern international criminal law. On first impression, the von Hagenbach trial appears to be a precedent for individual criminal responsibility before international courts and perhaps under a kind of internationalised law, but it is not possible to affirm this with any certainty. In particular, there was no continuity of practice: it cannot be said that this trial was followed by consistent practice for the judicial treatment of war criminals. The treatment of Napoleon at the beginning of the ninteenth century was summary punishment through political rather than judicial processes;[32] moreover the law of arms was virtually extinct by the seventeenth century. When the First World War broke out there was no developed conception of individual responsibility for international crimes under international law, nor any individual responsibility before internationalised judicial processes. The only developed individual responsibility was a matter for domestic law and domestic processes, consistent with the nineteenth century framework of the international legal system which suggested that individuals could only derive duties from domestic law.

4.3 The inter-war period: the Kaiser and the Leipzig trials

During the First World War there were calls for the prosecution of individuals committing offences against the laws and customs of

[30] Keen, *The Laws of War in the Late Middle Ages*, p. 53.

[31] *Ibid.* pp. 258–69.

[32] F. Giles, *Napoleon Bonaparte: England's Prisoner* (London, Constable, 2001), p. 6. See also F. L. Maitland, *Narrative of the Surrender of Buonaparte: And of his Residence on Board H.M.S. Bellerophon* (London, H. Colburn, 1826) and E.-A.-D. Las Cases, *Memoirs of the Life, Exile, and Conversations, of the Emperor Napoleon* (London, H. Colburn, 1836).

war:[33] the Allied governments committed to hold individuals 'personally responsible' for their crimes[34] but only the French government made an express reference to 'judicial' punishment.[35] At its first plenary meeting in January 1919, the Paris Peace Conference established a Commission to report on breaches of the laws and customs of war committed by German forces and their allies, responsibility for those offences attaching to individuals 'however highly placed', and the constitution and procedure of a tribunal appropriate to try these offences.[36] That Commission's Report, presented to the Peace Conference in March 1919, did not address the question whether individuals held direct obligations under international law, but implied that individuals were so obliged in suggesting that individuals were responsible for offences under the laws and customs of war without the interposition of domestic law. The Report concluded:

All persons belonging to enemy countries, however high their positions may have been, without distinction of rank, including Chiefs of States, who have been guilty of offences against the laws and customs of war or the laws of humanity, are liable to criminal prosecution.[37]

It noted that international law permitted states to try persons within their custody (regardless of their nationality) for certain offences and to set up courts and procedure under domestic law in order to do so.[38] The Commission recommended that an International High Tribunal be

[33] H. H. L. Bellot, 'War Crimes: Their Prevention and Punishment' (1916) 2 *Grotius Soc'y Transactions* 31, 37–8. An account of the Belgian atrocities is given in P. Northomb, *The Barbarians in Belgium* (Jean E. H. Findley (trans.), London, Jarrold and Sons, 1915); see also E. Verhaeren, *Belgium's Agony* (London, Constable, 1915). A defence of the German army in Belgium is recorded in E. Bennett, *The German Army in Belgium: The White Book of May 1915* (London, Swathmore Press Ltd, 1921).

[34] United Nations War Crimes Commission (UNWCC), *History of the United Nations War Crimes Commission and the Development of the Laws of War* (London, HM Stationery Office, 1948), p. 35.

[35] 'Conduct which is equally contrary to international law and the fundamental principles of all human civilization will not go unpunished . . . the authors and directors of these crimes will be held responsible morally, judicially, and financially. They will seek in vain to escape the inexorable expiation which awaits them.' *The Times*, 7 October 1918; *New York Times*, 5 October 1918.

[36] Minute No. 2 of the Preliminary Peace Conference Plenary Session on 25 January 1919, reprinted in 'Commission on the Responsibility of the Authors of War and on Enforcement of Penalties' (1920) 14 *AJIL* 95.

[37] 'Commission on the Responsibility of the Authors of War and on Enforcement of Penalties' (1920) 14 *AJIL* 95, 117.

[38] *Ibid.* 121.

formed to deal with charges against persons in positions of authority, including heads of state, and charges against persons who committed offences against nationals of multiple Allied states.[39] The US representatives appended a Memorandum of Reservations to the Commission's Report, disagreeing with the Commission on its central finding that individuals were responsible for offences under the laws and customs of war and the laws of humanity:

> The American representatives know of no international statute or convention making a violation of the laws and customs of war – not to speak of the laws or principles of humanity – an international crime, affixing a punishment to it, and declaring the court which has jurisdiction over the offence.[40]

The US memorandum suggested that this difficulty was not insurmountable because the relevant acts were rather violations of domestic law: they had 'declared certain acts violating the laws and customs of war to be crimes, affixing punishments to their commission, and providing military courts or commissions within the respective states possessing jurisdiction over such offence'.[41] It urged that an international tribunal ought not be created, and instead argued that existing military commissions or tribunals ought to be used 'with a law and a procedure ... known in advance'.[42]

The Treaty of Versailles provided for the punishment of enemy nationals through two mechanisms: one for the Kaiser, a second for all other individuals.[43] Article 227 arraigned the Kaiser 'for a supreme offence against international morality and the sanctity of treaties' before a special tribunal composed of five judges to be appointed by the US, Great Britain, France, Italy and Japan. It implied that the Kaiser was liable for breaches of international law, although it did not expressly refer to the source of any individual obligations not to commit those breaches. No trial of the Kaiser ever took place: after abdicating, William II had entered the Netherlands under asylum.[44] The Secretary-General of the Peace Conference wrote to the Dutch Minister, asking for the ex-Kaiser to be handed over, specifying several crimes committed by the Germans for which William II held moral responsibility:

[39] *Ibid.* 121–2. [40] *Ibid.* Annex II, 146. [41] *Ibid.* Annex II, 146. [42] *Ibid.* Annex II, 141–2.
[43] Treaty of Versailles, Arts. 227–30, 28 June 1919, UKTS 4 (Cmd 153).
[44] On the Kaiser's decision to go to the Netherlands, see M. Baumont, *The Fall of the Kaiser* (E. Ibbetson James (trans.), London, George Allen & Unwin Ltd, 1930), pp. 241–7.

For all these acts, at least moral responsibility rises all the way to the supreme chief who ordered them or who abused his full powers to violate or to allow to be violated the rules which are most sacred to the human conscience.[45]

The Dutch Minister refused the request on the grounds that the Netherlands was not party to Art. 227 of the Versailles Treaty and that it could not 'associat[e] herself with an act of high international politics of the Powers'.[46] In response the Allied Powers wrote that the Dutch refusal would create an unfortunate precedent which would undermine the use of international tribunals to bring justice to 'highly placed' culprits.[47] The Dutch remained firmly opposed to the request:[48] ex-Kaiser Wilhelm was never extradited and remained in the Netherlands until his death in 1941, a year after the German invasion.[49]

The second mechanism established by the Treaty of Versailles was for all other individuals to be brought before military tribunals to be tried for 'acts in violation of the laws and customs of war'. Article 228 provided in part:

[45] The original French is reproduced in A. Mérignhac, 'De la Responsibilité Pénale des Actes Criminels commis au cours de la Guerre de 1914–1918' (1920) 8 *Revue du Droit International* 34, 38. Author's own translation.

[46] *Ibid.* 39–40. This summary is taken from M. Lachs, *War Crimes: An Attempt to Define the Issues* (London, Stevens & Sons, 1945), p. 57, which also sets out the relevant Dutch law on the granting of extradition requests. The Dutch government commissioned an expert opinion on the point from Clunet, editor of the *Journal de Droit International*, which appeared in the Journal on 17 January 1920 in support of the Dutch position. Mérignhac, 'De la Responsibilité Pénale des Actes Criminels commis au cours de la Guerre de 1914–1918', 40–2. Clunet argued that the charges specified in Art. 227 of the Treaty of Versailles were not pre-existing crimes and that to accede to the extradition request would be in violation of Holland's domestic law. An opposing view was put forward by Professors Larnaude and de La Pradelle: F. Larnaude and A. G. de La Pradelle, *Examen de la responsibilité pénale de l'Emperor Guillaume II* (Paris, Imprimerie Nationale, 1918).

[47] Mérignhac, 'De la Responsibilité Pénale des Actes Criminels commis au cours de la Guerre de 1914–1918', 42–4; see also Lachs, *War Crimes*, p. 58.

[48] Mérignhac, 'De la Responsibilité Pénale des Actes Criminels commis au cours de la Guerre de 1914–1918', 44–5.

[49] Lachs argues that the request was unfortunately framed incorrectly: the ex-Kaiser was charged with 'moral responsibility' when he ought to have been charged with murder, pillage, robbery and violence, which were punishable under foreign law: see also Lachs, *War Crimes*, pp. 58–9. For a different view, see Mérignhac, 'De la Responsibilité Pénale des Actes Criminels commis au cours de la Guerre de 1914–1918'. On the execution of Art. 227 generally, see G. Hankel, *Die Leipziger Prozesse: Deutsche Kriegsverbrechen und ihre strafrechtliche Verfolgung nach dem Ersten Weltkrieg* (Hamburg, Hamburger Edition, 2003), pp. 74–87.

The German Government recognises the right of the Allied and Associated Powers to bring before military tribunals persons accused of having committed acts in violation of the laws and customs of war. Such persons shall, if found guilty, be sentenced to punishments laid down by law. This provision will apply notwithstanding any proceedings or prosecution before a tribunal in Germany or in the territory of her allies.

Article 229 provided that persons guilty of criminal acts against the nationals of one of the Allied Powers would be brought before the military tribunals of that Power, while persons guilty of acts against the nationals of more than one Allied Power would be brought before military tribunals 'composed of members of the military tribunals' of the relevant Powers.[50] Similar provisions were inserted in the Treaty of Sèvres but it was never ratified. It was replaced with the 1923 Treaty of Lausanne which did not include provisions relating to individual criminal responsibility:[51] instead it was accompanied by a 'Declaration of Amnesty' for all offences between 1 August 1914 and 20 November 1922.[52]

Anxious to avoid execution of Articles 228–30 of the Treaty of Versailles, in January 1920 the Germans proposed, by way of 'compromise', that all persons accused by the Allied Powers of war crimes should be tried in proceedings before the Reich Supreme Court in Leipzig. The Allies consented to Germans trying the persons accused of war crimes but reserved the right to institute proceedings in accordance with the Versailles Treaty.[53] The trials were to be conducted under the ordinary domestic criminal law, observing the fundamental rules of criminal procedure.[54] The Court applied German law in assessing the charges and imposing sentences but it recognised that if an act were an offence against customary international law, its illegality would be established.[55] The Allied state instigating the prosecution was to send details of the evidence

[50] Treaty of Versailles, 28 June 1919, UKTS 4 (Cmd 153).

[51] Treaty of Lausanne, 24 July 1923, UKTS 16 (Cmd 1929). [52] UNWCC, *History*, p. 45.

[53] This letter is referred to in the Allied Note to President of German Delegation Respecting War Criminals, Paris, 7 May 1920, British Parliamentary Papers (1921, Cmd 1325), p. 110; reproduced in (1922) 16 *AJIL Supplement* 195.

[54] To carry out the terms of the agreement with the Allies, the German Parliament passed special laws giving jurisdiction to the Imperial Court of Justice: Reichsgesetzblatt, 1919, no. 247; Reichsgesetzblatt, 1920, no. 53 and Reichsgesetzblatt, 1921, no. 51, cited in C. Mullins, *The Leipzig Trials: An Account of the War Criminals' Trials and a Study of German Mentality* (London, H. G. & G. Witherby, 1921), p. 35.

[55] It is clear from the reports that the applicable law was German national law. This is affirmed in C. Dinstein, *The Defence of 'Obedience to Superior Orders' in International Law* (Leyden, A. W. Sijthoff, 1965), p. 19 n. 46, who notes that at least one jurist incorrectly asserted that the Leipzig judgments purported to express existing international law.

to the German State Attorney before the trial. During the trials, witnesses were called and questioned by the judge: the state attorney, defence counsel and the accused could put questions to the witnesses through the judge. During and after the examination of the witnesses, the judge could ask the accused to give his version of the relevant incident. The special German law permitted the Allies to participate as co-prosecutor, and they were urged to do so by the representative of the German Minister of Justice: but they declined, citing their view that these ought to be German trials, conducted entirely by the German government.[56]

Initially, the Allied governments submitted a list of 896 accused war criminals to the German government. After Germany stated it was 'impossible to deliver up' all persons on the list,[57] the Allies submitted a new list of some forty-five persons.[58] Initially, only twelve persons were tried: six were convicted and sentenced to terms of imprisonment between two months and four years.[59] The Leipzig Court held that the defence of superior orders excused breaches of the laws and customs of war.[60] Some convicted persons were not made to serve the imposed sentences;

[56] Allied Note to the German government, signed by M. Millerand, 7 May 1920; cited in Mullins, *The Leipzig Trials*, pp. 47–8.

[57] This letter is referred to in the Allied Note to President of German Delegation Respecting War Criminals, Paris, 7 May 1920, British Parliamentary Papers (1921, Cmd 1325), p. 110; reproduced in (1922) 16 *AJIL Supplement* 195.

[58] *Ibid.*

[59] Mullins, *The Leipzig Trials*, pp. 27, 191. Mullins, a London Barrister, accompanied the British Mission as interpreter. See generally, G. Hankel, *Die Leipziger Prozesse: Deutrche Kriegsverbrechen und ihre strafrechtliche Verfolgung nach dem Ersten Weltkrieg* (Hamburg, Hamburger Edition, 2003). The British cases are reported in British Parliamentary Command Paper no. 1450, reproduced in 'German War Trials' (1922) 16 *AJIL* 674. Summaries of the decisions are given in 'German War Trials: Report of Proceedings before the Supreme Court in Danzig' (1922) 16 *AJIL* 628. Of the six cases brought by the British, five were convicted; of France's five cases, one was convicted and Belgium's single case resulted in an acquittal.

[60] *Commander Karl Neumann, Hospital Ship 'Dover Castle'*, Judgment, 4 June 1921, reproduced in 'German War Trials' (1922) 16 *AJIL* 674, 707. The presiding judge stated that all civilised nations recognise the principle that a subordinate is covered by the orders of his superiors, adding that there was no doubt in the opinion of the Court that those orders were justified: this finding is disputed in contemporary critique of the decision: see G. A. Finch, 'Superior Orders and War Crimes' (1921) 15 *AJIL* 440. It is also difficult to reconcile with the Court's decision in the *Llandovery Castle* case, where it was held that the defence of superior orders did not apply where the accused knew that the order involved a violation of civil or military law: see *Lieutenants Dithmar and Boldt, Hospital Ship 'Llandovery Castle'*, Judgment, 16 July 1921, reproduced in 'German War Trials' (1922) 16 *AJIL* 674, 722. Dinstein argues that overall, the decisions of the Leipzig Court demonstrate a unified approach to the question of obedience to superior orders: see Dinstein, *The Defence of 'Obedience to Superior Orders' in International Law*, pp. 10–20.

others escaped and the prison guards who assisted them were publicly congratulated. In protest at the conduct and results of the trials, the Allied mission attending the trials withdrew and the German Supreme Court thereafter proceeded to enter acquittals and dismiss cases on the basis that there was a failure to identify crimes covered by German law or for a lack of sufficient evidence.[61] Subsequently, the Conference of Ambassadors threatened to execute Articles 228–30 of the Versailles Treaty; in response, the Leipzig Court decided to continue with the trials, but in the vast majority of cases there was no public hearing and only six resulted in convictions.[62] By the close of the Leipzig trials, from a total of 901 cases brought before the court, 888 accused were acquitted or summarily dismissed and only 13 were convicted.[63] Although the Allies never followed through on their threat to execute the provisions of the Versailles Treaty with any joint action, France and Belgium undertook trials themselves under domestic law, dealing with more than 1,200 accused.[64]

The Treaty of Versailles implied that individual responsibility could arise directly under international law: in the case of the Kaiser this responsibility was stipulated for an offence 'against the sanctity of treaties'; in the case of other individuals, it was for having committed 'acts in violation of the laws and customs of war'.[65] Germany acknowledged that individuals in the latter category could be tried by military tribunals of the Allied Powers. These provisions of the Treaty of Versailles suggested that individuals held direct obligations under international law, obligations which could be enforced in domestic courts. In this way, the provisions are consistent with the post-1945 framework of the international legal system, which provides that individuals may be subject to international duties and commit international wrongs.

However, Articles 228–30 of the Treaty of Versailles were effectively abandoned and the only individuals tried were prosecuted in German courts under German domestic law. Where an act was an offence under customary international law, presumably including the laws and

[61] W. B. Simons, 'The Jurisdictional Bases of the International Military Tribunal at Nuremberg' in G. Ginsburgs and V. N. Kudriavtsevs (eds.), *The Nuremberg Trial and International Law* (Dordrecht, Martinus Nijhoff, 1990), pp. 39, 41. See generally, Mullins, *The Leipzig Trials*.

[62] UNWCC, *History*, p. 48. [63] *Ibid.*

[64] Some cases are reported: see (1921) *Journal de Droit International* 781, 781–2, 1076–7 and see generally, N. J. B. Jørgensen, *The Responsibility of States for International Crimes* (Oxford, Oxford University Press, 2000), pp. 6–7.

[65] Treaty of Versailles, Arts. 227–8, 28 June 1919, UKTS 4 (Cmd 153).

customs of war, it was taken to be illegal under German domestic law. Thus the practice after the First World War was consistent with the nineteenth century framework of the international legal system because individual responsibility was ultimately determined under domestic law and through domestic processes.

Individual responsibility under the Treaty of Versailles sat alongside the criminalisation of the state of Germany, the Treaty of Versailles expressly referring to Germany's responsibility for the war and imposing punishment in the form of curtailed sovereign authority:[66] Germany was required to pay punitive damages and to undergo a process of demilitarisation.[67] The Versailles model of state criminality was criticised: the US was reluctant to support the more punitive aspects of the settlement and the effects on the German population at large were felt to be unjust. Many blame the treatment of Germany for the breakdown of the European order leading to the Second World War.[68]

4.4 Individual responsibility after 1945

(a) Post-Second World War prosecutions

(i) The Nuremberg Tribunal

During the Second World War, the Allies made statements which referred to the punishment of war criminals through judicial processes but did not foreshadow the use of an international tribunal.[69] On 13 January 1942, nine states signed the Declaration of St James, which referred to the 'punishment, through the channel of organised justice, of those guilty of or responsible for' crimes against the civilian population as a principal war aim.[70] On 7 October 1942, the Lord Chancellor announced the establishment of a United Nations War Crimes Commission (UNWCC) for the Investigation of War Crimes, to name

[66] *Ibid.* Art. 231. [67] *Ibid.* Arts. 231–47.

[68] J. M. Keynes, *The Economic Consequences of the Peace* (New York, Harcourt, Brace, and Jovanovich, 1920), pp. 32–5, 226–51; G. Simpson, *Law, War and Crime* (Cambridge, Polity Press, 2007), p. 61.

[69] See Statements of Roosevelt and Churchill, 25 January 1941, reproduced in UNWCC, *History*, pp. 89–90. In his declaration Churchill stated '[r]etribution for these crimes must henceforward take its place among the major purposes of the war'.

[70] *Punishment for War Crimes*, the Inter-Allied Declaration signed at St James' Palace London on 13 January and Relative Documents, reproduced in UNWCC, *History*, pp. 89–90. (It was signed by Belgium, Czechoslovakia, France, Greece, Luxembourg, Norway, the Netherlands, Poland and Yugoslavia.)

and identify persons responsible for Nazi atrocities, and in particular organised atrocities; he also stated that surrender of named criminals wanted for war crimes should be a condition of the Armistice.[71] On the same day, President Roosevelt indicated an intention to cooperate with the UNWCC and stated that provision should be made for surrender of war criminals to the UN.[72] A week later, the Soviet government stated that it 'share[d] the just desire ... that those guilty of the [atrocities perpetrated by the Hitlerites] shall be handed over to judicial courts and prosecuted, and that the sentence passed on them shall be put into execution'.[73] On 1 November 1943, the Moscow Declaration of Stalin, Roosevelt and Churchill suggested that these prosecutions would occur through domestic processes and through the application of national law;[74] but it expressly reserved 'the case of the major criminals whose offences have no particular geographical location and who will be punished by a joint decision of the Governments of the Allies'.[75]

[71] Parliamentary Debates, House of Lords, vol. 124, no. 86, col. 563. The UNWCC was established on 20 October 1943 to accomplish the broad functions outlined by the Lord Chancellor: to investigate war crimes, to record available evidence and to name and identify persons responsible for those crimes. It was required to make recommendations to governments concerning the tribunals in which war criminals should be tried (see generally UNWCC, *History*; M. E. Bathurst, 'The United Nations War Crimes Commission' (1945) 39 *AJIL* 565. Initially the Commission was ineffectual, but by June 1945 it was issuing substantial fortnightly bulletins listing names, last known addresses and charges against suspects: A. Tusa and J. Tusa, *The Nuremberg Trial* (London, Macmillan, 1983), p. 96. See also UNWCC Report of 16 November 1946, cited in Q. Wright, 'The Law of the Nuremberg Trial' (1947) 41 *AJIL* 38; *Ex Parte Quirin*, 317 US 1 (1942) and *In re Yamashita*, 196, 66 Sup. Ct 340 (1946).

[72] Inter-Allied Information Committee, London, *Punishment for War Crimes*, (2) Collective Notes presented to the Governments of Great Britain, the USSR and the USA and Relative Correspondence, reproduced in UNWCC, *History*, pp. 105–6.

[73] See Reply of the Soviet Government, 14 October 1942, annexed to 'I. Memorandum to President Roosevelt from the Secretaries of State and War and the Attorney General, January 22, 1945', *Report of Robert H. Jackson, United States Representative to the International Conference on Military Trials, London, 1945* (Department of State, Publication 3080, 1949), pp. 3, 13–17.

[74] Reported in *The Times*, 3 November 1943, reproduced in UNWCC, *History*, pp. 107–8. That these crimes could be tried by national courts was consistent with the interim report of the Cambridge Commission on Penal Reconstruction and Development, see *Confidential Report of the International Committee for Penal Reconstruction and Development*, reproduced in UNWCC, *History*, p. 95. A Sub-committee subsequently examined the jurisdiction of municipal courts in order to ascertain whether existing law permitted them jurisdiction over these crimes committed in Germany and occupied Europe, and made suggestions for amendments to national codes to remedy defects in existing law: see UNWCC, *History*, pp. 95–9.

[75] Reported in *The Times*, 3 November 1943, reproduced in UNWCC, *History*, pp. 107–8.

Initially, both the British and the Americans were reluctant to commit to a judicial process for the treatment of the major war criminals.[76] In September 1944, Churchill and Roosevelt agreed to propose to Stalin that a number of the top Nazi leaders be executed, including Hitler and Himmler.[77] On 22 October, Churchill reported that Stalin was not amenable to a political disposition of the Nazi leaders and was firmly insistent on a trial if death sentences were to be imposed.[78] But the British continued to reject the prospect of establishing an international court by treaty, preferring trial before national military courts.[79] At the same time, a preference was emerging in the US government for the establishment of an international court to try the highest ranking German leaders and their organisations. It was proposed that a first stage of prosecution would be before an international tribunal created by executive agreement, which would adjudge the guilt of the individual defendants, the organisations and the complicity of members of those organisations. Thereafter, other individuals who were members of the convicted organisations could be tried before occupation courts, where the only necessary proof of guilt was membership of a convicted organisation.[80] It was not until the San Francisco Conference that the British Cabinet instructed

[76] An aide-mémoire from the British government to the US State Department on 19 August 1944 expressed this view; the State Department agreed: (1944) 1 FRUS 1351. See B. F. Smith, *The Road to Nuremberg* (London, Basic Books, 1981), pp. 18–19. Documents relating to the developments in the US on the question of the major war criminals are found in B. F. Smith, *The American Road to Nuremberg: The Documentary Record 1944–1945* (Stanford, Hoover Institution Press, 1982).

[77] Foreign Relations of the United States (FRUS), *The Conference of Quebec 1944* (Washington, DC, 1972), p. 467. In Britain, the Lord Chancellor, Lord Simon, had been advocating this position for two years with the support of Churchill. In 1944, a Cabinet Decision directed Simon to prepare a draft proposal, which advanced arguments as to why trials were inappropriate, and argued that the Moscow Declaration implied that the major war criminals could be dealt with politically, not judicially: Memorandum 'Major War Criminals', 4 September 1944, FRUS, *The Conference of Quebec 1944* (Washington, DC, 1972), pp. 91–3. In the US, the State Department prepared a memorandum to similar effect: Memorandum for the Cabinet Committee on Germany, 5 September 1944, *ibid.* p. 96.

[78] Churchill to Roosevelt, 22 October 1944, FRUS, *The Conferences at Malta and Yalta, 1945* (Washington, DC, 1955), p. 400.

[79] British Aide-Mémoire, 30 October 1944, (1944) 1 FRUS 1389–91.

[80] This proposal originated in the 'Bernays plan': see B. F. Smith, *The Road to Nuremberg* (London, Basic Books, 1981), pp. 50–1. See also 'I. Memorandum to President Roosevelt from the Secretaries of State and War and the Attorney General, January 22, 1945', *Report of Robert H. Jackson, United States Representative to the International Conference on Military Trials, London, 1945* (Department of State, Publication 3080, 1949), p. 3 and in 'Memorandum for the President', 22 January 1945, FRUS, *The Conferences at Malta and Yalta, 1945* (Washington, DC, 1955), pp. 402–11.

its delegation that there was no utility in continuing to oppose a trial if the US and the USSR were committed to it. In early May 1945, at the San Francisco Conference, Judge Rosenman (representing the US) presented a draft agreement on the setting up of an international tribunal[81] to try the major war criminals[82] and organisations.[83] In principle, the US, UK, USSR and France agreed to a trial of the major war criminals before an international military tribunal, rather than political disposition (i.e. summary execution).[84] Subsequently, representatives of the four states met in London to reach agreement on a Charter.[85] The resulting London Agreement and the Charter of the International Military Tribunal of 8 August 1945, entered into by the UK, US, France and USSR,[86] in principle reflected the first US draft.[87] It listed crimes for which there would be individual responsibility,[88] and provided that at the trial of any individual member of any group or organisation the tribunal could declare that the group or organisation was a 'criminal organisation';[89] in the event that a group or organisation was declared criminal by the tribunal the competent national authority of any signatory to the Agreement had the

[81] 'IV. American Draft of Definitive Proposal Presented to Foreign Ministers at San Francisco, April 1945', *Report of Robert H. Jackson, United States Representative to the International Conference on Military Trials, London, 1945* (Department of State, Publication 3080, 1949), p. 22. See also 'V. American Memorandum Presented at San Francisco, April 30, 1945', *ibid.* p. 28.

[82] Article 6, 'IV. American Draft of Definitive Proposal Presented to Foreign Ministers at San Francisco, April 1945', *ibid.* p. 24.

[83] *Ibid.* p. 25, Art. 12(c) and (d).

[84] *Ibid.* p. 22. See also 'VI. British Memorandum of May 28, 1945', *ibid.* p. 39. The acceptance in principle is recorded in 'VII. Aide-Mémoire from the United Kingdom, June 3, 1945', *ibid.* p. 41. Jackson's report on his May discussions in London are recorded in 'VIII. Report to the President by Mr Justice Jackson, June 6, 1945', *ibid.* p. 42.

[85] The documentary history of the London Conference and the plenary discussions is reproduced in *ibid.* The drafting history from the original US proposal is also discussed in Report of Rapporteur Spiropoulos, Document A/CN.4/22, reproduced in (1950) II *Yearbook of the International Law Commission* 181, 182.

[86] 1945 London Agreement for the Prosecution and Punishment of the Major War Criminals of the European Axis Powers and Charter of the International Military Tribunal, 8 UNTS 279. The drafting history of the Charter is recounted in (1950) II *Yearbook of the International Law Commission* 182–7. See T. Taylor, *The Anatomy of the Nuremberg Trials: A Personal Memoir* (London, Bloomsbury, 1933).

[87] For detailed drafting and documentary history, see *Report of Robert H. Jackson, United States Representative to the International Conference on Military Trials, London, 1945* (Department of State, Publication 3080, 1949).

[88] London Agreement for the Prosecution and Punishment of the Major War Criminals of the European Axis Powers and Charter of the International Military Tribunal, Art. 6, 8 August 1945 (entry into force 8 August 1945) 8 UNTS 279.

[89] *Ibid.* Art. 9.

right to bring any individual to trial for membership of that group or organisation, and in those trials the criminal nature of the group or organisation 'is considered proved and shall not be questioned'.[90]

Article 6 of the Charter outlined crimes within the jurisdiction of the tribunal 'for which there shall be individual responsibility' as follows:

> (a) Crimes Against Peace: namely, planning, preparation, initiation or waging of a war of aggression, or a war in violation of international treaties, agreements or assurances, or participation in a common plan or conspiracy for the accomplishment of any of the foregoing;
> (b) War Crimes: namely, violations of the laws or customs of war. Such violations shall include, but not be limited to, murder, ill-treatment or deportation to slave labor or for any other purpose of civilian population of or in occupied territory, murder or ill-treatment of prisoners of war or persons on the seas, killing of hostages, plunder of public or private property, wanton destruction of cities, towns or villages, or devastation not justified by military necessity;
> (c) Crimes against humanity: namely, murder, extermination, enslavement, deportation, and other inhumane acts committed against any civilian population, before or during the war; or persecutions on political, racial or religious grounds in execution of or in connection with any crimes within the jurisdiction of the Tribunal, whether or not in violation of the domestic law of the country where perpetrated.

Article 6 also provided that leaders, organisers, instigators and accomplices participating in a common plan or conspiracy to commit any of these crimes 'are responsible for all acts performed by any persons in execution of such plan'. Article 7 provided that any official position of defendants, as heads of state or otherwise, would not free them from responsibility nor mitigate punishment. Article 8 stated that superior orders was not a defence to charges under the Charter, but might be considered in mitigation of punishment. The provisions for declaring a group or organisation 'criminal' and its consequences were set out in Articles 9 and 10.

The Nuremberg Tribunal received the indictment on 10 October 1945 and hearings commenced on 20 November. The indictment contained four main charges based on Article 6 of the Charter: conspiracy, crimes against peace, crimes against humanity and criminal organisations.[91]

[90] *Ibid.* Art. 10.

[91] Count one, overall conspiracy, was prosecuted by the US; count two, crimes against peace, was dealt with by the UK; and the remaining counts were dealt with by France and the USSR, France dealing with the western zone of conflict and the USSR dealing with the eastern.

Twenty-four defendants and six organisations were charged on the indictment. Twenty defendants appeared before the Tribunal on its first day of hearing and entered pleas of not guilty, with Goering attempting to make a speech to the effect that he was perfectly willing to stand trial before a German court, but not before the Tribunal.[92] After a trial lasting ten months, the Tribunal delivered its judgment and sentences on 1 October 1946: of the twenty-two defendants who were prosecuted, twelve were sentenced to death; seven to terms of imprisonment between ten years and life; and three were acquitted;[93] and of the six indicted organisations, three were declared criminal.

In its judgment, the Tribunal explained the right of the Allies to try the major war criminals as a delegation of legislative power from Germany to the Allied Powers:

> The Making of the Charter was the exercise of the sovereign legislative power by the countries to which the German Reich unconditionally surrendered; and the undoubted right of these countries to legislate for the occupied territories has been recognized by the civilized world. The Charter is not an arbitrary exercise of power on the part of the victorious nations . . . The Signatory Powers created this Tribunal, defined the law it was to administer, and made regulations for the proper conduct of the trial. In doing so, they have done together what any one of them might have done singly, for it is not to be doubted that any nation has the right to set up special courts to administer law.[94]

At an early stage of the proceedings a defence motion raised the question whether the provisions of the Charter were consistent with international law. The Tribunal dismissed the motion insofar as it constituted an objection to the Tribunal's jurisdiction, holding that '[t]he law of the Charter is decisive and binding upon the Tribunal'.[95] However, the Tribunal indicated that it was prepared to hear arguments as to the compatibility of the provisions of the Charter with international law and examined this question in relation to the application of specific provisions of the Charter. The issue was raised repeatedly in

92 V. H. Bernstein, *Final Judgment: The Story of Nuremberg* (London, Latimer House, 1947), p. 21.

93 One of the remaining indicted defendants was declared unfit for trial and the other committed suicide before the trial began.

94 International Military Judgment (Nuremberg), Judgment and Sentences, 1 October 1946, reproduced in (1947) 41 *AJIL* 172, 216. A description of the proceedings can be found in R. West, *A Train of Powder* (London, Macmillan, 1955) and Bernstein, *Final Judgment*.

95 International Military Judgment (Nuremberg), Judgment and Sentences, 1 October 1946, reproduced in (1947) 41 *AJIL* 172, 216.

respect of the charge of waging a war of aggression or in violation of international treaties. The Tribunal's position was twofold: first, that since the Charter made such an act a crime, it was not necessary to consider whether and to what extent it constituted a crime before the Charter;[96] and second, that the Charter was 'the expression of international law existing at the time of its creation', i.e. that waging aggressive war was an international crime at the time of the Charter.[97]

A further challenge was made by the defence to the terms of the Charter in imposing international responsibility.[98] The defence argued first that 'international law is concerned with the actions of sovereign States and provid[es] no punishment for individuals' and second that 'where the act in question is an act of State, those who carry it out are not personally responsible, but are protected by the doctrine of the sovereignty of the State'.[99] These questions were addressed by Sir Hartley Shawcross, prosecuting for the UK. He argued that, although the procedure and the indictment were 'novel', there was nothing new in the principles the Tribunal was seeking to enforce.[100] He continued:

> The Charter lays down expressly that there shall be individual responsibility for the crimes, including the Crimes against the Peace, committed on behalf of the State. The State is not an abstract entity. Its rights and duties are the rights and duties of men. Its actions are the actions of men. . . .
>
> [T]he principle of individual international responsibility for offences against the law of nations [is not] altogether new. It has been applied not only to pirates. The entire law relating to war crimes, as distinct from the crime of war, is based upon the principle of individual responsibility.[101]

The Tribunal's judgment echoed Shawcross's submissions:

> That international law imposes duties and liabilities upon individuals as well as upon States has long been recognized. In the recent case of Ex Parte Quirin (1942 317 U.S. 1), before the Supreme Court of the United States, persons were charged

96 *Ibid.* 217. 97 *Ibid.* 218–20.

98 1945 London Agreement for the Prosecution and Punishment of the Major War Criminals of the European Axis Powers and Charter of the International Military Tribunal, Art. 6, 8 UNTS 279.

99 International Military Judgment (Nuremberg), Judgment and Sentences, 1 October 1946, reproduced in (1947) 41 *AJIL* 172, 220.

100 *The Trial of German Major War Criminals: Proceedings of the International Military Tribunal Sitting at Nuremberg Germany*, Part 2, *3rd December 1945 to 14th December 1945, Taken from the Official Transcript* (London, HM Stationery Office, 1946), Transcript Twelfth Day, p. 46.

101 *Ibid.* p. 56.

during the war with landing in the United States for purposes of spying and sabotage. The late Chief Justice Stone, speaking for the Court, said:

> From the very beginning of its history this Court has applied to the law of war as including that part of the law of nations which prescribes for the conduct of war, the status, rights, and duties of enemy nations as well as enemy individuals.

He went on to give a list of cases tried by the Courts, where individual offenders were charged with offenses against the laws of nations, and particularly the laws of war. Many other authorities could be cited, but enough has been said to show that individuals can be punished for violations of international law. Crimes against international law are committed by men, not by abstract entities, and only by punishing individuals who commit such crimes can the provisions of international law be enforced.

The provisions of Article 228 of the Treaty of Versailles already referred to illustrate and enforce this view of individual responsibility.[102]

The Tribunal held further that individual responsibility was not precluded because the conduct amounted to an act of state, referring to Article 7 of the Charter and stating that 'the very essence of the Charter is that individuals have international duties which transcend the national obligations of obedience imposed by the individual state'.[103]

The judgment reads as though the Tribunal sought to place a bet each way: on the one hand, it claimed to be bound by its Charter, which established individual responsibility for the crimes enumerated therein; on the other hand, it claimed that it was long-established that 'international law imposes duties and liabilities upon individuals'. There is little to quarrel with in respect of the first point: the Tribunal

[102] International Military Judgment (Nuremberg), Judgment and Sentences, 1 October 1946, reproduced in (1947) 41 *AJIL* 172, 220–1. Shawcross's submissions and the judgment reflected the essence of a statement made by Hersch Lauterpacht in his famous 1944 article on the punishment of war crimes: 'The rules of warfare, like any other rules of international law, are binding not upon impersonal entities, but upon human beings. The rules of law are binding not upon an abstract notion of Germany, but upon members of the German government, upon German individuals exercising governmental functions in occupied territory, upon German officers, upon German soldiers.' See H. Lauterpacht, 'The Law of Nations and the Punishment of War Crimes' (1944) 21 *BYBIL* 58, 60. This is not surprising given that Lauterpacht assisted Shawcross in drafting his speeches before the tribunal: see 'Introduction' to the Part on the 'Law of War', E. Lauterpacht (ed.), *International Law, Being the Collected Papers of Sir Hersch Lauterpacht* (Cambridge, Cambridge University Press, 2005), vol. V.

[103] International Military Judgment (Nuremberg), Judgment and Sentences, 1 October 1946, reproduced in (1947) 41 *AJIL* 172, 220–1.

was no doubt bound by its Charter which clearly stated that such individual responsibility existed. The Tribunal pointed out that any state could legislate to allow an international tribunal to prosecute its nationals: since the German Reich had surrendered its sovereign power to the Allied Powers, they could legitimately exercise that power.[104] In respect of the second point, the Tribunal's appeal to precedents is open to criticism.[105] The Tribunal referred to *Ex Parte Quirin* and to other cases where individuals were prosecuted for violations of the law of war, but without inquiring as to whether those prosecutions were based on domestic law or international law. The Tribunal also referred to Article 228 of the Treaty of Versailles: it has already been explained that this provision was never executed and that post-First World War prosecutions were conducted on the basis of domestic (German) law. Moreover, these precedents related exclusively to war crimes and did not cover either crimes against humanity or crimes against peace. Nevertheless the Tribunal's approach was suggestive of a reluctance to characterise its jurisdiction as new or as expanding individual responsibility under international law, explicable by its anxiety to avoid criticism for having violated the *nullem crimen* principle.[106]

(ii) The Tokyo Tribunal

An International Military Tribunal was also set up in Tokyo to try those accused of war crimes in the Pacific.[107] The Tribunal was established by General MacArthur to whom the US, UK and the Soviet Union had

[104] On that basis, Schwarzenberger argued that the IMT was merely a court run by the government of Germany, a municipal war crimes court rather than an international tribunal: G. Schwarzenberger, 'The Problem of an International Criminal Law' (1950) *Current Legal Problems* 263, 290–1; Schwarzenberger, 'The Judgment of Nuremberg', 333–4. Cf. Wright, 'The Law of the Nuremberg Trial', 48–51.

[105] See e.g., H. Ehard, 'The Nuremberg Trial Against the Major War Criminals and International Law' (1949) 43 *AJIL* 223, 240–1.

[106] Subsequently there was less reluctance: Telford Taylor (assistant and then Chief Prosecutor for the US at the Nuremberg Trials) stated some twenty-five years after the judgment that the trials 'brought about a great expansion of the principle that individuals may be held liable under international law': T. Taylor, *Nuremberg and Vietnam: An American Tragedy* (Chicago, Ill., Quadrangle, 1970), p. 82. For a different view, see J. J. Paust, 'The Reality of Private Rights, Duties, and Participation in the International Legal Process' (2003–4) 25 *J In'l* 1229, 1234–41.

[107] Special Proclamation, Establishment of an International Military Tribunal for the Far East, 19 January 1946, IAS no. 1589, 3.

delegated power to implement the Potsdam Declaration, Principle 10 of which promised 'stern justice' for war criminals.[108] The Tokyo Tribunal consisted of eleven judges drawn from victor nations in the Pacific sphere: it was presented with an indictment on 29 April 1946 which contained fifty-five counts against twenty-eight defendants,[109] including military men, career diplomats, leading politicians (including the Prime Minister at the time of the attack on Pearl Harbour) and one civilian who had acted as a propagandist (although the latter was eventually held unfit for trial).[110] The trial took more than two and a half years, and all those tried were found guilty.[111] The judgment records seven grounds of challenge to the jurisdiction of the Tribunal by the defence, including that war was an act of the nation for which there is no individual responsibility under international law.[112] The majority judgment of the Tribunal expressly adopted the Nuremberg Tribunal's reasoning with respect to the binding character of the Charter, the criminality of aggressive war and the dismissal of the defence of superior orders.[113]

Two major dissenting judgments were given by judges from the Netherlands (Röling) and India (Pal). Judge Röling considered that there was no individual responsibility for the crime of aggression, but accepted that there was individual responsibility for war crimes.[114] Judge Pal essentially accepted an act of state defence, holding that individuals constituting the government and functioning as its agents could not be held criminally responsible for their acts.[115] Judge Pal was

[108] (1945) 13 *US Dept of State Bulletin* 1027 (27 December 1945); Special Proclamation, Establishment of an International Military Tribunal for the Far East, 19 January 1946, IAS no. 1589, 3. The Potsdam Declaration is reproduced in (1945) 13 *US Dept of State Bulletin* 364, (9 September 1945), Annex A-2, 7–11.

[109] The indictment is reproduced in N. Boister and R. Cryer (eds.), *Documents on the Tokyo International Military Tribunal: Charter, Indictments, Judgments* (Oxford, Oxford University Press, 2008).

[110] See generally, B. V. A. Röling, *The Tokyo Trial and Beyond: Reflections of a Peacemonger* (Cambridge, Polity Press, 1993), pp. 3–4.

[111] The Tokyo Tribunal judgment is reproduced in B. V. A. Röling and C. F. Rüter, *The Tokyo Judgment of the International Military Tribunal for the Far East (IMTFE) 29 April 1946–12 November 1948* (Amsterdam, APA University Press, 1977), vols. I–XII. The trial proceedings are usefully digested in Arnold C. Brackman, *The Other Nuremberg: The Untold Story of the Tokyo War Crimes Trials* (London, Collins, 1989).

[112] Röling and Rüter, *The Tokyo Judgment of the International Military Tribunal*, p. 27.

[113] *Ibid.*

[114] Dissenting Opinion of the Member from the Netherlands, reproduced in Boister and Cryer, *Documents on the Tokyo International Military Tribunal*, pp. 684–704.

[115] Dissentient Judgment of Justice Pal, reproduced in *ibid.* p. 809.

criticised by another judge for failing to accept the Charter's provisions as establishing individual responsibility while Pal had accepted his own appointment under the same Charter.[116]

Although there were provisions for the conduct of a fair trial in the Tokyo Charter, the trial was not carried out in accordance with these limited rights and considerable doubts have been expressed about the conduct of the proceedings. The trial is now almost 'totally ignored', perhaps because of embarrassment about the process on the part of prosecuting states.[117]

(iii) Control Council Law No. 10 trials and military commissions in the Pacific

In addition to the Nuremberg Tribunal, the Allied Powers occupying Germany established occupation courts for the prosecution of war crimes in their respective occupation zones. To 'establish a uniform legal basis in Germany for the prosecution of war criminals' other than those dealt with by the Nuremberg Tribunal, the four occupying powers enacted 'Control Council Law No. 10'.[118] Article II recognised the following as crimes: (a) crimes against peace, including initiating or waging a war of aggression; (b) war crimes; (c) crimes against humanity; and (d) membership of a group or organisation declared criminal by the Nuremberg Tribunal. Article III empowered each of the occupying powers to designate a tribunal to prosecute these crimes, with rules and procedure to be determined by the Zone Commander.[119] The US trials under Law No. 10 focussed on defendants who were involved in

116 Concurring Opinion of the Member from the Philippines, reproduced in *ibid.* pp. 656–8.

117 Cryer, *Prosecuting International Crimes*, pp. 46–7; J. Shklar, *Legalism: Law, Morals and Political Trials* (Cambridge, Mass., Harvard University Press, 1986), p. 180; M. C. Bassiouni, 'Nuremberg: Forty Years After' (1986) 80 *ASIL Proceedings* 59, 60; see generally, R. H. Minear, *Victor's Justice: The Tokyo War Crimes Trial* (Princeton, NJ, Princeton University Press, 1971). The ICTY Appeals Chamber was critical of the Toyko Tribunal's interpretation of command responsibility: see *Prosecutor* v. *Delalic, Mucic, Delic and Landžo* (*Celebici* case), Case no. IT-96-21-A, Appeals Chamber, 20 February 2001, para. 259. A qualified defence of the Tribunal's legacy is made in N. Boister and R. Cryer, *The Tokyo International Military Tribunal: A Reappraisal* (Oxford, Oxford University Press, 2008), pp. 325–7.

118 Reproduced in T. Taylor, *Final Report to the Secretary of the Army on the Nuernberg War Crimes Trials under Control Council Law No. 10* (Washington, DC, Government Printing Office, 1949).

119 Control Council Law no. 10, Art. III, reproduced in *ibid.*

Nazi economic, political, racial, medical and legal policies.[120] Often reference was made to the findings of the Nuremberg Tribunal[121] and the US trials affirmed that individuals were responsible directly under international law.[122] Trials in the British zone were carried out under the authority of the Royal Warrant 'for the trial and punishment of violations of the laws and usages of war'.[123] In the French occupation courts, 2,107 individuals were tried on all three counts of crimes and the courts issued several hundred sentences *in absentia*.[124] It is estimated that some 20,000 individuals were convicted in Soviet courts but there is no reliable record of those proceedings.[125]

In the Pacific sphere, a large number of trials were conducted by the Allies in domestic military tribunals or courts.[126] There was no equivalent to Law No. 10 enacted by the Allies in respect of the Pacific; rather, these trials were exclusively governed by domestic war crimes law.

The prosecutions by occupation and domestic tribunals were pursued expeditiously: by 31 October 1946, 1,108 war criminals had been tried in Europe and 735 had been tried in the Far East, in addition to those tried

[120] W. A. Zeck, 'Nuremberg: Proceedings Subsequent to Goering et al.' (1948) 26 *NCL Rev.* 350; M. Lippman, 'The Other Nuremberg: American Prosecutions of Nazi War Criminals in Occupied Germany' (1992–3) 3 *ICLQ* 1.

[121] See e.g., *United States* v. *Altstoetter* (1951) III Trials of War Criminals Before the Nuernberg Military Tribunals under Control Council Law no. 10, 968 (*Justice* case). See generally, A. Basak, 'The Influence of the Nuremberg Judgment on the Practice of the Allied Courts in Germany' (1977–8) *Polish Yearbook of International Law* 161.

[122] For example, the tribunal for the US zone rejected the proposition that international obligations apply only to 'abstract entities called states' since states could only act through 'human beings' and each combatant was obliged to respect international law: *United States* v. *Otto Ohendorf* (1950) VI Trials of War Criminals Before the Nuernberg Military Tribunals under Control Council Law no. 10, 411, 460 (*Einsatzgruppen* case). The Tribunal also held that international law imposed direct obligations on private individuals: see *United States* v. *Freidrich Flick* (1950) VI Trials of War Criminals Before the Nuernberg Military Tribunals under Control Council Law no. 10, 1187, 1192. See also *United States* v. *Wilhelm von Leeb* (1950) XI Trials of War Criminals Before the Nuernberg Military Tribunals under Control Council Law no. 10, 462, 489.

[123] See generally, A. P. V. Rogers, 'War Crimes Trials under the Royal Warrant: British Practice 1945–1949' (1990) 39 *ICLQ* 780.

[124] I. A. Lediakh, 'The Application of the Nuremberg Principles by Other Military Tribunals and National Courts' in G. Ginsburgs and V. N. Kudriavtsevs, *The Nuremberg Trial and International Law* (Dordrecht, Martinus Nijhoff, 1990), pp. 263, 276–7.

[125] A. Rückerl, *The Investigation of Nazi Crimes 1945–1978* (Derek Rutter (trans.), Hamden, Conn., Archon Books, 1980), pp. 20–31.

[126] H. Levie, *Terrorism in War: The Law of War Crimes* (New York, Oceana Publications, 1993), pp. 155–83; Robert Miller, 'War Crimes Trials at Yokohama' (1948–9) 15 *Brooklyn Law Review* 19. In the UK, trials were undertaken on the basis of the Royal Warrant: Rogers, 'War Crimes Trials under the Royal Warrant'.

in US military commissions.[127] These trials were conducted in domestic and occupation tribunals and the basis for individual responsibility was domestic criminalisation of violations of the laws of war. These trials may be reconciled with the nineteenth century framework of the international legal system, as individual responsibility arose under domestic law and was punished by domestic courts. Nevertheless, both Control Council Law No. 10 and some of the decisions of the domestic tribunals suggested that individual criminal responsibility could arise under international law.

In contrast to the post-First World War prosecutions, the treatment of individuals after the Second World War suggested that international law imposed duties upon individuals for which those individuals may be punished. This was most significantly implemented by the Nuremberg Tribunal, which suggested that individual responsibility arose either under its Charter or more generally under the rules of international law prohibiting international crimes. The Tribunal's explanation of the source of the relevant obligations is open to criticism, but on any view individual responsibility was considered as arising directly under international law without interposition of domestic law.

(b) The 'Nuremberg Principles'

The day after the opening meeting of the General Assembly, the Secretary-General of the UN suggested that 'the principles which were implied in the Nürnberg trials' be 'made a permanent part of the body of international law as quickly as possible'.[128] On 11 December 1946, the General Assembly adopted a resolution affirming 'the principles of international law recognized by the Charter of the Nürnberg Tribunal and the judgment of the Tribunal';[129] subsequently the General Assembly directed the International Law Commission (ILC) to:

> (a) formulate the principles of international law recognized by the Charter of the Nürnberg Tribunal, and in the judgment of the Tribunal, and

[127] UNWCC Report of 16 November 1946, cited in Wright, 'The Law of the Nuremberg Trial'. See also *Ex Parte Quirin*, 317 US 1 (1942) and *In re Yamashita*, 66 Sup. Ct 340 (1946).

[128] 35th Plenary Meeting, Verbatim Record of the General Assembly, pp. 699–700. Opening the first meeting, President Truman had referred to the Nuremberg Charter and judgment: see 34th Plenary Meeting, Verbatim Record of the General Assembly, p. 684.

[129] GA/Res/95(I), 11 December 1946.

(b) prepare a draft code of offences against the peace and security of mankind, indicating clearly the place to be accorded to the principles mentioned in sub-paragraph (a) above.

The different language used in reference to the Nuremberg judgment is interesting: while the Secretary-General's statement suggested that the principles be 'made a part' of international law (the inference to be drawn is that they were not existing principles of international law), the General Assembly resolutions affirmed the principles 'recognised' by the Nuremberg Tribunal (suggesting that those principles were pre-existing). This suggest that there was no clear view as to whether the Nuremberg judgment involved a recognition of pre-existing principles of international law or whether they were new principles which ought to become part of international law. All that was clear was the wish to ensure that the Nuremberg Principles were part of positive international law.

The ILC adopted the Nuremberg Principles in 1950.[130] It did not engage with the question whether the Nuremberg Principles were principles of positive international law; since the General Assembly had already affirmed the principles, the Commission's only task was to formulate them.[131] However, different views were expressed as to whether the principle of individual responsibility formed part of existing positive international law.[132] For example, Amado argued that the principle of individual responsibility formed the basis of the Charter and the judgment of the Nuremberg Tribunal, but that individual responsibility 'was a new concept, for up to then the individual had not been considered as capable of being guilty of an international crime',[133] dismissing analogies with piracy and slavery.[134] In contrast, Scelle argued that the principle of individual responsibility 'was only the application of a more general principle ... that the individual was subject to international law' which was a pre-existing general

130 Report of the International Law Commission to the General Assembly covering its second session, 5 June–29 July 1950, Doc. A/1316, reproduced in (1950) II *Yearbook of the International Law Commission* 364, 374.

131 See discussion at the 17th Meeting, (1949) I *Yearbook of the International Law Commission* 129, 129–3.

132 See e.g., 45th Meeting, 13 June 1950, (1950) I *Yearbook of the International Law Commission* 30, paras. 1, 2; discussion at the 25th and 26th meetings, (1949) I *Yearbook of the International Law Commission* 182, 186 and 188.

133 26th Meeting, 24 May 1949, (1949) I *Yearbook of the International Law Commission* 185, 186, para. 11.

134 *Ibid.* 186, para. 12.

principle.[135] Since the ILC interpreted its mandate as merely formulating the principles rather than deciding whether they were consistent with positive international law, no conclusion was reached; moreover, it was evident from the discussions that there was no general consensus.[136]

On second reading, it was proposed to add to the general principle of individual responsibility (Principle I) a statement that 'the individual is subject to international law, at least in criminal law'.[137] The amendment was defeated by five votes in favour and six against:[138] the Rapporteur argued in favour of conservative drafting because '[i]f an individual could be regarded as subject to international penal law, it was a theoretical and doctrinal question on which there was no likelihood of unanimity in the Commission'.[139] As adopted[140] and presented to the General Assembly, Principle I and the Commentary read:

> Any person who commits an act which constitutes a crime under international law is responsible therefor and liable to punishment.
>
> 98. This principle is based on the first part of article 6 of the Charter of the Nürnberg Tribunal which established the competence of the Tribunal to try and punish persons who, acting in the interests of the European Axis countries, whether as individuals or as members of organizations, committed any of the crimes defined in sub-paragraphs (a), (b) and (c) of article 6. The text of the Charter declared punishable only persons 'acting in the interests of the European Axis countries' but, as a matter of course, Principle I is now formulated in general terms.
>
> 99. The general rule underlying Principle I is that international law may impose duties on individuals directly without any interposition of internal law. The findings of the Tribunal were very definite on the question whether the rules of international law may apply to individuals. 'That international law imposes duties and liabilities upon individuals as well as upon States', said the judgment of the Tribunal, 'has long been recognized'. It added: 'Crimes against international law are committed by men, not by abstract entities, and only by punishing individuals who commit such crimes can the provisions of international law be enforced.'[141]

135 *Ibid.* 186, para. 13. 136 *Ibid.* 190–1, paras. 72–84.

137 45th Meeting, 13 June 1950, (1950) I *Yearbook of the International Law Commission* 30, 35, para. 90, see also para. 94.

138 *Ibid.* 36, para. 103 *et seq.* See also a point raised by Alfaro, that the words 'at least . . . etc.' weakened the point: '[t]he fundamental principle to be affirmed was that the individual was subject to international law': *ibid.* 35, para. 90, see also para. 94.

139 *Ibid.* 35–6, para. 93. 140 *Ibid.* 36, para. 103 *et seq.*

141 *Report of the International Law Commission to the General Assembly Covering its Second Session, 5 June–29 July 1950*, UN Doc. A/1316, reproduced in (1950) II *Yearbook of the International Law Commission* 364, 374.

The Commentary thus avoided stating expressly that individuals were 'subject to' international law, but admitted that international law 'may impose duties on individuals directly'.

Principle II as adopted provided:

> The fact that internal law does not impose a penalty for an act which constitutes a crime under international law does not relieve the person who committed the act from responsibility under international law.[142]

The Commentary to Principle II noted that the Tribunal held 'that international law can bind individuals even if national law does not direct them to observe the rules of international law'.[143]

The remaining principles dealt with the defences of act of state[144] and superior orders;[145] the right to a fair trial on the facts and the law;[146] crimes punishable under international law;[147] and complicity.[148] Principle VI, setting out the punishable crimes, covered crimes against peace (including initiating or waging a war of aggression), war crimes and crimes against humanity.[149]

These Nuremberg Principles were acknowledged by the General Assembly in Resolution 488(V) on 12 December 1950, which also invited member states to provide the ILC with observations which would be considered in the drafting of a code of offences against the peace and security of mankind.[150] No further action was taken by the General Assembly on the Nuremberg Principles. Very few states sent comments, and those which did offered only brief remarks.[151] Discussion of the Principles in the Sixth Committee[152] evidenced general support for Principle I affirming individual responsibility for international crimes. However, the implications for the status of individuals in the international system were contested. As representative for Brazil, Amado took the same position he had taken in the ILC: he suggested that this 'was a crystallization of the efforts made by a great many jurists to weaken the traditional doctrine under which States were the only subjects of international law'.[153] Similar comments were made by representatives of

142 *Ibid.* 374–5. 143 *Ibid.* 374–5. 144 Principle III, *ibid.* 374. 145 Principle IV, *ibid.* 375.
146 Principle V, *ibid.* 375. 147 Principle VI, *ibid.* 376–7. 148 Principle VII, *ibid.* 377.
149 *Ibid.* 376–7. 150 GA/Res/488(V), 12 December 1950.
151 *Observation of Governments of Member States relating to the Formulation of the Nürnberg Principles Prepared by the International Law Commission*, UN Doc. A/CN.4/45, (1950) II *Yearbook of the International Law Commission* 104.
152 The comments were canvassed in *Second Report* (Mr J. Spiropoulos, Special Rapporteur), UN Doc. A/CN.4/44, reproduced in (1951) II *Yearbook of the International Law Commission* 43.
153 *Ibid.* 49, paras. 53–9, esp. para. 53, view of Amado (Brazil).

Greece, Uruguay, Egypt and France: that the individual was 'subject to international law'[154] and consequently individuals had legal personality in international law.[155] On the other hand, the representative for the UK (Fitzmaurice) argued that individuals could be subject to trial and punishment for international crimes 'without adopting the theory of the responsibility of the individual under international law'. In the summary of the debate his view is summarised as follows:

> All that was in fact necessary was to establish the position in which the State admitted that the individuals under their jurisdiction would be subject to punishment for certain acts recognized as crimes under international law ... [Fitzmaurice's comments] related solely to the *modus operandi*, to the legal methods to be used in attaining the generally desired objective. He had simply said that, in order to punish the individual, there was no need at all to regard him as being subject to international law, and that the desired result could be attained without affecting the classic concept that international law solely governs relations between States.[156]

The basic rule underlying Principle I of the Nuremberg Principles, as reflected in the Commentary, was that 'international law may impose duties on individuals directly without any interposition of internal law'.[157] However, the ILC was reluctant to engage in discussion of the consequences of recognising that individuals had duties directly under international law, a reluctance which could be explained either by the Commission's limited mandate, or by the absence of a clear agreement amongst the members of the Commission as to those consequences. Taking the basic rule identified as underlying Principle I, it seems difficult to sustain the view that individuals are not responsible under international law, and that international law governs solely relations between states, as Fitzmaurice suggested. For Fitzmaurice's claim to be sustained, it would be necessary not only to conceive the jurisdiction of an international tribunal as a delegation of domestic jurisdiction from the relevant state of nationality of the accused, but also that the applicable law be domestic law: that individual responsibility arises not under international law, but under domestic law. A mere concession of jurisdiction to an international tribunal to enforce individual responsibility from a

154 *Ibid.* 50–1, paras. 68 (Spiropoulos, Greece), 69 (Arechaga, Uruguay), 70 (Sultan, Egypt) and 75 (Chamont, France).

155 *Ibid.* 50, para. 68 (Spiropoulos, Greece).

156 *Ibid.* 50, paras. 63–4.

157 *Report of the International Law Commission to the General Assembly Covering its Second Session, 5 June–29 July 1950*, UN Doc. A/1316, reproduced in (1950) II *Yearbook of the International Law Commission* 364, 374, para. 99.

domestic authority would not be sufficient to displace the relevant applicable law, which was, according to the Nuremberg Tribunal and the Nuremberg Principles, international law. Recognition that individuals had duties under international law may not have entailed acknowledgement of their status as subjects of international law, since in 1946 there may have been no established understanding that the conferral of rights and obligations on an entity had the effect of designating that entity as a subject of international law. But it necessarily entailed acknowledging that individuals were subject to international law and that individuals were responsible under international law.

The Nuremberg Principles were a significant development of international criminal law because they expressed the clear desire of the international community to make individual responsibility for specified crimes a 'permanent part' of positive international law.[158] Although the Principles did not form part of an international convention, they at least indicate *opinio juris* in support of customary international law. It is possible, of course, that this was initially driven by a desire on the part of the Allied Powers to avoid criticism of the Nuremberg Trial, but whatever the motivation, the Nuremberg Principles were a strong indication that individuals could be held responsible directly under international law for certain violations of international law.

(c) Development of substantive international criminal law in the United Nations

Immediately after the Nuremberg judgment and the formulation of the Nuremberg Principles, there was a general drive towards the development of procedural and substantive international criminal law - an attempt in effect to justify Nuremberg by filling the legal gap which the Nuremberg Tribunal denied existed. In terms of procedural law, in 1948 the ILC was directed to examine the prospect of an international criminal tribunal,[159] but the project was postponed in 1954 and was

[158] In the words of the Secretary-General of the UN: 35th Plenary Meeting, Verbatim Record of the General Assembly, pp. 699–700.

[159] GA/Res/260B(III), 9 December 1948. The Genocide Convention of 1948 expressly contemplated the establishment of an international criminal court: Convention on the Prevention and Punishment of the Crime of Genocide, Art. VI, 1 January 1948 (entry into force 12 January 1951), 78 UNTS 277. The Torture Convention also implicitly referred to individual responsibility by requiring states to criminalise acts of torture: see Convention Against Torture and Other Cruel, Inhuman or Degrading Treatment or Punishment, Art. 4, 10 December 1948 (entry into force 26 June 1987), 1465 UNTS 85.

only taken up again in 1989. That process will be considered in the following section.[160]

Conventions from the post-war period which referred to international crimes suggested that individuals were responsible for international crimes, although their language was ambiguous as to whether that responsibility arose directly under international law or whether it arose under domestic law. For example, in December 1946, the General Assembly affirmed that genocide was a crime under international law;[161] and subsequently the Genocide Convention required states to make provision for the punishment of individuals who committed genocide and associated acts enumerated in the Convention.[162] The Genocide Convention did not expressly refer to individual obligations but rather used language suggestive of state obligations to give effect to the prohibition in domestic law.

In contrast, the ILC Draft Code of Crimes against the Peace and Security of Mankind suggested that international crimes entailed individual responsibility without the interposition of domestic law. In the first phase of work (1949–54), Article I as adopted provided that offences defined in the Draft Code 'are crimes under international law, for which the responsible individuals shall be punished'.[163] The Commentary referred to 'the principle of individual responsibility for crimes under international law' recognised by the Nuremberg Tribunal.[164] In the second phase of work (1982–96), there was unanimous support for the principle of individual responsibility for international crimes.[165] The principle was included in a Draft Article 3 (adopted on first reading

160 Pending a definition of aggression: GA/Res/897(IX), 4 December 1954; GA/Res/898(IX), 14 December 1954.

161 GA/Res/96(I), 11 December 1946.

162 Convention on the Prevention and Punishment of the Crime of Genocide, 1 January 1948 (entry into force 12 January 1951), 78 UNTS 277.

163 Article I was discussed and adopted at 106th Meeting, 19 June 1951, (1951) I *Yearbook of the International Law Commission* 210, 212, para. 143. A minor amendment was made before the Draft Code was adopted: see *Report of the International Law Commission to the General Assembly on the Work of its Sixth Session*, (1954) II *Yearbook of the International Law Commission* 49, para. 46.

164 *Report of the International Law Commission to the General Assembly on the Work of its Third Session*, UN Doc. A/1858, reproduced in (1951) II *Yearbook of the International Law Commission* 122, ch. IV, 134–5. The ILC discussed adding the words 'by an international court' after the words 'shall be punished', but decided against their inclusion: 266th Meeting, 12 July 1954, (1954) I *Yearbook of the International Law Commission* 123, 124–5, paras. 6–32, 63–76.

165 Report of the International Law Commission on the Work of its 35th Session, (1983) II *Yearbook of the International Law Commission* Pt 2, 3, ch. II, 14, para. 51.

in 1991[166] and on second reading there were no material changes). Article 2, entitled 'individual responsibility', affirmed[167] that an international crime 'entails individual responsibility' and set out modes of participation including committing; ordering; failing to prevent or repress commission; aiding, abetting or assisting in commission; direct participation in planning or conspiracy; direct and public incitement; and attempt.[168] The Commentary to Article 2 noted that '[t]he principle of individual criminal responsibility for crimes under international law was clearly established at Nürnberg' and that the Tribunal 'confirmed the direct applicability of international criminal law with respect to the responsibility and punishment of individuals for violations of this law'.[169] Like the Nuremberg Principles, the Draft Code made no reference to how this 'direct applicability' affected the position of individuals in the international legal system or whether it had the consequence of conferring legal personality on individuals. Although the Code was never adopted by the General Assembly and has not formed the basis of an international convention, the provisions relating to individual responsibility were 'generally well received' by states.[170]

(d) International criminal tribunals and courts

The end of the Cold War and subsequent internal conflicts turned international attention to the establishment of international criminal tribunals.[171] In 1989, the General Assembly requested the ILC to

166 Report of the International Law Commission on the Work of its 43rd Session, (1991) II *Yearbook of the International Law Commission* Pt 2, 1, ch. IV, 79–107, 98. See also *Eighth Report on the Draft Code of Crimes Against the Peace and Security of Mankind* (Mr Doudou Thaim, Special Rapporteur), UN Doc. A/CN.4/430 and Add. 1, (1990) II *Yearbook of the International Law Commission* Pt 1, 27–39.

167 The Commentary notes that the ILC considered it important to reaffirm the principle to avoid any question of its application to all crimes, not only those listed in Part 2 of the Code: see *Report of the International Law Commission on the Work of its 48th Session*, (1996) II *Yearbook of the International Law Commission* Pt 2, 1, 19.

168 *Report of the International Law Commission on the Work of its 48th Session*, (1996) I *Yearbook of the International Law Commission* Pt 2, 1, 18–19.

169 *Ibid.* 19.

170 *Ibid.* 78, para. 126; Draft Code of Crimes Against the Peace and Security of Mankind, UN Doc. A/CN.4/448 and Add. 1, Comments and Observations received from Governments, (1993) II *Yearbook of the International Law Commission* Pt 1, 59–109.

171 See generally, J. Crawford, 'The Work of the International Law Commission' in A. Cassese, P. Gaeta and J. R. W. D. Jones, *The Rome Statute of the International Criminal Court: A Commentary* (Oxford, Oxford University Press, 2002), vol. I, pp. 23, 24–25.

consider the establishment of a permanent international criminal court,[172] a project which had been postponed in 1954. The work of the ILC moved quickly (relative to some other projects) but before it reached fruition, the UN Security Council had established two ad hoc tribunals: for the former Yugoslavia in 1993 and for Rwanda in 1994. The ILC adopted a Draft Statute for a permanent court in 1994[173] and in 1998 states participated in a Conference in Rome which resulted in the Rome Statute for the International Criminal Court, which came into force on 1 July 2002. In addition, since 2000 several 'hybrid' courts have been established, which combine aspects of international criminal law with national mechanisms and law to prosecute offences including international crimes. The contribution of each of these mechanisms to the development of individual responsibility under international law will now be reviewed.

(i) Ad hoc international tribunals

The UN Security Council set up two ad hoc tribunals to prosecute international crimes: in 1993, the International Criminal Tribunal for the former Yugoslavia (ICTY) and in 1994, the International Criminal Tribunal for Rwanda (ICTR).[174]

172 The General Assembly also requested the ILC to consider the inclusion of international drug trafficking in the Draft Code: GA/Res/44/39, 4 December 1989.

173 *Report of the International Law Commission on the Work of its 46th Session*, (1994) II *Yearbook of the International Law Commission* Pt 2, 1, 25–6, paras. 79–88. See also *Observations of Governments on the Report of the Working Group on a Draft Statute for an International Criminal Court*, UN Doc. A/CN.4/458 and Add. 1–8, (1994) II *Yearbook of the International Law Commission* Pt 1, 21–96; *Report of the International Law Commission on the Work of its 46th Session*, (1994) II *Yearbook of the International Law Commission* Pt 2, 1, 26, para. 90. J. Crawford, 'The Drafting of the Rome Statute' in P. Sands (ed.), *From Nuremberg to The Hague: The Future of International Criminal Justice* (Cambridge, Cambridge University Press, 2003), p. 109.

174 The establishment of these tribunals was arguably *ultra vires*: see J. Crawford, 'International Law and International Crimes: Comments on a Developing Relationship' in Società Italiana di Diritto Internazionale, *Cooperazione fra Stati e Guistizia Penale Internazionale. II Convegno, Siena, 12–13 giugno 1998* (1999), p. 147. The ICTY Appeals Chamber held that it was constitutionally established: *Prosecutor* v. *Tadić*, Case no. IT-94-1-AR72, Appeals Chamber, Judgment on Jurisdiction, 2 October 1995. For a view in support of the Tribunals, see Meron, *War Crimes Law Comes of Age*, p. 186. See generally, C. L. Blakesley, 'Atrocity and Its Prosecution: The Ad Hoc Tribunals for the Former Yugoslavia and Rwanda' in T. H. McCormack and G. Simpson (eds.), *The Law of War Crimes: National and International Approaches* (The Hague, Kluwer, 1997), p. 189; and M. P. Scharf, *Balkan Justice: The Story Behind the First International War Crimes Trial Since Nuremberg* (Durham, NC, Carolina Academic Press, 1997).

The establishment of the ICTY was preceded by a series of statements by the Security Council asserting that persons perpetrating grave breaches of the Geneva Conventions and other crimes were 'individually responsible' and would be called to account.[175] On 22 February 1993, the Security Council decided, in principle, to establish an international tribunal to prosecute 'persons responsible for serious violations of international humanitarian law';[176] Resolution 827 of 25 May 1993 established the Tribunal and annexed its Statute.[177] Article 1 of the Statute provided that the ICTY had 'power to prosecute persons responsible for serious violations of international humanitarian law committed in the territory of the former Yugoslavia since 1991 in accordance with the provisions of the present Statute'. The jurisdiction of the Tribunal was not dependent on criminalisation of the same offences under domestic law; rather, the Tribunal was given jurisdiction to determine individual responsibility for violations of international law. Articles 2–5 specified crimes within the jurisdiction of the Tribunal as including grave breaches of the 1949 Geneva Conventions; violations of the laws and customs of war; genocide; and crimes against humanity. The principle of individual criminal responsibility and modes of participation were set out in Article 7(1) as follows:

> A person who planned, instigated, ordered, committed or otherwise aided and abetted in the planning, preparation or execution of a crime referred to in articles 2 to 5 of the present Statute, shall be individually responsible for the crime.[178]

The formulation of Article 7 does not appear to have drawn upon the work of the ILC on either the Nuremberg Principles or the Draft Code of Crimes (which by 1993 had been adopted on first reading).[179]

175 See SC/Res/764, 13 July 1992; SC/Res/771, 13 August 1992; SC/Res/780, 6 October 1992.

176 SC/Res/808, 22 February 1993. The record of debate leading to its adoption is reproduced in V. Morris and M. P. Scharf, *An Insider's Guide to the International Criminal Tribunal for the Former Yugoslavia: A Documentary History and Analysis* (New York, Transnational Publishers, 1995), vol. II, p. 159.

177 The Statute was adopted from *Report of the Secretary-General pursuant to Paragraph 2 of Security Council Resolution 808 (1993)*, UN Doc. S/25704 (3 May 1993) and corrigendum, UN Doc. S/25704/Corr.1 (30 July 1993). Subsequently, the Security Council amended the Statute to add a third Trial Chamber and three new judges by SC/Res/1166, 13 May 1998.

178 ICTY Statute, reproduced at www.un.org/icty/legaldoc-e/basic/statut/statute-feb08-e.pdf. For the various proposals put forward by states and organisations to the formulation of this principle, see Morris and Scharf, *An Insider's Guide to the International Criminal Tribunal for the Former Yugoslavia*, vol. II, pp. 383–7.

179 The Secretary-General's Report annexing the Draft Statute only refers to the Nuremberg Charter and Judgment to assert that conventional international

In April 1994, the Tutsi-dominated Rwandan Patriotic Front (RPF) began to press the Security Council to set up a war crimes tribunal for Rwanda similar to the ICTY.[180] In May 1994, the High Commissioner for Human Rights emphasised the need for the 'authors of the atrocities [to be] made aware that they cannot escape personal responsibility for criminal acts carried out, ordered or condoned',[181] but recommended the use of national mechanisms for prosecutions, rather than an international tribunal. On 30 June 1994, the US publicly called for the establishment of a war crimes tribunal,[182] and soon after the UN High Commissioner for Human Rights, the European Parliament, the Secretary General of the OAU and the Chief Prosecutor of the ICTY made similar statements.[183] On 8 November 1994, the Security Council established the ICTR; the Rwandan (RPF) government voted against the Resolution because it considered such a court ought to be based in Rwanda, but stated that it would cooperate fully with the Tribunal if it was established despite Rwanda's objections.[184] The ICTR was given jurisdiction to prosecute genocide, crimes against humanity and violations of common Article 3 of the Geneva Conventions and Additional Protocol II.[185] The principle of individual criminal responsibility and modes of participation were incorporated in Articles 5 and 6 of the ICTR Statute in the same terms as the ICTY Statute.[186] Like the ICTY, the ICTR's jurisdiction made no reference to

humanitarian law has become part of customary law: see *Report of the Secretary-General pursuant to Paragraph 2 of SC/Res 808 (22 February 1993)*, UN Doc. S/25704 (3 May 1993) and corrigendum, UN Doc. S/25704/Corr.1 (30 July 1993), p. 9, para. 35.

180 The RPF sent a letter to the Security Council on 13 April 1994: see discussion in Morris and Scharf, *An Insider's Guide to the International Criminal Tribunal for the Former Yugoslavia*, vol. II, p. 62.

181 Commission on Human Rights, Resolution S-3/1, The Situation of Human Rights in Rwanda, adopted on 25 May 1994; UN, *Report of the Commission on Human Rights on its Third Special Session*, UN Doc. E/1994/24/Add.2, p. 4.

182 Cited in Morris and Scharf, *An Insider's Guide to the International Criminal Tribunal for the Former Yugoslavia*, vol. II, pp. 64–5.

183 *Ibid.*

184 SC/Res/955, 8 November 1994. After coming to power in July 1994, the Tutsi-dominated Rwandan Unity government was initially opposed to an international tribunal but it subsequently agreed to defer domestic trials pending the creation of an international tribunal: UN SCOR 49th Sess., 3453d mtg, UN Doc. S/PV.3453 (1994), p. 16. In a formal letter to the Security Council, Rwanda requested the establishment of an international tribunal (Letter dated 28 September 1994 from the Permanent Representative of Rwanda to the United Nations addressed to the President of the Security Council, S/1994/1115, 29 September 1994) and on 6 October 1994 the President reiterated this request before the General Assembly: UN GAOR, 49th Sess., 21st Plenary Meeting, pp. 3, 5, UN Doc. A/49/PV.21 (1994).

185 ICTR Statute, arts. 3–5, available at www.un.org/ictr/statute.html.

186 *Ibid.*

domestic law; rather, it had jurisdiction to determine responsibility for violations of international law.

Both the ICTY and the ICTR addressed the principle of individual criminal responsibility in dealing with objections to their jurisdiction. In the ICTY, a Defence Motion on Jurisdiction in *Tadić* argued, *inter alia*, that the Tribunal was not duly established by law since the Security Council could not 'create criminal liability on the part of individuals'.[187] The Trial Chamber held that it had no authority to investigate the legality of its creation by the Security Council, but considered it would be inappropriate to dismiss the contentions of the accused without comment.[188] It noted the broad discretion of the Security Council to act under Chapter VII,[189] and concluded that the Security Council was not prevented from establishing the Tribunal, 'by providing for the prosecution of individuals who violate well-established rules of international law',[190] nor was there a basis 'for denying to the Security Council the power of indirect imposition of criminal liability upon individuals through the creation of a tribunal having criminal jurisdiction',[191] since the establishment of the Tribunal fell within the Security Council's powers under Article 41 of the Charter.[192] The Trial Chamber did not therefore take a position on the question whether individual responsibility existed independently of the Statute's provisions on jurisdiction. On the one hand, it suggested that by creating the ICTY, the Security Council provided a means by which individuals could be prosecuted for violations of international law; on the other hand, it suggested that the Security Council could indirectly impose liability on individuals for those violations. The Appeals Chamber considered that it had *la compétence de la competence*, enabling it to address the question of the legality of the creation of the Tribunal,[193] but dismissed the objection on the ground that the Tribunal was established in accordance with the UN Charter and according to law,[194] without commenting on the source of individual responsibility for violations of international law. However, in examining a defence objection to holding individuals responsible for violations in internal armed conflict, the Appeal Chamber held that 'customary international law imposes criminal liability [on individuals]'

[187] *Prosecutor* v. *Tadić*, Case no. IT-94-1-AR72, Trial Chamber, Decision on Defence Motion on Jurisdiction (Rule 73), 10 August 1995, para. 2.

[188] *Ibid.* paras. 5–6. [189] *Ibid.* para. 7. [190] *Ibid.* para. 18. [191] *Ibid.* para. 36.

[192] *Prosecutor* v. *Tadić*, Case no. IT-94-1-AR72, Appeals Chamber, Judgment on Jurisdiction, 2 October 1995, paras. 39–47.

[193] *Ibid.* paras. 18–22. [194] *Ibid.* paras. 47–8.

for violations of international humanitarian law, including serious violations of common Article 3[195] and consequently the Tribunal had 'jurisdiction over the acts alleged in the indictment, regardless of whether they occurred within an internal or an international armed conflict'.[196] The Appeals Chamber decision suggests that individual responsibility arises under international law independently of any international instrument conferring jurisdiction on a tribunal.

The ICTR took a rather different approach. In *Kanyabashi*,[197] the defence objected to the jurisdiction of the Tribunal on the basis that 'the Security Council has no authority over individuals'.[198] The Trial Chamber dismissed the objection, but it recalled that 'the question of direct individual criminal responsibility under international law is and has been a controversial issue'. It held that this controversy was resolved by the Security Council's creation of the ad hoc tribunals:

> By establishing the [ICTY and the ICTR], however, the Security Council explicitly extended international legal obligations and criminal responsibilities directly to individuals for violations of international humanitarian law. In doing so, the Security Council provided an important innovation of international law, but there is nothing in the Defence Counsel's notion to suggest that this extension of the applicability of international law against individuals was not justified or called for by the circumstances, notably the seriousness, the magnitude and the gravity of the crimes committed during the conflict.[199]

Thus, the ICTR relied exclusively on its Statute to justify individual criminal responsibility, stating that individual criminal responsibility arose under the provisions of its Statute, rather than under international humanitarian law, treaties or customary international law. Its statement that its Statute 'explicitly extended international legal obligations' directly to individuals suggests that no such obligations existed prior to or independently of its Statute. Although the prosecution had argued that the Nuremberg trials 'established that individuals who have committed crimes under international law can be held criminally responsible directly under international law',[200] the Tribunal did not rely on the Nuremberg judgment nor the Nuremberg Principles: rather, it suggested that the Security Council's creation of the ad hoc tribunals had extended international legal obligations to individuals.

195 *Ibid.* para. 134, see also paras. 128–37. 196 *Ibid.* para. 137.
197 *Prosecutor* v. *Kanyabashi*, Case no. ICTR-96-15-T, Decision on the Defence Motion on Jurisdiction, 18 June 1997.
198 *Ibid.* para. 33. 199 *Ibid.* para. 35. 200 *Ibid.* para. 34.

The ICTR's approach in *Kanyabashi* takes an extremely limited view of individual criminal responsibility. If international legal obligations were merely extended to individuals by the Security Council in creating the Tribunal's charter, then individuals would only be obliged not to commit international crimes (by international law) in circumstances where there was an international tribunal having jurisdiction. This approach also denies that the Nuremberg Principles, which were affirmed by the General Assembly, reflect international law, since they provide that any person who commits an international crime 'is responsible therefor and liable to punishment'.[201] The ICTR's approach also fails to take account of the Security Council's practice prior to the establishment of the ad hoc tribunals. The language of the relevant Security Council Resolutions prior to the establishment of the ICTY and the ICTR implied that individuals were responsible for relevant violations of international humanitarian law and that responsibility existed independently of the provisions of the Statutes conferring jurisdiction on the Tribunal. The approach of the ICTR has the consequence that individuals are only obliged not to commit international crimes in circumstances where there is a Statute establishing the jurisdiction of an international tribunal – a circular and question-begging formulation which conflates jurisdiction and substantive legislative authority.

In this context a comparison with the conferral of rights in international law may be helpful. When the PCIJ first recognised that individuals could be granted rights under treaty, in the *Danzig* Opinion, the only enforcement mechanism it referred to was enforcement in national courts.[202] Individual rights existed despite any provision by which individuals could enforce those rights in an international court. In another context, some five years later, the PCIJ confirmed that capacity to bear rights was distinct from capacity to enforce those rights. In examining the capacity of Peter Pázmany University of Budapest to submit a claim under the Treaty of Trianon, the PCIJ held that 'the capacity to possess civil rights does not necessarily imply the capacity to exercise those rights oneself'.[203] In large measure, individuals have been given international law rights without

201 See Principle I, reproduced in *Report of the International Law Commission to the General Assembly Covering its Second Session, 5 June–29 July 1950*, UN Doc. A/1316, reproduced in (1950) II *Yearbook of the International Law Commission* 364, 374.

202 *Jurisdiction of the Courts of Danzig (Pecuniary Claims of Danzig Railway Officials who have Passed into the Polish Service, Against the Polish Railways Administration)*, PCIJ Rep. ser. B no. 15 (1928) 3, 17–18.

203 *Appeal from a Judgment of the Hungaro-Czechoslovak Mixed Arbitral Tribunal (Peter Pázmány University* v. *State of Czechoslovakia)*, PCIJ Rep. ser. A/B no. 61 (1933) 231.

having any direct access to a remedy, or the means to enforce those rights in an international court. Thus, in the context of rights, the bearing of rights is not dependent on any provision conferring jurisdiction to enforce.

It seems uncontroversial that obligations could be extended to individuals by international law without necessarily requiring that those obligations be enforceable in an international court - indeed, without requiring that they be enforceable in any court. Inter-state obligations are created without necessarily conferring jurisdiction to enforce on an international tribunal; more often than not, international treaties impose obligations on states without providing any compulsory mechanism for enforcement. Why should the position be different for individuals?

Taking into account the affirmation of the principle of individual responsibility in the Nuremberg judgment and Principles, and the practice of the Security Council which refers to existing individual obligations in respect of international crimes, the preferable view is that expressed by the ICTY Appeals Chamber: that customary international law imposes criminal responsibility on individuals for international crimes. This is consistent with international practice and is supported by analogy with inter-state obligations under international law, which exist irrespective of any international enforcement mechanism. It can also be noted that even if the ICTR's approach was acceptable, it too confirms that individual responsibility arises under international law, without the interposition of domestic law, since the ICTR held individual responsibility arose under the terms of its Statute, which is clearly an international instrument.

(ii) The International Criminal Court

The prospect of establishing an international court for the trial of persons charged with genocide or other crimes was referred to the ILC in 1948 but for a variety of reasons the Draft Statute was only adopted in 1994.[204] The Draft Statute implicitly limited the Court's jurisdiction *ratione personae* to individuals and its jurisdiction *ratione materiae* to

[204] Draft Statutes were produced in 1951 and 1953 (*Report of the Committee on International Criminal Jurisdiction*, UN Doc. A/2136 and *Report of the 1953 Committee on International Criminal Jurisdiction*, UN Doc. A/2638) but work was deferred pending the adoption of a definition of aggression and was only referred back to the ILC in 1989 (GA/Res/44/39, 4 December 1989). Following the adoption of a definition of aggression by consensus in 1974 (GA/Res/3314(XXIX), 14 December 1974) there was little impetus for pursuing the question of an international criminal court and although the General Assembly requested the ILC to continue work on the Draft Code (GA/Res/36/106, 10 December 1981), the General Assembly did not immediately request the ILC to continue work on an international criminal court.

genocide; aggression; serious violations of the laws and customs applicable in armed conflict; crimes against humanity; and crimes established by treaties listed in the annex to the Statute.[205] Subsequently, work was continued by a Preparatory Committee established by the General Assembly,[206] which recommended that the fundamental principles of criminal law ought to be set out in the Statute,[207] including the principle of individual criminal responsibility.[208] The Preparatory Committee's draft contained a single Article 23 dealing with the principle of individual criminal responsibility as follows:

> 1. The Court shall have jurisdiction over natural persons pursuant to the present Statute.
> 2. A person who commits a crime under this Statute is individually responsible and liable for punishment.[209]

There were few changes from the Preparatory Committee's draft to what eventually became Article 25 of the ICC Statute.[210] Paragraphs (1),

[205] *Report of the International Law Commission on the Work of its 46th Session*, Draft Article 20, (1994) II *Yearbook of the International Law Commission* Pt 2, 1, 38.

[206] GA/Res/50/46, 11 December 1995.

[207] *Report of the Preparatory Committee on the Establishment of an International Criminal Court*, UN Doc. A/51/22 (1996), vol. I, *Proceedings of the Preparatory Committee during March-April and August 1996*, pp. 41–2, para. 181.

[208] *Ibid.* p. 44, para. 191. [209] *Ibid.* p. 48.

[210] Rome Statute of the International Criminal Court, 17 July 1998 (entry into force 1 July 2002), 2187 UNTS 3. On the Rome Conference generally, see P. Kirsch QC and D. Robinson, 'Reaching Agreement at the Rome Conference' in A. Cassese, P. Gaeta and J. R. W. D. Jones (eds.), *The Rome Statute of the International Criminal Court: A Commentary* (Oxford, Oxford University Press, 2002), vol. I, p. 67; on the contribution of NGOs see W. R. Pace and J. Schense, 'The Role of Non-Governmental Organizations' in A. Cassese, P. Gaeta, and J. R. W. D. Jones (eds.), *The Rome Statute of the International Criminal Court: A Commentary* (Oxford, Oxford University Press, 2002), vol. I, p. 105; on Article 25, see V. Militello, 'The Personal Nature of Individual Criminal Responsibility and the ICC Statute' (2007) 5 *JICJ* 941; S. Manacorda, 'The Principle of Individual Criminal Responsibility: A Conceptual Framework' (2007) 5 *JICJ* 913; P.-M. Dupuy, 'International Criminal Responsibility of the Individual and International Responsibility of the State' in A. Cassese, P. Gaeta and J. R. W. D. Jones (eds.), *The Rome Statute of the International Criminal Court: A Commentary* (Oxford, Oxford University Press, 2002), vol. I, p. 1085; A. Eser, 'Individual Criminal Responsibility' in A. Cassese, P. Gaeta and J. R. W. D. Jones (eds.), *The Rome Statute of the International Criminal Court: A Commentary* (Oxford, Oxford University Press, 2002), vol. I, p. 767; K. Ambos, 'Article 25: Individual Criminal Responsibility' in O. Triffterer (ed.), *Commentary on the Rome Statute of the International Criminal Court: Observers' Notes, Article by Article* (Baden Baden, Nomos Verlagsgesellschaft, 1999), p. 475; G. Werle, 'Individual Criminal Responsibility in Article 25 ICC Statute' (2005) 5 *JICJ* 953; P. Saland, 'International Criminal Law Principles' in R. S. Lee, *The International Criminal Court: The Making of the Rome Statute – Issues, Negotiations, Result* (The Hague, Kluwer, 1999), p. 189.

(2) and (3)(a) of Article 25 reflect the general principle of individual criminal responsibility for crimes within the jurisdiction of the Court, while the remaining sub-paragraphs of Article 25 deal with forms of participation.[211] Paragraph (3)(a) expressly provides for individual responsibility for commission or perpetration by action which is either individual, jointly with another person, or through another person.[212] Although the French delegation pushed for the extension of criminal responsibility to 'juridical persons', on the basis that it was important for restitution and compensation for victims,[213] no consensus was reached on the inclusions of persons other than natural persons and it was dropped by the Working Group.[214] The provisions of the Statute defining crimes specify that the Court has jurisdiction 'with respect to the [specified] crimes';[215] they do not use the language of 'international crimes' or refer to any individual obligations under international law.

Other provisions of the Statute set out the circumstances in which the Court may exercise its jurisdiction: where a situation is referred by a state party or by the Security Council acting under Chapter VII, or where the prosecutor has initiated an investigation.[216] Where a situation is referred by a state party or where the prosecutor has initiated an investigation, the Court may exercise its jurisdiction if that state on whose territory the conduct in question occurred is a party to the Statute (or the registration state where the crime is committed on a vessel or aircraft) or if the national state of the accused is a party to the Statute.[217]

211 These include ordering, soliciting or inducing the commission or attempt of a crime; aiding, abetting or otherwise attempting the commission or attempt of a crime; contributing to the commission or attempt of a crime by a group of persons acting with a common purpose; direct and public incitement of genocide; and attempt. For an analysis of these sub-paragraphs, see Eser, 'Individual Criminal Responsibility', 795–803.

212 For an analysis of the elements of each of these forms of perpetration, see Eser, 'Individual Criminal Responsibility', 789–95.

213 See French Proposal for Article 23, UN Doc. A/CONF.183/C.1/L.3 (1998), paras. 5 and 6. The failure to include a power to order forfeiture against corporate entities might significantly curtail the effectiveness of the reparations regime established in the ICC Statute.

214 See *Report of the Working Group on General Principles of Criminal Law*, UN Doc. A/CONF.183/C.1/WGGP/L.4/Add.1 (29 June 1998); *Report of the Working Group on General Principles of Criminal Law*, UN Doc. A/CONF.183/C.1/WGGP/L.4/Add.2 (2 July 1998); *Report of the Working Group on General Principles of Criminal Law*, UN Doc. A/CONF.183/C.1/WGGP/L.4/Add.3 (7 July 1998).

215 Rome Statute of the International Criminal Court, Art. 5, 17 July 1998 (entry into force 1 July 2002), 2187 UNTS 3; see also Arts. 6–9.

216 *Ibid.* Art. 13. 217 *Ibid.* Art. 12.

The Statute does not take a position on the question whether individuals are bound under customary international law not to commit international crimes; one would not expect it to as it is a court of limited jurisdiction, defined by the terms of its Statute. However, it is interesting in this context to observe that the material jurisdiction of the Court under the terms of its Statute is more limited than the prohibited conduct and individual responsibility under customary international law. One example is the war crime relating to attack of civilians and civilian objects, which incorporates a proportionality test of 'clearly excessive',[218] a more limited offence than that which would arise under the customary law rule which prohibits attacks which are 'excessive'.[219] Another example is the Statute's provisions on command responsibility, which distinguish between military commanders and other superiors, requiring a stronger connection for command responsibility in the case of the latter;[220] whereas in customary international law there is no relevant distinction between commanders and superiors.[221]

The ICC Statute also provides for two forms of incidental responsibility or punishment of individuals, apart from responsibility for crimes enumerated under the Statute. The first is the Court's jurisdiction over offences against the administration of justice, broadly including contempt offences and other offences of misconduct.[222] Thus, individuals may be held responsible for offences which do not derive more generally from violations of international law or international crimes.[223] The second are the

218 *Ibid.* Art. 8(b)(iv).

219 See Protocol I Additional to the Geneva Conventions of 12 August 1949 and Relating to the Protection of Victims of International Armed Conflicts, Art. 51(5)(b), 8 June 1977, 1125 UNTS 3 and J.-M. Henckaerts and L. Doswald-Beck, *International Committee of the Red Cross: Customary International Humanitarian Law*, vol. I, *Rules* (Cambridge, Cambridge University Press, 2005), Rule 14, p. 46.

220 Rome Statute of the International Criminal Court, Art. 28, 17 July 1998 (entry into force 1 July 2002), 2187 UNTS 3.

221 Henckaerts and Doswald-Beck, *International Committee of the Red Cross: Customary International Humanitarian Law*, vol. I, *Rules*, Rule 153, pp. 558–9.

222 Rome Statute of the International Criminal Court, Arts. 70–1, 17 July 1998 (entry into force 1 July 2002), 2187 UNTS 3; see also International Criminal Court, *Rules of Procedure and Evidence*, ICC_ASP/1/3, adopted by the Assembly of State Parties, 3–10 September 2002, Rules 162–72.

223 Both the ICTR and the ICTY have held individuals responsible for contempt based on the inherent power of the Tribunal derived from its judicial function, since no equivalent provision appears in either Statute: see ICTY, Rules of Procedure and Evidence, IT/32/Rev 42 (4 November 2008), Rule 77; ICTR Rules of Procedure and Evidence (14 March 2009), Rule 77; *Prosecutor* v. *Tadić*, Case no. IT-94-1-AR72, Appeals Chamber, Judgment on Jurisdiction, 2 October 1995, para. 13.

provisions on forfeiture of proceeds of crime, which imply that the Court has power to order the forfeiture of proceeds of crime possessed by *male fide* associates of the accused.[224] One view of these provisions is that they permit punishment to be imposed on individuals who hold proceeds of crime without requiring that the Court determine that they have any responsibility for that crime as contemplated by Article 25 of the Statute.

The ICC Statute also provides the Court with a power to order reparations. Article 75(2) of the ICC Statute provides:

> The Court may make an order directly against a convicted person specifying appropriate reparations to, or in respect of, victims, including restitution, compensation and rehabilitation.

This provision is separate from the Statute's specification of penalties and is not conceived of as an additional or separate element of individual punishment for international crimes. Like reparations in general international law,[225] the ICC reparations regime is rather concerned with addressing the harm caused by the internationally wrongful acts, rather than punishing the perpetrator. Outside of Article 75, there has been no development in general international law of an obligation on the perpetrator of international crimes to provide reparation to victims; while the ICC Statute may lead to further development of this concept, there are situations in which reparations will be materially impossible or where it is difficult to causally attribute harm to the perpetrator.[226]

(iii) International crimes before 'hybrid' and domestic courts

In the last decade hybrid courts have been created which prosecute individuals for international crimes; and in addition there have been prosecutions of individuals for international crimes in domestic courts.[227] The contribution of these courts to the development of the

[224] Rome Statute of the International Criminal Court, Art. 77(2)(b), 17 July 1998 (entry into force 1 July 2002), 2187 UNTS 3; International Criminal Court, *Rules of Procedure and Evidence*, ICC_ASP/1/3, adopted by the Assembly of State Parties, 3–10 September 2002, Rules 147 and 218. The Court has issued a freezing order in anticipation of reparations orders being made in proceedings against Jean-Pierra Bemba Gombo, see ICC, *Decision et demande en vue d'obtenir l'identification, la localisation, le gel et la saisie des biens et avoirs adressées a la république Portguaise*, ICC-01/05-01/08, 27 May 2008.

[225] *Factory at Chorzów (Claim for Indemnity)*, Merits, PCIJ Rep. ser. A no. 17 (1928) 47.

[226] See generally, C. McCarthy, 'Reparations under the Rome Statute of the International Criminal Court and Reparative Justice Theory' (2009) *ICTJ* 1, 10.

[227] On hybrid courts generally, see L. Dickinson, 'The Promise of Hybrid Courts' (2003) 97 *AJIL* 295; C. Romano, A. Nollekemper and J. Kleffner, *Internationalized Criminal Courts* (Oxford, Oxford University Press, 2004); S. Nouwen, '"Hybrid Courts": The Hybrid

principle of individual criminal responsibility under international law cannot be generalised because usually there is a mix of international and domestic law in their applicable law; they will be briefly sketched in this section.

Courts which apply domestic law do not contribute to the development of the principle of individual criminal responsibility under international law, whether they are domestic courts or international courts. For example, the Special Tribunal for Lebanon is an international court which applies exclusively domestic law (the relevant applicable law does not reflect any substantive international criminal law);[228] although it is an international forum, it determines individual responsibility under domestic law. Where the applicable domestic law in substance incorporates international crimes, these courts may contribute indirectly to the development of substantive law on international crimes, but without exception individual responsibility is imposed by domestic law. Since the applicable law is domestic law, even in a formal sense, these courts are enforcing individual obligations and responsibility which arise under domestic, not international, law. Ordinary domestic courts prosecuting war crimes fall into this category (for example, the Israeli court prosecuting *Eichmann*),[229] as do special domestic courts or panels established with jurisdiction over acts which in substance amount to international crimes (such as the 'Regulation 64' Panels in Kosovo;[230] the War Crimes Chamber in Bosnia and Herzegovina;[231] and the Iraqi High Tribunal).[232]

Category of a New Type of International Crimes Courts' (2006) *Utrecht Law Review* 190, esp. 206–9.

228 The Agreement is contained in SC/Res/1664, 29 March 2006, and was endorsed in SC/Res/1757, 30 May 2007, after it was signed by the Lebanese Government on 6 February 2007. See in particular Art. 2 of its Statute.

229 *Attorney General (Israel)* v. *Adolf Eichmann*, Israeli Supreme Court sitting as a Court of Criminal Appeal (1962) 36 ILR 5.

230 The Panels may apply a new Criminal Code which incorporates genocide, crimes against humanity and war crimes. The more favourable (to the accused) of existing law or the new Criminal Code apply: UNMIK/REG/2000/64, ss. 1 and 2; UNMIK/REG/1999/1, 10 June 1999. UNMIK/REG/2000/6 granted the UN Special Representative the authority to appoint and remove international judges and prosecutors to the courts in Mitrovica; subsequently this was applied to all five district courts in Kosovo under UNMIK/REG/2000/34.

231 War Crimes Balkan Investigative Reporting Network, *In Pursuit of Justice: Guide to the War Crimes Chamber of the Court of BiH*, www.birn.eu.com. See SC/Res/1503, 28 August 2003 (on the completion strategy).

232 The Iraqi High Tribunal is a domestic tribunal with jurisdiction over genocide, crimes against humanity and war crimes defined in domestic law: see I. Bantekas, 'The Iraqi Special Tribunal for Crimes Against Humanity' (2004) 54 *ICLQ* 237; C. Garraway,

In contrast, courts which apply international law directly may contribute to the development of individual responsibility under international law. There are three courts in this category. The Extraordinary Chambers of Cambodia have jurisdiction over genocide; crimes against humanity; grave breaches of the Geneva Conventions; the destruction of cultural property; and crimes against internationally protected persons, as well as three specific crimes under domestic law (homicide, torture and religious persecution).[233] The Special Court for Sierra Leone has jurisdiction over crimes against humanity, violations of common Article 3 of the Geneva Conventions and of Additional Protocol II and other serious violations of international humanitarian law, as well as for crimes under Sierra Leonean law.[234] The Serious Crimes Panels of the District Court in Dili (East Timor) have jurisdiction for international crimes including virtually all those covered in the ICC Statute and the international crime of torture, as well as murder and sexual offences under the applicable domestic law.[235] The constituent documents of

'The Statute of the Iraqi Special Tribunal' in S. Breau and A. Jachec-Neale (eds.), *Testing the Boundaries of International Humanitarian Law* (London, BIICL, 2006), p. 155. Jurisdiction of the Tribunal is set out in SICT Statute, Arts. 11–14, available at www.ictj.org/static/MENA/Iraq/iraq.cpaorder48.121003.eng.pdf. See Y. Shany, 'Does One Size Fit All?' (2004) 2 *JICJ* 338. The Tribunal has concurrent jurisdiction with other domestic courts but also primacy: see SICT Statute, Arts. 29–30. Another example is the War Crimes Chamber of the Belgrade District Court, which is a national court with jurisdiction over war crimes committed in the former Yugoslavia: see M. Ellis, 'Coming to Terms with its Past: Serbia's New Court for the Prosecution of War Crimes' (2004) 22 *Berkeley Journal of International Law* 165.

233 The crimes covered are genocide under the 1948 Genocide Convention; crimes against humanity as defined in the ICC Statute; grave breaches of the Geneva Conventions; and certain other crimes under Cambodian law: Arts. 3–8 of the UN-Cambodia Agreement, annexed to GA/Res/57/228B, 13 May 2003. The Extraordinary Chambers do not have jurisdiction over war crimes in non-international armed conflicts as Cambodia was not a party to the Additional Protocols before 1980 and there is doubt that these crimes were customary when they were committed: see *Report of the Group of Experts for Cambodia Established Pursuant to General Assembly Resolution 52/135*, UN Doc. A/53/850, paras. 72–5.

234 SCSL Statute, Arts. 2–5, available at www.sc-sl.org/LinkClick.aspx?fileticket=uClnd1MJeEw%3d&tabid=176. Owing to the character of the conflict, the subject-matter jurisdiction of the Special Court covers crimes against humanity and war crimes committed in a non-international armed conflict (SCSL Statute, Arts. 2–4) and some specified crimes under Sierra Leonean law (SCSL Statute, Art. 5). The Special Court has held, however, that the war crimes within its jurisdiction may be prosecuted whether the conflict is international or non-international: *Prosecutor* v. *Moinina Fofana*, Case no. SCSL-2004-14-AR72(E), Appeals Chamber, Decision on Preliminary Motion on Lack of Jurisdiction *Ratione Materiae*: Nature of the Armed Conflict, 25 May 2004.

235 UNTAET Reg. 2000/15, 5 July 2000, ss. 4–9, 10–21. The applicable law being the UNTAET Regulations, domestic law and, where appropriate, applicable treaties and recognised principles of international law: UNTAET Reg. 2000/15, s. 3. The UN handed over

these three courts suggest that individuals are responsible for violations of international law, and by implication that individuals have duties directly under international law.

4.5 Conclusions: the position of the individual in international criminal law

Prior to the Nuremberg Tribunal, there was no developed conception of individual responsibility under international law. Rather, individual responsibility for acts which might have amounted to a breach of international law only arose under domestic law. This was consistent with the nineteenth century framework of the international legal system, because individual duties and responsibility could only be imposed through domestic law, and individuals were not directly subject to or subjects of international law. The penal provisions of the Treaty of Versailles implied that individual responsibility for acts in violation of the laws and customs of war (or international treaties) could arise directly under international law. These provisions were consistent with the post-1945 framework of the international legal system, because they stipulated that individuals had duties directly under international law. However, these penal provisions were never executed, and individual responsibility was only pursued (and only then faintly) through domestic processes and through the application of domestic law.

Since 1945, the principle of individual criminal responsibility has become entrenched in international law. This is most often traced to the Nuremberg Tribunal: the Charter of the Tribunal provided that 'there shall be individual responsibility' for specified crimes and the judgment of the Tribunal applied the Charter as establishing that individual responsibility, while also maintaining that it had long been

administration to East Timor on 20 May 2002 and UNTAET was replaced by UNMISET, which continued to provide the Serious Crimes Panels with practical support. The project formally ended with the departure of UNMISET in May 2005 and in October 2005, the Commission for Reception, Truth and Reconciliation recommended the establishment of an international tribunal to investigate the violence in East Timor, and also the renewal of the mandate of the Serious Crimes Panels: see *Chega! Final Report of the Commission for Reception, Truth and Reconciliation in East Timor*, Pt 11, Recommendations, p. 26, available at www.cavr-timorleste.org/en/chegaReport.htm. The Commission of Experts established by the UN Secretary-General also recommended (in 2005) that an international tribunal be established. In August 2006, the Security Council provided for the completion of investigations by a unit within the current UN mission, UNMIT.

recognised that individuals had direct obligations under international law not to commit certain acts. Nevertheless, the Tribunal's attempt to appeal to precedent was unconvincing and it may be justifiably cited as the first express recognition of individual criminal responsibility under international law.

Despite criticisms on this ground, the Nuremberg judgment was on the whole accepted and steps were taken to make the principles of the Tribunal 'a permanent part of ... international law'. But although the principle that individuals were responsible for acts constituting international crimes was accepted, there was some reluctance to admit that this necessarily had the consequence that individuals were subjects of or subject to international law. This reservation was most clearly enunciated by Fitzmaurice (for the UK) when the Nuremberg Principles were discussed in the Sixth Committee: he argued that the individual could be punished for international crimes without 'regard[ing] him as being subject to international law' and in particular without displacing 'the classic concept that international law solely governs relations between States'.[236] These statements are reminiscent of the arguments made by the defence against the imposition of responsibility by the Nuremberg Tribunal, arguments which were rejected by that Tribunal. It seems that there is little practical difference between admitting that international law 'may impose duties on individuals directly', as the Commentary to the Nuremberg Principles stated, and admitting that individuals are 'subject to' international law. If individuals may be punished for crimes without the interposition of domestic law, their responsibility must arise under international law. In those circumstances the suggestion that individuals were not 'subject to international law' and that international law continued to 'solely govern relations between States' is unsustainable. On the other hand, if an international tribunal exercises delegated domestic jurisdiction to punish individuals, this interpretation might be consistent with the nineteenth century framework of the international legal system, as individual responsibility would arise under domestic law but be enforced, for practical or other reasons, by an international tribunal. This was not the case with the Nuremberg Tribunal, the ICTY and the ICTR. It is not the case with the ICC. Rather, those tribunals are determining individual responsibility under international law.

[236] *Second Report* (Mr J. Spiropoulos, Special Rapporteur), UN Doc. A/CN.4/44, reproduced in (1951) II *Yearbook of the International Law Commission* 43, 50, paras. 63–4.

Even if the Nuremberg judgment and Principles could be interpreted in a manner consistent with the nineteenth century framework of the international legal system, subsequent development of individual criminal responsibility has precluded that interpretation. Individual criminal responsibility has been imposed in international tribunals without the interposition of domestic law, and without being interpreted as a delegation of domestic jurisdiction and enforcement of responsibility under domestic law. Nevertheless, the question of the source of individual obligations - obligations which give rise to individual responsibility which may be enforced by international courts without regard to domestic law - has been contested. While the ICTY suggested that individual responsibility derived from obligations imposed on individuals by treaty and customary international law, the ICTR held that individual responsibility was effectively imposed on individuals by instruments giving an international tribunal jurisdiction to enforce that responsibility - that those jurisdictional provisions effectively extended international obligations to individuals. Surprisingly, neither tribunal gave much attention to the Nuremberg Principles, which must have as much precedential value at least as the Nuremberg Tribunal and judgment, and which clearly expressed *opinio juris* in support of a customary principle of individual criminal responsibility for specified crimes. The Statute of the ICC has not addressed the question of the source of the individual obligation either: it merely gives the Court jurisdiction over crimes defined in its Statute and provides that a person who commits a crime so defined 'is individually responsible and liable to punishment'.

For present purposes the question is moot. Under either interpretation individual responsibility derives directly from international law, either from the substantive rules or from the jurisdictional provisions of the relevant international tribunal. It is suggested, however, that individual responsibility does arise under customary international law and that it exists independently of any jurisdiction to enforce before an international tribunal. This is for three reasons. First, the Nuremberg Principles, which were affirmed by the General Assembly which intended to make them part of international law, provide that any person who commits an international crime 'is responsible therefor and liable to punishment'.[237] The Nuremberg Principles did not

[237] *Report of the International Law Commission to the General Assembly Covering its Second Session, 5 June–29 July 1950*, UN Doc. A/1316, reproduced in (1950) II *Yearbook of the International Law Commission* 364, 374 (Principle I).

establish the jurisdiction of any international tribunal over international crimes; rather, individual responsibility stood separately from jurisdiction to enforce. In this respect it can be noted that individual rights commonly exist irrespective of any jurisdiction to enforce, and that inter-state obligations are commonly imposed without conferring jurisdiction to enforce on any international tribunal. There is no reason to suggest that individual responsibility could not arise under international law absent jurisdiction to enforce, when international law does not operate in that manner with respect to states. Second, international practice, particularly since the 1990s, supports the principle of individual criminal responsibility under customary international law, as reflected in the Nuremberg Principles. The Security Council has stated that individuals committing international crimes are 'individually responsible'[238] and has suggested that individuals may be responsible for serious violations of international humanitarian law.[239] These statements have been made in circumstances where no international tribunal has jurisdiction to prosecute. Third, it is untenable that individuals would only be obliged not to commit international crimes in circumstances where there is a statute establishing an international tribunal's jurisdiction to prosecute. This would run counter to the underlying purpose of individual criminal responsibility; moreover, it would mean that unless an international tribunal was created in advance, international law tolerated breaches of the *nullum crimen* principle, imposing retrospectively responsibility for conduct for which there was no individual international responsibility at the time it was committed. The preferable interpretation is that individual responsibility exists under customary international law for established international crimes. Individual responsibility for international crimes has been affirmed by international prosecutions: in circumstances where an international tribunal has jurisdiction to prosecute, its jurisdiction is limited *ratione materiae*, *ratione temporis* and *ratione personae* by its constituent statute. But individual criminal responsibility exists absent any jurisdiction to enforce, in the same way that state responsibility and individual rights exist absent jurisdiction to enforce.

[238] See SC/Res/764, 13 July 1992; SC/Res/771, 13 August 1992; SC/Res/780, 6 October 1992.
[239] SC/Res/808, 22 February 1993.

5 The individual in international human rights law

5.1 Introduction

International human rights law is widely acknowledged as having had a transformative effect on the position of the individual in the international legal system in the post-1945 period.[1] But while there is widespread acceptance of the importance of human rights protection in international law, there is considerable confusion about its basis and role in international law.[2] It is often suggested that human rights are defined as those fundamental rights to which every person is entitled to 'merely by virtue of having been born a human being';[3] the character of human rights is commonly explained by reference to individual integrity and human dignity.[4] From a rhetorical point of view, the reference to human dignity may be powerful, but it suggests that human rights adhere to individuals through some inherent capacity and fails to acknowledge that international human rights law is tied to the state system of international law: that human rights were initially (at least) conceived as rights held by individuals as against the state, without horizontal effect as between non-state actors.

This chapter explores the extent to which international human rights law has engaged individuals. Of interest here is not the content of the rights in question, but how human rights law structurally treats

[1] See e.g., R. Higgins, *Problems and Process: International Law and How We Use It* (Oxford, Oxford University Press, 1994), p. 95; R. Mullerson, 'Human Rights and the Individual as Subject of International Law: A Soviet View' (1990) 1 *EJIL* 33.

[2] M. Moskowitz, *The Policies and Dynamics of Human Rights* (London, 1968), pp. 98–9.

[3] See e.g., Higgins, *Problems and Process*, p. 96.

[4] *Ibid.* p. 96; M. S. McDougal, H. Lasswell and L. Chen, *Human Rights and World Public Order: The Basic Policies of an International Law of Human Dignity* (New Haven, Yale University Press, 1980), pp. 82–93.

individuals. The first section of the chapter considers the development of the abolition of slavery. There are, of course, other antecedents which could be considered, such as early protection of religious freedom, provisions in the laws of war directed to humanitarian ends or natural law theories in political philosophy. However, the focus here is on slavery because it is the most often cited antecedent of international human rights law in the nineteenth and early twentieth centuries, coinciding with the time when international law is generally recognised as cohering around a body of rules and forms of conduct. The second section examines the rules and mechanisms developed in the inter-war period to protect certain groups of individuals which exhibit characteristics of modern international human rights law. The third section of the chapter examines the development of international human rights law after 1945, with focus on the structural engagement of individuals.

In addition to the rights given to individuals under international human rights law, individuals may also be entitled to human rights or civil liberties under domestic law: though there may be common features, this protection will vary from state to state. Individuals may also benefit from domestic law which incorporates international human rights law.[5] In substance, the rights to which individuals are entitled under domestic law may correspond to their international law rights. However, in principle the extent to which domestic law has developed to protect individuals is beyond the scope of this chapter.

5.2 Antecedents: the case of slavery

The most often cited antecedent of international human rights is the abolition of slavery. The movement for the abolition of slavery began in Britain in the eighteenth century. The first Act regulating the slave trade was passed in Britain in July 1788;[6] subsequently, involvement in the slave trade was criminalised.[7] Similar legislation was passed in

[5] For example, in the UK, Human Rights Act 1998, s. 7 (cap. 42) allows an individual to claim before a domestic court that a public authority has acted unlawfully by reason of the violation of specified ECHR rights.

[6] J. Bandinel, *Some Account of the Trade in Slaves from Africa as Connected with Europe and America* (London, Frank Cass & Co. Ltd, 1968), pp. 93–8.

[7] *Ibid.* pp. 116–24, 146. See Act 47 Geo. III cap. 36, 25 March 1807; Acts 51 Geo. II cap. 53; 53 Geo. III cap. 93; 58 Geo. III cap. 49; and 58 Geo. III cap. 98; Act 5 Geo. IV cap. 17; Act Vic. cap. 91.

Denmark and Sweden; legislation was also enacted in the US but was not enforced.[8] Britain also sought to conclude treaties aimed at abolishing the slave trade.[9] By 1839, it had concluded bilateral conventions with almost every leading maritime state, permitting reciprocal search and seizure on the high sea for vessels suspected on reasonable grounds of being engaged in the African slave trade;[10] it also negotiated treaties with rulers in Africa prohibiting the slave trade.[11] In execution of these bilateral treaties, the British Royal Navy acted as a *de facto* police force on the high seas.[12]

While Britain had success in making bilateral arrangements, it was difficult to reach agreement on a multilateral convention.[13] At the Congress of Vienna, Lord Castlereagh (for Great Britain) sought agreement on some kind of international enforcement machinery but none was agreed: the Final Act of 9 June 1815 merely noted that 'the universal abolition of the Slave Trade [w]as a measure particularly worthy of ... attention'.[14] Castlereagh continued to pursue agreement on an international naval police force at Aix-la-Chappelle in 1818 and Verona in 1822, without success.[15] After Castlereagh's untimely death in 1822, the British focussed their efforts on bilateral arrangements and it was not until the Conference of Berlin in 1885 that progress was made on a multilateral instrument. States participating in the Conference of Berlin committed 'to help in suppressing slavery and the Slave Trade'[16] and in 1889, the Brussels Conference General Act provided

[8] Bandinel, *Some Account of the Trade in Slaves from Africa*, p. 305, produces a list of dates of abolition of the slave trade in various states.

[9] *Ibid.* p. 125.

[10] H. H. Wilson, 'Some Principal Aspects of British Efforts to Crush the African Slave Trade, 1807–1929' (1950) 44 *AJIL* 505. A list of treaties is found in C. Lloyd, *The Navy and the Slave Trade: The Suppression of the African Slave Trade in the Nineteenth Century* (London, Longmans, 1949), p. 287.

[11] Most of these were concluded in 1841: see Bandinel, *Some Account of the Trade in Slaves from Africa*, p. 297.

[12] Under some of these treaties vessels were tried by courts of mixed commission at Sierra Leone: see e.g., HM Commissioners at Sierra Leone, 'Annual Report, 1838', XXVII BFSP 209, 214.

[13] Bandinel, *Some Account of the Trade in Slaves from Africa*, pp. 148–9.

[14] Final Act of 9 June 1815; H. Fischer, 'The Suppression of Slavery in International Law' (1950) 3 *ICLQ* 28, 44.

[15] C. K. Webster, *The Foreign Policy of Castlereagh 1812–1815: Britain and the European Alliance* (London, Bell & Sons, 1925), p. 454.

[16] Chapter II, Articles 4, 6, 9, General Act of Berlin, 26 February 1885, *Hertslet's Commercial Treaties* (London, 1827–1925), vol. XVII, p. 66 *et seq.*

for general cooperation in abolition of the African Slave Trade.[17] Under the auspices of the League of Nations, the 1926 Slavery Convention imposed obligations on states parties (a) '[t]o prevent and suppress the slave trade'; and (b) '[t]o bring about, progressively and as soon as possible, the complete abolition of slavery in all its forms'.[18] The Convention did not purport to confer rights on individuals; rather, it imposed obligations on states to take certain steps. In 1956, a Supplementary Convention was opened for signature affirming the obligations specified in the 1926 Convention and requiring states to criminalise participation in the slave trade.[19] States parties were required to take all measures to 'bring about progressively and as soon as possible the complete abolition or abandonment' of specified practices.[20] Again, like the 1926 Convention, it referred only to state obligations and did not purport to confer rights on individuals.

In marked contrast to the measures taken in international law, in domestic law slavery was treated consistently with inherent individual rights. For example, in Britain it was held that slaves were entitled to freedom, under English law. Chief Justice Holt held in 1705 that 'As soon as a negro comes into England he becomes free'.[21] In the famous decision in *Somerset's Case* (1772), Lord Mansfield held that when a slave came to England, he fell under the protection of English law and thus became free.[22] That freedom was not conceptualised as an obligation on the state; it was not something needing to be done by Parliament or government, but rather it was a consequence of an *existing* legal situation, a status of freedom intrinsically connected to the common law.

The claim of the abolition of slavery as an antecedent of international human rights is thus open to challenge. In contrast to the post-1945 conception of international human rights and the post-1945 right to

[17] Article 3 of Chapter I of the General Act of Brussels, *Hertslet's Commercial Treaties* (London, 1827–1925), vol. XIX, p. 282 *et seq*. The Convention of St Germaine-en-Laye of 1919 purported to abrogate the Berlin and Brussels Act.

[18] Slavery Convention, 25 September 1926 (entry into force 9 March 1927), 60 LNTS 253. Discussion as to the scope of the definition can be found in Wilson, 'Some Principal Aspects of British Efforts to Crush the African Slave Trade, 1807–1929', 522–3.

[19] Supplementary Convention on the Abolition of Slavery, the Slave Trade, and Institutions and Practices Similar to Slavery, 7 September 1956 (entry into force 30 April 1957), 266 UNTS 3. See generally, J. A. C. Gutteridge, 'Supplementary Slavery Convention, 1956' (1957) 6 *ICLQ* 449.

[20] Supplementary Convention on the Abolition of Slavery, the Slave Trade, and Institutions and Practices Similar to Slavery, Art. 1, 7 September 1956 (entry into force 30 April 1957), 266 UNTS 3.

[21] *Smith* v. *Brown* (1705) 91 ER 566. [22] *Somerset* v. *Stewart* (1772) 98 ER 499.

freedom from slavery as articulated in modern human rights treaties,[23] in this early period the abolition of slavery operated exclusively through inter-state obligations. The evil of treating the slave as an object of property was combatted through the normal mode of a treaty in which the individual was an object of (in this case beneficial) regulation. Furthermore, such international regulation did not depart from the general prohibition of intervention in the domestic jurisdiction of states, since it was directed primarily against acts taken on the high seas, outside the jurisdiction of any state.

5.3 Protection of individuals during the inter-war period

The League of Nations Covenant made no reference to individual rights. Although Japan had attempted to secure a racial equality clause in the Covenant, it did not succeed.[24] The Covenant expressed a commitment to principles of respect for humanity in Article 23 in two contexts: 'fair and humane conditions of labour'; and 'just treatment of the native inhabitants of territories under their control'.[25] But Article 23 did no more than impose general obligations on states intended to benefit individuals.

However, under the auspices of the League, groups of individuals were given protection in three contexts: minorities; the inhabitants of mandated territories; and refugees. In addition, the International Labour Organisation concluded conventions which operated to benefit individuals during the inter-war period.

(a) Minorities

In the Peace Treaties of Versailles, St Germain-en-Laye, Trianon and Neuilly, Poland, Czechoslovakia, Romania, Yugoslavia and Greece each agreed to sign a treaty with the Allied Powers 'to protect the *interests* of the inhabitants ... who differ from the majority of the

[23] See e.g., Universal Declaration of Human Rights, Art. 4, 10 December 1948, GA/Res/217A (III); European Convention for the Protection of Human Rights and Fundamental Freedoms (ECHR), Art. 4, 4 November 1950 (entry into force 3 September 1953), 87 UNTS 103; International Covenant on Civil and Political Rights (ICCPR), Art. 8, 16 December 1966 (entry into force 23 March 1976), 999 UNTS 171.

[24] P. G. Lauren, *The Evolution of International Human Rights: Visions Seen* (2nd edn, Philadelphia, Pa., University of Pennsylvania Press, 2003), p. 99.

[25] Covenant of the League of Nations, Art. 23, 28 June 1919 (entry into force 10 January 1920), 108 LNTS 188.

population in race, language, or religion'.[26] These treaties and declarations were signed between 1919 and 1934;[27] the Polish Minorities Treaty[28] was used as a template for subsequent treaties. Virtually all the minorities treaties and declarations included provisions:

(a) for the acquisition of nationality by persons belonging to a minority, including a right to opt for nationality of the state to which they formerly belonged;[29]
(b) to secure for minorities legal equality with the national majority, including full protection of life and liberty, enjoyment of equal civil and political rights, and free exercise of any creed, religion or belief not inconsistent with public order or public morals;[30]
(c) regarding the use of minority languages in private relations, before courts and in primary education, and the establishment of educational, religious and welfare institutions.[31]

The minorities treaties imposed obligations on contracting states which were to be recognised as 'fundamental laws', invalidating all laws, regulations or official action inconsistent with them.[32] The substantive provisions were expressed as conferring rights on 'all

[26] Treaty of Versailles, Art. 93, 28 June 1919, UKTS 4 (Cmd 153) (emphasis added). See also Treaty of St Germain-en-Laye, Art. 51, 10 September 1919, UKTS 11 (Cmd 400); Treaty of Neuilly, Art. 46, 27 November 1919, UKTS 5 (Cmd 522); Treaty of Trianon, Art. 44, 4 June 1920, UKTS 10 (Cmd 896).

[27] J. Robinson, *Were the Minorities Treaties a Failure?* (New York, Institute of Jewish Affairs, 1943), pp. 19–20; I. L. Evans, 'The Protection of Minorities' (1923) 4 *BYIL* 95, 104; see United Nations Economic and Social Council, Commission on Human Rights, *Study of the Legal Validity of the Undertakings Concerning Minorities*, E/CN.4/367 (7 April 1950), pp. 2–3. The territorial settlement of the area of Upper Silesia was the subject of extended controversy. The decision of the Peace Conference to arrange a plebiscite was incorporated in the Treaty of Versailles, but it was not until 20 October 1921 that the Conference of Ambassadors decided to implement a territorial division proposed by a committee of small powers, and a definitive boundary settled: see (1921) *League of Nations Official Journal* (December) 1220–32, esp. 1230–1. The Polish portion of Upper Silesia included approximately 300,000 persons of German origin and Poland asserted that German Upper Silesia contained an even greater number of persons of Polish origin: J. Stone, *Regional Guarantees of Human Rights: A Study of Minorities Procedure in Upper Silesia* (New York, Macmillan, 1933), p. 3.

[28] Treaty of Peace between the United States, the British Empire, France, Italy, Japan and Poland, 28 June 1919 (entry into force 10 January 1920), 225 CTS 412 (hereinafter 'Polish Minorities Treaty').

[29] Polish Minorities Treaty, Arts. 3–6. [30] *Ibid.* Arts. 2, 7–8, 11.

[31] *Ibid.* Arts. 7, 9–10. The Convention relating to Upper Silesia contained additional protection: (1921) *League of Nations Official Journal* (December) 1220–32, esp. 1230–1. See discussion in H. Rosting, 'Protection of Minorities by the League of Nations' (1923) 17 *AJIL* 641, 652–3.

[32] Polish Minorities Treaty, Art. 1.

inhabitants' of the contracting state,[33] on 'nationals'[34] generally or on 'nationals who belong to racial, religious or linguistic minorities'.[35] These provisions used language of direct rights: for example, they provided that individuals are 'entitled to'[36] or 'have a right'.[37] Although these rights were in effect conferred upon a category of persons, the language indicated that the rights were conferred directly on individuals, rather than on a minority as a group.

The treaties provided further that the stipulations 'so far as they affect persons belonging to racial, religious or linguistic minorities' were to be secured by the guarantee of the League of Nations.[38] The treaties provided that any member of the Council could bring an infraction or danger of infraction to the attention of the Council.[39] But the treaties did not prescribe any particular procedure. The Council commissioned the Tittoni Report to consider the character of the League's guarantee.[40] That Report suggested that the right of members to bring a matter to the attention of the Council did not 'in any way exclude the right of the Minorities themselves, or even of States not represented on the Council, to call the attention of the League of Nations to any infraction, or danger of infraction'.[41] But this latter complaint would not have the 'legal effect of putting the matter before the Council and calling upon it to intervene'; rather, it was in 'the nature of a petition, or a report pure and simple'.[42] When a petition was addressed to the League it was to be circulated to the members of the Council for their information, and the Council would only be competent to deal with the question if a member of the Council drew attention to it. On 22 October 1920, the Council adopted the Tittoni Report's recommendations.

The Council subsequently established a Minorities Committee to examine petitions;[43] if the Committee was unable to settle a matter, it could recommend that the question be referred to the Council.[44] Petitions could be submitted either by individuals or groups; it appears that the Commission did not distinguish between group and individual

[33] *Ibid.* Art. 2. [34] *Ibid.* Art. 7. [35] *Ibid.* Art. 8. [36] For example, *ibid.* Art. 2.
[37] For example, *ibid.* Art. 8. [38] *Ibid.* Art. 12. [39] *Ibid.*
[40] (1920) *League of Nations Official Journal* (November/December) 8–9.
[41] *Ibid.* [42] *Ibid.*
[43] Resolution adopted by the Council on 25 October 1920; see also Resolutions of 10 June 1925 and 13 June 1929.
[44] See discussion of practice in O. I. Janowsky, *Nationalities and National Minorities* (New York, Macmillan, 1925), pp. 117, 120. The PCIJ found that the Committee procedure was a means by which the Council's attention could be drawn to a matter in *German Settlers in Poland*, Advisory Opinion, PCIJ Rep. ser. B no. 6 (1923) 21–2.

petitions, nor did it examine the question whether the minorities treaties created group rights in addition to individual rights. Between 1929 and 1939, the Minorities Committee received 642 petitions; of these approximately 35 per cent were held to be 'non-receivable' and approximately 60 per cent were examined.[45] There is no comprehensive report of the petitions which were settled by the Committee or referred to the Council and no minutes of the Committee meetings were kept.[46] Between 1923 and 1935, the Council referred eight questions relating to minorities to the PCIJ;[47] of these, four were initiated by individual or group petition.[48] Subsequent to Germany's withdrawal from the League in 1933, the system of minorities protection effectively broke down.[49]

At various times proposals for generalising or broadening minority protection were discussed in the Assembly of the League. In a Resolution of 21 September 1922, the Assembly expressed the hope that states not bound by the minority clauses 'would nevertheless observe in the treatment of their own minorities at least as high a standard of justice and toleration as required' by those clauses.[50] Proposals that all member states of the League be bound by the minorities clauses were rejected in 1925, 1930 and 1932.[51] In 1933, in the Sixth Committee, the representative of Haiti proposed that the rights of

45 Robinson, *Were the Minorities Treaties a Failure?*, p. 252. 46 *Ibid.* p. 110.

47 Some commentators categorise *Exchange of Greek and Turkish Populations*, Advisory Opinion, PCIJ Rep. ser. B no. 10 (1925) as an advisory opinion relating to the minorities treaties, but the Opinion concerned the interpretation of the 1923 Convention Concerning the Exchange of Greek and Turkish Populations, a convention which came into effect after ratification of the Treaty of Peace of 24 July 1923 (which incorporated provisions concerning minority rights). The Opinion did not address minority rights or the minority provisions of the 1923 Treaty of Peace. Similarly, although the Opinion in *Interpretation of the Greco-Turkish Agreement of December 1st, 1926*, PCIJ Rep. ser. B no. 16 (1928) related to the conditions for reference of questions to the Greco-Turkish Mixed Arbitral Tribunal established under the 1923 Treaty of Peace (which contained provisions for the protection of minorities), it did not originate from a complaint or petition made under the League Guarantee for the protection of minority rights and the Court did not have occasion to comment on minority rights.

48 These were: *German Settlers in Poland*, Advisory Opinion, PCIJ Rep. ser. B no. 6 (1923); *Acquisition of Polish Nationality*, Advisory Opinion, PCIJ Rep. ser. B no. 7 (1923); *Access to German Minority Schools in Upper Silesia*, PCIJ Rep. ser. A/B no. 40 (1931); and *Minority Schools in Albania*, PCIJ Rep. ser. A/B no. 64 (1935).

49 See generally, Robinson, *Were the Minorities Treaties a Failure?*

50 Resolution of 21 September 1992, reproduced in A. Mandelstam, 'La protection des Minorités' (1923) *RdC* 363, 499 (author's own translation).

51 J. H. Bergers, 'The Road to San Francisco: The Revival of the Human Rights Idea in the 20th Century' (1992) 14 *HRQ* 447, 450. See also Proposal before the Sixth Committee, League of Nations, Special Supplement no. 120, Records of the Fourteenth Ordinary

minorities be extended to all people, whether they belonged to a minority or a majority, arguing that 'the generalisation of the protection of the rights of men and of citizens is highly desirable'.[52] There was only limited support for this proposal,[53] which was not put to a vote.[54]

In 1948, ECOSOC requested that the Secretary-General initiate a study examining 'whether and to what extent' the minorities treaties and declarations 'should be regarded as being still in force'.[55] In 1950, the Secretariat produced a report which concluded that the minorities obligations had ceased to exist on the basis of *rebus sic stantibus*.[56] It suggested that the principle of the system established after the First World War 'was that certain States ... should be subject to obligations and international control in the matter of minorities', but that 'this whole system was overthrown by the Second World War'.[57] '[R]eviewing the situation as a whole', the Study concluded 'that between 1939 and 1947 circumstances as a whole changed to such an extent that generally speaking, the system should be considered as having ceased to exist'.[58]

The Study is open to criticism for at least two reasons. First, the *rebus sic stantibus* principle does not automatically bring a treaty to an end; it only allows a party to invoke it as justification for termination.[59] Second, since 'human rights' were not identical to 'minority rights', it is difficult to argue that the incipient recognition of a category of human rights effected a fundamental change of circumstances. Even if the development of a category of human rights had effected such a change, it is difficult to sustain the finding that this had occurred by 1947, even before the Universal Declaration had been adopted. In 1947, the UN Charter was the only instrument which mentioned universal

Session of the Assembly, Meetings of the Committees, Minutes of the Sixth Committee (Political Questions), 3 October 1933, p. 31.

52 League of Nations, Special Supplement no. 120, Records of the Fourteenth Ordinary Session of the Assembly, Meetings of the Committees, Minutes of the Sixth Committee (Political Questions), 4 October 1933, p. 34.

53 *Ibid.* 5 October 1933, pp. 45, 52.

54 A resolution was put forward which provided for the principles to be applied to all minorities in member states, but it was defeated: see *ibid.* Annex 6, p. 72.

55 ECOSOC Resolution 116 C(VI), Resolutions adopted by the Economic and Social Council during its Sixth Session, 1 and 2 March 1948, p. 28.

56 United Nations Economic and Social Council, Commission on Human Rights, *Study of the Legal Validity of the Undertakings Concerning Minorities*, E/CN.4/367 (7 April 1950).

57 *Ibid.* pp. 70–1. 58 *Ibid.* p. 71.

59 See J. L. Kunz, 'The Present Status of the International Law for the Protection of Minorities' (1954) 48 *AJIL* 282, 284; Vienna Convention on the Law of Treaties, Art. 62, 26 May 1969 (entry into force 27 January 1980), 1155 UNTS 331.

human rights, and it did not even impose any general obligations on states in that respect. In 1950, it could not be said that universal human rights obligations had displaced legal obligations relating to protection of minorities, much less in 1947.[60]

(b) Inhabitants of mandated territories

Article 22 of the League of Nations Covenant provided that the colonies and territories which had ceased to be under Turkish and German control and were inhabited by peoples unable to govern themselves would be placed under 'a sacred trust of civilisation' under the League, which would delegate their governance to 'advanced nations'.[61] 'A' mandates were applied to Palestine, Syria and Mesopotamia (Iraq), those territories whose inhabitants were considered least in need of assistance. They required the mandatory to ensure 'complete freedom of conscience and the free exercise of all forms of worship' and non-discrimination on the basis of race, religion or language to all inhabitants.[62] 'B' mandates, which applied to territories in Central Africa,

[60] It was argued on other grounds that the minorities system did not cease to exist. See generally, A. Renouf, 'The Present Force of the Minorities Treaties' (1950) *Can. Bar Rev.* 804; J. W. Bruegel, 'A Neglected Field: The Protection of Minorities' (1971) 4 *Revue des droits de l'homme* 413. Greece and Turkey proceeded on the basis that the minority provisions in the Treaty of Lausanne continued to apply: L. Sohn and T. Buergenthal, *International Protection of Human Rights* (Indianapolis, Bobbs Merrill, 1973), p. 304. In relation to Finland (who was party to a declaration not a treaty) it was argued that the obligations undertaken by Finland continued to exist but were suspended pending an express decision by the UN to apply those obligations: see T. Modeen, *The International Protection of the National Identity of the Aaland Islands* (Stockholm, Almqvist and Wiksell International, 1973), p. 210.

[61] Covenant of the League of Nations, 28 June 1919 (entry into force 10 January 1920), 108 LNTS 188. On the origin of Art. 22 see P. B. Potter, 'Origin of the System of Mandates under the League of Nations' (1922) 16 *American Political Science Review* 563, 563–83 and P. B. Potter, 'The Origin of the System of Mandates under the League of Nations: Further Notes' (1926) 20 *American Political Science Review* 842, 842–6. See also J. C. Smuts, *The League of Nations: A Practical Suggestion* (London, Hodder and Stoughton, 1918); on mandates generally, see the excellent works of Q. Wright, *Mandates under the League of Nations* (Chicago, Ill., University of Chicago Press, 1930) and N. Bentwich, *The Mandates System* (London, Longmans, 1930). See also A. Berriedale Keith, 'Mandates' (1922) 4 *Journal of Comparative Legislation and International Law* 71, 71–83; W. E. Rappard, 'The Practical Working of the Mandates System' (1925) 4 *Journal of the British Institute of International Affairs* 205, 205–26; T. Baty, 'Protectorates and Mandates' (1921–2) 2 *BYIL* 109; N. Bentwich, 'Colonial Mandates and Trusteeships' (1946) 32 *Transactions of the Grotius Society* 121, 121–34.

[62] See Palestine Mandate, Art. 15, reproduced in Wright, *Mandates under the League of Nations*, p. 603. In fact only Iraq approached the anticipated degree of independence and between 1930 and 1932 Great Britain and Iraq made a series of agreements as to the

were those where the mandatory was responsible for the administration of the territory subject to conditions intended to safeguard certain interests of the inhabitants. 'C' mandates, which included South West Africa and the Pacific Islands, were those administered under the laws of the mandatory 'as integral portions of its territory', subject to the same safeguards for inhabitants as 'B' mandates.[63] In respect of all mandates, Article 23 of the League Covenant imposed a general undertaking by member states 'to secure and maintain fair and humane conditions of labour' and 'to secure just treatment of the native inhabitants of territories under their control'. Article 23 did not use language which suggested individual rights, but rather referred to state obligations to accord standards of treatment or establish certain conditions. Moreover, there was no distinction in Article 23 between group and individual rights.

Most of the provisions of the mandates likewise indicate that the mandatory was obliged to accord certain treatment to inhabitants: for example, to 'ensure to all complete freedom of conscience',[64] although some of the provisions refer to 'rights'[65] and one of the mandates, that for Tanganyika, refers to the 'rights conferred by this article' in a provision which requires the mandatory to 'secure to' aliens national treatment.[66] The question whether the mandates conferred rights on the inhabitants of mandated territories was not addressed by either the Permanent Mandates Commission established under Article 22 or by the Council of the League, which had oversight responsibility for the

formal independence of Iraq: see J. Crawford, *The Creation of States in International Law* (2nd edn, Oxford, Oxford University Press, 2006), p. 575. In Syria, France in effect exercised direct rule and in the case of Palestine the mandatory was given 'full powers of legislation and administration', so that it resembled the 'B' category of mandates: *ibid.* pp. 596–570; J. Stoyanovsky, *The Mandate for Palestine* (London, Longmans & Co., 1928), p. 40.

63 See generally, R. Gordon, 'Mandates' in R. Wolfrum (ed.), *The Max Planck Encyclopedia of Public International Law* (Oxford, Oxford University Press, 2008, online edition, www.mpepil.com); Crawford, *The Creation of States in International Law*, pp. 566–74; C. Stahn, *The Law and Practice of International Territorial Administration* (Cambridge, CUP, 2008), pp. 73–91.

64 Reproduced in Wright, *Mandates under the League of Nations*, p. 583 *et seq.*: Syria and the Lebanon Mandate, Art. 8 (p. 609); Palestine Mandate, Art. 15 (p. 603); see also Iraq Mandate, Art. 11 (p. 597); Tanganyika and Ruanda-Urundi Mandate, Art. 5 (p. 613) and Art. 7 (p. 615); Nauru Mandate, Art. 3 (p. 620); British Cameroons, British Togo Mandate, Art. 2 (p. 617).

65 Reproduced in *ibid.*: Syria and the Lebanon Mandate, Art. 8 (second paragraph) (p. 609); Palestine Mandate, Art. 15 (second paragraph) (p. 603).

66 Reproduced in *ibid.*: Tanganyika and Ruanda-Urundi Mandate, Art. 7 (p. 614).

observance of the mandates.[67] The leading authority on the mandates system, Quincy Wright, argued that the 'peculiar conditions of the mandatory system' gave the inhabitants of the territory a special status under international law which accorded them rights against the mandatory corresponding to all of the duties imposed upon the mandatory states.[68] But he also argued that since the mandated communities 'were not parties to the peace treaties they could not acquire rights from them', and on that basis the Commission had 'properly refused to consider petitions from the inhabitants' concerning incompatibility of the mandates with Article 22 of the Covenant.[69] Consistently with the first part of Wright's argument (but not the second), a 1931 Resolution of the Institute of International Law asserted that '[t]he communities under mandate are subjects of international law', and that they could acquire rights and obligations in accordance with the terms of the mandate.[70] There was no clear delimitation in this context between group rights and individual rights.

In 1950, the International Court of Justice referred to the 'international status' of the communities under the mandates and to the 'right of the population to have the territory administered in accordance with' the mandate,[71] statements which suggests that all the obligations imposed on the mandatory state were owed directly to the inhabitants. This view was heavily influenced by Article 80 of the UN Charter, which contained a savings provision referring to 'the rights ... of ... any peoples' under existing arrangements for the administration of territory. So although the mandates were later interpreted as conferring rights on inhabitants, either as individuals or as members of a group, during the inter-war period there was no unequivocal statement that the mandates had this effect.

The mandatory states were required to provide annual reports to the Permanent Mandates Commission, which would 'advise' the Council.[72]

[67] The related question of the entitlements of the inhabitants of the territories when in the territory of the mandatory state was raised before the Commission but was not decided: *ibid.* p. 462; Stoyanovsky, *The Mandate for Palestine*, p. 278.

[68] Wright, *Mandates under the League of Nations*, p. 473. See also Stoyanovsky, *The Mandate for Palestine*, p. 53.

[69] Wright, *Mandates under the League of Nations*, pp. 119, 458.

[70] (1932) 26 *AJIL* 87, 91 (point 4).

[71] *International Status of South-West Africa*, Advisory Opinion [1950] ICJ Rep. 128, 132–3.

[72] Covenant of the League of Nations, 28 June 1919 (entry into force 10 January 1920), 108 LNTS 188, Art. 22. The mandates remained in force pursuant to Art. 80 of the UN Charter.

The Commission saw its role as 'determin[ing] how far the principles of the Covenant and the mandates have been truly applied' and 'assist[ing] the mandatory Governments in carrying out' the task entrusted to them by the League.[73] The Council had power to pass binding resolutions concerning the mandates but it rarely did so; the fulfilment of a mandate was broadly considered to be a political rather than legal responsibility.[74] At its first session, the Commission reported that it had received a number of individual petitions from inhabitants of the mandated territories.[75] In January 1923, the Council authorised the Commission[76] to receive petitions from persons or bodies in the mandated territories submitted by the mandatory state, for purposes of information about the situations in the mandated territories. Unlike the minorities petitions, the mandates petitions were used only as a source of information for the Commission and did not invoke a dispute settlement procedure.[77] Although the Commission regularly heard a representative of the mandatory state during private sittings, it did not allow petitioners to appear or attend;[78] neither was the Commission given power to make on-site inspections. Petitions were filed by inhabitants of all of the mandated territories; the greatest number were received from inhabitants of the A mandates.[79] It appears that petitions were submitted by both individuals and groups of individuals. On the whole, the petitions were a useful tool for the Commission to fulfil its supervisory responsibilities although they did not provide individuals with any direct rights to enforce obligations of the mandatory states.[80] The Commission produced reports which censored policies of oppression and supervised labour, health and education standards. But it referred in general terms to obligations of the mandatory towards the League, rather than obligations towards inhabitants, still less any rights of the inhabitants.[81]

[73] Wright, *Mandates under the League of Nations*, p. 196.
[74] C. Stahn, *The Law and Practice of International Territorial Administration* (Cambridge, Cambridge University Press, 2008), p. 85.
[75] Wright, *Mandates under the League of Nations*, p. 169; D. Hall, *Mandates, Dependencies and Trusteeship* (London, Stevens, 1948), p. 203.
[76] This followed a British proposal, whose colonial practice allowed a petition to the Secretary of State through the local governor: Wright, *Mandates under the League of Nations*, p. 174.
[77] *Ibid.* pp. 170–1, 194. [78] *Ibid.* p. 194.
[79] Hall, *Mandates, Dependencies and Trusteeship*, p. 198.
[80] Stahn, *The Law and Practice of International Territorial Administration*, p. 86.
[81] Wright, *Mandates under the League of Nations*, pp. 190–262.

The terms of the mandates also gave the PCIJ jurisdiction over any dispute between a mandatory state and another member state of the League concerning the mandates.[82] Thus, the obligations under the mandates could be said to be owed *erga omnes* to the international community as a whole (or at least to those members of the international community who were members of the League). This procedure was only used twice: once for a contentious case between Greece and Palestine concerning concessions;[83] and once for an advisory opinion on the Mosul frontier between Iraq and Turkey.[84] Neither case shed any light on the question whether inhabitants of the mandated territories derived rights from the mandates. Domestic courts also found the mandates to be directly enforceable in the mandated territory in several cases and undertook judicial review of domestic acts.[85] But on the whole, domestic courts recognised a broad discretion on the part of the mandatory state.[86]

(c) *Refugees*

In 1921, following a request from the President of the ICRC to help deal with the Russian refugee problem,[87] the Council of the League appointed a High Commissioner for Russian refugees and defined the activities of

[82] The British government admitted in the *Mavrommatis* case that it was 'open to any member of the League to question' actions 'which infringed the international obligations [of the mandatory state]': *Mavrommatis Palestine Concessions*, PCIJ Rep. ser. A no. 2 (1924) 22, 445; Stoyanovsky, *The Mandate for Palestine*, p. 145. The Court considered that the additional paragraph in the dispute settlement provisions of the mandates (providing that 'states members of the League of Nations may likewise bring any claims on behalf of their nationals for infraction of their rights under the mandate before the court for decision') added nothing to the article providing for submission of 'any dispute whatever' with the mandatory by another member of the League 'relating to the interpretation or application of the provisions of the mandate'.

[83] *Mavrommatis Palestine Concessions*, PCIJ Rep. ser. A no. 2 (1924) 22.

[84] *Interpretation of Article 3, Paragraph 2, of the Treaty of Lausanne*, PCIJ Rep. ser. B no. 12 (1925) 33.

[85] Questions of interpretation of the mandates were also determined by the local courts: see *Jerusalem, Jaffa District Governor* v. *Suleiman Murra* (1926) ER-Appeal Cases 321; *Rex* v. *Christian* (1924) South African Law Reports 101; and *Cape Law Society* v. *Van Aardt* (1926) South African Law Reports CPD 312; (1925–6) 3 ILR 43; see N. Bentwich, *The Mandates System* (London, Longmans, 1930), pp. 126–8.

[86] Q. Wright, 'Some Recent Cases on the Status of Mandated Areas' (1926) 20 *AJIL* 768, 770.

[87] Letter by Gustave Ador, (1921) *League of Nations Official Journal* (March/April) 227–8. See also C. M. Skran, *Refugees in Inter-War Europe: The Emergence of a Regime* (Oxford, Clarendon Press, 1995), pp. 84–5; G. S. Goodwin-Gill and J. McAdam, *The Refugee in International Law* (3rd edn, Oxford, Oxford University Press, 2007), esp. pp. 16–20.

its office as including protection for refugees.[88] The Council initially was reluctant to become involved and suggested that the ICRC and the League of the Red Cross form a joint body to address the problems.[89] The Secretary-General also requested that member states comment on the extent to which the League could contribute to this 'international problem'.[90] Subsequently, the Council established the Office of the High Commissioner[91] and provided for a Conference to settle a programme of work.[92] The Conference passed eleven resolutions, including measures directly relevant to Russian refugees: issue of passports; a prohibition on forcible return; special measures of protection for refugees who were intellectuals; the provision of special education for children; and protection for women. The following year the High Commissioner secured agreement on a system of identity certificates to facilitate freedom of movement of Russian refugees.[93] These arrangements operated on the basis of collectivised surrogacy: individual refugees benefited from arrangements secured by the High Commissioner but they were not considered to hold specific rights. Rather, states agreed to permit representatives of the High Commissioner to put arrangements in place[94] or to carry out functions in respect of qualifying refugees.[95]

There was a shift with the 1933 Convention Relating to the Status of Refugees, which purported to confer rights on qualifying refugees.

88 *Resolutions Adopted by the Council of the League of Nations at its Thirteenth Session in Geneva, 17–27 June 1921*, p. 37.
89 (1921) *League of Nations Official Journal* (March/April) 225–6 (cf. Memorandum on the Possible Action of the League in Connection with Russian Refugees, NBKR 4/472).
90 (1921) *League of Nations Official Journal* (March/April) 226.
91 *Resolutions Adopted by the Council of the League of Nations at its Thirteenth Session in Geneva, 17–21 June 1921*, p. 37.
92 *Ibid.*
93 Arrangement with Regard to the Issue of Certificates of Identity to Russian Refugees, 5 July 1922, 355 LNTS 238. Subsequently the work of the High Commissioner and the League was extended to additional categories of refugees: see Arrangement Concerning the Extension to Other Categories of Refugee of Certain Measures Taken in Favour of Russian and Armenian Refugees, 30 June 1928, 2006 LNTS 65. The identity certificate programme was extended to cover Armenian, Greek, Assyrian, Assyro-Chaldean and Turkish refugees: see (1927) *League of Nations Official Journal* 155; *Report by High Commissioner*, League of Nations Doc. 1927.XIII.3 (1927), p. 14; *Report by the Secretary-General on the Future Organisation of Refugee Work*, League of Nations Doc. A.28.1930.XIII (1930), pp. 2–4.
94 See e.g., Arrangement of 1928, 89 LNTS 53.
95 See generally, J. C. Hathaway, *The Rights of Refugees under International Law* (Cambridge, Cambridge University Press, 2005), pp. 83–7; R. Jennings, 'Some International Law Aspects of the Refugee Question' (1939) 20 *BYIL* 98.

In 1931, the Assembly of the League had resolved to see the adoption of a binding international convention as part of its programme to ensure that the work of the League would only be temporary.[96] The 1933 Convention applied to specified refugees; it did not set out generalised criteria for refugee status. Its provisions incorporated earlier agreements relating to identity certificates and imposed obligations on contracting states to accord refugees the same treatment as aliens in respect of employment, education, taxation and welfare.[97] It also incorporated an obligation not to expel authorised refugees and to avoid *refoulement*.[98] The conventions used language suggestive of the direct conferral of rights: for example, Article 9 provided that refugees were entitled to 'the most favourable [medical] treatment'. Also in 1933, the Assembly established an office to deal specifically with German refugees[99] and subsequently it concluded agreements which applied the same criteria as the 1933 Convention to German refugees.[100] During the War these agreements were extended to protect persons who had not yet left their country of origin but who were forced to emigrate on account of their political opinions, religious beliefs or racial origin.[101] In 1938, these arrangements were consolidated in a Convention Concerning the Status of Refugees Coming from Germany, which entitled refugees to travel documents and conferred upon them rights to national treatment.[102] Although these arrangements referred to 'refugees' in general rather than to individuals, it appears that the term 'refugees' was used in this context to refer to qualifying individuals rather than a group of individuals: that is to say, the arrangements conferred rights on individuals rather than on groups.

96 (1931) *League of Nations Official Journal*, Spec. Supp. 92, p. 38. On the temporary character of the League's undertaking, see e.g., *League of Nations Questions, No. 9: The Refugees* (1938), pp. 29, 51.

97 Convention Relating to the International Status of Refugees, 28 October 1933 (entry into force 13 June 1935), 159 LNTS 3663, esp. Arts. 7–12.

98 *Ibid.* Art. 3.

99 *Report by the Second Committee to the Assembly*, League of Nations Doc. 1933.XIII.2 (1933).

100 Provisional Arrangement Concerning the Status of Refugees Coming from Germany, 4 July 1936, 3952 LNTS 77; Convention Concerning the Status of Refugees Coming from Germany, 10 February 1938, 4461 LNTS 61; Additional Protocol Concerning the Status of Refugees Coming from Germany, 14 September 1939, 4634 LNTS 142.

101 *Report Submitted by the Director*, ICR Doc. (25 July 1944), p. 2.

102 Convention Concerning the Status of Refugees Coming from Germany, 10 February 1938, 4461 LNTS 61.

(d) The International Labour Organisation

The International Labour Organisation (ILO) was not an organ of the League of Nations; it had a separate constitutional basis in the Treaty of Versailles.[103] However, it worked in partnership with the League in the inter-war period and produced conventions which promoted social justice and human rights in the field of labour and employment. Its activities are worth recalling in this context.

The ILO produced specific conventions dealing with subjects such as the minimum age for child labour, compensation, repatriation of seamen and protection from accidents.[104] Its most general convention in the inter-war period was the 1930 Forced Labour Convention: building upon the 1926 Slavery Convention, the 1930 Convention sought to suppress the use of forced or compulsory labour but it had significant exclusions for labour for public purposes.[105] It imposed obligations on states which operated to benefit individuals; its provisions did not suggest that it conferred rights on individuals: for example, Article 10(1) provided that '[f]orced or compulsory labour exacted as a tax . . . shall be progressively abolished'. The 1930 Convention was subject to the ILO's reporting system for supervision and monitoring compliance which operated between member states and the ILO, and which did not provide for individual petitions or communications.[106] This convention provided benefits for individuals without conferring upon them

[103] Treaty of Versailles, Art. 387, 28 June 1919, UKTS 4 (Cmd 153).

[104] Once a draft convention was accepted by a two-thirds majority of the Conference, the text was settled and there was no need for each state to sign the convention in the case of a multilateral treaty. All members were then under an obligation to submit the convention to their legislature, and conventions became binding on ratification: J. F. McMahon, 'The Legislative Techniques of the ILO' (1965–6) *BYIL* 31. See generally, A. W. B. Simpson, *Human Rights and the End of Empire: Britain and the Genesis of the European Convention* (Oxford, Oxford University Press, 2001), pp. 149–51; D. A. Morse, *The Origin and Evolution of the I.L.O. and Its Role in the World Community* (New York, Humphrey Press, 1969); W. C. Jenks, *Human Rights and International Labour Standards* (London, Stevens, 1960); J. T. Shotwell, *The Origins of the International Labour Organization* (New York, Columbia University Press, 1934). In its first half-century the ILO produced some 130 specific conventions which built up what might be viewed as an international code on labour law: McMahon, 'The Legislative Techniques of the ILO'.

[105] Convention no. 29 Concerning Forced Labour, 28 June 1930 (entry into force 1 May 1932) (Forced Labour Convention) (available at www.unhchr.ch/html/menu3/b/31.htm); see also the more comprehensive Convention no. 105 Concerning the Abolition of Forced Labour, 25 June 1957 (entry into force 17 January 1959) (available at www.unhchr.ch/html/menu3/b/32.htm).

[106] Jenks, *Human Rights and International Labour Standards*, pp. 16–22; W. C. Jenks, *The International Protection of Trade Union Freedom* (London, Stevens, 1951), pp. 68–87.

international rights; rather, it imposed obligations within an inter-state framework.

(e) Conclusions

In the inter-war period, measures taken to benefit or protect individuals introduced innovative elements into the international legal system. The first such element was that specific categories of individuals were granted international protection against treatment by their own state. This was inconsistent with the pre-1945 account of the international legal system. International rules dictated treatment of individuals: those rules were not concerned exclusively with inter-state relations, but rather set standards of treatment for individuals within state borders. Thus, these rules are distinguishable from rules regarding treatment of aliens because they represented an incursion into matters traditionally conceived as within the exclusive domestic reserve of states. This is particularly evident in the rules for protection of minorities and those concerning inhabitants of mandated territories, but also find resonance in the rules relating to refugees and those developed under the auspices of the ILO.

The second innovative element in the inter-war period was that direct rights were conferred on certain categories of individuals, most clearly in the case of the minorities treaties and in some of the later conventions dealing with refugees. In relation to minorities, individuals were treated as beneficiaries of direct individual rights although the question whether minorities as groups also were beneficiaries of group rights was never resolved. It was suggested that the mandates system conferred direct rights on individuals: while this was not the clear effect of the relevant instruments, after 1945 it appears to have been accepted that such rights were conferred on inhabitants under the mandates arrangements, although it was not entirely clear whether these were individual rights or group rights The conferral of direct rights on individuals under treaties was acknowledged by the PCIJ in 1928,[107] but during the inter-war period it was not the established understanding that individuals could derive rights directly from treaties. Other rules imposed obligations on states which were directed to the benefit of individuals without conferring direct rights on individuals. The early rules for the protection of refugees and the ILO Conventions fall within this category: they are consistent with the nineteenth century

[107] See 1.2(c) above.

framework of the international legal system, which continued to form the basis of the orthodox account of the system during the inter-war period. Yet, the system of refugee protection developed after 1945, whereas the system of minorities protection was suppressed.

5.4 International protection of human rights after 1945

The development of international human rights law after 1945 is often presented as both historic inevitability and instantaneous creation, urged by outrage at Nazi atrocities and resulting from the efforts of activists.[108] The picture which emerges from an examination of the historical record is more complex: although there is no doubt that the horrors of the Second World War and the campaigns of human rights advocates made a significant contribution to the commitment of states to international recognition and protection of human rights, that recognition and protection has occurred as a rather more incremental process, from loose political commitments, to rhetorical moral imperatives, to legal obligations, and eventually tending in the direction of enforceable rights. This section explores that incremental development. Since the issue under examination is the structural engagement of individuals in international law, a catalogue of rights is not presented; rather, the emphasis is on the extent to which human rights law has engaged individuals.

(a) Human rights rhetoric during the Second World War

During the Second World War, the Allied Powers made reference to defence of the rights of individuals as a war aim. In 1939, addressing Parliament on the imposition of Defence Regulations, British Prime Minister Churchill referred to the war aims as the establishment of 'the rights of the individual' and to 'revive the stature of man'.[109] In 1941, US President Roosevelt declared that '[f]reedom means the supremacy of human rights everywhere. Our support goes to those who struggle to gain those rights and keep them.' He identified 'Four Freedoms': speech, religion, freedom from fear (of external invasion)

[108] See e.g., Lauren, *The Evolution of International Human Rights*, 147 *et seq.*

[109] Simpson, *Human Rights and the End of Empire*, p. 158; see also the statement of Lord Halifax, British Foreign Secretary, on 7 November 1939: H. H. E. Craster (ed.), *Speeches on Foreign Policy by Viscount Halifax K. G., D.C.L.* (Oxford, Oxford University Press, 1940), nos. 47 and 48.

and want.[110] That same year, the Atlantic Charter defined more clearly the war aims of the Allies. It contained a reference to 'the right of all peoples to choose the form of government under which they will live' and expressed the hope of establishing a peace which would permit all men to 'live out their lives in freedom from fear and want'.[111] A further reference to human rights appeared in the Declaration of the United Nations signed on 1 January 1942 by twenty-six states supporting the purposes and principles of the Atlantic Charter. The Declaration stated that signatories pledged themselves 'to preserve human rights and justice in their own lands as well as in other lands'.[112] These generalised references to human rights did not necessarily indicate that human rights protection was a matter of legal obligation, but they did suggest that the treatment of nationals within state boundaries was becoming a matter of international concern.

The inclusion of protection of human rights as justification for involvement in the war created a dilemma for Allied governments. On the one hand, discussions about rights helped the Allied states to distinguish themselves from their adversaries and to inspire genuine sacrifices in support of the war effort. At the same time, discussions about rights threatened to highlight the hypocrisy of Allied governments in the treatment of their own subjects.[113] Churchill expressly referred to

110 Address of 6 January 1941, S. Rosenman (ed.), *The Public Papers and Addresses of Franklin D. Roosevelt* (New York, Random House, 1938), vol. IX, p. 672.

111 Reproduced in D. Brinkley and D. R. Facey-Crowther (eds.), *The Atlantic Charter* (Basingstoke, Macmillan, 1994), p. xvii. Apparently Roosevelt attached importance to the Atlantic Charter as an endorsement of the aims he had outlined in his Four Freedoms speech earlier in 1941: see M. G. Johnson, 'The Contribution of Eleanor and Franklin Roosevelt to the Development of International Protection for Human Rights' (1987) 9 *HRQ* 19, 22. Since freedom of the press and religion were not referred to, news of the Atlantic Charter prompted some reporting that these freedoms were lost: Roosevelt responded when he reported to Congress on his meeting with Churchill, stating (S. Rosenman (ed.), *Public Papers and Addresses of Franklin D. Roosevelt: The Call to Battle Stations, 1941* (New York, Harper & Bros, 1950), p. 334): 'It is also unnecessary for me to point out that the declaration of principles included of necessity the world need for freedom of religion and freedom of information. No society of the world organized under the announced principles could survive without these freedoms which are a part of the whole freedom for which we strive.'

112 Other signatories were: Australia, Belgium, Canada, Costa Rica, Cuba, Czechoslovakia, Dominican Republic, El Salvador, Greece, Guatemala, Haiti, Honduras, India, Luxembourg, the Netherlands, New Zealand, Nicaragua, Norway, Panama, Poland, South Africa and Yugoslavia.

113 Churchill made several statements about not permitting principles such as the right of self-determination to precipitate the liquidation of the British empire: cited in League of Nations Union, *The Atlantic Charter* (London, Hodgson, 1942), p. 1.

his desire not to allow human rights principles to impact upon British imperial interests and in that context described the Atlantic Charter as a wartime statement of a goal rather than a firm commitment.[114]

Wartime intellectual discussion, especially in the Anglophone world, was broadly in support of human rights. British writer H. G. Wells led a campaign to put human rights at the centre of the Allied war aims and for their expression in some form of charter.[115] He assembled a committee to draft the text of a Declaration which was published in 1940.[116] Subsequently, he published a book entitled *The Rights of Man or What Are We Fighting For?*, which was widely distributed.[117] From Cambridge, Hersch Lauterpacht also advocated human rights, publishing his proposals in 'An International Bill of the Rights of Man'.[118] Similar campaigns emerged in the US. The Commission to Study the Organization of Peace, composed of scholars and foreign policy experts, released a report arguing that it was necessary to address the problem of human rights across borders.[119] In a subsequent report, the Commission argued that there was an intimate connection between respect for human rights and international peace, and suggested an international bill of rights be incorporated into domestic law of every state, with a right of individuals to petition a Human Rights Commission in case of violations.[120] An international bill of rights was pressed by the International Bill of Rights Committee of the Twentieth Century Association, which produced a draft text in collaboration with representatives of forty-seven universities,[121] and the American Law Institute, which published a 'Statement of Essential Human Rights' calling on leaders of the world

114 Lauren, *The Evolution of International Human Rights*, p. 155. See also statement by Deputy Prime Minister Clement Attlee on 5 December 1940, which indicated concern about attempting to impose regulation on other states: Simpson, *Human Rights and the End of Empire*, p. 160.

115 H. G. Wells, *The Times*, 23 October 1939, cited in Bergers, 'The Road to San Francisco', 464.

116 Bergers, 'The Road to San Francisco', 465.

117 Lauren, *The Evolution of International Human Rights*, p. 147.

118 H. Lauterpacht, *An International Bill of the Rights of Man* (New York, Columbia University Press, 1945).

119 Q. Wright, 'Human Rights and the World Order' (1943) 389 *International Conciliation* 238.

120 Commission to Study the Organization of the Peace, *International Safeguard of Human Rights*, reproduced in (1944) 403 *International Conciliation* 554; P. G. Lauren, 'First Principles of Racial Equality: History and the Politics and Diplomacy of Human Rights Provisions in the United Nations Charter' (1983) 5 *HRQ* 1, 6.

121 I. Isaacs, *The International Bill of Rights and Permanent Peace Concordance* (Boston, NJ, Twentieth Century Association, 1943); C. Bayliss, 'Towards an International Bill of Rights' (1944) 8 *Public Opinion Quarterly* 244.

to recognise that 'at this crucial moment in human history ... new concepts [of human rights] affecting the future development of man and society are being crystallized'.[122]

Some critiques of human rights also emerged in this period but there was little serious criticism until work of codification was begun in the UN;[123] moreover, these critiques did not go to the question of reconciling international protection of human rights with the established understanding of the international legal system or the domestic reserve of states. George Orwell criticised the work of Wells in numerous pieces, the most damaging entitled 'Wells, Hitler and the World State' (1941).[124] His critique was, however, more directed to Wells' world view than to the concept of human rights. He disputed that the protection of human rights was a war aim: he argued that the chief motive for English involvement in the Second World War was patriotism – 'the ingrained feeling of English-speaking peoples that they are superior to foreigners'.[125]

(b) Preparation for an international bill of rights

Most Allied governments created committees during the war charged with anticipating future peace and security and preparing for institutional post-war arrangements.[126] The most elaborate of these was in the US. A Special Subcommittee on Legal Problems drafted a statement of principles reflecting individual rights and recommended that these rights should be made 'part of the supreme law of each state' and

122 American Law Institute, *Report to the Council of the Institute and Statement of Essential Human Rights* (New York, American Law Institute, 1944), p. 5. See also L. Sohn, 'How American International Lawyers Prepared for the San Francisco Bill of Rights' (1995) 89 *AJIL* 546. It appears that the debate between Orwell and Wells led to some personal antagonism: S. Orwell and I. Angus (eds.), *The Collected Essays, Journalism and Letters of George Orwell*, vol. II, *My Country Right or Left, 1940–1943* (London, Secker and Warburg, 1968), p. 415.

123 See e.g., cultural relativism as was promoted by the American Anthropological Association during the drafting of the UDHR: Executive Board of the American Anthropological Association, 'Statement on Human Rights' (1947) 49 *American Anthropologist* 539.

124 Reproduced in G. Orwell, *Critical Essays* (London, Secker & Warburg, 1946), pp. 83–8. See also J. S. Partington, 'The Pen as Sword: George Orwell, HG Wells and Journalistic Parricide' (2004) 39 *Journal of Contemporary History* 45.

125 Orwell, *Critical Essays*, p. 84. See generally, L. Sohn, 'How American International Lawyers Prepared for the San Francisco Bill of Rights' (1995) 89 *AJIL* 546.

126 Lauren, *The Evolution of International Human Rights*, p. 156. See also Simpson, *Human Rights and the End of Empire*, pp. 221–75.

enforced by its administrative and judicial authorities.[127] They recommended further that the international bill of human rights should not establish any procedures for enforcement at the international level, in order to avoid opposition by states.[128] Underlying the Subcommittee's reservations was a broader concern about the principle of non-interference in domestic matters.[129] This preparatory work indicated that what was preferred was only rhetorical international declarations, with obligations and rights to be derived only through domestic law processes, in substance preserving the reserved domain.

Between August and October 1944, representatives of the US, Great Britain, the Soviet Union and China met at Dumbarton Oaks to negotiate an 'in principle' agreement on post-war international organisation. The US proposed on two occasions that the organisation be required to promote the observance of human rights but these proposals were rejected by the Soviet Union and Britain: the former wanting to link any such requirement to 'fascist' states; the latter perceiving a contradiction between the promotion of human rights and the principle of non-intervention in the domestic affairs of states, and also concerned to preserve its imperial interests.[130] It was agreed, however, to give the organisation 'a simple authorization ... to promote respect for human rights'.[131] China sought to give the organisation authority to enforce racial equality and non-discrimination, but by the time it had joined the talks in their second phase, the other three states had agreed to eliminate any mention of racial equality in the Charter;[132] moreover, there was no general support for giving the organisation power to enforce any individual rights.[133] The Dumbarton Oaks drafts did not

[127] See generally, United States Department of State, *Postwar Foreign Policy Preparation, 1939–1945* (Washington, DC, Government Printing Office, 1949); Lauren, 'First Principles of Racial Equality', 7.

[128] Lauren, 'First Principles of Racial Equality', 8–9.

[129] Lauren, *The Evolution of International Human Rights*, pp. 159–60.

[130] R. Russell and J. Muther, *A History of the United Nations Charter* (Washington, DC, Brookings Institute, 1958), pp. 423–4. See also F. Jhabvala, 'The Drafting of the Human Rights Provisions of the UN Charter' (1997) XLIV *Netherlands International Law Review* 1, 3–4; M. G. Johnson, 'The Contribution of Eleanor and Franklin Roosevelt to the Development of International Protection for Human Rights' (1987) 9 *HRQ* 19, 24.

[131] Russell and Muther, *A History of the United Nations Charter*, p. 424.

[132] See 'Tentative Chinese Proposals for a General International Organization, 23 August 1944' (1944) FRUS 718.

[133] Lauren, *The Evolution of International Human Rights*, p. 161. See also H. Kelsen, 'The Old and the New League: The Covenant and the Dumbarton Oaks Proposals' (1945) 39 *AJIL* 45.

purport to impose obligations on states in respect of human rights and nor did they purport to confer direct international law rights on individuals.

In contrast, support for a mechanism of international enforcement came from Latin America and from numerous NGOs. In February 1945, representatives of twenty Latin American states met at Chapultepec in Mexico and passed resolutions endorsing 'the rights of man' and declaring support for 'a system of international protection of these rights'.[134] NGOs, including the Joint Committee on Religious Liberty, the American Jewish Congress, the Synagogue Council of America and the Commission to Study the Organization of Peace, called for a human rights agency in the organisation.[135] Added to these critiques of the Dumbarton Oaks proposals was 'a vast movement of public opinion' which expressed the idea that 'the future peace would not be complete if it did not consecrate the principle of international protection of human rights in all States and if it would not guarantee this protection in an effective manner'.[136]

(c) *The United Nations Charter: a promise postponed*

The San Francisco Conference opened on 25 April 1945, with 4 May as a deadline for the submission of formal amendments to the Dumbarton Oaks proposals.[137] In the wake of vigorous lobbying by NGOs,[138] the US delegation agreed amendments with the UK, the USSR and China to

[134] Lauren, *The Evolution of International Human Rights*, pp. 171–2. Argentina was not invited as being pro-Axis: see Bergers, 'The Road to San Francisco', 475. See generally, M. C. Canyes, 'The Inter-American System and the Conference of Chapultepec' (1945) *AJIL* 504.

[135] Bergers, 'The Road to San Francisco', 476. The contribution of various individuals is summarised in Lauren, *The Evolution of International Human Rights*, pp. 173–4; see also Commission to Study the Organization of the Peace, *International Safeguard of Human Rights*, reproduced in (1944) 403 *International Conciliation* 554, 569. As to criticism of the Dumbarton Oaks Proposals generally, see Simpson, *Human Rights and the End of Empire*, pp. 250–4 and C. Eagleton, 'International Law and the Charter of the United Nations' (1945) 39 *AJIL* 751.

[136] R. Brunet, *La garantie internationale des droits de l'homme* (Genève, Ch. Grasset, 1947), pp. 93–4, translated in Bergers, 'The Road to San Francisco', 474. See e.g., 'Welles Warns', *New York Times*, 25 October 1944; and generally, Simpson, *Human Rights and the End of Empire*, pp. 250–4.

[137] See C. K. Webster, 'The Making of the Charter of the United Nations' (19478) 32 *History* 16, 23; Simpson, *Human Rights and the End of Empire*, pp. 259–60.

[138] A letter on behalf of twenty-one NGOs was presented to Secretary of State Stettinius on 2 May 1945. It was apparently pointed out to Stettinius that the consultants (representing NGOs) participating in the San Francisco Conference represented

include promoting respect for human rights as a purpose of the UN and to establish a human rights commission under the Economic and Social Council.[139] Several states pushed for the inclusion of a bill of rights in the text of the Charter.[140] The US delegate stated that this was impracticable but suggested that the proposed Human Rights Commission should prepare an international bill of rights 'which can be accepted by all the member states as an integral part of their own system of law, just as our Bill of Rights has been an integral part of our system of law'.[141] The UK delegation agreed that the organisation ought not to guarantee individual rights but was in principle supportive of undertakings by states - rather than enforceable obligations - to observe rights.[142] The drafting committee of the purposes provision concluded that it would not be practical, in the time available, to include a draft 'bill of rights for nations and individuals' in the Charter, but recommended that the General Assembly give effect to the proposal of a bill of rights.[143] Article 1(3) of the Charter as adopted referred to promotion of respect for human rights as a purpose of the UN without defining the human rights whose existence it presupposed:

> 3. To achieve international cooperation in solving international problems of an economic, social, cultural, or humanitarian character, and in promoting and encouraging respect for human rights and for fundamental freedoms for all without distinction as to race, sex, language, or religion;[144]

The Charter contains seven additional references to human rights. First, the Preamble states that 'the people of the United Nations determined ... to reaffirm faith in fundamental human rights, in the

organisations which controlled four million votes in the US: Simpson, *Human Rights and the End of Empire*, p. 253, n. 154.

139 Bergers, 'The Road to San Francisco', 476. There had been discussion of the need to include a reference to human rights in the Preamble in the House of Lords in Britain on 17 April 1945: see Simpson, *Human Rights and the End of Empire*, p. 253, citing a speech of Lord Cranborne. British and continental European organisations played virtually no part in the San Francisco Conference, due in large part to the difficulty of foreign travel for individuals.

140 See e.g., proposals from Panama and Cuba: Russell and Muther, *A History of the United Nations Charter*, p. 778.

141 Simpson, *Human Rights and the End of Empire*, p. 262.

142 *Ibid.* p. 262.

143 *Report of the Rapporteur of Committee 1 to Commission I*, cited in Jhabvala, 'The Drafting of the Human Rights Provisions of the UN Charter', 13.

144 See also generally, B. Simma (ed.), *The Charter of the United Nations: A Commentary* (2nd edn, Oxford, Oxford University Press, 2002), pp. 39–44.

dignity and worth of the human person, in the equal rights of men and women of nations large and small'.[145] Second, Article 55 provides that the Organisation shall promote, *inter alia*, 'universal respect for, and observance of, human rights and fundamental freedoms for all without distinction as to race, sex, language, or religion'.[146] Third, Article 56 contains a pledge by all members to take joint and separate action 'for the achievement of the purposes set out in Article 55'.[147] Fourth, in respect of the powers of the Economic and Social Council, Article 62(2) provides that the Council 'may make recommendations for the purpose of promoting respect for, and observance of, human rights and fundamental freedoms for all'.[148] Fifth, in respect of the functions and powers of the General Assembly, Article 13(1) provides that the Assembly will initiate studies and make recommendations for, *inter alia*, 'assisting in the realization of human rights and fundamental freedoms for all without distinction as to race, sex, language, or religion'.[149] Sixth, in respect of the machinery of the Organisation, Article 68 provides that the Economic and Social Council 'shall set up commissions in economic and social fields and for the promotion of human rights'.[150] Finally, Chapter XII establishing an international trusteeship system includes in Article 76 a reference to 'encourag[ing] respect for human rights and fundamental freedoms without distinction as to race, sex, language, or

[145] Jhabvala, 'The Drafting of the Human Rights Provisions of the UN Charter', 7–8. See also generally, Simma, *The Charter of the United Nations*, pp. 33–7.

[146] During negotiation of the text of Art. 55 the US requested the Committee reconsider the text 'in order to eliminate certain forms of wording subject to misconstruction as being in support of intervention in the domestic affairs of members of the Organization'. The proposed draft was strongly opposed and the US agreed to withdraw it subject to a statement in the Committee's report expressing full agreement that 'nothing contained in Chapter IX can be construed as giving authority to the Organization to intervene in the domestic affairs of members states'. Jhabvala, 'The Drafting of the Human Rights Provisions of the UN Charter', 14–20. See also generally, Simma, *The Charter of the United Nations*, pp. 917–41.

[147] An Australian proposal to enumerate purposes in Art. 56 as including improved labour standards, social security and full employment and calling for annual reports as to fulfilment of the pledge was not accepted: cited in Jhabvala, 'The Drafting of the Human Rights Provisions of the UN Charter', 21. See also generally, Simma, *The Charter of the United Nations*, pp. 941–3.

[148] Cited in Jhabvala, 'The Drafting of the Human Rights Provisions of the UN Charter', 23–4. See also generally, Simma, *The Charter of the United Nations*, pp. 991–5.

[149] For the drafting history see Jhabvala, 'The Drafting of the Human Rights Provisions of the UN Charter', 25–6; Simma, *The Charter of the United Nations*, pp. 299–301.

[150] Jhabvala, 'The Drafting of the Human Rights Provisions of the UN Charter', 28; Simma, *The Charter of the United Nations*, pp. 1027–57.

religion' as a basic objective of the system.[151] In addition to these references, Article 8 of the UN Charter provides for non-discrimination on the grounds of gender in participation in the Organisation itself, the result of campaigning by a number of feminists working with the Inter-American Commission on the Status of Women.[152]

There is no express provision in the Charter obliging states to respect or protect human rights. The only provision which implies any obligation to act in accordance with the purposes and principles of the Charter is Article 6, which provides that members who have 'persistently violated the Principles' of the Charter may be expelled. No action has ever been taken under Article 6.[153] Furthermore, Article 56 refers to a 'pledge' - not an obligation - by members to take cooperative action 'for the achievement of the purposes set forth in Article 55'. The ICJ has referred to this pledge and to the compatibility of acts with the principles of the Charter, but it has never held that a state has violated a specific obligation imposed by Article 55 or 56 of the Charter. For example, in *Tehran Hostages* the ICJ referred to certain acts which might be 'incompatible with the principles of the Charter of the United Nations',[154] but did not draw from this a conclusion that Iran had violated any obligation under the Charter. Similarly, in its Advisory Opinion on the *Legal Consequences for States of the Continued Presence of South Africa in Namibia* in 1971, the Court referred to the 'pledge' of the mandatory to observe and respect human rights and fundamental freedoms, noting that the policy of apartheid 'is a flagrant violation of the purposes and principles of the Charter'.[155] But the Court's findings in the *dispositif* were based not on this pledge, but on other considerations. Rather than imposing a specific obligation to respect or protect human rights, it is more plausible that Articles 55 and 56 impose a good faith

[151] Jhabvala, 'The Drafting of the Human Rights Provisions of the UN Charter', 29–30; Simma, *The Charter of the United Nations*, pp. 1105–17.

[152] See Simma, *The Charter of the United Nations*, p. 231. Eleanor Roosevelt in her 'Open Letter to Women of the World' noted that at the time of the first General Assembly session, no more than seventeen women representatives and advisers were to be found: UN Doc. A/PV.29 (12 February 1946), cited in Simma, *ibid.* p. 231.

[153] T. D. Grant, *Admission to the United Nations: Charter Article 4 and the Rise of Universal Organization* (Leiden, Martinus Nijhoff, 2009), pp. 273–4.

[154] *United States Diplomatic and Consular Staff in Tehran (United States* v. *Iran)*, Merits [1980] ICJ Rep. 3, 42 (para. 91).

[155] See *Legal Consequences for States of the Continued Presence of South Africa in Namibia*, Advisory Opinion, [1971] ICJ Rep. 6, 57 (para. 131). The Trusteeship obligations are contained in Arts. 75–85 of the UN Charter.

obligation on member states to act in support of the purposes of the Charter, including promoting respect for human rights.[156]

The UN Charter also expressly recognised the principle of non-interference in domestic jurisdiction as a basic principle of the UN, in Article 2(7). Unlike the provision of the League Covenant dealing with the domestic reserve, which applied only to activities of the Council of the League, Article 2(7) applies to all organs of the UN and to all of their activities.[157] This was justified on the basis of the increased competence of the UN compared to the League, and in particular in the economic, social and cultural fields.[158] At the time of the Charter it was not clear how Article 2(7) would interact with the provisions of the Charter which referred to human rights or with any subsequent agreements relating to human rights.[159] This relationship was clarified in the late 1950s when the General Assembly passed resolutions calling upon the government of South Africa to observe the obligations contained in Article 56 of the UN Charter. South Africa's contention that these Resolutions violated Article 2(7) was rejected by overwhelming majorities.[160]

The Charter effectively postponed any commitment to human rights, with work on a bill of rights deferred and the text of the Charter containing no express obligations on states to respect or protect human rights. In other words the Charter did not confer rights on individuals. Discussion of rights at San Francisco indicated a willingness to engage in hortatory statements at the international level, with some measure of incorporation of those commitments in domestic law - but little more. The UN Charter is consistent with the pre-1945 framework of the international legal system, as it imposed no express obligations

156 See e.g., R. Jennings and A. Watts, *Oppenheim's International Law* (9th edn, London, Longmans, 1992), p. 989; cf. L. Sohn, 'The Human Rights Law of the Charter' (1977) 12 *Texas Intl L J* 129.

157 *Interpretation of Peace Treaties with Bulgaria, Hungary and Romania*, Advisory Opinion, [1950] ICJ Rep. 71. See also *Nationality Decrees Issued in Tunis and Morocco*, Advisory Opinion, PCIJ Rep. ser. B no. 4 (1923). See Simma, *The Charter of the United Nations*, pp. 150–1. See also generally, F. Ermacora, 'Human Rights and Domestic Jurisdiction (Article 2(7) of the Charter)' (1968-II) *Recueil des Cours* 375.

158 Simma, *The Charter of the United Nations*, pp. 150–1; Ermacora, 'Human Rights and Domestic Jurisdiction'.

159 Simma, *The Charter of the United Nations*, p. 160; H. Kelsen, *The Law of the United Nations* (London, Stevens, 1950), p. 29; R. Higgins, *The Development of International Law through the Political Organs of the United Nations* (London, OUP, 1963); see also L. Henkin, *The Age of Rights* (New York, Columbia University Press, 1990), esp. 50–64.

160 See GA/Res/1016(XI), 30 January 1957; GA/Res/1178(XII), 26 November 1957; GA/Res/1248(XIII), 30 October 1958.

on states with respect to treatment of persons within their jurisdiction, and it conferred no direct international rights on individuals.

(d) The Universal Declaration of Human Rights

At its first session the General Assembly referred the matter of the bill of rights to the Economic and Social Council (ECOSOC), for submission to the Commission on Human Rights.[161] ECOSOC mandated the Commission to work towards proposals, recommendations and reports on an international bill of rights and any other matter concerning human rights. It was urged to submit suggestions 'for the effective implementation of human rights and fundamental freedoms' at an early date. At its first session, the Human Rights Commission sought to produce a draft which would be 'acceptable to all Members of the United Nations'; on the basis that it would be simpler to reach agreement on a non-binding declaration, the Commission decided to work first on a declaration and to take up immediately afterwards the preparation of one or more treaties.[162]

The Universal Declaration of Human Rights (UDHR), the hortatory part of the Commission's venture, was adopted by the General Assembly in December 1948.[163] It was the first universal human rights instrument proclaimed by an international organisation. The Preamble suggests that the UDHR is a 'common standard of achievement' and that every individual and organ of society 'shall strive ... by progressive measures, national and international, to secure their universal and effective recognition and observance'. As noted by Hersch Lauterpacht, the unanimity of member states in noting the importance of the UDHR was accompanied by an equally unanimous repudiation of the idea that the Declaration imposed any legal obligation to respect the human rights it enumerated.[164] Both national and international measures are referred to as possible and desirable means for securing their recognition and observance, but no obligations are imposed in either respect.

161 GA/Res/43(I), 11 December 1946.

162 See discussion in J. T. Möller, 'The Universal Declaration of Human Rights: How the Process Started' in A. Eide, G. Alfredsson, G. Melandr, L. A. Rehof and A. Rosas (eds.), *The Universal Declaration of Human Rights: A Commentary* (Oslo, Scandinavian University Press, 1992), pp. 1, 1–3. See also N. Robinson, *The Universal Declaration of Human Rights: Its Origin, Significance, Application and Interpretation* (New York, Institute of Jewish Affairs, 1985).

163 Universal Declaration of Human Rights (UDHR), GA/Res/217A(III), 10 December 1948.

164 H. Lauterpacht, 'The Universal Declaration of Human Rights' (1948) 25 *BYIL* 354, 356 *et seq.*; see e.g., the statement of Eleanor Roosevelt: reproduced in M. M. Whiteman, *Digest of International Law* (Washington, DC, Department of State, 1965), vol. V, p. 243.

The Declaration proclaims two broad categories of rights: civil and political rights, and economic, social and cultural rights.[165] The UDHR expressly recognises that states may enact laws limiting the exercise of rights, provided their sole purpose is to secure the rights and freedoms of others and 'just requirements of morality, public order, and the general welfare in a democratic society'.[166] It provides that each individual 'has duties to the community', but does not elaborate on their content.[167] The articulation of rights in the UDHR is consistent with the conferral of direct rights: it states that 'everyone is entitled' to certain rights[168] and that 'no one shall' be subject to certain conditions.[169] On the one hand, the language of universal rights is significant: the UDHR is the first international instrument to refer to the direct conferral of individual rights on a universal basis. On the other hand, this language of 'rights' must be considered in light of the status of the UDHR as a soft law instrument, and in particular of the fact that it is not intended to impose any correlative legal obligations on states. In this respect it is rhetoric: there is no obligation on states to respect or ensure respect for the Declaration rights, nor to incorporate them into their domestic law.[170]

(e) From moral imperative to legal articulation: state obligations, individual rights and international enforcement in the European system

The first international convention which expressly imposed obligations on states in respect of human rights was the European Convention for the Protection of Human Rights and Fundamental Freedoms (ECHR), which opened for signature in 1950 and entered into force in 1953. Concluded under the auspices of the Council of Europe, the ECHR covers civil and political rights and some economic, social and cultural rights. Article 1 imposes an obligation on contracting states to 'secure to everyone within their jurisdiction the rights and freedoms' defined in the Convention. It uses declaratory language which indicates the direct conferral of rights on individuals: 'everyone has the right'[171] or 'no one shall' be subjected to certain treatment.[172]

[165] See generally, J. Morsink, 'The Philosophy of the Universal Declaration' (1984) 9 *HRQ* 309 and S. Waltz, 'Universalizing Human Rights: The Role of Small States in the Construction of the Universal Declaration of Human Rights' (2001) 23 *HRQ* 44.
[166] UDHR, Art. 29(2). [167] *Ibid.* Art. 30. [168] See e.g., *ibid.* Arts 2, 3, 8.
[169] See e.g., *ibid.* Arts. 4 and 5.
[170] Whether the UDHR, or specific rights enumerated therein, have over time acquired the status of customary international law is discussed below (see 5.4(g) below).
[171] For example, see *ibid.* Art. 5. [172] For example, see *ibid.* Art. 3.

The ECHR was the first instrument to impose generalised obligations in respect of human rights, although earlier instruments relating to the Council of Europe had made reference to aspirations of human rights. The Preamble to the Brussels Treaty, signed in March 1948, 'reaffirm[ed the parties'] faith in fundamental human rights, in the dignity and worth of the human person and in other ideals proclaimed in the Charter of the United Nations'.[173] The Statute of the Council of Europe, adopted on 5 May 1949, included two references to human rights: in Article 1 stating its purpose as achieving greater unity through 'the maintenance and further realisation of human rights and fundamental freedoms'; and in Article 3 which provided that members 'must accept the [principle] ... of enjoyment by all persons within its jurisdiction of human rights and fundamental freedoms'.

It is too simplistic to attribute the development of state obligations in respect of human rights in Europe exclusively to the atrocities of the Second World War, but undoubtedly the experience of the war was a central motivating factor. The debate in the Consultative Assembly in August 1949 is revealing: the French representative, Teitgen, expressly linked the development of human rights in Europe to Nazism:

> Mr. President, while I was in the Gestapo prisons, while one of my brothers was at Dachau and one of my brothers-in-law was dying at Mauthausen, my father ... was interned at Buchenwald. He told me that on the monumental gate of the camp was this outrageous inscription: 'Just or unjust, the Fatherland.'
>
> I think that from our First Session we can unanimously proclaim that in Europe there will henceforth only be *just* fatherlands.
>
> I think we can now unanimously confront 'reasons of State' with the only sovereignty worth dying for, worthy in all circumstances of being defended, respected and safeguarded – the sovereignty of justice and of law.[174]

Moreover, there was a definite and express desire to conclude a legally binding instrument. In the same session, the Danish representative argued that human rights in Europe was not a mere duplication of UN efforts since in Europe agreement on obligations was more realistic:

> [A]lthough the question of human rights had been discussed at length by the United Nations, it had not yet been possible to draft a text which held good in International Law. The universal declaration lacked precision. It could not be

[173] Simpson, *Human Rights and the End of Empire*, pp. 574–5.

[174] Council of Europe, *Collected Edition of the 'Travaux Préparatoires' of the European Convention on Human Rights* (The Hague, Martinus Nijhoff, 1975), vol. I, pp. 48–50.

otherwise in view of the differences in civilization and forms of Government existing in different Member States of the United Nations. It would be a very different matter if the question was reconsidered on a purely Western European basis, in which case a text might be elaborated which would be binding in the legal sense.[175]

The need for concrete and binding obligations was also emphasised by the Swedish representative:

Mankind today has had more than enough of high-sounding principles and beautiful declarations. Willingness and ability to make something real out of those declarations has too often been lacking ...

When I cast my vote for concrete measures to secure for the men and women of the European countries their human rights and fundamental freedoms, I shall do it with a fervent desire, first, that the definition of those fundamental freedoms will be so clearly formulated as to leave no room for doubts about their meaning, and secondly, that the Charter of Human Rights ... will be regarded as supreme and binding upon all Governments which adopt it.[176]

Another motivating factor was the threat posed by communism in general, and the Soviet Union in particular. The Belgian Prime Minister, Paul-Henri Spaak, remarked that the most influential person in the union of Europe was Stalin, for it was the challenge of communism which made European countries acutely aware of the need to reaffirm the principles of their political faith.[177] This was also a factor motivating European integration in general, but more specifically it was thought that effective protection of human rights lay the foundations 'to defen[d] ... human personality against all tyrannies and against all forms of totalitarianism'.[178]

The ECHR was also the first human rights convention to incorporate a petition system for individuals, conditional on a declaration of acceptance by a state.[179] The European Commission of Human Rights, which was created by the Convention, had mandatory jurisdiction for inter-state complaints and opt-in jurisdiction for individual petitions.[180] Petitions could be brought by 'any person, non-governmental

175 *Ibid.* p. 24. 176 *Ibid.* p. 78.

177 See generally, J. G. Merrills and A. H. Robertson, *Human Rights in Europe* (4th edn, Manchester, Juris Publishing, 2001), pp. 4–5.

178 Robert Schuman, cited in A. H. Robertson and J. G. Merrills, *Human Rights in the World* (4th edn, Manchester, Manchester University Press, 1996), p. 120. See generally, Simpson, *Human Rights and the End of Empire*, pp. 587–9.

179 ECHR, Arts. 24, 25.

180 The individual petition became operative in 1955: Merrills and Robertson, *Human Rights in Europe*, p. 14.

organization or group of individuals claiming to be the victim of a violation' of a Convention right, provided that local remedies had been exhausted and conditions for admissibility were met.[181] The Commission held a hearing with representatives of the parties; if a friendly settlement was not reached[182] the Commission issued a report to the relevant state and to the Committee of Ministers, stating whether there had been a breach of the Convention, together with any proposals for remedying a breach.[183]

A second supervisory body, the European Court of Human Rights (ECtHR), was created in September 1958, after eight states accepted its jurisdiction.[184] The ECtHR did not have competence to receive petitions directly from individuals, but once a petition had been considered by the Commission, either the respondent state or the Commission (provided the relevant state had accepted the jurisdiction of the Court) could refer the matter to the Court.[185] If a petition was referred to it, and the Court found that a state party had violated its obligations under the Convention, the Court was to 'afford just satisfaction to the injured party'.[186]

The individual right of petition was included in the Legal Committee's draft to the Consultative Assembly, submitted in September 1949. The Legal Committee argued that an individual right of petition to a judicial body was necessary:

> After a long debate, the Committee rejected as completely insufficient a proposal granting the victim of a violation of the Convention a simple right of petition, whether to the Committee of Ministers or to a Commission of Enquiry. It is in fact well known that any authority which, in such circumstances, receives a petition, may quite likely decide to ignore it.
>
> After this the Committee decided that the guarantee should include a judicial ruling preceded by a preliminary investigation of the complaint, followed, if necessary, by an enquiry, and then an attempt at conciliation, to be carried out by a special Commission.[187]

The Legal Committee's proposals for individual petition to a Commission, and for the establishment of a Court, both encountered opposition, particularly from representatives of France and the UK, who

[181] ECHR, Art. 26. [182] *Ibid.* Art. 28.
[183] *Ibid.* Art. 31. These procedures were streamlined by Protocol no. 3.
[184] Merrills and Robertson, *Human Rights in Europe*, p. 14.
[185] ECHR, Arts. 32, 44, 48. [186] *Ibid.* Art. 50.
[187] Council of Europe, *Collected Edition of the 'Travaux Préparatoires' of the European Convention on Human Rights* (The Hague, Martinus Nijhoff, 1975), vol. I, p. 224.

opposed permitting private individuals to 'bring one of the States to trial even after examination and with the authority of a "sorting organization"'.[188] A proposal to reject a European Court of Human Rights was, however, itself rejected,[189] and a British proposal to delete the right of individuals to petition the Commission was also rejected.[190] With some minor amendments, the Legal Committee's draft was adopted by the Consultative Assembly in September 1949;[191] and in November 1949, the Committee of Ministers referred the matter to a Committee of Experts.[192] The Committee of Experts' Report was then considered by a Conference of Senior Officials, which noted that the creation of an optional Court was supported by eight countries (Belgium, France, Greece, Ireland, Italy, Luxembourg, Sweden and Turkey), opposed by two (the Netherlands and the UK) and supported by two if supported by a majority (Denmark and Norway).[193] Nine countries supported the right of individual petition to the Commission (Belgium, Denmark, France, Ireland, Italy, Luxembourg, Norway, Sweden and Turkey) while three reserved their position (Greece, the Netherlands and the UK).[194] In August 1950, the Committee of Ministers decided to make both the jurisdiction of the Court and the right of individual petition optional;[195] in substance the text then adopted was the same as that signed in November 1950.

That individuals hold direct and substantive rights under the European Convention has been affirmed by the ECtHR's treatment of the question of waiver. The Court has held that individuals may validly waive their entitlement to certain of the rights specified in the Convention (such as the right to a public hearing under Article 6(1)),[196] a finding consistent with the direct conferral of rights on individuals. Any waiver must be 'established in an unequivocal manner'[197] and 'not run counter to any important public interest';[198] in the case of procedural rights, a

[188] *Ibid.* p. 242.
[189] Council of Europe, *Collected Edition of the 'Travaux Préparatoires'*, vol. II, pp. 156–8.
[190] *Ibid.* p. 202. [191] *Ibid.* pp. 274–86. [192] *Ibid.* p. 290.
[193] Council of Europe, *Collected Edition of the 'Travaux Préparatoires'*, vol. IV, pp. 250–2.
[194] *Ibid.* p. 252.
[195] Council of Europe, *Collected Edition of the 'Travaux Préparatoires'*, vol. I, pp. xxvi–xxviii.
[196] *Albert and LeCompte* v. *Belgium*, Judgment, 10 February 1983, ECHR ser. A no. 58, para. 35; *H* v. *Belgium*, Judgment, 30 November 1987, ECHR ser. A no. 127-B, para. 54.
[197] *Barberà, Messengué and Jabardo* v. *Spain*, Judgment, 6 December 1988, ECHR ser. A no. 146, para. 82; *Oberschlick* v. *Austria*, Judgment, 23 May 1991, ECHR ser. A no. 204, para. 51.
[198] *Håkansson and Sturesson* v. *Sweden*, Judgment, 21 February 1990, ECHR ser. A no. 171-A, para. 67; *McGonnell* v. *United Kingdom*, Judgment, 8 February 2000, ECHR Rep 2000-II,

waiver may not detract from 'minimum guarantees commensurate to its importance'.[199] This stands in contrast to the position taken on waiver of state's rights to exercise diplomatic protection; as noted in Chapter 2, the ILC's treatment of the Calvo clause suggests that individuals cannot waive their state of nationality's right of recourse in respect of an internationally wrongful act.[200]

The European system for the protection of human rights was innovative at the time in two respects: it expressly imposed obligations on states in respect of human rights; and it contemplated individual mechanisms of enforcement in an international forum. The latter seems to have followed from the former; from an acknowledgement that some kind of individualised judicial procedure was necessary to accomplish the objective of concrete state obligations and individual rights.

(f) Human rights and state obligations in the UN system

At the universal level human rights conventions incorporating state obligations took longer to achieve, the first appearing in the mid-1960s. The catalogue of UN human rights treaties incorporates two forms of conventions: subject-specific conventions and the two Covenants, on Civil and Political Rights (ICCPR), and on Economic, Social and Cultural Rights (ICESCR). In addition to these conventions, the General Assembly and other organs of the UN have made declarations of specific rights. Structurally, where these instruments impose obligations on states and confer rights on individuals, they are analogous to the ECHR, although they lack the opportunities for enforcement afforded to individuals in that system; they are sketched in this section briefly because, unlike the ECHR, they are not limited to a single region.

In addition to these conventions, some of which provided for optional complaints procedures, since the late 1960s the Human Rights Commission has developed procedures to assess compliance with humans rights standards in execution of its mandate under the UN Charter. These procedures, which are now undertaken in a modified form by the Human Rights Council, are summarised in this section.

para. 44; *Lundevall* v. *Sweden*, Application no. 38629/97,ECtHR, Judgment, 12 November 2002, para. 34.

199 *Pfeifer and Plankl* v. *Austria*, Judgment, 25 February 1992, ECHR ser. A no. 227, para. 37; *Pailot* v. *France*, Judgment, 22 April 1998, ECHR Rep. 1998-II, para. 52; *Schöps* v. *Germany*, Judgment, 13 February 2001, ECHR Rep. 2001-I, para. 48.

200 See 2.4(a)(i) above.

(i) Subject-specific conventions

The first of the subject-specific conventions was the Convention on the Elimination of Racial Discrimination (CERD).[201] Although the Genocide Convention[202] is sometimes referred to as the first universal human rights convention, it can be distinguished from the catalogue of UN human rights conventions under examination on several grounds, including, *inter alia*, that it does not articulate specific rights for individuals. The CERD originated from a recommendation of the Sub-Commission on Prevention and Protection of Minorities: it suggested that the General Assembly prepare an international convention which would impose specific legal obligations on parties to prohibit manifestations of racial and national hatred.[203] The General Assembly decided to pursue both a declaration and a convention on racial discrimination;[204] the UN Declaration on the Elimination of All Forms of Racial Discrimination was proclaimed by the General Assembly on 20 November 1963.[205] The Declaration refers to both state obligations and individual rights. Obligations are cast in very general terms. For example, Article 2 provides that '[n]o State, institution, group or individual shall make any discrimination whatsoever in matters of human rights and fundamental freedoms' on grounds of race, colour or ethnic origin and that '[n]o State shall encourage, advocate or lend its support ... to any [such] discrimination'. Article 3 requires states to 'take effective measures' to revise policies and laws 'which have the effect of creating and perpetuating racial discrimination'. In terms of individual rights, the Declaration uses language similar to the UDHR: it stated that '[e]veryone has the right to equality before the law and to equal justice under the law' and that '[e]veryone shall have the right to an effective remedy and protection' against discrimination.[206]

The Convention, which was adopted by the General Assembly on 21 December 1965, enumerates state obligations in much more specific

[201] International Convention on the Elimination of all Forms of Racial Discrimination (CERD), 21 December 1965 (entry into force 4 January 1969), 660 UNTS 195.

[202] Convention on the Prevention and Punishment of the Crime of Genocide, 1 January 1948 (entry into force 12 January 1951) 78 UNTS 277.

[203] *Report of the Thirteenth Session of the Sub-Commission on Prevention of Discrimination and Protection of Minorities*, UN Doc E/CN.4/815 (1961), paras. 176 and 185.

[204] GA/Res/1780(XVII), 7 December 1962; GA/Res/1781(XVII), 7 December 1962.

[205] GA/Res/1904 (XVIII), 20 November 1963. [206] *Ibid.* Art. 7.

terms.[207] In Article 2, states parties undertake 'to engage in no act or practice of racial discrimination', 'not to sponsor, defend or support racial discrimination', to take effective measures to review policies, laws and regulations which have the effect of creating or perpetuating racial discrimination, and to 'prohibit and bring to an end ... racial discrimination by any persons, group or organization'. These undertakings are elaborated in Articles 3–7, and particularly by Article 5, which contains an undertaking to guarantee the right of everyone without distinction to equality before the law. In terms of individual rights, Article 5 refers to the right 'to equality before the law' in the enjoyment of rights, and includes a non-exhaustive list of the those rights, including the right to security of person, political rights, civil rights and economic, social and cultural rights. The majority of those rights also appear in the UDHR. On its terms, Article 5 appears to confer direct rights on individuals to equality before the law in the enjoyment of their rights, commensurate with the state's obligation to 'guarantee' that right.

The CERD established a Committee on Racial Discrimination[208] with compulsory competence to receive inter-state complaints[209] and optional competence in respect of individual communications (i.e. provided the relevant state recognised the Committee's competence to do so).[210] The Committee was to include a summary of communications and the action taken in its annual reports to the General Assembly.[211]

The CERD was the first of a catalogue of subject-specific human rights conventions adopted by the UN and its organs. They all follow the same structure: many impose obligations on states to prevent and suppress acts in contravention of human rights, to adopt measures to give effect to those rights and to observe, respect and ensure respect for those rights.[212] Some of these conventions articulate individual

207 See generally, E. Schwelb, 'The International Convention on the Elimination of All Forms of Racial Discrimination' (1966) 15 *ICLQ* 996.
208 CERD, Art. 8. 209 *Ibid.* Art. 11.
210 *Ibid.* Art. 14. At least ten acceptances were required to make the Committee competent to receive individual communications.
211 *Ibid.* Art. 14(8).
212 See e.g., *ibid.* Arts. 2, 3, 5, 6, 7; Convention on the Elimination of All Forms of Discrimination Against Women (CEDAW), Arts. 2, 5, 18 December 1979 (entry into force 3 September 1981), 1249 UNTS 13; Convention Against Torture and Other Cruel, Inhuman, or Degrading Treatment or Punishment (CAT), Art. 2(1), 10 December 1984 (entry into force 26 June 1987), 1465 UNTS 85; Convention on the Rights of the Child (CROC), Art. 2(1), 20 November 1989 (entry into force 2 September 1990), 1577 UNTS 3.

rights[213] while others appear to assume that individuals are granted rights corresponding to the obligations imposed on states. Several conventions provide an opt-in individual complaint mechanism for individuals who claim to be a victim of a violation of the convention,[214] under the same model as the CERD Committee. The conventions also impose reporting requirements on states.[215]

(ii) The International Covenants

Structurally, the two International Covenants follow the same pattern as the CERD. Both the ICCPR and the ICESCR were opened for signature in December 1966 and entered into force a decade later, on 23 March 1976 and 3 January 1976, respectively.[216] The ICCPR currently has 164 states parties; the ICESCR has 160 states parties.[217]

Like the ECHR, the ICCPR imposes legal obligations on states parties: in Article 2 of the ICCPR, each state party 'undertakes to respect and to ensure to all individuals within its territory and subject to its jurisdiction' the rights in the Covenant without discrimination, and to take the necessary steps 'to adopt such legislative or other measures as may be necessary to give effect' to those rights. Part III of the Covenant sets out the relevant rights which build upon the civil and political rights declared in the UDHR.[218] Its language suggests that corresponding

213 See e.g., International Convention on the Protection of the Rights of All Migrant Workers and Members of Their Families, Art. 18, 18 December 1990 (entry into force 1 July 2003), 2220 UNTS 93 (Migrant Workers Convention).

214 See CERD, Art. 14; Optional Protocol to the Convention on the Elimination of Discrimination against Women, 10 December 1999 (entry into force 22 December 2000), GA/Res/54/4; CAT, Art. 22; Migrant Workers Convention, Art. 77; Optional Protocol to the International Convention on the Protection and Promotion of the Rights and Dignity of Persons with Disabilities, 13 December 2006 (not yet in force), 46 ILM 443.

215 CERD, Art. 9; International Convention on the Suppression and Punishment of the Crime of Apartheid, Arts. VII and IX, 30 November 1973 (entry into force 18 July 1976), 1015 UNTS 243; CEDAW, Art. 17; CAT, Art. 19; CROC, Art. 44; Migrant Workers Convention, Art. 73; International Convention on the Protection and Promotion of the Rights and Dignity of Persons with Disabilities, Art. 35, 13 December 2006 (not yet in force), 46 ILM 443. See generally, *Effective Functioning of Human Rights Mechanisms Treaty Bodies*, E/CN.3/2004/98; and *Report of the UN Secretariat on Guidelines for an Expanded Core Document*, HRI/MC/2004/3 (2004); see also P. Alston and J. Crawford (eds.), *The Future of UN Human Rights Treaty Monitoring* (Cambridge, Cambridge University Press, 2000).

216 ICCPR; International Covenant on Economic, Social and Cultural Rights (ICESCR), 19 December 1966 (entry into force 3 January 1976), 993 UNTS 3.

217 See http://treaties.un.org/Pages/Treaties.aspx?id=4&subid=A&lang=en.

218 The ICCPR includes a right to enjoy property, to seek and enjoy asylum and to nationality, which do not appear in the UDHR: see generally, L. Henkin (ed.),

rights are directly conferred on individuals. It states, for example, that 'everyone shall have the right'[219] and that 'no one shall be subjected' to certain conditions.[220]

The ICCPR established a Human Rights Committee to administer the reporting system and inter-state complaint mechanism.[221] The Committee developed a proactive of adopting 'General Comments' addressed to all states parties to provide guidance to them in discharging their obligations.[222] This has evolved into a quasi-judicial advisory opinion, providing interpretation of provisions of the Covenant. The Committee often relies upon the General Comments in evaluating the compliance of states with their obligations. The Covenant also provides for an optional inter-state complaint mechanism,[223] which has not yet been used.

Initially there was no provision for an individual complaint mechanism, but the First Optional Protocol to the ICCPR, which came into force in 1976, permits individuals who are victims of a violation of the Covenant to file an 'individual' communication with the Committee, provided they have exhausted local remedies.[224] Complaints may only be filed against states which have ratified the Protocol: currently 111 of the 164 states parties to the Covenant have done so.[225] Communications are dealt with on the papers: on receipt of a communication the state party is given two months to make an objection to admissibility or six months to submit arguments on the merits;[226] the complainant is given an opportunity to reply within a fixed period. The Committee then adopts its decision in the case, designated as 'Views'.[227] The Views of

The International Bill of Human Rights: The Covenant on Civil and Political Rights (New York, Colombia University Press, 1981). The Second Optional Protocol to the ICCPR, which entered into force in 1991, is directed to the abolition of the death penalty: Second Optional Protocol to the International Covenant on Civil and Political Rights, Aiming at the Abolition of the Death Penalty, Arts. 1, 6(2), 15 December 1989 (entry into force 11 July 1991), 29 ILM 1464.

219 ICCPR, see e.g., Art. 9. 220 *Ibid.* see e.g., Art. 7. 221 *Ibid.* Arts. 40–1.

222 This is anticipated by ICCPR, Art. 40(4).

223 See generally, M. Nowak, *UN Covenant on Civil and Political Rights: CCPR Commentary* (Kehl, NP Engel, 1993), pp. 580 and 604.

224 (First) Optional Protocol to the International Covenant on Civil and Political Rights, Art. 1, 16 December 1966 (in force 23 March 1976) 999 UNTS 171.

225 See www.treaties.un.org/Pages/ViewDetails.aspx?src=TREATY&mtdsg_no=IV-5&chapter=4&lang=en.

226 Rules of Procedure of the Human Rights Committee, adopted 24 April 2001, UN Doc. CCPR/C/3/Rev.6 (1994), Rule 91.

227 See generally, P. R. Ghandhi, *The Human Rights Committee and the Right of Individual Communication: Law and Practice* (Aldershot, Ashgate, 1998).

the Committee are not expressed to be binding on states and the Committee has no specific mandate to ensure compliance. The Committee has established a Special Rapporteur for the Follow-Up of Views and has required states to indicate in their periodic reports what measures they have taken to give effect to the Committee's Views.[228] This is not a judicial procedure;[229] but it permits individuals access to an international forum to seek redress for violations of their rights, albeit non-binding on the relevant state. In general, state compliance with optional protocol Views has been poor[230] and compared to the judicial procedures in other regional systems, the individual communications procedure only provides individuals with very weak means of enforcement for individual rights.

In contrast to the ICCPR, the ICESCR does not impose obligations to 'respect and ensure' rights; rather, it imposes a general obligation of conduct on contracting states:

> to take steps ... to the maximum of its available resources, with a view to achieving progressively the full realization of the rights recognized in the present Covenant by all appropriate means, including particularly the adoption of legislative measures.[231]

Further, states 'undertake to guarantee' that the Covenant rights 'will be exercised without discrimination'.[232] Part III of the Covenant sets out a more extensive catalogue of economic, social and cultural rights than the UDHR. However, its language differs from the ICCPR: in general its provisions provide that states parties 'recognise' certain rights rather than providing that individuals have the relevant right. One exception is Article 8 relating to trade unions, which provides that states parties 'undertake to ensure' the rights of everyone to form and join trade

228 Rules of Procedure of the Human Rights Committee, adopted 24 April 2001, UN Doc. CCPR/C/3/Rev.6 (1994), Rule 95.

229 The New Zealand Supreme Court held in *Wellington District Legal Services Committee* v. *Tangiora* (1997) 115 ILR 655 that the Human Rights Committee was not an 'administrative tribunal or judicial authority' within the meaning of the Judicial Services Act. That decision was upheld by the Privy Council on appeal: *Tangiora* v. *Wellington District Legal Services Committee* (1999) 124 ILR 570.

230 S. Joseph, J. Schultz and M. Castan, *The International Covenant on Civil and Political Rights: Cases, Materials, and Commentary* (2nd edn, Oxford, Oxford University Press, 2005), p. 46; H. J. Steiner, 'Individual Claims in a World of Massive Violations: What Role for the Human Rights Committee?' in P. Alston and J. Crawford (eds.), *The Future of UN Human Rights Treaty Monitoring* (Cambridge, Cambridge University Press, 2000), pp. 15, 36–7.

231 ICESCR, Art. 2(1). 232 *Ibid.* Art. 2(2), see also Art. 3.

unions.[233] To the extent that the terms of the Covenant confer rights on individuals, these must be limited to the corresponding obligations imposed on states, which are expressed in more limited terms than the ICCPR.[234]

The ICESCR did not establish a Committee to supervise its implementation; it only required each state party to submit reports on its measures and progress 'in achieving the observance' of the Covenant Rights[235] to the Secretary-General of the UN, who was to transmit copies to the Economic and Social Council (ECOSOC) and to relevant specialised agencies.[236] In 1985, ECOSOC established a Committee on Economic, Social and Cultural Rights (ESCR Committee) to consider reports submitted by states and to make 'recommendations of a general nature' to assist the Council to fulfil its responsibilities under the Covenant.[237] Like the Human Rights Committee, the ESCR Committee issued general comments. In 1990, it adopted General Comment no. 3 on the 'nature of State parties obligations', which suggests that the Covenant imposes various obligations of immediate effect on states. The Committee singled out the undertaking of states parties to guarantee that the rights set out in the Covenant will be exercised without discrimination and the undertaking in Article 2(1) 'to take steps'. It expressed the view that 'a minimum core obligation to ensure the satisfaction of, at the very least, minimum essential levels of each of the rights is incumbent upon every State party'[238] and that, even though any assessment of a state's compliance with this minimum core obligation must take account of resource constraints, 'the obligation remains

[233] *Ibid.* Art. 8. It also provides that states undertake to ensure rights of trade unions to establish federations and to function freely, and the right to strike, subject to lawful restrictions.

[234] In the *Wall* Opinion, the ICJ noted that Israel was bound by the ICESCR in the occupied territories and noted that several provisions were relevant (para. 130). It drew a general conclusion that the construction of the wall was in breach of human rights treaties (para. 136) but did not refer specifically to breaches of the ICESCR: *Legal Consequences of the Construction of a Wall in the Occupied Palestinian Territory*, Advisory Opinion, [2004] ICJ Rep. 36. See generally, R. Higgins, 'Human Rights in the International Court of Justice' (2007) 20 *LJIL* 745; S. R. S. Bedi, *The Development of Human Rights Law by the Judges of the International Court of Justice* (Oxford, Hart, 2007).

[235] ICESCR, Art. 16(1). [236] *Ibid.* Art. 16(2).

[237] ECOSOC Resolution 1985/17, esp. para. (f), adopted 22nd Plenary Meeting, 28 May 1985.

[238] Human Rights Committee, General Comment 3, 14 December 1990, UN Doc. HRI/GEN/1/Rev.1 (1994), p. 4, para. 10. See also P. Alston and G. Quinn, 'The Nature and Scope of State Parties' Obligations under the International Covenant on Economic, Social and Cultural Rights' (1987) 9 *HRQ* 156.

for a State party to strive to ensure the widest possible enjoyment of the relevant rights under the prevailing circumstances'.[239] The Committee has found that states parties have acted inconsistently with Covenant rights: for example, it stated that 'the guarantees in article 11 of the Covenant had not been respected' by the Dominican Republic;[240] it has also found certain actions to be 'incompatible with respect for the right to housing'.[241] It has made recommendations urging repeal of legislation,[242] encouraging implementation of legislation,[243] encouraging preventive action to avoid violations[244] and recommending that states make certain efforts to fulfil their obligations.[245]

Although the ICESCR did not establish any inter-state or individual complaint system, since 2000 the Committee has invited NGOs to submit information to be included in country files and taken into account in the preparation of the Committee's reports.[246] This information has provided scope for an 'ad hoc complaints procedure'.[247] In 2008, an Optional Protocol was adopted by the UN General Assembly and will open for signature in 2009:[248] it gives the Committee competence to receive communications 'by or on behalf of individuals or groups of individuals, under the jurisdiction of a State Party, claiming to be victims of a violation' of any Covenant rights.[249] Its procedures are similar to those of the Human Rights Committee under the ICCPR; the

239 Human Rights Committee, General Comment 3, 14 December 1990, UN Doc. HRI/GEN/1/Rev.1 (1994), p. 4, paras. 10–11.

240 Dominican Republic, UN Doc. E/C.12/1990/8, para. 249.

241 Philippines, UN Doc. E/C.12/1995/18.

242 See e.g., Philippines, UN Doc. E/C.12/1995/18; Dominican Republic, UN Doc. E/C.12/1990/8.

243 See e.g., Belgium, UN Doc. E/C.12/1994/20.

244 See e.g., Dominican Republic, UN Doc E/C.12/1991/4, para. 330; see also Mexico, UN Doc. E/C.12/1993/3.

245 See e.g., Canada, UN Doc. E/C.12/1993/3; Dominican Republic, UN Doc. E/C.12/1990/8; Mexico, UN Doc. E/C.12/1993/3.

246 *NGO Participation in Activities of the Committee on Economic, Social and Cultural Rights*, UN Doc. E/C.12/1993/WP.14; 'Substantive issues arising in the implementation of the ICESCR: NGO participation in the activities of the Committee', Note by the Secretariat, 7 July 2000, UN Doc. E/C.12/2000/6.

247 See M. Craven, 'Towards an Unofficial Petition Procedure: A Review of the Role of the Committee on Economic, Social and Cultural Rights' in C. Krause and A. Rosas (eds.), *Social Rights as Human Rights: A European Challenge* (London, Martinus Nihoff, 1994), p. 91; M. Craven, *The International Covenant on Economic, Social and Cultural Rights: A Perspective on its Development* (Oxford, Clarendon Press, 1995).

248 GA/Res/63/117, 10 December 2008.

249 Optional Protocol to the International Covenant on Economic, Social and Cultural Rights, Art. 2, 10 December 2008 (not yet in force), GA/Res/63/117.

Committee is to submit its views to the parties, together with any recommendations.[250] The Optional Protocol also provides for an opt-in inter-state complaints procedure.[251]

Both UN Covenants confer direct rights on individuals; those rights correspond to the obligations of states: in the case of the ICCPR, states are obliged to 'respect and ensure' the relevant rights; whereas in the case of the ICESCR, states are obliged to a lesser degree, to take steps with a view to achieving the realisation of the relevant rights and to recognise rights. The ICCPR provides an optional procedure for individual complaints and a similar procedure is contemplated for the ICESCR. These processes do not result in binding judgments but they do give individuals a right of access to an international complaints procedure to seek redress for violations of their rights.

(iii) Declarations of specific rights

Apart from these Conventions, the General Assembly and other organs of the UN have, from time to time, made declarations of specific rights, such as the right to a clean environment;[252] the right to development;[253] and the right to peace.[254] To the extent that these declarations purport to impose obligations on states, those obligations are cast in terms which seek realisation of the right, rather than an obligation to respect and observe the right. For example, the 1986 Declaration on the Right to Development notes that 'States have the primary responsibility for the creation of national and international conditions favourable to the realisation of the right to development'[255] and provides that states 'should' take all necessary measures 'for the realisation of the right to development'.[256] While the General Assembly's practice has led some scholars to argue that, in practice, 'a claim is an international human right if the United Nations General Assembly says it is',[257] others have

[250] *Ibid.* Art. 9. [251] *Ibid.* Art. 10.

[252] *Report of the UN Conference on the Human Environment, Stockholm, 5–16 June 1972*, p. 4; endorsed in GA/Res/2994(XXVII), 15 December 1972.

[253] GA/Res/34/46, 23 November 1979; GA/Res/35/174, 15 December 1980; GA/Res/36/133, 14 December 1981; GA/Res/37/199, 18 December 1982; GA/Res/37/200, 18 December 1982; GA/Res/41/128, 4 December 1986.

[254] Commission on Human Rights Resolution 5 (XXXII) (1976), para. 1; Declaration on the Preparation of Societies for Life in Peace, Pt 1, para. 1, GA/Res/33/73, 15 December 1978.

[255] GA/Res/41/128, 14 December 1986, Art. 3(1). [256] *Ibid.* Art. 8(1).

[257] See e.g., R. B. Bilder, 'Rethinking International Human Rights: Some Basic Questions' (1969) 71 *Wis. L Rev.* 171, 173.

contested the authority of the General Assembly to 'literally conjur[e] up' these rights, in the absence of any established procedure for scrutinising the rights.[258] It must also be noted that in the absence of any meaningful state obligations, the declarations cannot be said to vest individuals with meaningful legal rights. But to the extent that they might do so, they are structurally equivalent to other human rights treaties.

(iv) Special procedures before the Human Rights Commission (now the Human Rights Council)

The Human Rights Commission, in pursuance of the obligations imposed on the UN and its members to 'promote' respect for and observance of human rights, has established various procedures to monitor and assess compliance with human rights standards. These procedures initially took two forms: country-specific and thematic. In 1967, ECOSOC Resolution 1235 authorised the Commission to 'examine information relevant to gross violations of human rights' and to 'make a thorough study of situations which reveal a consistent pattern of violations of human rights'.[259] This authorisation formed the basis of the Commission's public procedure for the investigation of allegations against a state. In 1970, ECOSOC Resolution 1503 authorised the Commission to consider communications from individuals and non-governmental organisations. It authorised the Sub-Commission on the Promotion and Protection of Human Rights to examine in private communications received by the UN Secretary-General, with a view to referring to the Commission 'situations which appear to reveal a consistent pattern of gross and reliably attested violations of human rights'.[260] If a situation was referred to the Commission, it provided the relevant state with an opportunity to be heard, and announced publicly the names of the states examined annually under Resolution 1503. Apart from this naming, the 1503 Procedures are kept confidential.

In 2006, the General Assembly created the Human Rights Council,[261] which replaced the Commission. The General Assembly mandated the Council to assume, review, and where necessary improve the existing special procedures within a year of its first session.[262] In execution of

[258] See P. Alston, 'Conjuring up New Human Rights: A Proposal for Quality Control' (1984) 78 *AJIL* 607, 607–8.
[259] ECOSOC Resolution 1235 (XLII), 42 UN ESCOR Supp. (no. 1) 17.
[260] ECOSOC Resolution 1503 (XLVII), 48 UN ESCOR (no. 1A) 8.
[261] GA/Res/60/251, 3 April 2006. [262] *Ibid.* para. 6.

that mandate the Council adopted, on 18 June 2007, Resolution 5/1 which established, *inter alia*, a complaints procedure for individuals and NGOs to replace the Resolution 1503 procedure.[263] The new complaints procedure is similar to the 1503 procedure. It is established to address consistent patterns of gross and reliably attested violations of human rights. Communications are referred to either a Working Group on Communications or a Working Group on Situations, and either Working Group may refer situations to the Council for a decision. Procedures before the Working Group and before the Council remain confidential. The Council may decide to discontinue review of the situation; to continue review of it (in which case it may request more information from the relevant state); to discontinue and take up a public consideration of the situation; or to discontinue review and refer it to the Office of the High Commissioner for Human Rights to provide technical cooperation, capacity-building assistance or advisory services to the relevant state.

While the new Human Rights Council complaints procedure purports to be victim-oriented, these procedures provide individuals with little capacity for redress in case of violations. But they are nevertheless of interest: first, the procedures before the Human Rights Commission were based on its mandate under the UN Charter, which did not purport to impose obligations on states in respect of human rights. Moreover, both the Resolution 1235 procedure and the Resolution 1503 procedures were established in 1967, before either of the UN Covenants came into force. While these procedures can hardly be said to have provided individuals with capacity to practically and legally enforce their existing rights, they demonstrate that even in the late 1960s, there was momentum towards universal human rights obligations, although at that time these obligations were not expressly recorded in an international convention.

(g) *Customary international human rights law: from soft to hard law?*

Against the development of human rights treaty law, a debate has occurred as to whether human rights as a whole or in part have become part of customary international law. This is particularly significant for domestic law outcomes, since a number of domestic systems provide for automatic incorporation of customary international law as part of the law of the land; and a few even rank it superior to domestic

[263] HRC Resolution 5/1: Human Rights Council Institution-building Package, 18 June 2007.

legislation.[264] Some writers argue that the entire substance of the UDHR has acquired the status of customary international law.[265] These arguments are commonly based on the invocation of the UDHR by officials[266] and in UN bodies, and tend to de-emphasise traditional state practice.[267] Other writers take a more nuanced[268] approach and conclude that a limited selection of the rights enunciated in the UDHR, the International Covenants and human rights treaties reflect customary international law.[269] This approach finds some support in decisions of the ICJ which refer to certain fundamental human rights as reflecting customary international law.[270] Although the rights put forward by various writers have been criticised on the basis that it seems to reflect the rights considered important under domestic law,[271] in principle this is a sound approach as it takes account of the extent to which particular human rights norms are realised in practice. Oscar Schachter argued that on that basis, a number of the rights enunciated in the UDHR have sustainable claims to the status of customary law:

264 B. Simma and P. Alston, 'The Sources of Human Rights Law: Custom, *Jus Cogens*, and General Principles' (1988–9) 12 *Aust. YBIL* 83, 86.

265 For example, L. Sohn, 'The Human Rights Law of the Charter' (1977) 12 *Texas Int'l LJ* 129, 133; J. P. Humphrey, 'The Universal Declaration of Human Rights: Its History, Impact and Juridical Character' in B. G. Ramcharan (ed.), *Human Rights: Thirty Years After the Universal Declaration* (The Hague, Martinus Nijhoff, 1979), pp. 21, 37; McDougal, Lasswell and Chen, *Human Rights and World Public Order*, pp. 273–4, 325–7; L. Henkin, *The Age of Rights* (New York, Columbia University Press, 1990), p. 19. Some suggest that the UDHR is an authoritative interpretation of the obligations of states under Arts. 55 and 56 of the UN Charter: L. Sohn, 'The New International Law: Protection of the Rights of Individuals Rather than States' (1982) 32 *Amer. Univ. LR* 1, 17; T. Buergenthal, 'International Human Rights Law and Institutions: Accomplishments and Prospects' (1988) 63 *Washington LR* 1.

266 See e.g., L. C. Chen, 'Restatement: Protection of Persons' (1989) 14 *Yale JIL* 542, 546–7.

267 B. Simma and P. Alston, 'The Sources of Human Rights Law: Custom, *Jus Cogens*, and General Principles' (1988–9) 12 *Aust. YBIL* 83, 99.

268 *Ibid.* 92.

269 O. Schachter, 'International Law in Theory and Practice: General Course in Public International Law' (1982-V) 178 *RdC* 21, 334; T. Meron, *Human Rights and Humanitarian Norms at Customary Law* (Oxford, Clarendon Press, 1989), pp. 97, 134; American Law Institute, *Restatement (Third) of the Foreign Relations Law of the United States* (St Paul, Minn., American Law Institute, 1987), para. 701, n. 2; H. Hannum, 'The Status of the Universal Declaration of Human Rights in National and International law' (1995–6) 25 *Ga. J Int'l and Comp. Law* 287, 319–51.

270 See e.g., *Barcelona Traction, Light and Power Co. Ltd (Belgium* v. *Spain)* [1970] ICJ Rep. 4, 32; *United States Diplomatic and Consular Staff in Tehran (United States* v. *Iran)* [1980] ICJ Rep. 3, 42.

271 Simma and Alston, 'The Sources of Human Rights Law', 94–5.

General statements by international bodies that the 'Universal Declaration constitutes an obligation for the members of the international community' are not without significance, but their weight as evidence of custom cannot be assessed without considering actual practice. National constitutions and legislation similarly require a measure of confirmation in actual behaviour. One can readily think of numerous constitutions that have incorporated many of the provisions of the Universal Declaration or other versions of human rights norms, but these provisions are far from realization in practice. Constitutions with human rights provisions that are little more than window-dressing can hardly be cited as significant evidence of practice or 'general principles' of law.[272]

Whatever the content of customary international human rights law, structurally it has the same implications for individuals as human rights treaties: individuals have particular international rights which correspond to obligations imposed upon states. Some of the academic discourse has, however, indicated a potential role for individuals in the application of more flexible arrangements for the creation of custom. Schachter argued that the usual process of customary law formation – state practice accompanied by *opinio juris* – is inapt in the human rights context, since states do not usually make claims on other states or protest violations against another state's nationals.[273] Taking up this line of argument and progressing it, some have argued that a 'modernised view of customary international law' ought to be applied to human rights, such that non-state actors such as international organisations and NGOs would have the ability to contribute to create custom.[274] This more flexible approach to the determination of a particular claim to customary status has the potential to engage individuals in international law-making, either through their participation in NGOs[275] or through a further extension of this approach to take account of an individual's claims or views in respect of customary human rights. Although there is a large measure of support for approaching customary human rights with some flexibility, the determination of rules of custom has remained primarily focussed on the actions and interactions

[272] O. Schachter, 'International Law in Theory and Practice: General Course in Public International Law' (1982-V) 178 *RdC* 21, 335.

[273] *Ibid.* 334.

[274] I. R. Gunning, 'Modernizing Customary International Law: The Challenge of Human Rights' (1991) 31 *Virgina JIL* 211, 213, 221–2, 227–8.

[275] Alternatively NGOs might have a claim to legal personality as a separate entity: see A.-K. Lindblom, *Non-Governmental Organisations in International Law* (Cambridge, Cambridge University Press, 2005).

of states. While it might be argued that NGOs and other organised non-state groups have influenced states to accept the customary status of human rights norms, that influence seems to have occurred through an informal process (i.e. by lobbying) and the crucial actors in relation to the creation of human rights law continue to be states.[276]

One practical impact which the recognition of customary international human rights law may have is where it gives rise to a right of enforcement in domestic law. In some states, domestic law provides for automatic reception of customary international law as the law of the land, or provides a statutory remedy for violations of customary international law through domestic courts. The only state which has any developed practice in respect of customary international human rights law is the US, where individuals may be permitted to bring an action in tort alleging a violation of the law of nations.[277] Such provisions in effect permit an individual to enforce their customary international law human rights through domestic processes. This possibility is, of course, to be distinguished from a situation where treaties provide individuals with capacity to claim a violation of human rights before an international body, on the basis that the latter provides individuals with standing under international law, whereas the former provides a right of enforcement in domestic law where the substance of the claim is to be determined by reference to customary international law.[278] Further, since states will in most cases be afforded immunity in domestic courts against any such action, the only possibility is to bring claims against individuals, either because of their role in an official state function or because human rights obligations are considered as extended, through customary international law, to other individuals and non-state entities. The extent to which international law recognises

[276] For example, see C. Ochoa, 'The Individual and Customary International Law Formation' (2007) 48 *Virginia JIL* 119.

[277] The Alien Tort Claims Act gives such a power to aliens (28 USC s. 1350). See *Sosa* v. *Alvarez-Machain*, 124 S. Ct 2739 (2004). See also the Torture Victims Protection Act 1992 (codified as a note to 28 USC s. 1350), under which both citizens and aliens may bring more limited claims against designated 'rogue' states. In respect of the US practice, the dissenting judges in the *Arrest Warrant* case noted that this may be seen as 'the beginnings of a very broad form of extraterritorial jurisdiction' in civil matters: *Arrest Warrant of 11 April 2000 (Democratic Republic of Congo* v. *Belgium)*, Preliminary Objections and Merits [2002] ICJ Rep. 3, Separate Opinion of Judges Higgins, Kooijmans and Buergenthal, para. 48. They commented that although 'this unilateral exercise of the function of guardian of international values has been much commented on, it has not attracted the approbation of States generally'.

[278] See discussion in 4.4(d)(iii) above.

such obligations is open to question. But these domestic processes are notable because in effect they provide individuals with an opportunity to enforce their customary international law rights - which has the potential to give greater significance to the question which human rights have acquired the status of customary law.

(h) Jus cogens *human rights norms*

While it is clear that not all human rights have the status of *jus cogens*, a number of human rights norms may have a valid claim to *jus cogens* status.[279] There is judicial practice asserting that human rights norms which have *jus cogens* status include the right to life,[280] the prohibition of torture,[281] prohibitions of summary execution, disappearance and arbitrary detention,[282] prohibitions of forced labour, torture and slavery,[283] equal protection before the law and non-discrimination,[284] and *non-refoulement.*[285] Treaty provisions which designate particular norms as non-derogable can provide an indication that a particular norm is *jus cogens.*[286] The Human Rights Committee expressed its view as follows in its General Comment no. 29:

[279] They may also have claims as obligations *erga omnes*: *Barcelona Traction, Light and Power Co. Ltd (Belgium* v. *Spain)* [1970] ICJ Rep. 4, 32, paras. 33–4. See generally, A. Orakhelashvili, *Peremptory Norms in International Law* (Oxford, Oxford University Press, 2006).

[280] *Victims of the Tugboat '13 de Marzo'* v. *Cuba*, Case no. 11.436, Inter-American Commission of Human Rights, 16 October 1996, Report no. 47/96, Inter-Am.CHR, OEA/Ser.L/V/II.95 Doc. 7 rev. 127 (1997), para. 79.

[281] *Prosecutor* v. *Furundžija*, Case no. IT-95-21-T, Judgment, 10 December 1998, (1999) 38 ILM 317, paras. 147–55; *Prosecutor* v. *Delalić, Mucić, Delić and Landžo*, Case no. IT-96-21-T, Judgment, 16 November 1998, para. 466; *Prosecutor* v. *Kunarac, Kovać and Vuković*, Case no. IT-96-23-T, Judgment, 22 February 2001, para. 454. See also *Siderman de Blake* v. *Republic of Argentina*, US Court of Appeals (Ninth Circuit), 22 May 1992, 103 ILR 472; *Bouzari* v. *Islamic Republic of Iran*, Court of Appeal of Ontario, 30 June 2004, 128 ILR 586, para. 36; *Suresh* v. *Canada*, Supreme Court of Canada, 11 January 2002, 124 ILR 344, paras. 61–5.

[282] *Xuncax* v. *Gramajo*, District Court, District of Massachusetts, 12 April 1995, 104 ILR 165, 184.

[283] *Doe* v. *Unocal Corp.*, 110 F. Supp 2d 1294, 1304 CD Cal. 2000, US Court of Appeals (Ninth Circuit), 18 September 2002.

[284] *Juridical Condition and Rights of the Undocumented Migrants*, Case no. OC-18/03, Inter-American Court of Human Rights, Advisory Opinion, 17 September 2003, para. 101.

[285] UNHCR Executive Committee, Conclusion no. 25 (XXXIII-1982), para. (b); see also J. Alain, 'The *Jus Cogens* Nature of Non-refoulement' (2002) 13 *Int'l Journal of Refugee Law* 538 (cf. Goodwin-Gill and McAdam, *The Refugee in International Law*).

[286] E. De Wet, 'The Role of Human Rights in Limiting the Enforcement Power of the Security Council: A Principled View' in E. De Wet and A. Nollkaemper (eds.), *Review of the Security Council by Member States* (Oxford, Intersentia, 2003), p. 22.

> The enumeration of non-derogable provisions in article 4 [ICCPR] is related to, but not identical with, the question whether certain human rights obligations bear the nature of peremptory norms of international law ... [T]he category of peremptory norms extends beyond the list of non-derogable provisions given in article 2, paragraph 2. States-parties may in no circumstances invoke article 4 of the Covenant as justification for acting in violation of humanitarian law or peremptory norms of international law, for instance by taking hostages, by imposing collective punishments, through arbitrary deprivations of liberty or by deviating from fundamental principles of fair trial, including the presumption of innocence.[287]

One consequence of recognition of the *jus cogens* status of a particular human rights norm is that the right it secures to individuals has guaranteed intractability; it cannot subsequently be set aside or modified by agreement between states.[288] The position of individuals might therefore be described as more secure in relation to *jus cogens* human rights in comparison with other human rights, which are more susceptible to amendment, withdrawal or termination by states, albeit encumbered by political opposition.

Whether *jus cogens* norms have effects outside of the law of treaties is more controversial. It has been argued that *jus cogens* norms may have an operative effect on the powers of international organisations, international tribunals and even national courts.[289] The extent to which a broad view of the effects of *jus cogens* human rights norms would impact upon the status of individuals in international human rights law is not clear. It may be that any such impact would be a knock-on effect rather than a direct effect: for example, if *jus cogens* human rights norms are considered to broaden the extent to which the Security Council can authorise the use of force, there is no direct impact on the position of the individual vis-à-vis the international legal system, although the end result may be that there is greater protection of individual human rights in practice.

(i) The evolution of enforcement mechanisms: the regional systems

In addition to the European human rights system, regional systems for protection of human rights exist in Latin America and Africa; there is

287 Human Rights Committee, General Comment 29, States of Emergency (Art. 4), UN Doc. CCPR/C/21/Rev.1/Add.11 (2001).

288 O. Schachter, 'International Law in Theory and Practice: General Course in Public International Law' (1982-V) 178 *RdC* 21, 340.

289 See generally, Orakhelashvili, *Peremptory Norms in International Law.*

also an Arab Charter on Human Rights, which was adopted by the Council of the League of Arab States in 1994 but is not yet in force.[290] Like the European system, the Inter-American and African systems developed from region-specific concerns. The Organisation of American States was motivated by concern about lack of representation in the UN and defence of the region.[291] The Organization for African Unity was primarily concerned with the unification of Africa and prohibiting colonialism. Both the 1978 American Convention on Human Rights (ACHR)[292] and the 1981 African (Banjul) Charter[293] impose obligations on member states with respect to the rights enumerated therein. In this way they are similar to the ECHR and the UN Covenants and Conventions. They also use language which indicate that rights are conferred directly on individuals.[294]

In their mechanisms for enforcement, the Inter-American and African systems have similar structures to the original system established by the ECHR. But in the Inter-American system in particular, these provisions have been interpreted liberally and in favour of recognising individual rights to participate in enforcement procedures. For example, initially the Inter-American Commission was not given competence to receive individual communications,[295] but in practice it did

[290] Arab Charter on Human Rights, adopted by the Council of the League of Arab States by Resolution 5437, 15 September 1994 (not yet in force), reproduced in (1997) 18 *HRLJ* 151.

[291] An antecedent existed in the International Union of American Republics: see generally, S. Davidson, *The Inter-American Court of Human Rights* (Dartmouth, Aldershot, 1992), pp. 7–27; C. G. Fenwick, *The Organization of American States* (Washington, DC, self-published, 1963). The International Union of American Republics comprised the US, Argentina, Bolivia, Brazil, Chile, Colombia, Costa Rica, Ecuador, El Salvador, Guatemala, Haiti, Honduras, Mexico, Nicaragua, Paraguay, Peru, Uruguay and Venezuela. See C. Medina Quiroga, *The Battle of Human Rights: Gross, Systematic Violations and the Inter-American System* (Dordrecht, Martinus Nijhoff, 1988), pp, 21–3.

[292] American Convention on Human Rights (ACHR), Art. 1, 22 November 1969 (entry into force 18 July 1978), 1144 UNTS 123. See generally, T. Buergenthal and R. E. Norris (eds.), *Human Rights: The Inter-American System* (New York, Oceana Publications, 1993), vol. I, Booklet 2.

[293] 1981 African (Banjul) Charter, Art. 1.

[294] For example, ACHR, Arts. 6, 7(1); African (Banjul) Charter on Human and Peoples' Rights (ACHPR), Arts. 5–7, 27 June 1981 (entry into force 21 October 1986), 21 ILM 58.

[295] See A. P. Schreiber, *The Inter-American Commission on Human Rights* (Leiden, Sijthoff, 1970), pp. 31–40, who recounts the discussion about a right of petition in the Committee and the Council. Eleven affirmative votes were needed for approval of each provision in the Council: the articles which would have given the Commission power to examine petitions were defeated. The provision which would permit the Commission to receive petitions from individuals, groups and organisations received nine votes in favour (Chile, Colombia, Cuba, Ecuador, El Salvador, Honduras, Mexico,

receive individual communications and it used those communications to make recommendations to particular member states in its reports.[296] In 1965, this *de facto* expansion of jurisdiction was normalised in amendments to its Statute.[297] In 1969, the ACHR gave the Commission compulsory jurisdiction for individual complaints and optional jurisdiction for inter-state complaints;[298] in this way it operated differently from the European Commission, which had compulsory jurisdiction for inter-state complaints and optional jurisdiction for individual petitions.

A similar approach has been taken by the Inter-American Court of Human Rights, which was established by the ACHR, in favour of allowing individuals to participate in proceedings. The Court was given jurisdiction similar to the ECtHR in its first incarnation: either the Commission or the respondent state could submit a case to the Inter-American Court, provided that the respondent state has accepted the Court's jurisdiction.[299] The Court adopted measures to give individual petitioners wide scope for involvement. When the Commission refers a case to the Court, it is required to notify the petitioner.[300] If a

Peru and Venezuela) and two against (the US and Bolivia), with ten abstentions. A weaker alternative provision which would have permitted the Commission to 'act upon' communications relating to some human rights was defeated with ten in favour, two against and nine abstentions.

296 Medina Quiroga, *The Battle of Human Rights*, p. 70. At its first session, the Commission requested the OAS Council to amend its Statute to permit it to receive individual communications, arguing that its mandate to defend human rights required it to see that those rights were not violated. Not all the members of the Commission agreed with this request: US representative Dr Duward Sandifer argued that a right to determine individual petitions would create resentment and a lack of confidence in the Commission: see Schreiber, *The Inter-American Commission on Human Rights*, pp. 45–6; OAS, Inter-American Commission on Human Rights, *Report on the Work Accomplished during its First Session: October 3 to 28, 1960*, OEA/Ser.L/V/II. 1 (Doc. 32) (14 March 1961), p. 13, cited in Schreiber, *The Inter-American Commission on Human Rights*, p. 45.

297 1965 Statute, Art. 9*bis*. See generally, C. Medina, 'The Inter-American Commission on Human Rights and the Inter-American Court of Human Rights: Reflections on a Joint Venture' (1990) 12 *HRQ* 439. Subsequently, the Commission established two separate procedures for individual communications: the first used communications to inform general requests to states to provide reports on measures it was taking with respect to human rights; the second was a special procedure for 'examining' individual petitions relating to a specified list of rights or relating to reprisals against complainant individuals.

298 ACHR, Arts. 44 and 45.

299 *Ibid*. Art. 51(1), 62; see discussion of the Inter-American Court below.

300 Rules of Procedure of the Inter-American Commission on Human Rights, Rule 71, approved by the Commission at its 109th Special Session, 4–8 December 2000, last amended on 7–24 October 2003. The executive secretary is also to provide the petitioner with all the elements necessary for the preparation and presentation of the application. This seems to imply that the petitioner is involved in drafting the

petitioner requests, he or she may act as a delegate representing the Commission before the Court.[301] When an application is filed, the Court's Rules of Procedure also require that the original complainants be notified;[302] the alleged victim, next of kin or their designated representative is permitted to present written pleadings, motions or evidence.[303] Once the application is admitted, the victims or their representatives may 'submit their pleadings, motions and evidence, autonomously, throughout the proceedings'[304] and they are permitted to examine witnesses, experts and any other persons the Court decides to hear.[305] Further, victims may present a request for provisional measures.[306] Where the Court finds a violation of the Convention, it may order remedies including assurance of restoration of the right and compensation for pecuniary and non-pecuniary loss.[307] In its annual reports to the OAS General Assembly, the Court specifies cases where a state has not complied with a judgment; compliance then becomes a matter to be pursued through the political processes of the Organization of American States.[308]

In the African system, initially the African Commission of Human and Peoples' Rights[309] was competent to receive communications from individuals, provided a simple majority of the members of the Commission agreed.[310] Since 1994, the Commission has permitted individuals to be represented before it, either by legal representatives or by

application: Rule 72 of the Rules provides, however, that the application is submitted by the Commission, in accordance with Art. 61(1) of the Convention.

301 Rules of Procedure of the Inter-American Commission on Human Rights, Rule 69, approved by the Commission at its 109th Special Session, 4–8 December 2000, last amended on 7–24 October 2003.

302 Rules of Procedure of the Inter-American Court of Human Rights, rule 35, *Annual Report of the Inter-American Court of Human Rights, 1991*, OAS Doc. OEA/Ser.L/V/III.25 doc.7 (1992), p. 18.

303 *Ibid.* Rule 36. 304 *Ibid.* Rule 23.

305 *Ibid.* Rule 42(2). Where there is more than one victim or representative they must designate a 'common intervenor' who is authorised to present pleadings, motions and evidence during proceedings, including during the hearing: see Rule 23(2).

306 *Ibid.* Rules 22 and 28(2). See generally, J. M. Pasqualucci, *The Practice and Procedure of the Inter-American Court of Human Rights* (Cambridge, Cambridge University Press, 2003), pp. 20–1.

307 See S. Davidson, *The Inter-American Court of Human Rights* (Dartmouth, Aldershot, 1992), pp. 87–8; on pecuniary loss see *Mapiripán Massacre* v. *Colombia*, Merits, Reparations and Costs, 15 September 2005, Inter-Am. Ct HR ser. C. no. 134; on non-pecuniary loss see *Aloeboetoe et al.* v. *Suriname*, Reparations and Costs, 10 September 1993, Inter-Am. Ct HR ser. C no. 15, para. 62.

308 ACHR, Art. 63; see also *Velásquez Rodríguez (Interpretation of Compensatory Damages)*, Judgment, 17 August 1990, Inter-Am. Ct HR ser. C no. 9 (1990), paras. 30–2.

309 ACHPR, Art. 30. 310 *Ibid.* Arts. 55 and 56.

NGOs.[311] In 2004, the Protocol on the African Court of Human and Peoples' Rights entered into force,[312] which established a second supervisory body for the African Charter. On 2 July 2006, eleven judges of the Court were sworn in and the Court began operating in late 2009. It has compulsory contentious jurisdiction[313] for cases submitted by the Commission, states and African intergovernmental organisations and optional jurisdiction for cases submitted by individuals and by NGOs with observer status before the Commission.[314] The Protocol establishing the Court indicates that the Court should bear in mind the complementarity between the Commission and the Court in dealing with questions of admissibility;[315] but the Court's Interim Rules do not shed light on the question whether the Court should effectively act as an appeal court in matters which fall within the jurisdiction of the Commission.[316] This may be dealt with more comprehensively in the forthcoming review of the Court's rules.[317]

It will be recalled that in the European system, initially there were two supervisory bodies: the Commission, which had optional jurisdiction for individual petitions; and the Court, to which only the Commission and states could refer cases. In 1994, Protocol no. 9 enabled individuals to bring cases before the Court, using a preliminary screening procedure. However, in November 1998, its provisions were overtaken by Protocol no. 11, which replaced the Commission and the Court with a new single organ, the European Court of Human Rights. The new Court has competence to receive applications directly from individuals: Article 34 entitles 'any person, non-governmental organisation or a group of individuals claiming to be the victim of a violation' by a state party to make

[311] Rules of Procedure of the African Commission on Human and Peoples' Rights, adopted 6 October 1995, ACHPR/RP/XIX, Rule 120(1).

[312] Protocol to the African Charter on Human and People's Rights on the Establishment of an African Court on Human and Peoples' Rights, 9 June 1998 (entry into force 25 January 2004), OAU Doc. OAU/LEG/EXP/AFCHPR/PROT (III).

[313] *Ibid.* Arts. 3–4.

[314] *Ibid.* Art. 5; see also Art. 34(6). The provision for individuals and NGOs to file cases was drafted taking into account the models from the Inter-American system, the European system and the UN system under the First Optional Protocol to the ICCPR: V.O. Orlu Nmehielle, *The African Human Rights System: Its Laws, Practice, and Institutions* (The Hague, Martinus Nijhoff, 2001), pp. 266–7.

[315] Protocol to the African Charter on Human and People's Rights on the Establishment of an African Court on Human and Peoples' Rights, Art. 10, 9 June 1998 (entry into force 25 January 2004), OAU Doc. OAU/LEG/EXP/AFCHPR/PROT (III).

[316] See Interim Rules of Court, 20 June 1998, available at www.african-court.org/en/.

[317] See www.african-court.org/en/news/latest-news/.

an application. Under the amendments effected by Protocol no. 11, the right of individual application is automatic and mandatory; it does not require the respondent state to have opted-in. An application is only admissible where local remedies are exhausted.[318] When an application is declared admissible, the hearings are normally held in public;[319] if no friendly settlement is reached, a reasoned judgment is given.[320] A judgment by a Chamber may be referred 'in exceptional circumstances' by a party to a Grand Chamber, whose judgment is final.[321] If the Court finds a violation of the ECHR has occurred, there is no express power to order remedial measures, only a power to award just satisfaction in circumstances where the internal law of the respondent state 'allows only partial reparation'.[322] In practice, the ECtHR has awarded compensation for pecuniary loss provided that the loss is proved and that it was caused by a breach of the Convention.[323] The Court may also order compensation for non-pecuniary loss, particularly in the case of violation of the right to life.[324]

In the regional systems, there has been a move towards individual rights of enforcement in international forums which has not been imitated or reproduced in the universal human rights treaties. Particularly in the Inter-American system, the evolution of the enforcement mechanisms has been driven by the institutions themselves: by involving individuals as far as possible in their proceedings, and arguably to the extent that the institutions have overstepped their jurisdictional competence. In all three regional systems there seems to have been a move towards strengthening individualised claims processes, at least until 1998.

Since 1998, the European system has witnessed a move towards the resolution of human rights violations through domestic processes and law. This has been caused by the massive number of applications received by the ECtHR: as at 1 May 2009, there were 105,450 pending applications before the Court.[325] To try to address

[318] Protocol no. 11 to the Convention for the Protection of Human Rights and Fundamental Freedoms, Restructuring the Control Machinery Established Thereby, Art. 35(1), 11 May 1994 (entry into force 1 November 1998), ETS no. 5.

[319] *Ibid.* Arts. 40(1) and 38(2). [320] *Ibid.* Art. 45. [321] *Ibid.* Arts. 43–4. [322] *Ibid.* Art. 41.

[323] See e.g., *Akdivar* v. *Turkey, Just Satisfaction*, ECtHR Grand Chamber, 1 April 1998, 23 EHRR 365.

[324] See e.g., *Salman* v. *Turkey*, Merits, ECtHR Grand Chamber, 27 June 2000, 34 EHRR 17, para. 140. See generally, C. D. Gray, 'Remedies for Individuals under the European Convention on Human Rights' (1981) HRR 153.

[325] See www.echr.coe.int/NR/rdonlyres/BBFE7733-3122-40F5-AACA-9B16827B74C2/0/Pending_applications_chart.pdf.

the great number of repetitive applications arising from systemic violations, in September 2003, the Court implemented a 'pilot judgment' procedure. This involved issuing a lead judgment once a particular systemic issue had been identified, which triggers an accelerated execution procedure before the Committee of Ministers to require the state to provide domestic redress with retroactive effect. Individual applications raising the same issue are stayed pending domestic redress, although the stay is lifted if no redress is provided within a reasonable time.[326] The pilot procedure was first used by the Court in 2004 in *Broniowski* v. *Poland*, to address claims for the failure to provide compensation for the loss of land and property after the Second World War (the so-called 'Bug River' claims). A Chamber judgment was issued in June 2004;[327] at that time, 167 related applications were pending before the Court and it noted that some 80,000 people were affected by the same issue. In July 2004, the Court adjourned all pending and future Bug River applications 'pending the outcome of the lead case and the adoption of the measures to be taken at national level'.[328] In Poland, a domestic compensation scheme was established which the Court held 'made its further examination of ... other similar applications no longer justified'.[329] In September 2008, the Court struck out all the remaining applications and closed the pilot judgment procedure, in respect of Bug River claims.[330]

Another proposed reform to deal with the number of applications has been to impose additional admissibility criteria. Protocol no. 14, which entered into force on 1 June 2010,[331] will amend the Convention to

326 See *Position Paper of the European Court of Human Rights on Proposals for Reform of the European Convention on Human Rights and Other Measures as Set Out in the Report of the Steering Committee for Human Rights of 4 April 2003 (CDDH(2006)006 final)*, ECtHR, CDDHGDR(2003)024 (26 September 2003), paras. 43–6.

327 *Broniowski* v. *Poland*, Application no. 31443/96, ECtHR, Judgment, 22 June 2004.

328 See 'Bug River cases adjourned', European Court Press Release, 31 August 2004.

329 *Wolkenberg and others* v. *Poland*, Application no. 50003/99, ECtHR, 4 December 2007; *Witkowska-Tobola* v. *Poland*, Application no. 11208/02, ECtHR, 4 December 2007.

330 *EG* v. *Poland*, Application no. 50425/99, ECtHR, 23 September 2008, striking out all 176 pending like applications. See generally, P. Leach, 'Beyond the Bug River: A New Dawn for Redress before the European Court of Human Rights?' (2005) *EHRLR* 148. The same procedure was applied in *Sejdovic* v. *Italy*, Application no. 56581/00, ECtHR, 10 November 2004.

331 See status of signatures and ratifications: www.conventions.coe.int/Treaty/Commun/ChercheSig.asp?NT=194&CM=1&DF=9/3/2007&CL=ENG. Russia ratified Protocol no. 14 in January 2010.

provide that a case may be declared inadmissible by the Court if it considers that:

> the applicant has not suffered a significant disadvantage, unless respect for human rights as defined in the Convention and the Protocols thereto requires an examination of the application on the merits and provided that no case may be rejected on this ground which has not been duly considered by a domestic tribunal.[332]

The effect of this provision will be to limit the right to bring an application to individuals who are victims of a violation of the Convention and who have also suffered a 'significant disadvantage', unless 'respect for human rights' requires the ECtHR to examine the application.

Further proposals for reform are now pending before the Committee of Ministers, including establishing the competence of a single judge to declare applications admissible or strike them out, and to empower committees of three judges to declare admissible and rule on the merits of applications which raise questions that are already the subject of well-established case law.[333] Like Protocol no. 14, these proposals have the potential to limit the scope of the right of individual application. The extent to which they will effectively abrogate the right of individuals to achieve redress for violations will depend on their form: frequent reference has been made to the right of individual application as 'being the distinctive and unique achievement of the Convention system';[334] and a number of recent opinions of the EctHR have emphasised the centrality of the right of individual application.[335] In 2002 the then-President of the Court noted that without reform, in any event 'the right of individual

[332] Protocol no. 14 to the Convention for the Protection of Human Rights and Fundamental Freedoms, Amending the Control System of the Convention, done at Strasbourg, 13 May 2004, ETS no. 194.

[333] See Report of the Committee of Wise Persons, 15 November 2006 (available at https://wcd.coe.int/ViewDoc.jsp?Ref=CM(2006)203&Sector=secCM&Language=lan English&Ver=original&BackColorInternet=9999 CC&BackColorIntranet=FFBB55& BackColorLogged=FFAC75); European Court of Human Rights, Opinion of the Court on the Wise Persons' Report, 2 April 2007; Council of Europe, Comments on Reflection Group Discussions on Enhancing the Long-term Effectiveness of the Convention System, AI Index: IOR 61/002/2009, March 2009 (available at www.londonmet.ac.uk/ londonmet/library/m35690_3.pdf). See generally, P. Leach, 'Access to the European Court of Human Rights: From a Legal Entitlement to a Lottery?' (2006) *HRLJ* 11; L. Wildhaber, 'A Constitutional Future for the European Court of Human Rights?' (2002) *HRLJ* 161.

[334] See e.g., Reflection Group on the Protection of the Reinforcement of the Human Rights Protection Mechanism, *Activity Report*, CDDH-GDR (2001) 010 (15 June 2001).

[335] See e.g., *Mamatkulov and Askarvo* v. *Turkey*, Applications nos. 46827/99 and 46951/99, ECtHR Grand Chamber, 4 February 2005, para. 122.

application will in practice be . . . seriously circumscribed by the material impossibility of processing them in anything like a reasonable time'.[336]

While it is possible to view these amendments to the individual claims procedures as a move away from automatic individual rights of enforcement, with emphasis instead on improving processes within the state, the primacy of domestic processes has been a constant feature in the decisions of the ECtHR. Moreover, the Court has been in dire need of reforms which will significantly ease its workload, else it would face collapse under the sheer number of cases. The emphasis placed in reforms on the right of individual application as a core feature of the European system suggests that these reforms do not herald a move away from individualised rights of enforcement.

(j) Conclusions

Universal and regional treaties for the protection of human rights in the period since 1945 have conferred direct rights on individuals and imposed corresponding obligations on states to respect and protect those rights. Initially there was a marked reluctance to impose obligations on states in respect of human rights: the UN Charter did not contain any such obligations and the UDHR, although it used language which suggested the direct conferral of individual rights, did not impose any legal obligations on states. The first human rights treaty (properly so-called) to directly confer rights on individuals and corresponding legal obligations on states was the ECHR, in 1950. Other regional systems in the Americas and Africa developed later, but along similar lines. In the UN system, a number of subject specific conventions and the two 1966 UN Covenants conferred rights on individuals and imposed obligations on states, although these were more limited in the case of the ICESCR. These treaties are consistent with the post-1945 framework of the international legal system, which acknowledges that individuals may acquire direct rights from international law.

There has also been progressive and significant development of individual rights to seek redress for violations in international forums. In the regional systems, these mechanisms provide individuals with access to judicial procedures before international bodies. There has been a steady development of these enforcement procedures in favour of individualisation of claims. Recent reforms and current proposals for

[336] Wildhaber, 'A Constitutional Future for the European Court of Human Rights?', 161, 164.

reforms in the ECtHR have emphasised the centrality of the right of individual application in the European system, and measures taken to ease the workload of the Court are better viewed as practical steps to ensure the feasibility of the Court going forward, rather than as signifying a trend away from individualised rights of enforcement.

The UN Conventions have not provided for the same methods of enforcement as those established in the regional systems; rather, they have generally adopted a model of an opt-in individual communication procedure, which enables a supervisory committee to adopt 'Views' in respect of particular violations. These procedures provide individuals with a right of access to an international forum to complain of violations of the relevant rights. In general these individual rights of redress to an international forum are consistent with the post-1945 framework of the international legal system, in that they provide individuals with a means to enforce their international rights in their own name before international tribunals. The extent to which that 'enforcement' is meaningful varies.

There has been limited development of the notion of individual responsibility under international human rights law, although the notion of responsibility for non-state actors generally has generated much discussion in the literature.[337] Some international treaties have purported to impose duties on individuals, but these have been cast in broad and generalised terms.[338] None of these provisions are subject to enforcement in an international forum. While individual responsibility under international law for international crimes is now entrenched in the international legal system, there has been no development of any other form of responsibility of individuals for breaches of international human rights law. Article 58 of the ILC's Articles on State Responsibility reserves, in general terms, the possibility of 'individual responsibility under international law of any person acting on behalf of a State', a reservation which is not limited to criminal responsibility. In domestic legal regimes, only the US has legislation dealing (in a very uneven way) with this issue,[339] and in some civil law countries, an *action civile* might be

[337] See e.g., A. Clapham, 'Human Rights Obligations of Non-state Actors in Conflict Situations' (2006) 88 *IRRC* 491; P. Alston (ed.), *Non-State Actors and Human Rights* (Oxford, Oxford University Press, 2005); S. R. Ratner and J. S. Abrams, *Accountability for Human Rights Atrocities in International Law: Beyond the Nuremberg Legacy* (2nd edn, Oxford, Oxford University Press, 2001).

[338] See e.g., UDHR, Art. 30; ACHR, Arts. 29–38; and ACHPR, Arts. 27–9.

[339] Private parties (US or foreign) can be sued for torts occasioned 'in violation of the law of nations' anywhere committed against aliens, under the unusual jurisdiction created

attached to criminal prosecutions for international crimes.[340] In the UK, implementation of the ECHR through the Human Rights Act 1998 imposed an obligation on courts to decide cases compatibly with the Convention,[341] and this has resulted in human rights being taken into account in the determination of disputes between private parties, the so-called 'horizontal effect' of the Human Rights Act. However, this does not amount to the direct imposition of human rights obligations on individuals, but instead it has resulted in the Convention being used as a means to interpret the common law consistently with the human rights obligations of states.[342] In addition, the UN Human Rights Committee,[343] the UN Committee on the Elimination of Discrimination Against Women,[344] the Inter-American Court of Human Rights[345] and the European Court of Human Rights[346] have held states liable for failing to take measures to prevent human rights violations by non-state actors within their jurisdiction, suggesting that any individual liability in respect of human rights is a matter to be secured by states under domestic law, rather than an obligation imposed on individuals by international law.

5.5 Conclusions: the position of the individual in international human rights law

Prior to 1945 there was no general international law of human rights nor was there an exception to the general prohibition of interference in

by the Alien Tort Claims Act (28 USC s. 1350). See *Sosa* v. *Alvarez-Machain*, 124 S. Ct 2739 (2004). The US cases distinguish between corporate complicity with governmental violations of human rights, and those violations (e.g., torture, slavery) which do not require any governmental involvement or state action.

340 K. Parlett, 'Universal Civil Jurisdiction for Torture' (2007) *EHRLR* 385.

341 Human Rights Act 1998 (cap. 42), s.6(3)(a).

342 See e.g., *Douglas* v. *Hello!; Venables* v. *News Group* [2002] 2 WLR 992, and *Campbell* v. *MGN* [2003] 1 WLR 740.

343 For example, *Delgado Paéz* v. *Colombia*, Human Rights Committee, Communication no. 195/1985, 12 July 1990; *Santullo* v. *Uruguay*, Human Rights Committee, Communication no. 9/1977, 20 February 1977. See also Human Rights Committee, General Comment no. 20 (44) 1992, Art. 7, CCPR/C/21/Rev.1/Add.3.

344 UN Committee on the Elimination of Discrimination Against Women, General Recommendation 19, 'Violence Against Women', UN Doc. A/47/38 (30 January 1992), para. 9.

345 *Velásquez Rodríguez* v. *Honduras*, Inter-American Court of Human Rights, 29 July 1988, ser. C no. 4, para. 172.

346 *Costello-Roberts* v. *United Kingdom*, ECtHR, 1993, ser. A no. 247-C, para. 27; *Waite and Kennedy* v. *Germany*, Application no. 26083/94, ECtHR, Judgment, 18 February 1999; *Denise Matthews* v. *United Kingdom*, Application no. 24833/94, ECtHR, 18 February 1999.

matters within the reserved domain of states in respect of human rights. Although there were rules of international law which sought to benefit individuals and to protect them dating back to at least the nineteenth century, these rules imposed obligations on states to accord certain standards of treatment on individuals without conferring upon those individuals international rights.

In the inter-war period, measures taken in international law to protect individuals can be characterised under two models: the first, like other rules of the nineteenth and early twentieth centuries, benefitted individuals without conferring upon them direct rights; the second conferred direct rights on certain groups of individuals under treaties, most clearly in measures for the protection of minorities and refugees.[347] Thus, although some rules conferred direct rights upon individuals, consistently with the post-1945 framework of the international legal system (and with the PCIJ's Opinion in *Danzig*), structurally other rules benefiting individuals were consistent with the nineteenth century framework.

Measures taken to benefit or protect individuals in the inter-war period were also significant because they gave individuals international protection against treatment by their own state. These measures represented a significant incursion into the traditional reserve of domestic jurisdiction, in a way which is analogous to the operation of post-1945 human rights law. They were inconsistent with the pre-1945 framework of the international legal system, which considered the relationship between a state and its nationals to be a matter beyond the remit of international law.

Since the Second World War, human rights have come to occupy a more prominent place in international law and to form part of general international law. Initially, there was little support among states for transforming rhetoric and declarations of human rights into legal rights and obligations: the UN Charter imposed no express obligations on states to respect or protect human rights, and conferred no international law rights on individuals and the UDHR declared individual rights but did not impose correlative legal obligations on states. Structurally and formally, these statements were consistent with the pre-1945

[347] In addition to individual rights, these measures may have conferred rights on groups as such. Consideration of the position of groups (including groups of individuals) in international law is beyond the scope of this thesis; for present purposes it is sufficient to note that these measures at least (if not also) conferred rights on individuals.

framework of the international legal system, since they conferred no international rights on individuals. The first international human rights convention to confer obligations on states and rights on individuals was the ECHR in 1950; in the 1960s the two UN Covenants also established rights for individuals and corresponding obligations for states; other international human rights treaties in the UN and regional systems have followed this same structural pattern. These treaties are consistent with the post-1945 framework of the international legal system, in that they confer international law rights on individuals. Many of the rights proclaimed in these treaties are also now reflected in customary international law; and further, may have acquired the status of *jus cogens* norms. In relation to rights which are reflected in *jus cogens* norms, individuals have relatively intractable rights; their position can be said to be more secure than the position in relation to other treaty or customary rules which may be more easily revoked or terminated.

Mechanisms have also been put in place to provide individuals with the possibility of appeal to an international forum (a commission, court or committee) to seek redress for violation of their rights. Individuals thus have means to enforce rights in their own name before an international forum, without the interposition of municipal law: consistent with the post-1945 framework of the international legal system. The efficacy of the international forum, and the extent to which it provides individuals with an effective means of enforcement, varies greatly, but structurally these mechanisms treat individuals as having independent and autonomous rights in the international legal system. In general, there has been a steady progression towards individualised claims, particularly in the regional systems. In the European system, reforms have been implemented and proposed which would have the effect of limiting the right of individual application, while placing emphasis on the need for domestic processes and laws to address violations of human rights (or to prevent them from occurring). These reforms have been motivated by a dire need to ease the workload of the ECtHR, and are better viewed in that way, rather than as indicating a move away from individualised claims processes.

PART III
Reassessing the Framework

6 Reflections on the structures of the international legal system

6.1 Introduction

As has been seen, the international legal system has changed from a nineteenth century system focussed exclusively on inter-state relations to a system of law which covers a wider range of entities, including individuals. The shift from a system which conceived of individuals as mere objects to a system in which individuals have a certain status and capacity has been traced in Part II of the thesis. In each of the areas examined - international claims, humanitarian law, criminal law and human rights law - provisional conclusions have been drawn concerning the position of the individual in that particular field. It remains to draw together themes and observations about the individual in the international legal system. The second section of the chapter examines the extent to which the doctrine and practice examined in Part II reflect the orthodox accounts of the structure of the international legal system in the periods set out in Part I. The third section discusses the doctrine of subjects, engaging with critiques of the doctrine and placing the individual in terms of international legal personality. In a final section, discussion centres on what the case of the individual reveals about transition in the international legal system, and what it reveals about the position of states.

6.2 Historical development of the position of the individual in the international legal system

(a) The nineteenth century international legal system

In the nineteenth and early twentieth centuries, the established understanding of the international legal system was that its exclusive concern was relations between states, and that individuals were not subjects of, and could derive no rights or obligations directly from, international law.[1] The examination of doctrine and practice in Part II, across the four areas, broadly supports this orthodox account. In general, international law did not engage individuals as right-holders or duty-bearers; nor did it recognise individual capacity to participate in the international system by bringing international claims. To the extent that the purpose was to protect or benefit individuals, this was achieved through the imposition of obligations on states, rather than by the conferral of international law rights on individuals.

Consistent with the orthodox account of the international legal system, two oft-cited antecedents for the direct engagement of individuals in the international legal system appear on closer inspection better characterised as arrangements regulating the conduct of individuals through the imposition of obligations on states. Piracy *jure gentium* was a special source of national jurisdiction which permitted states to prosecute individuals under their municipal law; international law did not directly impose obligations on individuals in respect of piracy; rather, it endorsed the power of states to prosecute individuals.[2] The abolition of slavery also operated exclusively through inter-state obligations imposed by treaty, in which the individual was an object of beneficial regulation.[3]

There were, however, a few exceptions. One was the Central American Court of Justice which permitted individuals to seise the Court with questions of 'violations of treaties or conventions'.[4] The Court, which was in operation for a decade, examined five cases brought by individuals; the one case held admissible was decided in favour of the respondent state. There was no specific requirement that the relevant treaty or convention ascribe a particular right to an individual to form the basis of a claim; rather, the Court's approach suggested that individuals had standing to complain that a state had violated an obligation characterised as an inter-state violation. The single case brought by an individual which proceeded to the merits focussed on the question whether the respondent state had complied with inter-state obligations of treatment and did not refer to individual

[1] See 1.2(b) above.

[2] 'Harvard Research Draft on Piracy' (1932) 26 *AJIL Supplement* 739, 759; see 4.2 above.

[3] Slavery Convention, 25 September 1926 (entry into force 9 March 1927), 60 LNTS 253, no. 1414; see 5.2 above.

[4] El Salvador–Nicaragua–Costa Rica–Honduras–Guatemala, Art. 2, 20 December 1907, (1908) 2 *AJIL* 231.

international law rights. The Central American Court of Justice was the only functioning international tribunal which permitted individuals to pursue claims independently. It treated individuals as having the capacity to bring international claims, but that capacity was not specifically linked to individuals as substantive right-bearers.[5]

A second exception was the treatment of armed opposition groups in civil conflict. Civil conflict caused problems for naval states when either or both of the lawful government and the insurgents claimed belligerent rights at sea. In response to these practical problems, maritime powers began to recognise belligerent rights. Initially, recognition of belligerency was linked to recognition of at least *de facto* independence, since it was thought that only states could be the subject of belligerent (international law) rights. From around the middle of the nineteenth century, recognition of belligerency was detached from recognition of independence. Thus, belligerent (international law) rights were recognised for groups and individuals who did not necessarily have a valid claim to statehood. It was not clear whether rights adhered to the group as such or to its individual members, but in practice individual members were treated as possessing rights. The possession of belligerent rights was linked to an express intentional act of recognition, either by the state in whose territory the conflict occurred, or by foreign states. The engagement of individuals in the international legal system was thus controlled exclusively by states. Individuals had no entitlement to international law rights unless and until a state expressly conferred or recognised them. Although it was argued that a duty of recognition arose in circumstances where the group or the conflict fulfilled certain criteria, this was never generally accepted and in practice states retained a wide measure of discretion in whether to recognise belligerent rights in the context of a particular conflict. In this way, states remained gatekeepers of the international legal system: the ability of individuals to acquire international law rights was dependent on a specific intentional act by a state adopted as a matter of policy.

At the time when recognition of belligerency and insurgency was detached from recognition of independence, the practice bore a marked uncertainty as to how it could be reconciled with the orthodox account of the international legal system: how entities which were not states could be granted belligerent rights under international law. It appears that governments had an appreciation of the problem but did not fully

[5] See 2.2(b)(ii)(D) below.

engage with it. Rather, they responded to a practical problem by recognising that international law rights accrued to non-state entities, without confronting the question of reconciling that recognition with the established understanding of the international legal system. The engagement of the individual in the international legal system was not the end to which the recognition of belligerency and insurgency was directed; rather, it was a by-product of a limited practice developed in response to a practical problem.

Even at the height of the practice at the end of the nineteenth century, recognition of belligerency and insurgency was not necessarily considered to be linked to recognition of legal personality. In 1890, Hall argued that the recognition of belligerent rights did not connote legal personality on the part of the rebels; rather that it was 'from the legal point of view a concession of pure grace'.[6] It was only after 1945, when a more flexible notion of legal personality had begun to be accepted, that scholars suggested that legal personality necessarily flowed from the recognition of belligerent rights.[7] In the period from the nineteenth century through to 1914, there was no conception of individuals possessing international legal personality, even where there had been recognition of belligerency or insurgency.

In contrast to these exceptional elements of international law during the nineteenth century, the vast majority of doctrine and practice supported the established understanding of the framework of the international legal system at that time. Before 1919, there was no developed conception of individual criminal responsibility under international law; rather, individual responsibility was a matter for domestic law and domestic processes. In this period there was no notion of a general international law of human rights and where measures were taken in international law to benefit or protect individuals (such as the abolition of slavery and rules of warfare to alleviate the suffering of victims), they were effected through inter-state obligations in which the individual was an object of regulation, rather than a right-holder.

(b) The inter-war period

In the inter-war period the established understanding of the international legal system was effectively unchanged: the theory held that

[6] W. E. Hall, *A Treatise on International Law* (3rd edn, Oxford, Clarendon Press, 1890), p. 35.

[7] See e.g., T.-C. Chen, *The International Law of Recognition* (London, Stevens & Sons Ltd, 1951), p. 306; E. Castrén, *Civil War* (Helsinki, Soumalainen Tiedeakatemia, 1966), pp. 136–67.

individuals could not bear rights and duties under international law directly; nor was it possible for individuals to be characterised as subjects of international law. During this period there was significant development in respect of individual rights, but it effected no immediate transformation of the orthodox account of the international legal system. In 1928, the PCIJ held that the object of a treaty 'may be the adoption by the Parties of some definite rules creating individual rights and obligations and enforceable by the national courts'.[8] While the *Danzig* Opinion is now commonly cited as recognising that individuals could hold international law rights and obligations, at the time this was not generally accepted as an accurate analysis – not least by influential members of the PCIJ itself.[9] International legal doctrine maintained that individuals could not bear rights or obligations directly under international law, and that individuals were objects, not subjects, of international law.

But in practice, the idea of individuals being granted rights under treaties was taken up across several fields. This can be seen in relation to claims, where international claims tribunals and commissions were about evenly split between those processes in which individuals pursued claims directly, claims over which they had exclusive control, and those processes which operated on the basis of diplomatic protection, brought by a state in respect of injury to its national.[10] It is also seen in some of the often-cited antecedents of international human rights law, most clearly in the arrangements for protection of minorities and some of the rules relating to the treatment of refugees.[11] Further, some of the rules of humanitarian law treaties referred to rights for individuals, although it was unclear whether these rights were derived from international rather than national law.[12]

The extent to which individuals derived rights and capacities from international law depended on an express and clear grant of such right or capacity by states. In the *Danzig* Opinion, the Court expressed a requirement of a clear intention on the part of states. In practice, the *Danzig* Opinion was often cited by tribunals dealing with claims brought directly by individuals, and the requirement of a clear intention was not

[8] *Jurisdiction of the Courts of Danzig (Pecuniary Claims of Danzig Railway Officials who have Passed into the Polish Service, Against the Polish Railways Administration)*, PCIJ Rep. ser. B no. 15 (1928) 3, 17–18.

[9] D. Anzilotti, *Cours de droit International* (Paris, Librairie de Recueil Sirey, 1929), pp. 407–8, 133–4; see 1.2(c) above.

[10] See 2.3(b) above. [11] See 5.3 above. [12] See 3.1(b) above.

questioned. Thus, the position of states as the exclusive gatekeepers of the international legal system was preserved: states retained a monopoly on access to rights, obligations and capacities.

The record also reveals that the conferral of direct rights on individuals was used as a means to some other particular end, rather than reflecting a conscious attempt to transform the structures of the international legal system. The development of rules concerned with the treatment of individuals within state borders, for example to protect minorities, was driven by concerns arising from the significant reorganisation of boundaries following the First World War, and was not the manifestation of an attempt to extend international law to an area traditionally considered as reserved to domestic jurisdiction.[13] The engagement of individuals as rights-holders was the by-product of particular forces, not an end in itself.

In respect of the protection of individuals during the inter-war period, international law continued largely to express rules which benefited or protected individuals by the imposition of obligations on states, and without conferring direct rights on individuals. For example, the vast majority of the rules governing the conduct of international armed conflict continued to operate in terms of obligations imposed upon states to protect and benefit individuals, and were not expressed in terms of rights.[14] Some of the early arrangements for refugees and the ILO conventions also imposed obligations upon states without conferring correlative rights on individuals.[15] Individuals were therefore protected in two ways: either as indirect beneficiaries of obligations imposed upon states, or as direct right-bearers under international treaties. These structural devices do not appear to have been applied in accordance with any overarching sense that one or the other was more appropriate in a given situation; indeed it seems that little attention was given to which was more effective or appropriate for a particular rule or set of rules. So, for example, arrangements for the protection of refugees in the early part of the inter-war period generally imposed obligations upon states without conferring rights on individuals, whereas later arrangements were expressed to confer rights on individuals. Minorities were protected by treaties which conferred direct rights upon them subject to the oversight of the League of Nations, whereas the inhabitants of mandated territories were protected by arrangements which did not appear and were not interpreted,

[13] See 5.3(a) above. [14] See 3.1(b) above. [15] See 5.3(d) above.

at least at that time, as conferring upon them direct rights. There is no discernible pattern or distinction between the application of one or other of these normative frameworks, and in particular there seems to have been no consideration given to the question of which normative framework was better suited to the type of benefit or protection.

In this period, a principle of individual responsibility under international law was implied by the Treaty of Versailles: for the Kaiser, responsibility was foreshadowed for violations of the 'sanctity of treaties',[16] whereas for all other individuals, responsibility was envisaged for violations of the laws and customs of war. Prior to the Treaty of Versailles, the only developed conception of individual responsibility for war crimes was that arising under domestic law. However, these provisions of the Treaty of Versailles were not executed and in practice individual responsibility was only enforced under domestic law, through (manifestly defective) domestic processes.[17] No conception of individual obligations directly under international law arose in this period in any other context: a convention for an international criminal court was drafted but was abortive.

In general, the developments in the inter-war period reflect a sense of transition and change in the structures of the international legal system. This is particularly evidenced in the reluctance of some commentators to accept the apparent consequences of the PCIJ's Opinion in *Danzig*. Yet in practice - on the part of states and tribunals - that reluctance was not manifested; *Danzig* was frequently cited in support of individual rights under treaties, enforceable before international tribunals, and a significant proportion of the arrangements for the protection of individuals under the auspices of the League used the structural device of individual rights to achieve that protection.

(c) The post-1945 international legal system

In the period between 1945 and the present day, it has come to be accepted in orthodox doctrine that individuals may derive rights and obligations directly under international law, which may be enforced in international tribunals. The effect of *Danzig* was only realised in this period; and eventually the ICJ held that treaties may confer rights on individuals by plain language.[18] In doctrine the bearing of rights and obligations has been more closely linked with international legal

[16] Treaty of Versailles, Art. 227, 28 June 1919, UKTS 4 (Cmd 153). [17] See 4.3 above.
[18] *LaGrand (Germany* v. *United States)*, [2001] ICJ Rep. 466, 492–4 (para. 77).

personality: it has come to be acknowledged that to the extent that individuals possess rights and duties, they are subjects of international law.

In practice, individuals have been accorded rights under treaties across a range of areas of international law. This is most clearly the case in international human rights law: universal and regional conventions treat individuals as holding rights which they may enforce in an international tribunal having jurisdiction, or through an international forum with an established complaint mechanism.[19] In internal armed conflict, individuals may possess both rights and obligations under common Article 3 of the Geneva Conventions and Additional Protocol II, or applicable customary international humanitarian law.[20] In the context of protection of foreign investment, although it depends on the particular BIT, it has been accepted that the terms of a BIT, interpreted in their context and in light of the treaty's object and purpose, may confer substantive rights on individual investors coterminous with the host state's obligations of treatment. In addition, it is also more common for states to establish treaty mechanisms which confer on individuals capacity to enforce their own rights before international tribunals or to seek redress through international complaint mechanisms. It is generally accepted that individuals have at least a procedural right to seek international arbitration claiming for violation of a BIT, provided it contains a relevant dispute resolution clause.[21] Both individual rights and individual capacities to enforce rights are dependent on a specific grant of right or capacity by states which might be given prospectively (as in the case of an offer to arbitrate in a BIT) or retrospectively (as in the case of the Iran–US Claims Tribunal and the UN Compensation Commission): access to the international legal system has remained within the exclusive control of states.

Although it is common to accord direct rights to individuals, rules for the protection of individuals do not operate exclusively through this structural device. A number of rules aimed to benefit individuals impose obligations on states without conferring rights on individuals. For example, international humanitarian law applicable in international armed conflict generally establishes standards of treatment as obligations on individuals and does not confer direct rights on individuals. While in the inter-war period it appeared that the choice between one or other of these structural devices was not reasoned, in this period

[19] See 5.4 above. [20] See 3.3(c) above. [21] See 2.4(c) above.

it has been argued that one or other normative framework may be used because it is better adapted or more effective in relation to the particular rule.[22] It has been suggested that in international armed conflict, a normative framework of standards is more effective than an individual rights framework in ensuring the protection of individuals. This may explain why international humanitarian law has retained its inter-state normative framework, rather than operating within an individual rights framework.[23] The sense that a particular normative framework is applied to a given situation because it was considered to be better tailored to the type of benefit or protection, or to the circumstances in which that benefit or protection was applied, was not present in the inter-war period; rather, a kind of coherence in the application of normative frameworks is a post-1945 development.

While individuals are given rights across a range of fields, the only developed conception of individual obligations has occurred in relation to international crimes. After Nuremberg, the principle of individual responsibility for international crimes was generally accepted but there was some reluctance to accept that this necessarily entailed that individuals were directly subject to international law. This reluctance is reminiscent of the reluctance which surrounded individual rights in the inter-war period, the full ramifications of the PCIJ's Opinion in *Danzig* only forming part of the orthodox account some twenty years later. With the work of the ICTY, ICTR and now the ICC, there can now be no question that individual responsibility for international crimes is imposed by international law and without the interposition of domestic law. However, the question of the source of the obligations remains unclear: the ICTY held that individual responsibility arose under treaty and customary international humanitarian law; the ICTR held that individual responsibility was imposed through the jurisdictional provisions of its Statute; and the ICC has not yet taken a position on the question. Although under either interpretation individual responsibility arises under international law directly, the better interpretation is that individual responsibility arises under customary international law and exists independently of jurisdiction to enforce in an international tribunal.[24]

The development of individual responsibility for international crimes (which is rightly traced to Nuremberg) occurred in response to the

[22] R. Provost, *International Human Rights and Humanitarian Law* (Cambridge, Cambridge University Press, 2002), pp. 54–6; see 3.3 above.

[23] See 3.3 above. [24] See 4.4 above.

practical question of what ought to be done with the major war criminals. While it is common to present the Nuremberg Charter and trial as a kind of inevitability in response to the horrors of the Second World War, the historical record presents a rather different picture. For the British and the Americans, there was a reluctance to commit to a judicial process rather than summary executions, and judicial treatment was pursued because Stalin was not amenable to a political disposition. Again, an international military tribunal was a political solution to a practical problem, and individual responsibility under international law was a by-product of that solution. The surge of enthusiasm for international criminal law around the 1990s was also motivated by a search for practical solutions in post-conflict reconstruction and development. In general, there is a sense that the development of individual responsibility under international law for international crimes was a graft onto the international legal system motivated by practical and political concerns and that it was not inevitable even in September 1944, less than twelve months before the Nuremberg Charter was signed.[25]

Notable by its absence is any capacity for individuals to formally participate in the process by which they acquire rights and obligations, or more generally in the making of international law. To the extent that individuals acquire rights, obligations and capacities, it is through a passive process, directed primarily, if not exclusively, by states. Individuals cannot agree to the conferral of rights or the imposition of obligations, for example, through participating in international treaties. In general, there has been little concern as to whether individuals consent to bearing rights, obligations and capacities. In the context of armed opposition groups in internal armed conflict, it has been suggested that these groups and individuals acquire rights and obligations through a process of consent, similar to that required for third party states to acquire rights and obligations under treaties. In other contexts there has been no consideration of whether individuals so consent. This absence might be explained in some circumstances by considerations of beneficence which imply that consent is irrelevant; in other contexts, particularly where obligations are imposed on individuals, the question of consent may be more significant. Moreover, this demonstrates the differential treatment of states and individuals: between active subjects

[25] See 4.4(a)(i) above.

and passive recipients of rights and obligations in the international legal system.

In the extent to which individuals exercise rights, individuals have a more active role, but even in this context the exercise of rights is dependent on a pre-existing grant (which like any treaty is revocable in certain circumstances). In international claims practice, whether an individual submits a claim to arbitration (for example, in relation to foreign investment) is a question solely within that individual's control and dependent on its resources. In this sense, the individual is not completely passive, but the extent to which it is capable of acting in the international legal system is still conditioned on a grant of capacity by a state. So, while the post-1945 period may be perceived as one which has witnessed the rise of the individual, it must be emphasised that states have remained central and in control of the extent to which individuals may engage in the international legal system: the extent to which individuals are given rights, obligations and capacities is dependent on a specific grant from the primary actors in the international legal system, dominated by states.

6.3 International legal personality as the measure of engagement: the case of the individual

(a) 'Subjects' versus 'objects'

As discussed in Part I,[26] since at least the end of the nineteenth century the device used to explain the relationship of entities to the international legal system has been the doctrine of the subjects of international law, which divides entities into binary categories of 'object' and 'subject'. In the nineteenth century international legal system, it was said that subjects of international law were states 'solely and exclusively'.[27] In the inter-war period the possibility of the League of Nations being a subject of international law since it had 'distinctive international rights and duties' was raised but not resolved.[28] In the post-1945 international legal system it has been accepted that to the extent that entities other than states 'directly possess' rights, powers and duties in international

[26] See discussion at 1.4 above.

[27] L. Oppenheim, *International Law: A Treatise* (1st edn, London, Longmans, Green & Co., 1905), pp. 18–19, para.13.

[28] A. McNair, *Oppenheim's International Law* (4th edn, London, Longmans, 1928), vol. I, pp. 133–4.

law they may be regarded as subjects of international law.[29] The opening of the doctrine of subjects is generally traced to the 1949 *Reparations* Opinion, where the ICJ introduced a variegated approach to the subject categorisation, holding that the extent of a subject's rights, duties and capacities in the international legal system 'depends on the needs of the [international] community'.[30] Thus, the subjects of international law are not identical: states possess the full range of rights, duties and attendant capacities, whereas other subjects may have more limited rights, obligations and capacities.

As noted in Part I, the variegated approach to subjects of international law has the consequence that there are qualitatively different subjects. At one end of the spectrum, a state, which has a complete ability to acquire rights, obligations and capacities and to enter into legal relations, is apt to be described as a subject of international law; while at the other end of the spectrum, a non-governmental organisation which is recognised by a single intergovernmental organisation as having standing before it is also apt to be described as a subject of international law. There must be significant qualitative differences between the two ends of the spectrum. Yet in orthodox doctrine there are no criteria for locating subjects according to the measure of their rights, obligations and capacities. Thus, the variegated approach to the doctrine of subjects has exposed a fundamental deficiency of the doctrine: that the identifier 'subject' has no objective and meaningful content, since it denotes no particular capacities: hence it fails to provide any revealing description of the relationship of the entity to the international legal system. As Eli Lauterpacht has noted:

> there is no definition of personality in international law which is sufficiently comprehensive to apply in some constructive or realistic way to all the different types of entities which operate in the international field.[31]

It has been suggested, for good reason, that using the term 'international legal personality' to refer to a particular bundle of rights, obligations and capacities or to refer to subjects which qualify to a certain threshold of capacities is undesirable. D. P. O'Connell

[29] R. Jennings and A. Watts, *Oppenheim's International Law* (9th edn, London, Longmans, 1992), p. 16, para. 7.

[30] *Reparations for Injuries Suffered in the Services of the United Nations*, Advisory Opinion, [1949] ICJ Rep. 178.

[31] E. Lauterpacht, 'The Development of the Law of International Organization by the Decisions of International Tribunals' (1976-IV) 152 *RdC* 377, 403.

suggested that it was more meaningful to inquire into the particular legal capacities of entities in relation to the international system, rather than limiting the identifier 'personality' to entities holding a certain level of capacities.[32] Referring to the *Reparations* Opinion, O'Connell suggested that 'personality' was only a shorthand term for the proposition that an entity has specific legal capacities. Whereas states might possess the full range of legal capacities, other entities which had more limited capacities could still be considered as having legal personality:

> So a State may have the capacity to do acts X, Y and Z, the United Nations to do acts Y and Z, the International Labour Organisation to do act X, and the human being to do acts X and Y. All four entities have capacities. To deny that the last three have personality is to argue that only entities with all capacities are persons, an argument that removes all meaning from the term 'personality'. This was the error of generations of international lawyers who asserted that 'States only are the subjects of international law'.[33]

In addition to the term 'capacity', various alternatives for describing the relation of individuals to the international legal system have been proposed. For example, Roslyn Higgins rejects the subject/object dichotomy as having 'no credible reality and ... no functional purpose'.[34] Drawing upon the New Haven process approach, she suggests that within the process of international law there are a variety of 'participants' who make claims corresponding to their values.[35] Within this framework, what matters is not the designated status of an entity but its actual exercise of functions.[36]

Higgins' notion of participation is elaborated by Robert McCorquodale, who argues that the notion can be divorced from Higgins' broader conception of international law as process.[37] He suggests that 'participation' connotes greater flexibility than the binary categories

[32] D. P. O'Connell, *International Law* (2nd edn, London, Stevens and Sons, 1970), vol. I, p. 83.
[33] *Ibid.* p. 82.
[34] R. Higgins, *Problems and Process: International Law and How We Use It* (Oxford, Oxford University Press, 1994), p. 49.
[35] *Ibid.* p. 50.
[36] R. Higgins, 'Conceptual Thinking about the Individual in International Law' (1979) *New York Law School Law Review* 11, 16.
[37] R. McCorquodale, 'The Individual and the International Legal System' in M. Evans (ed.), *International Law* (2nd edn, Oxford, Oxford University Press, 2006), pp. 307, 311; R. McCorquodale, 'An Inclusive International Legal System' (2004) 17 *LJIL* 477, 481.

of subjects and objects, and that this flexibility reflects current doctrine, as reflected in the ICJ's treatment of international legal personality.[38]

A similar approach is advocated by Christoph Schreuer, who prefers to examine the relationship of entities to the international system by an examination of their 'functions'. He argues that the gradual diffusion of powers amongst different participants has challenged the dominance of sovereign states in the international legal system. He concludes:

> we should adjust our intellectual framework to a multi-layered reality consisting of a variety of authoritative structures. Under this functionalist approach what matters is not the formal status of a participant ... but its actual or preferable exercise of functions.[39]

The notions of capacities, participation and functions are conceptually useful because they suggest that what is significant is not the formal status of an entity, but its actual ability to engage in the international legal system in a given context. Whether an entity can act in the international legal system in a particular way is dependent not on its formal status, but rather it depends on that entity's capacities and functions. Since the generalised identifier of 'subject' is not revealing of any particular ability to act in the international legal system, an examination of the capacities, participations or functions of an entity must be undertaken to determine whether and to what extent an entity is able to act or engage in the international legal system.

Where the notions of capacities, participation and functions do not assist is in locating entities in the international legal system: in distinguishing between qualitatively different subjects, from those entities bearing a single international right or obligation at one end of the spectrum, to entities with the full range of rights, responsibilities and capacities at the other.

The qualitative difference between different subjects was reflected, in early treatises, in the use of the term 'subject' to denote full members of the international community (i.e. states) and the use of the term 'international person' to refer to a broader category of entities which were engaged in the international legal system to a more limited

[38] *Reparations for Injuries Suffered in the Services of the United Nations*, Advisory Opinion, [1949] ICJ Rep. 178.

[39] C. Schreuer, 'The Waning of the Sovereign State: Towards a New Paradigm for International Law' (1994) 4 *EJIL* 447, 453.

extent.[40] But as noted in Part I, any distinction between the concept of a subject of international law and international legal persons was conflated at least with the ICJ *Reparations* Opinion, where it was held that the UN was an 'international person', meaning that 'it is a subject of international law'.[41] In some contexts, a distinction is drawn between 'full' and 'partial' subjects, or 'full' and 'partial' international legal personality, but even this fails to achieve much differentiation: rather, it only serves to divide the subjects of international law into binary categories of 'states' and 'others'.

While dividing the subjects of international law into 'states' and 'others' might seem overly simplistic, it is nevertheless helpful to identify which capacities distinguish subjects at one end of the spectrum from subjects at the other end of the spectrum. In particular, two capacities would appear to distinguish entities which have autonomy and independence in the international legal system (termed, for convenience, 'autonomous subjects') from entities which have only limited and passive capacities in the international legal system ('passive subjects'). The first is the extent to which an entity has control over its own receipt of rights, obligations and capacities: whether it receives capacities only when it consents or whether capacities are imposed upon it without regard for its consent. An entity which has this type of control would have capacity to prevent international law from being imposed upon it by other international law-makers, without its consent. The second capacity is an entity's control over the delegation of functions and capacities to other entities: the extent to which it can control access to the international legal system. Entities which enjoy this capacity may be described as 'gatekeepers'. Entities which have both these capacities have an independent capacity to participate in the international legal system, whereas entities which possess neither may only participate in the international legal system at the instigation of and with the consent of these independent subjects. The latter are passive to the extent that they have no independent capacity to participate or exercise functions in the international legal system.

In sum, the doctrine of subjects in international law no longer provides a revealing description of the relationship of entities to the

[40] See e.g., 'Full Sovereign States are perfect, not-full Sovereign States are imperfect International Persons, for not-full Sovereign States are for some parts only subjects of International Law': Oppenheim, *International Law*, p. 99; see 1.4 above.

[41] *Reparations for Injuries Suffered in the Services of the United Nations* [1949] ICJ Rep. 174, 179.

international legal system. The formal status of an entity does not assist in explaining the reality of its ability to engage and act in the international system. Rather, that ability can only be discerned by examining an entity's particular capacities and functions in the international legal system. The notions of functions, participation and capacities suggest that it is necessary to lift the 'veil' of formality surrounding the doctrine of subjects, but they do not assist in qualitatively distinguishing between entities in the international legal system, and in particular they do not distinguish between entities which have autonomy and independence and those which have a more passive role: entities which acquire rights, obligations and capacities by consent, and which control access to the international legal system, on the one hand; and entities which may only participate in the international legal system at the instigation of and with the consent of the more independent and autonomous entities. Entities which possess these two capacities enjoy qualitatively meaningful participation in the international legal system, whereas entities which possess neither have significantly less meaningful capacity to participate in that system.

(b) Locating individuals: rights, obligations and capacities

Applying the doctrine of subjects to the question of the position of the individual in the international legal system reveals a shift from the international legal system of the nineteenth century to that of the present day. From the nineteenth century to 1914, the orthodox account of the framework of the international legal system held that individuals were objects, not subjects, of international law, since international law conferred no rights or duties on individuals.[42] In general this was reflected in the doctrine and practice during this early period, although there were certain limited exceptions which acknowledged rights to individuals. The established understanding of the international legal system in the inter-war period also maintained that individuals were not subjects of international law, since it was 'untenable as a general proposition' that individuals could acquire rights and duties under international law.[43] It will be recalled that although the PCIJ held in 1928 that it was possible for international treaties to confer rights on

[42] Oppenheim, *International Law*, pp. 18–19, para. 13; G. Manner, 'The Object Theory of the Individual in International Law' (1952) 46 *AJIL* 428, 428–9.

[43] McNair, *Oppenheim's International Law*, vol. I, p. 520.

individuals,[44] during the inter-war period the Opinion did not effect a shift in traditional doctrine.[45] During the inter-war period, doctrine and practice followed the trend reflected in the PCIJ's Opinion: individuals were given direct rights under international law where states so intended. But it was not generally acknowledged in doctrine that this meant that individuals had become subjects of international law, instead of objects. In the period since 1945 it has become part of the orthodox understanding of the international legal system that (a) individuals can have rights and duties flowing directly from international law; and (b) to the extent that individuals have rights, duties and capacities under international law, individuals are subjects of international law.[46] In 2002, Judge Cançado Trinidade, in a separate opinion in the Inter-American Court of Human Rights, emphasised that it was now impossible to sustain the opposite view, that individuals were not subjects of international law:

> The doctrinal trend which still insists in denying to individuals the condition of subjects of International Law is based on a definition of these latter, requiring from them not only to possess rights and obligations emanated from International Law, but also to participate in the process of creation of its norms and of the compliance with them. It so occurs that this rigid definition does not sustain itself.[47]

So individuals are subjects of international law to the extent that they derive rights, obligations and capacities directly from international law. But qualitatively the capacities of individuals have been limited to receiving rights, obligations and particular capacities through processes in which they have no formal rights of participation. Thus, the way in which individuals may participate and exercise functions in the international legal system operates on a kind of dependency: it only occurs at the instigation and with the consent of other subjects of international law which control access to the international legal

[44] *Jurisdiction of the Courts of Danzig (Pecuniary Claims of Danzig Railway Officials who have Passed into the Polish Service, Against the Polish Railways Administration)*, PCIJ Rep. ser. B no. 15 (1928) 3, 17–18.

[45] See 1.2(c) above.

[46] Jennings and Watts, *Oppenheim's International Law*, p. 16, para. 7. See also O'Connell, *International Law*, pp. 107–8; Higgins, 'Conceptual Thinking about the Individual in International Law', 16; McCorquodale, 'The Individual and the International Legal System', 329; McCorquodale, 'An Inclusive International Legal System'.

[47] *Legal Status and Human Rights of the Child*, Inter-American Court of Human Rights, Advisory Opinion OC-17/02, 28 August 2002, (2004) 11 IHRR 510, concurring opinion of Judge Cançado Trinidade, paras. 26–7.

system. Thus, individuals remain subordinated in the international system, suspended between object and independent or autonomous subject.

This is clear when the means by which individuals obtain rights, obligations and capacities is considered. In 1928, the PCIJ held that individuals could obtain rights and obligations under an international treaty where the states parties to the treaty clearly intended to create those rights.[48] The ICJ subsequently affirmed that individuals can derive rights directly under international treaties, based on an examination of the clear text of the treaty, and without requiring an inquiry into the intention of the states parties to the treaty.[49] Also since 1945, the principle of individual responsibility for international crimes has affirmed that individuals may acquire obligations directly under international law – international law created by states. In a number of different contexts, individuals have acquired capacities to enforce their rights under international law and processes: although individuals have no inherent rights to participate in enforcement processes, those rights may be created by treaty. But all individual rights, obligations and capacities are imposed on individuals without particular regard for their consent in the process. Individuals have control to the extent that they may choose to exercise rights to enforce their rights, but the ability to exercise rights is preconditioned on a conferred capacity. Individuals have no meaningful or formal capacity to participate in the process by which international law is created. Thus, the way in which individuals obtain rights, obligations and capacities is to be contrasted with the way in which states receive them: for states, consent is required, either by participation in an international treaty, consenting as a third party beneficiary of a treaty, or acquiescence in the development of a customary rule. Thus, states have control over their rights, obligations and capacities under international law, whereas individuals have no such control.

It is relevant that in international criminal law, where there has been development of individual responsibility, there has been no concern as to whether individuals consent to the imposition of obligations upon them. In international humanitarian law applicable in internal armed

[48] *Jurisdiction of the Courts of Danzig (Pecuniary Claims of Danzig Railway Officials who have Passed into the Polish Service, Against the Polish Railways Administration)*, PCIJ Rep. ser. B no. 15 (1928) 3, 17–18.

[49] *LaGrand (Germany* v. *United States)* [2001] ICJ Rep. 466, 492–4 (para. 77).

conflict, it has been questioned how obligations can be imposed on a non-assenting entity – individuals participating in armed opposition groups – but there has been no generally accepted answer. While it has been argued that Additional Protocol II applies to armed opposition groups on the basis of their consent to be bound,[50] in practice it is treated as applicable without requiring that the groups (still less their composite individual members) consent.[51] Thus, in practice, rights and obligations are conferred on individuals without their consent. They are objects when it comes to acquiring rights, though they seem to be subjects for the purposes of exercising them.

McCorquodale acknowledges that individual capacities are largely tied to state consent, stating that for individuals, 'participation in the system could be viewed as largely dependent on State consent'.[52] But he suggests that, to a certain extent, individuals do have an independent role in the international legal system; that they 'do have considerable international rights and responsibilities in the system, a number of which are independent from a State's ability to control or determine them'.[53] In the context of rights, McCorquodale refers to customary international human rights and *jus cogens*, suggesting that these norms may have developed 'without a State having an express practice on the issue'.[54]

While it is increasingly common for individuals to be given rights and obligations (the latter at least in respect of conduct amounting to international crimes), in each of the situations examined in Part II, the conferral of rights and obligations has been exclusively dependent on the consent of states and has occurred independently of any consideration of whether individuals consent to the acquisition thereof. Where rights are conferred by treaty, they are created by the states parties to the treaty. Where rights are created by customary international law, that custom is the consequence of state practice – or at least failure of states to persistently object to the formation of a customary rule. And while certain rules in the field of human rights have claim to *jus cogens* status, they have originated in a rule agreed to or acquiesced in by states. They may not (as noted by McCorquodale) result from generally consistent state practice, but they result from either practice or acquiescence, including by an absence of protest. There are no *jus cogens* rules which

50 A. Cassese, 'The Status of Rebels under the 1977 Geneva Protocol on Non-International Armed Conflicts' (1981) 30 *ICLQ* 416, 423.

51 See 3.2(c)(ii) above.

52 McCorquodale, 'The Individual and the International Legal System', 311.

53 *Ibid.* 328. 54 *Ibid.* 313.

have developed to protect individuals over vigorous protest by a majority (or even a significant proportion) of states. The picture which emerges from Part II is that the role of individuals in the international legal system has remained heavily, if not exclusively, dependent on state consent.

Higgins also suggests a kind of independent participation of individuals in her construct of a symmetry between the subject matter of the field in which an entity participates and the interests of that entity. She suggests:

> In the way our world is organized, it is states who are most interested in, for example, sea-space, boundaries or treaties. It is thus states who advance claims and counter-claims concerning the values contained therein. Individuals' interests lie in other directions: in protection from the physical excesses of others; in their personal treatment abroad; in the protection abroad of their property interests; in fairness and predictability in their international business transactions; and, in securing some external support for the establishment of a tolerable balance between their rights and their duties within the national state. Thus, the topics of minimum standards of treatment of aliens, requirements as to the conduct of hostilities, and human rights, are not simply exceptions conceded by historical chance within a system of rules that operate as between states. Rather they are simply part and parcel of the fabric of international law, representing the claims that are naturally made by individual participants in contradistinction to those presented by state participants.[55]

While this notion is appealing, this symmetry does not appear to be reflected in international doctrine and practice: an interest in the subject matter of a field does not necessarily correspond to a capacity to participate in that field. Rather, capacity to participate is dependent on a specific grant of capacity by subjects which have autonomy and law-making capacity, primarily states. A clear example is found in the rules applicable in international armed conflict for the benefit of individuals: these rules are best characterised as inter-state obligations to accord certain standards of treatment which do not confer international rights on individuals directly. While individuals might be particularly interested in their protection from the effects of warfare which fails to distinguish between civilian and military targets, individuals have no rights under that law and no capacity to participate; rather, individuals are indirect beneficiaries of inter-state obligations – objects of the law.

In general, it does appear that there is a connection between the capacity of individuals to participate in a particular field of international

[55] Higgins, 'Conceptual Thinking about the Individual in International Law', 16.

law and their interest in that field: for example, individuals have significant capacities in relation to human rights (as noted by Higgins), international crimes and their treatment by foreign states (particularly in respect of investment). It is logical that there be such a connection. But there is not necessarily any symmetry between individual interests and individual capacities to participate.

Moreover, this conception of a symmetry between interests and direct capacity does not take account of the possibility that individual interests in a particular field may be best protected by a normative framework which does not necessarily accord them rights of participation: in relation to humanitarian law, it has been suggested that a normative framework of standards of treatment functions more effectively than a framework of individual rights. Direct participation by individuals is one model which operates to protect individual interests, but the assumption that it is the preferable model for that protection is open to question – and it can certainly not be assumed to be the exclusive model. Individuals might have direct interests in having the standard of minimum treatment of aliens respected, but this is not to say that individuals should have standing to bring claims which traditionally belonged to the realm of diplomatic protection to the ICJ. Individuals might well have direct interests in respect of the rules of warfare, but this does not necessitate that those individuals have substantive rights which would entitle them to reparation in case of violation. In those contexts, the state construct still serves some useful purpose. Furthermore, individuals may have rights – and effective remedies – through domestic law. The primacy of domestic law and remedies has been emphasised in recent times: it is reflected in the complementarity provisions of the ICC Statute, and it has been mentioned in the context of reforms to the European Court of Human Rights, an institution which is struggling to deal with the number of individual applications pending before it. In the end it may be more beneficial to individuals to focus efforts on improving domestic rights and remedies – and making them more consistent with international law standards – than to seek elevated standing in the international legal system in respect of each and every area in which individuals have interests.

(c) Moving from the actor to the action? The notion of international law relationships

Other critiques of international legal personality have taken a more reformist approach, suggesting that the doctrine places undue emphasis on the relevant actor, whereas what should be relevant is the action itself.

Referring to the qualitative differences between capacities to act in the international legal system, and noting that these are traditionally explained by differentiating between full and partial international legal personality, Walters argues that the link between capacities and legal personality should be questioned. He suggests that what should be relevant in determining whether an entity has capacity to act is not the particular status of that entity, but what the relevant act is. He argues:

> Whether or not a person can act in a specific manner depends on the applicable norms which allow or prohibit a certain action, not on his or her legal personality. [This] idea could be transferred to international law. One would then have to ask which norms govern a specific behaviour. The question would not be who acts, but rather whether the action in question is governed by international law or not. The focus consequently shifts from the international legal personality to what could be called an international law relationship.
>
> If the observation is correct that the reason for the primordial relevance of the notion of subjects of international law is the actor-centred structure of traditional international law, and if it is equally correct that the traditional actor-centred order is currently being, perhaps not really replaced, but at least supplemented and in part modified by a subject-oriented structure, then it may help as a first step to give up the notion of international legal personality as the corner stone of international law and replace it with the notion of an international law relationship. This would most probably change little as to the answers to specific legal questions, but it would contribute to a re-conceptualization of international law which takes into account the proliferation of its subjects which has taken place throughout the 20th century.[56]

While this might at first glance seem attractive, what Walters is proposing is not only an adjustment of the notion of international legal personality, but rather to do away with the established notions of explaining the relation of entities to the international legal system and to replace them with a new conception of international law. In that conception, international obligations would be imposed not be directed to specific entities, but rather would prohibit or permit certain action. Violations of human rights would be unlawful if committed by any entity, be it a state, corporation or individuals. Violations of international criminal law could be committed by individuals, corporations, states or state-owned entities. While this might be viewed as one way to more fully achieve the objectives to which international rights and

[56] C. Walters, 'Subjects of International Law' in R. Wolfrum (ed.), *The Max Planck Encyclopedia of Public International Law* (Oxford, Oxford University Press, 2008, online edition, www.mpepil.com), pp. 30–1.

obligations are directed, it would be a complete reconceptualisation of the way international law works.

Moreover, this study of the position of the individual demonstrates the extent to which the rules of international law are focussed on particular actors and that they are not in general subject-matter oriented. Rights and obligations in treaties are conferred or imposed on specific entities and not declared to exist in the abstract or at large. Rules of custom and general principles of law operate in the same way. In the existing international legal system, capacity to act is directly linked to possessing legal personality, even if the doctrine of international legal personality might not adequately distinguish between qualitatively different capacities.

6.4 Reflections on structural transition in the international legal system: the case of the individual

Part II of the thesis has traced the development of the position of the individual in the international legal system, from a system which was relatively closed to the individual to a system in which individuals have particular rights, obligations and capacities. From this examination, it is possible to venture some general observations about structural change in the international legal system. In this section two matters are discussed: first, the movement of the international legal system from a relatively inflexible and closed system to one which is more flexible and open; second, the way in which structural change occurs: in particular, how the structures of the international legal system have changed by the application of practical solutions to manage particular problems, rather than by reference to some overriding theoretical framework or pursuit of a structurally different system.

(a) Relative openness and flexibility of the system

Structurally the international legal system is now open to any entity on whom rights, obligations and capacities to function and participate are conferred. The post-1945 international legal system thus reflects an openness in strong contrast to Vattel's law of nations and the international law of the nineteenth century. The expansion of the doctrine of subjects and the provision of international rights and obligations for individuals represent only one aspect of this relative openness.[57]

[57] J. Crawford, *International Law as an Open System* (London, Cameron May, 2002), pp. 19–37.

This openness is a recurring theme in the material examined in Part II. The 1907 Central American Court of Justice and the treatment of insurgent groups and individuals in civil conflict from around the middle of the nineteenth century were exceptional at the time, but they are examples of states using international law to apply a solution to a practical problem with the result that the international legal system was adapted to engage other entities, including individuals. The particular solutions were creative at the time, given that they were not consistent with the traditional conception of international law as the law applicable to inter-state relations. These examples and others demonstrate that the international legal system has been used to serve changing needs without being constrained by the established understanding of the limits of the international legal framework. The same pattern can be discerned in the measures taken for the protection of individuals in the inter-war period, for minorities, inhabitants of mandated territories and refugees. It can also be seen in the development of individual criminal responsibility under international law and in other post-1945 developments, including claims mechanisms for human rights treaties and in the context of protection of foreign investment.

That the international legal system has been opened to other entities and devices created to provide those entities with capacities to act in the international system has not however replaced other devices in international law which protect or benefit those entities. The system of diplomatic protection has not been outright replaced by regimes for protection of foreign investment or human rights; rather those newer regimes continue to operate alongside the existing regimes. It seems unlikely that diplomatic protection will be replaced by these regimes or others; it continues to serve a useful purpose in the international system. In this way new developments in the international legal system can be seen to have resulted in a series of grafts onto the existing structure of the international legal system, rather than a replacement of the existing structure. Thus, the international legal system has developed multiple structural devices which can be used in a particular situation to address particular problems. In any given situation, more than one structural device may offer possible answers to those problems.

This examination of the position of the individual shows that while the structural limits of the system are de-emphasised, the way international law works has remained unchanged – that is, it operates to confer rights and impose obligations on specified entities, rather than declaring rights and obligations to exist in abstract terms. Where individuals are the subject of rights or obligations, they result from the imposition of a right or obligation which is directed at individuals. The way international law works has remained essentially unchanged, even if its reach has been extended beyond the traditional parameters of inter-state relations.

Another aspect of the enduring sub-structure of the international legal system is the centrality of states. The flexibility and openness of the international legal system has coexisted with the enduring centrality of states as the principal subjects and near-exclusive makers of international law.[58] States have retained the monopoly on access to the international legal system by their exclusive control over the creation of new international legal persons; additionally, states are the primary legislators of the international legal system, and thus have control over the delegation of rights, obligations and capacities to other potential actors, including individuals. States have retained exclusive or near-exclusive status as autonomous subjects of international law, while other entities might be considered passive subjects of international law, since they have no control over the way in which they receive rights and obligations and they have no capacity to control access to the international legal system by other entities.

(b) Forces for structural change: solutions above theories

A second observation is that the international legal system has experienced structural transition as a result of the need to manage and address practical problems rather than resulting from any deliberate attempt to effect a structural transformation. The international legal system does not appear to be developing along a smooth trajectory from a state-centric international law to a more inclusive international legal system.[59] The picture which emerges is rather that states manage practical questions as they arise by adaptation of the international legal system, and as a result of those practical solutions the international legal system may be transformed. That transformation does not seem to inhere in

[58] Spiermann suggests that international law is 'concerned not merely with relations between states, but more generally with issues affecting the interests of a plurality of states': O. Spiermann, 'Individual Rights, State Interests and the Power to Waive ICSID Jurisdiction under Bilateral Investment Treaties' (2004) 20 *Arbitration International* 179, 186.

[59] See e.g., the discussion in C. Grossman and D. D. Bradlow, 'Are We Being Propelled Towards a People-Centred Transnational Legal Order?' (1993–4) 9 *Am. U J Int'l L and Pol'y* 1.

any particular theoretical framework or any preconceived notions of a fixed set of goals for international law.

One example is the development of individual criminal responsibility. In an orthodox account of international criminal law, the move from the concept of war crimes prosecuted in national courts to international crimes prosecuted in an international court at Nuremberg is presented as if it were a *fait accompli*, a natural progression for an international law concerned with the commission of appalling crimes on a mass scale. But the historical record reveals that it was only at the last gasp that it was agreed to deal with the major war criminals through a judicial process, and an internationalised one at that. The Allies had made no commitment to judicial treatment of the major war criminals: in September 1994, less than a year before the Nuremberg Charter was signed, Churchill and Roosevelt agreed that the top Nazi leaders would be summarily executed. Only when it became apparent that the Soviets were firmly opposed to political disposition was it agreed that these persons should be dealt with by judicial process. Thus, the Nuremberg Tribunal, subsequently understood as having a transformative effect on the structures of the international legal system, came into being because it represented a political solution to a practical problem.[60] The transformation of the structures of the international legal system was a side-wind.

The same general point may be made in respect of the development of international human rights law. Since 1945, there has been incremental development in that field in response to a range of factors, including the atrocities of the Second World War. But that international conventions would impose binding obligations on states corresponding to individual rights enforceable in international fora was in pursuit of generalised goals, including the protection of the individual from ill-treatment by his or her own state. Human rights law is acknowledged as having had a transformative effect on the international legal system, yet it came about because of steps taken to address the problem of protection of individuals within domestic jurisdiction (and in the context of the failure of the minorities system), not because of a conscious decision to change the structures of the international legal system.

The same might be said of the device of diplomatic protection, and of the more recent developments in the law relating to the protection of foreign investments. An increase in the movement of persons across

60 See 4.4(a) above.

borders and the need to protect those persons and property resulted in the development of an international standard of minimum treatment of aliens, which essentially gave states of nationality an actionable interest in the treatment of their nationals. In more recent times a desire to more effectively protect foreign investment (and thus to encourage foreign investment) has resulted in treaty regimes for the protection of foreign investments. These developments were the consequences of addressing particular problems, rather than a desire to elevate the individual to a particular status in international law, or to transform the international legal system. The ensuing structural transformation was a by-product, not a cause.

To suggest that the international legal system has developed in the absence of a coherent theoretical framework is not to say that theorising serves no useful purpose or that the international legal system at any particular point in time cannot be explained by reference to theory. It is rather to suggest that there are (and have been) a range of possible futures for the international legal system, and that the extent to which those futures are realised is highly contingent, and in the end dominated by the interests of states. There is a kind of unpredictability inherent in the development of the international legal system, but that unpredictability reflects a strength in the system's potential to flexibly respond to the needs of the international community.

(c) States in the international legal system

In Part I, some of the challenges to state-centrism in international law were set out, organised in categories corresponding to theoretical approaches which address, in some meaningful way, the question of actors in the international legal system.[61] Although often these claims are made *de lege ferenda*, an examination of the development of the position of the individual may shed light on the extent to which challenges to state-centrism are reflected in existing law and practice.

A commonly given account of the development of the position of the individual in the international legal system begins with a Vattelian state-centric structure, and suggests that the system is moving towards a system in which individuals have a more prominent and active status, and in consequence, the international legal system is now a less 'state-centric' system than that of the nineteenth century. This might be associated with 'cosmopolitanism' as a general approach to international

[61] See 1.5 above.

law.[62] As a general proposition this argument no doubt holds true, but it ought to be qualified. There is no doubt that individuals can have rights and obligations conferred on them by international treaties and by general international law, and while this might have been exceptional in the period before 1945, it has become normalised practice since 1945. But this does not necessarily mean that the international legal system is no longer a 'state-centric' system. This study of the individual in international law shows that, while individuals have a kind of status as passive subjects of international law, individuals do not have independence or autonomy in the international legal system to any meaningful extent. In particular, individuals have no control over the way in which they receive rights and obligations, and they have no capacity to allow any other entities access to the international legal system. These capacities are limited to states (and perhaps to some international organisations).[63] The conferral of rights and obligations on individuals might, on one view, be seen as a move away from a state-dominated international legal system. But another view might be that the conferral of rights and obligations on individuals - which is exclusively controlled by states - actually reinforces the dominant position of states in the international legal system, to an extent which might not have been possible without some concessions or participatory rights granted to individuals. The point is that the former view may be an overly simplistic approach.

Moreover, while it is common to suggest that it benefits individuals to be given direct rights and obligations under international law, rather than to make provision for the imposition of obligations on an interstate basis which operate to protect or to some other beneficial end for individuals, this assumption is open to challenge. This may be the case, for example, for the protection of individuals in humanitarian law, which operates under a framework consistent with Vattelian statecentrism. As discussed above, an inter-state normative framework may be more effective and result in better protection of individuals in the context of armed conflict than an individual rights framework. Claims that the international legal system is moving away from a state-centric model and that better protection of individuals is necessarily achieved through a framework of individual rights overlook the

[62] See discussion in 1.5(c) above.

[63] The extent of the legal personality of international organisations is outside the scope of this book.

possibility that in a particular context, a normative framework closely associated with a state-centric international legal system may be more effective in achieving benefits for and protection of individuals. In consequence, the pejorative use of state-centrism is also open to question.[64]

In respect of the individual at least, it can be noted that states continue to dominate law-making. Individuals have no capacities to enter into treaties, or to create or to contribute to the creation of customary international law.[65] While it is clear that customary international law now may be found by taking into account a broader range of actions than only inter-state legal relations, and there is a large measure of support for approaching the determination of the rules of customary international law with some flexibility, the determination of rules of custom has remained primarily focussed on the actions and interactions of states.[66] While it might be argued that NGOs and other organised non-state groups have influenced states to accept the customary status of certain norms (particularly human rights norms), that influence seems to have occurred through an informal process (i.e. by lobbying) and the crucial actors in relation to the creation of international law continue to be states.[67] To that extent the claims (whether normative or otherwise) of various theoretical schools to the effect that individuals contribute to the creation of international law have little support in existing law and practice. Thus, at least as far as the creation of international law is concerned, the international legal system has remained dominated by states.

Undoubtedly the international legal system of the twenty-first century is less state-centric than the international legal system of the nineteenth century, and the individual has a more prominent role in international law today than in the time of Vattel. However, even today, states still have a dominant role in the international legal system, as autonomous and independent subjects of international law, while individuals, although also subjects, have much more limited capacities to engage in the international legal system. Furthermore, while individuals have some direct rights in international law in various (and ever-expanding)

[64] See S. Marks, 'State-Centrism, International Law, and the Anxieties of Influence' (2007) 19 *LJIL* 339 and discussion in 1.5 above.
[65] Cf. some claims of the process approaches: see 1.5(b) above.
[66] See discussion of modified positivism, 1.5(a) above.
[67] For example, see C. Ochoa, 'The Individual and Customary International Law Formation' (2007) 48 *Virginia JIL* 119.

fields, it should not be assumed that direct rights necessarily connote better protection in a particular context, than would be possible under a state-centred model of international law. Despite the structural transformation of the international legal system, the state is not about to 'wither away'.[68] Rather, its dominating position in the international legal system has been reinforced while some limited rights and obligations have been developed for individuals, who remain subordinated in the international legal system.

Martii Koskenniemi has written of the 'turn to history' in international law, a movement he sees as inspired by a sense that 'some aspect of today's policy is best understood as a washed-up version of some past pattern of privilege'.[69] No doubt this may be true, but an examination of the history can do much more than demonstrate that there are quickly forgotten precedents and antecedents in genuine enthusiasm for the new. In the context of the position of the individual, this historical review has revealed that generally accepted accounts of structural change in the international system are often based on myth and that the movement towards a more inclusive system (and the rise of the individual) has represented a possible but not inevitable future for international law. Moreover, though the trend towards increased participation of and capacities for individuals seems set to continue, states continue to dominate the international legal system, particularly in respect of international law-making, and access of other entities to the system. And while there is a modern tendency to use 'state-centrism' in a pejorative way[70] and to celebrate individualism in all its forms, it seems legitimate to question whether some of these aspects of the structures of international law, which have withstood the test of time, still serve a useful purpose, and should be celebrated rather than condemned.

[68] E. Stein, 'International Law in Internal Law: Towards Internationalization of Central-Eastern European Constitutions?' (1994) 88 *AJIL* 427, 450.

[69] M. Koskenniemi, 'The Politics of International Law: 20 Years Later' (2009) 20 *EJIL* 7, 17–18.

[70] Marks, 'State-Centrism, International Law, and the Anxieties of Influence'.

Bibliography

Abbott, Kenneth W., 'International Relations Theory, International Law, and the Regime Governing Atrocities in Internal Conflicts' (1999) 93 *AJIL* 361

Abi-Saab, Georges, 'Wars of National Liberation' (1979-IV) 165 *RdC* 353

'*Non International Armed Conflicts*' in UNESCO, *International Dimensions of Humanitarian Law* (Geneva, Henry Dunant Institute, 1988), p. 217

Abi-Saab, R., '*Humanitarian Law and Internal Conflicts: The Evolution of Legal Concern*' in Astrid J. M. Delissen and Gerard J. Tanya (eds.), *Humanitarian Law of Armed Conflict: Challenges Ahead, Essays in Honour of Frits Kalshoven* (Dordrecht, Martinus Nijhoff, 1991), p. 211

Alain, J., 'The *Jus Cogens* Nature of Non-refoulement' (2002) 13 *Int'l Journal of Refugee Law* 538

Alston, Philip, 'Conjuring up New Human Rights: A Proposal for Quality Control' (1984) 78 *AJIL* 607

'The 'Not-a-Cat' Syndrome: Can the International Human Rights Regime Accommodate Non-State Actors?' in P. Alston (ed.), *Non-State Actors and Human Rights* (Oxford, Oxford University Press, 2005), p. 3

Alston, Philip (ed.), *Non-State Actors and Human Rights* (Oxford, Oxford University Press, 2005)

Alston, Philip and Crawford, James (eds.), *The Future of UN Human Rights Treaty Monitoring* (Cambridge, Cambridge University Press, 2000)

Alston, Philip and Quinn, Gerard, 'The Nature and Scope of State Parties' Obligations under the International Covenant on Economic, Social and Cultural Rights' (1987) 9 *HRQ* 156

Ambos, Kai, 'Article 25: Individual Criminal Responsibility' in Otto Triffterer (ed.), *Commentary on the Rome Statute of the International Criminal Court: Observers' Notes, Article by Article* (Baden Baden, Nomos Verlagsgesellschaft, 1999), p. 475

American Law Institute, *Report to the Council of the Institute and Statement of Essential Human Rights* (New York, American Law Institute, 1944)

Restatement (Third) of the Foreign Relations Law of the United States (St Paul, Minn., American Law Institute, 1987)

Anzilotti, Dionisio *Cours de droit International* (Paris, Librairie de Recueil Sirey, 1929)

Arangio-Ruiz, G., 'On the Nature of the International Personality of the Holy See' (1996) 29 *Revue Belge de Droit International* 354
Arend, Anthony Clark, *Legal Rules and International Society* (Oxford, Oxford University Press, 1999)
Aust, Anthony, *Modern Treaty Law and Practice* (Cambridge, Cambridge University Press, 2000)
Bandinel, James, *Some Account of the Trade in Slaves from Africa as Connected with Europe and America* (London, Frank Cass & Co. Ltd, 1968)
Bantekas, Ilias, 'The Iraqi Special Tribunal for Crimes Against Humanity' (2004) 54 *ICLQ* 237
Basak, Adam, 'The Influence of the Nuremberg Judgment on the Practice of the Allied Courts in Germany' (1977–8) *Polish Yearbook of International Law* 161
Bassiouni, M. Cherif, 'Nuremberg: Forty Years After' (1986) 80 *ASIL Proceedings* 59
Crimes Against Humanity in International Law (Dordrecht, Martinus Nijhoff, 1992)
Bathurst, M. E., 'The United Nations War Crimes Commission' (1945) 39 *AJIL* 565
Baty, T., 'Protectorates and Mandates' (1921–2) 2 *BYIL* 109
Baumont, Maurice, *The Fall of the Kaiser* (E. Ibbetson James (trans.), London, George Allen & Unwin Ltd, 1930)
Bayliss, Charles, 'Towards an International Bill of Rights' (1944) 8 *Public Opinion Quarterly* 244
Beaulac, Stéphane, *The Power of Language in the Making of International Law : The Word 'sovereignty' in Bodin and Vattel and the Myth of Westphalia* (Leiden, Martinus Nijhoff, 2004)
Beckett, W. E., 'Decisions of the Permanent Court of International Justice on Points of Law and Procedure of General Application' (1930) 11 *BYIL* 1
Bedi, Shiv R. S., *The Development of Human Rights Law by the Judges of the International Court of Justice* (Oxford, Hart, 2007)
Bekker, Peter H. F., *The Legal Position of Intergovernmental Organizations: A Functional Necessity Analysis of their Legal Status and Immunities* (Dordrecht, Martinus Nijhoff, 1994)
Bellot, Hugh H. L., 'War Crimes: Their Prevention and Punishment' (1916) 2 *Grotius Soc'y Transactions* 31
Bennett, Ernest, *The German Army in Belgium: The White Book of May 1915* (London, Swathmore Press Ltd, 1921)
Bentwich, Norman, *The Mandates System* (London, Longmans, 1930)
'Colonial Mandates and Trusteeships' (1946) 32 *Transactions of the Grotius Society* 121
Bergers, Jan Herman, 'The Road to San Francisco: The Revival of the Human Rights Idea in the 20th Century' (1992) 14 *HRQ* 447
Bernstein, Victor H., *Final Judgment: The Story of Nuremberg* (London, Latimer House, 1947)
Berriedale, Keith A., 'Mandates' (1922) 4 *Journal of Comparative Legislation and International Law* 71
Bilder, Richard B., 'Rethinking International Human Rights: Some Basic Questions' (1969) 71 *Wis. L Rev.* 171

Bishop Jr, J. W., *Justice Under Fire: A Study of Military Law* (New York, Charterhouse, 1974)
Blakesley, Christopher L., 'Atrocity and Its Prosecution: The Ad Hoc Tribunals for the Former Yugoslavia and Rwanda' in T. H. McCormack and G. Simpson (eds.), *The Law of War Crimes: National and International Approaches* (The Hague, Kluwer, 1997), p. 189
Bluntschli, Kaspar, *Le Droit International codifié* (M. C. Lardy (trans.), Paris, Guillaumin, 1870)
Boister, Neil and Cryer, Robert, *The Tokyo International Military Tribunal: A Reappraisal* (Oxford, Oxford University Press, 2008)
Boister, Neil and Cryer, Robert (eds.), *Documents on the Tokyo International Military Tribunal: Charter, Indictments, Judgments* (Oxford, Oxford University Press, 2008)
Borchard, Edwin M., 'The Protection of Citizens Abroad and Change of Original Nationality' (1933–4) 43 *Yale Law Journal* 359.
Boucher, David and Kelly, Paul, 'The Social Contract and its Critics: An Overview' in D. Boucher and P. Kelly (eds.), *The Social Contract from Hobbes to Rawls* (London, Routledge, 1994), p. 1
Brackman, Arnold C., *The Other Nuremberg: The Untold Story of the Tokyo War Crimes Trials* (London, Collins, 1989)
Brauer-Gramm, Hildburg, *Der Landrogt Peter von Hagenbach: Die burgundische Herrschaft am Oberrhein 1469–1474* (Musterschmidt-Verlag, Göttingen, 1957)
Breycha-Vauthier, Arthur C., 'The Order of St. John in International Law: A Forerunner of the Red Cross' (1954) 48 *AJIL* 554
Brierly, J. L., 'The Covenant and the Charter' (1946) 23 *BYIL* 83
Brinkley, Douglas and Facey-Crowther, David R. (eds.), *The Atlantic Charter* (Basingstoke, Macmillan, 1994)
Brownlie, Ian, *Principles of Public International Law* (7th edn, Oxford, Oxford University Press, 2008)
Bruegel, J. W., 'A Neglected Field: The Protection of Minorities' (1971) 4 *Revue des droits de l'homme* 413
Brunet, René, *La garantie internationale des droits de l'homme* (Genève, Ch. Grasset, 1947)
Buergenthal, Thomas, 'International Human Rights Law and Institutions: Accomplishments and Prospects' (1988) 63 *Washington LR* 1
Buergenthal, Thomas and Norris, Robert E. (eds.), *Human Rights: The Inter-American System* (New York, Oceana Publications, 1993), vol. I
Butte, George C., 'The "Protocole Additionell" to the International Prize Court Convention' (1912) 6 *AJIL* 799
Byers, Michael, *Custom, Power and the Power of Rules: International Relations and Customary International Law* (Cambridge, Cambridge University Press, 1999)
Canning, George, *The Speeches of the Right Honourable George Canning with a Memoir of his Life* (R. Therry (ed.), 2nd edn, London, J. Ridgway, 1830)
Canyes, Manuel C., 'The Inter-American System and the Conference of Chapultepec' (1945) *AJIL* 504

Cassese, Antonio, 'The Status of Rebels under the 1977 Geneva Protocol on Non-International Armed Conflicts' (1981) 30 *ICLQ* 416
'The Martens Clause: Half a Loaf or Simply Pie in the Sky?' (2000) 11 *EJIL* 187
Castrén, Erik, 'Recognition of Insurgency' (1965) *Indian Journal of International Law* 443
Civil War (Helsinki, Soumalainen Tiedeakatemia, 1966)
Charlesworth, Hilary, 'Feminist Methods in International Law' (1999) 93 *AJIL* 379
Charlesworth, Hilary and Chinkin, Christine, *The Boundaries of International Law: A Feminist Analysis* (Manchester, Manchester University Press, 2000)
Chen, L. C., 'Restatement: Protection of Persons' (1989) 14 *Yale JIL* 542
Chen, Ti-Chiang, *The International Law of Recognition* (London, Stevens & Sons Ltd, 1951)
Claerr-Stamm, Gabrielle, *Pierre de Hagenbach: Le destin tragique d'un chevalier sundgauvien au service de Charles le Téméraire* (Altkirch, Société d'Histoire du Sundgau, 2005)
Clapham, Andrew, 'Human Rights Obligations of Non-State Actors in Conflict Situations' (2006) 88 *IRRC* 491
Human Rights Obligations of Non-State Actors (Oxford, Oxford University Press, 2006)
Clark, Grover, 'The English Practice with regard to Reprisals by Private Persons' (1933) *AJIL* 694
Coing, Helmut, 'Bank for International Settlements' in R. Bernhardt (ed.), *Encyclopedia of Public International Law* (Amsterdam, Elsevier Science Publishers, 1992), vol. I, p. 342
Commission to Study the Organization of the Peace, *International Safeguard of Human Rights*, reproduced in (1944) 403 *International Conciliation* 554
Corbett, P. E., 'What is the League of Nations?' (1924) 5 *BYIL* 119
Council of Europe, *Collected Edition of the 'Travaux Préparatoires' of the European Convention on Human Rights* (The Hague, Martinus Nijhoff, 1975)
Cox, N., 'The Acquisition of Sovereignty by Quasi-States: The Case of the Order of Malta' (2002) 6 *Mountbatten J of Legal Studies* 26
Craster, H. H. E. (ed.), *Speeches on Foreign Policy by Viscount Halifax K.G., D.C.L.* (Oxford, Oxford University Press, 1940)
Craven, Matthew, 'Towards an Unofficial Petition Procedure: A Review of the Role of the Committee on Economic, Social and Cultural Rights' in C. Krause and A. Rosas (eds.), *Social Rights as Human Rights: A European Challenge* (London, Martinus Nijhoff, 1994), p. 91
The International Covenant on Economic, Social and Cultural Rights: A Perspective on its Development (Oxford, Clarendon Press, 1995)
Crawford, Emily, 'Unequal Before the Law: The Case for the Elimination of the Distinction between International and Non-International Armed Conflicts' (2007) 20 *LJIL* 441
Crawford, James, 'Decisions of British Courts during 1985–6' (1986) *BYIL* 410
'International Law and International Crimes: Comments on a Developing Relationship' in Società Italiana di Diritto Internazionale, *Cooperazione fra*

Stati e Guistizia Penale Internazionale. II Convegno, Siena, 12–13 giugno 1998 (1999), p. 147
'The ILC's Articles on Responsibility of States for Internationally Wrongful Acts: A Retrospect' (2002) 96 *AJIL* 874
'The Work of the International Law Commission' in A. Cassese, Antonio, P. Gaeta and J. R. W. D. Jones, *The Rome Statute of the International Criminal Court: A Commentary* (Oxford, Oxford University Press, 2002), vol. 1, p. 23
The International Law Commission's Articles on State Responsibility: Introduction, Text and Commentaries (Cambridge, Cambridge University Press, 2002)
International Law as an Open System (London, Cameron May, 2002)
'The Drafting of the Rome Statute' in P. Sands (ed.), *From Nuremberg to The Hague: The Future of International Criminal Justice* (Cambridge, Cambridge University Press, 2003), p. 109
The Creation of States in International Law (2nd edn, Oxford, Oxford University Press, 2006)
'Treaty and Contract in Investment Arbitration' (2008) 24 *Arbitration International* 351
Cryer, Robert, *Prosecuting International Crimes: Selectivity and the International Criminal Law Regime* (Cambridge, Cambridge University Press, 2005)
D'Oliver Farran, C., 'The Sovereign Order of Malta in International Law' (1954) 3 *ICLQ* 211
Davidson, Scott, *The Inter-American Court of Human Rights* (Dartmouth, Aldershot, 1992)
Davis, George B., 'Doctor Francis Lieber's Instructions for the Government of Armies in the Field' (1907) 1 *AJIL* 13
de Barante, A. G., *Histoire des Ducs de Bourgogne de la Maison de Valois, 1364–1477* (Brussels, J. P. Meline, 1839)
de Clerq, Alexandre (ed.), *Recueil des Traités de la France* (Paris, Arynot, 1864)
de la Brière, Yves, 'Évolution de la Doctrine et de la Pratique en Matière de Représailles' (1928-II) *RdC* 237
de la Pradelle, A. G. and Politis, N. S., *Recueil des arbitrages internationaux* (Paris, Editions Internationales, 1955)
De Wet, Erika, 'The Role of Human Rights in Limiting the Enforcement Power of the Security Council: A Principled View' in E. De Wet and A. Nollkaemper (eds.), *Review of the Security Council by Member States* (Oxford, Intersentia, 2003), p. 22
Dickinson, Laura, 'The Promise of Hybrid Courts' (2003) 97 *AJIL* 295
Dinstein, Claud, *The Defence of 'Obedience to Superior Orders' in International Law* (Leyden, A.W. Sijthoff, 1965)
Dominicé, C., 'La personalité juridique internationale du CICR' in C Swinarski (ed.), *Studies and Essays on International Humanitarian Law and Red Cross Principles in Honour of Jean Pictet* (The Hague, Martinus Nijhoff, 1984), p. 663
Doswald-Beck, Louise and Vité, Sylvain, 'International Humanitarian Law and Human Rights Law' (1993) *IRRC* 94
Douglas, Zachary, 'The Hybrid Foundations of Investment Treaty Arbitration' (2003) 74 *BYIL* 151

The International Law of Investment Claims (Cambridge, Cambridge University Press, 2009)
Draper, G. I. A. D., 'The Geneva Conventions of 1949' (1965) 114-I *RdC* 60
Dugard, John, 'Diplomatic Protection and Human Rights: The Draft Articles of the International Law Commission' (2005) 24 *Australian YIL* 75
Dunn, Frederick Sherwood, *The Diplomatic Protection of Americans in Mexico* (New York, Columbia University Press, 1933), p. 98
Dupuy, Pierre-Marie, 'International Criminal Responsibility of the Individual and International Responsibility of the State' in A. Cassese, P. Gaeta and J. R. W. D. Jones (eds.), *The Rome Statute of the International Criminal Court: A Commentary* (Oxford, Oxford University Press, 2002), vol. I, p. 1085
Duursma, J., *Fragmentation and the International Relations of Microstates* (Cambridge, Cambridge University Press, 1996)
Eagleton, Clyde, 'International Law and the Charter of the United Nations' (1945) 39 *AJIL* 751
Ehard, Hans, 'The Nuremberg Trial Against the Major War Criminals and International Law' (1949) 43 *AJIL* 223
Elder, David A., 'The Historical Background of Common Article 3 of the Geneva Conventions of 1949' (1979) 11 *Case Western Reserve Journal of International Law* 37
Ellis, Mark, 'Coming to Terms with its Past: Serbia's New Court for the Prosecution of War Crimes' (2004) 22 *Berkeley Journal of International Law* 165
Ermacora, Felix, 'Human Rights and Domestic Jurisdiction (Article 2(7) of the Charter)' (1968–II) *Recueil des Cours* 375
Eser, Albin, 'Individual Criminal Responsibility' in A. Cassese, P. Gaeta and J. R. W. D. Jones (eds.), *The Rome Statute of the International Criminal Court: A Commentary* (Oxford, Oxford University Press, 2002), vol. I, p. 767
Evans, Ifor L., 'The Protection of Minorities' (1923) 4 *BYIL* 95
Evans, Malcolm (ed.), *International Law* (2nd edn, Oxford, Oxford University Press, 2006)
Executive Board of the American Anthropological Association, 'Statement on Human Rights' (1947) 49 *American Anthropologist* 539
Feldman, N., 'Cosmopolitan Law?' (2006) 116 *Yale Law Journal* 101
Feller, A. H., 'Some Observations on the Calvo Clause' (1933) 27 *AJIL* 461
The Mexican Claims Commissions 1923–1934: A Study in the Law and Procedure of International Tribunals (New York, Macmillan Company, 1935)
Fenwick, C. G., *The Organization of American States* (Washington, DC, self-published, 1963)
Finch, George A., 'Superior Orders and War Crimes' (1921) 15 *AJIL* 440
Fischer, H., 'The Suppression of Slavery in International Law' (1950) 3 *ICLQ* 28
Foreign Relations of the United States, *The Conferences at Malta and Yalta, 1945* (Washington, DC, 1955)
The Conference of Quebec 1944 (Washington, DC, 1972)
Freeman, A. V., 'Recent Aspects of the Calvo Doctrine and the Challenge to International Law' (1946) 40 *AJIL* 121

Gaja, Giorgio, 'Positivism and Dualism in Dionisio Anzilotti' (1992) 3 *EJIL* 123
Garraway, Charles, 'The Statute of the Iraqi Special Tribunal' in S. Breau and A. Jachec-Neale (eds.), *Testing the Boundaries of International Humanitarian Law* (London, BIICL, 2006), p. 155
'War Crimes' in E. Wilmshurst and S. Breau (eds.), *Perspectives on the ICRC Study on Customary International Humanitarian Law* (Cambridge, Cambridge University Press, 2007), p. 377
Gasser, Hans-Peter, 'International Humanitarian Law' in H. Haug (ed.), *Humanity for All: The International Red Cross and Red Crescent Movement* (Berne, P. Haupt, 1993), p. 491
Ghandhi, P. R., *The Human Rights Committee and the Right of Individual Communication: Law and Practice* (Aldershot, Ashgate, 1998)
Giles, Frank, *Napoleon Bonaparte: England's Prisoner* (London, Constable, 2001)
Goldsmith, J., 'Liberal Democracy and Cosmopolitan Duty' (2002–3) 55 *Stanford Law Review* 1667
Goodwin-Gill, Guy S. and McAdam, Jane, *The Refugee in International Law* (3rd edn, Oxford, Oxford University Press, 2007)
Gordon, Ruth, 'Mandates' in R. Wolfrum (ed.), *The Max Planck Encyclopedia of Public International Law* (Oxford, Oxford University Press, 2008, online edition, www.mpepil.com)
Graham, R. A., *The Rise of the Double Diplomatic Corps in Rome: A Study in International Practice* (The Hague, Martinus Nijhoff, 1952)
Grant, Thomas D., *Admission to the United Nations: Charter Article 4 and the Rise of Universal Organization* (Leiden, Martinus Nijhoff, 2009)
Gray, C. D., 'Remedies for Individuals under the European Convention on Human Rights' (1981) *HRR* 153.
Grewe, Wilhelm G., *The Epochs of International Law* (Michael Byers (trans.), Berlin, Walter de Gruyter, 2000)
Grossman, Claudio and Bradlow, Daniel D., 'Are We Being Propelled Towards a People-Centred Transnational Legal Order?' (1993–4) 9 *Am. U J Int'l L and Pol'y* 1
Grotius, Hugo, *The Rights of War and Peace* (1625, R. Tuck (ed.), Indianapolis, Liberty Fund, 2005)
Gunning, Isabelle R., 'Modernizing Customary International Law: The Challenge of Human Rights' (1991) 31 *Virgina JIL* 211
Gutiérrez, Carlos José, *La Corte de Justicia CentroAmericana* (Tegucigalpa, Biblioteca del Pensamiento Centroamericano, 1957)
Gutteridge, Joyce A. C., 'Supplementary Slavery Convention, 1956' (1957) 6 *ICLQ* 449.
Hackworth, G. H., *Digest of International Law* (Washington, DC, US Government Printing Office, 1943), vol. V
Haggenmacher, Peter, *Grotius et la doctrine de le guerre juste* (Paris, Presses Universitaires de France, 1983)
Hall, Duncan, *Mandates, Dependencies and Trusteeship* (London, Stevens, 1948)
Hall, W. E., *A Treatise on International Law* (3rd edn, Oxford, Clarendon Press, 1890)

Hampson, Françoise, 'Human Rights Law and Humanitarian Law: Two Coins or Two Sides of the Same Coin?' (1991) 1 *Bull. Hum. Rts* 46
Hankel, Gerd, *Die Leipziger Prozesse: Deutrche Kriegsverbrechen und ihre strafrechtliche Verfolgung nach dem Ersten Weltkrieg* (Hamburg, Hamburger Edition, 2003)
Hannum, Hurst, 'The Status of the Universal Declaration of Human Rights in National and International Law' (1995–6) 25 *Ga. J Int'l and Comp. Law* 287
Hathaway, James C., *The Rights of Refugees under International Law* (Cambridge, Cambridge University Press, 2005)
Henckaerts, Jean-Marie and Doswald-Beck, Louise, *International Committee of the Red Cross: Customary International Humanitarian Law*, vol. I, *Rules* (Cambridge, Cambridge University Press, 2005)
Henkin, Louis, *The Age of Rights* (New York, Columbia University Press, 1990)
Henkin, Louis (ed.), *The International Bill of Human Rights: The Covenant on Civil and Political Rights* (New York, Colombia University Press, 1981)
Higgins, A. Pearce, *The Hague Peace Conferences* (Cambridge, Cambridge University Press, 1909)
Higgins, Roslyn, *The Development of International Law through the Political Organs of the United Nations* (London, Oxford University Press, 1963)
'Conceptual Thinking about the Individual in International Law' (1979) *New York Law School Law Review* 11
Problems and Process: International Law and How We Use It (Oxford, Oxford University Press, 1994)
'Human Rights in the International Court of Justice' (2007) 20 *LJIL* 745
Hobbes, Thomas, *Leviathan* (R. Tuck (ed.), Cambridge, Cambridge University Press, 1996)
Hollis, Martin and Smith, Steve, *Explaining and Understanding International Relations* (Oxford, Clarendon Press, 1990)
Hudson, Manley O., *The Permanent Court of International Justice: A Treatise* (New York, Macmillan, 1934)
International Tribunals (Washington, DC, Carnegie, 1944)
Humphrey, J. P., '*The Universal Declaration of Human Rights: Its History, Impact and Juridical Character*' in B. G. Ramcharan (ed.), *Human Rights: Thirty Years After the Universal Declaration* (The Hague, Martinus Nijhoff, 1979), p. 21
ICRC, *Official Records of the Diplomatic Conference on the Reaffirmation and Development of International Humanitarian Law Applicable in Armed Conflicts, Geneva, (1974–1977)* (Bern, Federal Political Department, 1978)
Interpretive Guidance on the Notion of Direct Participation in Hostilities under International Humanitarian Law (Geneva, ICRC, 2009)
Institute of International Law, *Manual of the Law of War on Land* (Oxford, Institute of International Law, 1880)
Resolutions of the Institute of International Law Dealing with the Law of Nations: With an Historical Introduction and Explanatory Notes (J. B. Scott (ed.), New York, Oxford University Press, 1916)
Isaacs, Irving, *The International Bill of Rights and Permanent Peace Concordance* (Boston, NJ, Twentieth Century Association, 1943)

Janowsky, Oscar I., *Nationalities and National Minorities* (New York, Macmillan, 1925)

Jellinek, Georg, *Die Rechtliche Natur der Staatenvertrage* (Vienna, Alfred Hölder, 1880)

Jenks, Wilfred C., *The International Protection of Trade Union Freedom* (London, Stevens, 1951)

Human Rights and International Labour Standards (London, Stevens, 1960)

Jennings, Robert, 'Some International law Aspects of the Refugee Question' (1939) 20 *BYIL* 98

Jennings, Robert and Watts, Arthur, *Oppenheim's International Law* (9th edn, London, Longmans, 1992)

Jhabvala, Farrokh, 'The Drafting of the Human Rights Provisions of the UN Charter' (1997) XLIV *Netherlands International Law Review* 1

Johnson, M. Glen, 'The Contribution of Eleanor and Franklin Roosevelt to the Development of International Protection for Human Rights' (1987) 9 *HRQ* 19

Jørgensen, Nina J. B., *The Responsibility of States for International Crimes* (Oxford, Oxford University Press, 2000)

Joseph, Sarah, Schultz, Jenny and Castan, Melissa, *The International Covenant on Civil and Political Rights: Cases, Materials, and Commentary* (2nd edn, Oxford, Oxford University Press, 2005)

Jouannet, Emmanuelle, *Emer de Vattel et l'émergence doctrinale du droit international classique* (Paris, Pedone, 1998)

Kaeckenbeeck, Georges, 'The Character and Work of the Arbitral Tribunal of Upper Silesia' (1935) 21 *Transactions of the Grotius Society* 27

The International Experiment of Upper Silesia: A Study in the Workings of the Upper Silesian Settlement 1922–1937 (London, Oxford University Press, 1942)

'Upper Silesia under the League of Nations' (1946) 243 *Annals of the American Academy of Political and Social Science* 129

Kant, I., *Political Writings* (H. Reiss (ed.), H. B. Nisbet (trans.), 2nd edn, Cambridge, Cambridge University Press, 1991)

Keen, Maurice H., *The Laws of War in the Late Middle Ages* (London, Keegan Paul, 1965)

Chivalry (New Haven, Conn., Yale University Press, 1984)

Nobles, Knights and Men-At-Arms in the Middle Ages (London, Hambledon Press, 1996)

Kelsen, Hans, 'The Old and the New League: The Covenant and the Dumbarton Oaks Proposals' (1945) 39 *AJIL* 45

The Law of the United Nations (London, Stevens, 1950)

Kennedy, David, 'Primitive Legal Scholarship' (1986) *Harvard International Law Journal* 1

'A New Stream of International Law Scholarship' (1988–9) 7 *Wisconsin International Law Journal* 1

'A New World Order: Yesterday, Today, and Tomorrow' (1994) 4 *Transnat'l Law and Contemporary Problems* 329

Kennedy, David and Tennant, Chris, 'New Approaches to International Law: A Bibliography' (1994) 35 *Harvard Int'l LJ* 417

Keynes, John Maynard, *The Economic Consequences of the Peace* (New York, Harcourt, Brace and Jovanovich, 1920)
Kirsch QC, Philippe and Robinson, Darryl, 'Reaching Agreement at the Rome Conference' in A. Cassese, P. Gaeta and J. R. W. D. Jones (eds.), *The Rome Statute of the International Criminal Court: A Commentary* (Oxford, Oxford University Press, 2002), vol. I, p. 67
Klabbers, Jan., *An Introduction to International Institutional Law* (Cambridge, Cambridge University Press, 2002)
'The Concept of Legal Personality' (2005) *Ius Gentium* 35
Koh, Harold, 'Transnational Legal Process' (1996) 75 *Nebraska Law Review* 181
Komarow, Gary, 'Individual Responsibility under International Law: The Nuremberg Principles in Domestic Legal Systems' (1980) 29 *ICLQ* 21
Koskenniemi, Martii, *From Apology to Utopia* (Cambridge, Cambrige University Press, 2005)
'International Legal Theory and Doctrine' in R. Wolfrum (ed.), *The Max Planck Encyclopedia of Public International Law* (Oxford, Oxford University Press, 2008, online edition, www.mpepil.com)
'The Politics of International Law: 20 Years Later' (2009) 20 *EJIL* 7
Kunz, Josef L., 'The Present Status of the International Law for the Protection of Minorities' (1954) 48 *AJIL* 282
Lachs, Manfred, *War Crimes: An Attempt to Define the Issues* (London, Stevens & Sons, 1945)
Larnaude, F. and de La Pradelle, A. G., *Examen de la responsibilité pénale de l'Emperor Guillaume II* (Paris, Imprimerie Nationale, 1918)
Las Cases, Emmanuel-Auguste-Dieudonné, *Memoirs of the Life, Exile, and Conversations, of the Emperor Napoleon* (London, H. Colburn, 1836)
Lasswell, Harold D. and McDougal, Myres S., *Jurisprudence for a Free Society: Studies in Law, Science and Policy* (Dordrecht, Nijhoff, 1992)
Lauren, Paul Gordon, 'First Principles of Racial Equality: History and the Politics and Diplomacy of Human Rights Provisions in the United Nations Charter' (1983) 5 *HRQ* 1
The Evolution of International Human Rights: Visions Seen (2nd edn, Philadelphia, Pa., University of Pennsylvania Press, 2003)
Lauterpacht, Elihu, 'The Development of the Law of International Organization by the Decisions of International Tribunals' (1976–IV) 152 *RdC* 377
Lauterpacht, Elihu (ed.), *International Law, Being the Collected Papers of Sir Hersch Lauterpacht* (Cambridge, Cambridge University Press, 2005), vol. V
Lauterpacht, Hersch, *The Development of International Law by the Permanent Court of International Justice* (London, Longmans, 1934)
'The Law of Nations and the Punishment of War Crimes' (1944) 21 *BYBIL* 58
An International Bill of the Rights of Man (New York, Columbia University Press, 1945)
'The Grotian Tradition in International Law' (1946) 23 *BYIL* 1
'The Subjects of the Law of Nations (Part I)' (1947) 63 *LQR* 460
Recognition in International Law (Cambridge, Cambridge University Press, 1947)

'The Subjects of the Law of Nations (Part II)' (1948) 64 *LQR* 97
'The Universal Declaration of Human Rights' (1948) 25 *BYIL* 354
Lauterpacht, Hersch (ed.), *International Law: A Treatise, by L. Oppenheim* (8th edn, London, Longmans, 1955)
Leach, Philip, 'Beyond the Bug River: A New Dawn for Redress before the European Court of Human Rights?' (2005) *EHRLR* 148
'Access to the European Court of Human Rights: From a Legal Entitlement to a Lottery?' (2006) *HRLJ* 11
League of Nations Union, *The Atlantic Charter* (London, Hodgson, 1942)
Lediakh, I. A., 'The Application of the Nuremberg Principles by Other Military Tribunals and National Courts' in G. Ginsburgs and V. N. Kudriavtsev, *The Nuremberg Trial and International Law* (Dordrecht, Martinus Nijhoff, 1990), p. 263
Lesaffer, Randall, 'The Grotian Tradition Revisited: Change and Continuity in the History of International Law' (2002) 73 *BYIL* 103
Levie, Howard, *Terrorism in War: The Law of War Crimes* (New York, Oceana Publications, 1993)
Lillich, Richard B. (ed.), *The United Nations Compensation Commission: Thirteenth Sokol Colloquium* (New York, Transnational, 1995)
Lindblom, Anna-Karin, *Non-Governmental Organisations in International Law* (Cambridge, Cambridge University Press, 2005)
Lippman, Matthew, 'The Other Nuremberg: American Prosecutions of Nazi War Criminals in Occupied Germany' (1992–3) 3 *ICLQ* 1
Lipstein, K., 'The Place of the Calvo Clause in International Law' (1945) 22 *BYIL* 130
Lloyd, Christopher, *The Navy and the Slave Trade: The Suppression of the African Slave Trade in the Nineteenth Century* (London, Longmans, 1949)
Lorimer, James, *The Institutes of the Law of Nations* (Edinburgh, Blackwood, 1883)
Maitland, Frederick L., *Narrative of the Surrender of Buonaparte: And of his Residence on Board H.M.S. Bellerophon* (London, H. Colburn, 1826)
Malloy, William M., *Treaties, Conventions, International Acts, Protocols and Agreements between the United States of America and Other Powers 1776–1909* (Washington, DC, Government Printing Office, 1910)
Manacorda, Stefani, 'The Principle of Individual Criminal Responsibility: A Conceptual Framework' (2007) 5 *JICJ* 913
Mandelstam, André, 'La protection des Minorités' (1923) *RdC* 363
Manner, George, 'The Object Theory of the Individual in International Law' (1952) 46 *AJIL* 428
Marks, Susan, 'State-Centrism, International Law, and the Anxieties of Influence' (2006) 19 *LJIL* 339
Martin, Christopher, 'The Declaration of London: A Matter of Operational Capability' (2008) *Historical Research* 1
McCarthy, Conor, 'Human Rights and the Laws of War under the American Convention on Human Rights' (2008) *EHRLR* 762

'Legal Reasoning and the Applicability of International Human Rights Standards during Military Occupation' in N. Quenivet and R. Arnold (eds.), *International Humanitarian Law and Human Rights Law: Towards a New Merger in International Law* (Leiden, Martinus Nijhoff, 2008), p. 121

'Reparations under the Rome Statute of the International Criminal Court and Reparative Justice Theory' (2009) *ICTJ* 1

McCormack, T. H., 'From Sun Tzu to the Sixth Committee: The Evolution of an International Criminal Law Regime' in T. H. McCormack and G. Simpson (eds.), *The Law of War Crimes: National and International Approaches* (The Hague, Kluwer, 1997), p. 31

McCorquodale, Robert, 'An Inclusive International Legal System' (2004) 17 *LJIL* 477

'*The Individual and the International Legal System*' in M. Evans (ed.), *International Law* (2nd edn, Oxford, Oxford University Press, 2006), p. 307

McDougal, M. S., Lasswell, H. and Chen, L., *Human Rights and World Public Order: The Basic Policies of an International Law of Human Dignity* (New Haven, Yale University Press, 1980)

McLachlan, Campbell, Shore, Laurence and Weiniger, Matthew, *International Investment Arbitration: Substantive Principles* (Oxford, Oxford University Press, 2007)

McMahon, J. F., 'The Legislative Techniques of the ILO' (1965–6) *BYIL* 31

McNair, Arnold, *Oppenheim's International Law* (4th edn, London, Longmans, 1928), vol. I

'The Law Relating to the Civil War in Spain' (1937) 53 *LQR* 471

International Law Opinions: Selected and Annotated (Cambridge, Cambridge University Press, 1956)

Medina Quiroga, Cecilia, *The Battle of Human Rights: Gross, Systematic Violations and the Inter-American System* (Dordrecht, Martinus Nijhoff, 1988)

'The Inter-American Commission on Human Rights and the Inter-American Court of Human Rights: Reflections on a Joint Venture' (1990) 12 *HRQ* 439

Menon, P. K., 'The International Personality of Individuals in International Law: A Broadening of the Traditional Doctrine' (1992) *Journal of Transnational Law and Policy* 151

The Law of Recognition in International Law: Basic Principles (New York, Edwin Mellen Press, 1994)

Mérignhac, A., 'De La Responsibilité Pénale des Actes Criminels commis au cours de la Guerre de 1914–1918' (1920) 8 *Revue du Droit International* 34

Meron, Theodor, *Human Rights and Humanitarian Norms at Customary Law* (Oxford, Clarendon Press, 1989)

'The Continuing Role of Custom in the Formation of International Humanitarian Law' (1996) 90 *AJIL* 238

War Crimes Law Comes of Age: Essays (Oxford, Clarendon Press, 1998)

'The Martens Clause, Principles of Humanity, and Dictates of Public Conscience' (2000) 94 *AJIL* 78

Merrills, J. G. and Robertson, A. H., *Human Rights in Europe* (4th edn, Manchester, Juris Publishing, 2001)

Militello, Vincenzo, 'The Personal Nature of Individual Criminal Responsibility and the ICC Statute' (2007) 5 *JICJ* 941
Miller, Robert, 'War Crimes Trials at Yokohama' (1948–9) 15 *Brooklyn Law Review* 19
Minear, Richard H., *Victor's Justice: The Tokyo War Crimes Trial* (Princeton, NJ, Princeton University Press, 1971)
Modeen, T., *The International Protection of the National Identity of the Aaland Islands* (Stockholm, Almqvist and Wiksell International, 1973)
Moir, Lindsay, *The Law of Internal Armed Conflict* (Cambridge, Cambridge University Press, 2002)
Möller, Jakob Th., 'The Universal Declaration of Human Rights: How the Process Started' in A. Eide, G. Alfredsson, G. Melandr, L. A. Rehof and A. Rosas (eds.), *The Universal Declaration of Human Rights: A Commentary* (Oslo, Scandinavian University Press, 1992), p. 1
Moore, J. B., *History and Digest of the International Arbitrations to which the United States has been a Party* (Washington, DC, Government Printing Office, 1898)
A Digest of International Law (Washington, DC, Government Printing Office, 1906)
Moreillon, J., *Le CICR et la protection des détenus politiques* (Geneva, Henry Dunant Institute, 1973)
Morse, David A., *The Origin and Evolution of the I.L.O. and Its Role in the World Community* (New York, Humphrey Press, 1969)
Morris, Virginia and Scharf, Michael P., *An Insider's Guide to the International Criminal Tribunal for the Former Yugoslavia: A Documentary History and Analysis* (New York, Transnational Publishers, 1995), vol. II
Morsink, Johannes, 'The Philosophy of the Universal Declaration' (1984) 9 *HRQ* 309
Moskowitz, M., *The Policies and Dynamics of Human Rights* (London, 1968)
Mosler, H., 'Subjects of International Law' (1984) IV *MPIL* 710
Mullerson, R., 'Human Rights and the Individual as Subject of International Law: A Soviet View' (1990) 1 *EJIL* 33
Mullins, Claud, *The Leipzig Trials: An Account of the War Criminals' Trials and a Study of German Mentality* (London, H. G. & G. Witherby, 1921)
Neff, Stephen C., 'A Short History of International Law' in M. Evans (ed.), *International Law* (2nd edn, Oxford, Oxford University Press, 2006), p. 29
Northomb, Pierre, *The Barbarians in Belgium* (Jean E. H. Findley (trans.), London, Jarrold and Sons, 1915)
Nouwen, Sarah, '"Hybrid Courts": The Hybrid Category of a New Type of International Crimes Courts' (2006) *Utrecht Law Review* 190
Nowak, Manfred, *UN Covenant on Civil and Political Rights: CCPR Commentary* (Kehl, NP Engel, 1993)
Nussbaum, Arthur, *A Concise History of the Law of Nations* (New York, Macmillan, 1964)
O'Connell, D. P., *International Law* (2nd edn, London, Stevens and Sons, 1970), vol. I

O'Connell, Mary Ellen, 'New International Legal Process' (1999) 93 *AJIL* 334
O'Rourke, Vernon A., 'Recognition of Belligerency and the Spanish War' (1937) 31 *AJIL* 398
Ochoa, C., 'Towards a Cosmopolitan Vision for International Law: Identifying and Defining CIL Post *Sosa v Alvarez-Machain*' (2005–6) 74 *University of Cincinnati Law Review* 105
'The Individual and Customary International Law Formation' (2007) 48 *Virginia JIL* 119
Oellers-Frahm, Karin and Wülher, Norbert, *Dispute Settlement in Public International Law: Text and Materials* (Berlin, Springer-Verlag, 1984)
Oglesby, Roscoe, *Internal War and the Search for Normative Order* (The Hague, Martinus Nijhoff, 1971)
Okowa, Phoebe, 'Issues of Admissibility and the Law of International Responsibility' in M. Evans (ed.), *International Law* (2nd edn, Oxford, Oxford University Press, 2006), p. 479
Oppenheim, Lassa, *International Law: A Treatise* (1st edn, London, Longmans, Green & Co., 1905)
'The Science of International Law: Its Task and Method' (1908) 2 *AJIL* 313
'Le Caractère essentiel de la Société des Nations' (1919) *RGIDP* 234
Orakhelashvili, Alexander, *Peremptory Norms in International Law* (Oxford, Oxford University Press, 2006)
Orlu Nmehielle, Vincent O., *The African Human Rights System: Its Laws, Practice, and Institutions* (The Hague, Martinus Nijhoff, 2001)
Orwell, George, *Critical Essays* (London, Secker & Warburg, 1946)
Orwell, Sonia and Angus, Ian (eds.), *The Collected Essays, Journalism and Letters of George Orwell*, vol. II, *My Country Right or Left, 1940–1943* (London, Secker and Warburg, 1968)
Otto, Diane, 'Holding up Half the Sky, But for Whose Benefit?' (1996) 6 *Australian Feminist Law Journal* 7
Pace, William R. and Schense, Jennifer, 'The Role of Non-Governmental Organizations' in A. Cassese, P. Gaeta and J. R. W. D. Jones (eds.), *The Rome Statute of the International Criminal Court: A Commentary* (Oxford, Oxford University Press, 2002), vol. I, p. 105
Parker, Geoffrey, '*Early Modern Europe*' in M. Howard, G. J. Andreopoulos and M. Schulman (eds.), *The Laws of War: Constraints on Warfare in the Western World* (New Haven, Conn., Yale University Press, 1994), p. 40
Parlett, Kate, 'Universal Civil Jurisdiction for Torture' (2007) *EHRLR* 385
'The PCIJ's Opinion in *Jurisdiction of the Courts of Danzig*: Individual Rights under Treaties' (2008) 10 *JHIL* 119
Partington, John S., 'The Pen as Sword: George Orwell, HG Wells and Journalistic Parricide' (2004) 39 *Journal of Contemporary History* 45
Pasqualucci, Jo M., *The Practice and Procedure of the Inter-American Court of Human Rights* (Cambridge, Cambridge University Press, 2003)
Paust, Jordan J., 'The Reality of Private Rights, Duties, and Participation in the International Legal Process' (2003–4) 25 *Mich. J Int'l L* 1229

Phillimore, Robert, *Commentaries upon International Law* (3rd edn, London, Butterworths, 1879), vol. I

Pictet, Jean (ed.), *Commentary of the Geneva Conventions of 12 August 1949, vol. I, Geneva Convention I for the Amelioration of the Condition of the Wounded and Sick in Armed Forces in the Field* (Geneva, ICRC, 1952)

Commentary of the Geneva Conventions of 12 August 1949, vol. IV, *Geneva Convention IV Relative to the Protection of Civilian Persons in Time of War* (Geneva, ICRC, 1958)

Commentary of the Geneva Conventions of 12 August 1949, vol. II, *Geneva Convention II for the Amelioration of the Condition of Wounded, Sick and Shipwrecked Armed Forces at Sea* (Geneva, ICRC, 1960)

Commentary of the Geneva Conventions of 12 August 1949, vol. III, *Geneva Convention III Relative to the Treatment of Prisoners of War* (Geneva, ICRC, 1960)

Plattner, Denise, 'The Penal Repression of Violations of International Humanitarian Law' (1990) 30 *IRRC* 409

Pogge, T., 'Cosmopolitanism and Sovereignty' (1992) 103 *Ethics* 48

Potter, Pitman B., 'Origin of the System of Mandates under the League of Nations' (1922) 16 *American Political Science Review* 563

'The Origin of the System of Mandates under the League of Nations: Further Notes' (1926) 20 *American Political Science Review* 842

Provost, René, *International Human Rights and Humanitarian Law* (Cambridge, Cambridge University Press, 2002)

Pufendorf, Samuel, *De Jure Naturae et Gentium Libra Octo* (J. B. Scott (ed.), C. H. and W. A. Oldfather (trans.), Oxford, Clarendon Press, 1934)

Purvis, Nigel, 'Critical Legal Studies in Public International Law' (1991) 32 *Harvard Int'l L J* 81

Rappard, W. E., 'The Practical Working of the Mandates System' (1925) 4 *Journal of the British Institute of International Affairs* 205

Rasmussen, Gustav, *Code des Prisonniers de Guerre: Commentaire de la Convention du 27 Juillet 1929 Relative au Traitement des Prisonniers de Guerre* (Copenhagen, Leven and Munksgaard, 1931)

Ratner, Steven R. and Abrams, Jason S., *Accountability for Human Rights Atrocities in International Law: Beyond the Nuremberg Legacy* (2nd edn, Oxford, Oxford University Press, 2001)

Ratner, Steven R. and Slaughter, Anne-Marie, 'Appraising the Methods of International Law: A Prospectus for Readers' (1999) 93 *AJIL* 291

Reisman, Michael W., *Jurisprudence: Understanding and Shaping Law* (New Haven, Conn., New Haven Press, 1987)

Remec, Peter, *The Position of the Individual in International Law according to Grotius and Vattel* (The Hague, Martinus Nijhoff, 1960)

Renouf, A., 'The Present Force of the Minorities Treaties' (1950) *Can. Bar Rev.* 804

Reuter, P., 'La personalité juridique internationale due Comité de la Croix-Rouge' in C. Swinarski (ed.), *Studies and Essays on International Humanitarian Law and Red Cross Principles in Honour of Jean Pictet* (The Hague, Martinus Nijhoff, 1984), p. 783

Reuter, Paul, *Introduction to the Law of Treaties* (London, Pinter, 1989)

Riedel, Eibe H., 'Recognition of Insurgency' in Rudolf Bernhardt, *Encyclopedia of Public International Law* (Amsterdam, Elsevier, 2000)
Robertson, A. H. and Merrills, J. G., *Human Rights in the World* (4th edn, Manchester, Manchester University Press, 1996)
Robinson, Jacob, *Were the Minorities Treaties a Failure?* (New York, Institute of Jewish Affairs, 1943)
Robinson, Nehemiah, *The Universal Declaration of Human Rights: Its Origin, Significance, Application and Interpretation* (New York, Institute of Jewish Affairs, 1985)
Rodley, Nigel, 'Can Armed Opposition Groups Violate Human Rights Standards?' in K. H. Mahoney and P. Mahoney (eds.), *Human Rights in the Twenty-First Century* (The Hague, Martinus Nijhoff, 1993), p. 307
Rogers, A. P. V., 'War Crimes Trials under the Royal Warrant: British Practice 1945–1949' (1990) 39 *ICLQ* 780
Röling, B. V. A., *The Tokyo Trial and Beyond: Reflections of a Peacemonger* (Cambridge, Polity Press, 1993)
Röling, B. V. A. and Rüter, C. F., *The Tokyo Judgment of the International Military Tribunal for the Far East (IMTFE) 29 April 1946–12 November 1948* (Amsterdam, APA University Press, 1977), vols. I–XIII
Romano, C., Nollekemper, A. and Kleffner, J., *Internationalized Criminal Courts* (Oxford, Oxford University Press, 2004)
Rona, Gabor, 'The ICRC Privilege not to Testify: Confidentiality in Action' (2002) 845 *IRRC* 207
Rosenman, Samuel (ed.), *The Public Papers and Addresses of Franklin D. Roosevelt* (New York, Random House, 1938), vol. IX
Public Papers and Addresses of Franklin D. Roosevelt: The Call to Battle Stations, 1941 (New York, Harper & Bros, 1950)
Rosting, H., 'Protection of Minorities by the League of Nations' (1923) 17 *AJIL* 641
Rubin, Alfred P., *The Law of Piracy* (2nd edn, Newport, Naval War College Press, 1998)
Rückerl, Aldalbert, *The Investigation of Nazi Crimes 1945–1978* (Derek Rutter (trans.), Hamden, Conn., Archon Books, 1980)
Ruda, José María, 'The Opinions of Judge Dionisio Anzilotti at the Permanent Court of International Justice' (1992) 3 *EJIL* 100
Russell, R. and Muther, J., *A History of the United Nations Charter* (Washington, DC, Brookings Institute, 1958)
Saland, Per, 'International Criminal Law Principles' in R. S. Lee, *The International Criminal Court: The Making of the Rome Statute – Issues, Negotiations, Result* (The Hague, Kluwer, 1999), p. 189
Sandoz, Yves, *The International Committee of the Red Cross as Guardian of International Humanitarian Law* (Geneva, ICRC, 1998)
Sandoz, Yves, Swinarski, Christophe and Zimmermann, Bruno (eds.), *Commentary on the Protocol Additional to the Geneva Conventions of 12 August 1949, and relating to the Protection of Victims of International Armed Conflicts* (Geneva, ICRC/Martinus Nijhoff, 1987)

Sands, P., Shany, Y. and Mackenzie, R. (eds.), *The Manual on International Courts and Tribunals* (London, Butterworths, 1999)
Sassoli, M. and Bouvier, A. (eds.), *How Does Law Protect in War* (2nd edn, Geneva, ICRC, 2006)
Schachter, Oscar, 'International Law in Theory and Practice: General Course in Public International Law' (1982-V) 178 *RdC* 21
Scharf, Michael P., *Balkan Justice: The Story Behind the First International War Crimes Trial Since Nuremberg* (Durham, NC, Carolina Academic Press, 1997)
Schindler, Dietrich and Toman, Jirí (eds.), *The Laws of Armed Conflicts: A Collection of Conventions, Resolutions and Other Documents* (3rd edn, Dordrecht, Nijhoff, 1988)
Schlögel, A., 'La guerre civile' (1970) 617 *Revue International de la Croix-Rouge* 137
Schreiber, Anna P., *The Inter-American Commission on Human Rights* (Leiden, Sijthoff, 1970)
Schreuer, Christoph, 'The Waning of the Sovereign State: Towards a New Paradigm for International Law' (1994) 4 *EJIL* 447
Schwarzenberger, George, 'The Judgment of Nuremberg' (1947) 21 *Tulane L Rev.* 329
'The Problem of an International Criminal Law' (1950) *Current Legal Problems* 263
International Law (3rd edn, London, Stevens, 1957), vol. I
International Law as Applied by International Courts and Tribunals, vol. II, *The Law of Armed Conflict* (London, Stevens, 1968)
Schwelb, Egon, 'The International Convention on the Elimination of All Forms of Racial Discrimination' (1966) 15 *ICLQ* 996
Scott, J. B., 'The International Court of Prize' (1911) 5 *AJIL* 302
'The Declaration of London of February 26, 1909' (1914) 8 *AJIL* 274
Scott, J. B. (ed.), *The Hague Convention and Declarations of 1899 and 1907* (New York, Oxford University Press, 1915)
Seidl-Hohenveldern, Ignaz, *The Austrian-German Arbitral Tribunal* (New York, Syracuse University Press, 1972)
Sereni, Angelo Piero, *The Italian Conception of International Law* (New York, Columbia University Press, 1943)
Seyersted, F., 'International Personality of Intergovernmental Organizations: Do their Capacities Really Depend upon their Constitutions?' (1964) 4 *Ind. JIL* 1
Shany, Yuval, 'Does One Size Fit All?' (2004) 2 *JICJ* 338
Shaw, Malcolm, *International Law* (6th edn, Cambridge, Cambridge University Press, 2008)
Shea, D. R., *The Calvo Clause: A Problem of International Law and Diplomacy* (Minneapolis, Minn., University of Minnesota Press, 1955)
Shklar, Judith, *Legalism: Law, Morals and Political Trials* (Cambridge, Mass., Harvard University Press, 1986)
Shotwell, James T., *The Origins of the International Labour Organization* (New York, Columbia University Press, 1934)
Silvanie, Haig, 'Responsibility of States for Acts of Insurgent Governments' (1939) 33 *AJIL* 78

Simma, Bruno (ed.), *The Charter of the United Nations: A Commentary* (2nd edn, Oxford, Oxford University Press, 2002)
Simma, Bruno and Alston, Philip, 'The Sources of Human Rights Law: Custom, *Jus Cogens*, and General Principles' (1988–9) 12 *Aust. YBIL* 83
Simma, Bruno and Paulus, Andreas L., 'The Responsibility of Individuals for Human Rights Abuses in Internal Conflicts: A Positivist View' (1999) 93 *AJIL* 302
Simons, William B., 'The Jurisdictional Bases of the International Military Tribunal at Nuremberg' in G. Ginsburgs and V. N. Kudriavtsevs (eds.), *The Nuremberg Trial and International Law* (Dordrecht, Martinus Nijhoff, 1990), p. 39
Simpson, A. W. Brian, *Human Rights and the End of Empire: Britain and the Genesis of the European Convention* (Oxford, Oxford University Press, 2001)
Simpson, Gerry, *Law, War and Crime* (Cambridge, Polity Press, 2007)
Sinclair, A. C., 'The Origins of the Umbrella Clause in the International Law of Investment Arbitration' (2004) 20 *Arbitration International* 411
Singh, N., *Enforcement of Human Rights in Peace and War and the Future of Humanity* (Dordrecht, Nijhoff, 1986)
Sire, H. J. A., *The Knights of Malta* (New Haven, Conn., Yale University Press, 1994)
Sivakumaran, Sandesh, 'Binding Armed Opposition Groups' (2006) 55 *ICLQ* 369
Skran, Claudena M., *Refugees in Inter-War Europe: The Emergence of a Regime* (Oxford, Clarendon Press, 1995)
Slaughter, Anne-Marie, 'International Law and International Relations Theory: A Dual Agenda' (1993) 87 *AJIL* 205
Smith, Bradley F., *The Road to Nuremberg* (London, Basic Books, 1981)
The American Road to Nuremberg: The Documentary Record 1944–1945 (Stanford, Hoover Institution Press, 1982)
Smith, H. A., 'Some Problems of the Spanish Civil War' (1937) 18 *BYIL* 17
Smith, H. A. (ed.), *Great Britain and the Law of Nations*, vol. I, *States* (London, P. S. King & Son Ltd, 1932)
Smuts, J. C., *The League of Nations: A Practical Suggestion* (London, Hodder and Stoughton, 1918)
Sohn, Louis, 'The Human Rights Law of the Charter' (1977) 12 *Texas Int'l L J* 129
'The New International Law: Protection of the Rights of Individuals Rather than States' (1982) 32 *Amer. Univ. L R* 1
'How American International Lawyers Prepared for the San Francisco Bill of Rights' (1995) 89 *AJIL* 546
Sohn, L. and. Buergenthal, T., *International Protection of Human Rights* (Indianapolis, Bobbs Merrill, 1973)
Spiegel, Hans W., 'Origin and Development of Denial of Justice' (1938) *AJIL* 64
Spiermann, Ole, 'Individual Rights, State Interests and the Power to Waive ICSID Jurisdiction under Bilateral Investment Treaties' (2004) 20 *Arbitration International* 179
'Twentieth Century Internationalism in Law' (2008) 18 *EJIL* 785
Spiro, P. J., 'Globalization, International Law, and the Academy' (2000) 32 *New York University Journal of International Law and Politics* 852

Stahn, Carsten, *The Law and Practice of International Territorial Administration* (Cambridge, Cambridge University Press, 2008)

Stein, Eric, 'International Law in Internal Law: Towards Internationalization of Central-Eastern European Constitutions?' (1994) 88 *AJIL* 427

Steiner, Henry J., 'Individual Claims in a World of Massive Violations: What Role for the Human Rights Committee?' in P. Alston and J. Crawford (eds.), *The Future of UN Human Rights Treaty Monitoring* (Cambridge, Cambridge University Press, 2000), p. 15

Stone, J., *Regional Guarantees of Human Rights: A Study of Minorities Procedure in Upper Silesia* (New York, Macmillan, 1933)

Stoyanovsky, J., *The Mandate for Palestine* (London, Longmans & Co., 1928)

Suárez, Francisco, *On Laws and God the Lawgiver* (1612, G. L. Williams (trans.), Oxford, Clarendon Press, 1944)

Swisher, Carl B., *The Taney Period* (New York, Macmillan, 1974)

Taylor, Telford, *The Anatomy of the Nuremberg Trials: A Personal Memoir* (London, Bloomsbury, 1933)

Final Report to the Secretary of the Army on the Nuernberg War Crimes Trials under Control Council Law No. 10 (Washington, DC, Government Printing Office, 1949)

Nuremberg and Vietnam: An American Tragedy (Chicago, Ill., Quadrangle, 1970)

Tomuschat, Christian, 'International Law: Ensuring the Survival of Mankind on the Eve of a New Century' (1999) 281 *RdC* 9

'*The Applicability of Human Rights Law to Insurgent Movements*' in H. Fischer, U. Froissart, U. Heintschel von Heinegg and C. Raap (eds.), *Krisensicherung und Humanitärer Schutz (Crisis Management and Humanitarian Protection): Festschrift für Dieter Fleck* (Berlin, Berliner Wissenschafts-Verlag, 2004), p. 573

Trindade, A. A. Cançado, 'Origin and Historical Development of the Rule of Exhaustion of Local Remedies in International Law' (1976-I) XII *Revue Belge de droit International* 499

Tusa, Ann and Tusa, John, *The Nuremberg Trial* (London, Macmillan, 1983)

United Nations War Crimes Commission, *History of the United Nations War Crimes Commission and the Development of the Laws of War* (London, HM Stationery Office, 1948)

van Harten, Gus *Investment Treaty Arbitration and Public Law* (Oxford, Oxford University Press, 2007)

Van Wynen Thomas, Ann and Thomas Jr, A. J., '*International Legal Aspects of the Civil War in Spain, 1936–1939*' in R. A. Falk (ed.), *The International Law of Civil War* (Baltimore, Johns Hopkins Press, 1971), p. 111

Vattel, Emmerich de, *The Law of Nations or, Principles of the Law of Nature Applied to the Conduct and Affairs of Nations and Sovereigns* (1758, B. Kapossy and R. Whatmore (eds.), Indianapolis, Liberty Fund, 2008)

Vaughan, Richard, *Charles the Bold: The Last Valois Duke of Burgundy* (London, Longman, 1973)

Vázquez, Carlos Manuel, 'Treaty Based Rights and Remedies of Individuals' (1992) 92 *Colum. L Rev.* 1083

Verhaeren, Emile, *Belgium's Agony* (London, Constable, 1915)
Vitoria, Francisco de, *Political Writings* (A. Pagden and L. Jeremy (eds.), Cambridge, Cambridge University Press, 1991)
von Clausewitz, Carl, *On War* (J. J. Graham (trans.), London, Kegan Paul, 1908)
Waldock, Humphrey (ed.), *J L Brierly, The Law of Nations: An Introduction to the International Law of Peace* (6th edn, Oxford, Clarendon Press, 1963)
Walter, C., 'Subjects of International Law' in R. Wolfrum (ed.), *The Max Planck Encyclopedia of Public International Law* (Oxford, Oxford University Press, 2008, online edition, www.mpepil.com)
Waltz, Susan, 'Universalizing Human Rights: The Role of Small States in the Construction of the Universal Declaration of Human Rights' (2001) 23 *HRQ* 44
Warbrick, Colin, 'States and Recognition in International Law' in M. Evans (ed.), *International Law* (2nd edn, Oxford, Oxford University Press, 2006), p. 217
Webster, Charles K., *The Foreign Policy of Castlereagh 1812–1815: Britain and the European Alliance* (London, Bell & Sons, 1925)
'The Making of the Charter of the United Nations' (1947–8) 32 *History* 16
Weil, Prosper, 'Towards a Relative Normativity in International Law' (1983) 77 *AJIL* 415
Weiss, Edith Brown, 'Invoking State Responsibility in the Twenty-First Century' (2002) 96 *AJIL* 798
Werle, Gerhard, 'Individual Criminal Responsibility in Article 25 ICC Statute' (2005) 5 *JICJ* 953
West, Rebecca, *A Train of Powder* (London, Macmillan, 1955)
Wharton, Francis, 'Insurgents as Belligerents' (1886) 33 *Albany Law Journal* 125
Wheaton, Henry, *Elements of International Law 1866 Edition* (Richard Henry Dana (ed.), Oxford, Clarendon Press, 1936)
Whiteman, Marjorie M., *Digest of International Law* (Washington, DC, Department of State, 1965), vol. V
Wiessner, Siegfried and Willard, Andrew R., 'Policy-Oriented Jurisprudence and Human Rights Abuses in Internal Conflict: Toward a World Public Order of Human Dignity' (1999) 93 *AJIL* 316
Wildhaber, Luzius, 'A Constitutional Future for the European Court of Human Rights?' (2002) *HRLJ* 161
Wilhelm, René-Jean, 'La Caractère droits accordés à l'individu dans les Conventions de Genève' (1950) *Revue international de la Croix-Rouge* 561
Williams, J. Fischer, *Some Aspects of the Covenant of the League of Nations* (London, Oxford University Press, 1934)
Wilmshurst, Elizabeth, '*Conclusions*' in E. Wilmshurst and S. Breau (eds.), *Perspectives on the ICRC Study on Customary International Humanitarian Law* (Cambridge, Cambridge University Press, 2007), p. 401
Wilson, George, *The Hague Arbitration Cases* (Boston, Ginn and Co., 1915)
Wilson, H. A., *International Law and the Use of Force by National Liberation Movements* (Oxford, Clarendon Press, 1988)
Wilson, Howard Hazen, 'Some Principal Aspects of British Efforts to Crush the African Slave Trade, 1807–1929' (1950) 44 *AJIL* 505

Woetzel, Robert K., *The Nuremberg Trial in International law* (London, Stevens & Sons Ltd, 1962)

Wolff, Christian, *Jus Gentum Methodo Scientifica Pertractatum* (J. B. Scott (ed.), Joseph H. Drake (trans.), Oxford, Clarendon Press, 1934), vol. II

Wright, Quincy, 'Some Recent Cases on the Status of Mandated Areas' (1926) 20 *AJIL* 768

Mandates under the League of Nations (Chicago, Ill., University of Chicago Press, 1930)

'Human Rights and the World Order' (1943) 389 *International Conciliation* 238

'The Law of the Nuremberg Trial' (1947) 41 *AJIL* 38

'The American Civil War, 1861–1865' in R. A. Falk (ed.), *The International Law of Civil War* (Baltimore, Md, Johns Hopkins Press, 1971), p. 30

Wühler, Norbert, 'Mixed Arbitral Tribunals' in R. Bernhardt, *Encyclopedia of Public International Law* (Amsterdam, Elsevier Science, 1997), vol. III, p. 433

Zeck, William A., 'Nuremberg: Proceedings Subsequent to Goering et al.' (1948) 26 *NCL Rev.* 350

Zegfeld, Lisbeth, *Accountability of Armed Opposition Groups in International Law* (Cambridge, Cambridge University Press, 2002)

Zimmern, A., *The League of Nations and the Rule of Law 1918–1935* (London, Macmillan and Co., 1936)

Index

access of claimants
in international claims, 55–7
Iran-US Claims Tribunal and issue of, 98–101
ACHR (American Convention on Human Rights), 328–30
Additional Protocols. *See under* Geneva Conventions
ADM (Archer Daniels Midland Company) and Tate & Lyle Ingredients Americas, Inc. v. United Mexican States, 116–19
administration of justice, International Criminal Court jurisdiction and, 270
admissibility criteria, regional enforcement of human rights and, 333
Africa
Central Africa, mandates in, human rights laws for inhabitants under, 287
human rights enforcement in, 327, 330
South West Africa, mandates in, human rights laws for inhabitants under, 288
African [Banjul] Charter, 328–30
African Commission of Human and Peoples' Rights, 330
African Court of Human and Peoples' Rights, 331
Alabama Claims arbitration, belligerent rights and, 201
Algiers Accords, Claims Settlement Declaration, 98, 100
Alien Tort Claims Act, 325n.278, 336n.330
aliens, international claims and, 48–50
diplomatic protection doctrine and, 87–8
Mexican Claims commissions provisions, 80
pre-1914 doctrine and practice, 48–50
Allied Powers
human rights law and
international bill of rights proposals, 299–301
World War I powers' discussion of, 282–7
World War II powers' discussion of, 296–9
war crimes proceedings and
Council Law No. 10 trials and military commissions, 251–3
inter-war legal theory and, 236–41
Nuremberg Tribunal prosecutions and, 241–9, 368
American Convention on Human Rights (ACHR), 328–30
American Institute of International Law, 68n.91
American Jewish Congress, 301
American Law Institute, 298
Anglo-German Tribunal, 73
Antoine Fabiani Case, binding effect of inter-state decisions in, 59–60
Anzilotti, Dionisio, 18, 23–4
appeal, right of, individual in international claims and, 60
applicable law principle
Common Article 3 of Geneva Convention and, 209
individual in international claims and, 60
international crime and individual responsibility, hybrid and domestic courts, provisions including, 271–4, 273n.235
treaty rights of individuals and, 21, 24
Arab Charter on Human Rights, 328
Arbitral Commission on Property Rights and Interests (Germany), 98

arbitration
  diplomatic protection claims, 52–4, 124–33
  investment treaties, 103–19
  mixed arbitral tribunals, inter-war period, 72–7
Archer Daniels Midland Company (ADM) and Tate & Lyle Ingredients Americas, Inc. v. United Mexican States, 116–19
armed conflict
  humanitarian law and
    customary international law and, 221
    Customary Law Study and, 191–3
    human rights law and, 193–6
    individual rights and responsibilities in, 177–96, 348, 352
    inter-war period developments, 180–96
    post-1945 legal theory and, 181–96
    pre-1914 regulation of, 177–80
  individual rights and responsibilities in
    civil war and, 198–206
    human rights law and, 222–4
    internal conflict, 177–224
    international conflict, 177–96
      human rights law and, 193–6
      pre-1914 regulation, 177–80
    inter-war period practice and doctrine, 180–96, 206–8
    post-1945 international armed conflict, 181–96
  internal. *See* internal armed conflict
  victims of. *See* victims of war
armed opposition groups. *See also* belligerency rights; insurgents, rights of; non-state entities
  Additional Protocol (Geneva Convention) obligations, 217
  customary law provisions concerning, 224
  as *de facto/de jure* government, 223n.210
  human rights obligations of, 222–3, 227
  humanitarian law concerning, 197–8, 361
  legislative jurisdiction concerning, 219
Atlantic Charter, human rights provisions, 297n.112, 297–8
Avena case
  individual rights in international claims and, 95–6, 123
  investment treaty arbitration, 112

Bank for International Settlements, 17
Barbasan, trial of, 233
Barcelona Traction case, 85, 88, 91
Beckett, W. E., 18, 23–4
Belgian-Mexican Administrative Arbitral Tribunal, 78, 85n.175
Belgrade District Court War Crimes Chamber, 273n.232
belligerency rights. *See also* armed opposition groups; insurgents, rights of
  in civil conflict, 198–206, 200n.110, 201n.114, 203n.126, 225–8, 345
  international criminal law and, 231
  inter-war period legal theory and, 206–8
  neutrality and, 199n.104, 200n.110, 207
  non-obligatory criteria for, 199n.104, 204n.129, 209
bilateral investment treaties (BITs), 4, 103–19, 350
Bosnia and Herzegovina War Crimes Chamber, 272
Brionowski v. Poland, 333
Britain. *See* Great Britain
British-Mexican Commission, international claims provisions, 81n.157, 82
Brussels Conference General Act (1889), 280
Brussels Treaty, 308
'Bug River' claims, 333

Calvo clause
  European human rights enforcement and, 312
  local remedies rule violations and, 92
  Mexican Claims commissions and, 79
capacities. *See under* subjects doctrine in international law
Cargill v. United Mexican States, 114
Central Africa, mandates in, human rights laws for inhabitants under, 287
Central American Court of Justice, 54
  individual claims in, 60–2, 64, 65, 121, 344–5
  insurgents' rights and, 366
Central American Peace Treaty of 1871, 62
CERD (Convention on the Elimination of Racial Discrimination), 313–15
Chattin case, 79
China, international bill of rights proposals and, 300
Chorzów Factory case, 70
Churchill, Winston, 242, 296–7, 297n.114, 368
civil conflict
  Additional Protocol II (Geneva Convention) provisions concerning, 213–19
  armed opposition groups and, 345
  Common Article 3 of Geneva Convention provisions concerning, 208–12

civil conflict (cont.)
customary international humanitarian law and, 219–22
early history of regulation, 176
humanitarian law and regulation of, 198–206, 225–8
inter-war period legal theory concerning, 206
post-1945 regulations on individuals in, 208–12
civil rights. *See also* human rights law
international criminal law and protection of, 336
in Universal Declaration on Human Rights, 307
Civilian War Claimants' Association v. The King, 72n.110
claims. *See* International claims
Claims Settlement Declaration (Algiers Accords), 98, 100
'clean hands' principle, Mexican Claims commissions provisions concerning, 79, 88n.186
codes of conduct, international criminal law and, 231
commissions for international claims. *See also* tribunals; *specific commissions*
arbitration, 54–62, 63
binding effects, inter-state decisions, 58–60
control of claim, 55–7
historical timeline (1792–1914), 134–61
International Prize Court and Central American Court of Justice, 60–2
inter-war period, 65–84, 162–75
legacy of, 63
Mexican Claims Commissions (1923–1932), 77–83
national issues, 68–71
payment of claims, 57–8
post-1945 practices, 97–103
communism, European human rights enforcement and impact of, 309
complicity in international law, Nuremberg Principles concerning, 256
Conciliation Commissions, international claims procedures, 97
Conference of Ambassadors, inter-war trials of German war criminals and, 240
Conference of Berlin (1885), 280
Congress of Vienna, 280
consent, individual rights and responsibilities and role of, 352, 360–3
conspiracy, Nuremberg Tribunal provisions concerning, 245
contempt offences, International Criminal Court jurisdiction and, 270n.223, 270
continuity of nationality. *See under* diplomatic protection, doctrine of
contract claims, 48n.1, 105n.262, 111
Convention on the Elimination of Racial Discrimination (CERD), 313–15
Convention on the Settlement of Investment Disputes between States and Nationals, 103–19
Convention on the Status of Refugees, 292
Corn Products International, Inc. v. United Mexican States (CPI), 116–19
corporations. *See also* foreign investment disputes
international claims by, 47–8, 102n.246
international rights of, 37n.145
cosmopolitanism, 43–4, 369
Costa Rica, Central American Court of Justice and, 61n.68, 61–2
Council Law No. 10 trials and military commissions in Pacific, individual responsibility for war crimes and, 251–3
Council of Europe, human rights enforcement and, 307
Council of the League of Arab States, 328
countermeasures, investment treaty arbitration and, 4, 114–19
CPI (Corn Products International, Inc.) v. United Mexican States, 116–19
crimes against humanity. *See* humanitarian law
crimes against peace
Council Law No. 10 trials and military commissions, 251–3
ILC code against, 259–60
Nuremberg Principles concerning, 256
Nuremberg Tribunal proceedings and, 245
criminal law. *See* international criminal law
criminal organisations
Council Law No. 10 trials and military commissions provisions on, 251–3
Nuremberg Tribunal provisions concerning, 245
customary international law principle
Customary Law Study and, 191–3
human rights and, 361–2
individual rights and responsibilities and, 371
internal conflict and, 219–22
Customary Law Study (ICRC)
Additional Protocol II analysis, 219

human rights law and, 322–6
international humanitarian law, 191–3
Czechoslovakia, minority rights in, 282

Dallal v. Bank Mellat, 100–1
Danzig, Poland
Danzig case on treaty rights of individuals, 17–26, 21n.77, 28, 29, 71, 218, 266, 347, 358–60
municipal jurisdiction of, 21n.77, 22n.78
railway treaty (1921 Agreement) and, 19–26
de facto government, belligerent rights of insurgency and, 202–5
death penalty, international claims, individual rights protections and, 94–6
Declaration of Amnesty, inter-war international criminal legal theory and, 238
Declaration of London (1909), 61
Declaration of St. James, 241
Declaration on the Right to Development (UN), 320
derivative rights theory, investment treaty arbitration, 109–12
Diallo case, diplomatic protection doctrine in, 93, 122
Dickson Car Wheel Co. case, 81
diplomatic protection, doctrine of
arbitration of specific claims, 52–4, 124–33
continuity of nationality
exceptions to, 90
ILC provisions on, 88–93
international claims and role of, 66–8, 67n.80, 67n.84, 90n.195
Mexican Claims commission provisions concerning, 81
unfairness, possibility of, 90
current and future issues, 120–3, 366, 368
historical evolution of, 47–50
individual claims under, 56
International Law Commission articles on, 86–93
inter-state law and, 50–62
in inter-war period, 65–84
investment treaty arbitration, 105n.262, 105–20
Iran-US Claims Tribunal rejection of, 99
legacy of, 62–5
Mexican Claims commissions 'Calvo clauses,' 79
Permanent Court affirmation of, 66n.76
post-1945 doctrine and practices, 85–120
pre-1914 doctrine and practice, 48–50
state protection of individuals and, 15n.50
state protection of natives, 15n.50
UN Compensation Commission and, 101–3
Vattel's discussion of, 49–50
direct rights
bilateral investment treaties, 113
human rights law
inter-war legal theory and, 338, 348, 349
minority rights, 284
investment treaty arbitration and, 105, 108, 118, 119–20
dispute resolution, investment treaty arbitration and, 106–19
doctrine, practice vs., 6
doctrine of subjects. *See* subjects doctrine in international law
domestic law. *See also* national law
abolition of slavery and, 281
human rights law and
customary international law principles and, 322–6
international enforcement and, 307–12
regional enforcement through, 332
UN human rights charter proposal and, 305
individual rights and responsibilities under, 18–26, 363
international claims and
binding effect of inter-state decisions and, 60
diplomatic protection and, 49–50, 51n.11
Iran-US Claims Tribunal and, 100–1
Serbian Loans and *Panevezys-Saldutikis Railway* cases, 66–71
international criminal law and, 234, 242n.74
Council Law No. 10 trials and military commissions use of, 252
hybrid and domestic courts, rulings before, 271–4
international tribunals and courts vs., 263
inter-war trials of German war criminals and, 240
Nuremberg Principles and, 257–8
Nuremberg Tribunal and, 242–9
summary of issues, 275–7
piracy prosecution under, 232
DRC v. Uganda, 193
drug trafficking, as international crime, 261n.172

Dumbarton Oaks, international bill of rights proposals at, 300–1
Dutch Government, trial of Kaiser Wilhelm II and, 236–7, 237n.46

ECHR (European Convention for the Protection of Human Rights and Fundamental Freedoms), human rights enforcement and, 307–12, 337
Economic and Social Council (ECOSOC) (United Nations)
  human rights initiatives
    human rights charter proposal, 302, 303
    international covenants, reports submitted to, 318
    minority rights study, 286–7
  Universal Declaration of Human Rights and, 306
economic rights, in Universal Declaration on Human Rights, 307
enforcement
  domestic law, customary international law principle and, 325
  European system for, 307–12, 335
  regional enforcement mechanisms, 327–35
England. *See* Great Britain
Eritrea-Ethiopia Claims Commission, 192
European Commission of Human Rights, 309, 327–35
European Convention for the Protection of Human Rights and Fundamental Freedoms (ECHR), human rights enforcement and, 307–12, 337
European Court of Human Rights, 310–12, 337, 363
  diplomatic protection doctrine and, 89, 93n.204
  formation of, 331
  non-international armed conflict issues and, 222–4
Ex Parte Quirin case, 247–9
Extraordinary Chambers of Cambodia, 273n.233, 273

fair trial in international crimes, Nuremberg Principles concerning, 256
Forced Labour Convention of 1930, 294
foreign investment disputes. *See also* investment treaties
  individual rights and responsibilities in, 350, 366, 368
  investment treaty arbitration, 103–19
forfeiture of proceeds of crime, International Criminal Court provisions for, 271
France, Council Law No. 10 trials and military commissions of, 251–3
fraudulent international claims, payment of, 57–8
freedom fighters, Additional Protocol II (Geneva Convention) civil conflict provisions and, 213
French-German Mixed Arbitral Tribunal, 73
Friendly Relations Declaration of 1970, 213
'fundamental laws' principle, minority rights and, 283

Gabcikovo-Nagymaros Project case, 114
gender rights
  UN Committee on the Elimination of Discrimination Against Women and, 337
  UN human rights charter proposal and, 304
Geneva Conventions, 182–9
  Additional Protocol I (1977), 189–90, 224, 227
  Additional Protocol II
    civil conflict regulation and, 213–19, 226–8
    customary international humanitarian law and, 219–22
    international tribunals and courts and violations of, 263
  Amelioration of the Wounded, 179n.12
  Common Article 3, 208–12, 221–2, 224, 226–8, 263
  Customary Law Study, 191–3
  Diplomatic Conference, 213
    Additional Protocol II and, 214
    humanitarian law and, 185
    ICRC commentaries and, 185
    national liberation movements and, 213
    parties to conflict designation and, 212
    reciprocity in civil conflict and, 208
    rights of insurgents and, 216
  'duty of commanders' provision, 190
  grave breaches doctrine and, 188–9
  ICRC and. *See under* International Committee for the Red Cross
  international criminal law and, 231
  1949 provisions, 182–9
  post-1945 international armed conflicts and changes to, 181–96
  on prisoners of war. *See* prisoners of war, Geneva Conventions concerning
  victims of war initiatives (1864 provisions), 178

genocide, as international crime, 258n.159, 259
Genocide Convention, 258n.159, 259
  human rights and, 313
  hybrid and domestic courts and, 273n.233, 273
German-American Mixed Claims Commission, 68n.88, 68
Germany
  mandated territories ceded from, human rights in, 283n.27, 284n.44, 287
  Nuremberg Tribunal provisions concerning legislative power of, 246
  refugees from, human rights for, 293
  war crimes by individuals, proceedings under law of, 237–40, 238n.54, 238n.55
globalisation, international law and, 44
grave breaches principle
  Additional Protocol I, (Geneva Convention), 190, 193n.81
  hybrid and domestic courts and, 273n.233
  individual criminal responsibility and, 188–9, 221–2
  international criminal tribunals and, 262
Great Britain
  abolition of slavery in, 279–82
  belligerent rights doctrine and, 203–5
  Council Law No. 10 trials and military commissions of, 251–3
  human rights law in, 279n.5, 336
  international bill of rights proposals and, 300, 302
  Jay Treaty provisions and, 50–2
  Nuremberg Tribunal prosecutions and, 239n.59, 243n.77, 243–5, 352
  Order of Malta and, 33n.125
  Tokyo Tribunal prosecutions and, 249
Greece
  mandate concessions dispute in, 291
  minority rights in, 282, 285n.47, 287n.60
Grotius, Hugo, 10, 177n.3
groups
  human rights provisions involving, 338n.348
  internal armed conflict and, 197–8

Hague Conventions
  Convention of 1899, 178–80
  Convention of 1907
    customary international humanitarian law and, 220
    International Prize Court and, 54, 60–1
    international regulation of armed conflict and, 178–80
  post-1945 armed conflicts and changes to, 181–96
historical development of international legal system, 3–5, 343–53. *See also* inter-war period, legal theory in; medieval legal theory; post-1945 period, legal theory in
  diplomatic protection doctrine, 47–50
  early period, 10–13
  human rights law, 6. *See also under* inter-war period, legal theory in; post-1945 period, legal theory in
  humanitarian law, 6, 177n.2
  individual rights and responsibilities concept, evolution of, 3–5, 343–53
  international claims law, 6, 162–75
    inter-state framework, 50–62
    mixed claims, evolution of, 47–50
    timeline of international commissions and tribunals (1792–1914), 134–61
  international criminal law, 6
  inter-state framework, 50–62, 344
  inter-war period, 16, 26n.87, 346–9
  law of nations as precursor, 10–13
  nineteenth century developments, 13–16, 343–6
  positive international law concept, 12
  post-1945 international legal system, 26–9, 349–53
  state-centered international law, evolution of, 5, 12–13, 343–6, 372
  structural framework, evolution of, 5–6
Hobbes, Thomas, 12
Holy See
  authority of, 32n.119
  as *sui generis* subject of international law, 32–4
host state obligations, investment treaty arbitration and, 103–19
hostis humani generis, pirates designated as, 232
Human Rights Act (UK), 279n.5, 337
Human Rights Commission. *See also* Human Rights Council
  establishment of, 302
  Somalian resolution of, 223n.211
  special procedures before, 321–2
  state human rights compliance assessment, 312
  Universal Declaration of Human Rights development and, 306
Human Rights Committee (UN)
  ICCPR establishment of, 316, 317n.230
  jus cogens human rights norms, 326
  non-international armed conflict issues and, 222–4, 223n.211
  state liability provisions, 337

Human Rights Council, 321–2
human rights law. *See also* civil rights
  Allied Powers and. *See under* Allied Powers
  customary law principles, hard vs. soft law, 322–6
  diplomatic protection doctrine, international claims and, 87–8
  direct rights
    inter-war legal theory and, 338, 348, 349
    minority rights, 284
  domestic law and. *See under* domestic law
  enforcement. *See* enforcement
  European state obligations, individual rights, and international enforcement, 307–12
  historical development of, 6. *See also under* inter-war period, legal theory in; post-1945 period, legal theory in
  humanitarian law and, 194–6, 225
  ICJ and. *See under* International Court of Justice
  individual rights and responsibilities in. *See under* individual rights and responsibilities in international law
  international armed conflict and, 193–6
  international bill of rights preparations, 299–301
  international tribunals and courts and, 266–7
  jus cogens human rights norms, 326–7
  League of Nations and. *See under* League of Nations
  mandated territories, rights of inhabitants in, 287–91
  minority rights, 282–7, 347–9
  national law and
    abolition of slavery, 281
    UN human rights charter proposal, 305
  non-international armed conflict and, 222–4
  PCIJ and. *See under* Permanent Court of International Justice
  refugees' rights, 291–3, 347–9
  regional enforcement mechanisms, evolution of, 327–35
  slavery, 279–82
  social and cultural rights, in Universal Declaration on Human Rights, 307
  state-centered approach to. *See under* state-centered international law
  summary of provisions and issues, 335–9
  UN charter, 301–6
  UN ECOSOC and. *See under* Economic and Social Council
  UN state obligations concerning, 312–22
    individual covenants, 315–20
    special procedures before Human Rights Commission (Human Rights Council), 321–2
    specific rights declarations, 320–1
    subject-specific conventions, 313–15
  Universal Declaration of Human Rights, 306–7
  World War II rhetoric on, 296–9
humanitarian law
  armed conflict and. *See under* armed conflict
  civil war and, 198–206
  Council Law No. 10 trials and military commissions provisions on, 251–3
  customary law as, 219–22
  Customary Law Study, 191–3
  historical development of, 6, 177n.2
  human rights law and, 194–6
  individual rights and responsibilities in. *See under* individual rights and responsibilities in international law
  inter-state framework for, 224–8, 351
  national law and
    Additional Protocol II (Geneva Convention) civil conflict provisions, 216–19
    civil conflict, 226–8
  Nuremberg Principles concerning crimes against, 256
  Nuremberg Tribunal provisions concerning crimes against, 245
  PCIJ and, 181
  post-1945 international armed conflict and, 181–96
  state-centered approach to, 181, 370
    Additional Protocol I (Geneva Convention) provisions, 189–90
    Additional Protocol II (Geneva Convention) civil conflict provisions, 215–19
    Common Article 3 of Geneva Convention on civil conflict and, 210–12
    Customary Law Study, 191–3
    Geneva Conventions of 1949 and, 182–9
    inter-war period legal theory, 206
  sui generis subject of international law and, 34–6

ICC. *See* International Criminal Court
ICCPR (International Covenant on Civil and Political Rights) (UN), 312, 315n.219, 315–20, 318n.234, 335

ICESCR (International Covenant on Economic, Social and Cultural Rights) (UN), 312, 315–20, 318n.235, 335
ICJ. *See* International Court of Justice
ICRC. *See* International Committee for the Red Cross
ICTR. *See* International Criminal Tribunal for Rwanda
ICTY. *See* International Criminal Tribunal for the former Yugoslavia
identity certificates, refugee rights and, 292n.93
ILC. *See* International Law Commission
ILO (International Labour Organization), 30n.113, 282, 294n.104, 294–5, 348
incidental responsibility, International Criminal Court jurisdiction and, 270
independence, belligerent rights doctrine and recognition of, 203–5
individual covenants, UN human rights provisions, 315–20
individual rights and responsibilities in international law
  armed conflict and. *See under* armed conflict
  in human rights law, 278–339, 347–9, 350–1, 368
    international covenants, 315–20, 339
    international enforcement, European system for, 307–12
    inter-war period legal theory, 282–96
    jus cogens human rights norms, 326–7
    limited development of, 336
    mandated territories, rights of inhabitants in, 287–91
    minority rights, 282–7
    post-1945 international protections, 296–337
    refugees' rights, 291–3
    regional enforcement, individual applications procedures, 327–35
    slavery, 279–82
    subject-specific UN conventions, 313–15
    summary of provisions and issues, 337–9
    UN-sponsored obligations, 312–22
  in humanitarian law, 176–228, 347, 360
    Additional Protocol I, (Geneva Convention), 189–90
    Additional Protocol II (Geneva Convention), 213–19
    civil war and, 198–206
    Common Article 3 of Geneva Convention, provisions on civil conflict and, 208–12
    current and future issues, 224–8
    Customary Law Study of, 191–3
    Geneva Convention 1949 provisions concerning, 182–9
    Geneva Convention inter-war provisions, 180–1
    internal armed conflict, 196–224
    international armed conflict, 177–96
    international crime, responsibility for, 236, 245, 262
    post-1945 international armed conflicts, 181–96
  in international criminal law, 229–77, 351–2, 366, 368
    Council Law No. 10 trials and military commissions, 251–3
    grave breaches doctrine, 188–9
    hybrid and domestic courts, rulings before, 271–4
    ILC Code of Crimes against Peace and, 259–60, 262
    International Criminal Court and, 267–71
    international criminal tribunals and court rulings, 260
    inter-war period legal theory, 234–41
    national law and. *See under* national law
    Nuremberg Principles and, 253–8
    Nuremberg Tribunal and, 229, 249n.106
    post-1945 legal theory and, 176, 188–9, 241–74
    pre-1919 legal theory, 230–4
    summary of, 274–7
    Tokyo Tribunal provisions, 249–51
    UN legal system and, 258–60
  international legal personality doctrine and. *See under* international legal personality doctrine
  national law and. *See under* national law
  structure of international legal system and. *See under* structure of international legal system
  war crimes. *See under* war crimes
Institute of International law, 90n.192
  belligerency rights and, 204n.129, 231
  civil war resolution, 203
  human rights laws, mandated communities, inhabitants' rights in, 289

insurgents, rights of. *See also* armed opposition groups; belligerency rights
 Additional Protocol II (Geneva Convention) civil conflict provisions and, 215–19
 in civil conflict, 225–8, 345
 Common Article 3 of Geneva Convention on civil conflict provisions and, 210–12
 human rights law and, 223–4
 humanitarian law and, 197–8, 202–5, 205n.132, 227–8
 inter-war period legal theory and, 206–8
 non-obligatory criteria for, 209
 operation as *de facto* government, 223n.210
 post-1945 recognition of, 205
Inter-American Commission on Human Rights, 328n.296
Inter-American Commission on the Status of Women, 304
Inter-American Court of Human Rights, 222–4, 329n.298, 329, 337, 359
interdependent rights, investment treaty arbitration, 112
Interhandel case, 85, 92n.200
internal armed conflict, 198–206. *See also* civil conflict
 Additional Protocol II (Geneva Convention) provisions, 213–19
 customary international humanitarian law and, 219–22
 human rights law and, 222–4
 individual rights and responsibilities in, 177–224, 350
 inter-war legal theory and, 206–8
 post-1945 legal theory and, 208–12
international bill of rights, post-1945 preparation for, 299–301
'An International Bill of the Rights of Man,' 298
international claims
 domestic law and. *See under* domestic law
 evidence, control of, 56, 80
 historical development of. *See under* historical development of international legal system
 individual rights and responsibilities in, 47
  arbitration of defined claims, 52–4
  binding effects on inter-state basis, 58–60
  continuity of nationality and, 66–8, 67n.80, 67n.84
  control of, 55–7
  control of claim, 53n.26, 55–7
  current and future issues, 120–3
  diplomatic protection doctrine and, 47–50
  International Court of Justice provisions concerning, 94–6
  inter-war period doctrine and practice, 65–84, 347
  investment treaty rights, 103–19, 122
  Iran-US Claims Tribunal and issue of, 98–101
  Mexican Claims Commissions and role of, 77–83
  mixed arbitral tribunals, proceedings involving, 72–3
  payment of awards, 57–8
  post-1945 doctrine and practices, 85–120
  practice of, 50–62
  pre-1914 doctrine and practice, 48–50, 134–61
  standing in International Prize Court and Central American Court of Justice, 60–2
  tribunals and commissions, 54–62, 97–103
  US Mixed Claims Commissions and status of, 73–4
  Vattel's articulation of, 49–50
 inter-state framework and. *See under* inter-state framework
 national law and. *See under* national law
 nationality and. *See under* nationality
 PCIJ and. *See under* Permanent Court of International Justice
 post-1945 period. *See under* post-1945 period, legal theory in
 state-centered international law and. *See under* state-centered international law
 tribunals and commissions. *See* commissions for international claims; tribunals
 Vattel's articulation of, 49–50
International Committee for the Red Cross (ICRC)
 civil war regulations and, 207–12
 Customary Law Study, 191–3, 219
 Geneva Conventions and
  Additional Protocol II (Geneva Convention) provisions on civil conflict and, 213–14, 216
  commentaries on 1949 provisions, 185–7
  commentaries on Common Article 3, 208–12
  provisions concerning, 35n.135
 human rights laws, refugee rights, 291
 as substitute protecting power, 35n.136

as *sui generis* subject of international law, 34–6
victims of war initiatives, 178
International Court of Justice (ICJ)
customary international humanitarian law and, 219
diplomatic protection doctrine and, 85, 88
human rights law and
in international conflict, 193–6
mandated communities, inhabitants' rights in, 289
UN human rights charter proposal and, 304
Wall opinion and, 318n.235
individual rights and responsibilities and, 94–6, 193–6, 349
international claims, post-1945 doctrine and practices, 85
international legal personality doctrine and, 356
investment treaty arbitration and, 105, 114, 120
Martens clause affirmation by, 191
Reparations opinion, 30–2, 354, 356
International Covenant on Civil and Political Rights (ICCPR) (UN), 312, 315n.219, 315–20, 318n.234, 335
International Covenant on Economic, Social and Cultural Rights (ICESCR) (UN), 312, 315–20, 318n.235, 335
International Criminal Court (ICC), 36
establishment of, 261, 267–71, 267n.204
individual criminal responsibility and, 221, 351
international vs. domestic law and, 275–6
international criminal law. *See also* war crimes
Council Law No. 10 trials and military commissions, 251–3
defined, 229
domestic law and. *See under* domestic law
grave breaches doctrine, 221–2
historical development of, 6
as humanitarian law violation, 225–8
hybrid and domestic courts for, 271–4
individual rights and responsibilities in. *See under* individual rights and responsibilities in international law
International Criminal Court and, 267–71
international criminal tribunals and courts, 260
inter-state framework and
debate concerning, 275
international tribunals and courts, 267
inter-war period legal theory, 234–41
national law and. *See under* national law
'Nuremberg Principles' and, 253–8
post-1945 legal theory and, 176, 188–9, 241–74, 351–2, 360
pre-1919 legal theory, 230–4
state-centered international law and
Geneva Conventions concerning, 231
Nuremberg Principles concerning, 252n.122, 256–8
summary of, 274–7
Tokyo Tribunal provisions, 249–51
tribunals. *See under* tribunals
United Nations development of, 258–60
International Criminal Tribunal for Rwanda (ICTR)
contempt offences and, 270n.223
establishment of, 261–7, 263n.184
individual criminal responsibility and, 221n.201, 221, 351
international vs. domestic law and, 275–6
Tadić decision and, 210
International Criminal Tribunal for the former Yugoslavia (ICTY), 36, 189
Common Article 3 of Geneva Convention and, 209
contempt offences and, 270n.223
customary international humanitarian law and, 220–2
establishment of, 261–7
individual criminal responsibility and, 221, 351
international vs. domestic law and, 276
Tadić decision and, 210
International Labour Organization (ILO), 30n.113, 282, 294n.104, 294–5, 348
International Law Commission (ILC), 85
Code of Crimes against Peace and Security of Mankind, 259–60, 262
diplomatic protection doctrine and, 86–93, 122
European human rights enforcement and, 312
individual responsibility for human rights and, 336
International Criminal Court establishment and, 267–71
international criminal tribunal and court proposals, 258, 260–1, 262
investment treaty arbitration, countermeasures, 114–16, 120
Nuremberg Principles and, 253–8

international legal personality doctrine
belligerency rights and, 205
defined, 7
engagement in international legal system and, 29–38
individual rights and responsibilities and, 353–65
international law relationships, actor-to-action, 363–5
rights, obligations, and capacities, 358–63
'subject' vs. 'object,' 36–8, 353–8
insurgents and armed opposition groups, 197–8
internal armed conflict, groups' rights and, 197
international law relationships, actor-to-action, 363–5
inter-war period interpretations of, 16–17
post-1945 doctrines concerning, 349
Reparations case and development of, 30–2
rights, obligations, and capacities, 358–63
'subject' vs. 'object,' 36–8, 353–8
sui generis subjects of international law, 32–6
international organisations
rights of, 36
as subjects of international law. *See under* subjects doctrine in international law
International Prize Court, 54, 60–2, 64, 121
international wrongs, by individuals, 28
internationalised courts, criminal law and establishment of, 230–4
Interpretation of the Statute of the Memel Territory, 24n.81
inter-state framework
international claims and
arbitration in diplomatic protection, 53–4
binding effect of decision, 58–60
commissions and tribunals for, 58–60, 71
control of claim, 55–7
historical practice, 50–62
inter-war period doctrine and practice, 65–84
Iran-US Claims Tribunal and issue of, 100
Mexican Claims Commissions and role of, 77–83
tribunals and commissions, 54–62
US Mixed Claims Commissions, 73–4
international crime
debate concerning, 275
international tribunals and courts, 267
investment treaty arbitration, 104, 109–12
laws of war and, 176, 180–1
medieval law of nations as, 11
structure of international legal system, historical development of, 344
inter-war period, legal theory in
armed conflict, 180–96
belligerency and insurgency rights, 206–8
diplomatic protection doctrine, 65–84
historical legal structures, 16, 26n.87
human rights law, 282–96, 338
mandated territories, rights of inhabitants in, 287–91
minority rights, 282–7, 366
refugees' rights, 291–3, 366
individual rights and responsibilities and, 65–84, 234–41, 346–9
international claims
commissions and tribunals, 65–84
individual rights and responsibilities, 65–84
international criminal law, 234–41
international legal personality doctrine, 16–17
mixed arbitral tribunals, 72–7
investment treaties
arbitration, 103–19
current and future issues, 122
individual rights and, 5n.6
Iran-US Claims Tribunal, 98–101
Iraq, mandate of, human rights laws for inhabitants under, 287n.62, 287, 291
Iraqi High Tribunal, 272n.232, 272
Italian-Mexican Commission, 82, 84

Japan
League of Nations racial equality clause proposed by, 282
Tokyo Tribunal on war crimes by, 249–51
Jay Treaty, 50–2, 57
Joint Committee on Religious Liberty, 301
judicial punishment principle, international criminal law, individual responsibility and, 235
Jurisdiction of the Courts of Danzig
Anzilotti's interpretation of, 18, 22–4
belligerency and insurgency rights and, 206, 218
failure to comply with international law obligations, 21–2, 23–4
intention to create individual treaty rights, 25

international claims tribunals and, 71, 84
international crimes and, 351–2
international law rights, 23, 26, 37
mixed arbitral claims tribunals and, 73
1921 Agreement, 19–22
treaty rights of individuals and, 17–26, 28, 29, 96, 266, 347, 349
jurisdictional issues. *See also* legislative jurisdiction principle; territorial jurisdiction
International Criminal Court rulings on, 267–71
international criminal law, role of tribunals and courts and, 263, 265–6
international criminal law, summary of, 275–7
Mexican Claims Commissions and role of, 77–83
treaty rights of individuals and, 23–4
jus cogens, human rights norms and, 326–7, 361–2
jus gentium
international law and concept of, 10
piracy law and, 232, 344
'justice and equity' provisions, international claims, 50n.10

Kant, Immanuel, 44
Kanyabashi case, International Criminal Tribunal for Rwanda and, 265–6
Kuwait, Iraqi invasion of, 101–3

La Abra international claims case, 57–8
labour unions, ICCPR provisions concerning, 318n.234
LaGrand case, 94–6
Latin America
human rights enforcement in, 327
international bill of rights proposals and, 301
Lausanne, Treaty of, 238
Lauterpacht, Hersch
on belligerency rights and neutrality, 200n.110
on human rights, 298
on insurgency rights, 205n.132
on national law vs. international law, 18, 25n.84
on Universal Declaration of Human Rights development, 306
on war crimes, 248n.102
law of arms, international criminal law and, 230, 233
law of nations
belligerent rights doctrine and, 199, 200–2
as historical precursor, 10–13
law of neutrality, belligerent rights doctrine and, 207
League of Nations
framework of international legal system, 16–17
human rights law and, 282
mandated territories, rights of inhabitants in, 287–91
minority rights, 284–6
refugee rights, 291–3
UN human rights charter proposal and, 305
International Labour Organization and, 294
international status of, 16–17
Slavery Convention of 1926 and, 281
as subject of international law, 30, 353
Lebanon, Special Tribunal for, 272
Legal Consequences for States of the Continued Presence of South Africa in Namibia, 304
legislative jurisdiction principle
Additional Protocol II (Geneva Convention) civil conflict provisions and, 211n.158, 218–19
international tribunals and courts and, 265–6
Nuremberg Tribrunal provisions concerning, 246
lex specialis derogate legi generali, international humanitarian law and, 194–6
Lieber Code of 1863, international criminal law and, 231
Llandovery Castle case, 239n.60
local remedies rule, international claims and exhaustion of, 92n.200, 92–3, 95–6
Loewen case, NAFTA Tribunal and, 107–9
London Agreement, Nuremberg Tribunal prosecutions and, 244
Lotus judgment (PCIJ), 40

Male fide associations, ICC provisions for, 271
Malta, Great Britain and, 33n.125
Maltese Knights. *See* Order of St. John of Malta
mandated territories, human rights of inhabitants in, 287–91, 366
marque, letters of, 48
Martens clause
Additional Protocol II and, 219–22
customary international law and, 191
in Hague Conventions, 179
Mavrommatis case, 65–6, 85, 291n.82

medieval legal theory
on civil war, 198, 226
claims arbitration and, 54
diplomatic protection doctrine and, 49–50, 62
international conflict regulation and, 177n.3, 177
international crime and, 230n.6, 230, 231n.7
inter-state law and, 11
natural law and, 11
origins of international law and, 10–13, 16
Mexico
Claims Commissions in, 55–8, 69, 71, 77n.139, 77–83, 84
international claims arising from Mexican Revolution, 71
NAFTA Tribunals and claims against, 114–19
US citizens' claims against, 55–6, 57
military forces. *See also* armed conflict; prisoners of war, Geneva Conventions concerning
Additional Protocol II (Geneva Convention) civil conflict provisions and, 196n.99, 214
humanitarian vs. human rights law and, 195
military tribunals. *See also specific tribunals*
Council Law No. 10 trials and military commissions use of, 252n.122, 252
individuals accused of international crimes, 231n.11, 237–40
minorities
human rights law involving, 282–7, 347–9
UN state obligations and individual responsibilities concerning, 313–15
mixed claims
historical evolution of, 47–50
mixed arbitral tribunals, inter-war period, 72–7
peace treaties and, 72–3
Upper Silesian Mixed Commission and Arbitral Tribunal, 74–7
US Mixed Claims Commissions, 73–4
post-1945 commissions and tribunals, 98
Moscow Declaration of 1943, 242
multilateral treaties
abolition of slavery and, 280
adoption procedures for, 294n.104
municipal law. *See* domestic law

NAFTA tribunal
investment treaty arbitration and, 107–9
Mexican countermeasures defence and, 114–19
Napoleon, trial of, 234
national law. *See also* domestic law
human rights law and
abolition of slavery, 281
UN human rights charter proposal, 305
humanitarian law and
Additional Protocol II (Geneva Convention) civil conflict provisions, 216–19
civil conflict, 226–8
international claims and
binding effect of inter-state decisions and, 60
diplomatic protection and, 49–50, 51n.11
Iran-US Claims Tribunal and, 100–1
Serbian Loans and *Panevezys-Saldutikis Railway* cases, 66–71
international crime, individual responsibility and, 234, 242n.74
hybrid and domestic courts, rulings before, 271–4, 273n.232
international tribunals and courts vs., 263, 266–7
inter-war legal theory and, 237n.46, 238n.54, 238n.55, 238–40
Nuremberg Principles and, 257–8
Nuremberg Tribunal and, 242–9
summary of issues, 275–7
piracy prosecution under, 232
treaty rights of individuals and, 18–26
national liberation movements. *See also* armed opposition groups; belligerency rights; insurgents, rights of
Additional Protocol II (Geneva Convention) civil conflict provisions and, 213–14, 217
as international conflict, 227
nationality
Additional Protocol II (Geneva Convention) civil conflict provisions and, 215–19
continuity of. *See* continuity of nationality
international claims and role of
arbitration of claims, 53
continuity of, 66–8, 67n.80, 67n.84
control of claims, 53n.26, 55–7, 90n.192
diplomatic protection doctrine, 50, 52–4
individuals and, 28–9
Mavrommatis case, 65–6
Mexican Claims Commissions provisions, 79–83
payment of awards, 57–8
investment treaty arbitration and, 105

natural law
  medieval concept of, 11, 13
  positivism and, 13
natural persons
  ICC referrals to, 268–9, 269n.211
  international claims by, 54n.31, 67n.82, 77n.139, 97n.220
naval states, civil conflict and, 198–206, 200n.110, 201n.114, 203n.126, 345
Neuilly, Treaty of, 282
neutrality, belligerency rights and, 199n.104, 200n.110, 207
New Haven school, 8, 42–3
NGOs. *See* nongovernmental organisations
Nicaragua
  Central American Court of Justice and, 61
  individual in international claims case and, 61
nineteenth century framework of international legal system, 14–16
nongovernmental organisations (NGOs)
  customary international law and human rights activities of, 324
  international bill of rights proposals and, 301n.139, 301
  international legal personality doctrine and role of, 354
  regional enforcement of human rights and, 330
  UN international covenants on human rights and, 319, 331n.315
non-international armed conflict. *See* civil conflict; internal armed conflict
non-intervention principles, international bill of rights proposals and, 300
non-obligatory criteria for belligerency rights, ICRC list of, 209
non-renunciation clause, in Geneva Convention 1949 provisions, 184–9
non-state entities
  Additional Protocol II (Geneva Convention) civil conflict provisions and, 213–14, 217–19
  belligerency/insurgency rights of, 346
  Common Article 3 of Geneva Convention on civil conflict and, 210–12
  rights and powers of, 353
normative framework
  claims, 8, 9, 44
  humanitarian vs. human rights law and, 195–6
  individual rights and responsibilities in, 224–8, 363
  international legal theory and, 8–9
  jus cogens status, human rights laws, 326–7
North American Dredging Company of Texas (United States) v. United Mexican States case, 80
North American Free Trade Association. *See* NAFTA tribunal
Nuclear Weapons Advisory Opinion (ICJ), 193–6
nullen crimen principle, individual criminal responsibility and, 277
Nuremberg Principles
  international criminal law and, 253–8, 351–2
  international criminal tribunal and court proposals and, 262, 265–6, 267
  legacy of, 274–7
  UN international criminal law following, 258
Nuremberg Tribunal, 28
  customary international humanitarian law and, 220
  international crimes, individual responsibility for, 229, 249n.106, 351, 368
  legacy of, 274–7
  post-World War II prosecutions, 241–9
  UN international criminal law following, 258–9

OAS (Organisation of American States), 328–30, 329n.297
OAU (Organisation for African Unity), 328
object theory of individual, international legal personality doctrine and, 36, 353–8. *See also* subjects doctrine in international law
observer status
  documentation granting, 34n.131
  sui generis subject of international law and, 32–4
Occidental v. Ecuador, 107–8
O'Connell, D. P., 354
opinio juris
  human rights law and, 324
  international criminal tribunals and, 276
  Nuremberg principles and, 258
Oppenheim's *International Law*, 14–16, 15n.50, 16n.56, 16, 26, 27
opposition groups, armed. *See* armed opposition groups
opt-in individual complaint mechanism, human rights law, UN conventions for, 315, 336
Order of St. John of Malta
  history and organisation of, 33n.120, 33n.125
  observer status of, 34n.131
  as *sui generis* subject of international law, 32–4

Organisation for African Unity (OAU), 328
Organisation of American States (OAS), 328–30, 329n.297

Pacific Islands, mandates in, human rights laws for inhabitants under, 288
Palestine, mandate of, human rights laws for inhabitants under, 287n.62, 287, 291n.82, 291
Panama-US Claims Tribunal, 71, 72n.110
Panevezys-Saldutikis Railway case, 66–8, 67n.84
papacy. *See* Holy See
Paraguay Navigation Company, 53n.26
Paris Peace Conference (1919), international criminal law, individual responsibility and, 235
participation, individual rights and role of, 355, 362. *See also* subjects doctrine in international law
'parties to the conflict' status, Additional Protocol II (Geneva Convention) civil conflict provisions and, 215
payment of awards, in international claims, 57–8
PCIJ. *See* Permanent Court of International Justice
peace, crimes against. *See* crimes against peace
peace treaties, mixed arbitral tribunals, inter-war period, 72–3
Permanent Court of International Justice (PCIJ), 65–71
  belligerency and insurgency rights and, 206
  Chorzów Factory case, 70
  Danzig opinion on treaty rights of individuals, 17–26, 21n.77, 28, 29, 71, 218, 266, 347, 358–60
  human rights law
    direct rights principles and, 295
    mandated communities, inhabitants' rights, rulings on, 291
    minorities petitions to, 284n.44, 285
  humanitarian law and, 181
  international claims doctrine and practice, 65–84
    diplomatic protection doctrine, 66n.76, 83–4, 121
    Mavrommatis case, 65–6
    mixed arbitral claims tribunals and, 73
    Serbian Loans and *Panevezys-Saldutikis Railway* cases, 66–8, 67n.84
  Lotus case, 40
  Panevezys-Saldutikis Railway case, 66–8, 67n.84
Peter Pázmany University of Budapest, 266
'pilot judgment' procedure, regional enforcement of human rights and, 333
piracy, individual responsibility for crime of, 230–4, 344
Poland. *See also* Danzig, Poland
  minority rights in, 75, 282, 283n.27
  regional enforcement of human rights in, 333
policy-oriented approach, state-centered international law, 42–3
Polish Minorities Treaty, 75, 283
Polish Railways Administration (PRA), 19
political rights, in Universal Declaration on Human Rights, 307
positive international law, historical concept of, 12
positivism. *See under* theoretical approaches
post-1945 period, legal theory in, 26–9, 349–53
  diplomatic protection doctrine, 85–120
  framework of international legal system, 26–9
  Geneva Convention of 1949 provisions, international armed conflicts, 181–96
  human rights law, 181–96, 296–337, 338–9, 350–1
    customary law principles, hard vs. soft law, 322–6
    European state obligations and enforcement, 307–12
    individual rights and responsibilities, 296–337
    international bill of rights preparations, 299–301
    jus cogens human rights norms, 326–7
    regional enforcement mechanisms, evolution of, 327–35
    state obligations and individual rights, 312–22
    summary of provisions and issues, 335–7
    United Nations charter, 301–6
    Universal Declaration of Human Rights, 306–7
    World War II rhetoric on, 296–9
  humanitarian law, international armed conflict, 208–12
  international claims law, 85–120
    mixed claims tribunals and commissions, 98
    state-centered practices, 97–103
  international criminal law, 176, 188–9, 241–74, 351–2
  war crimes, individual responsibility for, 176, 241–53
PRA (Polish Railways Administration), 19

practice, doctrine vs., 6
prisoners of war, Geneva Conventions concerning
1929 provisions
inter-war humanitarian law and, 180–1
sui generis principle, 35n.135, 35
1949 provisions, 182–9
Additional Protocol II, civil conflict provisions and, 213
private law disputes, international claims and, 59
prize claims, 48n.1
procedural rights, investment treaty arbitration and, 106–19
procedural-direct theory, investment treaty arbitration, 109–12, 116–19
Property Commissions, international claims procedures, 97n.223, 97
proportionality test, International Criminal Court jurisdiction relating to war crimes, 270
protected persons, Geneva Convention provisions concerning, 184–9
protecting Power, Geneva Convention provisions concerning, 186
Pufendorf, Samuel, 12
punishable crimes in international law
International Criminal Court jurisdiction and, 270
Nuremberg Principles concerning, 256
punitive damages, international war crimes trials and, 241

racial discrimination, UN state obligations and individual rights, 313–15
ratione materiae principle
individual criminal responsibility and, 277
International Criminal Court establishment and, 267, 270
ratione personae principle, 5n.6
individual criminal responsibility and, 277
International Criminal Court establishment and, 267
ratione temporis principle, individual criminal responsibility and, 277
reciprocity, principle of, civil conflict regulations, 208
refoulement principle
jus cogens human rights norms, *non-refoulement*, 326
refugee rights and, 293
refugees
human rights laws for, 291–3, 347–9
identity certificates for, 292n.93
Refugees Convention (1951), 6
'Regulation 64' Panels (Kosovo), war crimes jurisdiction, 272n.230, 272
relevant bound entity, insurgency rights and, 217, 227
reparations, ICC provisions for, 271
Reparations for Injuries Suffered in the Services of the United Nations, 30n.113, 30–2, 354, 355, 357
reprisals, pre-1914 international claims and letters of, 48
res judicata, international claims and issue of, 101, 103
responsible authority
Additional Protocol II (Geneva Convention) civil conflict provisions and, 214
of insurgents, Common Article 3 of Geneva Convention on civil conflict, 210–12
'The Rights of Man or What Are We Fighting For?' (Wells), 298
Rome Statute for the International Criminal Court, 261
Roosevelt, Eleanor, 304n.152
Roosevelt, Franklin D., 242, 296, 297n.112, 368
rule-based legal theory, 7–9
Additional Protocol II (Geneva Convention) civil conflict provisions and, 217
human rights, summary of inter-war principles, 295–6
positivism and, 41
Romania, minority rights in, 282
Russia. *See* Soviet Union
Rwanda, war crimes in, 261–7, 263n.184. *See also* International Criminal Tribunal for Rwanda
St. Germain-en-Laye, Treaty of, 281n.17, 282
St. Petersburg Declaration (1868), 178
San Francisco Conference
Nuremberg Tribunal prosecutions and, 243
UN charter on human rights and, 301n.139, 301–6, 302n.140
'Sanctity of Treaties' principle, 349
savings clause, in Geneva Convention 1949 provisions, 184–9
secondary rules of responsibility, investment treaty arbitration and, 109

self-determination, right of, Additional Protocol II (Geneva Convention) civil conflict provisions and, 213
Serbian Loans case, 66–8
Serious Crimes Panels of the District Court of Dili, 273n.235, 273
Sèvres, Treaty of, 238
SGS v. Philippines, 113
Shawcross, Hartley (Sir), 247
sick and wounded, Geneva Convention provisions concerning, 179n.12, 182–9
Sierra Leone, Special Court for, 273n.234, 273
slavery
  international human rights law and abolition of, 279–82
  International Labour Organisation and, 294
  inter-state obligations for abolition of, 344
Slavery Convention of 1926, 281, 294
social contract theory, diplomatic protection and, 50
Somerset's Case, 281
sources of international law, 8, 9
South America. *See* Latin America
South West Africa, mandates in, human rights laws for inhabitants under, 288
sovereignty
  Additional Protocol II (Geneva Convention) civil conflict provisions and, 215–19
  Common Article 3 of Geneva Convention on civil conflict provisions, 210–12
  diffusion of power as challenge to, 356
  diplomatic protection and, 49–50
  inter-war trials of German war criminals and issue of, 241
  Nuremberg Tribunal provisions concerning legislative power and, 246–9
Soviet Union
  international bill of rights proposals and, 300
  Nuremberg Tribunal prosecutions and, 244
  refugee rights in, 291, 292n.93
  Tokyo Tribunal prosecutions and, 249
Spain, United States treaty of 1795 with, 51, 57
Spanish Civil War (1936–1939), 206
Special Court for Sierra Leone, 273n.234, 273
Special Tribunal for Lebanon, 272
Stalin, Josef, 242, 309, 352
state model of criminality, Treaty of Versailles and, 236–41
state-centered international law
  alternative approaches to, 38–44
  belligerency rights and, 345
  continuity of nationality, international claims, 70
  cosmopolitanism and, 43–4
  critiques, 39–44
  diplomatic protection doctrine and, 49–50, 62, 87–8
  historical origins of, 5, 12–13, 343–6, 372
  human rights law and
    abolition of slavery, 280
    Human Rights commission special procedures, 321
    international covenants, UN provision of, 315–20
    international enforcement and, 307–12
    minority rights, 282–7
    subject-specific UN conventions and, 313–15
    summary of inter-war principles, 295–6
    UN human rights charter proposal and, 304–5
    UN-imposed state obligations, 312–22
  humanitarian law and. *See under* humanitarian law
  ICC jurisdiction and, 269
  individual rights in context of, 352–3, 360–3, 367, 369–72
  international claims and
    ILC provisions on, 88–93
    inter-war period, 83
    investment treaty arbitration, 103–19
    post-1945 practices, 97–103
    US Mixed Claims Commissions, 73–4
  international criminal law and
    Geneva Conventions concerning, 231
    Nuremberg Principles concerning, 252n.122, 256–8
  local jurisdiction vs., 22, 23–4
  nineteenth century dominance of, 13, 16
  positivism and, 7, 39–42
  post-1945 international legal system, 26–9
  process approaches, 42–3
  structure of international legal system and, 7, 26–9, 369–72
  sui generis subjects, 32–6
structure of international legal system
  individual responsibility and
    beneficiaries vs. right-holders, 6
    capacities and obligations, 358–63

changes in, forces for, 367–9
defined, 4
doctrine vs. practice, 6
historical development, 3–5, 343–53
international claims and, 53n.28
international wrongs committed by, 28
inter-war period legal theory, 346–9
nineteenth century view of, 14–16, 343–6
openness and flexibility in, 365–7
openness and flexibility of system, 365–7
passive acquisition of rights and obligations, 352–3
post-1945 system changes, 349–53
rights by treaty for, 17–26
state-centered international legal system and, 26–9, 352–3, 360–3, 367, 369–72
structural transition, 10–29, 365–72
subjects doctrine and, 30n.109, 36–8, 353–8, 358–63
themes and observations, 343
state-centered role in, 7, 26–9, 369–72
Suárez, Francisco, 11
subjects doctrine in international law, 29–38
capacities, 38
individual rights and responsibilities and, 358–63
international legal personality doctrine and, 355, 357, 363–5
state consent and, 361
functional approach, 31–2, 37
historical development of, 29
individual as subject in, 30n.109, 36–8, 353–8, 358–63
international legal personality, 29
international organisations
League of Nations, 14–15, 16, 26
Reparations opinion, 30n.113, 30–2, 354, 355, 357
object theory, 14–15, 16–17, 19, 26
participants, 8, 9, 38
Reparations case and development of, 30–2, 354, 355, 357
states as gatekeepers, 25, 33, 36
states exclusively, 14, 16, 18
sui generis subjects of international law, 32–6
Holy 32–4
ICRC, 34–6
Order of St. John of Malta, 32–4
variegated approach, 9, 31, 38
substantive-direct model, investment treaty arbitration, 109–12, 117–19
succession, principle of, Additional Protocol II (Geneva Convention) civil conflict provisions and, 218
superior orders defence
International Criminal Court jurisdiction and, 270
Nuremberg Principles concerning, 256
Nuremberg Tribunal provisions on, 239n.60, 245
Tokyo Tribunal provisions concerning, 250
Supreme Court (United States), Nuremberg Tribunal and rulings of, 247–9
Synagogue Council of America, 301
Syria, mandate of, human rights laws for inhabitants under, 287, 288n.62

Tadić case, 189, 209, 264
Tanganyika, mandate in, human rights laws for inhabitants under, 288
Taylor, Telford, 249n.106
Teheran Hostages case, 304
territorial jurisdiction
diplomatic protection and, 49–50
international human rights law and, 223
prejudice in claims, 73n.118
theoretical approaches
cosmopolitanism, 43–4, 369
New Haven school, 8, 42–3
normative claims, 8, 9, 44
positivism, 7–9, 13–16, 40–2
classical and modern forms of, 40–2
international legal theory and, 7–9
natural law and, 13
nineteenth century dominance of, 13–16
state-centrism vs., 39–42
process approaches, 42–3
third party states
Additional Protocol II (Geneva Convention) civil conflict provisions and, 217–19
investment treaty arbitration countermeasures and, 115–16
Tittoni Report, 284
Tokyo Tribunal, international criminal law and individual responsibility under, 249–51
torture
domestic law on, 273
as international crime, 258n.159, 273
trade unions, ICCPR provisions concerning, 318n.234
treaties. *See also* Versailles, Treaty of
human rights laws and, minority rights, 282–96
individual rights conferred by, 17–26, 28, 29, 96, 266, 347, 349, 361

treaties (cont.)
international regulation of armed conflict through, 178–80
Trial Chamber, international tribunals and courts and authority of, 264
Trianon, Treaty of, 266, 282
tribunals. *See also* military tribunals; *specific tribunals*
human rights proceedings and, 339
for international claims, 162–75, 345
arbitration procedures, 54–62
binding effects, inter-state decisions, 58–60
control of claim, 55–7
historical timeline (1792–1914), 134–61
International Prize Court and Central American Court of Justice, 60–2
inter-war period doctrine and practice, 65–84
legacy of, 63
mixed arbitral tribunals, inter-war period, 72–7
national issues, 68–71
payment of claims, 57–8
post-1945 practices, 97–103
for international crimes
international criminal tribunals and courts, 233n.29, 260, 275–6
inter-war legal theory and, 235, 237–40
post-1945 prosecutions, 241–53
UN proposals for, 258–60
Trinidade, Cançado (Judge), 359
truth and reconciliation commissions, international human rights law and, 223–4
Turkey, mandated territories ceded from, human rights in, 285n.47, 287n.60, 287, 291
Twentieth Century Association, International Bill of Rights proposal, 298

umbrella clause, bilateral investment treaties, 104
unions, ICCPR provisions concerning, 318n.234
United Kingdom. *See* Great Britain
United Nations
ad hoc criminal tribunals established by, 261–7
Committee on the Elimination of Discrimination Against Women, 337
Compensation Commission, 101–3, 102n.246, 120
ECOSOC. *See* Economic and Social Council
Human Rights Committee. *See* Human Rights Committee
human rights initiatives
ECOSOC study on minority rights, 286–7
individual covenants, 315–20
mandated communities, inhabitants' rights in, 289
proposed UN charter, 301–6
special procedures before Human Rights Commission (Human Rights Council), 321–2
specific rights declarations, 320–1
state obligations in, 312–22
subject-specific conventions, 313–15
human rights law , UN state obligations concerning. *See under* human rights law
ICCPR, 312, 315n.219, 315–20, 318n.234, 335
ICESCR, 312, 315–20, 318n.235, 335
International Criminal Court established by, 267–71
international criminal law development by, 258–60
international person status of, 30–2
'Nuremberg Principles' adopted by, 253–8
UNWCC, 241, 242n.71
United States
abolition of slavery in, 280
belligerent rights doctrine and, 203–5
civil war in, 199, 200–2
claims against Mexico by, 55–6, 77–83
Commission to Study the Organization of Peace, 298, 301
Council Law No. 10 trials and military commissions of, 251–3
international bill of rights proposals in, 299–301, 302
Jay Treaty provisions concerning, 50–2
Mixed Claims Commissions, 73–4
Nuremberg Tribunal prosecutions and, 243–5, 252n.122, 352
Spanish Treaty of 1795 with, 51, 57
Tokyo Tribunal prosecutions and, 249
tort laws in, human rights enforcement using, 325n.278, 325, 336n.340, 336
Universal Declaration of Human Rights, 297
customary international law principles and, 322–6
evolution of, 306–7
legacy of, 335–7

UNWCC (United Nations War Crimes Commission), 241, 242n.71
Upper Silesia territorial settlement controversy, Treaty of Versailles provisions on, 74–7, 283n.27
Upper Silesian Mixed Commission and Arbitral Tribunal, 74–7
US-France Air Services case, 114
US-Mexican General Claims Convention, 77–83, 78n.147
US-Mexican Special Claims Convention, 78n.147, 78
USSR. *See* Soviet Union

Vatican. *See* Holy See
Vattel, Emer de, 10–13, 49
  on civil war, 198, 226
  claims arbitration and, 54
  diplomatic protection doctrine and, 49–50, 62
  international conflict regulation and, 177n.3, 177
  origins of international law and, 10–13, 16, 365
Venezuelan Claims Commission, 57
Versailles, Treaty of, 19
  human rights provisions, 282, 283n.27
  individual rights and responsibilities and, 349
  international criminal law and, 236–41, 274
  International Labour Organisation and, 294
  mixed arbitral claims tribunals and, 72n.110, 73
  Nuremberg Tribunal provisions and, 248
  state model of criminality and, 236–41
  Upper Silesia territorial settlement controversy, 283n.27
vessel seizure and capture, Jay Treaty provisions concerning, 50–2
victims of war
  Additional Protocol I, Geneva Convention (1977), 189–90
  international regulations concerning, 178
Vienna Convention on Consular Relations, 94–6
Vienna Convention on the Law of Treaties, 25n.83, 217
Vitoria, Francisco de, 11
voluntarism, positivism and, 40
Von Hagenbach, Peter, trial of, 232–4, 233n.23

waiver by protected persons
  European human rights enforcement and, 311–12
  Geneva Convention 1949 non-renunciation provision, 185
Wall case
  ICESCR provisions and, 318n.235
  international humanitarian law and, 194
war crimes
  Allied Powers and. *See under* Allied Powers
  individual responsibility for
    Council Law No. 10 trials and military commissions, 251–3
    current developments in theory of, 368
    hybrid and domestic court provisions for, 272
    inter-war legal theory and, 234–41, 349
    military tribunals and, 231n.11, 252n.122, 252
    Nuremberg Principles concerning, 256
    Nuremberg Tribunal provisions, 241–9
    post-1945 legal theory concerning, 176, 241–53
    pre-1919 legal theory, 230–4
    Tokyo Tribunal provisions, 249–51
  International Criminal Court jurisdiction relating to, 270
  Lauterpacht's discussion of, 248n.102
War Crimes Commission, United Nations (UNWCC), 241, 242n.71
Warfare. *See* armed conflict
Weil international claims case, 57–8
Wilhelm II (Kaiser), criminal liability of, 236–7, 237n.49, 349
William A Parker case, 81
Wolff, Christian, 12, 177, 198
World War II. *See also* post-1945 period, legal theory in
  European human rights enforcement and impact of, 308–9
  human rights rhetoric during, 296–9
  international criminal law discussions during, 241–9
wounded and sick, Geneva Convention provisions concerning, 179n.12, 182–9
Wright, Quincy, 289

Yugoslavia, minority rights in, 282. *See also* International Criminal Tribunal for the former Yugoslavia

Zoppot Street Crossing case, 22

CAMBRIDGE STUDIES IN INTERNATIONAL AND COMPARATIVE LAW

Books in the series

The Individual in the International Legal System: State-Centrism, History and Change in International Law
Kate Parlett

The Participation of States in International Organisations: The Role of Human Rights and Democracy
Alison Duxbury

'Armed Attack' and Article 51 of the UN Charter: Evolutions in Customary Law and Practice
Tom Ruys

Science and Risk Regulation in International Law: The Role of Science, Uncertainty and Values
Jacqueline Peel

Theatre of the Rule of Law: The Theory, History and Practice of Transnational Legal Intervention
Stephen Humphreys

The Public International Law Theory of Hans Kelsen: Believing in Universal Law
Jochen von Bernstorff

Vicarious Liability in Tort: A Comparative Perspective
Paula Giliker

Legal Personality in International Law
Roland Portmann

Legitimacy and Legality in International Law: An Interactional Account
Jutta Brunnée and Stephen J. Toope

The Concept of Non-International Armed Conflict in International Humanitarian Law
Anthony Cullen

The Challenge of Child Labour in International Law
Franziska Humbert

Shipping Interdiction and the Law of the Sea
Douglas Guilfoyle

International Courts and Environmental Protection
Tim Stephens

Legal Principles in WTO Disputes
Andrew D. Mitchell

War Crimes in Internal Armed Conflicts
Eve La Haye

Humanitarian Occupation
Gregory H. Fox

The International Law of Environmental Impact Assessment: Process, Substance and Integration
Neil Craik

The Law and Practice of International Territorial Administration: Versailles, Iraq and Beyond
Carsten Stahn

Cultural Products and the World Trade Organization
Tania Voon

United Nations Sanctions and the Rule of Law
Jeremy Farrall

National Law in WTO Law: Effectiveness and Good Governance in the World Trading System
Sharif Bhuiyan

The Threat of Force in International Law
Nikolas Stürchler

Indigenous Rights and United Nations Standards
Alexandra Xanthaki

International Refugee Law and Socio-Economic Rights
Michelle Foster

The Protection of Cultural Property in Armed Conflict
Roger O'Keefe

Interpretation and Revision of International Boundary Decisions
Kaiyan Homi Kaikobad

Multinationals and Corporate Social Responsibility: Limitations and Opportunities in International Law
Jennifer A. Zerk

Judiciaries within Europe: A Comparative Review
John Bell

Law in Times of Crisis: Emergency Powers in Theory and Practice
Oren Gross and Fionnuala Ní Aoláin

Vessel-Source Marine Pollution: The Law and Politics of International Regulation
Alan Tan

Enforcing Obligations Erga Omnes in International Law
Christian J. Tams

Non-Governmental Organisations in International Law
Anna-Karin Lindblom

Democracy, Minorities and International Law
Steven Wheatley

Prosecuting International Crimes: Selectivity and the International Law Regime
Robert Cryer

Compensation for Personal Injury in English, German and Italian Law: A Comparative Outline
Basil Markesinis, Michael Coester, Guido Alpa, Augustus Ullstein

Dispute Settlement in the UN Convention on the Law of the Sea
Natalie Klein

The International Protection of Internally Displaced Persons
Catherine Phuong

Imperialism, Sovereignty and the Making of International Law
Antony Anghie

Necessity, Proportionality and the Use of Force by States
Judith Gardam

International Legal Argument in the Permanent Court of International Justice: The Rise of the International Judiciary
Ole Spiermann

Great Powers and Outlaw States: Unequal Sovereigns in the International Legal Order
Gerry Simpson

Local Remedies in International Law
C. F. Amerasinghe

Reading Humanitarian Intervention: Human Rights and the Use of Force in International Law
Anne Orford

Conflict of Norms in Public International Law: How WTO Law Relates to Other Rules of Law
Joost Pauwelyn

Transboundary Damage in International Law
Hanqin Xue

European Criminal Procedures
Edited by Mireille Delmas-Marty and John Spencer

The Accountability of Armed Opposition Groups in International Law
Liesbeth Zegveld

Sharing Transboundary Resources: International Law and Optimal Resource Use
Eyal Benvenisti

International Human Rights and Humanitarian Law
René Provost

Remedies Against International Organisations
Karel Wellens

Diversity and Self-Determination in International Law
Karen Knop

The Law of Internal Armed Conflict
Lindsay Moir

International Commercial Arbitration and African States: Practice, Participation and Institutional Development
Amazu A. Asouzu

The Enforceability of Promises in European Contract Law
James Gordley

International Law in Antiquity
David J. Bederman

Money Laundering: A New International Law Enforcement Model
Guy Stessens

Good Faith in European Contract Law
Reinhard Zimmermann and Simon Whittaker

On Civil Procedure
J. A. Jolowicz

Trusts: A Comparative Study
Maurizio Lupoi

The Right to Property in Commonwealth Constitutions
Tom Allen

International Organizations Before National Courts
August Reinisch

The Changing International Law of High Seas Fisheries
Francisco Orrego Vicuña

Trade and the Environment: A Comparative Study of EC and US Law
Damien Geradin

Unjust Enrichment: A Study of Private Law and Public Values
Hanoch Dagan

Religious Liberty and International Law in Europe
Malcolm D. Evans

Ethics and Authority in International Law
Alfred P. Rubin

Sovereignty Over Natural Resources: Balancing Rights and Duties
Nico Schrijver

The Polar Regions and the Development of International Law
Donald R. Rothwell

Fragmentation and the International Relations of Micro-States: Self-determination and Statehood
Jorri Duursma

Principles of the Institutional Law of International Organizations
C. F. Amerasinghe